TEACHER'S MANUAL

IMMIGRATION AND REFUGEE LAW AND POLICY

FIFTH EDITION

by

STEPHEN H. LEGOMSKY
The John S. Lehmann University Professor
Washington University School of Law

CRISTINA M. RODRÍGUEZ
Professor of Law
New York University School of Law

FOUNDATION PRESS
2009

195 Broadway, 9th Floor
New York, NY 10007
Phone Toll Free 1–877–888–1330
Fax (212) 367–6799
foundation–press.com

Printed in the United States of America

ISBN 978–1–59941–614–4

SUMMARY OF CONTENTS

INTRODUCTION

Too many Teacher's Manuals seem to have been written just for the sake of "having" a Teacher's Manual. The authors went through the motions because, as every publisher tells every casebook author, "teacher's manuals sell books."

In writing this particular teacher's manual, we tried to do two things to make the effort worthwhile. One was to think seriously about what features would be of real, practical use to people who teach immigration law. Those features are described below. The other was to write the Teacher's Manual and the coursebook at the same time -- chapter by chapter, section by section, case by case, question by question. This was the process from the first edition on. One way not to make a teacher's manual an afterthought is not to write it afterwards.

That latter decision profoundly affected the coursebook itself. As law students, we hated casebooks that contained long lists of clever- *sounding* questions to which there really wasn't much to say in response. So, in writing this book, every time we thought of questions that sounded provocative, we forced ourselves to write out what one might say by way of response. If we felt we could say something interesting or meaningful or useful, we did so. The question or fact problem then appeared in the coursebook, and the analysis that we had written out went into the teacher's manual. If we couldn't think of anything worthwhile to write, the question never made it into the book.

By writing the coursebook and the teacher's manual simultaneously, we were also better able to make the policy materials *teachable*. We have tried to introduce the students both to big picture policy questions (What are we really trying to accomplish with an immigration system, or with expulsion, or with asylum, or with citizenship?) and to little picture policy questions. (Why would Congress include a provision like that? Does it make sense to grant relief to X but not to Y?) The coursebook contains a fair amount of both kinds of policy and theoretical material, but we try not to give away the store. When teaching other courses from casebooks that are rich in policy material, instructors often find that the class discussion starts with questions like "What do you think about X?" and too frequently ends up degenerating into "Well, what arguments does the author make on that point?" Rather than provide all the arguments in the coursebook, we prefer to have the book raise the issue, sometimes get the ball rolling by posing arguments that invite counterarguments, and then use the Teacher's Manual to discuss all the considerations that we can think of. That way, the students are forced to create and develop their own positions rather than regurgitate arguments that others have made. If class discussion bogs down, the teacher can draw on arguments from the Teacher's Manual and solicit responses to them.

This Teacher's Manual also contains synopses of all the cases that are reproduced in the coursebook. (We thank Linda Rose for the suggestion.) The synopses have only two very limited purposes. One is to assist in preparing a syllabus. Scanning the synopses might be a way to weed out cases that you can see right away don't particularly interest you. The other purpose is for review before class.

Like the coursebook itself, this teacher's manual reflects our conscious recognition of the diversity that we law teachers bring to our work. We differ in our backgrounds, in our coverage priorities, in our substantive values and ideologies, in our teaching methods, and in our classroom personalities. Other than at the highest levels of generality, we even differ in our ultimate pedagogical goals. The suggestions and analyses that appear in this Teacher's Manual attempt to provide ideas that will be of use to a broad range of teachers, but we appreciate that these materials cannot entirely avoid reflecting our own values and preferences.

With that disclaimer, we hope this Teacher's Manual will serve some useful functions. Teachers of some law school courses have the luxury of being able to consult knowledgeable specialists on their own faculties, but two or more immigration specialists on the same law faculty are still the exception, not the norm. A Teacher's Manual, while no substitute for a live conversation, might be the next-best thing. If the authors have carefully thought through the organization, functions, and uses of the materials in the coursebook, then there can be some benefit in learning what the authors had in mind with particular materials.

We hope this Teacher's Manual will also aid instructors in making coverage decisions (apart from the case synopses discussed above). By skimming it, an instructor can narrow the choices, quickly screening out many cases and other materials that he or she would prefer not to cover. Since the vast bulk of the material has been classroom-tested, we have also acquired a general sense of how much class time given material will require. Those estimates are reflected in the sample syllabi below (more on those in a moment).

This Teacher's Manual also includes our own analyses of (a) all the questions that appear in the Notes and Questions segments (and most of the questions that appear in other miscellaneous spots) and (b) all the fact Problems. Most of the Questions and Problems require policy analysis, interpretation, or strategy. We do not claim our analyses to be "right" – much less, uniquely so. Rather, we expect most instructors will agree with some arguments and disagree with others. We have also included analyses of all the Simulation Exercises, along with logistical suggestions for conducting them.

One particular feature of the coursebook bears emphasis. For reasons that are more fully discussed in item (4) of the coursebook Preface, the Notes and Questions are extensive. The strategy described in the Preface assumes the students make good faith efforts to map out their analyses of those Questions (and the fact Problems) *in advance of class* . It is recommended that the instructor make clear to the students on the first day of the course that a standing part of every assignment is to outline, on paper, specific responses to all the questions in the Notes and Questions, and to all the Problems, that are contained in the day's reading. In class, the instructor can then specifically raise many of those

Questions and generally all the assigned Problems, using them as the starting points for a good chunk of the discussion.

The original author has long used this combination of imparting a clear expectation of fully-thought-out answers to some prearranged questions and then fairly consistently making those questions the nucleus of the class discussion. Many of the questions that appear in the book are ones that he accumulated over the years and asked in class before developing his own materials. He therefore had the opportunity to compare the effectiveness of some of the same questions (a) when the students hear them for the first time in class and (b) when they have seen them in print and have mapped out tentative responses before class. He reports that the difference has been night and day. Questions that formerly had brought simplistic, superficial responses now often (not always) generate some of the most thoughtful and sophisticated classroom dialogue that he has experienced.

A few words on coverage: This coursebook is long; it contains *much* more material than could reasonably be covered even in the rare four-unit course. This is deliberate. First, instructors have widely varying coverage preferences; we wanted to be sure there were enough choices that instructors could select the kinds of materials they personally prefer. Second, we wanted there to be enough material to allow any instructor who wishes to do so to change the coverage from year-to-year (in part to stay fresh, and in part to defeat the practice of students relying on the class notes of their predecessors).

Different instructors cut pages in different ways. Some might wish to cover a broad range of subject matter and to excise particular cases, passages, fact problems, etc. Others might prefer simply to cut entire chapters or sections. The materials have been designed to make either approach feasible.

At the end of this Introduction are two sample syllabi – one for a three-unit course, the other for a two-unit course. In each one we have attempted to include the major components of immigration and refugee law and policy and a mix of theoretical and practical materials. None of the included readings depends on coverage of the omitted readings.

Both syllabi reflect the following assumptions about the amount of class time required:

(1) 14 contact hours for each unit of course credit (i.e., 42 class hours for a three-unit course, 28 for a two-unit course);

(2) Instructors taking up in class all the fact Problems and Simulation Exercises that appear in the day's assignment, but only selected Notes and Questions that appear in the day's assignment; and

(3) Occasional carry-over of material to succeeding lessons if there is not enough class time.

The developments of the past few years have required significant changes to the coursebook. Much of the explanatory text has been heavily rewritten, as have many of the questions and fact problems. Several of the cases had to be replaced or supplemented. Several new sections have been added, and a few old ones discarded. Chapter 12, which covers undocumented immigrants, has been reorganized and heavily rewritten.

Still, recognizing that users of past editions have invested considerable preparation time, we retained as much of the existing organizational structure as we could. The chapter sequence remains the same.

We are always grateful for any feedback that users of either the coursebook or this Teacher's Manual are willing to provide. Many of you supplied valuable comments on previous editions. Any questions, comments, criticisms, etc. will again be very welcome. You can reach Steve Legomsky at the Washington University School of Law, One Brookings Drive, CB1120, St. Louis, MO 63130, tel 314-935-6469, e-mail legomsky@wulaw.wustl.edu. You can reach Cristina Rodríguez at the New York University School of Law, 40 Washington Square South, New York, NY 10012, tel 212-992-8827, e-mail cristina.rodriguez@nyu.edu.

SAMPLE SYLLABUS

3-Unit Course

NOTE TO INSTRUCTORS: Classes 25 and 26 of this sample syllabus are devoted to the simulated removal hearing on coursebook pages 790-806. Some instructors might prefer to skip this exercise and, instead, reserve the same amount of class time for the simulated attorney-client initial asylum interview on coursebook pages 1085-94 (i.e., the two classes immediately following the one currently designated class 36). Instructors who choose to do either of these simulations should assign the student (and any other) roles several classes in advance. This Teacher's Manual provides detailed logistical suggestions for both exercises.

Class 1	Overview of Immigration Law; Moral Dimensions of Immigration Control.	Preface; pages 1-13, 24-37. [Optional: Skim pp. 13-24.]
Class 2	Immigration, Race, Culture, and Language; Politics of Immigration; Immigration and National Security; Immigrants, Self-identity, and Home.	Pages 38-56, 59-70 (except omit items 9 and 10 on page 62); pages 91-97; skim pp. 97-112.
Class 3	Immigration and the Constitution: Sources of the Federal Immigration Power.	Pages 113-32.
Class 4	Immigration and the Constitution: Limits to the Federal Immigration Power: The Foundation Cases.	Pages 132 to bottom of 133, 136 to top of 155.
Class 5	Immigration and the Constitution: Limits to the Federal Immigration Power: Modern Developments (begin).	Top of page 155 to p.166; item 3 on pp. 169-71; pp. 177 to top of 195.
Class 6	Immigration and the Constitution: Limits to the Federal Immigration Power: Modern Developments (finish).	Pages 206 to bottom of 225; pp. 242-44. [Instructor's option: Simulation Exercise on pp. 245-47.]
Class 7	Immigrant Priorities: Historical Background; Fundamentals of Quotas and Preferences.	Pages 250-61.

Class 8	Immigrant Priorities: Family: The Basics; Spouses (including same-sex marriages and marriage fraud).	Pages 262-76, 282-86, 302-04.
Class 9	Immigrant Priorities: Employment-Based Immigration: The First Three Preferences (including labor certification).	Pages 304-24. [Optional (and very enjoyable) reading: pages 324-27.]
Class 10	Immigrant Priorities: Fourth and Fifth Employment-Based Preferences; Diversity Immigrants; Nonimmigrant Priorities (begin).	Pages 344-54 (except omit Problem 16 on page 350); pages 355 through Problem 3 on page 368.
Class 11	Nonimmigrant Priorities (finish).	Pages 368-69; bottom of p.371 to p.383; middle of p.386 to middle of p.388; pp. 393 to bottom of 398; Problem 8 on p.403 to p.404 (including introduction to section C); bottom of p.407 to p.408; p.411 (starting with section E) to bottom of p.419.
Class 12	Exclusion Grounds: Historical Background; Grounds Related to Immigration Control; Political and National Security Grounds (begin).	Page 420 through Problem 8 on p.443. (But pages 422-31 can be skimmed.)
Class 13	Exclusion Grounds: National Security Grounds (finish); Criminal; Economic; Public Health and Morals.	Pages 443-62.
Class 14	Admission Procedure: History; Modern Procedure: Visa Petitions; Visa Applications.	Skim pages 463-69; study pages 469-87.
Class 15	Admission Procedure: Actual Admission; Adjustment of Status; Deportability Grounds: History; Theory of Deportation; Current Grounds.	Pages 503-19.

Class 16	Deportability Grounds: Meaning and Significance of "Entry" and "Admission."	Pages 522-23, p. 529 through Problem 6 on p.544.
Class 17	Deportability Grounds: Immigration Control Grounds; Criminal Grounds (begin).	Pages 544-52 (except omit Problems 11-13 on page 547); pages 557 to top of 561; p.570 (starting with subsection b) to p.574 (except omit Problems 20-21 on pp. 573-74).
Class 18	Deportability Grounds: Criminal (Aggravated Felonies).	Page 574 through Problem 24 on page 585.
Class 19	Deportability Grounds: Criminal (finish); Political and National Security; Other Deportability Grounds; Relief from Removal: Cancellation of Removal Part A (begin).	Page 585 (starting with Problem 22) through section F on p.589; page 593 through subsection iv on p.600.
Class 20	Relief from Removal: Cancellation of Removal Part A (finish); Cancellation of Removal Part B.	Pages 601-08, middle of 617 to 625.
Class 21	Relief from Removal: Registry; Legalization; Adjustment of Status; Private Bills; Deferred Action; Voluntary Departure; Objections to Destination; Stays of Removal; Miscellaneous; Perspective on Relief. Deportation Procedure: Introduction; Overview.	Pages 625-39, 644 (starting with subsection 4) to 659.
Class 22	Deportation Procedure: Independence; Representation (begin).	Item 3 on page 665 to page 673; pages 680-98.
Class 23	Deportation Procedure: Representation (finish); Evidence and Proof; Administrative Review; Motions to Reopen.	Pages 698-713, first 2 paragraphs of item 9 on page 740; bottom of p.743 (starting with Problem 1) to top of p.756.

Class 24	Deportation Procedure: Judicial Review.	Page 756 through Question on page 790.
Class 25	Deportation Procedure: Phase I of Simulated Removal Hearing.	Pages 790-806.
Class 26	Deportation Procedure: Phase II of Simulated Removal Hearing.	Continue preparation for hearing.
Class 27	Immigration and National Security: Detention; Intelligence-Gathering; Expansion of Removal Grounds; Shrinking Procedural Rights.	Page 816-44.
Class 28	Immigration and National Security: Visas; Enhanced Border Enforcement; Profiling; Perspective.	Pages 844-68.
Class 29	Refugees: Overseas Refugees.	Pages 869-91.
Class 30	Refugees: Asylum and Withholding: Introduction; Meaning of "Persecution."	Pages 892-907, p. 913 to bottom of p.915.
Class 31	Refugees: Race; Religion; Nationality; Political Opinion.	Page 916 (starting with subsection 2) to middle of p.931.
Class 32	Refugees: Social Group: Introduction; Sexual Orientation; Gender (begin).	Pages 931-50.
Class 33	Refugees: Social Group and Gender (finish).	Pages 950-74.
Class 34	Refugees: Non-State Actors; "On Account of;" Problems; Standard of Proof.	Pages 974-76, 983-90 (but omit items 2 and 4 on pp. 983-84); question 6 on p.997 to top of p.1002.
Class 35	Refugees: Methods of Proof; Exceptions to Eligibility.	Pages 1002 (starting with subsection 4) to 1018.
Class 36	Refugees: Asylum Procedure.	Page 1029 to top of p.1041; pp. 1044 (starting with subsection b) to p.1065.

Class 37	Refugees: Convention Against Torture.	Pages 1095 through Problem 3 on p. 1114.
Class 38	Undocumented Immigrants: Introduction; Enforcement.	Pages 1140-64; page 1167 (starting with first full paragraph) through first paragraph of subsection b on p.1171.
Class 39	Undocumented Immigrants: Legalization; Rights and Self-Deportation Strategy (begin).	Page 1178 to top of p.1187; pp. 1190-93; p.1209 (starting with Post-Secondary Education) to middle of p.1225 (except omit Question 3 on p.1212).
Class 40	Undocumented Immigrants: Rights (finish); Creating Alternatives to Illegal Immigration; Federalism.	Pages 1225-43; pp. 1251-59; p.1274 to bottom of p.1275; bottom of p.1281 through last full paragraph on p.1282.
Class 41	Citizenship: Introduction; Acquiring Citizenship.	Page 1288 through Problem 3 on page 1296; top of p.1300 to middle of p.1302; bottom of p.1305 to p.1308; pp. 1313-21.
Class 42	Citizenship: Loss of Citizenship; Significance of Citizenship.	Pages 1336-38, 1357 to top of 1360, 1373-82; item 7 on pp. 1395-96.

SAMPLE SYLLABUS

2-Unit Course

Class 1	Overview of Immigration Law. Immigrant Priorities: Historical Background; Fundamentals of Quotas and Preferences.	Preface; pages 1-11; pp. 250-61.
Class 2	Immigrant Priorities: Family: The Basics; Spouses (including same-sex marriages and marriage fraud).	Pages 262-76, 282-86, 302-04.
Class 3	Immigrant Priorities: Employment-Based Immigration: The First Three Preferences (including labor certification).	Pages 304-24. [Optional (and very enjoyable) reading: pages 324-27.]
Class 4	Immigrant Priorities: Fourth and Fifth Employment-Based Preferences; Diversity Immigrants; Nonimmigrant Priorities (begin).	Pages 344-54 (except omit Problem 16 on page 350); pages 355 through Problem 3 on page 368.
Class 5	Nonimmigrant Priorities (finish).	Pages 368-69; bottom of p.371 to p.383; middle of p.386 to middle of p.388; pp. 393 to bottom of 398; Problem 8 on p.403 to p.404 (including introduction to section C); bottom of p.407 to p.408; p.411 (starting with section E) to bottom of p.419.
Class 6	Exclusion Grounds: Historical Background; Grounds Related to Immigration Control; Political and National Security Grounds (begin).	Page 420 through Problem 8 on p.443. (But pages 422-31 can be skimmed.)
Class 7	Exclusion Grounds: National Security Grounds (finish); Criminal; Economic; Public Health and Morals.	Pages 443-62.
Class 8	Admission Procedure: History; Modern Procedure: Visa Petitions; Visa Applications.	Skim pages 463-69; study pages 469-87.

Class 9	Admission Procedure: Actual Admission; Adjustment of Status; Deportability Grounds: History; Theory of Deportation; Current Grounds.	Pages 503-19.
Class 10	Deportability Grounds: Definition of "Admission;" Immigration Control Grounds; Criminal Grounds (begin).	Pages 522-23; item 9 on p. 539; INA § 101(a)(13); items 16 and 17 on p.543; pp. 544-52 (except omit Problems 11-13 on page 547); pages 557 to top of 561; p.570 (starting with subsection b) to p.574 (except omit Problems 20-21 on pp. 573-74).
Class 11	Deportability Grounds: Criminal (Aggravated Felonies).	Page 574 through Problem 24 on page 585.
Class 12	Deportability Grounds: Criminal (finish); Political and National Security; Other Deportability Grounds; Relief from Removal: Cancellation of Removal Part A (begin).	Page 585 (starting with Problem 22) through section F on p.589; page 593 through subsection iv on p.600.
Class 13	Relief from Removal: Cancellation of Removal Part A (finish); Cancellation of Removal Part B.	Pages 601-08, middle of 617 to 625.
Class 14	Relief from Removal: Registry; Legalization; Adjustment of Status; Private Bills; Deferred Action; Voluntary Departure; Objections to Destination; Stays of Removal; Miscellaneous; Perspective on Relief. Deportation Procedure: Introduction; Overview.	Pages 625-39, 644 (starting with subsection 4) to 659.
Class 15	Deportation Procedure: Independence; Representation (begin).	Item 3 on page 665 to page 673; pages 680-98.

Class 16	Deportation Procedure: Representation (finish); Evidence and Proof; Administrative Review; Motions to Reopen.	Pages 698-713, first 2 paragraphs of item 9 on page 740; bottom of p.743 (starting with Problem 1) to top of p.756.
Class 17	Deportation Procedure: Judicial Review.	Page 756 through Question on page 790.
Class 18	Refugees: Overseas Refugees.	Pages 869-91.
Class 19	Refugees: Asylum and Withholding: Introduction; Meaning of "Persecution."	Pages 892-907, p. 913 to bottom of p.915.
Class 20	Refugees: Race; Religion; Nationality; Political Opinion.	Page 916 (starting with subsection 2) to middle of p.931.
Class 21	Refugees: Social Group: Introduction; Sexual Orientation; Gender (begin).	Pages 931-50.
Class 22	Refugees: Social Group and Gender; Non-State Actors; "On Account of;" Problems; Standard of Proof.	Pages 950-59, 974-76, 985-90; Problems 1-5 on pp. 997-99; p.999 through Question 3 on pp. 1000-01.
Class 23	Refugees: Methods of Proof; Exceptions to Eligibility.	Pages 1002 (starting with subsection 4) to 1018.
Class 24	Refugees: Asylum Procedure.	Page 1029 to top of p.1041; pp. 1044-64.
Class 25	Undocumented Immigrants: Introduction; Enforcement.	Pages 1140-64; page 1167 (starting with first full paragraph) through first paragraph of subsection b on p.1171.

Class 26	Undocumented Immigrants: Legalization; Rights and Self-Deportation Strategy; Federalism.	Page 1178 to top of p.1187; pp. 1192-93; p.1209 (starting with Post-Secondary Education) to p.1213 (except omit Question 3 on p.1212); p.1225 to top of p.1232; p.1274 to bottom of p.1275; bottom of p.1281 through last full paragraph on p.1282.
Class 27	Citizenship: Introduction; Acquiring Citizenship.	Page 1288 through Problem 3 on page 1296; top of p.1300 to middle of p.1302; bottom of p.1305 to p.1308; pp. 1313-21.
Class 28	Citizenship: Loss of Citizenship; Significance of Citizenship.	Pages 1336-38, 1357 to top of 1360, 1373-82; item 7 on pp. 1395-96.

OVERVIEW CHAPTER

One difficulty in teaching immigration law is that the various parts of the subject are hopelessly interrelated. Concepts involving relief from removal, inadmissibility grounds, adjustment of status, asylum, and judicial review all surface constantly in both the admission cases and the deportation cases. Students are often befuddled by the constitutional materials when the court distinguishes admissibility from deportability. Many instructors feel that a knowledge of basic citizenship principles is vital to understanding the materials on the admission process as well as the materials on deportation, yet it is hard to comprehend the process for becoming a citizen before one understands the concept of lawful permanent residence. Like most immigration law teachers, we constantly find ourselves wishing the students knew subject A before they studied subject B, and B before they studied A.

With that dilemma in mind, we have included a brief overview of current immigration law. The overview is superficial, but it includes enough information about basic concepts and connections that the students should be able to follow the rest of the book without the teacher having to provide frequent distracting background explanations and asides in class. This approach permits time for deeper analysis of individual items later. It also helps students synthesize the various units at the end of the course and learn a little bit about areas the instructor decides not to cover.

This material is intended solely as background reading. We recommend including the Overview in the first day's assignment but not taking it up in class.

CHAPTER 1
THE IMMIGRATION DEBATE: GOALS, STRATEGIES, AND IMPACT

SECTION A. HISTORICAL BACKGROUND

We generally assign section A only as background reading. If you want to take up this material in class, however, there are at least two possibilities:

First, before the students have been exposed to the materials on the actual operation of the current family-sponsored and employment-based preference system, you can ask the students what they think the criteria for admitting immigrants ought to be. Based on the historical readings, the students might focus on family, on occupational credentials, on refugee protection, on investment, on new seed immigrants, or on ethnicity. Perhaps some students will favor open borders at this point, particularly if they are simultaneously assigned the material in section B below on the morality of immigration restrictions. Engaging the students in a preliminary discussion now might enable you to see later whether the readings and class discussions have influenced their ideas.

Second, you might wish to focus specific attention on the national origins quota system that persisted in one form or another until 1965. Much of this discussion can be deferred until the coverage of diversity immigrants in chapter 3, section D. But if you want to pursue this subject at this point, you can simply ask the students to argue the pros and cons of a national origins quota system. Possibly the students will cite as advantages the benefits of cultural assimilation, the natural human preference for cultural affinity, the desire to favor those to whom we feel closest, the avoidance of domestic unrest, etc. The arguments against a national origins quota system include avoiding inevitable bigotry, the moral obligation to admit people who are in need, and the benefits of cultural, linguistic, and ethnic pluralism. You might also introduce a twist on this discussion at this stage by asking whether it would be desirable to allow the admission of more immigrants from higher demand countries than from lower demand countries, e.g., should more visas be available to immigrants from Mexico than to those from other countries, or should we retain the presumption of equality/neutrality when setting visa ceilings? This question could also be asked in relation to note 7 in Part C of the chapter.

SECTION B. THE MORAL DIMENSIONS OF IMMIGRATION CONTROL

Because some of the arguments contained in these readings make assumptions about the economic impacts of immigration, instructors might choose to assign Sections B and D together.

This entire question of whether a nation can morally restrict immigration at all might strike many of the students as unreal, since today the question of literally open borders is not seriously debated as a real-world issue. The instructor might observe that the question has more practical relevance than the students might think, however, because many of the arguments for and against restricting immigration are ones that they will see later in less radical form when they evaluate the policy justifications for certain specific programs and provisions of the current immigration laws. For the same reason, this material is useful background for later discussions of immigration policy.

If you wish, you can defer this section until either (a) the end of chapter 3, when the students will have acquired a better practical understanding of actual U.S. immigration criteria (though discussing this chapter before the students have become bogged down in detail is also a positive advantage) or (b) chapter 13, when they could discuss this material in conjunction with an analogous discussion of citizenship. Some of the questions raised by this material lend themselves more easily to sophisticated discussion after a study of the law that governs acquisition and loss of citizenship, because the question who <u>is</u> a citizen affects the moral issue whether those who are <u>not</u> citizens should be subject to exclusion.

One option is to structure the discussion along the lines suggested by the Notes and Questions that follow Nett and Macedo. An alternative, however, is simply to ask the open-ended question whether there is a moral justification for immigration restrictions and to permit a free, relatively unstructured discussion in which the instructor and the students bring out points raised in Nett and Macedo or the Notes or Questions to the extent they are relevant. An unstructured discussion of this material might be more likely to engage the students' attention but less likely to survey all the important arguments.

<u>Notes and Questions Following Nett and Macedo</u> (page 31):

Q1: Obviously there is no "correct" answer here, but the question does serve to alert students to the premises on which their arguments are based. Scanlan and Kent, in the cited article, argue that the moral considerations relevant to immigration -- those concerning the treatment of individual interests and rights--are rooted elsewhere in the United States legal system and in established "general norms of 'acceptable' political behavior." See page 64 of the cited article. Those principles, according to the authors, include rational laws and the political equality of all humans. They cite Bruce Ackerman, Social Justice in the Liberal State 89-95 (1980). Others, in contrast, believe that moral principles are not universal -- i.e., that they are confined by national boundaries not only because of varying cultural norms, but also because of state sovereignty.

Q2: It is not entirely clear whether Nett has in mind a national utilitarianism or a global utilitarianism. Many of the advantages he claims for open borders -- reducing misunderstandings, blunting nationalism, and avoiding social waste -- would seem applicable to every nation (the receiving nation, the sending nation, and even third nations). Thus that discussion would be consistent with both global and national utilitarianism. The costs that he acknowledges support either assumption. The temporary disequilibrium that cultural clashes could engender seems limited to the receiving nation. So, too, do the housing and employment problems that he cites. The disadvantages he acknowledges for *emigration*, in contrast, seem limited to the sending nation.

As to which approach is more appropriate, global utilitarians would argue that no nation's citizens have interests that are morally superior to those of the citizens of other nations; the interests of each individual should be weighed equally, regardless of citizenship. Proponents of national utilitarianism might argue (a) that it is human nature to feel diminishing concern for others as relationships with them become more remote; (b) that it is good for a nation to encourage loyalty; (c) that citizens owe a nation a duty of allegiance and therefore have a superior right to claim protection from that nation; and (d) that there are limits to one's obligation to render affirmative assistance, and that for this purpose national boundaries are one reasonable dividing line.

The Macedo excerpt can be used to raise the question: even if we prioritize the welfare of citizens, what constitutes welfare? If certain immigration policies improve economic prosperity as a whole but impose distributional costs, with whose welfare should we be concerned? Perhaps it is possible to reconcile Schuck's argument–that immigration policy should promote economic growth–with Macedo's concern about the impacts of immigration on the least well-off Americans. For example, the government could compensate the least well-off through tax transfers or investment of resources in other social programs, rather than restrict immigration. The Chang excerpt in Section D raises similar possibilities. Another issue that could be raised in discussing whether economic growth ought to be the overriding goal of U.S. immigration policy is the impact such a focus would have on sending societies, who would lose the human capital that they have invested in their own educational and social welfare systems to the United States. Are there ethical implications to promoting one's own prosperity through the recruitment of workers from less well-off societies?

Q3: The greatest hurdle for those who argue that immigration restrictions are morally justifiable is that these restrictions inherently discriminate on the basis of circumstances of birth. They do this by discriminating on the basis of citizenship, which in the overwhelming majority of cases (not all) is, in turn, legally determined solely by place of birth and identity of parents. Those born in the United States (or to United States citizen parents) normally receive citizenship and, with it, the legal rights to enter and to remain in the United States at will. Others are denied that right unless they meet the nation's immigration criteria and subsequently become naturalized. In most other contexts, our society condemns discrimination based on birth-determined classifications such as race, ethnicity, or gender. Yet place of birth and identity of parents are the official legal criteria for determining whether an individual will be subject to immigration restrictions. The question for the class is why such discrimination is morally permissible in the immigration context when it is impermissible in other contexts.

Some students will argue that the answer lies in either freedom of association or freedom of contract. The instructor might ask, however, why employers cannot justify racial discrimination on that basis. Here the student might take either of two tacks. First, the student might assert that the nation is qualitatively different from private employers. As to this, the instructor might observe that by law even the government may not generally discriminate on the basis of race. The second tack that the student might take, however, is that racial discrimination is different from citizenship discrimination. It is true that both are generally determined by circumstances of birth, but one might find persuasive some of the factors listed in item 3, subsections a-f. The instructor might wish simply to begin with those arguments.

a. The argument that "we were here first" does not seem morally defensible at first glance, but in other legal contexts precisely such a criterion is used. Homestead claims in property law and national claims of newly discovered territory in international law are examples. Moreover, one might argue that, if there is not enough room for everyone, those who arrived first should receive priority because they have developed deeper roots and consequently have stronger reliance interests. On the other hand, a similar argument would *not* generally be accepted as a justification for racial discrimination in employment. If the all-white management of a company refused to hire African-Americans, few today would suggest that the refusal is justified because the company was originally started by white employees or owners. Why is immigration different? Moreover, the chronological argument has not been accepted in other race discrimination contexts. That the European ancestors of many Americans arrived before the African slaves does not entitle the descendants of Europeans to discriminate against the descendants of Africans. In the U.S. context, the "we were here first" argument also ignores the historical reality that the Native Americans, and not the European immigrants, were "here first," as Professor Michael Olivas helpfully pointed out in an e-mail to the authors.

b. Counter-arguments might include these: (i) This rationale merely perpetuates a system of wealth based on blood lines. (On the other hand, is it really any different from laws that permit children to inherit property from their parents?) (ii) Although the parents contributed to their society, they also benefitted from it, and there is no systematic reason to assume that their contributions exceeded their benefits. (iii) It is wrong to relegate people to third world conditions simply because their parents were so relegated, especially if the particular receiving nation became wealthy by economically exploiting less developed countries.

c. There is some merit to this argument. If there is not enough room for everybody, it makes more sense to turn people away than to expel people from their homes to make room for others. Counter-arguments, however, would include the following: (i) People should share the bounty; it is better to give everyone a turn than to award permanent stay to some and no stay to others. (ii) The real question is what is meant by the premise that there is not enough room for everyone. A nation can almost always make room with enough sacrifice. The ultimate issue is how much sacrifice, if any, is morally required. (iii) It is not true that everyone now here has stronger ties to the United States national community than do all who are not here. Compare, for example, the child who was born in the United States but abandoned at birth, with a foreign-born child whose parents are in the United States. (On the other hand, perhaps morality does not require a perfect correlation; a high correlation might be enough).

d. Opponents of immigration restrictions might respond as follows: First, as a factual matter, citizenship and allegiance cannot be equated. Not all people who were born here, and not all people who were born abroad to United States parents, are in fact loyal to the United States. Conversely, many who wish to come to the United States would in fact be loyal if they were admitted. (Response: At least citizenship is a *reasonably* accurate proxy for allegiance.) Second, why have a concept of citizenship in the first place? Counties, cities, and other political subdivisions exist without a citizenship concept. Why does a nation need it? And if the answer to that latter question is that a nation must somehow define those who are to govern it, citizenship could simply be replaced by residence. See, e.g., Gerald M. Rosberg, *Aliens and Equal Protection: Why Not the Right to Vote?*, 75 Mich. L. Rev. 1092 (1977). That subject is taken up in chapter 13 (citizenship). Third, the analog to this argument would certainly be rejected in the race context. An employer could not justify refusing to hire an African-American by asserting that African-Americans as a class are less loyal to white employers than whites as a class would be. That argument would be rejected not only for lack of factual support, but also because the law would not permit such action even if the premise could somehow be demonstrated empirically.

e. Responses might include the following: First, the correlation is weak. The instructor could ask the class with whom a United States citizen living in northern Minnesota would be more likely to have values in common -- a Canadian citizen living in southern Manitoba or a United States citizen living in Hawaii. Probably correlations concerning culture and values would be much more likely to exist when distinctions are drawn between urban and rural, or between professional and unskilled, or between family members and single individuals, or between rich and poor. These are more significant cultural differences than are United States citizens versus others, especially after the first generation. Second, it is not obvious that cultural homogeneity is a worthwhile goal. Diversity and pluralism arguably have spurred this country's economic, cultural, and spiritual growth. Third, many believe that it is unrealistic to talk about the freedom *not* to associate when the freedom is asserted by a group as large as the population of the United States. The freedom of association argument, they would say, should be limited to smaller groups in which face-to-face encounters are more likely. See Lichtenberg, in item 5 of the Notes and Questions. Fourth, this argument certainly would not be accepted as a defense to race discrimination. Cultural differences among African-Americans, whites, and Asians would be neither a legal nor a moral defense to job discrimination.

f. Assume *arguendo* that the factual premise is correct -- i.e., that the welfare of the receiving nation would indeed decrease, and that the result would be unfairness as between their citizens and those of other, more restrictive nations. Under those circumstances, the moral question would be whether it is even worse to close the borders and thereby to preserve the even greater disparity between the citizens of the sending countries and the citizens of the receiving country. In theory, the laws of supply and demand should operate, and people should continue to come to the prosperous nation until the gap between the sending nations and that receiving nation closed (or at least became small enough that it is not worth the transaction costs to move). If that were to happen, then it is not obvious that unilateral action by the receiving nation would be less fair to the citizens of that receiving nation than the status quo is to the citizens of the sending countries. The argument posited in item 3.f lacks a precise analog in the job discrimination context. National law, with only limited exceptions, uniformly prohibits employers from discriminating; therefore, there is no analogous competitive disadvantage. In contrast, there is no world order that can force all nations to open their borders.

Q4: Ackerman's position requires an assumption that the preservation of the liberal polity is more important than admitting those people who seek entry after the breaking point is reached. If one assumes that the collapse of the liberal polity would mean the end of open borders, then perhaps one can justify temporary restrictions as an instrument for *maximizing* freedom of movement in the long run. The question could also be raised: what would it mean for the liberal polity to be threatened? As discussed in note 4 of Section C, evidence exists that ethnic diversity can undermine trust within communities. Does that fact alone threaten the liberal conversation enough to justify immigration restrictions?

Q5: Proponents of open borders would probably argue that immigration restrictions impede free association by preventing noncitizens from associating with United States family members, employers, and others with whom they seek to interact. Proponents would add that a majority of United States citizens have no right to deny to a minority of citizens the right to associate with whomever they wish. Restrictionists, in contrast, might argue that freedom of association includes a right to *limit* one's association to people of one's own choosing -- i.e., a right to exclude noncitizens. Existing members, in other words, should have a right to associate only with each other and with a legally limited population of new members. Proponents might respond, as noted earlier, that the freedom *not* to associate assumes less practical significance when the community is large. Lichtenberg, for example, argues that the emphasis on mutual commitment is strained when applied beyond the context of face-to-face encounters.

Q6: Differing views as to whether there is a moral duty to render reasonable assistance usually reflect the tension between personal autonomy, on the one hand, and the saving of life and limb, on the other hand. As for the applicability of Rawls to State action, one consideration is that a wider range of assistance is possible because the State has more resources than the individual. For example, a State might choose to help by dispensing foreign aid rather than by admissions (unless the noncitizen in question is a refugee). With respect to admission, however, the question on which students will differ is how great a sacrifice, if any, the receiving nation is morally required to make.

Q7: Proponents of open borders might respond as follows: First, this analogy simply exposes flaws in the entire notion of private ownership of property. Second, even if the system of private property ownership is accepted, the bundle of rights associated with property ownership is not unlimited. In torts, for example, a cause of action for trespass to property is subject to a necessity exception. (Response: This argument does not support the concept of open borders; it merely counsels some limitations on a nation's moral power to restrict immigration.) Third, proponents of open borders might reject the analogy on the basis that national territory differs from private property. The former is part of the jurisdiction exercised by a sovereign State. Opponents of open borders might respond by saying that in a country like the United States, where the citizenry is the sovereign, the distinction between jurisdiction and private ownership is not meaningful. Opponents of open borders might even argue that, if anything, the fact that the State is sovereign is an additional reason for recognizing a moral power to enact restrictions. Fourth, the anti-discrimination laws effectively limit one's property rights by prohibiting employers, hotel and restaurant owners, universities, and others from using their property in certain discriminatory ways. Why, then, is it morally permissible for nations to discriminate consciously on the basis of citizenship status?

Q8: Each of the regional arrangements mentioned in item 8 is, of course, sui generis, resting on historical, economic, and cultural ties among nations within the group. Moreover, migration issues between the United States and Canada differ significantly from those between the United States and Mexico. Mexico's population is much larger than Canada's, and Mexico is a much poorer country. Therefore the free migration of workers from Mexico to the United States could be a large-scale undertaking. In the long term, though, the historic links and geographic proximity of Mexico, the United States, and Canada, combined with the increasing difficulties of separating trade from labor migration, might well make the concept of a North American free migration zone politically realistic, as both Aleinikoff and Johnson have suggested.

The hope of many NAFTA supporters has been that it will spur long-term economic development in Mexico, thereby reducing the economic incentive for Mexicans to migrate to the United States. Then President Salinas of Mexico made this point graphically by suggesting that the United States must eventually choose between importing goods and importing people. The instructor could take up in class the question of what the impact of NAFTA has been on the United States. There are economic issues (effects on employment, consumer prices, and federal and state budgets); social issues; racial issues; environmental issues; and issues stemming from historical ties. (Much of the current United States territory formerly belonged to Mexico; in addition, as noted earlier, for many years the United States implemented farm labor policies specifically calculated to encourage large scale migration from Mexico).

SECTION C. IMMIGRATION, RACE, CULTURE, AND LANGUAGE

<u>Notes and Questions Following Schuck, Rodríguez, Brimelow, Johnson, and Perea</u> (page 59):

Q2: By definition, immigration fosters diversity with respect to nationality (in the sense of country of legal citizenship). The practical consequences of immigration also include diversity with respect to ethnicity, culture, language, religion, lifestyle, and politics/ideology. Since immigrants tend to be younger than the native population, immigration might also enhance age diversity. Students could be asked whether the government or other institutions ought to work to reduce the salience of certain types of diversity over time. Which is a greater threat to unity: religious or linguistic diversity? If it is the former–and an argument can be made that religion can create unbridgeable gaps between people–is it nonetheless desirable to tolerate or promote religious diversity?

Q3: Perhaps contemporary America is best described as an amalgam of all three. The melting pot metaphor seems unrealistic in a populous country in which people divide along so many lines – race, ethnicity, culture, language, religion, gender, sexual orientation, economic class, education level, politics, region, urban versus suburban and rural, and age, to name just some of the modern stress points. Yet the patchwork quilt model seems overstated too. Despite all the differences, many fundamental similarities bind the overwhelming majority of Americans – exposure to "American" media, rituals, customs, and lifestyle; a language that the vast majority speak; a commitment to the work ethic, democracy, and the rule of law; and a host of other commonly held values. The granola metaphor seems more convincing as an aspiration than as a description of either historical or contemporary reality; while the contributions of various ethnic groups have indeed inured to the benefit of the wider public, the degree of tolerance that the metaphor implicitly assumes surely has not yet been attained.

Q4: Brimelow offers examples of heterogeneous states that ultimately failed to withstand the stresses and strains of ethnic division. Julian Simon, however, observes that even states with relatively homogeneous populations have broken down. (He cites Yugoslavia.) See Brimelow, above, at 123-24. Brimelow responds that, if even homogeneous societies feel these sorts of strains, heterogeneous states have even less chance. Still, the fact that both relatively homogeneous and relatively heterogeneous states have sometimes succeeded and sometimes failed makes it difficult to read cause and effect into Brimelow's historical examples. At any rate, one can argue that the United States is an apt counterexample; for generations, the United States has been home not only to descendants of Europe, but also to millions of people of African, Asian, and Latino descent. The whole has held together, and America has prospered. Whether the success establishes that sovereign states generally do not need a common ethnic core to thrive, or whether it is a reflection of the "American exceptionalism" that Brimelow discusses, pluralism has not destroyed the United States yet. (Brimelow maintains that that is because, in the past, native-born and immigrant alike have shared a common commitment to "Americanism," a strategy that has now given way to affirmative action, multiculturalism, bilingualism, and other centrifugal forces. Perhaps he also believes that the United States simply hasn't reached the numerical breaking point yet but that that point will arrive soon if the immigration laws are not drastically altered.)

Students who express strong support for diversity, or skepticism of Brimelow's arguments, could be asked to grapple with the results of Putnam's research on the effects of ethnic diversity on trust and solidarity. Putnam himself contends that the response to such evidence should not be to promote homogeneity but to find ways of bridging the divides that diversity might create. What might some of those strategies be, and can you distinguish between the short-term costs and long-term benefits of diversity? Perhaps diverse societies over the long-haul are more likely to prosper, because a certain level of conflict and competition breeds innovation and ensures the constant influx of new ideas, generating awareness of the limitations (and contingencies) of one's own values and ways of living.

Q5: There is a broad social consensus that learning English is vital to immigrants' success in the United States. But should that consensus translate into policies that actively discourage the retention of the native language, that are agnostic as to whether immigrants retain their native language abilities, or that attempt to foster bilingualism? Instructors might focus this discussion on the education of English-language learners in the public schools, referencing note 16. Among the values of fostering bilingualism is that it promotes family values by enabling immigrant children to retain close bonds with their parents and grandparents, as well as larger ethnic communities. But if popular culture and public schooling both lead to quick language loss, is that really a cause for concern on the part of the state or society? Relatedly, what should be the goal of English-language instruction: teaching functional English and integrating students into the student body as quickly as possible, or ensuring long-term linguistic and cognitive development? Empirical evidence, some of which is cited in Note 16, suggests that the two goals are not necessarily compatible. At the same time, the same evidence underscores that keeping English-language learners segregated from their native-born peers can be damaging.

Instructors might also raise this question in the discussion of the Note on the English-only Movement. Perhaps the most important question to explore in relation to Official English is whether the adoption of a formal, official language will have any effect on the rate at which new immigrants integrate. Also, if an official language law includes restrictions on the ability of government officials to use languages other than English when dealing with the public, will the policy encourage integration by creating incentives for immigrants to learn English as quickly as possible, or will it make government inscrutable and services hard to deliver? Or both?

Q6: Brimelow argues that the 1965 repeal of the national origins quota system is responsible for Asian and Latino domination of immigrant visas in the past several decades. Actually, as Johnson points out, the 1965 law had nothing to do with the increased immigration of Latinos, who had been exempt from the quotas entirely before 1965. (The 1965 law, for the first time, put an annual numerical limit on the number of immigrants from the western hemisphere, which consisted mainly of North and South America.) It is true, however, that the 1965 law had the practical effects of increasing Asian immigration and decreasing European immigration. These results occurred because the immigration laws assigned highest priority to family reunification and because of various demographic and geographic factors. The real question is normative. The 1965 law simply repealed the affirmative preference that the national origins quotas had accorded immigrants from countries to whom large numbers of existing Americans had ancestral links. Its passage was part of the civil rights renaissance that the United States was then experiencing. If a premium on reuniting families is otherwise a valid and important goal, should that goal be sacrificed solely because it produces an ethnic balance of which Brimelow and others disapprove? To take that position would require the government to adopt, as an official position, the thesis that some ethnic backgrounds are more valued than others.

Q7: No. Supporters of the current policy did not arrive at their position out of an affirmative preference for nonwhite immigrants. To most supporters (certainly in 1965, and almost assuredly today as well), the fundamental value was racial neutrality. The philosophy of the immigration preference system, as modified by the 1965 reforms, was that it was important to reunify families and that that goal should not be constrained by racial preference. Since the current policy serves the goal of reunifying families (albeit inadequately), it is the critics of race neutrality who should have the burden of identifying the harm that results from disproportionate use of those preferences by immigrants of color. At this stage, you might raise the question of whether the principle of race neutrality should be rethought for other reasons–because it has a disparate impact on people from certain countries, such as Mexico, China, and India, where the demand for entry into the United States is particularly high.

Q8: Johnson marshals substantial evidence in support of his thesis. Brimelow's book, like much of the modern anti-immigration debate and in particular the rhetoric of the pro-Proposition 187 campaign, places great emphasis on the harm that Latino immigration supposedly has caused. Moreover, much of the criticism is directed at United States citizens of Latino descent rather than at Latino immigrants, often with little awareness of the differences. The conflation of the two groups supports Johnson's position that ethnicity, not immigration status, is often the true concern, or at least that the two concerns are closely intertwined.

Q9: As to the first part of the question, the Commission on Immigration Reform emphasizes the two-way nature of its proposed Americanization. Just as immigrants would be encouraged to learn English and to adapt to American institutions, so too native-born Americans would be reminded to respect such core values as democracy, equality, and tolerance. Brimelow, in contrast, envisions a one-way process that would seek to adapt immigrants to American values and institutions but not vice-versa.

As to the second part of the question, Perea points out that even United States citizenship has not always guaranteed people of color the rights traditionally associated with citizenship. Among the examples that he cites are the treatment of the Cherokees and the internment of the Japanese during World War II. Moreover, while he commends the Commission for including the education of native-born Americans in its proposed plan, he fears that in practice Americanization would be difficult to separate from its regrettable historical predecessors. In addition, he is concerned that, as Americanization develops, there will inevitably be pressures on immigrants (as well as citizens of color) to suppress their own languages and cultural practices. Thus, even the Commission's well intentioned brand of Americanization could ultimately harden into a renewed nativism. What is the alternative, however? Should the federal government not attempt to develop an integration policy? Should that task be left to private actors, the marketplace, or perhaps even to state and local governments?

Q10: Perea and the Commission accept that immigrants have an obligation to make certain adaptations. They stress the importance, for both the immigrant and the national community, of immigrants learning English, becoming involved in the political process, and acquiring an understanding of American civic and cultural values. Whether or not the sovereign prerogative of the state is alone enough to create such an obligation, almost all will agree that both the individual and the nation are better off when these basic tools are acquired. At the same time, Perea (and the Commission) think it crucial for native-born Americans to understand that "Americanization" is not inherently incompatible with learning and studying one's native language and continuing to value one's ethnic and cultural heritage. After all, cultural pluralism is also part of the American aspiration.

Q11: The irony is that the acquisition of citizenship is one of the most significant legal steps one can take on the road to what Brimelow would think of as assimilation. Yet he advocates new obstacles to naturalization. Some might regard the combination of positions as evidence that what Brimelow really fears is increased political power for immigrants of color. Chapter 10 of his book (not reproduced here) takes that tack more explicitly. On the other hand, Brimelow might respond that, while he would prefer to diminish immigration by people of color, he would also prefer that the law encourage those who are granted LPR status to do the sorts of things that will integrate them the most effectively into a common daily life. More rigorous English language and civic knowledge requirements, he might say, are part of that process.

Q16: For potential discussion topics, see suggestions for Q5.

SECTION D. THE ECONOMIC IMPACT OF IMMIGRATION

Because some of the issues raised in this section bear directly on the moral questions discussed in Section B–particularly the extent to which policy should account for the impact of immigration on the wages of United States citizens–instructors might wish to assign this section in tandem with Section B.

Notes and Questions Following Borjas, Chang, & The New Americans (page 81):

Q1: In favor of that position, one could argue that almost anything – including labor – can be purchased for the right price. Sometimes either the nature of the job duties or the amount of training time and expense can be great enough that native workers do not find employment in the particular occupation worthwhile. If neither the job duties nor the training investment can be reduced, perhaps a higher wage scale would solve the problem.

The opposing position might rely on free market globalization. The optimal wage scales should be determined like any other unregulated commodity – through the laws of supply and demand. Borders interfere with those laws. One might also argue that, if wages were permitted to soar to a level that would attract enough native workers, the prices of goods would be intolerable. All consumers benefit (albeit to differing degrees) when goods are priced low, and the higher levels of consumption will themselves stimulate further economic growth. Moreover, importing foreign workers for jobs that natives are unwilling to take (at the existing wage levels) frees up native workers to perform other economically productive work that they find preferable and that also contributes to the economy.

Q2: They seem inconsistent. If the net impact is a positive one, he should not use language that implies the opposite. His point is that, while the sum of the economic consequences is positive, there are winners and losers. His negative terminology, though misleading, is most likely a reference to the losers.

Q3: Yes. Borjas is referring to the differentials between high-wage and low-wage *native* workers. Chang is referring to *worldwide* wage differentials. Chang does not argue that immigration has no negative impact on native low-wage workers. But the two commentators' prescriptions differ considerably. For Borjas, the answer is to reduce immigration. For Chang, the answer is to continue high-level immigration because of its overall net positive economic impact (as well as its noneconomic benefits) but to address the possible negative impact on low-wage native workers through redistributive means such as tariffs.

Q4: The Borjas solution is to reduce immigration (or at least reduce immigration of unskilled or less skilled workers). Wage differentials are already undesirably wide, and a priority should attach to diminishing those differentials.

The utilitarian view is that the overall economic benefit is fairly universally assumed to be positive (as even Borjas acknowledges). Thus, the immigration laws should reflect what is best for the nation as a whole, not just for those who dropped out of high school. Moreover, immigration serves other social goals, including family unification, humanitarian relief for refugees, etc.

A third view, which also supports continued high-level immigration, is that with a net overall positive impact the priority should be on continuing immigration but finding ways to ameliorate any negative effect it might have on the lowest-waged earners. These strategies might include education, job training, and/or the tariff system proposed by Chang.

Q5: On the positive side, the proposed model simultaneously promotes a utilitarian immigration policy that generates a net economic benefit while nullifying or at least mitigating the undesirable redistributive effects of that policy. On the negative side, to the extent that the otherwise optimal tariffs reward high-wage immigrants and hurt low-wage immigrants, they constitute regressive taxes that transfer money from poor immigrants to wealthy ones. Whether that result is better or worse than the transfer of money from low-wage native workers to low-wage immigrants (assuming arguendo that that is indeed the case) hinges partly on the relative priorities one assigns to global justice and intra-state justice.

Q6: On the yes side, one might argue that native workers should not *have* to migrate in order to avoid losing job opportunities to foreign workers. And when firms relocate to take advantage of more plentiful and cheaper foreign labor, they reduce wages nationwide and damage the communities that they leave behind.

On the no side, immigration is, again, a net economic benefit for the native population as a whole. Moreover, labor mobility is not necessarily a bad thing and at any rate occurs all the time in the United States for reasons unrelated to immigration. As for the migration of firms, any harm to the community that is left behind must be balanced against the positive good to the new community. And, again, immigration serves other positive, noneconomic functions.

Q7: There is no doubt that immigrants are significantly younger than the native U.S. population or that an influx of young workers would have a positive fiscal effect on social security for the reasons explained by Simon. The counterarguments would be (a) the positives do not outweigh what immigration restrictionists perceive as the negative consequences of immigration; and (b) as Simon acknowledges, the effect on social security funds is a one-time event (while the other consequences of immigration persist forever). The first counterargument is of course a matter on which reasonable people disagree. Responses to the second counterargument might include (a) even a one-time effect can still be a very large effect, especially at a time when the future of social security is very much an issue; and (b) it is a one-time effect only in the sense that the effect occurs once *per immigrant cohort*. Simon, for example, would argue that substantial numbers of immigrants should be admitted continuously, so that the economic benefits could persist in the long term.

Q8: Simon's philosophical premises seem to be at least two-fold: First, he seems to assume that immigration policy is simply an instrument for achieving other ends, rather than a function of human rights or humanitarian compassion. Second, he seems to assume that the only ends worth considering are economic ones. See especially the first and fourth paragraphs reprinted in item 8. For example, he does not acknowledge any value either in promoting family unity or in conferring relief from persecution.

The most obvious problem with Simon's proposal is that not all have equal ability to pay. His answer would probably be that he is allowing successful bidders to pay their fees in future installments. But that answer is adequate only if either (a) those with lesser talents, experience, education levels, etc., were confident they could earn enough in the future in the United States to pay off what would certainly be a substantial debt, an assumption that seems unrealistic if the amounts they have to bid are formidable; or (b) the judgment were made that such people shouldn't be admitted, which assumes, again, that family unity programs, refugee programs, and other programs are worthless if not economically advantageous.

The analogous suggestion by economist Gary Becker suffers from similar flaws. He claims that the third world poor would not be excluded because they could either save the (for example) $50,000 or so or borrow it from a United States employer, a commercial lender, or the United States government (apparently without collateral). Many students and others assume Simon and Becker intended these proposals as satire. (They did not.)

SECTION E. IMMIGRATION, POPULATION, AND THE ENVIRONMENT

Notes and Questions Following The New Americans and Kraly (page 90):

Q1: If the two interests indeed conflict, one would expect a true environmentalist to feel more concern for the world environment than for the environment of one portion of the world - especially a portion defined solely by man-made boundaries. Considerations of environmental justice fortify that conclusion. One argument advanced by those Sierra Club members who favor liberal immigration laws is that, to the extent population correlates positively with resource consumption, it would be selfish and even unconscionable for the United States, a wealthy and powerful country with a relatively low population density but a high per capita consumption, to achieve environmental gains at the ecological expense of the poorer, less powerful, and already more densely populated states, typically in the third world.

The flip side of the coin is the familiar concept of sovereignty, coupled with the notion that a sovereign state has the right (or even the obligation) to press for maximum living standards for its own people - even when doing so disadvantages the people of other states. (Under either view, there remain the separate questions of (a) whether immigration in fact has such negative effects on the United States; and (b) if so, how those effects stack up against the social and economic gains associated with immigration.)

Q2: Kraly's main point is that the environmental impact of a given group is not necessarily proportional to its size. Different groups, for example, have different fertility rates (and, she might have added, mortality rates), as well as different levels of consumption. Therefore, one cannot simply translate given population increases into greater resource consumption. It matters who the additional people are, and one needs to know their environmentally relevant habits. In particular, one cannot assume that natural increases in the population (i.e., those due to births and deaths) have the same effects as increases attributable to net immigration.

More specifically, Kraly notes the following variables:

a. Where immigrants settle (for example, urban versus rural or suburban areas, which states within the United States, etc.) might differ from where the native-born settle and might therefore have different environmental consequences.

b. Population increases in some locations might affect resource availability in other locations.

c. Different migration categories - for example, permanent residents, temporary workers, tourists, and refugees - will obviously have different impacts.

d. Short-term and long-term environmental consequences must be distinguished.

e. Future advances in environmental technology (especially those that increase the efficient use of scarce resources) alter the impact of population increases. Some even believe that migration itself creates conditions that spur technological advances, presumably by increasing the incentive for further research, by stimulating the economic conditions that make additional research spending possible, and by adding talented foreign researchers to the population. (This is the third theory to which Kraly refers.)

The second part of the question is whether these various data are readily attainable. Certainly social science can (and to a large extent already has) compiled data on the fertility rates of various immigrant groups and their United States descendants, but the past does not necessarily reveal the future. Estimating consumption is also tricky, because so much depends on degree of economic success, a highly unpredictable variable in the long term even for the aggregate population - more so for particular ethnic groups.

Settlement patterns, at least for the short-to-medium term, might be more attainable. One can probably expect to find agricultural workers primarily in rural areas, unskilled workers primarily in urban areas, and professionals primarily in the suburbs. For work-related reasons, those patterns might be fairly durable, though forecasting which future immigrant groups are likely to fall into which category in the first place might be precarious. The same can be said of distribution by geographic region or state within the United States. Present patterns are known, but projecting future distributions is tricky. Predictions about the likely pace (and effect) of technological advance are unusually difficult; predicting how much of that pace will itself be triggered by migration is harder still.

Thus, one might be skeptical that serious research along the lines suggested by Kraly would unearth data capable of measurably improving the accuracy of the environmental predictions.

SECTION F. THE POLITICS OF IMMIGRATION

There are no Notes & Questions for this section. The instructor who wishes to discuss this material in class might simply begin with an open-ended question: What do you see as the major political forces or interest groups in play in the formulation of immigration policy? This discussion could cover not only the players and constituencies, but also the interests those players have in the outcome; how much sway the students believe the various players have; and what coalitions might emerge among these players.

SECTION G. IMMIGRATION AND NATIONAL SECURITY: AN INTRODUCTION

The instructor could either defer this entire subject until chapter 10 or solicit the students' initial thoughts on (a) how to reconcile national security needs with civil liberties generally and (b) more specifically, how to reconcile national security needs with the civil and human rights of non-U.S. citizens in an "immigration" country like the United States. The instructor could also invite preliminary discussion on the subject of ethnic profiling. See the Notes & Questions throughout chapter 10, and particularly those in section G of that chapter, for possible lines of inquiry.

SECTION H. IMMIGRANTS, SELF-IDENTITY, AND HOME

Notes and Questions Following Grunwald, Hernández-Truyol, Olivas, Saito, and Romero (page 107):

[Items 1 to 12 are informational.]

Q13: The Grunwald essay, despite limitations made evident by the writings that follow it, is a sensitive portrayal of many aspects of immigrant identity. Quite a number of students, especially those who are themselves immigrants or the children or grandchildren of immigrants, have said that Grunwald's essay does a remarkable job of articulating either their own deeply held feelings or those of their parents or grandparents about the identity changes that accompany immigration to a new and culturally different country. Even those who are not close to the immigrant experience have sometimes suggested that the essay helped them better understand what immigrating really signifies.

How universal are Grunwald's reactions? Some elements of Grunwald's United States experience -- especially those relating to his persistent feelings of dual identity -- would certainly seem universal, at least for those who immigrated after very early childhood. Other aspects -- the generally positive reception, the size of the gap between expectation and reality, his personal concern with mastery of the language, and the embracing of freedom -- depend much more heavily on the individual and, perhaps, on the culture from which that immigrant comes and American attitudes toward that culture.

Q14: Brimelow might either (a) contend that the negative experiences related by the minority writers are highly exceptional and that the pervasive attitudes they described are more imagined than real; or (b) argue that, to the extent the negative experiences are typical, they only confirm his point that multiethnic societies are not sustainable. Johnson and Perea might respond that (a) the stories are so common among so many people of color that it is impossible to dismiss them as anecdotal; and (b) that, at any rate, one does not solve problems of racial prejudice by blaming the victims.

Q15: Most students are likely to concede that they make precisely that assumption when they encounter people of Latino, Asian, or Arabic appearance, though many will answer that "it depends" on the presence of other cultural indicia, the physical surroundings, etc. Some will say that they simply make no assumptions at all. Rarely will a student make such an assumption about someone who looks African-American or white.

The second part of the question is why the assumptions are made for some ethnic groups but not others. Part of the answer is statistical. In the United States, the vast majority of those individuals whose appearance suggests either European or African descent are in fact native-born Americans. Given the current immigration patterns, the probability of native birth is not quite as high among individuals of Latino, Asian, or Arabic appearance. Still, the probability is high enough that the more logical reaction is to refrain from making any assumption at all. The authors whose excerpts you have just read suggest, at any rate, that it is not just a matter of demographics – that cultural differences, cultural unfamiliarity, and the psychological need for scapegoats all foster these presumptions of foreignness.

Q16: Storytelling is now a significant, and controversial, genre of academic scholarship. There are limits to the utility of stories. Because they are often hard to verify, their factual persuasiveness can hinge on the credibility of the storyteller (and that of the narrator, if the story is being related second hand). Assuming the story is true, the reader does not always know whether the experience was typical or aberrational. Moreover, it can be difficult to synthesize the stories into a coherent lesson.

Still, stories can accomplish things that traditional scholarship cannot, at least as easily. Since most rules of law reflect policy tradeoffs, stories help the reader understand the practical degree of harm that a given law or policy can cause. In the present context, for example, one can be against racial discrimination in the abstract but, without exposure to the everyday flavor of its manifestation, not fully appreciate how debilitating it can be when it is experienced by live, flesh-and-blood humans.

CHAPTER 2
IMMIGRATION AND THE CONSTITUTION

General Comments:

A. Covering Immigration and the Constitution: Consolidate or Spread Out?

Immigration law has its own unique constitutional principles. There are at least two fundamentally different ways to cover them. Approach #1 is to spread the constitutional cases throughout the book. One might, for example, include *Harisiades* in the section on speech-related deportation grounds, *Fiallo* in the section on the admission of children born out of wedlock, *Chadha* in the section on cancellation of removal, *Mezei* in the section on the exclusion of returning residents or in the section on detention, and so on. Approach #2 is to bring the important constitutional cases together into a single chapter.

This coursebook takes approach #2. Having taught the subject both ways, the original author has consistently found this approach more satisfying both for himself and for the students. Whenever he taught the constitutional cases in scattered form, he inevitably had to rehash repeatedly the constitutional principles the class had discussed at various earlier points in the semester, so that the students could discuss whatever refinement the new case adds. This was disruptive and a frustrating waste of class time. A single unit approach avoids that problem.

More important, the single-unit approach makes the study of these unique constitutional principles more coherent, better enables students to see the historical progression, and aids their understanding of the relationships between (a) substantive and procedural constitutional limitations and (b) exclusion and deportation. Finally, treating the constitutional cases as a unit permits and encourages the students to focus on the broad constitutional issues that these cases raise, rather than on the few specific substantive rules that the particular challenged statutes happen to embody. That emphasis seems appropriate. The statutory provisions at issue in most of the leading constitutional cases in immigration law are now repealed, modified, or of little importance today (e.g. the white-witness rule in *Fong Yue Ting*, the deportation ground for alien Communists in *Harisiades*, the illegitimate child rule in *Fiallo*, the legislative veto provision in *Chadha*, etc.). In contrast, the broad constitutional principles have had enduring impact.

There are a few exceptions. The importance of the *St. Cyr* case to the law of judicial review warrants placing that case in chapter 9, § B.6.b (habeas corpus). Also, apart from direct federal regulation of admission and expulsion, immigration lawyers and scholars have increasingly had to deal with other federal, and state, regulation of noncitizens. Common issues have concerned noncitizens' eligibility for various professions, government employment, welfare, and, given California Proposition 187 and related movements, public education. Those subjects are treated separately, in chapters 12 (undocumented migrants) and 11.C (significance of citizenship). At relevant points, the readings relate these issues to the plenary power doctrine cases of the present chapter.

B. Organizing Chapter 2.

Chapter 2 contains two parts. Section A addresses the sources of the congressional power to regulate immigration. Section B examines the limitations on those powers. Today the existence of a congressional power to regulate immigration is no longer in serious doubt; consequently, section A is short. It is a necessary section, however, because without it the cases that address the constitutional limitations on Congress's power to regulate immigration would be difficult to follow.

C. Helping Students Who Have Not Taken Constitutional Law

One additional advantage of consolidating the plenary power doctrine cases into a single chapter is that it becomes easy to include any general constitutional law information that the students need in order to understand and appreciate the immigration-related material. We try to keep these general constitutional law explanations short and simple. We also try to provide that information in connection with the specific cases to which it relates. For example, there are bare bones descriptions of the enumerated powers doctrine (section A); procedural due process (pages 154-55), including what it takes for something to be a liberty or property interest (*Roth*) and how you can tell how much process is due (*Mathews v. Eldridge*); substantive due process and "federal equal protection" (page 185); heightened ends and means scrutiny for equal protection purposes (page 188); and the usual first amendment standards (pages 190-91). In class, the instructor might wish to call specific attention to those textual discussions.

With this approach, we think the students who have not yet studied the Bill of Rights will still have enough information to be comfortable with the discussions in the book and in class. For those students who have studied the Bill of Rights, these bare bones summaries are useful refreshers.

D. How Much to Cover?

Some instructors might wish to cover this whole chapter, but most instructors in even three-unit courses will probably prefer selective coverage. See the sample syllabi.

SECTION A. SOURCES OF THE FEDERAL IMMIGRATION POWER

1. The Enumerated Powers

Subsection 1 lays out most of the arguments pro and con on the issue of whether any of the expressly enumerated congressional powers are broad enough to cover immigration. The text considers four arguably applicable sources – the commerce clause, the migration or importation clause, the naturalization clause, and the war clause (in each case, with the possible aid of the "necessary and proper" clause). This material is intended principally as background reading, but the instructor might wish to begin the discussion by summarizing, or having the class consider, these various arguments. That discussion sets the stage for the next subsection, which considers the implied constitutional powers and the *Chinese Exclusion Case*.

2. Implied Constitutional Powers

Chae Chan Ping v. United States [Chinese Exclusion Case] (page 120):

Chae Chan Ping, a Chinese laborer, entered the United States in 1875. In 1882, Congress enacted legislation excluding Chinese laborers, but the statute allowed those who were already living in the United States to leave and return, as long as they had obtained certificates attesting to their residence. Chae Chan Ping, armed with such a certificate, visited China. While he was en route back to the United States in 1888, Congress repealed the returning resident exemption, even for immigrants like Chae Chan Ping who had already obtained certificates and left. Consequently, he was excluded at the border. He challenged the 1888 law on the ground that it violated both an 1880 treaty with China and the Constitution. The Court acknowledged that the statute conflicted with the treaty but held that the statute would prevail because it was later in time.

As for the constitutional challenge, the immigrant argued Congress simply did not have the authority to pass the 1888 statute; it is not clear whether the argument was that Congress lacked any power to exclude noncitizens or merely that it lacked the power to exclude those noncitizens who had left the country in reliance on the certificate program. Although none of the congressional powers specifically enumerated in the Constitution refers explicitly to immigration, the Court held that the power to exclude noncitizens, being essentially the power of a nation to control its own territory, is inherent in the very notion of a sovereign state. Linking the exclusion of noncitizens to a nation's foreign policy, the Court then added that Congress's decision is "conclusive on the Judiciary."

Notes and Questions Following The Chinese Exclusion Case (page 123):

Q1: In one sense, Chae Chan Ping was not arguing that *any* specific provision had been violated; he did not, for example, invoke the due process clause or the federal equivalent of equal protection. Rather, his position was that Congress lacked any enumerated power that would affirmatively authorize this legislation. As to that, there are at least two possibilities. Possibly he was making the broad argument that there was no federal power to exclude noncitizens. Alternatively, he might have been arguing merely that there is no federal power to exclude those returning resident noncitizens who had left the United States and obtained certificates before the enactment of the challenged statute.

In another sense, Chae Chan Ping was implicitly invoking the Tenth Amendment. He was simply arguing that the Constitution nowhere delegated to Congress the power to exclude noncitizens. (Or at least he was arguing that the Constitution nowhere authorized Congress to exclude those returning resident noncitizens who were in possession of government-issued certificates of residence.) Of course, reliance on the Tenth Amendment would be tricky, since the implication would be that the individual states were meant to decide which immigrants to admit and which to exclude. On that point, see the subsequent discussion in section A.4 of this chapter and in chapter 12.

Q2: The seemingly innocuous word "it" has enormous importance here. The syntax suggests that the word "it" refers to the phrase "every independent nation." The Court, importantly, appears to have in mind the nation itself, not merely the Congress. The immigrant's argument might have been that the *nation's* power to exclude does not necessarily imply a *congressional* power to exclude. The Court seems here to be leaping from a principle of international law (a sovereign nation has a right to exclude noncitizens) to a conclusion about the allocation of power under United States domestic law (in the United States, that power rests with the federal government, not with the states). International law tells us nothing about how the United States, through its Constitution, allocates such power internally.

The Exchange, an important decision cited by Justice Field in the *Chinese Exclusion Case*, supports the above argument. Chief Justice Marshall's point in *The Exchange* was that only the nation itself can limit jurisdiction over its own territory; otherwise, the Chief Justice said, "A nation to that extent would be subject to a foreign power." Therefore, limitations on that power must be traced to the nation's consent. The instructor might ask whether the immigrant in the *Chinese Exclusion Case* could have accepted that principle and still prevailed. The answer to that question seems to be yes. He was arguing that the statute was unconstitutional. If he was right, then the nation, by adopting the Constitution, *has* consented to some limits on its own inherent power to control the use of its territory.

Q3: The Court further suggests, in the last paragraph of its opinion, in the first sentence, that this sovereign power is "delegated by the Constitution." That suggestion is important because the principle of enumerated powers requires that every federal action be affirmatively authorized by the Constitution. The question, of course, is *where* the Constitution provides a "sovereign" power of Congress to exclude noncitizens. The readings suggest three theories for finding an implicit delegation of such sovereign powers - a general power to regulate foreign policy (discussed in items 4 and 5 below); structural theories for finding a power over immigration (item 6 below); and an obviousness theory (item 7 and the excerpt that follows it).

Q4: As for the theory based on a general congressional power to regulate foreign affairs, there are at least two separate questions - whether such a power exists (taken up here) and, if it does, whether it encompasses the regulation of immigration (item 5). As to the former, Professor Henkin emphasizes that, although the Constitution contains a number of specific powers related to foreign affairs (war, treaties, international commerce, etc.), there is no provision expressly conferring a more general power to conduct foreign policy. The readings suggest the possibility that all belligerent actions might be brought within the war clause, while all peaceful overtures might be brought within the clause empowering Congress to regulate international commerce. The instructor might ask whether that viewpoint unduly stretches the constitutional language.

Q5: The Court in the *Chinese Exclusion Case* stresses that a foreign nation could invade the United States with hordes of its people and suggests that that possibility establishes a sufficient relationship between immigration and foreign policy. It is also possible to argue that an excluded immigrant could ask his or her country to intervene diplomatically with the United States. The instructor might ask the class how even a judicial decision to *admit* a given noncitizen or a given class of noncitizens could adversely affect foreign relations. For example, the person's admission could remove from the President an important bargaining chip that might otherwise have been used to obtain reciprocal concessions. (President Carter made this argument to justify selectively disadvantaging Iranian students in the United States during the 1980 hostage crisis.) Or, the admission of a given noncitizen might offend a third country that is an enemy of the admitted person's country or political movement.

There are real difficulties, however, in linking immigration to foreign policy. These difficulties will recur in the material in Section B on the limits of the federal power.

Q6: The structural arguments devised by Professors Aleinikoff and Martin are particularly thoughtful. The instructor can invite the students to argue against them. The students might argue, for example, that if the framers had intended to delegate a general sovereign power they would simply have said so. (They could still have listed certain specific powers as nonexclusive examples if they had wanted to do so.) Also, the assumption that the framers intended to delegate a general sovereign power would force the courts to decided what "sovereign" means; the instructor could ask the class how courts should decide which powers are "sovereign." Perhaps sovereign powers are those that sovereign States typically exercise. (And sovereign States do typically exercise the power to exclude noncitizens.)

Note on the Public Reaction to Asian Immigration (page 127):

This Note was included to give the students some of the flavor of the social and political environment in which the *Chinese Exclusion Case* was decided. It could be assigned solely as background reading or discussed in class. Questions that it raises might include: (1) Do you think public attitudes toward Asians actually affected the Court's opinion? (2) *Should* courts generally, or the Supreme Court in particular, consider contemporary public opinion when they decide important constitutional issues? (This question will enable students to think about whether judges "make" law or merely interpret it and, if they make law, what sorts of considerations they should factor in.) (3) Are there identifiable parallels between the anti-Asian sentiments that you just read about and the anti-immigrant sentiments emanating from California and some other border states today? Are there additional parallels with the modern treatment of Arab and Muslim immigrants? Earlier readings (chapter 1, sections C, F, and H) consider the links between race and immigration more directly.

3. Beyond the Constitution

This subsection is intended only as background reading. The instructor can either leave it at that or ask the students to work through the steps in Justice Sutherland's syllogism.

4. Residual State Power

This subsection too is intended principally as background reading. The issue of the permissible limits of state regulation of noncitizens will resurface in chapters 12 and 13. Nonetheless, the instructor might wish to get the students to articulate the difference between the uniformity argument of *Henderson* and the embroilment argument of *Chy Lung*. The instructor can also ask why uniformity is important in this context. The likely response is that, without uniformity, those noncitizens whose harmful qualities subject them to exclusion in one state might simply go to other, more liberal states. Moreover, once admitted to those latter states, the freedom of interstate travel will enable them to make their way to states that might have excluded them as an initial matter. Border Patrol officials do not police state lines.

SECTION B. LIMITS TO THE FEDERAL IMMIGRATION POWER

1. The Foundation Cases

General: In this section it will be assumed that Congress has the power to regulate immigration. The questions then become: (a) What, if any, are the constitutional limits to that power and (b) How much power do the courts have to pronounce those limits? The *Chinese Exclusion Case*, explored in the previous section for its analysis of whether *any* congressional power to regulate immigration exists, is also instructive here. The introductory paragraph of subsection B.1 asks the students to re-read the last three printed paragraphs of the opinion in the *Chinese Exclusion Case*. It is difficult to say whether the Court regarded the congressional decision as conclusive simply because the Court found the particular statute constitutional or, rather, because the Court believed it lacked power to decide the constitutionality of the statute. The language is probably consistent with either reading, but by that stage of the opinion the Court had already found the statute constitutional. There is at least a good chance, therefore, that the Court did not mean to imply that the constitutionality of immigration legislation is always nonjusticiable.

Nonetheless, the case has generally been read for the broader proposition that federal statutes excluding noncitizens are not subject to review for constitutionality. Under that assumption, the question is whether the decision is compatible with *Marbury v. Madison*, where the Supreme Court explicitly asserted the power to declare an Act of Congress unconstitutional. To see whether the two cases are reconcilable, the students must examine the last paragraph of the *Chinese Exclusion Case*. The instructor should ask the students to identify the rationales articulated in that paragraph for treating immigration cases differently and then to evaluate those rationales.

The first rationale contained in that paragraph is that the exclusion power is "an incident of sovereignty." Assuming *arguendo*, however, that the power is sovereign, does it follow that a court is barred from reviewing a particular exercise of that power? Interestingly, the Court adds that these sovereign powers are "delegated by the Constitution." Even if that is so, however, there seems at least as much reason to put constitutional restrictions on an implied sovereign power as there is to limit an express enumerated power.

A second rationale might be inferred from the Court's observation that noncitizens had been given a "license" to return to the United States after their departure. The Court says this license is held "at the will of the government, revocable at any time, at its pleasure." Perhaps the suggestion here is that remaining in the United States is, for a noncitizen, merely a privilege, not a right. The students will see later in the materials that labeling an interest a privilege rather than a right no longer conclusively determines whether constitutional safeguards apply.

A third rationale that might be inferred from this paragraph stems from the last sentence. The Court suggests that any complaint must be made to the *political* department of our government. The Court seems to imply here that any question as to the constitutionality of a federal immigration statute is inherently a political question. The Court does not explain in this paragraph why that is so. Perhaps the Court has in mind the connection between immigration and foreign affairs discussed earlier in the opinion. That rationale recurs in the readings that follow.

The instructor might wish to advise the students at this point that, despite what they might have assumed, the *Chinese Exclusion Case* has never been overruled. In fact, modern decisions have often cited it to support statements about the breadth of the congressional power to exclude noncitizens.

Ekiu v. United States (page 134):

Ekiu, a citizen of Japan, was excluded at the border on the ground she was likely to become a public charge. She said she was to meet her husband, but the immigration inspector did not believe her. She sought habeas relief, offering evidence of her ability to support herself. The district court denied relief, interpreting the statute as making the immigration inspector's factual findings unreviewable in court. She argued that, if so interpreted, the statute violates procedural due process. The Supreme Court acknowledged that an excluded immigrant has been restrained of liberty and therefore has the right to seek habeas relief. It held on the merits, however, that due process does not require an opportunity for judicial review of executive factfinding.

Questions Following Ekiu (page 135):

Q1: Here the students should distinguish three propositions: (a) As a matter of international law a *nation* has the power to exclude noncitizens; (b) As a matter of domestic United States constitutional law the *federal* government (as opposed to the states) possesses that power; and (c) Within the federal government, the power is entrusted to the two *political* branches, not the courts.

Q2: In this question the students have to figure out how far the Court meant to go. At the very least, the Court held that it is constitutional for Congress to entrust to administrative officers the final determination of the facts on which the exclusion of a noncitizen depends. The more difficult question, raised by the hypothetical statute that explicitly permits administrative officials to use whatever procedure they see fit, is whether the Court meant to go so far as to hold that the congressional choice of exclusion procedure is simply not reviewable for constitutionality. Here the students should be reminded that the breadth of the holding requires consideration of both the Court's *language* and the Court's *rationale*.

The pertinent language appears in the last reprinted sentence of the opinion. The Court says that, as to noncitizens who reside outside the United States, "the decisions of executive or administrative officers, acting within powers expressly conferred by Congress, *are* due process of law" (emphasis added). This language is absolute enough to suggest an unreviewable congressional power to exclude at least those noncitizens who do not yet reside in the United States.

Guidance can also be extracted from what the Court does *not* do. Nowhere in the opinion does the Court rely on the adequacy or fairness of the administrative process. Since the Court never examines whether the process was fair, it can be inferred that the Court considered that fact irrelevant and that, again, the Court simply will not review the constitutionality of the congressionally prescribed exclusion procedure.

Finally, the Court in *Ekiu* reaches its conclusion that Congress may entrust the final decision to administrative officers by reasoning that the exclusion power belongs to the *political* department because it involves international relations. That sounds like political question reasoning; combined with the fact that the Court does not examine the adequacy of the process given, it suggests a broad holding that the exclusion power belongs *exclusively* with Congress. If that is the case, and if the immigrant had challenged a statutory provision that dispensed with even administrative procedural safeguards, the Court would have reached the same result.

Q3: This question examines the adequacy of the precedent (two cases) that the Court cites to support its conclusion that the exclusion power rests with the political department of the federal government. The *Head Money Cases* clearly do not support that proposition. They held only that the commerce clause empowers Congress to regulate immigration. Nothing in those decisions spoke to the constitutional limits on that congressional power. The *Chinese Exclusion Case* arguably supports the result in *Ekiu*, but the plaintiff in the *Chinese Exclusion Case* had argued only that the statute was invalid because no constitutionally enumerated power affirmatively authorized it. The Court held that the power was inherent in sovereignty. In *Ekiu*, in contrast, the argument is based on procedural due process, an individual rights limitation. Ekiu might well have argued that the mere existence of a federal power to exclude noncitizens does not imply the absence of constitutional limits. The instructor can illustrate this distinction by hypothesizing a federal statute that prohibits nationally syndicated newspaper columns from containing statements critical of the government. Congress has the power to regulate interstate commerce, and without question this statute fits that description. But the statute is unconstitutional nonetheless because it fails to comport with the affirmative limitations contained in the Bill of Rights -- in this hypothetical, the First Amendment. So, from a case holding only that Congress needs no enumerated power, the Court progresses to a holding that Congress need not worry about procedural due process either.

Fong Yue Ting v. United States (page 136):

Under an 1892 statute, all Chinese laborers became deportable unless they were living in the United States on the date of enactment and could obtain a certificate attesting to that residence. If found without such a certificate, they were to be taken before a court and ordered deported unless they could show unavoidable cause for not having a certificate and could prove, by the testimony *of a white witness*, that they lived in the United States on the enactment date. Three resident noncitizens who were ordered deported for failure to produce a white witness sought habeas to challenge that requirement on procedural due process grounds.

The Court extended to deportation several of the principles announced in the *Chinese Exclusion Case* and *Ekiu* in the context of exclusion: that in international law every sovereign state has the power to deport noncitizens; that in the U.S. the Constitution vests that power in the federal government (not the states); and that within the federal government the Constitution vests that power in the political branches (not the courts). On the last point the Court suggests that the constitutionality of a federal deportation provision is a political question. The Court also holds that deportation is not punishment and that, *therefore*, these plaintiffs have not been deprived of due process. This is the first case to invoke the principle of plenary congressional power in the context of deportation. All three dissenters emphasized the differences between exclusion and deportation.

<u>Notes and Questions Following Fong Yue Ting</u> (page 147):

Q1: On the international law issue, Vattel emphasizes a nation's right to protect itself, while Ortolan stresses that the noncitizen's presence is purely by "permission," or by "tolerance." Ortolan's position appears to be a restatement of the right/privilege distinction.

Q2: The instructor here might explore how Congress's decision whom to deport might affect, or be affected by, foreign policy considerations. First, Congress might want to deport citizens of countries with which the United States is at war, or for that matter even citizens of countries that, although not at war with the United States, are nonetheless unfriendly. In that situation deportation is used as retaliation; *refraining* from deportation might remove a bargaining chip. Along the same lines, Congress or the executive might wish to please a third country by deporting a given noncitizen who is an enemy of that latter country, especially if the person in question is a government official. Second, Congress might, in order to build or preserve friendship with another nation, deliberately refrain from deporting someone who might otherwise have been deported.

The instructor can also question the propriety of deporting people to serve foreign policy needs. If the person entered the United States illegally, then such deportation is difficult to oppose unless it is meted out selectively. If the person is an LPR, however, then the idea of deportation designed solely to serve foreign policy needs is more problematic. Subsections (a) and (b) of question 2 raise possibilities for arguing that, given an exclusion power, a deportation power is needed for practical reasons. Both those arguments are probably best deferred until chapter 7, where the students will consider the purposes of deportation.

Q3: The hypothetical statute described in this question raises the issue whether there are *any* bases on which a court may invalidate a provision of a federal deportation statute. On the one hand, the language of the Court's opinion suggests that the Court cannot review a congressional decision concerning either the substantive criteria or the procedures for deportation. For example, on page 140, the Court says that the question is "one to be determined by the political departments of the government." The sentence does go on to speak of the judicial department's not being able to properly express an opinion upon "the wisdom, the policy, or the justice" of the statute. Taken alone, that latter language might be read merely to express the common sentiment that a court should distinguish between the constitutionality of a statute and the wisdom of that statute. In the context of the preceding clause, however, the paragraph should probably be read to mean that the congressional decision is not subject to judicial review even for constitutionality. That interpretation is fortified by the Court's earlier statement, see page 139, first paragraph, that Congress may expel noncitizens "whenever in its judgment their removal is necessary or expedient for the public interest." That language similarly implies an unfettered congressional power to deport.

On the other hand, the Court in this case ultimately reviews Congress's reason for the white-witness requirement. Possibly, therefore, the Court believes only that this particular procedure does not violate due process. Even on that latter assumption, however, the Supreme Court's scrutiny was not very assertive. The Court simply speculates that Congress's reason for the white-witness rule was that it believed Chinese witnesses were more prone to lie under oath. The Court then accepts that assumption at face value.

Q4: This question raises some issues that pervade the modern immigration cases as well. The instructor might wish to defer some of the discussion until later. The basic question is why the Court is showing so much deference to Congress. What is it about immigration regulation -- in this case deportation -- that has engendered this special restraint? One theme recurring in *Fong Yue Ting* is that the constitutionality of a deportation statute is a question for the political departments. This is the same as the Court's reason for assigning immigration to the federal government rather than to the states. As the Notes point out, however, it is difficult to apply this rationale to the statute challenged in *Fong Yue Ting*. The white-witness rule obviously was not enacted to enhance our foreign relations; it was antithetical to United States relations with China but was pursued nonetheless for domestic purposes. Whether that is the kind of judgment a court should make, however, is another question. Some might argue that a court has no way to predict the foreign policy consequences of a decision whether to deport a given class of noncitizens. Others, however, will say that at least sometimes the presence or absence of a foreign policy objective is too obvious to ignore. For this purpose, a court might wish to look at how selective the provision is with respect to the foreign countries involved, the legislative history of the provision, the prevailing political mood, etc.

Another theme apparently persuading the Court to display special deference is the idea that the immigration power is inherent in the very notion of a sovereign State. On that subject the dissenting opinion of Justice Field is quite interesting. The Notes ask whether his dissent can be reconciled with his majority opinion in the *Chinese Exclusion Case*. Two possibilities suggest themselves: One, compatible with the results he reaches in the two cases, is that he believes there is an inherent sovereign congressional power to exclude noncitizens but not to deport them. The problem with that reading, of course, is that in *Fong Yue Ting* Justice Field makes clear that he believes the federal government takes <u>no</u> power by virtue of sovereignty. A second possibility, again somewhat problematic in light of the broad language he uses, is that Justice Field believes in sovereign powers that are *delegated by the Constitution* (as he said in the *Chinese Exclusion Case*) but not in *extraconstitutional* sovereign powers. If that is his belief, however, it is not clear that he really differs from the majority in *Fong Yue Ting*.

Q5: This question asks how the Court that decided *Fong Yue Ting* would have responded to a substantive constitutional challenge -- for example, one based on the First Amendment or on equal protection grounds. The answer is not entirely clear from the opinion, but there are at least three indications that the Court would similarly have exhibited exceptional deference to Congress: First, the Court's reference to political questions (which it assumes the constitutionality of a deportation provision to be) suggests that the Court might view a substantive challenge as equally nonjusticiable. Second, the earlier discussed paragraph in which the Court says that Congress can constitutionally expel noncitizens whenever "in its judgment" removal is necessary or expedient would seem to apply with equal force to substantive constitutional challenges. Third, the Court in *Fong Yue Ting* does in fact uphold a racially discriminatory statute. It does so without seriously examining whether Congress had a valid justification for discriminating in this way. That fact again suggests that the Court did not intend to confine its holding to procedural challenges.

Q6: The key language in Justice Brewer's dissent appears on page 142, first full paragraph, first sentence: "I deny that there is any *arbitrary and unrestrained* power to banish *residents*" (emphasis added). Note first that he speaks only to the power to banish *resident* noncitizens, not to the power to banish either nonimmigrants or undocumented persons. Note also that he does not even go so far as to say Congress may not deport LPRs; his point is merely that such power is not unlimited. Even if the power can be implied, he says, it must be exercised compatibly with constitutional limitations.

Q7: The various parts of this question examine possible reasons for distinguishing between exclusion and deportation in the context of due process.

a. Without explanation, it is difficult to understand the basis for Justice Brewer's dissent in *Ekiu*. Possibly Justice Brewer considered Ekiu to be physically and lawfully within United States territory at the port of entry. Or maybe his dissent was based on statutory interpretation grounds.

The instructor might ask the students whether, assuming the Constitution has no extraterritorial effect, that fact adequately distinguishes the *Chinese Exclusion Case*. The immigrant in that case was physically within United States territory; he was in San Francisco Bay. Justice Brewer, of course, might respond by conceding that the person was physically within United States territory, but stress that this was so only for purposes of inspection. Constitutional rights arguably should not turn on whether the government sets up its inspection posts on one side of the boundary or another.

Students might wish to contrast the position of the three immigrants whose cases have now been studied. In *Fong Yue Ting*, a resident noncitizen was being deported. In the *Chinese Exclusion Case*, a returning resident noncitizen was being excluded. And in *Ekiu*, a noncitizen seeking initial entry was being excluded.

In the modern era, this extraterritoriality issue has come up in two important settings. First, the instructor might point out that many Haitian asylum-seekers have been intercepted by United States vessels on the high seas. Their challenges to the lawfulness of their exclusions have generally failed in the courts, specifically because the government actions take place outside United States territorial waters. This issue will be examined in more detail in the context of asylum (chapter 11). Second, in *Rasul v. Bush*, 542 U.S. 466, 124 S.Ct. 2686, 159 L.Ed.2d 548 (2004), the Supreme Court applied the federal habeas statute to the noncitizen detainees on Guantánamo.

b. Most of the possibilities are laid out in the question itself. Generally an excluded noncitizen has less at stake than does the deported LPR, but there are many variables. For example, the excluded individual might be either an initial entrant (Ekiu) or a returning LPR (Chae Chan Ping, the plaintiff in the *Chinese Exclusion Case*). Second, even an initial entrant can be a family member, a refugee, or some other person with important individual interests at stake. Third, a deported individual might be an LPR, a lawful nonimmigrant, or an undocumented migrant.

c. For present purposes, the most important part of this sub-question is the Court's reason for holding that deportation is not punishment. As the text observes, the Court's reasoning is not convincing. The instructor might ask the students, however, whether Justice Brewer's reasoning is any more convincing. Do consequences become punishment solely because they are harsh? Surely the answer to that question is no; a car accident can be at least as harsh but is not punishment. So the question becomes whether the *purposes* of deportation coincide with those of punishment. Students will be in a better position to address this question in depth once they have studied deportation in chapter 7. For now, the instructor could observe that today one of the main purposes of deportation is to remove from society those people whose presence Congress considers injurious to the common welfare. Certainly similar sentiments could be expressed about the incapacitation theory of criminal incarceration.

Q8: The instructor might briefly consider whether deportation constitutes a "liberty" interest, within the meaning of the *Roth* case. The test is whether remaining here is "essential to the orderly pursuit of happiness by free men." Certainly an LPR could claim to satisfy such a test, and probably others can as well. As the students will see later, modern courts assume that deportation implicates a liberty interest and focus principally on whether the process afforded was all that was due. The more troublesome question in this case is whether, assuming the due process clause applies, the white-witness rule satisfies due process. Such a conclusion seems doubtful. The personal stakes are quite high, and the factfinder could easily make individualized credibility judgments rather than rely on statutorily imposed racial stereotypes. To do so would not even require much more government time or expense. Hence, under the formulation contained in Mathews v. Eldridge, the white-witness rule would surely be struck down today.

2. Modern Developments

a. Procedural Due Process in Exclusion Cases

Shaughnessy v. United States ex rel. Mezei (page 156):

Mezei, a long-term LPR, left the United States to visit his ailing mother in Rumania. During the trip, he passed through Hungary. For about 20 months, the Hungarian officials would not allow him to leave. Eventually they granted him an exit visa, the U.S. consulate issued an entry visa, and he sailed to Ellis Island. There he was excluded on national security grounds. Under a special regulation, the Attorney General classified the information as confidential and thus declined to specify the basis for the charge or conduct a hearing. Because no other country would take Mezei, he was detained indefinitely on Ellis Island. He sought habeas to challenge both his detention and his exclusion on due process grounds. The Court held that, for an excluded noncitizen, due process is whatever Congress says it is. Neither the fact that he was a returning resident nor the fact that in his case the practical consequence of exclusion would be indefinite detention altered that basic principle. The Court distinguished on narrow grounds a case in which a returning resident had been assumed to be entitled to invoke the due process clause. The dissent would have held that the due process clause applies at least when exclusion is accompanied by detention, and that in this case the lack of a hearing violated due process.

General Notes and Questions Following Mezei (page 163):

Q2: As for the breadth of the Court's holding in *Mezei*, there are indications that the Court truly means to hold that a noncitizen may not challenge a congressional exclusion decision on due process grounds. At the bottom of page 157, for example, the Court states that the exclusion power is "a fundamental sovereign attribute exercised by the Government's political departments *largely immune from judicial control*" (emphasis added). In the next paragraph, second sentence, the Court quotes *Knauff*, stating: "Whatever the procedure authorized by Congress is, it is due process as far as an alien denied entry is concerned." Further, given the actual result the Court reaches, the holding extends to the case in which the practical consequence of exclusion is indefinite detention.

On the other hand, in the last paragraph of the majority opinion, the Court does rely on the fact that national security considerations were present. Possibly that fact limits the holding. Arguably too, the Court means to leave an out for returning residents. In quoting from *Knauff*, the Court qualifies its point by referring specifically to the person who is "on the threshold of initial entry." And on page 158 the Court concedes that "a lawful resident alien may not captiously be deprived of his constitutional rights to procedural due process." Despite these concessions, however, Mezei was held not entitled to procedural due process. Perhaps the Court considered him no longer to be a permanent resident? Or perhaps the Court felt simply that the deprivation of his due process rights was not "captious"?

Notes and Questions on the Exclusion of Returning Residents: Some Cracks in the Plenary Congressional Power (page 164):

Q1: The gut instincts of most students and of others is that returning residents should have broader procedural rights than initial entrants. This question, however, requires the students to decide whether that distinction should go to the very applicability of due process or merely to its content.

As to content, the *Mathews v. Eldridge* formulation includes consideration of the magnitude of the private individual interest at stake. Usually (but obviously not always), the interest at stake for a returning resident is greater than that for an initial entrant. Also, there is at least some reason to treat the exclusion of a returning resident as being similar to the deportation of a permanent resident. If the person had not made a temporary visit abroad, there is no question that procedural due process would have been a prerequisite to deportation, as the students will later see in *Yamataya*.

As to the applicability of due process, most of the reasons traditionally asserted for denying due process to excluded noncitizens are ones that would not seem to rest on the distinction between initial entrants and returning residents – the notion that the Constitution is inapplicable outside United States territory; the idea that the constitutionality of a law excluding noncitizens is a political question; the theory that the power to regulate immigration is "sovereign" and therefore unreviewable; and the tendency to label the admission of a noncitizen as a privilege rather than a right. Whatever the general merit of these theories, their logic does not seem to rest on the distinction between initial entrants and returning residents.

Q2: The counter-argument to Justice Jackson's objection to *in camera* proceedings would be that, even without counsel, the proceeding does *some* good. The judge might find the government argument unconvincing and order the government to choose between disclosing evidence and dropping the case. At least this procedure gives the individual more of a chance than holding no hearing at all. See also the discussion, in chapter 10, § D.2, of IIRIRA's in camera procedure for certain terrorism cases involving classified information.

Q3: Reconciling these cases is not easy, and the problem is further complicated by the decision in *Plasencia*, which is excerpted in item 4 of the Notes and Questions. The Court in *Mezei* distinguishes *Kwong Hai Chew* in four ways: (a) Chew received pre-clearance, whereas Mezei simply left on his own; (b) Chew was on a United States ship, while Mezei was behind the "Iron Curtain;" (c) Chew was gone only four months, whereas Mezei was gone nineteen months; and (d) In *Chew* there was the special consideration that under the 1940 Nationality Act maritime service didn't break the period of continuous residence for purposes of naturalization.

Q5: As for the question of which excluded noncitizens, if any, ought to receive procedural due process, there are a number of possible answers. They include the following:

a. None. The Constitution lacks extraterritorial force.

b. Returning residents who were absent only a short time. One could argue they should not lose rights simply because of short and otherwise innocuous visits. The instructor here might or might not wish to mention *Fleuti*, discussed in chapter 7, which considers an analogous statutory question.

c. All returning residents. Why should *any* visit that does not result in the loss of permanent resident status destroy due process rights? Also, such a test avoids the need for complex line-drawing.

d. All noncitizens. Some might say it would be too expensive to afford due process to all arriving passengers, but how many are really excluded at the border? Normally, except for asylum claimants (who obviously have important individual interests at stake), only those noncitizens who possess visas would have an incentive to appear at the border and apply for admission. The lack of a visa makes almost all other noncitizens inadmissible.

Notes and Questions on the Detention of Excluded Noncitizens (page 166):

Q1: The Court in*Mezei* refuses to distinguish exclusion from indefinite confinement. It regards the latter as just part and parcel of the admission process. Mezei is free to go anywhere except into the United States. (See Justice Jackson's sarcastic response). Should the prospect of indefinite detention have made any difference in this case? Some would argue that, no matter what the legal fiction, the government simply cannot imprison a person for life without a hearing. Others would argue that foreign countries should not, by the simple device of refusing admission, be able to force the United States to accept a noncitizen whom the United States does not want. The counter-argument would be that other countries should indeed be able to do precisely that if the person in question is a lawful permanent resident of the United States.

b. Procedural Due Process in Deportation Cases: More Cracks in the Plenary Congressional Power

Yamataya v. Fisher (page 171):

Four days after her admission, Yamataya was ordered deported on the ground that she had been inadmissible at entry as a pauper and as likely to become a public charge. She challenged her deportation on procedural due process grounds, arguing that she did not understand English, that she hadn't realized even that the proceedings involved deportation, and that therefore she had not had an adequate opportunity to be heard. The Court interpreted the statute as requiring notice of the charges and an opportunity to be heard, because it believed that executive officers could not constitutionally deprive a person of liberty without those basic safeguards. The Court went on to hold, however, that on these facts Yamataya had not been denied an opportunity to be heard and thus had received all the process that was due.

Notes and Questions Following Yamataya (page 173):

Q1: The statutory interpretation principle to be gleaned from *Yamataya* is that a court should not give a statute an interpretation that will render the statute unconstitutional, unless a contrary interpretation "plainly and palpably appears."

Q2: It seems likely that the Court in *Yamataya* intended its holding to encompass congressional action as well as executive action. The Court, after all, interpreted a *statute* so as to avoid constitutional objections. That rationale would not make sense unless the Court was assuming that Congress is in fact restrained by due process.

Q3: It is difficult to reconcile *Yamataya* with *Fong Yue Ting*, unless *Fong Yue Ting* is interpreted narrowly as holding only that procedural due process is not violated either (a) by reasonable government restrictions on the type of admissible evidence (and that the white-witness rule is reasonable); or (b) by the fact that administrators, rather than judges, do the fact-finding. As discussed earlier in connection with *Fong Yue Ting*, however, it seems unlikely that the holding was meant to be that narrow.

Q5: The Court acknowledges the difficulties but describes them as simply her "misfortune." Yet it is difficult to see how the procedure in this case could be said to have provided either notice of the charges or a reasonable opportunity to be heard, the two most fundamental elements of modern due process.

Q7: This question synthesizes the *Yamataya* and *Mezei* materials. In each case the noncitizen was a permanent resident who claimed a deprivation of procedural due process. Yamataya, who was in deportation proceedings, was held entitled to challenge Congress's decision on due process grounds. Mezei, who was in exclusion proceedings, appears to have been held *not* to have that right. Earlier, in the Notes and Questions following *Fong Yue Ting* (question 7), there was an opportunity to discuss the relevant differences between exclusion and deportation. At this stage the instructor could revisit that discussion, asking whether permanent resident status affects any of the rationales for distinguishing the constitutional safeguards required for exclusion proceedings from those required for deportation proceedings. There were four such rationales:

a. An excluded noncitizen is outside United States territory. This rationale would not be affected by the distinction between initial entrants and returning residents. In this respect, therefore, exclusion of a returning resident is more like the exclusion of an initial entrant than it is like deportation of a permanent resident.

b. Deportation takes away what was lawfully acquired. In this respect, in contrast, the exclusion of an LPR is more like deportation. Either event effectively eliminates a lawfully acquired residence.

c. A returning resident has greater individual interests at stake than does an initial entrant. Again, in this respect, the exclusion of an LPR is more like deportation.

d. It is difficult to see the exclusion, even of a returning resident, as punishment. In this respect, therefore, the exclusion of a returning resident is more like the exclusion of an initial entrant (although the majority in *Fong Yue Ting* at any rate disallowed the characterization of deportation as punishment).

c. Substantive Applications of the Plenary Power Doctrine

Harisiades v. Shaughnessy (page 177):

Three long-term LPRs were members of the Communist Party. They left the Party at a time when present membership, but not past membership, was a ground for deportation. Congress subsequently made past membership a deportation ground, and the former INS then brought deportation proceedings. All were ordered deported. They challenged the constitutionality of the new deportation ground on several fronts: that substantive due process bars the deportation of LPRs; that substantive due process at least requires a reasonable basis for the particular deportation ground; that this deportation ground violates the first amendment (freedoms of speech and assembly); and that the retroactive application of the new ground violates the ex post facto clause.

The Court rejected all those arguments and upheld the constitutionality of the challenged provision. As for substantive due process, the Court held that Congress's decisions whom to deport are "largely immune" from judicial review; in the process, it elaborated in some detail the reasons for such special judicial deference. As for the first amendment, the Court purported to apply the usual standards for restrictions on political speech, ruling that the first amendment does not protect advocacy of the violent overthrow of the government. And as for the ex post facto argument, the Court doubted that the statute could really be classified as retroactive but held that in any event the ex post facto clause doesn't apply to deportation because deportation is a civil sanction rather than a criminal punishment. Frankfurter's concurrence suggested that Congress's powers in this area are *entirely* immune from judicial review, not just *largely* immune. The dissent would have overruled *Fong Yue Ting* and held Congress's exercise of the deportation power subject to constitutional constraints.

<u>Notes and Questions Following Harisiades</u> (page 184):

General: The instructor might first ask the students to map out the various constitutional arguments that the plaintiffs were making. These included substantive due process, the First Amendment (which protects not only freedom of speech but also the freedom "peaceably to assemble"), and the ex post facto clause. As for substantive due process, there were two alternative sub-arguments: that an LPR has a vested right to remain and, alternatively, that a deportation ground must at least bear a "reasonable relation" to some valid congressional aim.

Q2: This question requires the students to decide how far the Court in *Harisiades* meant to go. The holding seems to suggest a minimal rationality test. First, the Court says that policies toward noncitizens are so related to foreign affairs that they are "largely immune from judicial inquiry or interference." The qualifier "largely" implies at least *some* review. Second, the Court actually applies this rule, deferentially. It says that congressional alarm about the Communist conspiracy is not a "fantasy or pretense." For the Court, it is enough that it cannot say there are "no possible grounds" for that belief. The objective -- preventing the violent overthrow of the government -- would obviously be important enough even if importance were required. But the Court does not evaluate the means by which that objective is realized. Congress assumed that, if a noncitizen is a member of the Communist Party, there is simply too great a chance that he or she will participate in efforts to overthrow the United States government. The Court does not consider whether Congress could have realized this objective through more narrowly tailored means.

Justice Jackson's description of the plaintiffs' fallback position is interesting. When the plaintiffs' argument is characterized as Justice Jackson does in this case, it sounds quite radical. *Of course* Congress's decision did not have to be concurred in by the courts. Broken down carefully, however, the argument he rejects here is really no different from the position he takes in *Mezei* – that Congress may not enact *unreasonable* legislation.

Justice Frankfurter appears to go even further than the majority. His absolute language implies a belief that the Court should not review even for reasonableness. Under that view the congressional decision is more than just *largely* immune; it is *entirely* immune. Presumably, under Justice Frankfurter's rule, a court would not search even for possible reasons for a congressional fear of Communist immigrants.

Q3: While the previous question focused on what the Court ultimately held in *Harisiades*, the present question asks *why* the Court would accord such exceptional deference to Congress in deportation cases. The reason *Harisiades* was included as a principal case is that it provides the Supreme Court's most comprehensive description of its reasons for such special judicial deference. Some of the rationales appear in earlier cases and have already been discussed. The instructor might wish, therefore, to focus solely on the two new considerations.

The plaintiffs' responses to the argument contained in part 3(a) could include (i) they couldn't have naturalized because the law withheld this option from members of the Communist Party; and (ii) even if they had been eligible for naturalization, their decision not to seek it was perfectly legal and not a reason to withhold constitutional protection.

The plaintiffs' responses to the argument contained in part 3(b) might include (i) it is doubtful these international law privileges are an adequate substitute for United States constitutional protection (e.g., for diplomatic intervention to be effective, the person's country would have to be willing to protest and the United States would have to be willing to grant that nation's request); and (ii) the plaintiffs recognize they are noncitizens and hence are not asking for the same package of rights that citizens have (e.g., noncitizens still would not be able to vote, would be less able to bring in their family members, etc.).

Q4: The values that generally support *stare decisis* do not seem weighty in the present context. Predictability in the law is of course essential to intelligent planning, but in the present case it is not clear who would be hurt by way of reliance if a court were to declare that, from this point on, Congress must observe due process when it regulates immigration. Perhaps Congress could be embarrassed if it were to pass an immigration law aimed at helping or hurting another country, and a court were to strike down the legislation, but that is not the case here. The goal of treating similarly situated litigants equally would theoretically be undermined by an overruling of the previous cases; perhaps the Court thought it unfair to let Galvan remain in the United States when Harisiades and others were deported for engaging in the same behavior. But such equal treatment is no more serious a concern than, for example, would be the congressional repeal of a deportation ground. Finally, *stare decisis* does promote judicial efficiency, but the system could probably handle the overruling of one immigration case every 100 years.

Q5: The Court does seem to suggest that the deportation of noncitizen Communists at a time when United States citizens are being drafted to fight Communism is poetic justice. That suggestion, however, makes it sound as if these noncitizens were asking to be treated *more* favorably than United States citizens. The implication is that the plaintiffs are arguing that it is permissible to uproot citizens (even to uproot citizens *because* of noncitizens like these) but not permissible to uproot noncitizens. In fact, of course, the plainfiffs are not seeking preferential treatment. First, United States citizens are free to join the Communist Party; these permanent residents ask only for the same privilege. Second, these LPRs, like United States citizens, could also have been drafted to fight against Communism. Probably the key here is that membership in the Communist Party is not tantamount to the type of Communist aggression that the Court observes United States citizens have been conscripted to combat.

Q8: Although the Supreme Court in section II of its opinion professed merely to be applying the usual First Amendment standards of *Dennis v. United States*, the case might be more important for what it does than for what it says. The *Dennis* test allowed government restriction on political expression only to the extent there is a "clear and present danger" of an important enough evil. The evil feared in *Harisiades* apparently is the overthrow of the United States government, obviously an important enough evil. There was, however, no evidence of a clear and present danger that allowing noncitizens to join the Communist Party would produce such an overthrow. But the Court does not require any such showing. That being the case, it is possible either to (a) agree with the district court in *American-Arab* that the Supreme Court, rightly or wrongly, at least purported to apply the usual standard of review even though this was an immigration case; or (b) disagree with *American-Arab*, on the basis that part of the Court's holding is its actual application of the standard and that, even allowing for the fact that this case was decided during the McCarthy era, the application of the *Dennis* test was clearly more deferential than usual. The Court, in fact, although citing the *Dennis* case, does not even state the *Dennis* test, much less apply it. Had the Court stated that*Dennis* requires a "clear and present danger," it might have been forced to examine whether the admission of noncitizen Communists truly posed a clear and present danger of overthrow.

Q9: The *ex post facto* argument is that it was not until after the plaintiffs had left the Communist Party that Congress made past membership in an organization advocating the overthrow of the United States government a deportation ground; i.e., their membership ended before the charged deportation ground was enacted. (The plaintiffs had also argued that they left the Communist Party before deportation proceedings were brought, and that by then they had reformed.)

The Court rejects the *ex post facto* argument, both because it believes the legislation was not truly retroactive and because it concludes that even retroactive immigration legislation would not be unconstitutional since the *ex post facto* clause is limited to *penal* legislation. With respect to the former, the Court might be saying either (a) that *present* membership has always been a deportation ground and nonetheless these noncitizens willingly joined the Communist Party; or (b) that even past membership has always been a deportation ground, but the Supreme Court in *Kessler v. Strecker* wrongly held otherwise and Congress amended the statute. The counter-argument to (a) would be that past membership is a more sweeping deportation ground than present membership, and past membership was not a ground until after the plaintiffs had left the Party. The counter-argument to (b) would be that the Court in *Kessler* was interpreting the then existing law; that Congress *later* amended the statute does not imply that the law originally covered past membership.

For present purposes, the more important reason the Court gives for rejecting the *ex post facto* argument is that, even if the 1940 Act were considered retroactive, it would not be unconstitutional. The *ex post facto* clause applies only to penal statutes and deportation is not penal. The students encountered that principle earlier in *Fong Yue Ting*. The instructor need not rehash this issue here, except possibly to inform the students that that aspect of the case is still good law.

<u>Substantive Cracks in the Plenary Congressional Power</u> (page 195):

Francis v. INS (page 195):

Under former INA § 212(c) [now recast as INA § 240A(a)], as interpreted by the BIA and the courts, an LPR who left the United States temporarily and then returned to a lawful unrelinquished domicile of seven consecutive years was eligible for discretionary relief from deportation (with some exceptions not pertinent here). Francis, an LPR, was convicted of a drug offense and found deportable on that ground. Because he had lived in the U.S. for more than the required seven years, he applied for 212(c) relief. The BIA denied relief because he had not left and returned to the United States. He challenged the constitutionality of the statute as interpreted, arguing that it was irrational, and therefore violative of equal protection (federal due process), to treat him less favorably than those who were similarly situated except for having left and returned to the United States. The court accepted the BIA interpretation of the statute and agreed with Francis that the distinction thus created was irrational. On that basis the court held the statute, as applied, violated equal protection. The court acknowledged that it could not review the validity of distinctions Congress draws *between groups* with respect to deportability, but it held that it could review the rationality of distinctions Congress draws *between individuals within a group*.

<u>Notes and Questions Following Francis</u> (page 197):

Q1: The court's attempt to distinguish the plenary power doctrine cases does seem clumsy. The court acknowledges that, if Congress decides to deport one group but not another group, a court cannot review that distinction to determine whether it is rational; the distinction, the court agrees, is "not a proper subject for judicial concern." Once Congress creates a particular group, however, the court says Congress may not distinguish between individuals within that group in ways a court finds irrational. The conceptual difficulty with that approach is that distinctions between groups and systematic, articulable (statutory) distinctions between individuals within a group are exactly the same thing. The latter type of distinction simply creates a new group. In *Francis*, the "group" to which the court implicitly refers would probably consist of LPRs who have lived in the United States at least seven years. Within that group, as the court sees it, those individuals who have left and returned are treated differently from those individuals who have stayed. Under that characterization, the court assumes it may review the latter distinction and strike it down if it is irrational (which it is). If the government counsel wished to use the court's formulation, however, he or she would simply argue that Congress has in fact distinguished between two groups: group one, eligible for section 212(c) relief, consists of those LPRs who have lived in the United States at least seven years and who have left and returned; and group two, ineligible for such relief, consists of those LPRs who have lived in the United States at least seven years and who have not left the country during that period. The distinction might well be irrational, but even if it is, government counsel would argue, a court may not strike it down because Congress, as the court acknowledges, may create different standards for different groups, and the validity of those distinctions "is not a proper subject for judicial concern."

Q2: There is no clear answer to this question. One remote possibility (and this is not an argument that the BIA itself has made) is that decisions of the courts of appeals partly reflect deference to the interpretation of the administering agency. If an agency changes its mind on a question of statutory interpretation, it is possible the court will do so also. Thus, even though both the Second Circuit and the Ninth Circuit interpreted the *statute* as inapplicable to noncitizens who have not yet left the United States, perhaps the BIA now takes the opposite view and feels justified in deviating from the decisions of the Second Circuit and the Ninth Circuit on the theory that, if those courts had known of the BIA view, they would have reached a different result.

Q5: Former INA § 242(a)(2), the challenged statutory provision, automatically required detention of aggravated felons. The plaintiffs challenged that provision, arguing that the Constitution requires individualized hearings to assess their chances of absconding and the degree of danger they would pose to the community. They would want to characterize that provision as procedural. The argument would be that the defect lies in the lack of opportunity to prove that the individual will not abscond or pose a danger. The government would want to characterize the provision as substantive. It would argue that Congress has simply made a determination that the likelihood of absconding or danger to the community is not the test; rather, the test is whether the person has been convicted of an aggravated felony. The individual *does* have an opportunity to litigate that fact question. There is no right to litigate facts that are substantively irrelevant. The instructor might ask the students whether the standard of judicial review for constitutionality should really be made to hinge on whether the challenged provision is called substantive or procedural.

d. Still More Cracks

INS v. Chadha (page 201):

Chadha was found deportable on overstay grounds, but the immigration judge granted suspension of deportation [today, cancellation of removal]. At the time, the suspension provision authorized either House of Congress to nullify a grant of suspension by passing a resolution to that effect. The House of Representatives did so, and the immigration judge therefore withdrew the grant of suspension. The BIA affirmed. Chadha challenged the constitutionality of the provision authorizing a one-House veto, on separation of powers grounds. (The INS agreed with Chadha, so the court of appeals invited the House and the Senate to file amicus briefs.) The Supreme Court ultimately agreed that one-House vetoes violate separation of powers and therefore struck down the statutory provision that authorized them. To reach the merits, however, the Court first had to resolve several preliminary issues, including whether Congress's plenary power over immigration made the issue a nonjusticiable political question. The Court conceded that Congress's power was plenary but held that it was still up to the courts to decide "whether Congress has chosen a constitutionally permissible means of implementing that power." The Court examined the factors (laid out in *Baker v. Carr*) that typically make questions political and found none of them present here.

Notes and Questions Following Chadha (page 204):

General: Before examining the merits of the decision, the instructor might wish to comment on the party alignment, which is interesting. The Justice Department is on the same side as Mr. Chadha. The instructor might ask the students why. The answer, of course, is that former INA § 244(c)(2) constrained the *executive* power to grant suspension of deportation. The Justice Department wanted to use *Chadha* as a test case for determining whether this and the many other legislative veto provisions Congress has enacted were constitutional. To make sure both sides of the issue would be forcefully presented, therefore, the Supreme Court invited the United States Senate and the United States House of Representatives to submit amicus briefs, which they did.

Q2: The Supreme Court in *Chadha* acknowledges the "plenary" congressional power over immigration but says that in this case the question is whether Congress has chosen a constitutionally permissible *means* of implementing that power. That view certainly raises the question of what the Court means, both in this case and in the previous cases, by the word "plenary." Conceivably the word simply means "full;" under that interpretation, "plenary" refers to the breadth of the congressional power. It covers the entire subject area, not just certain segments of it. Under that interpretation there could still be constitutional limitations on the exercise of a "plenary" power. But it seems difficult to explain the previous cases on that basis, since those cases often explicitly disclaimed either the power of the court to review or the existence of a broad standard of review.

Possibly the Court meant to distinguish substantive decisions from procedural ones. On that assumption, Congress may define the substantive criteria for deportation without fear of judicial reversal, but the procedure it chooses remains subject to constitutional constraints. Congress would argue that the challenged provision is a substantive one, simply another way of saying "We will not deport you as long as you meet the following substantive criteria: good moral character, continuous physical presence, extreme hardship, a favorable exercise of discretion by the immigration judge or the BIA, and the favorable exercise of discretion by both Houses of Congress." Those seem like substantive hurdles. Chadha and the executive branch might acknowledge that the requirement of favorable equities is a substantive criterion but argue that the choice of the two Houses of Congress as the assessors of those equities is a procedural decision subject to constitutional limits. Under that latter approach the opinion of the Court is consistent with previous plenary power doctrine cases, which recognize *procedural* constitutional limitations on *deportation*. It's just that this is separation of powers rather than procedural due process.

Q3: Had prior Supreme Court opinions utilized the *Baker v. Carr* analysis adopted in *Chadha* -- i.e., examining the applicability of the different reasons for holding constitutional challenges nonjusticiable -- perhaps they too would have been willing to review on the merits. In *Harisiades*, for example, the Court simply assumed that immigration policy was too bound up with foreign affairs to permit judicial intrusion. The Court in that case never asked, as this Court did, whether there was in fact a textually demonstrable constitutional commitment to Congress of the issue of whether to deport noncitizen communists, or whether there are discoverable standards, etc. If anything, in fact, it might be that foreign affairs considerations were *more* pervasive in *Chadha* than in some of the previous cases. Chadha's claim turned partly on discrimination by British society against individuals of Indian descent. In contrast, foreign affairs implications were missing in the vast majority of the cases discussed up to this point.

Q4: It is difficult to reconcile *Chadha* with some of the previous plenary power doctrine cases. Attempts to distinguish *Chadha* might take the following form:

a. The stated reasons for the plenary power doctrine rest ultimately on the view that the political branches, not the courts, should make decisions concerning the admission and the expulsion of noncitizens. To protect that aspect of separation of powers, the Supreme Court in *Chadha* could have allowed the statute to stand. Had it done so, however, it would have been sanctioning what it ultimately decided was another breach of separation of powers -- congressional usurpation of an executive power. Under this rationale, there is reason to distinguish between the justiciability of individual rights challenges to deportation statutes and the justiciability of separation of powers challenges to deportation statutes.

b. Again we might be back to the notion that, with respect to deportation, the plenary power doctrine is only substantive and this issue is procedural.

Zadvydas v. Davis (page 206):

In consolidated cases (*Zadvydas* and *Ma*), two noncitizens were found deportable on the basis of criminal convictions and were ordered removed. The government was unable to execute the removal orders, however, because no other country was willing to receive either plaintiff. INA § 241(a)(6) required removal within 90 days and prescribed detention pending removal. The statute authorizes further detention "beyond the removal period" when the person is inadmissible, or the person is deportable on certain crime-related or certain other grounds, or the Attorney General has found the person to be "a risk to the community or unlikely to comply with the order of removal." The detainees applied for habeas corpus under 28 USC § 2241, seeking their release from detention. Concluding that indefinite detention would create "a serious constitutional problem," the Court by a vote of 5-4 construed the statute as not authorizing it, absent a clear statement by Congress to the contrary. The Court ruled that detention was permissible only for a period reasonably necessary to secure the noncitizens' eventual removal and, therefore, that as soon as there was no reasonable likelihood of removal there was no basis for continued detention. The dissenters believed that Congress had expressed itself clearly enough and further doubted that a contrary interpretation would have rendered the statute unconstitutional.

<u>Notes and Questions Following Zadvydas</u> (page 218):

Q3: That hardly seems clear. Since the provision is part of the statutory removal scheme, construing it as designed to assure compliance with removal orders does not seem implausible. But Justice Kennedy does offer some substantial arguments for a contrary interpretation. First, he identifies contrasting language in other removal provisions as evidence that the contrast was deliberate. Second, he points out that the statutory text makes no distinction between inadmissible and deportable noncitizens and that, therefore, it is difficult to read a time limitation into the power to detain the former without doing so for the latter. (This last point resurfaces in *Clark v. Martinez*, the next case excerpted.)

Q4: Probably not. The fact that Congress entrusted the decisionmaking to administrative officials was an additional, independent irritant, but the Court seems more bothered by the substantive criteria themselves. The Court concludes that detention is constitutionally permissible only as a concomitant to removal, not merely to prevent absconding or to ensure public safety. As to the former, the noncitizen has little reason to abscond if removal itself is not a realistic possibility. As to the latter, the majority finds no more reason to detain a dangerous noncitizen (other than as part of a criminal sentence) than to detain a dangerous citizen; the law places stringent limits on civil commitment.

Q5: The hypothetical amendment leaves the statutory language clear enough to force the Court to reach the constitutional issue directly. Although the Court says only that a broad interpretation of the statute would raise a serious constitutional "problem," its reasoning suggests it would have found a constitutional violation had it been required to reach the issue. Even if the statute were amended as hypothesized, there would remain the problem of Congress allowing administrative officials to decide whether to lock people up for life, a scenario the Court found objectionable. Moreover, the Court commented that even the plenary power doctrine is "subject to important constitutional limitations," citing *Chadha* (excerpted in the coursebook starting on page 201).

Q7: The plaintiffs are claiming a constitutional right not to be detained indefinitely (except pursuant to a criminal sentence). In some cases, it is true, supervised release will be the only practical alternative to indefinite detention. That fact might well be one argument against recognizing a right not to be detained indefinitely, but the question is whether the argument is weighty enough to offset the individual liberty interest at stake. That is a different question from whether there is a general constitutional right to supervised release.

The quoted phrase also describes the release as being "into the United States." This language is misleading. Having formulated it, Justice Scalia draws on that phrase to suggest that the noncitizen who has been ordered removed has no more legal right to be released "into the United States" than does the noncitizen who stands on the threshold of initial entry. One might well disagree. The person who seeks initial entry is outside the United States and asking to be let in. The plaintiffs in *Zadvydas* are not requesting release "into" the United States, as Justice Scalia declares; they are already here. The only issue is where, *within the United States,* these persons will live, or – to put it another way – whether the government can constitutionally imprison them for the rest of their lives (other than as part of a criminal sentence).

Q8: Counsel should respond that Justice Scalia's question is interesting but irrelevant. Whether or not Congress *could* constitutionally make either a life sentence or indefinite detention part of the criminal sentence while citizen offenders are subject only to lesser sentences is not relevant, because Congress in fact has not done so. The indefinite detention challenged in this case was not part of the criminal sentence.

If Congress were to enact the hypothesized statute, would it be constitutional? On the one hand, the plenary power doctrine has long permitted Congress to treat noncitizens more harshly than citizens and has long prevented meaningful judicial review of most of Congress's immigration decisions. On the other hand, *Wong Wing* requires the observance of minimal constitutional safeguards in criminal proceedings, even for noncitizens, although the Court in *Wong Wing* was concerned only with procedural ingredients. Since the rationale for the harsher sentence would be immigration-related, however, perhaps the Court would uphold it.

Q9: It is true that the Court's ruling will sometimes require judges to evaluate the likelihood of success of international negotiations. Justice Kennedy feels that such evaluations exceed judicial competence, and he is probably right. But while the negotiations are ongoing, only a rare judge would order the noncitizen released on the ground that the negotiations are likely to fail. It is only after negotiations have terminated that the question of their resumption is likely to be assessed, and even in those situations the court may take into account whatever information the government supplies. Balanced against these potential difficulties are the substantial interests of noncitizens in being free of indefinite imprisonment.

Q10: Probably the 90-day period was a concession to the practical demands of the workload of the former INS. Any government agency with multiple responsibilities needs some amount of time just to process the paperwork, make travel arrangements, and begin negotiations with the country to which the person will be returned. The Court was not prepared to declare the 90-day period presumptively unreasonable for this purpose.

Clark v. Martinez (page 223):

Two Cuban Marielitos filed habeas applications in district court to challenge their indefinite detention by the former INS. Both had been found inadmissible (having been paroled in) and ordered removed, but in both cases the INS had been unable to execute the removal orders because the countries of origin refused to cooperate. Interpreting the same statutory language that it had construed in *Zadvydas* (which had involved deportable noncitizens), the Court held that indefinite detention was not permitted, extending the holding of *Zadvydas* to inadmissible noncitizens. The excerpts match Justice Scalia's opinion (for a 7-Justice majority) with Justice Thomas's dissenting opinion (which the Chief Justice joined).

There are no separate Notes and Questions following this opinion. Class discussion can focus on the dialogue between Justices Scalia and Thomas, which address two interesting questions: (1) Can a statutory phrase be interpreted differently in two cases when the constitutional avoidance principle applies differently to the two sets of plaintiffs? (2) Which Justice is more persuasive on the question whether the dissenters' positions in *Martinez* are consistent with the same dissenters' positions in *Zadvydas*? (Justice Thomas argues in the alternative for overruling *Zadvydas*.)

Demore v. Kim (page 226):

Kim, an LPR, was ordered removed on criminal grounds and was detained pursuant to INA § 236(c)(1)(B). That provision makes detention mandatory in almost all cases in which removal is predicated on crime-related grounds. Kim conceded the INS interpretation of section 236(c)(1)(B) and its applicability to him but applied for habeas corpus, arguing that mandatory detention violates due process. The district court agreed, and the INS subsequently held an individualized bond hearing at which it determined that Kim was neither a flight risk nor a danger to the community and, therefore, released him on bond. The Ninth Circuit, in accord with the holdings of all other circuits that had passed on the issue except one, affirmed the district court decision. At the request of the government, the Supreme Court granted certioriari.

The Court (by a 6-3 vote) first held that the district court had jurisdiction to decide Kim's habeas application. On the merits, a 5-4 majority upheld the constitutionality of mandatory detention. It distinguished Zadvydas on the bases that in that case (1) removal was no longer attainable; and (2) detention was indefinite. Justice Kennedy (one of the five majority Justices) wrote a separate concurring opinion to emphasize that the individual hearing originally offered to Kim (on the issue of whether he fit the statutory criteria for mandatory detention) was all the Constitution required. Justice Souter, dissenting (and joined by Justices Stevens and Ginsburg), would have held that due process requires individualized consideration of the reasons for detention. Justice Breyer, concurring and dissenting, agreed that mandatory detention of Kim violated due process, but only because, on Justice Breyer's reading of the record (unlike the majority's reading), Kim had not conceded deportability. Justice Breyer also urged the importation of the bail standards that are used during the pendency of appeals from criminal convictions.

Notes and Questions Following Demore v. Kim (page 239):

Q1: The cited article lays out the theories, benefits, and costs in some detail. Here is a summary:

As to preventive detention generally, the benefits might include preventing absconding, protecting public safety, and (subject to stringent limits) deterring immigration violations. The costs of detention include, first, the human costs – the deprivation of the detainee's liberty and the loss of opportunity to work, attend school, socialize, and interact with family and friends; the economic loss to the detainee and his or her dependents if the detainee is eligible to work (as well as the loss of income tax revenues for the federal and state governments in such cases); and serious practical obstacles to the detainees in the preparation of their removal cases (access to lawyers, witnesses, interpreters, documentary evidence, etc.).

As to mandatory versus discretionary detention determinations: The benefits of mandatory, categorical detention criteria might include avoiding the expense of individual bond hearings, avoiding false negatives (i.e., the fact-finder predicts a low risk of the person absconding or endangering public safety and therefore releases the person, and the person then absconds or commits a crime); and strengthening the deterrent to immigration violations by making the threat of detention absolute rather than speculative. The costs of mandatory, categorical detention criteria include false positives (i.e., the fact-finder predicts a high risk of the person absconding or threatening public safety and therefore orders the person detained, and the person in fact would have done neither, so that the human and monetary costs of detention are not offset by any corresponding benefit); inefficient use of bed space that could have been allocated to those who don't fit the mandatory detention criteria but who might nonetheless be dangerous and worthy of detention; discouraging immigration officials from initiating removal proceedings in cases where detention would be mandatory but bed space is scarce; and the fiscal costs of detention.

Q1: For the first part of the question the students might draw arguments pro and con from the article excerpts that follow the case. Much will turn on both (a) how heavily they weigh the individual liberty interests (including the impact of the detention on the person's practical ability to obtain counsel and prepare the case) relative to the government interests in assuring appearances and safeguarding the public; and (b) how heavily they weigh the advantages of a rule-bound detention determination system (avoiding false negatives, avoiding the expense of bond hearings, etc.) relative to the advantages of case-by-case adjudication (avoiding false positives, avoiding the expense of needless detention, etc.).

The second part of the question refers to Justice Souter's characterization of the majority holding. Because the district court in this case had found section 236(c) unconstitutional and thus had ordered the INS to evaluate Kim individually, the INS had to decide whether detention was warranted in Kim's case. It thought not. Thus, Justice Souter is able to emphasize that Kim is being detained even though the INS itself thinks there is no reason to do so. Of course, the government might argue that that characterization is unfair. It might say that, even though the INS decided to release Kim, it doesn't follow that there was *no* reason to detain him. The risk of his absconding or endangering the public might have been very low, but it wasn't zero. Also, they might say, even if one concludes that there was no reason to detain this particular individual, the proxy rule doesn't have to be perfect to be constitutional or desirable. If it results in preventing harm in numerous other cases, they might argue, then the fact that it sometimes requires the detention of someone who could safely have been released is a price that Congress could reasonably and constitutionally decide to pay.

Q2: The procedural due process argument is straightforward – that fairness requires an individual inquiry into whether detention is necessary before such an important liberty interest can be taken away. The substantive due process argument is that, by basing detention on what is merely a correlate of risk rather than on an actual finding of risk, an individual whom there is no need to detain will be unnecessarily deprived of his or her liberty.

The two arguments connect in an interesting way. Recall the majority's argument, made explicit by Justice Kennedy, that the person *is* receiving an individualized inquiry. It's just that it's a hearing on whether the person satisfies the congressionally prescribed criteria for detention rather than on whether the person is likely to abscond or endanger the public. Therefore, proponents of this argument would say, the person is not being denied *procedural* due process; a fair hearing is being provided. The real objection, they would then say, is to the substantive criteria that Congress has adopted for detention. And that objection is one of *substantive* due process.

When the lower courts were actively deciding the mandatory detention cases, the characterization of the argument as procedural or substantive often affected the outcome. Once a court decided it was dealing with a substantive due process issue, it was frequently inclined to invoke the plenary power doctrine and accord great deference to the government. In contrast, if it decided it was dealing with a procedural due process argument, it often invoked the procedural due process exception to plenary power. See, e.g., the cases digested on pages 93-95 (item 5) of the third edition of the coursebook.

Q3: The degree of ends scrutiny is virtually impossible to pin down. The Court credits the various governmental interests that the INS asserts, but it never comments on how important it thinks those interests are. The Court elaborates more fully with respect to means scrutiny. At the general level, the Court says (in the context of its discussion of *Zadvydas*) that "when the Government deals with deportable aliens, the Due Process clause does not require it to employ the least burdensome means to accomplish its goal." It adds that the evidence before Congress "certainly supports the approach it selected, even if other, hypothetical studies might have suggested different courses of action." That language and its application to the facts make clear that the Court is not employing any type of heightened means scrutiny even though the important liberty interest in being free of detention hangs in the balance. On the other hand, the Court spends quite a bit of time examining the empirical evidence the two sides have presented on (a) appearance rates of those released on bail; and (b) recidivism rates. (The full opinion contains even more discussion of the empirical questions; much was edited out for space reasons.) That the Court felt a need for that discussion suggests a standard of review akin to rational basis "with bite," to use Gerald Gunther's terminology - as distinguished from the kind of rational basis review the students have seen in other cases, where the Court has relied on theoretical or speculative rationales that Congress *might* have had in mind.

Q4: The majority distinguishes *Zadvydas* in two ways. First, it says, although the detainees in *Zadvydas* had already been ordered removed, there was no realistic likelihood of removal occurring because no other country would admit them. Therefore, they had no real incentive to abscond if released. Mr. Kim faced the real prospect of removal and thus had a greater incentive to flee. Second, the individual interest was far greater in *Zadvydas*, where the detention was potentially indefinite, than in *Kim*, where the detention is to last only for the duration of the removal proceedings.

The dissent acknowledges that the two cases present different specific issues - mandatory detention versus indefinite detention. Its point, however, is that *Zadvydas* stands for a larger principle that should also govern the present case. The Court in *Zadvydas*, the dissent points out, ordered individualized consideration of the detainees' claims. The same, it says, should be true here.

Q5: Justice Souter lays great emphasis on Kim's LPR status and the close resemblance between the rights of LPRs and the rights of citizens. A noncitizen's immigration status might rationally affect the outcome in two ways. First, an LPR's interests are greater. With time and legal status come deeper roots in the local and national communities. Still, while that point clearly holds with respect to the issue of remaining in the country, its relevance to detention is less clear. Roots or not, detention is still a deprivation of liberty. The person is being separated from *some* community, either one in the United States or one in a foreign state. The second way in which the noncitizen's immigration status might rationally affect the outcome, however, is that an LPR might be assumed to be less likely to flee pending the hearing. Having a legal residence, the person is more likely to have a home, a job, a family, etc.

Q6: It's hard to see why. Justice Breyer's reasoning (and apparently that of the majority as well) is that, if deportability is conceded, removal is both inevitable and not too distant, and thus the detention will be for a relatively short period. Moreover, the argument might run, the person who concedes deportability might anticipate removal and thus will have an incentive to abscond if released. As noted, however, deportability often does not result in actual removal, since in most removal hearings (and at any rate in this one) the person will apply for affirmative relief. Thus, there is every possibility of both (a) delay and (b) success.

Q7: The liberty interests at stake seem quite similar. The main difference between the removal setting and both the cited analogies is that the Court has consistently emphasized the special nature of immigration laws. Since the majority opinion expressly characterizes detention as part and parcel of the removal process, and since it points out that Congress has the power to make laws for noncitizens that it could not constitutionally make for citizens, it is not convinced by the analogies to either pretrial detention in criminal cases or involuntary civil commitment.

Q8: It seems misplaced. The reason the criminal law imposes such a tough standard in the appellate cases is that the person has already been convicted, after either a trial or a guilty plea. There is arguably good reason to impose a kind of rebuttable presumption of correctness once a full trial has been held or the person has waived it. Moreover, it is rational to think that the fact of the initial conviction increases the probability of the person ultimately having to face criminal punishment; thus, it enhances the incentive to flee. In the present setting, the person has not yet had his or her removal hearing, so there is no room for a presumption of correctness or a presumption that the person will lose his or her case in the first round and thus have an incentive to flee. It is true that in *Kim* the particular deportability ground was a criminal conviction; thus, it can be said that he has had one day in court already. But that day in court concerned only the questions of guilt and punishment (which he has now fully served). He has not yet had *any* hearing on either deportability or affirmative relief.

Most likely Justice Breyer's reason for wanting to require a showing that there is a substantial likelihood of success on the merits relates back to his focus on Kim not having conceded deportability. If Kim's arguments on the merits were frivolous, then perhaps Justice Breyer would regard Kim's position as functionally equivalent to that of a person who has conceded deportability.

Q9: On the one hand, the majority opinion does recite the maxim that "Congress may make rules as to aliens that would be unacceptable if applied to citizens." But that maxim alone is hardly tantamount to a plenary power doctrine. Indeed, few would dispute it. Congress, for example, may deport noncitizens, something it has long been assumed it may not do to citizens. The real question is one of limits. Some of the older plenary power decisions contained language that, if read literally, would suggest there are no limits on what Congress may do to noncitizens, at least in the exclusion setting. More modern cases (as well as many of the older cases) suggest merely that federal immigration statutes are due a greater *degree* of deference than other statutes. But even that formulation of the plenary power doctrine goes further than the Court's mild statement in *Kim* that some differences in treatment are permissible. Moreover, the Court appears to apply a fairly serious rational basis standard of review. (Query, again, whether even rational basis review should be enough when lengthy detention is at stake).

The status of the procedural due process exception is unclear. Although the Court does not cite *Mathews v.Eldridge* (discussed in the coursebook at 154-55), one might read *Kim* as applying the principle of that case, at least insofar as the Court considers both the government interests in detaining aggravated felons and the individual liberty interest. The Court attaches little weight to the latter, dismissing the detention as short-term, but at least it purports to consider it. (Of course, the third important *Eldridge* factor is the risk that the procedural deficiency - here, the lack of any inquiry into the likelihood of Kim's absconding or endangering the public - will cause an erroneous result. The Court defines that risk away by emphasizing that the result won't *be* erroneous as long as Kim is a noncitizen who has been convicted of an aggravated felony. And as to that, the Court observes, he can have a *Joseph* hearing. Not exactly textbook *Eldridge*, but it's close.)

Q10: As the text indicates, this question might be better left to chapter 10, when the students will have a better idea of the post-September 11 detention programs that have been devised.

e. Where Are We Now?

Simulation Exercise (page 245):

General: This exercise first appeared long before the September 11 terrorist attacks and the resulting wave of anti-Arab and anti-Muslim sentiment. One option, therefore, is for the teacher to modify the Problem by substituting the word "Arabic" for "Latino" or "Spanish" throughout the exercise (and making any other necessary adjustments). The instructor could also change the title of the Act and the conference committee report to refer not only to race relations, but also to national security. Alternatively, the instructor could have the statute discriminate against Muslims (or both Arabs and Muslims).

Note also: There are many ways to conduct this simulation exercise in class. It is probably best to have each of the four cases argued on each side by a different student, rather than have one student represent all four individuals and another student represent ICE in all four cases. As discussed below, however, there is considerable overlap between the issues presented in the first two cases. The instructor might, therefore, assign one student to represent noncitizens 1 and 2, a second student to represent noncitizen # 3, and a third student to represent noncitizen # 4. Similarly, one student would represent ICE in Cases 1 and 2 combined, a second in Case # 3, and a third in Case # 4. Alternatively, depending on the amount of time available, the instructor might wish to delete either Case # 1 or Case # 2.

Another option is to form teams of students -- e.g., two students representing the noncitizen in each case and two students representing ICE in each case. The instructor should also decide whether to do this simulation solely as a classroom exercise or, instead, to use it as the basis for a written exercise, requiring the students to submit in advance either actual briefs or outlines of the points they would make in their briefs. Even if no written briefs or outlines are required, the instructor should decide how much advance preparation to assign. The instructor could assign specific roles in advance of class, or could require all students to be prepared to assume any role, or as a middle ground could ask all students whose last names begin with A - M, for example, to be prepared to represent the noncitizen in any of these cases and all other students to be prepared to represent ICE in any of these cases. Or the instructor could simply line up volunteers in advance.

The instructor might also wish to have students play the roles of the Supreme Court Justices. The instructor could, at the time this exercise is played out, randomly select nine Supreme Court Justices (preferably people sitting near each other) and have them deliberate at the close of argument and/or decide the case. The students particularly relish playing the roles of the Justices, and they respond with insightful and creative questions. Questions might be designed simply to test the outer limits of the ICE position. The Justices might, for example, ask ICE counsel whether Congress could constitutionally enact an adjudication procedure that consists of the flip of a coin.

On the merits, the arguments might include the following:

For all four cases, common arguments can be constructed to the effect that the statutory provisions have no rational basis (as Chin argues) or, alternatively, trigger heightened judicial scrutiny that they cannot withstand. In all four cases the students might additionally argue that the international law developments cited by Chin are alone enough to prevent dismissal on plenary power grounds. As for the more specific arguments:

Case #1:

Arguments for the noncitizen:

a. As a matter of statutory interpretation, this person is not of "Latino" descent" because she is only half Argentinean. The statute nowhere defines Latino "descent." As in *Zadvydas* and *Martinez*, the saving interpretation should be adopted because the statute is not clear and a contrary interpretation would raise the serious constitutional problems outlined below.

b. This provision is impermissibly vague and therefore violative of procedural due process. What does "Latino" mean?

c. The Court should overrule the plenary power doctrine entirely, even with respect to exclusion. These issues are no more likely to present political questions than are other domestic issues (and this issue is domestic, not foreign policy). The rationales for the plenary power doctrine do not withstand scrutiny. (See discussion from preceding cases.)

d. At the very least, the Court should overrule the plenary power doctrine with respect to *racial* classifications. These are irrational and offensive. See the Chin article.

e. In *Fiallo*, the Court recognized some limited judicial responsibility. If even racial classifications don't fall within that dictum, then what does?.

f. This provision would fail even a minimal rationality test. The measures Congress has taken will not only fail to relieve racial tensions, but exacerbate them. Congress is punishing the victims, not the perpetrators.

Arguments for ICE:

a. The *Chinese Exclusion Case* is on point. The Court in that case made clear that even racial classifications are constitutional in the context of immigration.

b. The Court should preserve the plenary power doctrine. The exclusion of noncitizens necessarily involves foreign affairs because (assuming the person is not stateless) he or she is a citizen of a foreign country.

c. The precedent on this issue is too solid to dislodge at this point. See *Galvan v. Press*.

d. Whether the Court agrees with the congressional strategy or not, the strategy is at least rational. Congress is trying to avoid the public perception, right or wrong, that one particular ethnic group will swamp our culture. This will facilitate the peaceful and orderly integration of Latino immigrants into our society.

Case #2:

Arguments for the noncitizen:

a. [Same arguments for overruling the plenary power doctrine].

b. Even under existing law*Fiallo* recognizes some limited judicial role. Here the statute is irrational. If the purpose is to reduce the Latino population, it doesn't make sense to exclude a person of German ethnicity.

Arguments for ICE:

a. [Same arguments for keeping the plenary power doctrine.]

b. Country of nationality is *rationally* related to the congressional objective. If too many people come from Spanish-speaking countries, regardless of original ancestry, the United States population might perceive, rightly or wrongly, that its culture is being swamped. Also, the correlation need not be perfect. It might be administratively easier to base the exclusion on country of nationality than to base it on descent; this way the officials need only look at the individual's passport.

c. Nationality is more convincingly related to foreign affairs.

d. The *Chinese Exclusion Case* and *Nishimura Ekiu* both upheld similar statutes.

Case #3:

Arguments for the noncitizen:

a. [The same arguments for overruling the plenary power doctrine.]

b. The Court at least should overrule the doctrine as it applies to returning LPRs.

c. This provision violates the federal due process equivalent of equal protection because it applies only to Latinos. Whatever reasons ICE might assert for keeping down the numbers of Latinos, it is irrational to selectively deprive Latinos of the *procedural* safeguards that help determine eligibility.

d. Under *Plasencia*, a returning LPR is entitled to procedural due process if he or she is not gone too long. Eight months is much less than the 19-20 months for which Mezei was gone. Moreover, this person did not travel to a Communist country. Thus she is more like Kwong Hai Chew, who had been gone only 4-5 months, than like Mezei.

e. As to the process that was due, the permanent residence at stake in this case is an important private interest. Witnesses who might be able to identify her would produce highly probative evidence. And it is not that costly for an inspector to hear those witnesses.

Arguments for ICE:

a. [Same arguments for keeping the plenary power doctrine.]

b. In the *Chinese Exclusion Case*, a returning resident similarly asserted the absence of sufficient procedural safeguards (the statute did not permit the government to rely on Chinese witnesses), and the Court upheld even that provision.

c. With respect to the argument based on duration of absence, *Kwong Hai Chew* represents the outer limits. Here, the absence was even longer -- eight months. That fact makes this case more like *Mezei*.

d. With respect to the process due, the individual interest is not as important as the noncitizen makes it appear. She has been here only four years. Nor is the evidence that she seeks to introduce very probative; the witnesses she is willing to put on the stand will obviously be sympathetic to her. In the meantime, she will have to be detained at government expense and proceedings will be delayed while witnesses travel to the hearing.

Case #4:

Arguments for the noncitizen:

a. [Same arguments for overruling the plenary power doctrine.]

b. The Court should at least overrule the plenary power doctrine as it applies to *deportation*. The person is already here and is losing what has been lawfully acquired. See the Fuller dissent in *Fong Yue Ting*.

c. This provision violates the first amendment guarantees of free speech and free assembly. The Court in *Harisiades* applied the usual first amendment standards. See the district court decision in *American-Arab*. Today that means the *Brandenburg* test. The political activity must be calculated to, and likely to, incite imminent lawless action. This activity does not meet that test. (And the Supreme Court's arguably contrary statement in the *American-Arab* case was (i) dictum and (ii) confined specifically to the issue of selective prosecution, not the first amendment generally.)

d. This plaintiff is in a stronger position than the plaintiffs in *Harisiades*. The latter at least had joined a Party that Congress found advocated the overthrow of the United States government. The present individuals were merely attending a peaceful and lawful demonstration.

e. *Chadha* has weakened the plenary power doctrine in deportation. The deportation power extends to a broad range of fact situations but is still subject to constitutional restraints. Under *Baker v. Carr*, there is no reason here to find the issue nonjusticiable. The constitutional text does not commit the deportation decision to Congress; there would be no embarrassment or lack of finality if the Court were to strike this provision down; and there are no foreign policy effects other than the *negative* effects of enforcement on United States relations with Latin American countries.

f. This provision violates the *ex post facto* clause of the Constitution. The plaintiff attended a lawful demonstration, and *then* Congress made this a deportation ground. This case is different from *Harisiades*, in which present Communist Party membership had always been a deportation ground.

g. Deportation *is* punishment. The consequences mirror those of punishment and promote the goals of deterrence and incapacitation.

Arguments for ICE:

a. [Same arguments for keeping the plenary power doctrine.]

b. Deportation is just the flip side of the exclusion coin. Without it, once a noncitizen enters, he or she would be permanently immune from the immigration laws.

c. The district court in *American-Arab* was wrong to read *Harisiades* as applying the usual first amendment standards. It is true that the Supreme Court cited *Dennis*, but it never mentioned the "clear and present danger" test for which *Dennis* stands, and at no point did the Court apply the *Dennis* test. Moreover, membership alone certainly did not constitute a clear and present danger; yet the Court rejected the noncitizen's argument there.

d. The plaintiffs in *Harisiades* were no more dangerous than Ali is. They were just passive members of the Communist Party.

e. The *Chadha* holding was limited to separation of powers challenges, which are procedural. The Court there acknowledged that the congressional power was plenary. Further, this provision *does* affect United States relations with the governments of Spanish-speaking countries; thus, there is a need for our country to speak with a single voice and therefore the Court should not interfere.

f. As for the *ex post facto* argument, the point of both *Fong Yue Ting* and *Harisiades* is that deportation is not punishment. Therefore the *ex post facto* clause is inapplicable even though this legislation is retroactive.

g. The courts have been *right* to say that deportation is not punishment. The purpose of deportation is to rid the country of undesirable noncitizens, not to punish people for the commission of crimes.

Concluding Note on the Plenary Power Over Immigration: Historical Parallels from Across the Atlantic (page 247):

This concluding Note was intended as background reading to provide a comparative perspective.

CHAPTER 3
IMMIGRANT PRIORITIES

SECTION A. THE FUNDAMENTALS: QUOTAS AND PREFERENCES

This section consists of explanatory text and two Problems -- one concerning the total worldwide ceilings for the family-sponsored and employment-based programs (page 255), and the other concerning the ceilings on the individual preferences (page 258). At the end of the section are some policy and philosophical questions that explore the assumptions and values underlying the present quota system.

Both Problems contain numbers, and numbers tend to intimidate many students. However, the materials have been arranged so that those instructors who prefer to avoid the mathematics can easily do so without disruption, focusing instead on the broad policy and philosophical questions raised by the present quota system. If that is your preference, you can still assign all of section A but tell the students to skip both Problems (in which case I would recommend taking up in class the policy questions on pages 260-61).

I have found these mathematical exercises extremely useful. After occasional initial panic, the students actually seem to enjoy them -- especially Problem 2 (on page 258), which is more of a logic puzzle than anything else. More important, I have found these Problems to be helpful in aiding students to understand both the theory and the workings of the quota system. At any rate, even if you prefer to deemphasize the math, you might consider assigning at least Problem 1, which is fairly easy and illustrates how the quotas are determined for the broad overall programs. As the text indicates, calculators are not necessary.

In case the students ask, you can reassure them that the only other mathematical Problem in the book is Problem 16 on page 350, concerning diversity immigrants (which most instructors skip).

On page 254, the students are asked why Congress adopted the crisscross approach of adding unused employment-based visas to the family-sponsored ceiling, and vice-versa, rather than add family to family and employment to employment. The main reason, probably, is one best illustrated by the actual post-1990 Act experience. In every year that the new system has been in effect, the family program as a whole has been oversubscribed while the employment program as a whole has been undersubscribed. Had Congress assigned the unused employment visas to the following year's employment ceiling, and the unused family visas to the following year's family ceiling, those transfers would have accomplished nothing, because the employment-based applicants don't need any more visas and the family-sponsored applicants, who do need them, wouldn't get any. By criss-crossing, Congress avoids wasting the visas that people actually need. The same rationale would have applied had it turned out that family visas were underused and employment visas overused, as long as the patterns remained fairly steady for successive years. (Of course, if both family and employment programs were generally oversubscribed, there would be no issue because there wouldn't be any unused visas to distribute. Conversely, if *both* were generally undersubscribed, there would be no issue because extra visas wouldn't be needed.)

Problem 1 on page 255:

A student might notice that the first three figures for fiscal year 1 add up to more than 480,000. That is OK. It is the number of immediate relatives (and children born abroad to LPRs) who were admitted in the *prior* fiscal year that gets deducted from the 480,000.

As for the Problem:

For fiscal year 2: Since immediate relatives are not numerically restricted, all 275,000 will receive visas. The family-sponsored ceiling will equal 480,000 minus the 230,000 immediate relatives who were admitted in fiscal year 1, plus the 5,000 (i.e. 140,000 minus 135,000) employment-based visas not used during fiscal year 1, for a total of 255,000. Since more than that number of applicants qualify, all 255,000 visas will issue. The employment-based ceiling will be 140,000 (no more, since all family-sponsored visas were used in fiscal year 1). Thus, all 130,000 employment-based applicants will receive visas. So for fiscal year 2, the Visas Issued column reads: 275, 255, 130 (in thousands).

For fiscal year 3: All 290,000 immediate relatives will receive vias because they are not numerically restricted. The family-sponsored ceiling will be 480,000 minus the 275,000 immediate relatives who were admitted in fiscal year 2, plus the 10,000 (i.e., 140,000 minus 130,000) employment-based visas not used in fiscal year 2. This comes out to 215,000, but it must be bumped up to the statutory floor of 226,000. Since more than that number of applicants qualify, all 226,000 visas will be issued. The employment-based ceiling will be 140,000 (no higher, because in fiscal year 2 all the family-sponsored visas were used). Since more than 140,000 applicants qualify, all 140,000 visas will issue. So for fiscal year 3, the Visas Issued column reads: 290, 226, 140 (in thousands).

Incidentally, there is a possible complication that the students would not ordinarily spot at this juncture and that I think it best to ignore for purposes of this Problem: Even if the total number of qualified employment-based immigrants is within the program limit specified in INA § 201(d) (i.e., 140,000+), some of these immigrants might not be admitted, because the individual preference categories have their own limits. For example, if too many of the qualified employment-based applicants were 4th-preference or 5th-preference immigrants, some would miss out. Similarly, no employment-based category is authorized to use visas not required for the 3rd preference. Thus, if the 3rd preference were undersubscribed and the other employment-based preference categories were all oversubscribed, not all qualified applicants would be admitted, even if their total numbers were less than the overall limit on employment-based immigrant visas. Again, it is extremely unlikely that the issue will be raised, but if someone asks, the instructor should tell the students to assume for purposes of this Problem that the only operative constraint on the number of employment-based immigrants to be admitted worldwide is the *program* quota specified in INA § 201(d)—not the oversubscription of particular *preference categories.* (They'll have an opportunity to think about the latter issue if you assign Problem 2.)

<u>Problem 2 on page 258:</u>

Unlike the previous Problem, which was concerned only with the overall ceilings for the family and the employment programs, this Problem focuses principally on the allocation of visas among specific preference categories <u>within</u> each of those two programs. To perform the latter calculation, however, it is first necessary to figure out the overall ceilings (for year x + 1). Under INA § 201(c), the family-sponsored ceiling will be 480,000 minus the 220,000 immediate relatives who were admitted in year x, plus any employment-based visas not used in year x (here zero). This comes out to 260,000. The total employment-based ceiling for year (x + 1) will be 140,000 plus the 10,000 (i.e., 245,000 minus 235,000) family-sponsored visas not used in year x. This comes out to 150,000.

As for the chart:

a. The family-sponsored visas:

The first preference allows 23,400 *plus unused 4th's*. At first glance it might appear there will be no unused 4th's at all, since 67,000 have applied for 65,000 slots. But the 4th preference ceiling includes any visas not used by the first three preferences, and the third preference applicants will use only 18,400 of the 23,400 they are allotted. These 5000 unused third preference visas thus raise the 4th preference ceiling to 70,000. Since only 67,000 4th preference applicants qualify, that number of visas will issue and there will still be 3000 left over. Therefore the limit for the first preference becomes 23,400 plus 3,000, or 26,400. Since more than that number of applicants qualify, all 26,400 visas will be issued. Finally, the 2nd preference ceiling will be 114,200 plus any unused 1st's (none), plus the amount by which the 260,000 available family-sponsored visas exceed 226,000 (i.e. 34,000). Thus, the 2nd preference ceiling will be 148,200. Since more than that number of applicants qualify, all

148,200 visas will issue. For the four family-sponsored categories, the "Visas Issued" column will thus read: 26,400; 148,200; 18,400; 67,000. The total is 260,000.

b. The employment-based visas:

The ceiling for each of the first three employment-based preferences will be 28.6% of 150,000, or 42,900. The ceiling for each of the last two preferences (i.e., the 4th and 5th) will be 7.1% of 150,000, or 10,650.

The 4th preference demand is below its 10,650 ceiling, so all 5,650 qualified applicants will receive visas, and there will be another 5000 visas left over. The same is true of the 5th preference. The 1st preference ceiling is 42,900 plus the unused 4th's (5000) and unused 5th's (another 5000), for a total of 52,900. Thus, all 12,900 qualified 1st preference applicants will receive visas and there will still be 40,000 visas left over. The 2nd preference ceiling will be 42,900 plus the 40,000 unused 1st's, for a total of 82,900. Since only 22,900 applied, all will get in, and there will still be 60,000 left over. The 3rd preference ceiling will be 42,900 plus the 60,000 visas not needed by the first and second preference applicants, for a total of 102,900. (Some students might mistakenly assume that the third preference ceiling is increased by *both* the extra 40,000 1st preference visas and the extra 60,000 2nd's. Explain that that would be double-counting. The 40,000 extra 1st's are already reflected in the 2nd preference ceiling from which the 60,000 excess was obtained.) Since more than 102,900 applied, only 102,900 will receive visas. For the five employment-based preferences, the "Visas Issued" column will therefore read: 12,900; 22,900; 102,900; 5,650; 5,650.

Questions on page 260:

Q1: On the one hand, it might seem unfair that some qualified applicants are allowed to jump ahead of others in the queue. On the other hand, some of the preference categories reflect values, such as family unification, that make some people's *need* for immigration greater than others. The analogy in the book is that hospitals don't put emergency room patients in the same queue as those who are awaiting elective surgery. In addition, some preference categories reflect congressional findings that certain immigrants (for example, those in the employment-based categories) would particularly benefit the United States.

Q2: These questions require consideration of some of the same factors that are taken up more thoroughly in the later section on diversity immigrants. You might wish to defer this subject until then. If you decide to take up this subject at this time, however, you might begin by asking students what the purpose of the per-country limitations is. The likely answer will be that per-country limitations prevent a small handful of countries from monopolizing the finite number of immigrant visas. You might then ask why such a monopoly would be bad. Possible answers include (a) it would reduce the diversity of the immigrant stream and (b) allowing a few nations to dominate is unfair to prospective immigrants from other nations. With respect to the diversity argument, however, the question is why a diverse *immigrant stream* is desirable. The instructor might note, as is pointed out later in the chapter, that the present United States population already contains far more Americans of European ancestry, for example, than of Latino ancestry. Therefore, measures that make the immigrant stream *more* diverse might, ironically, make the resulting population *less* diverse. As for fairness, one can argue that the concern should be for fairness as between *similarly situated individuals*, not fairness as between *countries*. If two individuals are otherwise similarly situated, but one is from Mexico and the other from Monaco, why should the Monacan be permitted to jump ahead of the Mexican in the queue just because the other Mexicans who want to immigrate to the United States outnumber the other Monacans? For a fuller discussion of these arguments, see Stephen H. Legomsky, *Immigration, Equality, and Diversity*, 31 Columbia J. Transnat'l L. 319 (1993).

The other part of the question is whether, if there are to be per-country limitations, those limits should be the same for every foreign country. Some might say it is unrealistic to have the same quota for Mexico as for Monaco. Other options exist. They include, for example: (a) a generally uniform per-country limit that allows exceptions for selected countries with unusually high demands and in which the waiting times otherwise would be intolerable; (b) a system of varying per-country limits that take some account of the demand for visas from each country; and (c) a national origins quota system.

Q3: Here you can ask the students to accept per-country limitations as a given and to consider a country that has reached its limit. Assume, in other words, that in a particular country the number of people whose priority dates are early enough to place them within the worldwide limits exceeds the per-country limitations. Which of those people should get in? Question 3 identifies three options. Perhaps there are others.

The advantage of option (a) is that it enables Congress to prioritize among preferences -- i.e., to say that first preference applicants will receive top priority, that seconds will receive second priority, etc. The counter-argument would be that such a system permits the top preferences to monopolize all the visas while the bottom preferences get short-changed. That, in fact, is the only respect in which the old system of six preferences truly formed a hierarchy. An opponent of option (a) might also observe that this option is not essential to permitting Congress to prioritize because Congress already does so on a worldwide basis by setting different percentages for each preference category. Note that option (a) prevailed under the pre-1990 law except in any year following one in which the full national allotment of 20,000 visas had been used.

Option (b) (pro-rating) is the present system. Its advantage is that it accommodates *all* preference categories in every country, in whatever proportions Congress desires. Unlike in option (a), the bottom preferences are not squeezed out. In choosing between options (a) and (b), policymakers would certainly need to consider the backlogs in the various preference categories. This comparison should take into account not only the waiting times for the respective categories, but also whether a wait of x years for one group of people is more harmful than a wait of the same duration for another preference category. For example, it might be worse to separate the nuclear family than to separate family-sponsored fourth preference siblings for the same length of time.

Option (c) would equalize waiting times as among preference categories within each country. It would still allow Congress to prioritize among preferences *worldwide*, by assigning different percentage allocations to the various preference categories, though of course it would not allow prioritization to the same extent as would options (a) and (b).

Q4: *Family*-sponsored first preference immigrants have no built-in advantage over seconds, who in turn have no built-in advantage over thirds, etc. In some ways, in fact, the "top" preferences are worse off. The family-sponsored second preference, for example, gets many more visas than the family-sponsored first preference. In addition, the lower the category is in the hierarchy, the more latitude that preference category usually has in being able to use visas not required by categories above it in the hierarchy. Under the pre-1990 law there was one important respect in which first-preference immigrants were better off than seconds, etc. When a country reached its then per-country limit of 20,000, the visas within that country were distributed to all the otherwise current first preferences, then to the seconds, then to the thirds, etc. But even under the old law, the proration system would not kick in, within that country, until the following year. In contrast, under the new law, the firsts have no built-in advantage over the seconds, etc. Rather, the relative advantages of the individual preferences reflect their statutory sub-ceilings and the actual demand. As it turns out, the waiting times do tend to increase as one goes to the higher-numbered preferences, but the pattern is not perfect. The Visa Bulletin for April 2009, on page 266 of the text, reveals, for example, that for immigrants from almost all the world's countries, the wait for family-sponsored first preference immigrants is longer than the wait for 2A's.

The instructor might wish to point out that, for *employment*-based immigrants, at least the first three preferences are hierarchial in ways that will become evident in section C. (First preference applicants don't require labor certification. Second preference applicants generally require labor certification but sometimes qualify for national interest waivers of that requirement. Third preference applicants always need labor certification.)

SECTION B: FAMILY IMMIGRATION

1. The Basics

Problems 3-4 on page 266:

Problem 3: X could file a family-sponsored 2A visa petition for Y. Based on the April 2009 Visa Bulletin, the wait would be a little over 4 ½ years. Alternatively, in one year, X could apply for naturalization. Once he is naturalized, he can petition for Y as an immediate relative. The wait would thus be one year plus the processing times for (a) X's naturalization and (b) the immediate relative petition. Note that Y could not be admitted under INA § 203(d) as a spouse "accompanying or following to join" an LPR, because the marriage occurred after X's admission.

Y's sister, Z, will have a more difficult time. There is no provision for siblings "accompanying or following to join" the principal immigrants. For Z to be admitted, Y must first be admitted as an LPR (in one year plus processing time if X naturalizes, otherwise in about 4 ½ years). Y would then apply for naturalization herself five years later (three if X has naturalized). Only then could Y file a 4th preference visa petition for Z. Thus, Y will not be able even to start the process of petitioning for Z until at least 4 years from now (plus processing times for both of the naturalizations and the immediate relative petition). Once she files the petition for Z, the April 2009 Visa Bulletin shows a waiting period of approximately 11 additional years, for a total of more than 15 years (plus processing times) from now.

Z's husband will have no problem immigrating at the same time as Z, because he will qualify as a spouse "accompanying or following to join" her. The sons will be able to do the same, but only if they are still "children." For that, they must be unmarried and, important here, still under age 21. Depending on the speed with which sibling preferences are admitted, it is very likely that at least the older son (who is now 7), and perhaps even the younger son (who is now 2), will be over 21 by the time Z's priority date becomes current. If they reach age 21 before their priority dates, and the only additional delay resulted from administrative processing, then the aging-out legislation discussed in the readings would preserve their status.

But what happens when there is a 2A petition for a spouse and his or her child under 21, but the child turns 21 before the parent is admitted as an LPR, and administrative processing time was *not* the cause? The child is eligible for 2B status, but what is his or her priority date? In an unpublished decision, the BIA has held that the derivative status automatically converts to the appropriate category (here, accompanying child to 2B) and that the priority date will be the date the *original* petition was filed. Thus, the child does not have to go to the back of the queue upon the parent's admission as an LPR. See *Matter of Garcia*,

A79-001-587 (BIA June 16, 2006). Thanks to Kristen Stilt and her students for raising the issue.

Assuming X naturalizes at the earliest possible date, and also assuming six-month processing times each for naturalization and for immediate relative petitions (a favorable assumption at this writing), the total estimated time for everyone to immigrate would be as follows: 2 years for X to naturalize and bring in Y as an immediate relative, plus 3 ½ years for Y to naturalize, plus 11 years for Y to bring in Z and her family on a 4th preference petition – for a grand total of 16 ½ years.

An alternative, albeit convoluted, strategy is possible if one or both of the parents of Y and Z are alive and willing to immigrate to the United States in order to help Z and her family do so. Once Y has been admitted, she could apply for naturalization after 3 or 5 years (depending on whether X has naturalized) and, once it is granted, bring in one or both of her parents as immediate relatives. Once here, the parent(s) could wait five years, apply for naturalization themselves, and, once they receive it, file a family-sponsored 3rd preference petition for Z (married daughter of United States citizen). Z's husband (and her sons if they are still under 21 and unmarried) could accompany or follow to join her. The estimated waiting time (under the same assumptions as above) would be 2 years for X to naturalize and bring in Y as an immediate relative, plus 4 years for Y to naturalize and bring in her parents as immediate relatives, plus 5 1/2 years for one of the parents to naturalize, plus, according to the April 2009 Visa Bulletin, approximately 8 ½ years for Z and her family to come in under the third preference. This adds up to 20 years, which is even longer than under the other possible strategies.

The second part of Problem 3 asks the student how things change if the intending immigrants are from the Philippines. The change does not affect the immigration of Y. If she enters as an immediate relative, there will be no waiting time other than the time it takes X to obtain naturalization and the administrative processing time for an immediate relative petition -- and neither of these periods is nationality-dependent. If Y enters as a 2A, there will be quota-related waiting time, but the April 2009 Visa Bulletin shows the same priority date for the Philippines as for Costa Rica (the general chargeability column). The nationality change does, however, affect Z and her family. The April 2009 Visa Bulletin shows a 4th preference wait of 11 years for Costa Rica but almost 23 years for the Philippines. When added to the time needed for X to naturalize and bring in Y, and for Y to naturalize, Z's sons will both be well over 21 and therefore ineligible to enter as accompanying children.

Problem 4: A has several options. As the "child" of a United States citizen, she might seek admission as an immediate relative. She has to be a "child," and therefore under age 21, but that will not be a problem. Even if the administrative processing is not completed before her birthday, the aging out legislation preserves her immediate relative status. The problem is that she would have to defer her marriage until after her admission; otherwise she would no longer be a "child." And if she does that, then B will not be able to come in as a spouse "accompanying or following to join" (because he won't be her spouse). That is true both because there is no statutory provision for the spouses accompanying immediate relatives and because, if the marriage takes place after A's admission (and it would have to in order for A to enter as a "child" and therefore an immediate relative), B would not meet the definition of an accompanying spouse anyway; after-acquired spouses don't qualify as accompanying or following to join. Consequently, if A were to enter as an immediate relative, she would have to file a family-sponsored 2A petition. According to the April 2009 Visa Bulletin, that will leave the couple separated for more than 4 ½ years.

In theory, a second option is for A to ask her United States citizen father to file a family-sponsored first preference petition on her behalf. A is the unmarried daughter of a United States citizen. But there is no reason to do that. According to the April 2009 Visa Bulletin, the wait for the first preference petition would be over 6 ½ years. And she would still have to remain unmarried until her admission in order to qualify under the first preference. After her admission, she could marry, but she still would not be able to use section 203(d) to bring in her spouse who is "accompanying or following to join," because that provision applies only when the marriage takes place before the principal immigrant's admission. Thus, as with the immediate relative option, A would have to marry after she is admitted and then file a family-sponsored 2A petition for her husband. Therefore the first preference route has no advantage over the immediate relative route and it would delay A's admission for 4 ½ years.

A third option is for A and B to marry now and then have A's father file a family-sponsored third preference petition, since she will then be the married daughter of a United States citizen. The disadvantage is that the waiting period would now be more than 8 ½ years. At least when that time comes, however, her husband will be able to enter at the same time as she, and therefore separation will not be necessary.

In the end, A needs to make a personal decision. On the one hand, she can enter the United States soonest as an immediate relative. On the other hand, proceeding as an immediate relative would require her to go to the United States alone, then get married, then file a 2A petition, and to remain separated from her husband for the first 4 ½ years of their marriage. They must decide whether it is more important for her to enter sooner than for them to be together in the interim.

2. Spouses

a. Same-Sex Marriages

Adams v. Howerton (page 267):

A United States citizen and a noncitizen, both male, went through a marriage ceremony in Boulder, Colorado, and the City Clerk issued a marriage certificate. The citizen filed a visa petition to classify his noncitizen partner as an immediate relative (spouse). The INS denied the visa petition on the ground that the immigration laws do not recognize same-sex marriages. The BIA, and later a district court, affirmed. The court of appeals said it was not clear whether Colorado law recognized same-sex marriages. But even if it did, the court held, federal law determines the meaning of "spouse" for immigration law purposes. The court then held that Congress did not intend to include same-sex couples within the definition of spouses. The court also rejected the argument that, so construed, the statute violated equal protection. In the light of the plenary power doctrine, the court would review only under the rational basis test, even though the right to marry is normally regarded as fundamental. The court found several possible justifications rational: Same-sex marriages cannot produce offspring; most (at that time, all) states declined to recognize same-sex marriages; and such marriages violate traditional and prevailing societal norms.

Notes and Questions Following Adams (page 270):

General: This case raises basic questions about both (a) the role of marriage in immigration law generally and (b) the consequences of homosexuality under our immigration laws. The Notes and Questions that follow this case are intended to raise not only legal questions along the lines just suggested, but also policy questions about the nature of governmental and private discrimination based on sexual orientation.

Q1: Arguments in favor of recognizing every marriage that is legally valid in the jurisdiction in which it was celebrated might include the following:

a. Congress should respect the marriage decisions of other jurisdictions -- both individual states within the United States and foreign jurisdictions.

b. Congress should not penalize those who comply with the applicable local laws.

c. Under present law, compliance with the requirements of the particular state is necessary, albeit not sufficient, for immigration purposes. If federal law thus allows other jurisdictions to consider marriages invalid for federal immigration purposes, then why not permit those same jurisdictions to consider marriages valid for immigration purposes?

d. At least when the jurisdiction in which the marriage was celebrated is one of the fifty states of the United States, state law might be a better proxy than federal law for current social mores.

Counter-arguments might include the following:

a. To decide which relationships are deserving of immigration preference is exclusively a federal responsibility.

b. Individual states cannot realistically be expected to screen out sham marriages. Thus, it is necessary for the federal government to impose its own requirements for relationships deserving of immigration preference. (This argument does not apply to same-sex marriages.)

Q2: The statutory interpretation techniques invoked by this court include (a) a show of deference to the agency (INS) interpretation; (b) reliance on the "ordinary meaning" of a particular word (in this case, both the general and the law dictionary meanings of the word "spouse"); and (c) reading related statutory provisions compatibly (in this case, the statutory provision for the admission of "spouses" as immediate relatives and the then existing statutory section for the exclusion of homosexual noncitizens).

Q3: Congress obviously gave preference to "spouses" because it recognized that the separation of spouses can entail great hardship. Since there is no reason to think the hardship will be any less simply because the relationship is homosexual rather than heterosexual, a liberal interpretation would seem to further the broad congressional purpose. The counter-argument would be that, even when the statutory language is not dispositive and one interpretation would better advance the legislative purpose broadly defined, the *Kirby* case shows that a court need not choose that interpretation if there are countervailing costs that might have prompted the legislature not to go so far. The harms this court felt Congress might have had in mind (these considerations appear only in the constitutional portion of the case) include the absence of offspring and the violation of "traditional and often prevailing social mores" (more on that later).

Q4: The students' immediate answer might be that the Surgeon General's announcement should have no bearing on the *Adams* issue because (a) whether a party to a same-sex marriage is a "spouse" is a separate issue from whether homosexuality constitutes a "psychopathic personality or a sexual deviation;" and (b) the 1979 announcement tells us nothing about Congress's intent in either 1952 or 1965. It is possible, however, to argue the contrary. The court in *Adams* did, after all, rely on the existence of former INA § 212(a)(4). The court reasoned that Congress would not have wanted to give preference to the very class it was affirmatively excluding. If INA § 212(a)(4) were interpreted as inapplicable when either (a) medical or social norms have changed or (b) there is no PHS certificate, then that part of the court's rationale disappears. Although it is possible that Congress intended simply to exclude noncitizen homosexuals per se, it is also possible that Congress's intent was as follows: "Noncitizens with either a psychopathic personality or a sexual deviation are excludable, and at present we regard homosexuals as meeting that definition, but if medical norms were to change in that respect, these individuals would not be excludable." The issue is broadly analogous to the "original intent" issue that surfaces in constitutional interpretation.

Q5: Hard to say. Possibly one could argue that it is never certain that the consular officer abroad or the immigration officer at the border will actually invoke that ground (although same-sex marriages are not likely to escape the officer's attention). Also, as discussed in item 4 above, the PHS had stopped issuing medical certificates for homosexuality by that time. Perhaps the court assumed that without a medical certificate there was no exclusion ground. (The Ninth Circuit has so held, see item 6 below, but of course the court in *Adams* had no way to foresee that decision.)

All this might be giving the court in *Adams* too much credit. Most likely no one spotted the mootness issue.

Q6: On the first question, given the conflict between the two circuits, a well counseled noncitizen homosexual who wished to move to a city located within the Fifth Circuit might simply follow a roundabout route -- i.e., entering initially at a port of entry within the Ninth Circuit and then, after admission, moving to the Fifth Circuit.

As to the second question, now that INA § 212(a)(4) has been repealed, it is uncertain whether the court that decided *Adams* would have come out differently immediately after the Immigration Act of 1990. Possibly it would. The Court relied on the fact that Congress in 1965 had made clear it was excluding noncitizen homosexuals. Counter-arguments might include the following: First, that rationale was only one of the bases for the court's holding; the court also purported to rely on the "ordinary meaning" of the statutory language and on the principle of deference to the agency interpretation. Second, even with respect to this consistency rationale, the court in *Adams* was interpreting a statute passed in 1952 and amended in 1965. The 1990 Act does not change Congress's earlier intent. Thus, one would probably have to show that the 1990 Act itself should be interpreted as not only repealing the exclusion ground, but also changing the definition of "spouse." That showing would be difficult.

At any rate, DOMA (discussed in item 10) changes the picture considerably. If upheld as constitutional, its wording seems clear enough to dictate a similar statutory conclusion today.

Q13: Discussion on this question can be incorporated into the discussion of the Student Note, below.

Q14: Many of the arguments for recognizing same-sex marriages could also be made for recognizing polygamous marriages, assuming the marriages are valid under the laws of the jurisdiction in which they were celebrated, and further assuming all the parties are consenting adults:

1. Whether and whom to marry are essential components of personal liberty; the state should not effectively negate those choices by adopting laws that will separate the spouses.

2. The same family unification rationale offered to support recognition of monogamous marriages (whether opposite-sex or same-sex) for immigration purposes applies here. The polygamous family is indeed a family.

3. Separating the spouses also results in separating the children, if any, from at least one of the adults performing parental functions, just as is the case when monogamous same-sex partners are separated and the children cannot live with both their parents.

4. Disqualifying polygamous spouses represents nothing more than cultural or religious bias, just as disqualifying partners to monogamous same-sex marriages does.

5. Just as recognizing monogamous same-sex marriages won't harm monogamous opposite-sex marriages, so too, recognizing polygamous marriages won't harm monogamous marriages.

In response, an opponent of recognizing polygamous marriages for immigration purposes might argue as follows:

1. Rarely does a woman have multiple husbands; in practice, a polygamous marriage almost always entails a man having multiple wives. However theoretically symmetrical a law that recognizes polygamous marriages might be, therefore, in the real world these marriages oppress women.

2. Evolving western norms are slowly becoming more tolerant of same-sex relationships; there is no evidence that that is the case with polygamous marriages. The immigration laws should reflect the contemporary norms of the society into which the prospective immigrants want to enter. (Again, some might respond that what some call a norm, others call an irrational bias rooted in nothing more than religious dogma.)

3. It is one thing to allow a U.S. citizen (or an LPR) to bring in one immigrant with whom to share his or her life. The immigration laws should not allow one person to bring in several others. (The response here might be that our immigration laws do precisely that when they authorize the admission of multiple children, parents, or siblings. How is this different?)

4. Recognition of polygamous marriages would magnify the incentive for sham immigration marriages. A person could "sell" multiple marriages to

those who wanted to buy their way into the United States. In contrast, there is no particular reason that sham monogamous same-sex marriages should be any more likely than sham monogamous opposite-sex marriages.

Notes and Questions Following Student Note (page 278):

The excerpt from the student Note, like the Notes and Questions that follow it, are designed partly to provide some factual data and partly to raise the policy question whether the immigration laws should recognize same-sex marriages. That discussion could either be structured along the lines of the specific questions raised in items 4 and 5 or conducted in a more free-ranging way. Many of the questions in item 4 are rhetorical, and some students will take issue with some of them. The instructor could simply assign these materials and ask the students whether they think the immigration laws should recognize same-sex marriages.

b. Fraudulent Marriages

On page 286, the question is raised whether the addition of subparagraph (C) (waiver for battered spouses) is merely a subcategory of amended subparagraph (B) or whether, instead, subparagraph (C) covers any additional situations. Each of these subparagraphs requires both that the noncitizen spouse married in good faith and that he or she was not at fault in failing to meet the petition and interview requirements. (Subparagraph (C) additionally requires battery or extreme cruelty, not a requirement of subparagraph (B)).

The one requirement that appears in (B) but not in (C) is that the marriage be terminated (other than by the death of the spouse). Therefore, an example of someone who might receive a waiver under (C) but not (B) is the person who married in good faith, suffered battery or extreme cruelty, and was not at fault in failing to meet the petition and interview requirements, but whose marriage has not yet been terminated. Of course, if the marriage has not been terminated and the noncitizen spouse married in good faith, the question arises why the noncitizen spouse was unable to meet the petition and interview requirements. Maybe the citizen spouse is uncooperative, for example by refusing to join in the petition or to appear for the interview (as in Problem 7 below).

The last paragraph of the introductory text asks the students to speculate about the purpose of INA § 204(a)(2). The apparent purpose was to prevent the following scheme: Noncitizens A and B both wish to immigrate to the United States. They arrange for A to marry a United States citizen or an LPR solely for immigration purposes (either with or without the latter's knowledge that the marriage was a sham). Then, when the condition is removed two years later, the "couple" divorce and A files a family-sponsored 2A petition on behalf of B.

Imposing a five-year waiting period, during which time A and B will likely be separated (because, to keep his or her LPR status, A will probably have to remain in the United States, while B probably will be abroad until the immigration preference is obtained) dampens the incentive for A and B to attempt this scheme. Whether or not significant numbers of people have in fact attempted such a scheme is not known. In any event, even the theoretical rationale is much less convincing if the noncitizens are chargeable to a country like Mexico or the Philippines, where the family-sponsored second preference queue (and therefore the separation period for A and B) is so long that the incentive for such a scheme is minimal.

Problems 5-11 on pages 286:

General: Problems 5 to 9 deal with the core of IMFA, the conditional residence program for spouses. Problems 10 and 11 deal with the section 204(a)(2) restrictions on the filing of family-sponsored 2A petitions by remarried LPRs.

Problem 5: At the time B received a visa, A and B had been married only 21 months. Thus, if entry occurs within the next three months, LPR status will be subject to the IMFA conditions. If they are confident that the marriage will stay intact until two years after entry and that they won't have any trouble proving the marriage was genuine at its inception, there is no problem. They could avoid the risk by waiting 3 months (but not more than 6) before entering.

Problem 6: D is not subject to the two-year IMFA condition because the definition of "alien spouse" requires that the noncitizen enter as an immediate relative, a family-sponsored second preference immigrant, or a fiancé; the condition is inapplicable to spouses and children accompanying or following to join preference immigrants. INA § 216(g)(1). Of course, the divorce after one year might make ICE suspicious of the parties' original intentions (and under section 237(a)(1)(G)(i) will trigger a rebuttable presumption of marriage fraud), but if the evidence shows the marriage was genuine at its inception there should be no problem. Question 4, in the Notes and Questions below (why Congress would want to exempt accompanying and following-to-join spouses from the conditional resident requirements), could be raised here.

Problem 7: One option is for E to show up alone and try to persuade the USCIS examiner that her husband had "good cause" for failing to appear. If he had good cause, then under INA § 216(c)(2)(A)(ii) his failure to appear will not be a basis for terminating her LPR status. Alternatively, E might request a waiver of her husband's appearance under section 216(d)(3). Failing both, she might apply for a discretionary waiver under INA § 216(c)(4)(A). She would have to prove that removal would cause extreme hardship, which is difficult to show when she has been here such a short time; absent other facts, this waiver request would probably fail. Paragraph (B) would not apply since the marriage has not been terminated, and paragraph (C) would not apply since there is no battery and probably no extreme cruelty. She might just fall through all the holes.

Problem 8: Having entered as an immediate relative, G is subject to the IMFA conditions. Both the marriage fraud and the divorce will prevent him from meeting the conditions, and the fraud will preclude (B) and (C) waivers. His only chance is an (A) waiver for extreme hardship. As to that, however, there are two problems. First, the statute is ambiguous as to who must suffer the extreme hardship, and the former INS acknowledged only that hardships to him and to his spouse and children would count. He can argue (a) that the statute means extreme hardship to *anyone*, a plausible reading since the ultimate determination is still discretionary; (b) that the statute should apply at least to a dependent parent; or (c) that hardship to the parent causes hardship *to G himself*. Second, even for eligible noncitizens, waivers are discretionary. DHS will have to decide whether the hardship and G's beneficent motives together outweigh the marriage fraud.

The instructor can observe that G could initially have requested parole under INA § 212(d)(5) instead of entering by fraud. (Whether it would have been granted for this indefinite duration is another question.)

Problem 9: Since J is subject to the two-year IMFA conditions, and since K has said he won't join her petition to remove the conditions, J will eventually need a waiver. Absent extreme hardship, battery, or extreme cruelty (the last being arguable if K is vindictively using deportation as a threat), her only chance is a (B) waiver. As to that, she married in good faith and is not at fault in being unable to produce a joint petition, but paragraph (B) also still requires that the marriage have been terminated. *Judicial* termination is impossible if no one is willing to take the initiative, but it could be argued that *factual* termination is enough. Section 216(c)(4)(B) does not say "*judicially* annulled or terminated" as, for example, section 216(d)(1)(A)(i)(II) does. Perhaps she could argue that, if the statute is construed to require a judicial termination, it violates freedom of religion as applied to one whose sincere religious convictions preclude divorce or annulment.

Problem 10: Under INA § 204(a)(2), since L became an LPR by a prior marriage to a United States citizen, the government cannot approve the petition until 5 years after L first attained LPR status, unless L can prove by clear and convincing evidence that the prior marriage was not entered into in order to evade the immigration laws. Here, the facts look suspicious. She married a United States citizen, entered the United States soon thereafter, divorced him very soon after the conditions were removed (to get a divorce six months later she probably had to start the process almost immediately), and then married her old boyfriend. The government is unlikely to find clear and convincing evidence that the first marriage was genuine.

In this case, however, the five-year wait required by section 204(a)(2) is likely to be a moot point. Since L had already been an LPR for 2½ years by the time she filed the visa petition, section 204(a)(2) will still permit the Attorney General (now the Secretary of DHS) to approve the visa petition 2 ½ years after she files it (because by then she will have been an LPR for 5 years). Since the waiting period for 2A's is longer than 2 ½ years (more than 4 years according to the April 2009 Visa Bulletin), N's priority date won't become current until more than 5 years after L's acquisition of LPR status anyway. (Keep in mind that the priority date is the date the petition is filed, not the date it is approved. See INA § 203(e)(1); 22 CFR § 42.53(a) (2008)). Thus, unless the waiting times for 2A's diminish to less than 2 ½ years, section 204(a)(2) will be a moot point. But one caveat: If USCIS were to take the position that the visa petition is not even ripe for filing until L has been an LPR for 5 years (i.e., if it returns visa petitions filed by people like L and tells them to re-file once they've been LPRs for 5 years), then section 204(a)(2) would indeed delay N's ultimate admission. Thanks to Jonathan Weinberg for his insights on these issues.

Problem 11: Unlike her counterpart in Problem 10, P won't have to worry about section 204(a)(2) because it restricts only family-sponsored second preference petitions, not immediate relative petitions. So she won't need clear and convincing evidence that her first marriage was genuine. Nor is there any apparent reason to doubt the genuineness of the *second* marriage. (The instructor can note here that P might run into other problems, however, if the government finds the first marriage fraudulent. Such a finding would make her deportable on the ground that, at the time of admission, she had been inadmissible because of fraud, as the students will discover in chapter 7.)

Notes and Questions (on IMFA Conditional Residence) (page 288):

Q1: Proponents of the IMFA conditions might argue, first, that the breakdown evidences a high probability that the marriage was a sham at its inception and, second, that even if the marriage was originally genuine there is no longer a strong enough reason to give this beneficiary a preference over anyone else. Opponents of the IMFA conditions might argue, first, that the separation is not necessarily the fault of the noncitizen (or of anyone else for that matter) and, second, that ties develop in two years (jobs, friends, maybe children from the marriage), although if the ties are strong enough a waiver based on hardship might be possible.

Q2: An argument for starting the two-year period at the time of the marriage would be that the whole purpose of the IMFA conditions is to provide a means for determining whether the marriage will withstand the test of time. Consequently, time spent married in a foreign country should count for this purpose. To illustrate, under current law, if the couple is married for one and one-half years abroad and one and one-half years in the United States -- a total of three years -- a divorce will terminate immigration status. In contrast, if they are married for six months abroad and for two years in the United States -- a total of only two and one-half years -- then the noncitizen's status will become permanent even though this couple was married an even shorter time. This seems anomalous.

The argument for the present law, under which the clock does not begin to run until the noncitizen is admitted for permanent residence, would be that witnesses who could describe the couple's living arrangements and provide other evidence of the bona fides of the marriage are more accessible for the period spent in the United States. While in the United States, it is more difficult to conceal a sham marriage. (This argument, however, would not explain why the statute does not permit the counting of time spent in the United States in nonimmigrant status).

Q3: As to the first issue, suppose the marriage was clearly genuine at its inception but, less than two years after the person receives LPR status, the marriage breaks down and divorce proceedings are commenced. The original INS position -- that in such a case the petition to remove the conditions should be denied -- seems inconsistent with the statute. INA §216(c)(3)(B) requires approval if the section 216(d)(1) conditions are met, and INA § 216(c)(3)(C) requires termination if they are not. The only section 216(d)(1) condition arguably applicable is paragraph d(1)(A)(i)(II) -- i.e., that the marriage has not been "judicially annulled or terminated." Even that condition seems to be satisfied in the present case, but if the government wished to argue the contrary it might do so as follows: First, it might assert that "judicially" modifies only "annulled," not the whole phrase "annulled or terminated." Thus, if the marriage is factually dead, the government might consider it "terminated." Second, the government might argue that a literal interpretation produces a result Congress likely did not intend, since Congress would not have wanted to favor people who are merely about to divorce over those who have actually divorced. The noncitizen could respond that Congress might indeed have accepted such a distinction because people who are merely about to divorce still have time to change their minds.

The INS's second suggestion -- that, if the parties separate and there is no foreseeable reconciliation, it will be difficult (though not impossible) to prove that the marriage was genuine at its inception -- seems weaker still. This INS position, unlike the first one, at least acknowledges the need to moor the denial to a statutory ground. The INS purported to infer a sham marriage from the later fact of a separation without foreseeable reconciliation. The INS conceded the possibility that such a marriage could be found to have been genuine at its inception, but the clear import of the INS statement was that such a finding would be the exception rather than the norm. So strong a presumption seems unrealistic, given the generally high frequency of marital separation.

Q4: The exemption was clearly deliberate, but the rationale is not clear. Possibly Congress thought that the provision for spouses accompanying or following to join presents less incentive for fraud, because *the principal immigrant* would not want to jeopardize his or her own application or status. But (a) some principal immigrants would be willing to take that chance; (b) there could be a unilateral fraud by the accompanying or following-to-join spouse; and (c) Congress imposed the conditional residence requirements on family-sponsored second preference immigrants, for example, even though in those cases the petitioners similarly would not want to jeopardize their own statuses. Another possibility is that Congress thought the fraud incentive was weaker in accompanying spouse cases because the marriage must take place before the principal immigrant's admission; thus, parties contemplating a fraudulent marriage would have to tie the knot before they even know whether it will do them any good. Still, if the principal immigrant's case is otherwise cut and dried, the slight uncertainty does not seem like a significant deterrent.

<u>Notes and Questions on Marriages During Removal Proceedings</u> (pp. 290):

Q1: On the first question, the argument in favor of Kaplan's position is that a happily married couple might reluctantly conclude that, in light of the immigration laws, divorce is indeed the only way to save the marriage! Without a divorce and remarriage, if one of the partners must stay in the United States, the consequence would be two years of early separation. That could well jeopardize a marriage, especially if the marriage is recent and the couple are young. If there are children to the marriage, then an additional reason to divorce and remarry is to permit both parents to be with the children. An argument against Kaplan's position is that it proves too much. If it were accepted, a noncitizen would always be able to make that argument whenever a marriage occurred during removal proceedings. IMFA §5 would therefore never be effective against a couple who are willing to divorce and remarry. That, the argument would run, cannot have been the congressional intent.

The second question raised is whether even a divorce that is clearly designed solely to circumvent IMFA §5 should be recognized. One argument against recognizing such a divorce is that the law should not treat the couple who marry in the United States, and then divorce and remarry, more favorably than a couple who marry in the United States and remain married. There is, in other words, no reason that divorcing and then remarrying should improve a couple's status. A second argument against recognizing such a divorce would be that to do so would effectively gut IMFA § 5. The argument in favor of recognizing such a divorce is that there is no reason to treat a couple who marry outside the United States better than a couple who marry in the United States and then, once outside, undo the marriage and re-do it. There is no difference in the likelihood of a sham marriage, which after all is the evil that IMFA was designed to prevent. Note that either position creates an anomaly. The anomaly results because the statute itself, by treating the couple who marry in the United States during removal proceedings differently from a couple who marry outside the United States after the proceedings are over, creates a situation in which <u>any</u> answer to the divorce issue is anomalous.

The instructor might hypothesize a divorce that was intended solely to make the noncitizen a family-sponsored first or second preference unmarried son or daughter. The analysis of this question is very different. The reason the latter law favors unmarried noncitizens is that married people have their own families and therefore have less need to reunite with their parents. If the divorce is a sham, that rationale breaks down. Thus, in that context, there is good reason not to recognize a sham divorce.

Q3: Arguments in favor of the proposed change would include the following:

a. The change would deter the practice of marriage fraud, a practice that demeans the institution of marriage.

b. If the relationship is stable, the couple should not be penalized simply because they prefer not to formalize their relationship by obtaining government sanction through marriage. Their need to be together is just as compelling as it would be with a marriage certificate.

The arguments for the status quo would include the following:

a. Some might have a moral objection to the proposed change. The fact that the government recognizes and participates in marriages reflects society's view that intimate sexual relations should be formalized by marriage. The proposal thus demeans or trivializes the institution of marriage.

b. The proposal would create serious problems of proof. It is difficult to prove or disprove an intent to remain together permanently, and administrative difficulties would arise if the issue had to be adjudicated in every case. Privacy values are also implicated. Using marriage as a proxy for intent to remain together permanently avoids those problems; marriage is not a perfect indicator, but at least it is reasonably accurate. (Counter-argument: Under current law, the government has to make that kind of individualized judgment in every case anyway.)

c. It would be extremely hard to draft statutory language that reflects the proposed policy change. Should the statute refer to "sexual" relationships, or to "intimate" relationships, or to couples with "permanent" intentions?

3. Other Family Members

Matter of Mourillon (page 292):

Mourillon was born in the British West Indies. His parents never married. His mother deserted him, and his father raised him. When Mourillon was 13, his father married another woman, and they all lived together as a family. Later Mourillon was admitted to the United States for permanent residence and eventually naturalized. When he was 25, his father and stepmother had a daughter. The daughter came to the U.S. on a student visa and lived with Mourillon, who filed a petition to classify her as a family-sponsored 4th preference immigrant (sister of a U.S. citizen). The INS denied the petition on the ground that they did not qualify as brother and sister. Mourillon appealed to the BIA.

The BIA held that, for two people to be siblings, they had to have a common parent. The BIA agreed with the INS that they lacked a common father. The law at the time (since changed) did not recognize the relationship between a father and his child born out of wedlock. Nor did Mourillon qualify as the "legitimated" son of his father, because the BIA held that legitimation requires that the child have all the legal rights of children born in wedlock -- not the case under the foreign law applicable here. Thus, Mourillon and the beneficiary did not share a common father.

The BIA concluded, however, that they shared a common mother. Mourillon, having been under age 18 at the time his biological father married the beneficiary's mother, became that woman's stepchild and therefore the beneficiary's stepbrother. And that latter steprelationship, the BIA held, would continue as long as <u>either</u> the marriage creating the steprelationship persisted <u>or</u> the petitioner and the beneficiary in fact maintained a family relationship. There was no evidence of the former in this case, but there was enough evidence of the latter. Hence, the sibling relationship still existed and the visa petition was granted.

<u>Notes and Questions Following Mourillon</u> (page 295):

Q1: Two arguments are possible: First, it is easier to fake paternity than to fake maternity. Second, Congress might have assumed that, on average, fathers are less likely than mothers to maintain close ties to their children born out of wedlock. See *Fiallo v. Bell*, 430 U.S. at 799 & n.8 (1977). Both arguments surfaced in *Nguyen*; as to the latter argument, the Court's position was that Congress might have found the mother's carrying of the child and her necessary presence at the birth to be biological facts that make her more likely than the father to bond with the child. Justice O'Connor, dissenting in*Nguyen*, viewed the majority's reasoning as gender stereotyping rather than biological fact.

The new technologies do seem relevant to this subject. DNA testing, while expensive, can help solve the proof of paternity problem. Gestational surrogacy casts some doubt on the factual premise adopted in *Nguyen* - i.e., that the mother (unlike the father) is guaranteed to be present at birth. Since the genetic mother (the egg donor) might not be the birth mother, and since there are some difficult legal issues as to which "mother" has parental rights, the assumption that the mother is always present at the birth is not necessarily true. Still, the government might argue, the premise is true with respect to the overwhelming majority of births. The more dubious assumption made in *Nguyen* is probably the jump from "The mother is present at the birth" to the conclusion "Therefore, mothers are more likely than fathers to bond with their children."

Q2: Since Mourillon's father raised him from birth, there was clearly a bona fide parent-child relationship. Therefore, under current law, the petition would have been granted without any need to consider the step-sibling relationship.

Had Mourillon's father deserted him at birth and never seen or communicated with him again, then no bona fide parent-child relationship would have existed and Mourillon would not have been the "child" of his father. But as soon as his father married, Mourillon would immediately have become the wife's stepchild, and therefore the beneficiary's sibling -- even if there was no bona fide stepparent-stepchild relationship. Further, he would remain the "sibling" as long as either the marriage lasted or he and his stepsibling maintained a familial relationship.

Q3: Restrictions on children born out of wedlock mainly reflect Congress's fear of fraudulent paternity claims. See item 1 above. The parents' willingness to legitimate the child decreases the probability of fraud, but only if the legitimation confers real rights and is not just a paper formality. Thus, the parent's willingness to give the child full rights, such as intestate succession, increases the chance that the legitimation was bona fide.

<u>Problems 12-15 on page 297</u>:

General: Here again, the instructor might prefer to substitute a more recent Visa Office Bulletin for the one that appears in the book.

Note also: The Child Citizenship Act (discussed on coursebook pages 1315-16) does not affect any of these fact Problems, since none of the children is under age 18.

Problem 12: The mother, A, can enter on a family-sponsored 2A visa as C's spouse. If A is admitted for permanent residence before B turns 21 (unlikely, since the current wait for family-sponsored 2A's worldwide is more than 4 ½ years, according to the April 2009 Visa Bulletin), then B can enter as A's "child" accompanying or following to join. But if, as is likely, A is unable to secure admission before B turns 21, then A, after her admission, might file a family-sponsored second preference visa petition on behalf of B (if B is still not married). In such a case, B would be subject to the waiting period for 2B immigrants (about 8 ½ years) rather than 2A, since by that time B will be over 21. Alternatively, A might naturalize in three or five years (depending on whether, by then, her husband is a United States citizen) and then file either a family-sponsored first preference (a 4-year wait) or a family-sponsored third preference petition (about 6 ½ years) for B (depending on whether B is then married). Note that in any case B will<u>not</u> be able to enter as a stepdaughter of C because B was over age 18 when A and C married.

If C has been an LPR for five years or more, then C could naturalize and then petition for A as an immediate relative. The only waiting periods would be the processing times. A could arrive sooner that way, but B would not be able to come in as an accompanying child, even if she is still under 21, because there is no provision for anyone accompanying immediate relatives. Once admitted, A could file a 2B petition for her daughter (2B because her daughter would be over 21 by the time a 2A visa became available).

Problem 13: D can come in under the family-sponsored 2A preference as the spouse of an LPR. E, if she is still under 21 when D's priority date comes up, will be able to enter as an "accompanying child." That she was born out of wedlock will not alter that result because she is claiming "child" status through her mother, not through her father. As in Problem 12, however, it is likely that D's priority date will not become current until after E turns 21.

On that latter assumption, E will need some other route to admission. E will not qualify as the "child" of her biological father, F, who is a United States citizen. Even if he were willing to file an immediate relative petition on her behalf, he would be unable to do so because she was born out of wedlock and he and she never had a bona fide parent-child relationship. But there are two other options, even if D is not admitted until after E turns 21. The better option is for G to file a family-sponsored second preference petition for E as his "stepdaughter." The marriage occurred while E was under 18; it does not matter that she is now over 18. She will become ineligible for 2A status if she turns 21 before her priority date comes up, but in that (likely) event she will still qualify for 2B status. A second option, not as good, is for D, after her admission, to file a family-sponsored second preference petition for her daughter (assuming, again, that her daughter is still not married). The reason this option is less advantageous than the previous option is that G will be able to file the visa petition now, whereas D would not be able to file the petition until D herself is admitted as an LPR. Thus, immigration through G would be much faster.

One final possibility is for G to naturalize. (The facts state that G became an LPR about a year ago, so naturalization could not occur for at least four more years.) G could then file an immediate relative petition for D and a

1st or 3d preference petition for E, depending on whether she is then married. (Four years from now, E will be over 21. So she will not be a "child" and therefore will not be an immediate relative.)

Problem 14: H cannot come in as the parent of a United States citizen because L would have to have qualified as H's "child" at one time. Since she was born out of wedlock and they never had a bona fide parent-child relationship, she never qualified as his "child."

Believe it or not, however, J qualifies as L's stepmother under INA § 101(b)(1)(B). The marriage of H and J occurred before L turned 18 (in fact, before L was even born), and the statute expressly says "whether or not born out of wedlock." And the marriage of H and J continues, so it does not matter that there is no family relationship in fact between J and L. The BIA so held in Fong, cited in the text. (In *Fong* the BIA also insisted on a meaningful stepchild-stepmother relationship, but that part of the case has been superseded by *Palmer and McMillan*, discussed in item 5 of the preceding Notes and Questions.) All this, of course, assumes that L is willing to petition for J.

Once J is admitted to permanent residence, she can file a family-sponsored 2A petition for H as the spouse of a permanent resident. Then again, perhaps after arriving in the United States, J will write a "Dear H" letter saying "Having a great time. Wish you were here. As soon as I have a free moment, I'm going to rush to the mail and file a petition to enable you to immigrate to the United States so that you can reunite with the child whom you fathered while you were cheating on me. Don't worry if it seems to be taking a long time. You know how slow these bureaucracies are. Love, J."

Note, by the way, that there is no provision for a spouse "accompanying or following to join" an immediate relative, which is what J is.

Problem 15: N could file a family-sponsored fourth preference petition for Q as his "sister." For that petition to succeed, N and Q would have to have been "children" of a common parent. N was never P's (step)child, because N was over 18 when his father married P. But both N and Q were once children of M. N was M's biological child and born in wedlock. Q became M's stepchild when Q's mother married M, since Q was under age 18 at that time.

The instructor might ask the students whether it is a problem that there was never a single moment at which both N and Q were children of M. By the time Q became M's stepchild, N was already over age 21 and therefore not a child. Each of them was, however, the child of M at some point. In *Gur*, cited in the text, the BIA held that that was enough. As the text points out, *Mourillon* adopted the same interpretation sub silentio.

Note on Foreign Adoptions (page 298):

This material is intended as background reading.

4. Family Unification Policy

General: The instructor can either take up this material on family unification policy here or defer it until the end of the chapter, when the students will have an opportunity to combine the material on family unification policy with other broad policy considerations relating to the admission of immigrants.

Notes and Questions on Family Unification Policy (page 302):

Q1: Some of the analysis here will introduce (and rest on) the kinds of considerations explored earlier in chapter 1, § B (moral dimensions of immigration control). Is immigration policy instrumental, rights-based, or both? To the extent that it is instrumental, how much does society benefit from family unity? Many point out, for example, that reuniting families makes the family members better adjusted, and therefore more productive, members of society. Others feel that present and future labor needs are great enough to warrant increased priority for skills-based immigration. Still others feel either that the country needs both or that the country should not recognize either. Some argue that the population is already too large.

To the extent immigration has a rights component, some regard family unity as fundamental. See, e.g., the Guendelsberger articles cited in item 4 of these Notes and Questions. Restrictionist organizations sometimes say that family sponsorship is nepotism, and that it shuts out those who lack family connections. As for the hardship of family separation, some even say that immigrants brought it on themselves by choosing to immigrate. One response, of course, is that in many cases the immigrants had no choice; poverty, persecution, and other forces beyond their control might have eliminated all other realistic options. Also, many of the individuals affected by restrictions on family immigration are United States citizens or LPRs who marry *after* immigrating. The rationale that immigrants "brought it on themselves" would at any rate be inapplicable to those groups.

Q2: Some oppose these preferences out of a belief that, as a practical political matter, family-sponsored immigration is a zero-sum game in which awarding visas to siblings inevitably triggers a corresponding reduction in the ceilings for other family-sponsored categories. Even if family-sponsored immigration is not literally a zero-sum game in which the offset is one for one, there is a concern that awarding visas to siblings will reduce the availability of other family-sponsored visas by some significant amount. If that assumption is correct, the argument runs, then as long as there are backlogs in the nuclear family categories the law should increase the allotments for those nuclear family members rather than award visas to siblings. Proponents of the sibling preference (a) deny that family-sponsored immigration is a zero-sum game or close to it and (b) emphasize that in many cultures the extended family is much closer knit than it is in the United States.

Q3: This was a hotly debated issue during the period that led up to the enactment of the Immigration Act of 1990. It resurfaced after publication of the 1995 recommendations of the U.S. Commission on Immigration Reform. The instructor might wish to have the students discuss this issue in the format of simulated testimony before a congressional subcommittee. Those testifying in favor of the proposal might make the following arguments:

a. The long waiting periods for these close family members are cruel and inhumane, especially when one considers that they occur at the start of the relationship; i.e., they separate newlywed spouses from each other and parents from their new-born children, in each case for several years.

b. Requiring so long a wait is not in the national interest because the LPR sponsor will be less happy and productive. (Some will also send support money - i.e., remittances - back to the family abroad, thus affecting the United States balance of trade).

c. Whether the law permits it or not, the spouses and young children of LPRs in the United States will come in large numbers anyway, because the human instinct for family unity is so great. If that assumption is correct, then (i) spouses and children will have to live in the United States in fear and with insecurity; (ii) the effect will be to encourage disrespect for law; (iii) an underground subculture that is unhealthy for everyone will thrive; and (iv) the law will create additional and unnecessary enforcement problems.

Restrictionists might be expected to offer the following arguments in opposition:

a. We have too many immigrants already.

b. Putting LPRs on a par with United States citizens with respect to their ability to bring in family members would diminish their incentive for naturalization.

Proponents of this change might respond to the naturalization argument by asserting that, even if the implicit empirical assumption that the present system encourages LPRs to naturalize is correct, this is the wrong kind of incentive. First, they would argue, so long a wait poses an unacceptable degree of suffering. Second, they would argue, the present law sends the wrong message. The law should not encourage people to become United States citizens simply in order to obtain immigration benefits, any more than it should encourage people to marry in order to obtain immigration benefits. The "right" reasons for naturalization are to vote, to participate in a democracy, and to express loyalty to the United States. Finally, proponents would assert, many LPRs forego naturalization not because their loyalty to the United States is ambiguous, but because, rightly or wrongly, they believe that renouncing their existing nationality (a requirement for naturalization) would amount to a repudiation of family, ethnic, and cultural heritage. (Increasingly relaxed attitudes toward dual nationality worldwide diminish this deterrent but don't eliminate it.)

SECTION C. EMPLOYMENT-BASED IMMIGRATION

1. The First Three Preferences: Superstars, Stars and Others

a. General Eligibility Requirements

This material is intended as background reading. The instructor could, however, ask the class for their reactions to the major league baseball player example on page 306. Should the applicant have to be at the top level of the majors or simply the top tier of professional baseball players? The latter group arguably includes all major leaguers, since only a very small percentage of minor leaguers ever make it to "the show." But even if not all major leaguers qualify, what about a slightly above average major league outfielder?

b. Labor Certification

i. Displacing American Workers

Matter of Marion Graham (page 310):

After recruiting unsuccessfully for a live-in housekeeper/child monitor, Marion Graham applied for labor certification to hire a noncitizen for that position. The Labor Department regulations say that, if the advertisement requires the employee to live on the premises, the employer must demonstrate a "business necessity" for that requirement. The certifying officer denied labor certification for failure to make that showing.

On appeal, the Board of Alien Labor Certification Appeals (BALCA) first held that in the present context "business" refers to the business of running a household; the employer need not work outside the home. In this case, though, BALCA found that the employer had not adequately documented her need for a live-in, as opposed to a commuting, housekeeper/child monitor. Therefore, it concluded, labor certification was properly denied.

Notes and Questions Following Marion Graham (page 314):

Q1: Under INA § 212(a)(5)(A), the Labor Department must find an absence of United States workers who are able, willing, qualified, and available. Ordinarily, the employer makes that showing by documenting its unsuccessful attempt to recruit United States workers. But if the employer posts job requirements that are unduly restrictive, then the fact that no acceptable United States workers turned up will not prove there were none who were both qualified and willing. It might be that the only credentials they lacked were ones that weren't needed for the job anyway.

Q2: As to the first question (interpretation of *Information Industries* test), one possibility is that the two parts differ concerning what the job requirements must be reasonably related, or essential, *to*. The first part of the test requires that the job requirements be reasonably related to the occupation (in the context of the employer's business). Under the second part of the test, the requirements must be essential *to the performance of the job duties*. If the duties required for this particular position differ from those customarily required for this occupation, then there could be a case in which the employee must have a particular qualification in order to do *this job* well, even though ordinarily a person in *that occupation* would not need that qualification.

In the *Information Industries* case itself, the Board dropped an illustrative footnote. It offered the example of a law firm that wants to hire a lawyer and insists on the lawyer being able to play golf because many of the clients with whom this lawyer would work like to transact business on the golf course. Arguably, golf is essential to performing the *duties* this employee would have to perform. Thus, the second part of the *Information Industries* test is met. But golf is not ordinarily thought of as being reasonably related to the occupation of being a lawyer. Therefore the employer would fail the first part of the test.

There is a problem with that interpretation. The reasonable relation requirement in part I is modified by the phrase "in the context of the employer's business." So qualified, "occupation" is difficult to distinguish from "job duties." In the lawyer example one could probably say that, in *this* employer's business, golfing is reasonably related to lawyering.

There is no clear solution to that problem unless, as ALJ Brenner argued in a concurring opinion in *Information Industries*, the first part really means (despite the Board's insistence to the contrary) that the job duties (not just the posted employee qualifications, which is what the Board said) must be reasonably related to the occupation. If that is what the Board meant, then a case could arise in which the qualifications are reasonably related, and even essential, to the duties, but in which labor certification is denied because the duties themselves were not reasonable given the employer's needs.

That brings us to the second part of the question. Unlike the *Information Industries* formulation, which says the job "requirements" must relate to the occupation and be essential to performing the job duties, the PERM regulation refers to the "job duties and requirements." These must relate to the occupation and must be essential "to perform the job in a reasonable manner." ETA must have had a reason to insert the phrase "duties and" right before "requirements." Literally interpreted, the PERM regulation seems to require a showing that not only the job *requirements* (i.e. the person's credentials), but also the job *duties* (i.e., the tasks the employee will be performing) are reasonably related to the occupation). That latter showing does not seem to be required by the *Information Industries* test. Yet the agency insisted in the commentary that it was merely incorporating the *Information Industries* test and that the final rule "marks a return to the status quo." That being so, it is difficult to know what to make of the wording changes.

Q3: An argument against insisting that the job duties be reasonable would be that an employer should be able to decide what duties its employees should perform. Otherwise, the Labor Department would be judging the value of the work to be done -- a policy judgment within neither its jurisdiction nor its area of expertise. (In fact the Board so concluded in *Information Industries*). The argument in favor of imposing such a requirement would be that, were the law otherwise, an employer who wished to help a friend immigrate could simply specify work that the employer did not need or even want. In *Matter of Ching & Yeou Lin*, 89-INA-28 (BALCA, Feb. 14, 1990), parents wanted to hire a noncitizen to watch their children and to teach the children the Chinese language and culture. The certifying officer had denied labor certification on the ground that the parents did not *have* to provide such instruction for their children; it was merely a preference. The Board granted labor certification. It made clear that certifying officers may not examine the reasonableness of the job itself. They were to accept the job duties as a given and ask only whether the posted *requirements* for that job were unduly restrictive, given the job duties.

Q4: Requiring only that the job requirements be reasonable and that they tend to enhance the efficiency and quality of the business serves the needs of the employers and of the immigrant beneficiaries. It also benefits the consumer by keeping down the costs of products. The theory here is that the employer should be permitted to hire whichever person will best help its business.

In contrast, requiring that the restriction be necessary for protecting the essence of the business operation is extraordinarily demanding. Especially with a large company, it would be a rare case in which the essence of the business actually turned on a single hiring decision. This standard places little weight on the employer's needs and more on the needs of the United States labor force. It assumes that it is more important to employ an American over a noncitizen than it is for an employer to be able to hire the best person for the job.

As for the second question, in each context the goal is to prevent some social harm. There are, of course, two different sets of competing interests to balance. In the Title 7 cases, the business necessity requirement is strict because discrimination is considered a serious harm. But some would say the same thing about displacement of United States workers, particularly during times of high unemployment.

Q5: As to the Board's application of the "business necessity" requirement to the business of running a household: The alternative would have been to require a showing that the job requirement was necessary to enable the employer to carry on some outside commercial activity (rather than personal activities). Which interpretation makes more sense? On the one hand, "business" does not ordinarily mean running a house. On the other hand, it *can* include that activity and, if the congressional intent is simply to safeguard the United States labor force, it should not matter why the employer wants to hire a housecleaner or a child monitor. The fact that the employer's reason for hiring someone is to be able to leave the house for another job, rather than for some other reason, would seem irrelevant. Otherwise the Labor Department would be deciding which jobs were socially useful, a function that it is ill suited to perform, as discussed in item 3 above.

The language of the new regulation probably would not have altered the outcome in *Marion Graham*. The first part of the PERM rule for live-in housekeepers ("essential to perform," etc.) is exactly the same as the part of the *Information Industries* test that the Board applied in *Marion Graham*. The second part of the PERM rule (no "cost-effective alternatives") was something the Board in *Marion Graham* ended up requiring anyway; it faulted the employer for failing to show that other alternatives were unavailable.

Q6: The text notes that foreign language cases constitute a high proportion of BALCA's caseload. That is not surprising. One of the few generalizations that can be made about immigrants from the vast majority of countries is that they are likely to speak a language other than English. Therefore, requiring fluency in that language as a job specification would be an effective way to ensure that the person has qualifications most Americans don't possess.

Whether business necessity should be found when the employer's clientele speak that foreign language only out of preference can be debated. Those who would argue against finding business necessity might assert that fluency in a foreign language is not essential to doing the job in that case, as *Information Industries* requires. Clients could get by in English. Those who argue that business necessity should be found in such a case would point out that the employer might lose business if the clients' preference for communicating in the foreign language is strong enough. It won't matter to the employer whether the clients could speak English if in fact they are willing to take their business elsewhere rather than do so.

As for the Mexican restaurant: If many customers speak only Spanish, then there is clearly business necessity. The requirement is necessary to the duties of the employee and reasonably related to the employer's business. If there are not that many customers who speak *only* Spanish, but there are many who prefer to speak Spanish, then it is not clear yet how the Board would rule. It is easy to argue that customers' comfort with their surroundings, including language, is an important element of the ambience of the restaurant.

Q7: Hiring two separate individuals would very seldom be so impractical as to be "infeasible," since an employer can almost always hire two separate full-time individuals if absolutely necessary. It would simply be more costly or less efficient, and under the Board's test that seems not to be enough. The Board in *Lippert Theatres* did say in dictum that even this stringent test might be met, for example (a) if the employer wants to hire a truck driver who can also do light mechanical repairs; or (b) if a venture is so unique that no second worker could perform the duties. The editors of Interpreter Releases, 67 IR 1047 (1990), question whether hiring two people in that first example is "infeasible" rather than just costly, and they note that the second hypothetical case is extremely rare. Another possible example, though, is a small business in which the extra expense would be great enough to cause financial ruin.

Q9: Again there are competing values. The argument for changing the statute to require only a showing that no *equally* qualified workers are available would be that an employer should be allowed to base its hiring decisions on its own sound business judgment. It should not have to take a less qualified American over a more qualified foreigner. The argument for the status quo would be that the law must protect United States workers. If the law allowed an employer to take a more qualified noncitizen, it might become too easy to justify a hiring decision as proper when in fact it amounts to favoritism.

Q10: Trillin angered many members of the immigration bar with this article. Many attorneys feel he portrayed isolated excesses as if they were typical. That point aside, the two examples he gives -- the accountant/systems analyst and the babysitter/Muslim tutor -- illustrate the difficulty of drawing a principled line between the attorney's duty to represent the client zealously and the attorney's duty to avoid fraud.

In both examples, if the job duties are accurately described and the employer will indeed be requiring them, then it is difficult to see anything wrong with the lawyer's decision to emphasize those aspects of the job that are most likely to persuade the Labor Department. Some might object that the only reason the employer was specifying those job duties in the first place was to make the applicant's qualifications essential. That is perfectly permissible, however, as long as the employee will in fact be performing those duties. Again, the Labor Department is not permitted to examine the reasonableness of the job duties themselves, just the qualifications for those duties. (Of course, if the advertisement misrepresents the duties, and the attorney is aware of that fact, it would be unethical to assist the employer; there was no evidence of that in these cases.)

Q13: As for the on-the-job-experience issue, the Labor Department in such a case might wonder why, if this employee received the necessary experience on the job, the employer could not similarly train a United States worker. An immigration lawyer representing the employer might argue (a) that the job duties have changed since the initial hiring or (b) that the business has changed such that it is no longer financially feasible to train the employee on the job (because the work force is now too busy or because training personnel are no longer available).

Q14: The argument in favor of requiring the immigrant who is admitted on the basis of a labor certification to remain in the certified job for a specified length of time is that, without such a requirement, it would be too easy to defeat the protective function of the labor certification requirement. An argument against imposing such a requirement is that it would unduly constrain the freedom of movement of a lawful permanent resident. Moreover, an employer could more easily exploit its noncitizen workers. There would be little economic incentive to improve the wages or working conditions of noncitizen employees because they would have nowhere else to go.

In *Yui Sing Tse*, the argument for the majority was that, if the immigrant intended to work in the certified job for a reasonable time, that is all that can reasonably be demanded. And if more were demanded, people would simply lie about their intentions. Also, the employer needs the person, the employee wants to come in, and there is at least a temporary benefit for the consumer. The argument for the dissent emphasized the minimal nature of the suggested requirement: It would not prohibit later changes of mind, and it would not require even an initial intent to remain in a job forever. But if, at the time of admission, the employee already has definite plans to leave the job at a certain time, then arguably he or she should be excluded. Otherwise there is competition with United States workers, and the offsetting benefits are too short-term.

Isaacson article on page 324:

This colorful article is intended only as background reading, to acquaint the students with the flavor of the *Dictionary of Occupational Titles* (and thereby its electronic successor, O*NET) and with the variety of work that could conceivably become the subject of an application for labor certification. It's also a nice break.

ii. Adversely Affecting the Wages and Working Conditions of American Workers

Industrial Holographics, Inc. v. Donovan (page 327):

A manufacturer applied for labor certification on behalf of Yu, whom it wished to employ as an export manager. The Labor Department regulations then required the employer to advertise the job at the "prevailing wage" for 30 days, to post the job notice for internal recruitment, and to document the results of its recruitment efforts. The employer (after being told the proffered wage was below the prevailing wage) eventually advertised at the prevailing wage, but the Labor Department found that the employer had failed to observe the other requirements mentioned above, and accordingly denied labor certification. The district court affirmed, and the employer appealed.

The employer argued that the Labor Department had no authority to require advertisement at the prevailing wage in the first place. The court disagreed. It held that the regulation rested on the reasonable correlation between paying below-market wages and adversely affecting the wages or working conditions of domestic workers. Although an ideal assessment of the effect of a particular job offer would require consideration of benefits other than salary, the court concluded that the Labor Department could reasonably opt for a simpler test. The court also held that, in determining the prevailing wage, the Department could consider wages earned by employees in other industries as long as the job functions were comparable.

<u>Notes and Questions Following Industrial Holographics</u> (page 330):

Q1: The argument for *Ozbirman* is that an employer could offer less than the prevailing wage and still not adversely affect wages or working conditions because the fringe benefits are greater. Considering the entire package, rather than the wage level in isolation, would be more accurate. The argument for *Industrial Holographics* would be that, if other factors were considered, the process would be more costly and less efficient. Wages at least are *generally* a good indicator of the impact that the job offer will have on the labor market. Further fine-tuning, the argument would run, is not worth the administrative cost.

Q2: The regulation assumes that the job market is elastic -- i.e., that other employers will follow this example and seek to import foreign labor at lower wages. In fact, however, not all employers would be willing or able to do that. They might have no openings; they might prefer United States labor; or they might be unwilling to accept the expense, delay, hassle, and legal fees involved in obtaining labor certification.

Q3: This question goes in the opposite direction from question 2 by asking whether the prevailing wage standard is strict enough. If able, willing, and qualified United States workers are not available, it might be because the prevailing wage is too low given the demands of the job and the costs of the necessary training. If employers could not recruit foreign workers, they might have to bid up the wages until American workers became willing to qualify themselves for these jobs. Viewed in that light, perpetuating the status quo inhibits wage *increases*. For precisely that reason, some labor economists maintain there is no such thing as a true labor "shortage."

Q4: Suppose first that the local prevailing wage is *lower* than the national prevailing wage. One who favors requiring the employer to offer the higher national wage might argue that doing so would encourage United States workers outside the area to move into the area to take the job. By doing so, they might drive up the local prevailing wages. Opponents of such a position might question the premises of the incentive argument: that the labor force is mobile, and that recruiting is widespread enough to apprise others of the opportunity. Both assumptions are questionable. And, if the hoped-for labor migration does not occur, the noncitizen who is eventually hired will receive a windfall, getting higher pay than similarly situated American colleagues. If that happens, then the employer will be at a competitive disadvantage with respect to costs.

Now suppose the local prevailing wage is higher than the national prevailing wage. One who argues in favor of requiring the employer to offer the higher, local wage might make several arguments: First, if the employer did not have to offer the higher wage, the employment of the noncitizen would adversely affect local United States workers. Other employers in the locale could do the same thing, hiring noncitizens at wages lower than what they would have had to pay United States workers in that region. Eventually the local prevailing wage would drop. Second, geographic wage differentials often reflect differences in the cost of living; therefore no correction is needed. Third, requiring the employer to offer the higher wage might attract workers from low-wage areas, thus forcing employers in those areas to boost wages. (Whether that is good or bad depends, of course, on how one resolves the tension between wages and consumer prices.) An argument for allowing the employer to offer the lower, national wage is that doing so would achieve greater parity as among employers in the same industry nationally.

Q5: The court doesn't say whether there were other local manufacturers of rubber tire machinery that employed export managers. If there were, then there was no apparent reason to go outside the industry. If there were not, then the question is whether export managers for companies that manufacture different products perform "substantially comparable" jobs. As to that, the regulations permit consideration of whether these are "substantially similar skills." Possibly export managers in some industries have responsibility for greater sums of money, more employees to manage, more trade regulations to contend with, etc.

Q6: The general question is a difficult one. On the one hand, a central purpose of the labor certification requirement is to protect the wages and working conditions of the domestic labor force. Allowing some employers to hire foreign workers at wages lower than those of American workers with similar skills and job duties obviously runs counter to that goal. On the other hand, the reality is that some employers cannot pay more than what they are offering. So if there are no qualified United States workers who will take the job at that lower rate, the employer will have to hire unqualified people, go short-handed, or shut down. All those options are undesirable from society's standpoint, and the last option is specifically harmful to any American workers whom the company will have to lay off.

As for the Labor Department regulation, the real question is whether colleges and universities should receive special treatment. As in other contexts, the hiring of a foreign researcher at a salary lower than what Americans with similar credentials and similar research responsibilities are earning in private industry could potentially depress wages or working conditions generally. Yet the reality is that colleges and universities simply don't have the resources to pay industry-level wages. In addition to the arguments noted in the text, the higher education community argued (a) that Congress, by enacting special rules for members of the teaching profession, see INA § 212(a)(5)(A)(ii)(I), has recognized the special needs of colleges and universities; (b) that in essence the job duties of university researchers really do differ from those of industry researchers because of the inseparability of research from teaching; (c) that industry research is proprietary, not shared outside the company until the development stage and possibly not until a patent has been secured, while academic research is generally disseminated to the public for the good of society; and (d) that academic researchers receive other job rewards, such as autonomy, tenure, interaction with students, and a university setting, so that wages alone do not adequately measure the entire compensation package.

The specific situation of UNCF colleges remains problematic. All of the general considerations mentioned above apply here, and the proposed rule does not solve the problem presented in *Tuskegee University*. In that case the employer argued not merely that it could not afford to pay the salaries prevalent in industry; it could not pay even the salaries prevalent elsewhere in academia. On the one hand, it can be argued that teaching physics is teaching physics, whatever the particular college or university. On the other hand, since UNCF colleges serve predominantly African-American, low-income students, perhaps one can argue that the job duties, not just the nature of the employer, are distinguishable from those at other academic institutions. Moreover, since UNCF colleges are seeking to remedy the consequences of past discrimination, one can argue that the treatment should be special, regardless whether the employee job duties are similar to those at other colleges.

c. Perspective on Employment-Based Immigration

<u>Notes and Questions Following Papademetriou & Yale-Loehr</u> (page 342):

Q1: Long-term goals include national and world economic growth; supporting the needs of American industry; serving the American consumer; encouraging training and education for the American workforce; and protecting the jobs, wages, and working conditions of American workers. Short-term goals include enabling employers to fill immediate labor needs; creating and preserving jobs for American workers; and fostering short-term economic prosperity.

The Papademetriou/Yale-Loehr proposal addresses a range of long-term economic goals that the current labor certification system largely ignores. It does so by focusing on the more enduring attributes of prospective employment-based immigrants rather than on the extent to which the immigrants' attributes match employers' immediate hiring needs.

But short-term needs are important too. The instructor might ask the students whether the proposed system adequately addresses them. Here it is important to stress that the proposal for admitting people on the basis of their long-term skills is only for *immigrants*. For the employers' immediate needs, the proposal relies more heavily than the present system on *nonimmigrants*. The philosophy is that permanent residents should be chosen on the basis of what they will contribute in the long term, while temporary workers should be chosen on the basis of what they will contribute in the short term. One question to raise here is whether foreign workers who possess the sorts of job skills that are in immediate demand will have a sufficient incentive to come to the United States for that purpose if they know that their stay here is likely to be a dead end. Moving for the short term, and then having to move again to return home, might be considered too disruptive for young workers anxious to get started on career paths. On the other hand, the experience they accrue in the United States might well be valuable to them upon their return home; higher U.S. wages for even a temporary period might well be enough of a draw; and they might hold out hope that, by the time their nonimmigrant visas expire, their credentials and experience will in fact qualify them for permanent resident status even though there was no guarantee at the outset.

Q2: The system should be fair and accurate; cost-efficient; speedy enough to meet the hiring needs of employers and the job needs of prospective employees (both domestic and foreign); reasonably resistant to manipulation and abuse; and flexible enough to adapt to rapid economic change.

The Papademetriou/Yale-Loehr proposal is deliberately designed to fit the realities of the modern employment process. Few employers can afford to hold jobs open, and few employees can afford to await decisions, for the many months (today, years) that the current labor certification process entails. The proposal speeds up the process considerably. Moreover, the proposal replaces a process that is cumbersome and quite expensive for both the employer and the government with one that is simpler and cheaper for all concerned.

The main concern will be whether the proposed attestation procedure adequately protects American workers from any hidden preference that employers might have for foreign workers. This issue is considered specifically in question 3 below.

Q3:

a. Some employers will try to recruit foreign workers who will work for lower wages or lesser benefits than their American counterparts, even though this is contrary to the intentions and philosophy of the proposed system. The authors acknowledge the concern but make a strong case that there will be ways to minimize manipulation and abuse. They point out that the law could require employers to compile, and retain, detailed records available to the government and other interested parties (consistently with privacy demands). Even with paperwork requirements, though, there is room for manipulation. The employer must attest that it will pay the prospective immigrant at least the greater of the prevailing wage for the occupation in the area of employment and the actual wage that it pays other workers "who are similarly employed with similar qualifications." To identify both the generally prevailing wage and the relevant wage paid to the employer's other workers, the employer will have a certain amount of leeway in describing both the nature of the work and the relevance of particular qualifications to that work. Within limits, therefore, the employer could make a set of assumptions that would distort the wage scale. Perhaps the answer is that some government agency - for example, the Labor Department - would have the final say on whether the employer was comparing apples to apples. But that approach would impede one of the major objectives of the proposed procedure, which is to speed the process by reducing the number of steps that require government action.

Still, no system can be expected to be foolproof. The potential for manipulation is a relative concept; the authors reasonably believe that the proposed system is faster and less vulnerable to employer manipulation than the present system of labor certification.

Along the same lines, the proposed system does not appear to prevent an employer who *initially* complies fully with the letter and spirit of the equal pay requirement from allowing the person's pay to diminish over time, relative to American workers. Perhaps the various state and federal laws prohibiting national origin discrimination in employment could be invoked in such cases. (Refer the students especially to the material in chapter 12 on IRCA and the Civil Rights Act of 1964.) Moreover, once the person is admitted as an LPR, he or she in theory becomes as much a part of this employer's, and the market's, supply-demand calculations as any other U.S. worker; thus, special protection beyond that already provided by civil rights laws is perhaps unnecessary.

b. On the one hand, the two-year attestation is a speedy and cost-effective way for an employer to demonstrate a strong likelihood that it complies with the requirements for hiring foreign workers. And the authors offer several excellent suggestions for making the blanket attestations reliable – a formal, company-wide compensation scheme communicated to all employees, the use of market data to set wage and benefit levels, adequate human resources administration, etc.

Since employers' policies can change rapidly, there is no guarantee that an employer will keep its attested policies in place after receiving approval. But an employer would risk having future requests for blanket attestation (and maybe even individual attestation) denied if it reneges. At any rate the approval would expire after two years, so any damage would be minimal.

c. The simplest solution would be to confine the wage requirements to the original job. Once the person attains LPR status, he or she is essentially part of the United States workforce, and there seems no reason to treat him or her any differently from other U.S. workers, who do not enjoy this protection. (This last statement assumes the absence of otherwise prohibited job discrimination, such as that based on race, religion, gender, national origin, etc.).

Q4: The authors address this question explicitly. Before making an offer, the employer will have to assess the person's credentials, skills, and likelihood of success. This process is an additional screening device, and it comes at no cost to the government. Moreover, a job offer means that the immigrant will be able to work immediately upon admission to the United States. Thus, the immigrant will not require public assistance and is also likely to be economically, culturally, and socially integrated more quickly and more successfully.

Q5: The authors point out that a work experience requirement (a) enables the immigrant to make a more immediate contribution; and (b) avoids unnecessary competition with U.S. workers for entry-level positions. Arguments against such a requirement might include (a) the country would benefit long-term (the thrust of the proposal, after all) from the admission of talented, high-achieving young workers fresh out of university; and (b) nothing prevents anyone from switching immediately to a new occupation in which the prior work experience was irrelevant anyway (though one who has invested time in an occupation might be less likely to leave it).

Q6: Dispensing with a recruitment requirement poses a short-term cost to the United States workforce but is perfectly consistent with the underlying philosophy of the proposal. There might be an excess of qualified United States citizens and LPRs for the particular position today, but if the immigrant possesses the qualifications that make for long-term success, then the person's admission is still in the public interest. In the meantime, the employer is able to hire the person *it* believes is most likely to help it the most.

Q7: Arguments against awarding points for English language include (a) The criterion favors those from English-speaking countries and disproportionately disfavors immigrants from non-English-speaking countries, with both concrete and symbolic consequences; and (b) The criterion is unnecessary, because the highly educated and motivated immigrants who otherwise qualify under the proposed system would be extremely likely to learn English soon after arriving anyway. In the long term (which is the arena in which the proposal mainly operates), even those who arrive without English skills will bring a net benefit.

Arguments in favor of the English language criterion include: (a) It sends the message that the United States values having a common language and sees it as a way to build a national community. (b) It encourages intending immigrants to develop the English language skills they will need to succeed economically and socially in the United States. (c) Although the person might well learn English down the road, one can never be certain. And (d) Knowing English at the outset enables the person to make a more immediate contribution.

Q8: The proposal does delegate a great deal of policymaking authority to the executive branch. And the decisionmaking that it delegates is on fundamental questions of national policy. By selecting the attributes that govern admission, and by deciding both how many points to award and how many will be required for admission, the executive is effectively deciding how many employment-based immigrants the United States will admit and which ones. Arguably, these decisions are better left to the people's representatives in Congress.

But the authors identify solid reasons to delegate the decisions to an administrative agency. Shifting the policy decisions from Congress to an executive branch agency adds speed, expertise, and flexibility. (USCIS is not an agency normally associated with speed, but it is at least speedier than Congress, which was designed more for its deliberative qualities than for rapid decisions.) Moreover, the authors contemplate congressional committee oversight of executive policy formulation. Of course, if Congress is seriously dissatisfied with the agency's decisions, it can always supersede those decisions through either ad hoc or permanent legislation.

Q9: The main argument for eliminating such visas is that unskilled foreign workers take jobs from unskilled American workers, particularly minorities and the poor. In addition, it is argued, the importation of unskilled foreign workers can be a device used by employers to depress the wages and benefits of American workers. Finally, unskilled workers are less likely to contribute long-term economic benefit (and presumably more likely to require public assistance later).

Yet there are times when employers' genuine demand for unskilled workers exceeds supply, especially during periods of low unemployment. At the least, that shortfall can exist for selected occupations. As the *Marion Graham* case suggests, for example, there is a current shortage of live-in housekeepers. Some would argue, however, that such situations are not true labor shortages; they are merely instances in which the prevailing wages are too low and that, without access to foreign workers, employers would be forced to bid up the wages to true market levels. Moreover, since unskilled workers are seen as relatively unlikely to confer long-term economic gains, it might be that short-term needs for unskilled workers are better addressed through programs for temporary workers than through programs for permanent residents (as the authors suggest).

2. The Fourth Preference: Certain "Special Immigrants"

This is just background reading.

3. The Fifth Preference: Immigrant Investors

General: This material is intended to be self-explanatory, but at least two questions can be explored in class if the instructor wishes:

1. Should there be an investor preference and, if so, what should the parameters be? Is such a preference tantamount to allowing the rich to buy their way into the United States? If so, should it be sanctioned nonetheless because of the benefits for unemployed American workers? What about the third world capital drain? Consider also the other rationales mentioned in the text (speeding admission and making foreign investors "American").

2. Does the conditional status feature -- in particular, the requirement that the enterprise not be established for the purpose of "evading" the immigration laws -- make sense? There does seem something odd about deporting someone on the ground that he or she set up the company solely to obtain immigration to the United States, when Congress's very purpose in enacting this program was to dangle permanent residence as a carrot to encourage wealthy investors to set up companies in the United States.

SECTION D. DIVERSITY IMMIGRANTS

General: The statutory formula for the diversity program is complex. Problem 16 on page 350 is challenging, forces the students to apply an intricate statutory provision, and gives the students a better sense of how the diversity program works than would be possible through abstract explanations.

Most normal instructors skip the Problem and go directly to the Essay on page 351. There is not much loss in doing that. From the text, the students will get the flavor of the policy, the politics, and the basic structure of the diversity immigrant program.

If the Problem is assigned, it is best done before the policy issues raised in the essay. The latter will seem more concrete to the students once they have a feel for how the system actually works. With or without the Problem, however, the policy considerations relevant to the diversity program raise fundamental questions about the objectives and values that should inform a nation's immigration laws.

Problem 16 (page 350):

The first step is to classify the regions. One-sixth of the 3,000,000 immigrants of the preceding five years equals 500,000. Only two regions -- Asia and South America -- exceed that total. So they are high-admission regions and the others are all low-admission. See INA § 203(c)(1)(B)(i). The two high-admission regions together account for 2,400,000 of the 3,000,000 total, or 80%. That is the percentage referred to in section 203(c)(1)(C). The low-admission regions account for 20%.

The next step is to compute the population ratios described in section 203(c)(1)(D)(ii and iii). The numbers given in the column entitled "Population of Low-Admission States in Region" are those which subsection D(i) requires USCIS to tabulate. The total population of the low-admission states of the four low admission regions -- Africa, Europe, North America, and Oceania -- is 1,000,000,000. Thus the D(ii) ratios for those four regions are, respectively, 300/1000, 650/1000, 0, and 50/1000. These come out to 30%, 65%, 0%, and 5%. The total population of the low-admission states of the two high-admission regions -- Asia and South America -- is also 1,000,000,000. Therefore, the D(iii) ratios for those two regions are, respectively, 900/1000 and 100/1000. The corresponding percentages are 90% and 10%.

Under INA § 203(c)(1)(E)(ii), the four low-admission regions thus receive the following number of visas: Africa, 80% of 30% of 50,000, or 12,000; Europe, 80% of 65% of 50,000, or 26,000; North America 0; and Oceania, 80% of 5% of 50,000, or 2,000. Under section 203(c)(1)(E)(iii), the two high-admission regions -- Asia and South America (etc.) -- receive the following numbers of visas: Asia, 20% of 90% of 50,000, or 9,000; South America (etc.), 20% of 10% of 50,000, or 1,000.

The arithmetic will be simpler if the students proceed in the way suggested by the summary of section 203(c) in the text preceding the Problems. Once they determine that the low-admission regions get 80% of the visas and the high-admission regions get 20%, they can immediately allocate 80% of

50,000 -- i.e., 40,000 -- to the group of low-admission regions and the remaining 10,000 to the group of high-admission regions. Within the group of low-admission regions, the 40,000 visas can then be allocated among the four regions in proportion to the population figures of 300, 650, 0, and 50. Thus, Africa gets 300/1000 of 40,000, or 12,000; Europe gets 650/1000 of 40,000, or 26,000; North America gets 0; and Oceania gets 50/1000 of 40,000, or 2,000. Within the group of high-admission regions, Asia gets 900/1000 of 10,000, or 9,000, and South America gets 100/1000 of 10,000, or 1,000. The total comes out to 50,000.

Under either method the allotments for the six regions are as follows: Africa 12,000; Asia 9,000; Europe 26,000; North America 0; Oceania 2,000; and South America 1,000.

<u>Essay on Diversity Immigrants</u> (page 351):

This essay is obviously an editorial. It can be skipped entirely, or it can be assigned as outside reading, or it can be made the subject of an unstructured class discussion. Because of the fundamental racial and ethnic issues that this subject raises, the instructor might wish to relate this discussion to the earlier material, in chapter 1, section C, on multiculturalism (if that material was assigned). I like to revisit the subject at this stage (and cross-reference it earlier in the immigration and race discussion), because the issues require such fundamental value choices as whether an immigration program should reflect the needs of the intending immigrants or the national interest or both; whether immigrants should be visualized as individuals or as representatives of the countries and cultures that they leave behind; and, ultimately, what the composition of our society should ultimately be.

CHAPTER 4
NONIMMIGRANT PRIORITIES

The main purposes of this chapter are (1) to expose the students to the basics of nonimmigrant visas; (2) to enhance their understanding of how the various nonimmigrant categories interrelate; and (3) to develop statutory interpretation skills. The introductory pages (355-58) are background reading.

N.B.: If you plan to skip this chapter, or at least not to cover the *Bricklayers* case on page 358, you might nonetheless wish to assign item 2 of the Notes and Questions that follow *Bricklayers* (page 366). That item summarizes the three basic approaches to statutory interpretation – the Literal Plain Meaning Rule, the Golden Rule, and the Social Purpose Rule. Materials in later chapters often refer to that description.

SECTION A. COMMERCIAL CATEGORIES OF NONIMMIGRANTS

1. Business Visitors

International Union of Bricklayers v. Meese (page 358):

Homestake, which owns a gold mining project in California, bought a new gold processing system from a German company. Part of the deal was that employees of the German company would come to the U.S. to assemble the equipment. For this purpose, the INS admitted them as B-1 business visitors. In doing so, it relied on an INS Operations Instruction that purports to admit B-1's if they are coming to install or service equipment bought from a foreign company under a sales contract that specifically requires such service within a year, provided the visitors have specialized knowledge. A labor union and its local affiliate sued to invalidate the Operations Instruction and enjoin the INS from granting B-1 status under those circumstances. The court held that the INS Operations Instruction conflicts with two provisions of the INA: section 101(a)(15)(B)(i), which the court interpreted (with the help of the State Dept. regulations) as barring B-1 status for individuals who will be performing "local employment for hire;" and section 101(a)(15)(H)(ii), which admits temporary workers but only after they have applied for temporary labor certification. Accordingly, the court granted the requested injunction.

<u>Notes and Questions Following International Union of Bricklayers</u> (page 365):

General: This case is a good introduction to the interaction of B-1 and H-2B nonimmigrant visas. It also illustrates common statutory interpretation techniques, as discussed below.

Q1: Here the instructor might explain that the Operations Instructions are subordinate to the regulations, and that there has been some controversy over whether the Operations Instructions have the force of law. See, e.g., the discussion of the deferred action program in chapter 8, section B.1 of the coursebook.

Q2: The court says it must interpret the statute in light of its purpose, and in fact the court does later consider the legislative purpose. That discussion suggests the social purpose approach. But the court also says that the starting point is the statutory language. The students might think the court is thus applying the literal plain meaning rule. They should understand, however, that a court's desire to accommodate the legislative purpose does not mean that the statutory language is irrelevant. The language, though not conclusive, is itself a good guide to the purpose and at any rate a good starting point.

Q3: First, the court finds in both provisions a congressional purpose to protect the United States labor force. Second, the court appears to reason that the labor certification procedure built into H-2 and the regulations would be pointless if a noncitizen could avoid it simply by invoking B-1. The teacher might ask whether this is a good argument. Arguably, it is not. A court could treat the Operations Instruction concerning B-1 visas for construction workers as simply a limited exception to the labor certification requirement of H-2.

Q4: On this point, the court follows the literal language of the statute. The court says Congress expressly chose a policy of protecting the labor force. The teacher can use this question as a springboard for discussing the competing policies in more depth. The policy of promoting international trade helps the employer, but in the process it also creates U.S. jobs and stimulates the economy. The students encountered these policies earlier in the materials on the admission of employment-based *immigrants*.

Q5: The court's point here is to show a continuing legislative purpose of protecting labor. The idea is that if Congress had wanted to deviate from that purpose it would have done so expressly. To the contrary, the legislative history shows that the 1952 Congress expressly strengthened protections.

Q6: The commonly stated reasons for judicial deference to agency interpretations of the statutes they administer are (a) the specialized expertise of the agency; (b) the desire to promote coherence of agency policy; and (c) an assumption that such deference was specifically intended by Congress. As for the agency's application of those principles to the facts of *Bricklayers*, the court simply says the "administrative interpretation" (presumably meaning the Operations Instruction) is inconsistent with the statutory mandate and policy and thus must be rejected. The teacher and students might bring out two points. First, the agency interpretation is itself relevant to determining what those mandates and policies are. Second, the teacher might ask which agency interpretation should be consulted – the Operations Instruction or the BIA decision in *Hira*?

Q7: The main difficulties with arguments based on congressional acquiescence are (1) Congress might not have known of the particular case or Operations Instruction or other agency interpretation; (2) Congress might have been aware of the interpretation but might have failed to act simply because there were higher priorities; and (3) there is some doubt as to whether even intentional congressional inaction should be binding, since inaction by a single House gives neither the other House nor the President the opportunity to sign on to the legislation. In this case, the court simply says there is no indication the interpretation was ever considered.

Q8: Hard to say. The court states that the B-1 exclusion of individuals coming to perform labor "precludes *** [a] distinction between business and labor in this case" (page 365, second paragraph). What does the court mean?

If the quoted *Hira* requirements are applied to the facts of *Bricklayers*, B-1 visas seem appropriate (intent to continue foreign residence, etc.). Is the court rejecting the "necessary incident to international trade or commerce" test, or is it distinguishing *Hira* on the facts? If the latter, how? Was the work in*Hira* more like business (versus labor) than was the work in *Bricklayers*? If the students believe *Hira* is not disapproved, have them try to articulate a rule that is consistent with both cases and yet tangible enough to be of some practical use.

Q10(a): The students' immediate impulse might be to say that the policy considerations are indeed different. One who trains American workers benefits the American labor force. But note that the effect of allowing B-1 to be used in this way is to admit a noncitizen who lacks a labor certification. If there are enough United States supervisors, why not use them, as the law does for the construction workers themselves? And if there are not enough, what harm is there in requiring the employer to apply for labor certification and file an H-2B visa petition?

Q10(b): *Hira* did not involve building or construction, so the new regulation seemingly does not affect the result of that case. Thus, the continuing vitality of *Hira* depends on whether the court in *Bricklayers* meant to invalidate all labor or just building/construction.

Q10(c): The text does not call for any discussion, but if the teacher wishes, hypotheticals based on the cited material from Gordon, Mailman & Yale-Loehr could be used to illustrate the practical problems that arise in drawing the business/labor distinction.

<u>Problems 1-3</u> (page 368):

Problems 1 and 2: Both these Problems require discussion of how to draw the line between business and labor. In each case the truckdriving itself sounds like labor, but if *Hira* is still good law the question is whether the truckdriving is a necessary incident to trade. From a policy standpoint, does the activity affect either the United States labor force or United States business?

As between the two Problems, the activity might intuitively seem more like business when the individual is an owner-operator and more like labor when he or she is simply driving the truck as an employee. Both problems are based on real cases. Problem 1 is based on *Matter of Camilleri*, 17 I.& N. Dec. 441 (BIA 1980). Problem 2, where the individual is an employee, is based on*Matter of H and A*, 6 I. & N. Dec. 711 (BIA 1955). Both individuals were from Canada, and in both cases the BIA approved the B-1 visa petitions. In *Camilleri*, an added fact was that the trips were frequent.

The added element (in Problem 1) of picking up and dropping off goods within the United States (called "cabotage," or sometimes "point-to-point hauling," makes a B-1 visa problematic. The former INS, in a September 12, 2001 memo, clarified that noncitizen truck drivers may qualify for B-1 visas as long as they are merely picking up or delivering cargo "traveling in the stream of international commerce." For this purpose, however, cabotage is not considered a "necessary incident" of international commerce. See 79 IR at 303-07 (Feb. 25, 2002).

Problem 3: *In Matter of Minei*, 11 I. & N. Dec. 430 (Regional Comm'r 1965), an Italian citizen was selling his work in the United States and the Regional Commissioner held there was <u>not</u> international trade or commerce. The difference here is that the paintings will be sold in Belgium. The question is whether that fact injects a sufficient international element.

2. Treaty Traders and Investors

At this point the instructor might wish to remind the students of the analogous provisions for *immigrant* investors, discussed in chapter 3, § C.3.

<u>Question in text preceding Nice v. Turnage</u> (page 369, third full paragraph):

Intent to depart is easier to establish; for example, the person might intend to take up residence in a third country. Is it permissible for a court to read in even a requirement of an intent to depart? Arguably this is appropriate on policy grounds; an E-entrant is supposed to be a nonimmigrant, so once the reason for staying disappears, Congress might have intended that the individual leave. On the other hand, the statute says nothing about the temporary nature of an E-entrant's stay, in visible contrast to the requirements Congress expressly imposed on most other nonimmigrants.

Nice v. Turnage (page 369):

Nice applied for change of status to E-2 (treaty investor). He invested $25,000, but the source of the funds was not clear. (They appeared to have come from his father-in-law.) The INS denied the change of status on the ground that he had failed to prove he himself was the source of the funds. Nice argued that such proof was not required, and that it was enough to show he had possession and control of the funds and would be directing and developing a real operating enterprise. The district court held the INS acted properly in requiring proof that the investor was personally at risk.

<u>Notes and Questions Following Nice v. Turnage</u> (page 371):

Q1: The court didn't say that the regulation was unhelpful to Nice solely because he had not established that he possessed and exercised dominion. Rather, the court suggests that the rule itself is irrelevant. Later, however, the court says that other portions of the Circular require the investor to place his or her own funds at risk, the implication being that is the test. It is not clear whether the court intends to distinguish between an investor having possession and control over the funds and the investor being personally at risk. Either way, it is hard to see why it should matter how the person acquired the funds.

Q2: In a case where the investor's own funds are not at risk, would the purpose of E-2 be defeated? Presumably the purpose of the provision is to create jobs and to stimulate the economy. Both goals would seem to be met as long as the funds are properly invested. Perhaps, however, there would be affirmative costs in permitting a noncitizen to immigrate on the basis of some other noncitizen's investment. For example (a) perhaps the investor would not have the same incentive to manage the enterprise properly, or (b) without a specially needed skill, why couldn't United States workers be used instead?

Q4: Class discussion here should examine the inherent conflict between legal certainty and administrative flexibility. At stake are predictability, efficiency, and equal treatment.

Q7: The principal advantage of an E-1 visa (over a B-1) that the students will be able to notice by comparing the statutory language is that the E-1 nonimmigrant need not show an intent to resume his or her foreign residence.

The disadvantages of an E-1 visa compared to a B-1 visa are as follows:

(a) a treaty with the United States is necessary; (b) the trade must be principally with the trader's country; (c) the trade must be existing trade; (d) the trade must be substantial; and (e) the trader must direct and develop the enterprise.

3. Temporary Workers

a. "Specialty Occupations," Athletes, and Entertainers: H-1's, O's, and P's:

This material is intended as background reading.

b. Lesser Skills and Labor Shortages: H-2's:

This material also is intended as background reading.

Matter of Artee Corp. (page 383):

A job contractor in the United States hires workers with technical skills and supplies them to U.S. employers who need the workers for temporary assignments. For that purpose, the job contractor wanted to bring in foreign machinists on H-2 [now H-2B] visas. The INS Regional Commissioner denied the visa petitions on the ground that the machinists were not coming to the United States to perform temporary services, as the statute requires. Even though each individual employee would be working only temporarily, the job contractor's hiring needs were permanent, since it would be permanently continuing to supply temporary workers to its clients. Disapproving a prior INS ruling, the INS Commissioner held that the statutory requirement of temporariness referred to the employer's need for the work, not the duties of the particular employee's job. Applying that test, and relying on the widespread national shortage of machinists, the Commissioner found that the job contractor's needs were permanent and upheld the decision of the Regional Commissioner.

Notes and Questions Following Artee Corp. (page 384):

Q1: The three views are:

a. The *Contopoulos* view: The *work* to be done must be temporary. (In that case, someone -- either the petitioner or another person -- would have to do the child-rearing beyond the temporary two-year period.)

b. The *Artee* view: The need for employing someone to perform that work must be temporary. (The Artee Corporation had a permanent need for a cadre of employees that it could farm out.)

c. The petitioner's view rejected in *Artee*: This particular noncitizen will be needed only temporarily. After that employee's term expires, it is all right that another employee will take his or her place.

Q2: Contopoulos would have won. All she would have had to show was that her need for a mother's helper would end in the near, definable future.

Q3: The literal statutory language could probably have been interpreted in any of the three ways laid out in question 1 above.

Q4: Had Congress said "perform *temporarily* services or labor," the argument for the petitioner's view rejected in *Artee* would have been stronger. In that case, the word "temporarily" would more clearly modify the verb "perform." Thus it would have been clear that it is only this beneficiary's performance that has to be temporary; an individual coming temporarily to perform even labor or services for which there would be a permanent need might still be eligible.

Q5: On those facts it can be argued that everybody loses when an H-2 is denied. The employer needs these workers because there are insufficient American workers; the beneficiary wants to perform the particular labor; and the employer's clients will be able to use those workers. Maybe the concerns are as follows: First, if the need for *some* employees will continue, it might be hard to believe that the person will not just stay on. Second, a temporary employee might be more easily exploitable than would either a citizen or an LPR. If the need is truly permanent, the argument might run, let the employer petition for an employment-based immigrant preference. Third, the employer might well have been able to find permanent United States workers even though temporary ones are unavailable. If the employer is unsuccessful in recruiting permanent United States workers, it could then apply for labor certification on behalf of intending immigrants.

Q6: The requirement that the H-2B worker be "coming temporarily to the United States" would not be superfluous even under the petitioner's interpretation of the phrase "coming to perform temporary services or labor." Perhaps, for example, the individual is coming to take a particular temporary position but intends either to take another job or to retire when that temporary job ends.

Q8: The beneficiaries in *Artee* might well have qualified for H-1B status had they had college degrees. (That, in fact, was the case in *Ord.*) The noncitizens in *Artee* would of course have had to meet the other requirements for H-1B status. See INA §§ 101(a)(15)(H)(i)(b), 214(i). If so, however, they would not have had to show that the services they wished to perform were only temporary.

c. Trainees: H-3's:

This material is intended as background reading.

d. Miscellaneous Other Temporary Workers:

This material too is intended as background reading.

Problems 4-5 (page 388):

Problem 4: El Fantastico will not qualify for an H-1B visa because, among other things, singing is not a specialty occupation. It does not require a degree. See INA § 214(i)(1). He also does not qualify for an O-1 visa. His ability is not "extraordinary" and, further, he has not sustained national or international acclaim; he is merely beginning to acquire local acclaim. Category P-1 is inapplicable because El Fantastico is not part of a group (among other reasons). Category P-2 is not available because this project is not part of a reciprocal exchange program. Category P-3 is probably inapplicable as well. Most likely a court would say that X's act is not culturally unique.

Possibly El Fantastico will be able to secure an H-2B visa. As to that, however, there are two problems: First, there is an *Artee* issue. Is the position permanent or temporary? The employer needs a continuing stream of nightclub singers, even though this individual would be only temporary. Second, since El Fantastico is not nationally acclaimed, there will probably be many United States workers available. (But are singers unique?)

Problem 5: Again, H-1B is out because, among other things, tennis is not a "specialty occupation." No degree is required. Can Y qualify for an O-1 visa? Possibly she has extraordinary ability in athletics; she is tenth in her country. Is that high enough? It is also not clear whether two years of high rankings (twelfth, now tenth) make her national acclaim "sustained." As for a possible P-1 visa, she is entering to compete in the U.S. Open, a specific event. It is not clear, however, whether being ranked tenth in Argentina puts her "at an *internationally* recognized level of performance."

4. Intra-Company Transferees

Karmali v. INS (page 388):

Karmali, a Canadian citizen, worked in Canada for a company owned by his brother-in-law. While still employed by that company, he came to the United

States to buy a motel, restaurant, and campground in Idaho, and he stayed on to operate them. (The facts do not reveal how he entered the U.S.) His Canadian employer then petitioned for L-1 (intracompany transferee) status for him. The L-1 provision requires that the person be "employed continuously for one year" by the firm, or its affiliate, for which he is entering the United States to render services. By the time Karmali filed the visa petition he had been working for the Canadian company more than one year, but for less than a year in Canada. The INS denied the visa petition. Relying on the principle of deference to agency interpretations and reading the legislative history as supporting the INS interpretation, the court construed the statute to require one year of experience while abroad. It thus upheld the INS denial.

Notes and Questions Following Karmali (page 390):

Q1: Courts will sometimes find congressional acquiescence in a given judicial interpretation if Congress has altered parts of the interpreted provision but has not altered those particular parts that the court is construing. Here, Congress left the one-year continuous employment requirement intact. (Of course this argument assumes Congress knew of the interpretation and made a conscious decision not to alter it.)

Q2(a): There is no specific evidence of a congressional intent to delegate to the agency the interpretation of the one-year requirement. The only legislative history cited in this opinion suggests that Congress had decided the interpretation question itself by inserting the word "abroad" in the committee report. As for the relevance of agency expertise, one might argue that the agency is obliged at least to explain its reasoning, if it plans to deviate from the literal language. In this case, we do not know whether the INS did so, unless, like the court, it was relying solely on the word "abroad" in the committee report.

Q2(b): The argument would be that the committee was probably envisioning only those nonimmigrants who were outside the country and seeking entry, rather than those who were already here in other capacities. Thus, it was natural to assume that the employment had probably taken place abroad.

Q2(c): The court's contextual argument is not entirely clear. One possibility is that the language of the "temporary entry" requirement reveals a congressional focus on the person who had been outside the United States all along. How else, the argument runs, would it be possible for the person to "enter?" Thus, Congress must have been assuming that the employment must take place abroad. Of course, that reasoning does not help a court determine how to apply the one-year requirement to the fact situation presumably not considered by Congress -- the person who is already present in the United States. Perhaps the court was thinking that, once the person has been employed abroad for a full year, he or she would be more likely to have a permanent overseas home to return to.

Q3: One danger in relying on the language of committee reports is that legislative history often is not easily accessed by the general public or even by many lawyers without significant time and expense. Second, even if the history is accessible, the language of the committee report, while important, has never been formally approved by either House of Congress or by the Executive. None of those authorities necessarily signs on to every comment in the committee report.

Q4: The purpose of the L visa is to permit multi-national companies to conduct their international business. The one-year requirement, like the requirement that the person be employed in a "managerial or executive" capacity or have specialized knowledge, is presumably designed to ensure that those people who are brought in are integral parts of the company operation and are qualified to do important work. It is difficult to see how allowing the person to compile the relevant experience in the United States, rather than abroad, would impair those policies.

Perhaps there are countervailing interests. For example, the requirement that the experience be compiled abroad might be intended to deter fraudulent entries. If the individuals could gain the necessary experience while in the United States, the argument might run, they would have incentives to enter surreptitiously or on non-work visas, then work in the United States for one year, then leave the country and apply for L-status. Yet it would be perfectly feasible for a person to enter on a B-1 or H-2B visa, for example, and accumulate the necessary experience in a perfectly legal manner, if it were not for the agency interpretation requiring employment experience abroad.

Q5: The statute does not expressly prohibit such a person from entering, but the regulations do impose limitations. For example, one must be able to meet the administrative definition of "executive capacity," which requires actual direction or management of at least some company functions. 8 CFR § 214.2(l)(1)(ii)(C) (2008). Second, the person must be an employee of a "qualifying organization." *Id.* § 214.2(l)(1)(ii)(g). For that, the organization must be "doing business" in the United States. Id. § 214.2(l)(1)(ii)(G)(2). That, in turn, means "the regular, systematic, and continuous provision of goods and/or services." Id. § 214.2(l)(1)(ii)(H). Thus, a corporation that exists only on paper will not suffice. Third, an individual who is the owner or the major stockholder of the United States affiliate or subsidiary must submit evidence that he or she will be transferred abroad upon completing the temporary services in the United States. See *id.* §214.2(l)(3)(vii). Finally, if the person seeks to qualify by opening a *new* office in the United States, then the regulations impose a variety of other special requirements. See *id.* § 214.2(l)(3)(v,vi).

5. Comparing Commercial Categories

Problems 6-7 (page 391):

Problem 6:

a. X might apply for a B-1 visa. Here there is a*Bricklayers* issue: Is his work business, or is it labor? He will be solving product design problems; his work thus sounds like skilled "labor." Even if it is, he might argue that the labor is a necessary incident to international trade or commerce. The manufacturing will take place in the United Kingdom and the company will sell its products to a United States client.

b. Alternatively, X might seek an O-1 visa and claim "extraordinary ability" in either the sciences or business. His engineering work might well qualify as science, and his other responsibilities might even make his work "business," but his level of prominence probably doesn't qualify as "extraordinary." He speaks occasionally and is reasonably well-known, but "extraordinary" requires much more.

c. X might be able to qualify for an H-1B visa. There are several issues: First, is his a "specialty occupation?" Mechanical engineering certainly requires a "theoretical and practical application of a body of highly specialized knowledge," and either a bachelor's degree or its "equivalent," as a minimum for entry. Engineering is in fact listed as a "profession" by INA § 101(a)(32); thus it probably qualifies also as a "specialty occupation." There remains the question whether he is a "member" of that profession. He has no degree or license, but his experience is arguably equivalent to a degree. He has two years of university plus five years doing engineering work, followed by positions that have been at least partly technical. Moreover, he has been promoted to progressively more responsible positions in the company related to his specialty. See generally INA § 214(i). The government might feel that he is coming to perform services described in subsection O-1 and thus is ineligible for H-1B status. It is likely that his work would be characterized as either science or business, but since he is ineligible for O-1 status for failure to meet the requirement of "extraordinary" ability, O-1 should not preclude his eligibility under H-1B.

d. X might also be eligible for E-1 (treaty trader) status. The United Kingdom has a treaty with the United States, and being an employee of a treaty trader is enough. The questions, however, are whether what he is conducting is "trade" (rather than service) and, if so, whether that trade is "substantial." We would need more facts to resolve the latter question.

e. X might also apply for L-1 status. He has been employed abroad for the required year. He is probably performing in an executive capacity, and if not he might well qualify as a person with specialized knowledge, since his knowledge is unique to this particular client and therefore, probably, unique to the corporation. His problem is that he is not coming to a United States subsidiary or affiliate. There are possible ways around this problem. One solution is to open a United States office of the corporation. Again, there are special requirements for one who seeks L-1 status on the basis of his or her affiliation with a new United States office. See 8 CFR § 214.2(1)(3)(v,vi) (2008). Alternatively, X might enter the United States on a B-1 business visa to set up the office and then, after setting it up, change to L-1 status. The change would be beneficial because L's usually receive more liberal extensions of stay.

f. If all else fails, X might apply for H-2B status as a noncitizen whose skills are in demand.

Problem 7: The instructor could first encourage the students to identify Y's distinct skills. These include chess-playing, craftsmanship in building and in designing fine chess sets, and business and marketing skills. Possible nonimmigrant visas include the following:

a. B-1 business visitor? That the business she is setting up is new is clearly no barrier. The possible duration of stay permitted by a B-1 visa is probably long enough, since she can be admitted for one year with six-month extensions. There could be some inconvenience in having to rely on a series of extensions, but at least the total duration should not be a problem. Her main concern will be whether, while here in B-1 status, she will be permitted either to work for the new company or to compete in professional chess tournaments.

b. E-1 treaty trader? The instructor can note that there is in fact a United States-Italy treaty that covers both E-1's and E-2's. Problems here include whether she is coming "solely" to conduct "substantial" trade principally between the United States and Italy. First, she is coming for other purposes as well – to set up a corporation that will do other things, such as promote chess tournaments, and to compete personally in chess tournaments. Second, whether the trade is substantial will depend on the volume of sales of Italian chess sets to Americans.

c. E-2 treaty investor? Here the main question is whether $200,000 is a "substantial" amount of capital. As for that, see item 4 on coursebook page 371. But is she coming solely for the purpose of investing? She will be competing in chess tournaments and will be doing work for the company.

d. L-1? Her capacity is clearly executive or managerial, and in any event she has acquired specialized knowledge. She also satisfies the requirement of at least one year of service to the company. But one cannot enter on an L-1 visa when the United States subsidiary or affiliate does not already exist. So she might have to come in on a B-1 visa to set up the new corporation and then change her status to L-1 in order to achieve a longer stay.

e. O-1? Here it is necessary to define precisely what her field is. Whether it is the arts (crafting fine chess sets) or business (marketing them), her ability probably does not rise to the statutory level of "extraordinary." And chess-playing probably does not constitute athletics or science. Even if it did, she is not at an "extraordinary" level in chess-playing either.

f. H-1B? Probably none of her fields is a "specialty occupation." Each might require "theoretical and practical application of a body of specialized knowledge," but none of these occupations requires either a bachelor's degree or "equivalent" experience.

SECTION B. EDUCATIONAL CATEGORIES

1. Students

This is intended mainly as background reading. The instructor might wish to invite foreign students to comment on their reception by the community (to the extent they feel comfortable in discussing it).

2. Exchange Visitors

Sheku-Kamara v. Karn (page 398):

A noncitizen was admitted as a J-1 exchange visitor. Because his program was funded by the U.S. government, he was subject to INA § 212(e), which bars U.S.-government-funded (and certain other) exchange visitors from becoming LPRs (or H's or L's) until they return home for at least two years. Shortly after arrival, however, he received permission to change to a different, non-U.S.-funded, exchange visitor program. After that, his wife and child entered the United States on J-2 visas (spouse and child following to join J-1). His wife later applied for adjustment of status to permanent residence. The INS regulations interpret the statutory two-year rule as applying to any J-2 who is admitted to join a J-1 who is subject to the rule. Thus the INS denied adjustment on the ground that she was subject to, and had not satisfied, the two-year rule. She conceded that her husband was subject to the two-year rule and that the INS regulation was valid, but she argued that the INS regulation did not apply to her because she was admitted after her husband had left the U.S.-funded program. The court disagreed. It interpreted the INS regulation as applicable regardless of whether the J-1 was in a government-funded program at the time the J-2 was admitted.

Notes and Questions Following Sheku-Kamara (page 401):

The instructor might explain for the benefit of the students that adjustment of status, the benefit sought by the J-2's in this case, is a procedure whereby certain individuals who enter on nonimmigrant visas may, if otherwise eligible for LPR status, be able to obtain that status without leaving the country. The students will learn about adjustment of status in chapter 6 and will encounter it again in chapter 8. Unless the students are told that adjustment of status requires substantive eligibility for LPR status, they might erroneously assume that adjustment is simply a matter of filling out a form and that spouses of nonimmigrants therefore have an easy way of attaining permanent residence.

Q1: INA § 212(e) does begin with the language "No person admitted under § 101(a)(15)(J)" [which includes J-2], but this language is later qualified. A person is constrained by § 212(e) only if he or she fits within one of the subsections i, ii, or iii. Each of those, in turn, refers only to the J-1 nonimmigrant. Consequently, the literal language does not cover J-2's and the only question is whether for policy reasons the court should deviate from this literal language. As to that, see question 2 below.

Q2: Consider here not only the three separate policy reasons discussed in the text of the opinion, but also the practical consideration mentioned in original footnote 10.

Q3: Section 212(e) aims at the problem of "brain drain" -- the flow of educated people from developing countries that need them to more prosperous countries that need them less. One purpose of the exchange visitor program, therefore, is to enhance the skills of foreign visitors so that they can later put those skills to good use in their countries of origin. Another purpose, noted in *Sheku-Kamara*, is to improve United States foreign relations by exposing foreign nationals to life here and enabling them to convey those (hopefully positive) impressions when they return home. Neither purpose is served, the argument runs, when exchange visitors remain permanently in the United States at the conclusion of their training. In the case of exchange visitors whose skills are specifically needed in their home countries, the first purpose is directly implicated. For other exchange visitors, the prime benefit of the two-year rule would be better foreign relations. Moreover, proponents of the two-year rule would argue, in both cases the person knows of the restriction at the time he or she accepts exchange visitor status, and in both cases the combined interests of the two nations outweigh the noncitizen's individual interest.

Others might question whether it is justifiable for the United States government to tell an otherwise qualified noncitizen that he or she will not be admitted here because his or her own country has a greater need. One might emphasize the interests in free movement, the individual's desire to come, and the willingness of the United States otherwise to receive him or her. In addition, the admission of these highly skilled people will often be in the national interest of the United States as well. Finally, some exchange visitors whom the United States rejects for permanent residence because of the 2-year rule might decline to go home anyway, opting instead for a prosperous third country.

If the home country doesn't need the individual's skills, and the only trigger for section 212(e) is U.S. government or foreign government funding, the justification for the two-year rule is less compelling. Since only certain subcategories of exchange visitors are subject to the two-year rule, the real question is why the funding is relevant. As to that, the analysis probably depends on whether the funding source is the U.S. government or the foreign government. If it is the foreign government's funding that supported the person in the United States, then a strong moral argument can be made that the United States should not deprive that country (especially if it is a developing nation) of the fruits of its investment. But it is not clear why *United States* funding should activate the two-year rule. If anything, one might argue, United States funding gives the United States added justification for keeping a person who wants to stay and whose skills would be beneficial to the U.S. economy. Of course one might feel that even a U.S.-funded visitor whose skills are not specifically needed by his or her home country would still be of some benefit back home, but the real question is why there is any more reason to require that of such a person than to require it of an exchange visitor who did not receive government funding.

General: There are some other possible discussion points concerning *Sheku-Kamara.* First, is it clear from the statute that even the J-1 is still subject to the two-year requirement if he or she switched to a program not funded by the government? The answer to this question is probably yes. Applying the statutory language, such a person was "admitted" as a J-1, and his or her "participation in the program for which he [or she] came to the United States" was government-financed. From a policy standpoint, if the person were not subject to the two-year requirement, he or she could simply change to a non-government-financed program just before applying for adjustment of status.

Second, the instructor might make sure the students understand why the plaintiffs in this case were relying on *Tabcum*, in which the Regional Commissioner had rejected the argument that section 212(e) is inapplicable to J-2's.

Problems 8-9 (page 403):

Problem 8: The choice between an F-1 visa and a J-1 visa will not affect the permitted duration of X's stay. Either visa would permit him to remain for the duration of his full-time student status. Nor would entry on a J-1 visa prevent him from changing to an F-1 later.

The advantages of the J-1 are principally financial. First, he receives a grant. Second, the amount of the grant is sufficient to permit him, his spouse, and his children to live more comfortably while they are here. Third, the J-1 employment rules for himself and for his spouse are somewhat more liberal than those for F-1 visas.

The danger of a J-1 visa is that it could jeopardize X's future eligibility for adjustment of status. With a J-1 visa, X must consider INA § 212(e)(the two-year rule). He appears to fall under subsection (i). His funding by the United States is only indirect, and it is only partial, but under the express wording of the statute, that funding will still trigger the two-year limitation. X would also want to inquire whether subsection (ii) independently triggers the limitation. The question would be whether Ghana needs individuals skilled in chemistry. (According to the DHS Skills List, it does.)

Assuming the two-year limitation applies to X, the only remaining question is whether he might qualify for a statutory waiver. The "exceptional hardship" waiver has no apparent applicability because none of his family members is a United States citizen or an LPR. Possibly he could receive a no-objection letter from Ghana, but (a) that government is unlikely to write such a letter, given its need for someone with X's skills and (b) even if such a letter were to issue, the U.S. government would probably withhold the favorable exercise of discretion because of the government funding. Consequently X should probably assume that, if he were to enter the United States on a J-1 visa, he would then have to return to Ghana for two years before becoming eligible for permanent residence in the United States (or even for H or L status).

Problem 9: Since she possesses skills that her home country needs, she falls within subsection (ii) of INA § 212(e). Therefore, she needs a waiver. The only waiver provision potentially applicable is the one based on exceptional hardship. A careful reading of INA § 212(e) makes clear, however, that hardship *to her* does not suffice. The hardship must be to a citizen or LPR spouse or child. Y's spouse is a citizen, and her daughter is an LPR. Y's argument would have to be that her death, a likely event if she cannot remain, would cause exceptional hardship to her spouse and child, both emotionally and financially. (The fact that the spouse and child would have to go to India with her in order to keep the family united would probably not constitute "exceptional hardship.")

SECTION C. TOURISTS

The introduction to the section on tourists asks the students to imagine fact situations in which the consular officer is likely to conclude that the applicant intends to remain permanently. Factors likely to give rise to that belief fall into two groups: those related to the country from which the person is coming and those related to the individual's personal characteristics. Certain countries are thought by some consular officers to have high rates of visa abuse. This is particularly likely in a developing country that people have substantial economic incentives to leave. Personal characteristics that a consular officer might consider include the absence of a return ticket, the absence of funds with which to return, weak personal ties to the home country, strong family, employment, or other personal ties to the United States, a prior application for LPR status, and conflicting stories about the applicant's purpose in coming to the United States.

Matter of Healy and Goodchild (page 404):

Two holders of B-2 visitor-for-pleasure visas were stopped at the border because they planned to attend a school. The former INS had not approved the school for F-1 student purposes. As students, the INS argued, they were not eligible for B-2 status and thus lacked valid nonimmigrant visas. The immigration judges in the two cases agreed, and ordered both of them excluded. (One of the two was found additionally excludable on fraud grounds.) The BIA affirmed, partly on the assumption that the use of B-2 visas for purposes of school attendance would undermine the conditions Congress had attached to the issuance of F-1 visas.

<u>Notes and Questions following Healy and Goodchild</u> (page 407):

Q1: Perhaps the limitation simply reflects an assumption that employment is inherently inconsistent with the purpose of the tourism provision. If that is the rationale, it is not clear why it would apply with any more force to tourism than it would to many of the other non-immigrant activities. Perhaps, too, the idea is that because a visit for pleasure is less important than a visit for some of the other purposes, the person can respond to a change in economic circumstances simply by going home. (For students, intra-company transferees, etc., a return home might be perceived as more problematic.)

Q2: The advantage of a catchall provision is that Congress cannot realistically anticipate all possible legitimate purposes for which nonimmigrants might wish to enter the United States. Why limit ourselves?

The argument against a catchall provision is that its practical effect would be to destroy the utility of any conditions attached carefully to the other nonimmigrant categories. In this case, for example, the requirement of government approval of the school serves important policy goals. Of course, it would be possible to limit the B-entrant's permissible duration or activities under a catchall provision in order to minimize this problem. See also Question 3 below.

Q3: See generally original footnote 3 of the court's opinion. One possibility is that foreign students will be exploited; i.e., they might be charged tuition but given an inadequate education that does not meet proper standards. Response: Nothing prevents United States citizens from enrolling in these schools. Why should the government be more concerned about exploitation of foreign students than about exploitation of United States citizen students? A second possible reason for refusing approval might be the school's poor monitoring of its foreign students for compliance with legal requirements. Response: This is bootstrap reasoning. If there were no such requirements of tourists (e.g., full-time student status, etc.), then why would any monitoring be necessary? The government does not, for example, require anyone to monitor tourists.

SECTION D. FIANCÉS AND FIANCÉES

The introductory text preceding the *Moss* case asks the students about the statutory requirement, added by IMFA, that the two people have met each other during the two-year period leading up to the filing of the petition. The requirement was obviously intended to reduce the opportunity for marriage fraud, but it can create problems in cases of (genuine) arranged marriages, prevalent in many other cultures. As long as there is no reason to doubt the genuineness and likely stability of the particular marriage, the requirement seems unnecessary. Perhaps that is why Congress made the requirement waivable.

Moss v. INS (page 408):

A noncitizen entered on a valid K-1 fiancee visa, but the marriage did not take place until (according to the court) 92 days after her entry. Under INA § 214(d), the fiancee is required to depart if the marriage does not take place within "three months" of the entry. The court held that "substantial compliance" with the three-month rule was enough and that whether substantial compliance would be found depended on the reasons for the delay. It remanded to the BIA for an application of the substantial compliance test to the facts of the case.

<u>Notes and Questions Following Moss</u> (page 410):

Q1: Possible influences include (a) the maxim that doubts in deportation statutes should be construed favorably to the noncitizen; (b) the policy consideration that, if the marriage is truly bona fide and delay could not be helped, there is no reason to penalize; and (c) the statutory imprecision in using both 90 days and 3 months, which suggests an intent not to be rigid. Again the basic tension is between the comparative advantages of certainty and flexibility.

Q2: This question illustrates the difficulties of a flexible test. Where should the line be drawn? Of course, in addition to duration, a court might wish to look to other factors, such as the reason for the delay and whether delay could have been avoided.

<u>Problem 10</u> (page 411):

The marriage took place four months after the mother's admission but only two months after the son's admission. INA § 214(d) states that, if the marriage does not occur within three months "after the admission of the said alien *and* minor children" (emphasis added), then *they* must depart. Does this mean the marriage has to take place within three months of the admission of the K-1 fiancée, or within three months after the admission of the child, assuming (as here) that the child came in later? Either interpretation is grammatically possible, but if the statute means that the marriage must take place within three months of the admission of the fiancée, then the insertion of the phrase "and minor children" would be superfluous, because the K-2 child "accompanying or following to join" the K-1 will always have been admitted either with or after the K-1 – never before. Thus, one plausible interpretation is that in such a situation parent and child may remain in the United States, provided only that the marriage takes place within three months after the *child's* admission.

Another interpretation is that Congress inserted the phrase "and minor children" because it wanted to differentiate between the conditions that would impel the departure of the mother and the conditions that would impel the departure of the child. If that was the intended result, though, the language is inartful. Congress should have made a distinction in the "then" clause, not just the "if" clause. More important, that result seems wrong as a policy matter. If the mother is being required to depart, then (a) Why should the child be permitted to remain? and (b) Why would Congress have thought that the timing of the parent's marriage is a reason to separate parent from child?

Note: In an earlier edition of the coursebook, the Problem had assumed the mother was deportable and had asked only whether the child was also deportable. Thanks are due to Maria Frankowska for noticing that the statute is ambiguous even with respect to the mother.

SECTION E. A FEW OTHER NONIMMIGRANT CATEGORIES

This section is intended only as background reading.

SECTION F. OTHER NONIMMIGRANT PROBLEMS

1. Intent to Remain Permanently

The instructor might first wish to discuss with the class the practical problems faced by USCIS and EOIR in ascertaining a noncitizen's intent. First, there is the question whether an intent to remain permanently was preconceived or whether instead it simply reflected a genuine change of mind. Second, if the intent to remain permanently was preconceived, there is the question whether the intent was unqualified (not permitted) or, rather, contingent on the person being able to remain permanently on a lawful basis (permitted under the doctrine of dual intent). Variables that might influence the government's decision include (a) the timing of the change (immediately after entering, or after a respectable interval?); (b) whether the individual in fact overstayed; and (c) in the case of adjustment of status, whether the basis for permanent residence existed before the person's original nonimmigrant entry or extension or change of status, or whether, instead, that basis arose only after entry. Finally, it occasionally happens either that the person confesses a preconceived intent (knowingly or unwittingly) or that someone else turns the person in.

Weissbrodt & Danielson excerpt (page 415):

Before approaching Problems 11-13 (on page 416), the instructor might wish to ask the students whether they agree with Professors Weissbrodt and Danielson that the attorney can (a) ethically inform the client about the legal consequences of intent and (b) then explain to the client that it is up to him or her to decide what intent to form. Suppose the attorney says to a client desirous of obtaining nonimmigrant status: "If you intend to stay permanently, you are ineligible for this visa, but if you intend to leave after a temporary visit, then you are eligible. Now you decide what to intend." In such a case, is the client really deciding what to intend or what to say (to the attorney and to USCIS)? And is that the attorney's problem?

Problems 11-13 (Problems in Ethics) (page 416):

Problem 11: This is the clearest case because there is no factual ambiguity concerning the client's intent. Under Rule 1.2(d) it is clear that the attorney cannot fill out the application for this client. To do so would be to assist a client in conduct that the attorney knows is fraudulent, since under substantive law the person is ineligible for F-1 status if she is not coming temporarily or if she does not have a foreign residence that she has no intent of abandoning.

The harder question is which consequences the attorney should disclose to the client. Possibilities include the following:

a. The attorney simply tells the client the substantive law: "If you clearly intend to remain permanently, then you are ineligible for F-1 status."

b. The attorney describes the legal sanctions that the person could incur if he or she is found out. Under this scenario, the attorney tells the client that, if she applies for F-1 status, and all along her true intent is to remain, then (i) if she is caught, her application will be denied; (ii) if they miss it now, admit her, and discover the defect later, they could remove her at any time; and (iii) the government could prosecute her criminally for defrauding the United States.

c. The attorney explains that in both removal proceedings and criminal proceedings the government has the burden of proving fraud. Perhaps the attorney adds that fraudulent intent is not easy to prove.

d. The attorney describes the evidence on which ICE usually relies to establish fraud. The attorney mentions specifically that ICE ordinarily considers the amount of time that elapsed before the noncitizen's expression of a desire to remain.

The instructor could examine these questions in class by playing the role of the client and asking the student to play the role of the attorney. The instructor-client could ask the student-attorney a series of progressively more dubious questions to test the ethical limits. A possible version of that dialogue:

Client (teacher): Our conversation is confidential, right?

Lawyer (student): Right.

Client: So you won't tell the government what I'm now telling you, right?

Lawyer: Right.

Client: OK. If I send in this information, and I say I'm not planning to remain permanently, but I really am, how likely is it that I'll get caught?

Lawyer: (will probably say) I can't ethically answer that.

Client: Well, in your experience as an immigration lawyer, how many people do you know of who have done this and been caught? I'm just asking you for factual information.

Lawyer: (not clear whether this is a question the student attorney should answer; he or she might say anything at this point).

Client: Well, as a practical matter, how would they find out?

Lawyer: I'm getting a little uncomfortable with these questions.

Client: OK, let me shift gears here. If I were caught, what would the legal consequences be?

Lawyer: Well, of course they would deny your application. In addition, if they miss it now but discover the fraud later, they could remove you. Also, they could criminally prosecute you for defrauding the U.S. government. The point is, don't do it.

Client: Back again to the likelihood of my getting caught. As far as removal and criminal prosecution are concerned, would I have to prove I intended to leave, or would the government have to prove I intended to remain?

Lawyer: Again, I don't feel comfortable with this. I can see what you're trying to do here.

Client: I'm just asking you what the law is. Don't I have the right to know what the law says about burden of proof?

Lawyer: The government has the burden of proof.

Client: Now we're getting somewhere. How could they possibly prove what's in my head? I mean, if I say I intended to leave, how could they prove I'm lying?

Lawyer: You're really asking me to help you pull off a fraud. I can't do that.

Client: I'm just asking for information about the law. I want to know what kind of evidence will be enough to establish fraudulent intent. Don't I have a legal right to know that?

Lawyer: (might say) Well, maybe they'd look at how long you were in the U.S. before you "changed" your mind. Or maybe they'd consider any incriminating statements you made to other people about your intent. (Or the student might say) Forget it. You're obviously trying to use me to help commit a fraud. I'm not going to do that. If you want legal advice on this, go find some other lawyer.

Problem 12: Under the Model Rules, the attorney clearly is not permitted, much less required, to turn the client in. Rule 1.6(a) prohibits such disclosure without the client's authorization. Such authorization certainly cannot be inferred if the client expressly says no. There are exceptions contained in Rule 1.6(b), but they are confined to the contexts of death and substantial bodily harm, not the situations here.

In a state that retains DR 4-101(C), however, the attorney is permitted (though not required) to report the client. It is a crime to defraud the United States government, see 18 USC § 1001, and the client has revealed an intent to commit that crime. Whether the attorney "should" report the client will depend on how the attorney balances the harm from the client's proposed conduct against the harm from breaching what the client probably understood to be a confidential relationship.

Problem 13: Under Rule 1.2(d), the question is whether the attorney "knows" the conduct is fraudulent. How high a probability of fraud does the word "know" entail? Near certainty? A belief in a high probability? A belief that fraud is more likely than not? There are analogies here to both criminal law and torts. Note also that, even if the attorney knows the client plans to stay in the event USCIS grants permission, it is possible the client will leave if such permission is not given. If that is the client's intent, then under the doctrine of dual intent his or her actions are perfectly lawful.

Balanced against the attorney's duty not to assist in the commission of a fraud is the attorney's duty under Rule 1.3 to act with reasonable diligence. (Of course Rule 1.3 will be inapplicable if the attorney decides not to take the individual as a client in the first place). Is this zealous advocacy? Considering the language of the comment accompanying Rule 1.3, is this a case in which the lawyer's preference not to assist the client is within his or her "professional discretion" to determine the means by which a matter should be pursued?

2. Change of Nonimmigrant Status

Problem 14 (page 419):

The students might initially think that INA §§ 212(e) and 248 are logically contradictory. But they are not; they are merely silly. In this Problem, X is subject to the two-year rule as a result of INA § 212(e)(i). A J-nonimmigrant who is subject to the two-year requirement and who does not receive a waiver may not change status under INA § 248 to any other nonimmigrant category (except to A or G). Under INA § 212(e), however, all that a J-nonimmigrant who is subject to the two-year rule cannot do (without leaving the United States for two years) is change to permanent resident status, H-status, or L-status. It seems, therefore, that X could go home, obtain an F-1 visa without much trouble, and then return.

That being the case, why preclude change of status under INA § 248? The instructor might ask what Congress thought it was accomplishing. When there are reasons for requiring the person to return home for two years, then why allow him or her to come back immediately with another nonimmigrant visa? And when there are not reasons for requiring the person to go home for two years, then why make him or her buy a round-trip plane ticket in order to stay?

There is one possible argument for a different interpretation: INA § 248 refers only to the individual who is "subject to the two-year foreign residence requirement." Arguably, to be "subject" to that requirement, the person must be a J-entrant who falls within one of the three statutory groups on whom the two-year residence requirement is imposed, *and be a person who desires immigrant, H, or L status*. Under this interpretation, the person who wants only to convert to F-1 status is not "subject to" the two-year requirement and therefore is not disqualified by the language of section 248. But that interpretation is problematic. It would render superfluous the language in INA § 248 concerning A's and G's. Since the latter do not want H or L status, under this interpretation they would not be "subject to the two-year foreign residence requirement" under any circumstances, so mentioning them specially in section 248 was unnecessary.

It is also possible, of course, that the individual can obtain a no-objection letter from Australia. In that event, INA § 248 could be used.

CHAPTER 5
EXCLUSION GROUNDS AND WAIVERS

General: The introductory materials on pages 420-31 are intended as background reading. When assigning this material, the instructor might wish to flag the instruction on page 430 that the students skim INA § 212(a) to get a sense of its layout.

As with the other chapters, the coverage here is highly selective. In addition to the usual reasons for selectivity, many of the concepts relevant to the exclusion grounds -- e.g. fraud and criminality -- will surface again in the material on deportability grounds, where they will be explored in more detail.

SECTION A. GROUNDS RELATED TO IMMIGRATION CONTROL

General: This section contains information that the students will need in order to follow the discussion in subsequent chapters (e.g. the exclusion grounds for lack of proper entry documents, for prior removal orders, for fraud, and for being out of status). In addition, the fact Problems will require the students to spot statutory interpretation issues, enable them to apply the statute to fact situations, permit them to observe the practical impact of these exclusion grounds, and raise policy questions about the soundness of the results.

Problems 1-5 (page 435):

Problem 1: X does not appear to be inadmissible under section 212(a)(9)(A), because he has not been ordered removed. ICE might argue, however, that one who leaves the United States while his or her removal proceedings are ongoing is deemed removed.

Is he inadmissible under section 212(a)(9)(B)? Under section 212(a)(9)(B)(iii), time spent while under age 18 does not count as unlawful presence. X will be regarded, therefore, as having been unlawfully present from his 18th birthday, which is July 1, 2008, until his departure on March 1, 2009 – a total unlawful presence of 8 months. (Under the USCIS interpretation, his one month in removal proceedings counts as unlawful presence, but on these facts it doesn't matter; either way, X was unlawfully present more than 180 days but less than one year.) Thus, the exclusion ground to consult is 212(a)(9)(B)(i)(I) (unlawfully present between 180 days and one year). If that provision applies, then X will be inadmissible for three years from his March 1, 2009 departure, and so far only two years have elapsed. Under the literal language, however, X would have to have departed "prior to the commencement of [removal] proceedings." X left *after* ICE commenced removal proceedings. On its face, therefore, this exclusion ground is inapplicable. That result might at first seem anomalous, since there is no apparent reason to treat X any more favorably than the person who left before proceedings began. But that's what the provision says.

The explanation might lie in INA § 212(a)(6)(B), which supplies a possible alternative ground of inadmissibility, failure to attend the removal hearing. This provision might explain why Congress added to section 212(a)(9)(B)(i)(I) the qualifying language "prior to the commencement of proceedings." Maybe Congress assumed that, if the person departed after the commencement of proceedings but before the hearing, he or she would be inadmissible for five years under section 212(a)(6)(B), and thus the three-year exclusion imposed by 212(a)(9)(B)(i)(I) would be superfluous. In contrast, since the ten-year bar imposed by section 212(a)(9)(B)(i)(II) is greater than the five-year exclusion in 212(a)(6)(B), the ten-year ground doesn't contain the same qualifier.

Michael Scaperlanda, in an e-mail to the author, has raised the possibility of arguing that the proceeding to which section 212(a)(6)(B) refers is the actual removal hearing, in which case a departure after service of the notice to appear but before the removal hearing would not trigger inadmissibility.

Finally, X is a nonimmigrant. Thus, if he is found inadmissible on either of those grounds, X could apply for a discretionary waiver under section 212(d)(3)(A).

Problem 2: The pertinent inadmissibility ground is INA § 212(a)(9)(B)(i)(I), which says that a noncitizen who was unlawfully present for more than 180 days, and then voluntarily departs before the commencement of removal proceedings, becomes inadmissible for three years after the departure. Y's original visa expired on June 1, 2008, but she stayed on. Under INA § 212(a)(9)(B)(iv), the first 120 days (approximately four months) of her overstay do not count as unlawful presence, because Y was lawfully admitted, she filed an unfrivolous application for an extension before her stay expired (we can assume the application was unfrivolous, since USCIS has found serious issues), and there is no indication she has worked without authorization. Even with four months of tolling, however, her presence would be unlawful from October 1, 2008 (i.e., four months after her lawful stay expired) until her departure on May 1, 2009 -- a total unlawful presence of seven months. Under INA § 212(a)(9)(B)(i)(I), therefore, she would be inadmissible for three years starting May 1, 2009. As of now, only two of those years have elapsed. Thus she would seem to be inadmissible for one more year.

But the USCIS policy discussed in the text alters that result. By its terms, her presence did not become unlawful until USCIS denied her application for an extension on December 1, 2008. She left on May 1, 2009, just five months later. Thus her unlawful presence was for less than 180 days and she is not inadmissible under INA § 212(a)(9)(B)(i)(I).

INA § 212(a)(9)(B)(v) confers discretion on the Attorney General to waive this exclusion ground for an immigrant who has certain U.S. citizen or LPR family members who would suffer extreme hardship if the principal immigrant were refused admission. The medical risks that Y's exclusion would cause certainly seem to rise to the level of extreme hardship to Y's daughter, but the problem is that the list of family members is not broad enough to cover this case. The inadmissible person must be the "spouse or son or daughter" of the citizen or LPR; being the parent is not enough.

Virgil Wiebe has raised an interesting question. Suppose one concludes that the three-year bar applies and that so far only two years have elapsed. Could the person enter on an H-1B visa with a discretionary waiver under INA § 212(d)(3)(A) (for nonimmigrants only) and then, after one year in the United States in that status, achieve LPR status as an employment-based immigrant? In other words, would the year in the United States count toward the 3-year waiting period? (If so, the person could presumably start the labor certification process even before the end of the 3-year period.)

The language of INA § 212(a)(9)(B)(i)(I) poses no obvious obstacle to that strategy. The person is inadmissible if he or she "seeks admission within 3 years of the date of such alien's departure or removal." It does not say that the person has to spend the required waiting period "in the country of his nationality or his last residence," for example, as section 212(e) requires for exchange visitors.

Whether the person could become eligible for LPR status even <u>before</u> the end of that first year in the United States is less clear. By referring to someone who seeks "admission" to the United States, the statute would probably be interpreted to include someone who seeks admission in the sense of being "admitted" to LPR status, for example through adjustment of status.

Of course, if Y were to seek admission on an H-1B visa with a 212(d)(3)(A) waiver, there could also be an issue of whether she is "coming temporarily to the United States," as INA § 101(a)(15)(H)(i)(B) requires. Dual intent would be a question of fact.

<u>Problem 3</u>: Z has two separate ten-year exclusion provisions to worry about. Under INA § 212(a)(9)(A), removal renders noncitizens inadmissible for a certain number of years. How many years the inadmissibility lasts depends on the circumstances of the removal. Prong (i) of 212(a)(9)(A) applies to individuals who were removed upon arrival at U.S. ports of entry, while prong (ii) governs those who were removed under other circumstances (i.e., from the interior). Z would therefore be subject to prong (ii) and thus will be inadmissible for ten years. Under section 212(a)(9)(A)(iii), however, the Secretary of Homeland Security has the discretion to eliminate this barrier by consenting to Z's reapplying for admission.

Note that Z does not fall within INA § 212(a)(9)(B)(i)(I). That provision renders inadmissible any noncitizen who was unlawfully present more than 180 days but less than a year (arguably Z), but only if the person *voluntarily* departed *prior* to the commencement of removal proceedings. Z's departure was not voluntary. In addition it was after removal proceedings had commenced; in fact they had concluded. [Since only departures that are voluntary can trigger section 212(a)(9)(B)(i)(I), it is not clear why the drafters ended the provision with the phrase "departure *or removal*" (emphasis added). Removals are never voluntary.] Thanks to Huyen Pham and Leti Volpp for those observations on section 212(a)(9)(B)(i)(I).

But what about section 212(a)(9)(B)(i)(II), which excludes anyone who was unlawfully present for a year or more and who then seeks readmission within ten years of the date of departure or removal? It has now been only six years since Z's removal. The answer is not clear. Z's unlawful presence began on January 1, 2008, and he did not depart until February 5, 2009, more than a year later. The issue is whether the period from December 1, 2008 until his departure counts toward unlawful presence. If it doesn't, then his unlawful presence was only 11 months and 212(a)(9)(B)(i)(II) will be inapplicable. INA § 212(a)(9)(B)(ii) defines "unlawfully present" to mean present "after the expiration of the period of stay authorized by the [Secretary of Homeland Security] or present in the United States without being admitted or paroled." Since Z was present the entire time without having been admitted or paroled, a literal reading would result in more than a year of unlawful presence. Z could argue, however, that Congress did not intend a literal reading. Z*couldn't* have departed sooner, he would argue, because ICE was detaining him. Or, he might say, the only way he could have departed sooner would have been to waive his right to a removal hearing and ask ICE to allow him to depart voluntarily. There is no guarantee his request would have been granted, and it is debatable whether one should be expected to give up important rights in order to avoid future inadmissibility. Moreover, Z might argue, through detention the Secretary of Homeland Security was implicitly authorizing him – in fact, compelling him – to stay in the United States during the pendency of the removal hearing. Consequently, that portion of his stay should not be regarded as unlawful.

Under the USCIS interpretation discussed on pages 433-34, the fact that a person is in removal proceedings does not affect the lawfulness of his or her presence for purposes of section 212(a)9)(B)(i). On that assumption, Z would not prevail. Z could argue, however, that even under the USCIS view an exception should be made when the person is detained and thus *cannot* depart.

Problem 4: Under INA § 212(a)(9)(A)(i), a noncitizen who is removed upon arrival becomes inadmissible for five years. A was removed only five months ago. Under section 212(a)(9)(A)(iii), the Attorney General may consent to such a person reapplying for admission before the five years are up. On the one hand, since A is the beneficiary of an approved family-sponsored second preference petition, he must be the spouse or unmarried son of an LPR. That fact would be a positive equity. On the other hand, he did try to enter surreptitiously, and then he lied about it to a consular officer. Moreover, only five months have elapsed out of a waiting period of five years.

The second alleged exclusion ground will be INA § 212(a)(6)(C)(i). Here there are two separate incidents to consider. One was the attempted illegal entry. This act probably does not constitute an attempt to procure admission by "fraud." Entry without inspection is not generally regarded as a fraud because there is no misrepresentation. (Nor does any provision make prior entry without inspection a basis for inadmissibility.) The instructor might ask at this point why fraudulent entry (for example, through false documents) should be treated as being worse than surreptitious entry. If anything, the latter might seem worse because CBP gets no opportunity to inspect.

The second incident is his later statement denying his prior attempt to enter without admission. That latter statement is clearly a fraud and would seem to render him inadmissible as one who is "seeking" a visa by fraud or misrepresentation.

Assuming A is inadmissible, might he receive a waiver under section 212(i)? Since A is a family-sponsored second preference immigrant, he must be the spouse or (unmarried) son of an LPR. But section 212(i) also requires extreme hardship to the citizen or LPR. We would need more information to assess the degree of hardship that family separation would entail in this case.

To receive the waiver, A would also need the favorable exercise of discretion. See the earlier discussion of the positive and negative equities.

Problem 5: The first question is whether she is inadmissible under INA § 212(a)(6)(C)(i). As to that:

a. She never sought a "visa" by fraud.

b. Did she attempt to obtain "other documentation" by fraud? If that ground is charged, she might offer two responses: First, B might argue that the phrase "other documentation" contemplates only other kinds of admission documents; it is, after all, lumped together with words like "visa" and "admission." Second, she might argue that she did not seek to "procure" the counterfeit birth certificate by fraud. Had she obtained the birth certificate, possibly she would have *used* it to obtain future admission by fraud, but that does not mean she procured the documentation itself by fraud.

c. ICE might allege that she planned to use the false birth certificate in order to achieve "admission" by fraud. ICE would have to prove that she planned to leave the United States and then gain readmission by presenting the counterfeit document. By analogy to the criminal law of attempt, B might argue that, to prove she has "sought" admission by fraud, it is necessary to show some sort of dangerous proximity to success.

d. ICE will not be able to show that she sought some "other benefit" -- i.e. the counterfeit birth certificate -- by fraud. Again, there is no evidence she used fraud in order to procure the birth certificate itself. More important, the birth certificate is not a benefit "provided under this Act;" it is authorized only by state law.

A second exclusion ground to consider is INA § 212(a)(6)(C)(ii). This ground would apply only if she "has falsely represented . . . herself to be a citizen of the United States." Although she planned to do so, it seems she never actually got to that stage. Thus, this ground seems inapplicable.

If she is found inadmissible under either of the two grounds discussed above, she might seek a waiver under INA § 212(d)(3)(A). That provision will waive almost any exclusion ground for a nonimmigrant. (The few it will not waive are not relevant here.) Whether discretion would be favorably exercised is not clear.

SECTION B. POLITICAL AND NATIONAL SECURITY GROUNDS

Notes and Questions on Political and National Security Grounds (page 439):

Q1: Since all other parts of INA § 212(a)(3) deal with political and national security grounds for exclusion, a court might assume that the phrase "unlawful activity" similarly contemplates only those unlawful activities that relate to either national security or political ideology. Common crimes like burglary, for example, would not be encompassed by that interpretation. This approach is fortified both by the title of INA §212(a)(3) ("Security and Related Grounds") and by the fact that another subsection, INA § 212(a)(2), already deals with crime-related grounds for exclusion.

Q2: On the one hand, the State Department has a legitimate interest in promoting the foreign policy of the United States. Some have suggested that subsection 3(C)(ii) goes too far because it prevents the government from excluding a political candidate who is an enemy of the government of a United States ally that would be angered by our willingness to admit the person. On the other hand, it is not obvious why foreign policy interests should outweigh First Amendment concerns when domestic interests generally do not. And the standard for the second exception (subsection 3(C)(iii)) ("compelling") is vague enough that, if the State Department claims the foreign policy interest is a compelling one, courts might well think it inappropriate to disagree. Thus this provision could turn out to be a major opening for excluding political adversaries.

Q5: The instructor might here invite a brief discussion of how to balance the special needs of, and the benefits conferred by, academics, against the egalitarian goal of not treating the ideas of some people as being worthier or more deserving of protection than the ideas of others.

Q7: One possibility is that former terrorists can have a way of becoming heads of state with whom the U.S. government some day might have to negotiate (or even become allied). Given the breadth of the terrorist definition, another possibility is that Congress wanted to leave some discretionary wiggle room. Thanks are due to Peter Spiro and Richard Boswell, respectively, for those thoughts.

Q8: The classic statement of the purposes of the First Amendment is Thomas I. Emerson, *Toward a General Theory of the First Amendment*, 72 Yale L.J. 877 (1963). Some of the purposes that Emerson discusses are designed to benefit the individual who expresses the idea (or, in this case, joins the organization). Whether the rationale that the individual benefits from being able to express ideas and participate in a political dialogue applies to noncitizens seeking initial entry is a point on which students are likely to disagree. Other benefits discussed by Emerson accrue to the recipients of the ideas and to society generally. Neither category of benefits disappears simply because the individual is a noncitizen seeking entry. Proponents of repeal might also ask rhetorically what, exactly, the United States government is afraid of. The law should not assume Americans are too gullible to be exposed to ideas with which the United States government disagrees. Opponents of repeal might counter that membership in the Communist Party or some of the other proscribed organizations is a convenient proxy for otherwise hard-to-prove but strongly suspected terrorist leanings. It is like going after gangsters for not paying the taxes on their takings even though the government cannot prove in court that the takings were illegal. Proponents of repeal would likely find this argument overinclusive.

<u>Problems</u> <u>6-8:</u> (page 442):

Problem 6: On the assumption that she can qualify for H-1B status, for example, there should be no problem in getting admitted. There is no longer any Communist Party exclusion ground for *nonimmigrants*. The problem is her future. She might not want to come if it appears she will not eventually be eligible for permanent residence. As a member of the Communist Party, she would now be inadmissible as an immigrant under subsection 3(D).

She might argue that her association was not meaningful enough. In *Rowoldt*, discussed in item 3 on page 440-41 of the text, the individual paid dues and attended meetings. The participation was still held not to be meaningful enough. But that case was different, involving the *deportation* of an LPR who had lived in the United States for 43 years. Absent United States family ties or a showing of coercion, her only other hope is subsection 3(D)(iii)(I)(a). She could withdraw from the Communist Party and then become eligible for LPR status two years later. Note this two-year exception is automatic, not discretionary.

Problem 7: ICE would probably allege that Y is inadmissible under INA § 212(a)(3)(C). It would argue that the recall of an ambassador is a "serious" adverse consequence. Y, in turn, would invoke subsection 3(C)(ii), the exception applicable to candidates for office. He cannot be removed on the basis of statements that would be lawful if made in the United States. The statements in question certainly fit that description.

Z faces a tougher hurdle. Under subsection 3(C)(iii), she can be removed even for statements that would have been lawful in the United States, provided the Secretary of State personally determines that her admission would compromise a "compelling" United States foreign policy interest and is willing to so certify to Congress.

Neither person will qualify for a section 212(d)(3)(A) waiver, because inadmissibility under section 212(a)(3)(C) is expressly made non-waivable.

Problem 8: W falls within INA § 212(a)(3)(D)(i) as a member of the Communist Party. He is not currently eligible for a discretionary waiver under INA § 212(a)(3)(D)(iv), because the parent of an LPR is not one of the family relationships listed. If willing to do so, however, his daughter, who has been here more than five years as an LPR, could become naturalized. W would then become the parent of a United States citizen (rather than the parent of an LPR) and therefore eligible for a waiver. The waiver would still require the favorable exercise of administrative discretion, which is uncertain in light of W's strong adherence to the Communist Party. That factor would have to be balanced against his family equities and against the benefits that W's scientific prominence would bring to his United States employer and to the United States public.

THE TERRORISM EXCLUSIONS

Matter of S-K- (page 444):

S-K-, a Chin Christian from Burma, applied for asylum, withholding of removal, and relief under the Convention Against Torture. (The students will study all three remedies in chapter 11.) The immigration judge denied asylum and withholding on the ground that by donating 1100 Singapore dollars (then worth about US$685) she had provided "material support" to the Chin National Front (CNF), which the IJ found to be a terrorist organization. The IJ denied withholding of removal and relief under CAT for the additional reason that the evidence did not establish a clear probability of either persecution or torture.

S-K- first argued that the CNF was not a terrorist organization. She emphasized that the CNF was resisting a Burmese government that systematically violated human rights and that the U.S. itself did not recognize the Burmese government as legitimate. The BIA rejected her argument. It reasoned that, under INA § 212(a)(3)(B)(iii)(V), acts constitute a "terrorist activity" if the acts are unlawful in the place where they are committed and ... (b) involve the use of explosives, other than for personal monetary gain, with the intent to endanger safety or cause substantial property damage. Under INA § 212(a)(3)(B)(vi)(III), an organization that engages in such activities is a terrorist organization. The BIA held it had no authority to declare a government illegitimate or waive the terrorist exclusion; Congress had delegated the latter power only to designated Cabinet members.

S-K- also argued that she did not provide material support to the CNF. First, she maintained, there was no evidence that her contributions were used to further terrorist acts. The BIA held this does not matter; it is enough that she gave money to a terrorist organization, regardless of what the organization did with her particular contribution. She also argued that her contribution was too nominal to be material. The BIA found it unnecessary to decide whether even nominal assistance could be "material," since it found that this amount was substantial at any rate. It therefore affirmed the IJ's denials of asylum and withholding of removal. The Board noted that during oral argument DHS had agreed she was eligible for deferral of removal under the Convention Against Torture and possibly for a discretionary waiver under section 212(d)(3)(B)(I).

Board member (and Acting Vice-Chairman) Juan Osuna agreed with the Board's reading of the statute and therefore concurred in the result. He wrote separately to stress that the result does not further Congress's goal of excluding those who endanger national security, and he encouraged DHS to grant the necessary waiver.

As a result of subsequent DHS and congressional intervention, and the accompanying consideration by the BIA, S-K- ultimately received asylum, as explained in item 1 of the Notes and Questions following the case.

<u>Notes & Questions Following S-K-</u> (page 450):

Q3: Arguments in favor of treating organizations like the CNF as terrorist organizations might include the following:

1. The goals of an organization should be irrelevant. The ends do not justify the means. All that should matter is whether the organization commits particular unlawful acts in furtherance of those goals.

2. The question is a moral one. If we are otherwise prepared to condemn terrorism, we should not condone it simply because the targets are people or governments whom we oppose.

3. Once we try to distinguish "good" unlawful organizations from "bad" unlawful organizations, who is to decide which is which? Do we trust either the political branches or the courts to make their decisions on the merits rather than on the basis of political self-interest?

Arguments against treating organizations like the CNF as terrorist organizations might include the following:

1. "Good" and "bad" are *not* purely in the eye of the beholder. The world community, through a series of universal and generic human rights treaties and other instruments, now recognizes certain fundamental human rights that every state must respect, even though there is disagreement as to certain specific practices. Sometimes force is the only possible weapon against state-sponsored human rights violations.

2. If an undemocratic government closes off all lawful means of participation in public policymaking, force might be the only alternative.

3. It is inconsistent for the U.S. to aid organizations that are trying to dislodge repressive (even murderous) regimes, but then deny admission to any individuals who have done the same thing, often while they are fighting alongside U.S. armed forces.

Q4: That language does indeed give rise to some absurd results. Some might emphasize that allowing the country where the act is committed to define unlawfulness is acceptable because, for an act to qualify as a "terrorist activity," the U.S. statute also requires one of several specific actions, all of which involve the use of force. But even that latter requirement would not save the U.S. marines who rescued Private Lynch; the marines committed an act that violated Iraqi domestic law and involved the use of weapons. Nor would anything in the definition save groups that are acting in self-defense against a brutal government that does not recognize the lawfulness of their actions. The challenge lies in devising statutory language that would avoid these results but still cover the sorts of activities that are generally thought of as "terrorist." That problem is considered in item 6 of the Notes and Questions.

Q5: The Board's reasoning seems to be a nonsequitur. A country can recognize a particular sovereign state without necessarily recognizing the present government of the country as legitimate. Therefore, the fact that the U.S. maintains diplomatic relations with the Burmese government and maintains an embassy there does not mean it recognizes the present government (or its legislative acts) as legitimate. The more convincing answer, which the BIA provides next, is that it simply doesn't have the statutory authority to determine the legitimacy of a foreign government.

Q7: The argument in favor of such a requirement is that a consequence as grave as exclusion from the United States – particularly for refugees – would be disproportionate to a minor, insubstantial contribution to a terrorist organization. The counter-argument would be that (assuming the contribution was voluntary, a separate issue taken up in Question 8 below) the act evidences sympathy with a terrorist organization and makes the person an undesirable resident. A substantiality argument would also require some potentially arbitrary judgements as to the significance of a person's contribution to a terrorist cause.

Q8: The case in which the person is literally unable to avoid providing support is an easy one. Under those circumstances the provision of support tells us nothing about the person's character, values, or views on terrorism. There is simply no reason to view the person as a threat to public safety or national security. The other case is both legally and morally more complex. Suppose a person provides significant assistance to an organization that carries out terrorist murders of innocent civilians. Should it be a defense that the organization was holding a gun to the person's head? In criminal law, one is generally not justified in killing an innocent person to save his or her own life. On the other hand, should the law recognize human frailties? How many people would give up their own lives in order to avoid killing others?

Q9: Hard to say. In criminal law, a mistake of law can be a defense – at least in certain cases – when it prevents the actor from forming the required mens rea. If the actor's ignorance of U.S. law prevents him or her from knowing that the organization is a "terrorist organization," then the issue would be whether it can be said that the actor "should have known."

Q10: The main argument against the BIA interpretation would be that a person should not be penalized for assisting a lawful, typically charitable, activity, simply because the organization also does other things that are not lawful. Such a person, the argument runs, did nothing wrong and presents no danger. The counter-argument is provided by the BIA. From a legal standpoint, it finds the statutory language clear. From a policy standpoint, it argues that accepting S-K-'s argument would create a loophole for terrorist organizations. Since money is fungible, a terrorist organization could solicit and receive money for a benign purpose and then transfer to a terrorist purpose the funds that it would otherwise have used for the benign purpose.

SECTION C. CRIMINAL GROUNDS

General: The immigration consequences of criminal activity are developed in much more detail in the context of deportation. See chapter 7, section D. In particular, the interpretation of the phrase "moral turpitude" is deferred until then. This material does, however, familiarize the students with the crime-related exclusion grounds and give them additional practice in statutory interpretation.

Problems 9-12: (page 456):

Problem 9: She has been convicted of a non-political crime involving moral turpitude, so she is inadmissible under INA § 212(a)(2)(A)(i)(I) unless some exception applies.

The first exception, INA § 212(a)(2)(A)(ii)(I), applies. She committed only one crime involving moral turpitude, and she committed it while she was under age eighteen. It does not matter that the conviction came after she turned eighteen. Further, the crime was committed more than five years ago. It is true that on June 1, 2006 she received a one-year sentence, which would have been scheduled to end on June 1, 2007 (less than five years ago). That is not, however, a problem. It is enough that she was "released" from confinement more than five years ago.

Note that the second exception -- i.e., INA § 212(a)(2)(A)(ii)(II) -- would not apply here. The maximum penalty for her offense was more than one year, and at any rate the sentence "imposed" exceeded six months. The fact that she served only six months of it is irrelevant.

Since she seeks admission only as a nonimmigrant, she will also be statutorily eligible for a discretionary waiver under INA § 212(d)(3)(A). She will not be eligible for a waiver under INA § 212(h) because she is a nonimmigrant. (Anyway, she has no United States relatives and has not yet satisfied the 15-year requirement of section 212(h)).

Problem 10: W is not within INA § 212(a)(2)(B) because she has not been *convicted* of two or more offenses. Under that provision, it is not enough that she was convicted of one offense and admitted the other. Also, the aggregate sentences to confinement actually imposed were not five years or more.

Again, therefore, ICE will charge INA § 212(a)(2)(A)(i)(I). She will fall within this ground both because she has been convicted of burglary and, alternatively, because she admits the shoplifting. She might attempt to invoke the first statutory exception in order to waive the burglary and the second exception to waive the shoplifting. Some students might think that the second exception applies, because she has admitted the commission of a crime involving moral turpitude for which only a sentence of less than one year could have been imposed. (The maximum sentence was six months). But the problem, which will prevent her use of either exception, is that she has committed more than one crime. It does not matter that she has been convicted of only one.

There is the same possibility of a discretionary waiver under INA § 212(d)(3), but the additional conviction exacerbates her negative equities.

Problem 11: Y is inadmissible under INA § 212(a)(2)(A)(i)(II) because he admitted having violated a law "relating to a controlled substance" --

possession, and then sale, of marijuana. The exception contained in INA § 212(a)(2)(A)(ii)(II) will not save him, because that exception is inapplicable to charges based on INA § 212(a)(2)(A)(i)(II) (drug convictions). Y is also ineligible for a discretionary waiver under INA § 212(h) because that provision waives INA § 212(a)(2)(A)(i)(II) only in the case of simple possession (of not more than 30 grams of marijuana). Y has effectively admitted the elements of the crime of sale of marijuana.

Problem 12: There are three exclusion grounds to consider:

a. She is inadmissible under INA § 212(a)(9)(A)(ii) because she was "ordered removed" (other than upon arrival) less than ten years ago. DHS, however, has the discretion to let her reapply sooner. As to that, her perpetration of a serious immigration fraud will be a heavy negative factor. On the other hand, the fraud was committed 14 years ago, her husband needs to move to the United States now, and separation will entail hardship for both.

b. She is also inadmissible under INA § 212(a)(6)(C)(i), because she procured a visa and admission by fraud. Perhaps, however, she is eligible for a discretionary waiver of this ground under INA § 212(i). She is the spouse of a United States citizen. She will have to show that her husband would experience "extreme hardship." She could argue that, depending on how long her husband's mother survives, the marital separation might well last several years.

c. Z is also inadmissible under INA § 212(a)(2)(A)(i)(I) because she has been convicted of a crime involving moral turpitude. Z appears to be eligible for discretionary relief under INA § 212(h)(1)(B) as the spouse of a United States citizen, provided, as above, she can show extreme hardship to her husband. Even if the hardship is found not to be extreme, Z will be eligible in about one year for relief under section 212(h)(1)(A), because by then 15 years will have elapsed since the activities for which she is inadmissible.

At first glance the last paragraph of section 212(h) might appear to disqualify her from relief. If Z attempts to enter the United States, she could become the subject of a removal hearing, since she is inadmissible on the grounds discussed above. If so, and if she applies for a 212(h) waiver at that hearing, ICE might argue that she is ineligible as a former LPR who has not resided continuously in the United States for at least seven years "immediately preceding the date of initiation of proceedings to remove the alien from the United States" (meaning the very removal proceeding she is now undergoing). During the preceding three years she has lived in Ghana. But the seven-year provision should not be an obstacle. The regulations contemplate that the 212(h) waiver decision be made by the INS (now DHS), <u>not</u> by EOIR at a removal hearing. See 22 CFR § 40.21(a)(7) (2008). Therefore the only relevant removal proceeding in this Problem is Z's original removal proceeding in 2008. Since she had had more than seven years of lawful continuous residence immediately preceding that, her prior LPR status should not be an obstacle. Thanks to Professors Elwin Griffith and Maria Frankowska for their insights on this issue.

While on the subject of that last paragraph of section 212(h), the instructor might ask the students what anomalies it generates. First, all else equal, former LPR's are treated less favorably than both noncitizens with no prior connection to the United States and noncitizens who are undocumented. Second, even present LPR's who are returning to unrelinquished domiciles of less than seven years are treated less favorably than initial entrants. (This latter point assumes the person was away more than 180 days. If the absence was shorter than that, the person normally will not be regarded as seeking admission unless the crime was committed during the absence. See INA § 101(a)(13), which defines "admission.") Why Congress added the paragraph in question is not clear. The explanations offered in the cited court decisions seem embarrassingly flimsy as actual explanations, but in the view of those courts still plausible enough to satisfy the plenary power doctrine for constitutional purposes.

Finally, Z might argue that she procured her initial admission by fraud and therefore was never "lawfully" admitted as a permanent resident. The BIA specifically rejected this argument in *Ayala-Arevalo* (discussed in the coursebook's introduction to this section). Possibly a reviewing court would take a different view if given the opportunity, but the students will discover in chapter 9 that the 1996 court-stripping provisions, particularly INA § 242(a)(2)(C), *might* (but would not necessarily) prevent the issue from ever getting to court.

SECTION D. ECONOMIC GROUNDS

Notes and Questions on page 460:

Q1: In theory there is no conflict. The fact that a person is poor at the time he or she enters the United States does not necessarily make the person likely to require public assistance after entry. But the question remains whether a person who is likely to become a public charge should be inadmissible. The instructor can ask whether the United States should admit noncitizens who satisfy the categorical requirements for admission (e.g., family, occupation, refugee) but who will likely become public charges. The instructor might also note that, as the students will see in chapter 11, refugees are exempt from the public charge exclusion.

Q2: The argument for making affidavits of support binding is that otherwise they are worthless. Promises of support say less about the likelihood of the promisee becoming a public charge when the promisor knows that it will never be necessary to make good on the promise. Moreover, after the fact, when an LPR does fall into distress, the government saves money if the private sector provides the needed relief.

One response might be that affidavits of support can serve useful functions even if they are not binding. The sponsor might feel a moral obligation to come to the beneficiary's assistance, especially if he or she knows that the beneficiary will be unable to receive welfare because the sponsor's assets and income have been deemed available. The beneficiary might also feel a moral obligation to the sponsor to make every effort to remain self-sustaining. At any rate, one can argue, the deeming provision already makes it nearly impossible for the beneficiary to become a public charge for several years; thus the need for legally binding affidavits is lessened.

The main affirmative danger of making affidavits of support binding is that potential sponsors can be scared off. There might well be many individuals who would be willing to provide affidavits if they were not binding and who would have been willing in fact to come to the beneficiary's aid once the financial distress occurred, but who are afraid to make the long-term commitment that the law now requires when they cannot confidently forecast their financial situation many years down the road. In such cases, the beneficiaries will not be admitted even when they fit within the family categories Congress has thought it otherwise desirable to admit. When that happens, everyone loses.

Q3: Perhaps the rationale was that the willingness of a United States resident to support a noncitizen is a safety net for the government. If the job offer falls through, or the employment terminates, or the immigrant's assets disappear, and as a result the immigrant requires government assistance, then the government will have a more reliable source from which to receive reimbursement.

Yet the narrowness of the circumstances in which the immigrant will even be eligible for public benefits diminishes the need for this security. More serious, there might well be immigrants who are perfectly capable of sustaining themselves in the United States and as a result highly unlikely to become public charges, but whose American sponsors lack the income or assets to provide the required guarantee. In some cases, in fact, it might even be the immigrant who is coming to provide support for the citizen. Denying admission in such a case is self-defeating. Both the immigrant and the citizen lose the benefits of family reunification, the citizen loses a means of support, the government loses the income tax that the immigrant would have paid, and the government can end up paying benefits to the citizen that would have been unnecessary had the immigrant been admitted. In those cases, everyone loses.

Q4: It is difficult to identify Congress's reason for insisting that the petitioner be the sponsor. Perhaps Congress assumed that the petitioner, being a close family member or an employer, has an interest in the immigrant's successful adjustment to life in the United States. Consequently, affidavits of support from petitioners are likely to be more reliable than affidavits from others. But if that is what Congress was thinking, it could have restricted the class of sponsors to any individuals whose affidavits are credible, or possibly to designated family members. If the petitioner's parents, or grandparents, or spouse, or in-laws, or children, for example, are willing to execute legally binding promises of support, why not accept them?

Q5: The 125% requirement was hotly contested. Until days before passage, in fact, IIRIRA would have imposed a 200% requirement (except 140% for spouses and children of United States citizens or LPRs). A last-minute compromise, fashioned under threat of a presidential veto, resulted in the figure of 125%. Perhaps Congress felt it needed some margin for error; if the required income level were only 100% of the poverty level, either a slight dropoff in the immigrant's or the sponsor's income, or an increase in the federal Poverty Income Guidelines, could result in the immigrant qualifying for public benefits. Still, given the sweeping restrictions on even legal immigrants' eligibility for most public benefits, the danger does not seem large. Moreover, again, the result will be to deny admission to a certain number of worthy (and self-sufficient) immigrants with close family members in the United States.

SECTION E. PUBLIC HEALTH AND MORALS

Question on page 462:

The competing considerations include the health concerns of the public and the interests of both the noncitizen victims and the Americans whom they wish to visit or join. There is both more reason and less reason to treat HIV in the same manner as the law treats, for example, tuberculosis. On the one hand, the HIV virus is more difficult to transmit then tuberculosis, which is airborne. On the other hand, AIDS, once contracted, is virtually certain to require intensive lifelong treatment.

The distinction between immigrants and nonimmigrants is relevant here for at least three reasons:

1. If a person is in the U.S. on a permanent basis, there is a greater chance of eventual sexual contact with someone else who is in the U.S.

2. Since AIDS is not (yet) curable, an AIDS victim who intends to live permanently in the United States is nearly certain to incur huge hospital, medical, or pharmaceutical costs eventually. Some have even argued that this fact inherently makes the immigrant who contracts AIDS "likely to become a public charge" and therefore inadmissible on that ground alone.

3. Arguably, however, if anything the distinction between immigrants and nonimmigrants cuts the other way. For a person to be otherwise eligible for immigrant (LPR) status, the person has to have met stringent qualifying requirements related to family ties, occupational skills, or refugee status. In any of those cases, either the immigrant personally or his or her United States sponsor

or both will generally have an especially important interest in the person's admission.

CHAPTER 6
ADMISSION PROCEDURE

SECTION A. THE EARLY DAYS

These excerpts can be assigned as background reading. They are intended to give the students some historical perspective on admission procedure and to provide a human context.

SECTION B. MODERN PROCEDURE: PRELIMINARY COMMENTS

This section too is intended as background reading. Its purpose is to facilitate students' understanding of how the various steps in the admission process fit together and to help them follow the succeeding sections of the chapter.

The instructor might wish, however, to take up in class the question presented in the second paragraph on page 471. Do we really need four basic steps and three federal departments? There is good reason to involve the Labor Department at the initial stage. It has specific expertise on unemployment rates in various fields, wages, working conditions, etc. It is therefore the logical agency to decide applications for labor certification.

Still, the students might wonder, why have USCIS adjudicate visa petitions, rather than simply include in the consular process the assessments of all the determinations that USCIS now makes at the visa petition stage? Perhaps the reason is that a visa petition is normally used to establish a relationship between the noncitizen beneficiary and a person residing in the United States -- e.g., a relative or an employer. Thus USCIS can more easily investigate the petitioner.

Then why not eliminate visas and consign the entire inspection function to CBP at ports of entry? There seem to be several answers to this:

1. The visa process, in contrast to the visa petition process, focuses principally on the personal history and qualities of the noncitizen beneficiary. Thus, the pertinent information is more likely to be abroad.

2. The visa is important to the beneficiary, who, if inadmissible, will want to know that fact before burning his or her bridges at home and coming to the United States.

3. Immigration inspectors at the border cannot realistically perform thorough inspections of the many hundreds of passengers who arrive within a

short time period at an airport or at a land border. The consular officer abroad will be better situated to apply that degree of scrutiny. Conversely, even though in theory the noncitizen has been examined thoroughly by the consular officer, the border inspector might catch a problem the consular officer missed. In addition, circumstances can change between visa issuance and actual arrival at the United States port of entry.

SECTION C. VISA PETITIONS

Questions Following Linda Kelly's Excerpt (page 473):

The following answers are provided by Linda Kelly:

1. As to the demonstration of the abuse [immigration status aside], the fact that domestic violence so often goes unreported challenges the ability to secure such documentation as restraining orders, police reports, hospital records, and shelter letters. Her undocumented status compounds this challenge as her fear of being deported may prevent her from seeking any public assistance. In some cases, the battered woman's affidavit and testimony may be the only evidence of the abuse. Recounting the abuse in a clear, detailed manner may be difficult for the VAWA applicant and it is important to stress the need for advocates to demonstrate great patience and sensitivity in doing this work.

2. This focuses on the common difficulty a battered, undocumented woman experiences in collecting the type of documentation typically required to demonstrate "good faith" marriage. For example, while individuals in a non-abusive, healthy relationship will commonly have such documentation as joint leases, joint bank accounts, and joint car titles, a person in an abusive relationship often is not listed on such documentation as a result of the controlling dynamic of the violence. Her undocumented status makes it even less likely her name will appear on such documentation as she may fear any public record of her existence will result in INS [now ICE - Eds.] becoming aware she is here and moving to deport her. As a result, to prove good faith marriage, advocates must be more innovative, gathering other types of documentation such as children's birth certificates which indicate the names of both parents, the applicant's affidavit, affidavits of friends and family, joint photographs, etc. For various reasons related to the abuse this documentation may also be difficult to produce. Friends may be afraid to speak or unaware of the violence, photographs may have been destroyed by the abusive spouse, there may be no children.

Notes and Questions on page 475:

Q1: The instructor might randomly select one of the family-sponsored preferences and ask the students which documents they might supply to prove the needed facts. By way of example, a family-sponsored fourth preference petition on behalf of a sibling would require proof that the petitioner is a United States citizen and over age 21. Documents that could be furnished to prove those facts include a birth certificate, a passport, or a naturalization certificate. The petition must also prove that the claimed sibling relationship in fact exists. A common way to establish a sibling relationship is to supply birth certificates of the two siblings, showing common parentage. There are complications if the "siblings" have different mothers but the same father, etc.

An instructor who wishes to explore this further could also offer an example involving an employment-based preference. These exercises are a useful process for getting students to think in terms of (a) identifying the substantive facts needed for their case; and (b) using common sense to figure out how they would prove those facts to the satisfaction of USCIS. Documents suggested for the various visa petitions are described in 8 CFR §§ 204.1(g) (petitioner's citizenship or lawful permanent residence), 204.2(a)(1)(i)(B) (genuineness of marriage), 204.2(a)(2) (existence of marriage), 204.2(f)(2) (parenthood), and 204.5 (employment-based qualifications)(2008).

Q2: A complete list appears in 8 CFR § 205.1 (2008).

In the case of immediate relative or family-sponsored petitions, the common reasons for automatic revocation include the following: The petitioner or the beneficiary dies; the petitioner withdraws the petition; the petitioner and the beneficiary divorce; either the petitioner or the beneficiary attains an age that destroys the beneficiary's eligibility for the particular status; there is a change in the marital status of the beneficiary; or an LPR petitioner loses his or her own status.

In the case of the employment-based preferences, the common events include the following: The labor certification is invalidated for some reason; either the employer or the beneficiary dies; the employer withdraws the petition; or the employer's business terminates.

Florida Bar v. Matus (page 476):

The Florida Bar sued to enjoin Matus, an immigration consultant, from the unauthorized practice of law. He offered various services to an undercover State Bar investigator: extension of the agent's tourist visa, arranging a sham marriage to get LPR status for the agent, and legalization of the agent's friend. Matus also presented a business card in which he held himself out as a general immigration service. The court held that the preparation of forms to effect a change in one's immigration status, because it requires training and familiarity with the immigration laws, constitutes the practice of law. Since Matus was not a lawyer, the court enjoined him from continuing to perform these services.

General: This case should be assigned together with both the Notes and Questions on page 478 and Problems 1-3 on page 479. These materials are included to alert students to two kinds of unauthorized practice of law problems. First, they are not yet lawyers themselves but might be tempted to give advice to friends or others, either on their own or while working part-time at a legal clinic or elsewhere. Second, even after being admitted to the Bar, they will have an ethical duty to supervise their clerks and other employees closely enough to prevent the unauthorized practice of law.

<u>Notes and Questions Following Matus</u> (page 478):

Q2:

a. He falsely represented himself as qualified to render general immigration services.

b. He gave specific advice on legalization applications and offered to handle this person's legalization case.

c. He offered to extend a tourist visa.

d. He offered to arrange a sham marriage.

e. He offered to file a visa petition in a permanent resident case.

f. The court implies that Matus held himself out to be an attorney. (Actually, the allegation was that he held himself out to perform immigration services, which the court holds would constitute the practice of law.) Today, such a false representation would violate the specific regulation quoted in item 1.

Q5: *Cortez* might be consistent with the regulations. First, the court in *Cortez* might not have intended to address the nominal remuneration exception, since the issue was not before the court. Second, perhaps the court in *Cortez* might have believed that even a nominally remunerated nonlawyer could not legally help the client fill out a standardized form unless either the client or a lawyer had already selected the form.

<u>Problems 1-3</u> (page 479):

Problem 1: The rules that govern unauthorized practice of law are especially murky, as those students who have already taken a course in Professional Responsibility will know. The court in *Matus* did in fact enjoin him from all the acts complained of, and one of those acts was helping clients get residency. Here there are two favorable facts that might distinguish *Matus*: First, the student is handling only one case, not an entire caseload. Second, the student is performing the service only as a friend, not for financial gain. Much will depend on how the regulations and *Cortez* are interpreted and reconciled. See question 5 above. Under the regulations, it seems the assistance would be permissible because there presumably is no remuneration and the student is not purporting to be qualified in immigration law or procedure. Whether *Cortez* recognizes that exception, however, is not clear, as discussed above. Perhaps the best course would be for the petitioner to select the form herself and for the law student simply to help her fill it out.

Problem 2: The main prohibition contained in both Disciplinary Rule 3-101 and Rule 5.5 concerns aiding the law clerk in the unauthorized practice of law. The question presented is whether the activities of this law clerk constitute the practice of law. The lawyer here is involved in the case and providing some level of guidance to the law student, but it is not clear whether that is enough. There are state-to-state variations. Ethical Consideration 3-6 provides some guidance. Is the lawyer maintaining a "direct relationship" with the clients? The lawyer never actually meets the clients directly, but arguably he or she is meeting them through the law clerk as an intermediary. Second, is the lawyer properly supervising the delegated work? Here, the lawyer saw the intake memo and asked questions. In the more complex cases, the lawyer undoubtedly is more involved. Still, the lawyer never looked over the completed visa petitions before they went out to USCIS. The third requirement – that the lawyer have "complete professional responsibility for the work product" – seems conclusory and harder to apply.

Problem 3: The statute clearly requires knowledge on the part of the defendant that he or she had failed to disclose having prepared or assisted in preparing an application. The statute also clearly requires that the application in fact be "falsely made." But does the statute require that the defendant know that the application was falsely made? It is not clear whether "knowingly" modifies everything that follows it or just the fact that the identity of the preparer was not disclosed.

The literal language is ambiguous. X might argue that the broader construction should be rejected because it would result in strict liability, an unacceptable interpretation given the possible 5-year prison term. But that argument would probably fail, since even the broad interpretation would require proof that the defendant knew of the failure to disclose his or her role in preparing the document. Nonetheless, X should argue that the text at least permits the court to conclude that Congress meant to require knowledge of both the lack of disclosure and the falsity.

INA § 274C(f) complicates the issue. This subsection defines "falsely made" to require knowledge, or at least reckless disregard, of the falsity. Here, however, it was not the defendant but a third person (the defendant's client) who possessed the knowledge. The defendant might argue, therefore, that subsection (e) contemplates documents that *the defendant* knows contain false statements (or at least disregards the risk of there being false statements).

SECTION D. VISA APPLICATIONS

Note: The instructor can mention that, in addition to the Visa Waiver Program described in the text, common cases in which visas are not required include returning residents, refugees, Canadian nonimmigrants, and Mexicans with border-crossing cards.

Notes and Questions on page 484:

Q2: There are probably several reasons, including the deterrence of consul shopping (some consuls are more lenient than others) and the difficulty of verifying ties (the evidence is usually in the country where the applicant lives). In addition, Canadian and Mexican posts could be overwhelmed. (Of course staffing decisions could be made accordingly.) Finally, the consular officer stationed in a given country is more likely to be familiar with the culture, the legal system, and the language of the documents of his or her base country.

Q3: First, the Department wants the process to remain fast and informal. Second, the consular officer wants to control the questioning. Third, the consular officer does not want an attorney coaching the applicant. Fourth, the consular officer probably does not want to be exposed if he or she asks improper questions.

Nafziger article (page 487):

General: This article contains many of the arguments for and against some form of review of the consular officer's decisions denying applications for visas. The article should be assigned if the instructor plans to assign H.R. 2567 (the Gonzalez bill) on page 491 and the Simulation Exercise following it on page 493.

Simulation Exercise Following H.R. 2567 (page 493):

There are at least two logistical options for this exercise. One is to make the class the House of Representatives and to divide the class (either in advance or on the day of the discussion) into two groups – supporters and opponents. Students could then volunteer, or be called upon, to speak. A second option is to conduct a subcommittee hearing and to have selected students testify. They could either be instructed to take a particular position or given the freedom to testify in favor of the bill, to testify against it, or to offer amendments. To make the class discussion manageable, the instructor can organize it into two segments:

First, is the general concept of administrative review of visa denials a sound idea? Proponents might make the following points:

1. Important individual interests are at stake.

2. A certain number of mistakes at the consular level will be inevitable, especially given the heavy caseloads of consular officers.

3. It is pointless to allow administrative review of all the other steps in the admission process (labor certification, visa petitions, removal orders) when all these procedural safeguards will be meaningless in cases where visa applications are wrongly denied.

4. Unlike certain categories of immigration cases, most notably removal of deportable noncitizens, these cases present no incentives to delay. Thus there is no reason to fear a flood of frivolous appeals.

5. The volumes should be manageable. Few noncitizens who are denied visas will be both willing and able to incur the expense and delay that are inevitable when one litigates from abroad. (Asylum claimants do not need visas.) In any event, the categories of visa denials could be limited so as to make the volumes manageable.

Opponents of the bill might offer the following arguments:

1. Because consular officers are stationed overseas, the communications aspect of administrative review would be especially burdensome. (Nowadays, of course, correspondence could be by fax and e-mail.)

2. The volumes are too heavy.

3. The issues are too discretionary or at least credibility-dependent.

4. Consular officers are specially trained and thus do not need to be reviewed.

5. The foreign affairs considerations create a special need for both speed and finality.

6. It would be burdensome for the consular officers, whose caseloads are large, to have to compile the detailed administrative records that would be necessary in a system of administrative review.

7. The appellate process would be expensive.

Once the discussion of the general concept has been completed, the instructor might decide to focus on the specifics of the Gonzalez bill. These include the jurisdiction, the composition, and the procedures of the proposed Board.

As for jurisdiction, supporters would emphasize that only the most important visa categories are included, and that the B-visas, for example, which constitute approximately 70% of all nonimmigrants, have not been included. Opponents might think that no nonimmigrant visas should be included. Others might argue that, if anything, the covered nonimmigrants should include all students (not just those who are returning). Their interests can be important ones.

The composition of the Board raises additional issues. Should the Board members be independent of the State Department? There is a tension, familiar throughout administrative law, between the advantages of independence (and perceived independence) and the desire to coordinate the tribunal's policymaking with that of other Departmental agencies so as to leave the overall agency position coherent.

A further issue is whether consular officers should be allowed to serve on the panels. On the one hand, the consular officer will bring experience, knowledge, and perspective. On the other hand, there is the obvious danger of bias. Sympathy for the government's side is likely to occur both because the consular officer will be sympathetic to the demands placed on his or her colleagues, and also because he or she will know that other consular officers could be reviewing his or her cases in the future.

As for procedure, at least two questions might be raised. First, the bill would require the consular officer to prepare, at the request of the Board, a concise summary of the facts. Whether that responsibility will be burdensome will of course depend on the volume. Second, the bill allows the personal appearance and testimony of a government representative and the applicant's representative. Presumably the hearing will be held in Washington, D.C. Thus it will normally be easier and much less expensive for the government representative to attend than it will be for the applicant or counsel to attend. Yet the applicant will be at a disadvantage if only the government is represented. One possibility would be to amend the bill to provide that the government representative would be allowed to appear only if the applicant's representative requests to be heard.

Hermina-Sague v. United States (page 493):

A noncitizen married to a United States citizen applied for an immigrant visa as an immediate relative. The consulate denied the visa. (The opinion does not say why.) The petitioner and the beneficiary brought an action in federal district court seeking review of the consular decision. They argued that the denial unconstitutionally deprived them of a family life together and of "rights, privileges, and immunities" to which they were entitled. The court held that consular decisions denying visas are not subject to judicial review. It cited the sovereign nature of the federal exclusion power, the absence of a statutory provision specifically authorizing judicial review of visa denials, the fact that the beneficiary was outside the United States, and precedent.

<u>Notes and Questions Following Hermina Sague</u> (page 496):

Q2: Note: Constraints on judicial review are covered in more detail in chapter 9, § B.6. The REAL ID Act of 2005 adds some sweeping restrictions but doesn't speak directly to visa denials. (Since visa denials are not discretionary, see analysis of question 4 below, judicial review would not seem to be precluded by INA § 242(a)(2)(B)). See chapter 9, § B.6.a.ii of the text. The students are unlikely to raise this question at this stage of the course because they have not yet been exposed to the court-stripping provisions.

Consular visa refusals seem to fall squarely within the letter of INA § 279 (in its then existing form) and, today, 28 USC § 1331. If the jurisdictional problem is territorial rather than subject matter, then possibly visa denials are different from exclusions in that the latter are at least *physically* within United States territory. One might also argue that Congress had specifically provided for district court review in exclusion cases and yet said nothing specifically about judicial review of visa denials, thus evidencing a deliberate decision to insulate the latter. On the other hand, Congress did not refer specifically to judicial review of visa petitions, or to denials of labor certification, or to many other decisions that courts routinely reviewed under INA § 279. Probably the only reason for singling out the removal of arriving noncitizens was to clarify that in such cases the form of review was habeas corpus. (Today, removals are generally reviewed by petitions for review in the courts of appeals, as noted later.)

Q3:

a. All INA § 221(a) says is that, under certain circumstances, consular officers may issue visas. Nothing in that language implies that denials of visas are unreviewable.

b. The court's citation is extremely misleading. INA § 104(a) arguably bars the *Secretary of State* from reviewing visa denials (probably to enable the Secretary to disclaim the power to intervene when foreign government officials protest, as discussed earlier), but this provision says nothing about *judicial* review. When the court says a decision is not reviewable "even" by the Secretary of State, the implication is that the decision is not reviewable by others either. The statute says nothing of the sort.

c. The cited passage relates only to review by an administrative review board or by the Secretary of State. It sheds no light at all on Congress's intentions concerning judicial review.

d. This evidence, unlike that discussed above, is clearly relevant. On the one hand, this language could mean that Congress intended to bar judicial review. On the other hand, if taken literally, this language says only that the omission of restrictions on judicial review of exclusion should not be taken as positive evidence of an intent to make visa denials reviewable. The government might argue that this statement in the committee report would be odd if the Senate committee was assuming that visa denials were reviewable in court. Proponents of judicial review might respond, however, that (a) the language in any event is too ambiguous to be "clear and convincing;" (b) even if the language were clear, it is only the opinion of the Senate committee, not even the whole Senate, much less the entire Congress and the President; and (c) that language certainly cannot offset the express wording of 28 USC § 1331 -- at least not by enough to constitute "clear and convincing evidence."

e. The government would argue that, if general federal question jurisdiction were interpreted as still covering challenges to immigration decisions, then the amendment to section 279 would be meaningless. Why would Congress have bothered to make the change?

The visa applicant could begin by reminding a court of the general standard: As noted above, a court will not disturb the presumption of reviewability of agency action without "clear and convincing evidence" of a congressional intent to preclude review. Such evidence is lacking here, for several reasons: First, section 279 has been superfluous ever since Congress eliminated the amount-in-controversy requirement for general federal question jurisdiction. Nothing Congress did in 1996 changed that. Second, 28 USC § 1331 is explicit. It gives the federal district courts jurisdiction over "all civil actions arising under the . . . laws . . . of the United States (emphasis added)." Third, the last sentence of section 279 now reads: "Nothing *in this section* shall be construed as providing jurisdiction for suits against the United States or its agencies or officers (emphasis added)." The qualifier "in this section" would be strange if Congress intended to bar such suits under all statutory jurisdictional grants. Fourth, the quoted passage from the conference committee report on IIRIRA expressly disavows any "effect on other statutory or constitutional grounds for private suits against the government." Given these expressions of congressional intent, the visa applicant would argue, one cannot find "clear and convincing evidence" of a congressional intent to preclude review; if anything, the evidence convincingly demonstrates a congressional intent not to disturb existing grants of federal jurisdiction.

Q4: The question here is whether a court would have meaningful standards to apply. It is difficult to see why it would not. A consular officer may deny a visa only on the specific grounds set out in the statute or regulations. The exclusion grounds require interpretations of law and findings of fact, just like other agency decisions. It is true that some of those decisions will require subjective judgment, such as whether the person is "likely to become a public charge," but even there a court can assess the evidence on which the officer's prediction is based. The "reason to believe" language of some of the exclusion grounds requires an objective test of reasonableness, but a court is just as capable of reviewing that determination as a trial court or appellate court would be to review the evidence in a civil case to determine whether as a matter of law a reasonable jury could reach a particular conclusion. (The instructor might also mention that the BIA has to make the same judgments whenever it reviews removal orders of the immigration judges in cases of exclusion at ports of entry. The students will see more on this in the next section).

Q5: The quoted language clarifies that section 236 does not affirmatively provide authority for judicial review, but it does not purport to take away any authority that other laws might grant (something Congress could have done quite easily and clearly had it wanted to).

Q6: In theory these practices strengthen the characterization of visa decisions as discretionary. But the kind of discretion they illustrate is an unlawful discretion, as the court pointed out in *Olsen*. Surely, Congress cannot have intended to "commit" to the agency the discretion to engage in the very discrimination that the same statute expressly prohibits. Moreover, these practices demonstrate that the possibility of arbitrary decisions cannot be dismissed as theoretical.

Q7: No. The plenary power doctrine goes only to whether Congress (or the Executive) *has the power* to make visa denials unreviewable (or, alternatively, to whether a court has the power to make that determination). Here, in contrast, the question is one of statutory interpretation: *Has Congress done so*? For example, in*Loza-Bedoya* (cited in *Hermina Sague*), the consular officer denied the visa because the INS had advised that the applicant was inadmissible for having aided another noncitizen to enter the United States illegally. The court acknowledged that the denial was erroneous because nothing in the record suggested the aid had been given for gain, which was then a requirement of the particular exclusion ground. Yet the court still held that no judicial review was authorized. That holding has nothing to do with the scope of Congress's powers under the Constitution; it is just straight statutory interpretation. If anything, a court that refuses to review the decision of the consular officer when it is obvious from the record that the officer has violated the substantive law is doing further violence to Congress's plenary power by permitting administrative officials to contravene the congressional intent.

Q11: Those who argue that Congress has acquiesced in the judicial interpretations might rely on enactment of comprehensive immigration legislation in 1990 and again in 1996. The argument would be that Congress had to have been aware of the principle of consular absolutism when it enacted comprehensive reform legislation in 1990, and yet it chose not to make any change in the law that governs judicial review of visa denials.

Proponents of judicial review might make the following arguments: First, judicial review was not a battlefield in 1990 (except for aggravated felons), even though the substantive grounds for exclusion and deportation were. Congress simply did not address this issue. (This argument cannot be made, however, with respect to the 1996 legislation, which took dead aim at judicial review in ways that will be explored in chapter 9.)

Second, it is always problematic to read significance into congressional inaction. For one thing, the inaction might simply reflect a congressional decision to accord the issue a low priority, rather than congressional agreement with the status quo. For another, legislation requires approval by both Houses (and the consent of the President or a congressional override of a Presidential veto). Without the agreement of *all* these organs of government, the law cannot be changed, even though a prior statute might have intended to make visa denials unreviewable.

SECTION E. ACTUAL ADMISSION

1. At the Border

This subsection could be assigned solely as background reading. An instructor who wishes to take up this material in class, however, could engage the students in a discussion of detention policy (although detention is examined in more detail in the asylum context, in chapter 11, § B.7.b.v). To the extent that Congress has authorized detention of arriving noncitizens pending removal hearings, is it good policy to do so? The government will argue that detention pending removal discourages frivolous applications and appeals by noncitizens who could otherwise walk in, request a hearing, and then abscond while the decision is pending. In addition, it would say, some people are too dangerous to be at large.

Opponents of detention might respond that the policy discourages bona fide applications, especially asylum claimants (considered in chapter 11). If the problem is that some noncitizens would either abscond or pose a danger to society, opponents of detention would argue, then the solution is to hold individualized hearings, not to detain everyone on a blanket basis. The government might respond that the individualized hearings would be too expensive and, at any rate, not foolproof.

2. Hearings Before Immigration Judges

This brief subsection is intended as background reading.

3. Appeals from Immigration Judge Decisions

This brief subsection is also intended as background reading.

4. Expedited Removal

This brief subsection is also intended as background reading.

5. Other Special Removal Procedures

Most of the discussion in this subsection is best deferred. The special procedure for alleged terrorists is explored in chapter 10; expedited removal is presented in greater detail in chapter 11.

SECTION F. ADJUSTMENT OF STATUS

Notes and Questions on page 511:

Q2: As to the first question, the purpose of the disqualification is to penalize and to deter immigration violations. An argument against such disqualifications is that, if the applicant is substantively admissible even with them, there is little point in making him or her return home, obtain a visa, and then return. Both the applicant and the government incur unnecessary expense.

The penalty fee can be justified as an accommodation of the competing interests. It enables both the applicant and the government to avoid the wasteful expenses associated with an extra trip abroad and extra processing, while still penalizing the applicant for violating the immigration laws. In addition, it raises revenue. The argument against it is that it is large enough (an additional $1000 per family member) to create disproportionate hardship for low-income immigrants.

Q3: There is good reason to make INA § 245 mandatory. An immigrant who is admissible (which one would have to be in order to qualify for adjustment, subject to the possible qualification noted in the analysis of Problem 5 below) can go abroad, obtain a visa, and then return immediately. Thus, all USCIS (or an immigration judge) accomplishes by denying adjustment of status on discretionary grounds is expense, trouble, and disruption for the immigrant. In addition, when an immigrant uses the visa process rather than adjustment of status, life becomes more complicated for the government, which must act through multiple agencies and engage in international transactions. The substantive result is the same with or without adjustment of status.

One caveat: For an immigrant whose unlawful status exceeds 180 days, the difference between the visa route and the adjustment route has more bite. By leaving the United States, the person becomes inadmissible for 3 years (10 years if unlawfully present for one year or more). See INA § 212(a)(9)(B)(i)(I,II) and the analysis of Problem 5 below.

Others might argue nonetheless that adjustment should remain discretionary. They might see denial of adjustment as a form of punishment, calculated to discourage dishonesty and other forms of misconduct. Advocates of mandatory adjustment might respond that, if the misconduct is serious enough to make the person inadmissible, discretion to deny adjustment will not be necessary, and if the misconduct does not rise to that level then it is too harsh to deny adjustment. Proponents of discretion might reply that Congress can choose to be more lenient by making the misconduct simply one element of a discretionary decision, rather than making it an automatic bar to admissibility. They might argue too that adjustment could be abused as a mechanism for permitting the person to remain in the United States longer than would otherwise be possible. The filing of an adjustment application does not trigger an extension of stay, but the argument would be that the person might enter as a nonimmigrant while waiting for the adjustment application to be decided, rather than wait outside. Again, however, proponents of mandatory adjustment might assert that in such a case there is really no harm if the person waits in the United States as a nonimmigrant. During that time, he or she would still be subject to all the requirements for the particular nonimmigrant category, and those requirements were crafted with an eye toward protecting the American workforce. Nor will the individual attain LPR status any sooner.

Problems 4-7 (page 512):

Problem 4: She cannot apply for adjustment of status until a visa is "immediately available," and that will not happen for another seven years, when her priority date becomes current. By then her stay will long since have expired. She should now file her visa petition, however, to get the process started and the clock running. In the meantime, she can look for legitimate ways in which to extend her nonimmigrant status.

Moreover, she will have turned 21 and therefore will have fallen into 2B status, with its even longer waiting periods. The Child Status Protection Act will not prevent that result, since the Act relieves only those delays that are attributable to administrative processing, not those attributable to numerical ceilings.

If X's LPR parent is eligible for, and obtains, naturalization while X is still unmarried and under age 21, then X would become an immediate relative at that time and a visa would be "immediately available" within the meaning of section 245. The parent should file the visa petition and application for adjustment of status before X's 21st birthday. If that is done, then the Child Status Protection Act (discussed on pages 265-66 of the coursebook) would preserve her eligibility even if the administrative processing is not completed until after X's 21st birthday. Thanks to Victor Romero and his student, Ryan Bialas, for spotting this possibility.

Problem 5: Y is ineligible for adjustment of status for two reasons. First, under the opening sentence of INA § 245(a), adjustment is authorized only for "an alien who was inspected and admitted or paroled." Y has not been inspected or admitted (or paroled). Second, section 245(a)(2) requires that the person be "admissible." Since Y is present without having been "admitted or paroled," he is inadmissible under INA § 212(a)(6)(A).

Incidentally, even though he has been unlawfully present for more than a year, he is not yet additionally inadmissible for ten years under section 212(a)(9)(B)(i)(II), because the inadmissibility created by that provision does not begin until he departs from the United States. Nor is he additionally ineligible for adjustment of status under section 245(c)(2) on the basis of his current unlawful immigration status, because immediate relatives are specifically exempted from section 245(c)(2).

INA § 245(i) has long since expired for new applications, and it is not clear that the former version of section 245(i) would have helped Y anyway. On the one hand, section 245(i)(1)(A)(i) allowed a noncitizen who had entered the United States without inspection to *apply* for adjustment of status "notwithstanding the provisions of subsections (a) and (c)," provided the person paid a penalty fee. On the other hand, section 245(i)(2)(A) permitted adjustment only if the person was "admissible;" as noted above, Y's presence without admission makes him inadmissible. The two provisions appeared (and for any pending grandfathered petitions still appear) to be at cross-purposes. Thanks to David Hudson for noting that apparent contradiction.

So adjustment of status will be impossible. Can Y obtain a visa overseas? His problem is INA § 212(a)(9)(B)(i)(II). The moment he leaves the United States, he becomes inadmissible for ten years as a noncitizen who was unlawfully present for a year or more. His only hope is a waiver under INA § 212(a)(9)(B)(v). He is the spouse of a United States citizen. To prevail, he will have to establish that his exclusion would cause his wife "extreme hardship" and that the favorable exercise of discretion is warranted. More facts would be needed.

Problem 6: Z is substantively admissible, and there is no quota delay because this preference category is current.

His problem is procedural. He falls within section 245(c)(2) because he has overstayed and is not an immediate relative. (He is the *son* of a United States citizen but, being over age 21, he is not a *child*).

Without section 245(i), he faces a possible dilemma. Under United States law, in theory he may return home for a visa and then return. The problem is that his country probably will not let him out again. This fact situation used to raise the problem of the so-called orphaned immigrant, who for any of various reasons was not able to go home. In this case the difficulty is that his own country restricts emigration, but there are other common reasons as well: The United States might have no visa-issuing facilities in his country, or personal reasons might prevent his return.

The best remedy for Z is a State Department regulation, 22 CFR § 42.61(a) (2008). This regulation specifies that a visa application should ordinarily be filed with the United States consulate in the applicant's country of residence, but it authorizes the consular officer to accept the application nonetheless if the person is physically present within the territory of that consulate and expects to remain there until the processing is finished. If Canada will admit Z (and it will probably do so once the visa petition has been approved), his best option is to go there for a couple of months or so until the visa is ready.

Note that Z need not worry about INA § 222(g)(2), which bars nonimmigrants who have overstayed their visas from returning *as nonimmigrants* without visas issued by consulates in their countries of nationality, absent extraordinary circumstances. Z seeks LPR status, not nonimmigrant status.

Problem 7: The problem here is that there is no administrative appeal from a USCIS decision denying adjustment of status. See generally item 4 of the Notes and Questions that precede this set of Problems. W's options, therefore would include the following:

a. Now that W's status has expired, one option is to ask ICE to bring removal proceedings on overstay grounds, so that W can renew his adjustment application before an immigration judge. W would hope to persuade the IJ that the crime does not involve moral turpitude. Being out of status, W is prima facie ineligible for adjustment because of INA § 245(c), subsections 2, 7, and 8. Under section 245(k), however, W may apply notwithstanding those limitations. He is an employment-based preference immigrant who was lawfully admitted as a student and who has not been out of status more than 180 days, worked without authorization, or otherwise violated the terms of his admission.

Nonetheless, section 245(k)(2)(A) will likely be a problem. On the assumption that it will take at least 180 days to schedule a hearing (even assuming ICE obliges by promptly filing a notice to appear), W will have been out of status for 180 days by the time the IJ is in a position to grant adjustment, unless W can persuade the IJ to expedite the hearing for this purpose.

The main danger in asking ICE to commence removal proceedings is that the IJ might deny the adjustment application, either because the 180 days have elapsed or because the IJ agrees with USCIS that the crime involved moral turpitude and thus renders W inadmissible. In that event, W could be ordered removed. If so, the removal order will make him inadmissible for another ten years under INA § 212(a)(9)(A)(ii). (At this stage the students have not studied voluntary departure. If the IJ grants voluntary departure, then W will not have to worry about 212(a)(9)(A)(ii), but, assuming the hearing cannot be scheduled right away, might still be inadmissible for 3 years or 10 years for having been out of status for 180 days or one year, under INA § 212(a)(9)(B)(i) -- at least under the view of the former INS that time spent in removal proceedings counts toward unlawful presence.)

b. Another option is for Z to simply wait and see what ICE does. That course too has disadvantages. First, his funds are running out. Second, he is not authorized to work. If he were to try to obtain a job illegally, he would be at a disadvantage because employers would not want to risk sanctions (more on that in chapter 12), and in any event his working without authorization would be still another deportability ground and still another negative factor that could affect the likelihood of his receiving voluntary departure. Third, there are the same dangers that are discussed in paragraph (a) above. At any rate, it would obviously be unethical to counsel Z to work without authorization.

c. Z could go to Pakistan and apply for a visa, but this option entails great expense. In addition, it is doubtful that his priority date would still be valid. Finally, the consular officer might refuse a visa because of W's conviction, which W will not be able to avoid disclosing because the consular officer will ask questions about Z's prior applications and convictions. If the consular officer does deny a visa on the ground that W has been convicted of a crime involving moral turpitude, the doctrine of consular absolutism that the students encountered earlier will preclude judicial review.

d. Possibly W could seek judicial review of the USCIS decision denying adjustment of status. INA § 242(a)(2)(B)(i) might initially seem to preclude judicial review of adjustment denials, but INA § 242(a)(2)(D) (added by the REAL ID Act, § 106(a)(1)(A)(iii)) exempts questions of law from this bar, and the issue W seeks to raise is a question of law - whether the particular crime involves moral turpitude.

There is one wrinkle, however, which we are indebted to Huyen Pham for spotting. The language in INA § 242(a)(2)(D) that exempts questions of law from the bar on judicial review is itself limited by the phrase "raised upon a petition for review filed with an appropriate court of appeals." Does this mean that in district court actions (the only actions that would be available if removal proceedings have not been instituted) adjustment denials cannot be reviewed even with respect to questions of law? Arguably, it does not mean that. First, as Professor Pham suggested in an e-mail, perhaps section 242(a)(2)(D) should be interpreted as applying regardless of whether removal proceedings have been instituted, just as the paragraphs that it qualifies – 242(a)(2)(B and C) – have been interpreted. Second, even before the passage of the REAL ID Act, which added section 242(a)(2)(D), the courts had generally interpreted section 242(a)(2)(B) (the bar on judicial review of discretionary decisions) as limited to the discretionary components of the denials of discretionary relief, not to denials on statutory eligibility grounds. There is nothing in the REAL ID Act to suggest Congress meant to alter that rule. At any rate, the students will not be prepared to discuss this wrinkle in any depth until they study judicial review in chapter 9. We mention it here only to alert teachers to the issue. Thanks are owed to Michael Olivas, Huyen Pham, and Peter Antone for their thoughts on Problem 7.

e. Another (time-limited) option is for W to apply for "optional practical training" (OPT) after graduation. See the casebook at 397 for details. Thanks to Michael Olivas for that suggestion.

CHAPTER 7
DEPORTABILITY GROUNDS

SECTION A. GENERAL CONSIDERATIONS

General: The last paragraph of the introduction contains enough procedural information to enable the students to follow the cases contained in chapters 7 and 8. But if you would like the students to know more about the procedure before taking on these cases, one option is to assign the Overview section of chapter 9 (Deportation Procedure) as required background reading.

1. A Historical Overview of American Deportation Policy

This short section is intended as background reading.

2. The Theory of Deportation

This section too is intended generally as background reading. Its aim is to get students thinking about the justifications for expulsion and the hardships that can result. In answer to the questions at the end of the section, other arguable justifications include the following:

1. Deportation might be seen as performing a deterrent function. Criminal lawyers distinguish general deterrence (punishing one person in order to get the message across to others) from specific deterrence (punishing one person so that he or she will not repeat). Some might argue that general deterrence is a legitimate function of deportation. The role of specific deterrence is less clear. On the one hand, it might seem nonsensical to talk about threatening deportation as a deterrent to a noncitizen who is already out of the country by reason of deportation. But a deported noncitizen might return, either illegally (in which case his or her original removal order will be reinstated, INA § 241(a)(5)), or legally by waiting the required number of years or obtaining a waiver, in which case the prospect of future deportation might discourage repetition of whatever behavior led to the first deportation.

2. Some might argue that the prospect of deportation is an incentive for naturalization. The limitations of this argument are (a) not all noncitizens are eligible for naturalization and (b) even for those who are, the question remains whether it is wise policy to encourage people to naturalize solely to avoid deportation.

3. Current Deportability Grounds

Although this short section is also intended mainly as background reading, the instructor might observe that several of the modern deportability grounds encompass behavior or events in which United States citizens are free to engage without fear of punishment -- e.g., receiving welfare benefits, engaging in activities that have adverse foreign policy consequences, etc. The instructor might ask the students whether the law *should* remove noncitizens for doing things that citizens are permitted to do. Some students will say yes. They will assert that a higher standard is appropriate for one who wishes to join a new society. They might add that a country is better off when it insists on higher standards. Other students will answer no. If citizens are allowed to engage in particular behavior, it must be because society views the advantages of permitting that behavior as outweighing the disadvantages.

4. Deportation and Statutory Interpretation

Fong Haw Tan v. Phelan (page 519):

A criminal indictment contained two counts, charging the noncitizen defendant with the murders of two individuals. He was convicted on both counts and, in a single judgment, received concurrent life sentences. Deportation proceedings were later initiated. The charged deportation ground required that the person be "sentenced more than once." The Supreme Court resolved a circuit split by holding that a person is "sentenced more than once" when he or she is convicted, "called before the bar," and receives judgment, and then "that happens again." The Court reaches that conclusion first by consulting the (only marginally helpful) legislative history, and then by elaborating a broader principle of statutory construction: When interpreting a deportation statute, a court should "not assume that Congress meant to trench on [the noncitizen's] freedom beyond that which is required by the narrowest of several possible meanings of the words used."

Notes and Questions Following Fong Haw Tan (page 520):

Q1: The Court distills from the legislative history the principle that Congress was after the "confirmed criminal." Some might argue that the Court's specific interpretation does not follow, because the stated congressional goal could be achieved at least as well by an interpretation that requires two offenses committed at different times. Others, however, might argue that the statute requires the commission of a second crime after the person has actually been sentenced for the first crime. Such a person, even after learning and understanding first hand the consequences of the criminal activity, made a conscious decision to repeat.

As for the court's use of legislative history, the statements on the House floor are generally considered less probative than the statements in the committee report. The former might represent only the views of a handful of representatives and are often self-serving. At the same time, that forum often represents the only opportunity for those representatives who are not on the committee to express their views (other than by voting). The committee report, in contrast, is generally considered the best source of legislative history. It is better thought out, and there is a greater chance that it represents a consensus. Even still, it is only the views of the particular members of the committee.

Q2: The argument in favor of the principle is that the drastic nature of a deportation order makes it inappropriate to take any unnecessary chances of deporting people whom Congress did not intend to deport. The argument against the Court's conclusion is that the interest of the government is also substantial. The real question -- analogous to that presented when the issue concerns standard of proof -- is whether an erroneous interpretation in favor of the noncitizen is generally better or worse than an erroneous interpretation in favor of the government.

Q4: The BIA has certainly accumulated specialized expertise in immigration law. Its members and staff have the kind of repeated exposure that the authors describe; indeed, that is all they do. As a purely adjudicative tribunal, however, the BIA lacks the second kind of expertise to which the authors refer – i.e., the familiarity with the day-to-day practical implementation of the immigration laws. Only the service and enforcement authorities are immersed in that process.

When the BIA was in the same department as the INS (DOJ), perhaps one could have argued that the BIA was more likely to be aware of the practical problems INS was facing. Now that the prosecuting agency is DHS, the argument might run, there is less reason to attribute to the BIA any specialized knowledge of the day-to-day operations. The distinction seems less than compelling, however, because the BIA members, being adjudicators, learn of relevant enforcement considerations mainly through the briefing process, and that information should not differ as between ICE and the former INS. (At any rate, the repeat exposure component of the BIA's expertise remains constant.)

Q5: The Court seems to be taking a "clear statement" approach. It recognizes Congress's supremacy in the field of immigration law and therefore will defer to Congress's wishes, even though deportation is drastic. Before doing so, however, the Court wants to be sure that is what Congress truly intended. It wants to force Congress to be clear, precisely because deportation is a drastic sanction.

Q6: The literal plain meaning rule is inconclusive here. The phrase "sentenced more than once" could mean more than one sentencing *proceeding* (in which case the noncitizen wins), or it could mean more than one *sentence* (in which case ICE wins). The Golden Rule is similarly inconclusive. For the reasons given in the analysis of question 1 above, neither result would be absurd. Therefore a court that wishes to apply the Golden Rule would have to fall back on the literal meaning of the statutory language, and that is ambiguous. The Social Purpose Rule requires the Court to ascertain the congressional purpose. The language does not clearly reveal the congressional purpose, but the legislative history suggests the goal of deporting "confirmed criminals." For the reasons given in the analysis of question 1 above, that purpose is too generally framed to be conclusive here.

SECTION B. THE MEANING AND SIGNIFICANCE OF "ENTRY" AND "ADMISSION"

Matter of Ching and Chen (page 523):

Two Chinese nationals traveling from Hong Kong to Guatemala were part of a group changing planes in Los Angeles. They were denied admission under the transit-without-visa program and isolated in an airport lounge pending their removal back to Hong Kong. They managed to leave the airport and make their way to Texas, where they were apprehended by the former INS and placed in exclusion proceedings. They moved to terminate the proceedings on the ground that, having "entered" the United States, they could be removed only through deportation proceedings. The IJ agreed and terminated proceedings. The INS appealed to the BIA. [Note: Although IIRIRA has now consolidated exclusion and deportation into a single process known as removal, and has also substituted admission for entry as the determinant of which set of grounds applies, the "entry" issue is still important for reasons discussed in the text preceding this case.]

The Board applied the 3-element entry definition announced in a prior decision, *Matter of Pierre*: Entry requires (1) a physical crossing into the U.S.; (2) either (a) inspection and admission, or (b) intentional evasion of inspection; and (3) freedom from official restraint. The Board found an entry. Both individuals had clearly crossed, had evaded inspection (not initially, but after their original detention at the airport), and had become free of restraint.

<u>Notes and Questions Following Ching and Chen</u> (page 526):

Q2: This question illustrates why it is not always to the advantage of the noncitizen to establish entry. In this case, by arguing there is an entry, are the noncitizens opening themselves up to criminal liability? Arguably, "entry" won't affect their criminal liability because under section 275 even an attempted entry will suffice.

The noncitizens might argue that entry is not enough to establish their guilt under INA § 275(a). Under subsection (1) of that provision, the person must enter at a "time or place" not designated for entries; they entered at Los

Angeles airport. And subsection (2) does not mention "entry" at all. Besides, under that subsection they would have to have eluded examination or inspection. They can argue that, in fact, they were inspected. The government will respond that they were inspected the first time but not the second time. Subsection (3) is inapplicable.

Q3: In the view of the BIA, the two decisions in question are compatible. Lin was still *in* exclusion proceedings when he escaped from detention; an exclusion hearing was then pending. A, in contrast, had accepted exclusion and the proceeding was now over. When he escaped from LAX and made his way inland, he was making a second, new attempt.

One can accept that factual difference and still ask whether it should affect the outcomes of the cases. There is no apparent policy reason for letting A enjoy the benefits of a deportation proceeding over those of an exclusion proceeding, while denying those benefits to Lin. Rather, it would seem sensible to base the procedural conclusions on such factors as the length of time the individuals were here, the roots they have laid down, etc.

Today, as noted in the text, the distinction between exclusion and deportation proceedings has been abandoned. Still, as the text also notes, "entry" continues to affect the applicability of specific procedural rules.

Q4: Lin and the hypothetical noncitizen are difficult to distinguish. Maybe the idea is that the person who is caught once while trying to enter, and who then escapes from custody, is more culpable than the one who merely enters surreptitiously. But it is not clear that that is the case, and at any rate it is not obvious that the level of culpability should determine the scope of the procedural safeguards. Moreover, under this reasoning it would be difficult to see why Ching and Chen received a deportation hearing; after all, they also made two attempts.

Q5: The noncitizens clearly made a "crossing." They were inspected but not admitted; thus, part 2(a) is inapplicable. The Board must therefore be finding part 2(b) (evasion of inspection) applicable and must be basing that conclusion on their second attempt. And they were free of restraint once they escaped into the interior.

Q6: There is no satisfying answer here. One option would be to hold that <u>any</u> crossing constitutes an entry. The difficulty with that approach is that the border inspection almost always takes place on the United States side of the border. Thus, virtually every "excluded" noncitizen would in fact be eligible for a deportation hearing. A second option would be to hold that an entry takes place once there has been a crossing and the person is free of restraint. A third option, first suggested by T. Alexander Aleinikoff & David A. Martin in Immigration: Process and Policy at 342-47 (1st ed. 1985), and then adopted by Congress in 1996, is to establish a single "removal" proceeding for both exclusion cases and deportation cases, at which every noncitizen would have the burden of proving either admissibility or a prior admission. As noted on page 514 of the text, however, even under this option distinctions are still drawn between arriving noncitizens and those who entered without inspection.

Problems 1-3 (page 528):

Problem 1: X clearly made a "crossing." It also appears that she was "inspected and admitted." ICE might argue that the inspection was not complete until the second officer had finished, but at least the first officer seems to have made a final decision to admit. The real question is whether she became "free of restraint." She might argue that, in the light of the first officer's decision, she was indeed free to enter the United States. ICE will counter that she was still in the inspection area and that she was not free to leave until she had cleared Customs. ICE might also argue that, if "admitted" were enough to constitute "free of restraint," then the latter requirement of the *Pierre* test would be redundant. In the two cited cases (*Correa* and *Patel*), both of which took place at the Houston Airport, an official who had been cross-designated to perform both immigration and customs inspections stamped the passengers' passports "admitted" and waved them through. In the customs inspection area, however, they were then caught attempting to smuggle drugs and were excluded. Each person was held not to be free of restraint.

Problem 2: Y clearly "crossed." It is not clear whether he "evaded" inspection, although he tried. At any rate, he in fact was not free of restraint, even though he might have thought so. See *Chen Zhou Chai*, cited in item 1 of the Notes and Questions following *Ching and Chen*; it holds that surveillance precludes freedom from official restraint.

Problem 3: Now there appears to be an entry. There is clearly both a crossing and an evasion of inspection. Being three days and 120 miles away, he would also appear "free of restraint." See, e.g., *Matter of Application of Phelisna*, 551 F.Supp. 960 (E.D.N.Y. 1982), as well as the *Hernandez-Herrera* case cited in the text..

Rosenberg v. Fleuti (page 529):

Fleuti, an LPR, visited Ensenada, Mexico for "a couple of hours" and then returned. A few years later, the former INS brought deportation proceedings. The deportation charge was that Fleuti had been inadmissible when he "reentered" the United States upon his return from Mexico. The alleged ground for inadmissibility was that Fleuti, being gay, was on that basis "afflicted with a psychopathic personality" (then an exclusion ground). Since that particular exclusion ground had not been in effect at the time of Fleuti's original admission, the INS had to rely on his return from Mexico as the "entry" that triggered his inadmissibility.

At one time the courts held that any coming of a noncitizen into the United States was an entry. By way of exception, two court decisions had held that an LPR does not make an "entry" upon returning from a trip abroad if departure from the United States was either unintended (an overnight sleeper train unexpectedly passing through Canada) or involuntary (wartime torpedo attack necessitated bringing crew member to Cuba for medical attention). Congress then enacted an exception to the "entry" definition that codified at least the specific results of those cases, and arguably codified the general rationale on which those cases were based -- avoiding consequences that are both harsh and arbitrary. The Court in *Fleuti* interpreted the statutory exception as exonerating an LPR from the consequences of a "reentry" when the person's departure from the United States had not been intended to "meaningfully" interrupt his or her permanent resident status. Among the factors the Court found relevant to that determination were the duration of the absence, the innocence of the purpose of the trip, and whether the person had needed to assemble travel documents. Three Justices dissented.

Note: As the text suggests, the *Fleuti* materials are worth assigning even though IIRIRA § 301(a) substituted a new "admission" definition for the "entry" definition that had been interpreted in *Fleuti*, and even though the returning resident exception in the new definition uses bright-line rules rather than the multi-factor *Fleuti* test. The material is helpful for 4 reasons: (1) The policies that underlie the returning resident exception in the new "admission" definition will not be comprehensible without exposure to *Fleuti*; (2) the case is a historical landmark; (3) Fleuti is a wonderful vehicle for illustrating several different statutory interpretation techniques; and (4) most practically, the *Fleuti* doctrine should remain viable in several contexts (see items 11-15 of the Notes and Questions).

Notes and Questions Following Fleuti (page 537):

Q1: The principle is that a court should not pass on constitutional questions unless it has to. The principle reflects judicial sensitivity to the doctrine of separation of powers. Pronouncing a statute unconstitutional is a drastic step, one that thwarts the will of the people's representatives. Also, courts prefer to avoid confrontations with Congress if they can responsibly do so. It is better for the Court and the Congress to work harmoniously.

The instructor might want to make sure the students are clear as to precisely how the Court's resolution of the "entry" issue in fact avoids the constitutional decision. The deportation charge was that Fleuti was inadmissible at the time of entry. If there was no entry, then that charge fails regardless whether he was inadmissible. The constitutionality of the term "psychopathic personality" goes only to the latter issue.

Q2: Before addressing the specific question, the instructor might want to discuss the development of the law from *Volpe* to the enactment of INA § 101(a)(13). The students should be able to articulate the law as it stood after the *Volpe* decision, the law as it stood after *DiPasquale*, the law as it stood after *Delgadillo*, and the law as it stood upon the enactment of INA § 101(a)(13).

At issue in *Fleuti* is the meaning of the statutory exception to the "entry" definition. The dissent assumes the majority is interpreting the statutory word "intended;" the dissent says the majority's interpretation is contrary to "any definition of 'intent' that I was taught." The students will probably accept the dissent's characterization of the majority opinion at face value. In actuality, though, the majority and the dissent do not seem to disagree at all about the meaning of the word "intent." At issue, rather, is what, exactly, must be intended. The literal statutory language says the person's "departure" must be intended. The dissent reads that word literally, while the majority interprets "departure" to mean "meaningfully interruptive" departure.

Q3: A literal interpretation would have produced an absurd result. It is difficult to imagine Congress intending to make a sanction as harsh as deportation hinge on such "fortuitous and capricious" events as whether the person had once stepped across the border and back. The point here is not that a literal reading would have produced a harsh result, but that it would have produced an irrational result.

Maybe the Court was simply applying the Social Purpose Rule. Possibly the Court did not view the literal language as producing an absurd result, just one contrary to the rationale that had prompted Congress to enact this exception to the entry definition. Of course, under either approach there remains the question what the legislative purpose actually was. That is taken up in question 4 below.

Q4: The dissent says Congress wanted to codify only the specific results of the two cited cases -- i.e., to make sure that unintentional, unexpected, or involuntary departures did not give rise to reentry. The majority believes Congress wanted to codify the broader principle on which those results were based -- that Congress would not want a fate as extreme as deportation to hinge on an event unrelated to any conceivable congressional aim. In particular, deportation should not depend on whether the person had once made a visit abroad if that visit was not intended meaningfully to interrupt his or her permanent residence.

Q5: The argument would be that it is dangerous to attach significance to congressional inaction. Congress can have any number of reasons for failing to amend an existing statute:

a. Congress was more preoccupied with other work.

b. The particular committee did not want to call attention to the issue and jeopardize fragile coalitions.

c. Congress was not willing to accept further delay.

Q6: The majority argues that the same reasoning that led Congress to allow temporary breaks in continuous residence for naturalization purposes applies here. The idea is that a court can distill from one statutory provision a broad principle that logically applies to a related provision in which Congress was less explicit.

The dissent would argue that it is the contrast that is telling. If Congress had wanted to exempt temporary absences from the entry definition, it could and would have done what it did with INA § 316. The general principle is that, if there are two analogous provisions of the same statute and one of them expressly does something that the other does not, a court should assume that the contrast was deliberate.

Q7: The argument of the dissent is circular. Fleuti is indeed presumed to have known the "law." The question, however, is what law Fleuti is presumed to have known. If one assumes that the law is that a temporary visit abroad necessarily subjects a noncitizen to the consequences of entry upon his or her return, then it follows that Fleuti knew the consequences of leaving. But that argument requires one to assume the very conclusion that the argument is intended to produce. The question here is whether the law does subject a noncitizen who leaves temporarily to the consequences of entry upon his or her return. (In fact, as it turns out, if Fleuti had assumed what the dissent says he should have assumed, then he would have been wrong!)

Q10: The practical effect of that bill would have been to render the reentry doctrine entirely inapplicable to returning LPRs. Every LPR, therefore, would have become able to leave and return at will, and the Fleuti doctrine would have become unnecessary [as would the analogous exception built into new INA § 101(a)(13)]. The issue in most cases would be whether the person abandoned his or her permanent residence, not whether the visit constituted a meaningful interruption. [Note: New INA § 101(a)(13)(C)(i) explicitly recognizes such abandonment.]

The arguments in favor of the bill might be as follows:

a. This bill would avoid the inefficient and uncertain process required by *Fleuti*, which entails balancing and factfinding.

b. Without this bill, the LPR who is inadmissible but not deportable can never leave the United States and be assured of being permitted to return.

An argument against the bill might be that, if any noncitizen possesses qualities Congress has declared undesirable, then he or she should be denied admission. If the results of that approach are sometimes too harsh, the remedy lies in the proper use of discretionary waivers.

Q11: Of course, the present statutory provision defines "admission" rather than "entry." Correspondingly, as the students will see in the succeeding sections of this chapter, most of the deportability grounds that formerly referred to "entry" now refer to "admission."

Both the *Fleuti* decision and the new statutory definition of "admission" recognize that in certain circumstances an LPR's return from a temporary visit abroad will not trigger adverse consequences. But the set of such circumstances has changed:

(a) For the Court in *Fleuti*, the governing test was whether the person had intended a meaningful interruption of his or her permanent residence. Courts were to weigh several factors -- duration of trip, purpose of visit, the need for travel documents, and additional factors to be developed later -- in deciding whether a meaningful interruption was intended. The statutory "admission" definition, in contrast, creates a bright line test; it provides that a returning LPR will not be deemed to be seeking admission unless any one of several enumerated circumstances is present.

(b) The individual factors are now also more determinate. The duration factor has become a fixed 180-day rule, the particular criminal activities that will spoil the automatic exemption from the consequences of admission are now laid out more specifically, and the travel documents factor mentioned in *Fleuti* is now omitted.

(c) The unlawful activity factor is much broader now. See question 14 in the text.

(d) The statutory definition makes specific provision for returns without inspection.

Q12: On the one hand, the *Fleuti* decision was an interpretation of a statutory provision that no longer exists. Thus, the government might argue, there is no more *Fleuti* doctrine. The Supreme Court's pre-statutory holding in *Volpe*, the government might argue, should therefore be reinstated. Under that holding, a noncitizen made an "entry" every time he or she physically came into the United States.

On the other hand, since the INA continues to use the word "entry" but no longer defines it, the courts have to decide what that word means. Even before Congress added a statutory definition, lower courts declined to interpret *Volpe* literally. And in *Fleuti*, the Supreme Court rested its interpretation on the sound policy of avoiding irrational results in high-stakes cases. Absent a statutory direction to the contrary, the noncitizen might argue, it makes sense to adopt a common law rule that promotes that policy. Thus, *Fleuti* should still apply for purposes of determining whether a returning LPR has made a new "entry."

Q13: The applicable deportability ground still says "entry," and Congress's decision not to change that word to "admission" was surely deliberate. Congress picked and chose which deportability grounds would be changed in that way. And there is no longer a statutory alternative to the Supreme Court's interpretation of "entry." It is hard to imagine that the same Congress that adopted a *Fleuti*-like doctrine for most other entry contexts wanted the deportation of a long-term LPR to hinge on whether the person had once made a shopping trip to Ensenada.

Q14: The narrower interpretation seems more logical, for the same policy reasons that led up to *Fleuti* in the first place. Congress might or might not decide that a particular criminal act is serious enough to warrant deportation, but why would it want that determination to depend on whether the individual had once made an innocent, casual, and brief excursion unrelated to any conceivable congressional concern?

Q15: The answer seems to be yes. The new definition of "admission" applies in such cases, but again the charge is inadmissibility at the time of "entry," not "admission." And even when the particular deportability charge uses the word "admission," as noted earlier the new definition of "admission" in turn rests explicitly on the word "entry." Either way, the court must decide what "entry" means, and *Fleuti* has not been disapproved.

<u>Problems</u> <u>4-6</u> (page 543):

Problem 4: Because more than six years have elapsed since A's original admission, the only "admission" on which ICE could rely would be A's return from overseas. The question is whether that return constitutes an admission. Under INA § 101(a)(13), if A made a lawful "entry" into the United States, there will be an admission; under section 101(a)(13)(C)(ii), the returning resident exception is inapplicable because he was away more than 180 days. So did he make an "entry?" Assuming *Fleuti* applies, and see item 12 of the Notes and Questions as to that, the court would have to balance all the factors. On the one hand, seven months is a long absence. On the other hand, the purpose was innocent.

In addition to C(ii), ICE might argue that the returning LPR exception is unavailable because of C(v); he "has committed" a moral turpitude crime. A will respond that C(v) contemplates only crimes committed *before* the alleged readmission. That argument is plausible. The statute says the person won't be regarded as "seeking" admission (present tense) unless he or she "has committed" a crime (past tense).

Problem 5: The question is whether B's return from overseas amounted to an "entry." Since this deportability charge turns on entry and not admission, the returning LPR exception to the admission definition would seem to do B no good, even though the duration was less than 180 days and the purpose was innocent. If *Fleuti* applies, however, and see items 12 and 13 of the Notes and Questions as to that, the court again will have to weigh the various *Fleuti* factors. Here, they seem to coincide. The trip was short and the purpose was innocent. B seems not to have intended a meaningfully interruptive departure. Thus, B should not be found to have reentered and therefore should not be found deportable.

Problem 6: This Problem is intended only to emphasize that the entire exception to the admission definition is limited to LPRs. See INA § 101(a)(13). Since C is here only on a student visa, her return will be an admission whether the visit was meaningfully interruptive or not. The same would be true if the question were whether her return constituted an "entry," since the analogous exception to the statutory "entry" definition interpreted in *Fleuti* was likewise limited to LPRs.

SECTION C. DEPORTABILITY GROUNDS CONCERNED WITH IMMIGRATION CONTROL

1. Entry Without Inspection

This subsection is meant only as background reading.

2. Entry While Inadmissible and Related Issues

Notes and Questions (page 545):

These questions, and the Problem set that follows them, raise technical issues that require the students to follow the interaction of related statutory provisions.

Q1: Technically, all INA § 237(a)(1)(H)(i)(II) says is that inadmissibility under subsections 5A and 7A (directly resulting from the fraud) will not prevent the Secretary of Homeland Security from waiving deportability on the ground that the person had been inadmissible *under subsection 6(C)(i)*. But if ICE charges INA § 237(a)(1)(A) (inadmissibility at entry) on the basis that the person was inadmissible under INA § 212(a)(5)(A) or 7(A), then the last sentence would be needed to clearly waive those other grounds.

The student might suggest that the language of the last sentence is broad enough to waive even grounds other than subsections 5(A) or 7(A) to the extent that those other grounds also directly result from the fraud. But it seems doubtful such a waiver could be granted. The last sentence presupposes the granting of a waiver "under this subparagraph." The noncitizen who is inadmissible under some provision other than 6(C)(i), 5(A), or 7(A) will not meet the "otherwise admissible" requirement of section 237(a)(1)(H)(i)(II). Therefore a waiver could not be granted.

Q2: There are two reasons: First, INA § 212(a)(7)(A) requires a valid visa. A material fraud will make the visa invalid. Hence an exemption is necessary. Second, INA § 212(a)(7)(A) also requires a passport. INA § 237(a)(1)(H) does not.

Problems 7-13 (page 546):

Problem 7: X's first entry into the United States was not at a designated entry point. At that time, therefore, she was inadmissible under INA § 212(a)(6)(A) as a noncitizen "who arrives in the United States at" an undesignated point. Under the literal wording of INA § 237(a)(1)(A), she then became deportable, because she "at the time of entry . . . was within one or more of the classes of aliens inadmissible by the law existing at such time." No statute of limitations is mentioned, so she is still a noncitizen who "at the time of entry [her first entry] was inadmissible." The question is whether her second, otherwise proper, entry should erase the effects of her first, unlawful entry. *Gunaydin*, interpreting a different statutory scheme, held that the original deportability persists. The literal interpretation does, however, generate at least two anomalies, as discussed in the analysis of Problem 8 below.

Problem 8: At the time X arrived at a port of entry for her admission as an LPR, there was no apparent inadmissibility ground. INA § 212(a)(9)(B)(i) was not a problem, because her unlawful presence had been much shorter than 180 days. Nor was she *then* a person who "arrives [present tense] in the United States" at an undesignated place. On that assumption, she was rightly admitted. But as soon as she entered, the literal language of section 237(a)(1)(A) made her deportable as a noncitizen who "at the time of entry" [her original entry] "*was*" inadmissible. One way to avoid the literal interpretation would be to read the word "entry" in section 237(a)(1)(A) as referring only to the most recent entry. As you have seen in the *Fleuti* line of cases, however, the courts have rejected that interpretation in other contexts.

A second anomaly that the literal interpretation would create is that even a very brief unlawful stay following entry at an undesignated point would effectively render a person forever inadmissible. Yet, even for people whose unlawful stays were between 180 days and one year, INA § 212(a)(9)(B)(i)(I) makes the bar only 3 years. There would be no reason to limit the exclusion period under that section to 3 years if the person were going to be forever inadmissible under another exclusion ground. Moreover, if Congress thought the past act (entry at an undesignated point followed by a stay of one month) was not serious enough to justify even exclusion, they why would it want to deport? And why admit the person in the first place if, immediately upon admission, he or she will automatically be deportable?

Problem 9: The charge will be that A is deportable under INA § 237(a)(1)(A) because he was inadmissible at entry under both INA § 212(a)(6)(C)(i)(fraud) and INA § 212(a)(7)(A) (no valid immigrant visa).

It is not clear whether a waiver under INA § 237(a)(1)(H) is available. He has an immigrant visa, and he is the son of a United States citizen. But A must also be "otherwise admissible" except for any inadmissibility that arises under subsections 5(A) and 7(A) to the extent those are "a direct result of that fraud or misrepresentation." The issue is whether his inadmissibility under subsection 7(A) was "a direct result" of his misrepresentation. He will argue that it was. Had the representation been true -- i.e., had he been unmarried as he said -- he would have been admissible.

ICE would likely disagree. It would argue that, had A not <u>made</u> the misrepresentation -- i.e., had he told the truth -- he would have been ineligible for a family-sponsored first preference visa and therefore would still have been inadmissible under subsection 7(A). Therefore his inadmissibility under subsection 7(A) did not result from the fraud. Moreover, the ICE interpretation seems fairer since, whatever merit there might be in excusing his fraud and not holding it against him, there is no particular reason he should affirmatively benefit from it.

Two other immigration law teachers and scholars have suggested a contrary result in correspondence with the author. Elwin Griffith offers the counterargument that the statutory reference to section 212(a)(7)(A) was meant to cover instances in which the invalidity of the visa related to the fraud, seemingly the case here. And Stanley Mailman has suggested that that broader reading might flow from *INS v. Errico*, 385 U.S. 214 (1966). That decision, even as narrowed in *Reid v. INS*, 420 U.S. 619 (1975), stands for the proposition that, when the government could charge deportability based on inadmissibility at entry because of fraud, but instead elects to charge failure to comply with the quota requirements that the fraud was designed to circumvent, the waiver applies. Under that interpretation, A might well prevail. The marriage that he concealed was relevant precisely because it affected the quota under which he sought admission.

Problem 10: The deportability charge will be that B was inadmissible at entry, INA § 237(a)(1)(A), both because of her fraud, INA § 212(a)(6)(C)(i), and because of her conviction of a moral turpitude crime, INA §

212(a)(2)(A)(i)(I). If ICE charges both grounds, then she will be deportable on the latter unless she obtains a 212(h) waiver retroactively. This seems possible, since the crime was committed more than fifteen years before her entry (and presumably before the issuance of her visa).

There is one possible hitch: As a result of IIRIRA, a person who has previously been admitted as an LPR is ineligible for 212(h) relief for seven years. See page 436 of the text. B has previously been admitted as an LPR and since then has lived in the United States only one year. Arguably, however, section 212(h) is available here. B is seeking to invoke it retroactively, at the time of her admission. At that time, she was not a person who had "previously" been admitted.

But that still leaves the charge based on INA § 212(a)(6)(C)(i) (fraud). For that, she needs a 237(a)(1)(H) waiver, which in turn requires a showing that she was "otherwise admissible" except for subsections 5(A) and 7(A) of section 212(a). She will meet this requirement if and only if she obtains a 212(h) waiver of the criminal exclusion ground. In summary, therefore, a waiver under INA § 237(a)(1)(H) will be necessary for her to avoid removal, but it will not be sufficient. She also needs a 212(h) waiver.

Problem 11: INA § 212(a)(6)(C)(i) is clearly a waivable ground, and she was not excludable under any provision other than subsection 7(A) or possibly 5(A), neither of which destroys eligibility for a 237(a)(1)(H) waiver. Further, she is the daughter of a United States citizen.

But there is one problem: INA § 237(a)(1)(H)(i)(II) requires a showing that she "*was* in possession of an *immigrant* visa or equivalent document and was otherwise admissible to the United States *at the time of such admission* . . ." [emphasis added]. C never had an *immigrant visa*. Adjustment of status might be regarded as an "equivalent document," but she didn't have it at the time of admission. Literally, therefore, it seems this waiver is unavailable.

She might argue that the phrase "at the time of such admission" modifies only the phrase "otherwise admissible," not the immigrant visa language.

What result would make the best policy? Had she entered on an immigrant visa that she had obtained through some other material fraud, C would presumably have been eligible for relief under INA § 237(a)(1)(H). She should not be treated less favorably than a noncitizen who entered on an *immigrant* visa obtained by fraud just because it was her *nonimmigrant* visa that had been fraudulently obtained. She is now an LPR and is perfectly admissible but for the fraud.

Problem 12: D is not eligible for relief. It is true that he entered by fraud, had an immigrant visa (the statute couldn't mean that he had to have a valid immigrant visa, since material fraud will always render the visa invalid), and is otherwise admissible except for the permitted statutory exclusions. But he is not the "spouse" of a citizen because the marriage was invalid for immigration purposes. Moreover, even if D were statutorily eligible for a waiver, it is doubtful that administrative discretion would be favorably exercised when the only basis for his coming here at all was his sham marriage.

Problem 13: Since E entered the United States under a false citizenship claim, she arguably has not been "inspected," *Reid v. INS*, and therefore has not been "admitted," INA § 101(a)(13)(A). Consequently, ICE might allege she is present without admission and therefore inadmissible under INA § 212(a)(6)(A). Again, thanks are due to Gerald Neuman (see the text) for spotting this possibility.

If instead IIRIRA is read as superseding *Reid*, ICE can achieve the same result by alleging that E is deportable on any of four grounds:

a. INA § 237(a)(3)(D), for falsely representing herself to be a citizen of the United States;

b. INA § 237(a)(1)(A), for being inadmissible at the time of entry under INA § 212(a)(6)(C)(ii)(false citizenship claim);

c. INA § 237(a)(1)(A), for being inadmissible at the time of entry under INA § 212(a)(6)(C)(i)(procured admission by fraud); or

d. INA § 237(a)(1)(A), for being inadmissible at the time of entry under INA § 212(a)(7)(A)(immigrant not in possession of valid visa).

Nothing in INA § 237(a)(1)(H) waives either the inadmissibility ground of presence without admission or the first two of the above deportability grounds. For this provision to apply, she must be deportable because of inadmissibility at entry, and the inadmissibility must be on account of subsections 5(A), 6(C)(i), or 7(A) of INA § 212(a).

Even with respect to the last two grounds, it appears that INA § 237(a)(1)(H) would not apply here. First, the person must have an immigrant visa (she did not) or "equivalent document." Possibly she could argue that a U.S. passport is an equivalent document. ICE would respond that a *fake* U.S. passport could not possibly qualify. Second, she is not "otherwise admissible," even putting aside the exceptions for 5(A) and 7(A); here, ICE would point out, she is additionally inadmissible under INA § 212(a)(6)(C)(ii) (false citizenship claim) and possibly also 212(a)(6)(A) (presence without admission), as discussed above. Thus she is ineligible for relief under INA § 237(a)(1)(H).

3. Post-Entry Conduct Related to Immigration Control

This material is intended as background reading.

SECTION D. CRIME-RELATED DEPORTATION GROUNDS

1. What Is a Conviction?

General: This material addresses two kinds of questions – whether there was ever a conviction to start with, and, if so, whether subsequent events have erased that conviction for immigration purposes. The discussion in the text is meant to be self-explanatory as to the first question but a basis for class discussion as to the second.

a. Withdrawing Guilty Pleas

The facts of *Parrino* are compelling ones that get students excited and involved: A former INS commissioner represents a noncitizen in a criminal case, doesn't know that a kidnapping conviction might lead to deportation, doesn't bother to look it up, and tells the client (only after the client spots the issue) that a guilty plea will not lead to deportation! The client believes him and pleads guilty. And the court still denies relief.

United States v. Parrino (page 553):

Parrino, a noncitizen, pleaded guilty to conspiracy to kidnap. Before pleading, he had specifically asked his attorney (a former INS commissioner) whether a guilty plea would result in deportation. His attorney, without researching the issue, told him, erroneously, that deportation would not result. After the conviction was entered and his two-year sentence was served, the INS instituted deportation proceedings. Parrino moved to withdraw his guilty plea, invoking Fed.R.Crim.P. 32(d), which then allowed such withdrawals upon a showing of "manifest injustice." He represented that he would not have pleaded guilty but for his attorney's assurance that a guilty plea would not lead to deportation.

The court stated in dictum that the defendant's reasonable surprise as to the *sentence* might be ground for relief if the surprise stemmed from comments *of the judge or the prosecutor*. But surprise resulting solely from erroneous information supplied by the defendant's own attorney, the court held, would not be enough unless the defendant could show "unprofessional conduct." Moreover, the court added, the surprise must concern a "direct" consequence, not a "collateral" consequence, of the conviction; for this purpose, the court held, deportation is merely "collateral." The dissent would have held (a) that surprise as to deportation should be a basis for withdrawal of a guilty plea; and

(b) that this should be true even when the surprise resulted from the erroneous advice of the defense attorney, at least when the attorney's actions were "hopelessly incompetent" and prejudiced the defendant.

Notes and Questions Following Parrino (page 556):

Q1: The direct/collateral distinction seems defensible. There has to be some limit to what the court is required to tell every criminal defendant about the possible consequences of his or her plea. For purposes of that principle, a direct consequence is normally only the sentence that can be imposed. Yet one could also defend a rule that requires a court to advise the defendant not only of the potential sentence, but also of any other unusual important consequences that the court has reason to know about. See, e.g., the Chin & Holmes article cited in the text.

If a student argues that the trial judge should be required to warn of at least some collateral consequences, the instructor can recite many of the common collateral consequences of criminal convictions and then ask the student whether he or she really means to require the sentencing judge to mention all that might apply. Among them are the enhancing effects of a conviction upon subsequent convictions, loss of a driver's license, loss of a civil service job, civil proceedings for involuntary commitment to a mental health facility, loss of good time credit, loss of voting rights, restrictions on travel, military ineligibility or discharge, loss of job opportunities, disqualification from certain professions, and res judicata effects. (All but the last two are drawn from footnote 1 of the dissent in *People v. Pozo*, 746 P.2d 523 (Col. 1987). If the student responds that that would be unreasonable, the instructor should ask how a court should decide which adverse consequences the judge is required to mention.

Given the direct/collateral distinction, should deportation be regarded as a direct consequence or a collateral consequence? On the one hand, deportation is not part of a criminal sentence, and in addition the judge at the pleading stage ordinarily has no way to know that the defendant is a noncitizen. (At the sentencing stage, this information would usually emerge from the probation report.) On the other hand, the deportation consequence is of crucial importance to the defendant, and in many cases the noncitizen status will be an obvious enough possibility that the judge should think to warn the defendant of deportation. As noted in item 2 of the Notes and Questions, many states have now enacted legislation requiring the trial judge in a criminal case to ask whether the defendant is a noncitizen and, if the defendant says yes, to advise him or her of the potential immigration consequences.

b. Expungements

Questions on Page 560:

Q1: On the one hand, the individuals in question have committed serious criminal offenses. Some of the policies associated with criminal punishment apply to removal as well -- retribution, deterrence, and incapacitation. The students were exposed to that subject on pages 517-18 of the text and will encounter it again on pages 587-88.

On the other hand, expungement reflects the judgment of the sentencing jurisdiction that, in certain categories of cases, subsequent events such as rehabilitation and atonement warrant erasure of the conviction. If the jurisdiction that prohibited the conduct in the first place makes those judgments, then arguably the federal government should respect them.

Some of the cases contain language suggesting that liberal recognition of state expungements would impair the uniformity that only a federal standard can supply. It seems doubtful, though, that uniformity cuts either way here. As long as states are given the authority to define the proscribed conduct, adjudicate guilt, and decide on the appropriate sentence, then deportability for a given type of misconduct will inevitably vary with state law. It is hard to see how recognition of state expungement decisions adds to the inconsistency. Moreover, legislatures that authorize expungement presumably are aware of the possibility of expungement when they set the sentencing ranges for the qualifying crimes.

Q2: The "conviction" definition in INA § 101(a)(48)(A) requires an actual finding of guilt and the imposition of actual punishment -- and nothing else. In contrast, giving effect to expungement puts a premium on rehabilitation (and possibly other positive factors, such as a clean prior record).

Q3: As to the first question, the Board's reliance on the noncitizen's participation in the criminal proceeding would be relevant in both direct appeals and motions to reopen, but the "late stage" comment and the distinguishing of *Pickering* on motion to reopen grounds suggests a narrower holding. Of course, even the inapplicability of the "late stage" rationale doesn't mean the Board wouldn't extend its holding to direct appeals based on the first rationale; it just means we can't assume it would.

As to the second question, at least three factors might be relevant to assigning a burden of proof: (1) Which party wants to disturb the status quo? (2) Which party has better access to the evidence? And (3) would an error in favor of one party be worse than an error in favor of the other? Based on the first factor, one could argue either way. In a direct appeal (assuming the noncitizen is appealing from a decision of the immigration judge), the noncitizen is seeking to alter the status quo. On the other hand, by seeking to resurrect for immigration purposes a conviction that has already been vacated, the government is attempting to alter the status quo. Based on the second factor, since the only evidence the BIA would probably accept would be evidence from the records of the criminal proceedings, and since that evidence is public, the government can get access to it just as easily as the noncitizen can (except possibly the noncitizen could more easily obtain the testimony or affidavit of his or her defense attorney.) Based on the third factor, if the actual fact is that the person really wasn't convicted (because the original conviction was flawed), the noncitizen might well have done nothing wrong and would be wrongly deported if unable to meet an assigned burden of proving the reason for the vacatur.

c. Executive Pardons

This one-paragraph description is intended as background reading.

d. Miscellaneous Collateral Attacks

More background reading.

2. Crimes Involving Moral Turpitude

a. The Meaning of "Crime Involving Moral Turpitude"

Marciano v. INS (page 561):

Marciano, an LPR, was convicted in Minnesota state court of statutory rape. He had claimed to be unaware that the female with whom he had had sexual intercourse was then under age 18, the age of consent at the time. Minnesota, however, did not recognize mistake of age as a defense to statutory rape. The IJ and the BIA ordered him deported on the ground that he had been convicted of a crime involving "moral turpitude."

Marciano first argued that the phrase "moral turpitude" was unconstitutionally vague, but that argument had already been rejected by the Supreme Court in *Jordan v. DeGeorge*.

He next argued that statutory rape is not a crime of moral turpitude. The court held otherwise, quoting previous judicial language to the effect that this crime is "usually classed as rape." The dissent identified three possible options for identifying crimes that involve moral turpitude: (1) the traditional formula, under which a crime does not involve moral turpitude unless every hypothetical act that could violate the criminal statute necessarily involved moral turpitude; (2) a middle view, to the effect that the crime "in its general nature is one which in common usage would be classified as a crime involoving moral turpitude;" and (3) an examination of the facts of the particular case.

Characterizing the majority opinion as having implicitly applied the second view, the dissent argued for the third view. Under that view, the dissent would have remanded for a determination whether Marciano's specific acts involved moral turpitude.

Note: The steady expansion of the "aggravated felony" definition has severely narrowed the contexts in which ICE needs to charge deportability based on a moral turpitude crime, with all its requirements concerning timing and sentence. Nonetheless, the *Marciano* analysis is highly useful for the reason given in item 10 of the Notes and Questions.

<u>Notes and Questions Following Marciano</u> (page 567):

Q1: The most common rationale for the vagueness doctrine is that the individual needs fair notice of what is prohibited in order to conform his or her conduct to the law. That rationale is probably inapplicable here. The criminal law already gives notice that the specified conduct is proscribed. All that is arguably unknown is whether, in addition to criminal sanctions, the conduct could give rise to removal. Also, the courts have given meaning to this otherwise ambiguous expression.

A second purpose of the vagueness doctrine, however, is to avoid unequal enforcement of the law by the police, the prosecution, and the courts. That objection is as applicable here as it is to criminal legislation, although again the government's argument will be that the accumulated case law supplies adequate guidance.

Q2: Articulating the three views is essential to analyzing the more difficult questions that follow. The three views are:

a. The traditional view. The crime in the abstract -- defined by the statute, judicial interpretations of it, and the indictment -- must encompass <u>only</u> conduct that would involve moral turpitude. If it is possible for a person to violate the statute without exhibiting moral turpitude, then the crime defined by that statute will be held not to involve moral turpitude even if the conduct in the particular case is seen as immoral.

b. The *Pino* view (as applied by the majority opinion in *Marciano*). The crime in its general nature, in common usage, must be classified as involving moral turpitude.

c. The Eisele dissent. The conduct in the particular case must involve moral turpitude.

Once the class has articulated the three views, it is in a position to evaluate them. The instructor could structure the discussion somewhat by having the class debate the comparative merits of views (a) and (c) above -- i.e., the traditional view and the Eisele view, respectively. Once that is done, further argument can be taken on the extent to which the advantages and disadvantages of the two principles would apply to the intermediate position taken in *Pino*.

In terms of the mechanics, the instructor could either conduct this like any other class discussion or have the students engage in oral argument before a simulated appellate court. If the latter option is chosen, the instructor could appoint one or two attorneys to represent each side. (For the reasons discussed below, it is not clear which side ICE would favor.) Arguments for the traditional view might include the following:

a. The traditional view is administratively more convenient for the agency. It provides a standard for the agency to follow once case law begins to accumulate. The agency will not have to examine the evidence in each individual case.

b. This approach is more efficient for the additional reason that the agency will not have to re-examine the facts of the criminal case.

The arguments for the Eisele position would generally emphasize the shortcomings of the traditional view. Those might include the following:

a. The traditional view would allow those noncitizens who in fact acted with moral turpitude when they committed the particular crimes to stay in the United States simply because the statutes under which they were convicted happen to cover hypothetical others who did not act with moral turpitude. That result is irrational.

b. The traditional view undermines uniformity. If two noncitizens in different states commit the same act and both states make that act a crime, but the first statute also covers other acts that do not involve moral turpitude while the second statute covers only the act in question here, the first person escapes removal while the second does not.

c. The traditional view is practically impossible to apply honestly. For almost every criminal statute, it is possible to think of <u>some</u> scenario in which the violator lacked moral turpitude.

d. Under the traditional view, the specificity of the indictment can determine deportability.

The *Pino* view has most of the advantages, and most of the shortcomings, of the traditional view. One of the shortcomings it does not have, however, is the difficulty of finding that a crime literally involves moral turpitude in every conceivable fact situation that it covers. Under *Pino*, it is enough that the crime *generally* involves moral turpitude. Its negatives resemble those of the traditional view. If the act of the particular individual doesn't involve moral turpitude, he or she could be removed under the *Pino* view simply because hypothetical others who violate this statute will usually have acted with moral turpitude. Conversely, if most people who violate the particular statute do not act with moral turpitude, the person will escape removal even if he or she acted with moral turpitude.

Q3: The majority doesn't actually provide a general principle. It says only that the courts and the BIA hold statutory rape to be a crime involving moral turpitude. By process of elimination, however, the assumption that Judge Eisele makes about the majority opinion is probably accurate. The majority expressly rejects the view that a court should examine the facts of the particular case. By the same token, as Judge Eisele points out in footnote 4 of his dissent, the majority could not be applying the traditional view because it is impossible to say that statutory rape necessarily involves moral turpitude in all conceivable fact situations. For example, a mistake as to the age or marital status of the victim would be no defense in Minnesota. Nor can one say that all pre-marital and extra-marital sexual relations inherently involve moral turpitude, since the crime of fornication has specifically been held <u>not</u> to involve moral turpitude.

Q4: No. If the violation of this law "under any and all circumstances" involves moral turpitude, then how could the particular act ever *fail* to evidence immorality? (If the conduct the statute embraces always involves moral turpitude, then it must do so in the particular case.)

Probably the BIA was thinking of the converse proposition: If a violation of the law in question does *not* always involve moral turpitude, then the crime will be held not to involve moral turpitude even if the particular act of the defendant *does* evidence immorality.

Q5: There is no real answer to this question. The issue of which community the *Pino* Court had in mind is an important one because acts that are morally condemned in some circles might be acceptable or at least viewed less harshly in others. The instructor might wish to revisit this issue in the context of question 8 below.

Q6: Maybe "always" really means "almost always?"

Q7: It is doubtful that these words focus the inquiry in any meaningful way. Perhaps, however, they at least impart some sense of proportion. The strength of the words might indicate the level of immorality the phrase "moral turpitude" requires.

Q8: As to the first question, it seems clear that an unelected judge should at least attempt to discover the values of the community rather than to apply his or her personal values. To a certain practical degree, the judge will of course be unable to screen out his or her own beliefs, but that does not mean that an attempt should not be made.

As to the national/local distinction, the advantages of a national approach are uniformity and, hence, equality. The advantage of a local approach is that it would permit a judgment as to whether the particular individual tends to respect the customs of the culture in which he or she lives. A related question that the instructor might wish to raise at this point is what should happen when the particular *ethnic* community has cultural norms different from those of the mainstream. Suppose, for example, that a father has deserted his family and has refused to pay child support, and that in the particular country in which his actions took place, society accepts that behavior. Some might argue that it is crucial to treat all ethnic groups alike, either in the interest of fairness or in the interest of encouraging assimilation. Others might disagree, maintaining that a court should take ethnic norms into account because, again, the ultimate judgment is whether the particular person is likely to respect the customs of the culture in which he or she lives.

As to the time dimension, different views are possible. An argument for focusing on the values that existed at the time of the original enactment of the "moral turpitude" clause (i.e., 1891) would be that Congress had specific activities in mind as grounds for deportation. An argument for going by the time of the most recent amendment (of either the INA or the specific deportability provision) is that that expression is most likely to reflect Congress's most recent view of which conduct should give rise to removal. (Of course, if Congress left the phrase "moral turpitude" intact, perhaps Congress simply did not address the issue at all.) An advantage of going by the time of the commission of the crime is that the person who violated the then existing norms might be perceived as likely to violate today's existing norms. Finally, the advantage of going by the time of the removal hearing is that, if society does not now view what the person did as being particularly socially harmful, then removal is simply too harsh.

<u>Problems 14-16: (page 570)</u>:

Problem 14: Under the traditional view, the result is uncertain. In theory, a court applying that view should ask whether voluntary manslaughter always involves moral turpitude. Here is the case where it arguably does not. Thus, a court that truly subscribes to the traditional view should hold that voluntary manslaughter does not involve moral turpitude, either here or in other cases. In fact, however, those courts that purport to follow the traditional view hold that voluntary manslaughter involves moral turpitude. It is much easier to find that the crime involves moral turpitude under the *Pino* test, since, in common usage, voluntary manslaughter is *usually* thought of as involving moral turpitude. Under the<u>Eisele</u> view, there is certainly a strong argument that there was no moral turpitude on the facts of this case.

This example illustrates well the difficulty of applying the traditional view. In theory, the traditional view is more favorable to the noncitizen than is the view of Judge Eisele; the traditional view enables the person to escape removal whenever a court finds that it is possible to commit the charged crime without moral turpitude. The Eisele view, in contrast, enables the person to escape removal only if committing the crime without moral turpitude is not only possible but is in fact what actually occurred. In this Problem, however, the person most likely prevails under Judge Eisele's view, whereas under the traditional view the court has to strain to say that voluntary manslaughter always involves moral turpitude. A contrary conclusion would allow not only this individual, but all noncitizens convicted of voluntary manslaughter, to avoid removal.

Problem 15: Under this statute, the defendant can be convicted without actual knowledge. It is enough that the perpetrator "should have known" that the property was stolen. Mere carelessness or thoughtlessness could suffice. Under those circumstances, it would seem too harsh to find moral turpitude. Since the traditional test requires moral turpitude in all possible scenarios covered by the statute, the result thus seems to be that this crime does not involve moral turpitude. The result is less clear under the *Pino* test. In common usage, the crime that is called "receiving stolen property" might well be thought of as involving moral turpitude. Under the Eisele view, the result turns on whether the defendant actually knew the property was stolen. Probably the immigration judge would have to make that judgment. The verdict is not revealing, since the jury might have found only that the defendant had reason to know. The trial transcript might be helpful, but even here the evidence is conflicting. Possibly the immigration judge could call the noncitizen and any other available witnesses and make an independent finding of fact.

Problem 16: The traditional view is somewhat confusing to apply on these facts. On the one hand, simple assault is not a crime involving moral turpitude, and thus it might seem the noncitizen prevails. But the traditional rule requires consideration not only of the statute, but also of the indictment or information. In this case the charge was assault with intent to kill, a crime that does involve moral turpitude. Perhaps the traditional view assumes that information in the indictment should be ignored to the extent it differs from the actual conviction.

Under the *Pino* formulation, the person almost certainly has not been convicted of a crime involving moral turpitude. In common usage, simple assault would *usually* not be held to involve moral turpitude.

The Eisele position would require consideration of the specific facts. If the defendant intended to kill or at least to do serious bodily harm, then moral turpitude was clearly present. Even without such an intent, a court might find spousal battery pernicious enough to imply moral turpitude. A difficult question is whether, under the Eisele view, it is open to the immigration judge to make a finding that the defendant intended to kill even though the jury did not make such a finding. There would be no logical contradiction, because the jury might have believed there was an intent to kill but not "beyond a reasonable doubt," the standard of proof in a criminal case. (In chapter 9 the students will encounter the slightly lower "clear and convincing" standard of proof for deportability.) Alternatively, perhaps the jury believed the defendant intended to kill but was willing to slough off the case as a "mere" domestic dispute and decided to be lenient.

b. "Committed Within Five Years After the Date of Admission"

Problems 17-18 (page 570):

Problem 17: X is clearly deportable. The conviction was entered slightly more than five years after his admission, but that is irrelevant. Under INA § 237(a)(2)(A)(i)(I), it is only the commission of the crime that has to occur less than five years after admission. Here, it did.

As discussed in the next subsection, it also does not matter that a sentence of less than one year was actually imposed. Under INA § 237(a)(2)(A)(i)(II), it is enough that a sentence of one year or longer "may" be imposed.

To avoid aggravated felony issues (which the students will not yet have studied), the crime chosen was state income tax fraud, which does not constitute an aggravated felony as long as the amount is under $10,000. See INA § 101(a)(43)(M).

Problem 18: Again the question is whether the crime was committed "within five years after admission." Y will argue that the indictment is not precise enough. It says only that the crime was committed "on or about" November 15. The timing is crucial. If the alleged time was off by just one day -- if, for example, the crime was actually committed on November 16 -- then it would have been committed more than five years after Y's original admission. Thus, he will argue, ICE needs to prove the timing of the commission of the offense.

ICE will argue that his return from his visit abroad constituted a second admission. Did it? Under INA § 101(a)(13)(C), a returning LPR is not regarded as seeking admission "unless the alien ... (ii) has been absent . . . in excess of 180 days." Y has been away longer -- ten months. Therefore, it seems (though for reasons discussed in the *Fleuti* materials it is not entirely clear) that he does not get the benefit of that statutory exemption. As also discussed, however, it is possible that Fleuti still applies for purposes of determining "entry," an essential element of "admission." If it does, the question is close. Ten months is a fairly long period, and the purpose of the trip, though innocent, was a significant one. Perhaps, too, Y needed to procure travel documents, although under the regulations he can return to the United States by presenting a passport and green card within one year.

Assume, though, that his return constituted a second "admission." Is he deportable? The statute requires that the crime be committed "within five years after the date of admission," and presumably any admission will do. Y will argue nonetheless that that requirement has not been met because, even if his return is treated as an admission, his crime was committed *before* that admission -- not "within five years *after*" the date of admission. ICE will argue that the phrase "within five years after the date of admission" means the point in time *no later* than a time five years after admission. The instructor here might point the students to INA § 237(a)(1)(E), the provision that makes the smuggling of other noncitizens into the United States a deportability ground, and then ask them whether that provision gives them any ideas for arguing in favor of Y's interpretation. Y's argument will be that, if in INA § 237(a)(2)(A)(i)(I) Congress had intended the phrase "within five years after the date of admission" to mean what ICE says it means, then Congress would have said "prior to the date of admission, at the time of admission, or within five years after the date of admission," as it essentially did in INA § 237(a)(1)(E). The argument would emphasize the contrast in the wording of those two deportability grounds.

ICE, in response, might support its interpretation by identifying an anomaly that Y's interpretation would produce. The instructor might elicit this argument by asking the students whether, in the event Y's return is considered an admission, he would be deportable under INA § 237(a)(1)(A) (inadmissible at entry for having committed a crime involving moral turpitude). The students should figure out that Y would not be deportable on that ground because, at the time of his return, he had not yet been convicted of the crime and had not admitted the essential elements of the crime. Therefore he was not inadmissible at the time he returned. Y's interpretation therefore produces the following anomaly: If a noncitizen both commits a crime involving moral turpitude and is convicted of it, and then leaves the United States and returns, he or she will be deportable for having reentered the United States while inadmissible for having previously been convicted of a crime involving moral turpitude. Similarly, if a noncitizen leaves the United States and returns, and *then*, less than five years later, commits a crime involving moral turpitude and is convicted, he or she will be deportable under INA § 237(a)(2)(A)(i) for having been convicted of a crime involving moral turpitude committed within five years after admission. Either way, the person is deportable. Yet if the situation is in between -- i.e., if the person commits the crime in the United States, then leaves and returns, and *then* is convicted -- there will be no deportability ground under Y's interpretation. There is no reason Congress would want to treat that individual more favorably than the other two.

As in Problem 17, it does not matter that the sentence actually imposed was only six months. The possible sentence was exactly one year, which is enough.

c. Sentencing Requirements:

This paragraph is intended only as background reading.

d. Two Crimes Involving Moral Turpitude

Problem 19 (page 571):

Bribery is clearly a crime involving moral turpitude because it involves dishonesty.

The analysis will hinge on precisely when the crime was committed. X entered the United States on June 14, 2000 and committed the two crimes some time in June 2005. If ICE can establish that he committed the crime before June 14, 2005, then it will charge that he is deportable as one who was convicted of a crime involving moral turpitude that was committed less than five years after admission. Since the potential sentence is much longer than one year, X would thus be deportable.

If the crime was committed after June 14, 2005, then the only possible deportability ground would be conviction of two crimes involving moral turpitude. If that charge is filed, the main issue would be whether X's activities constituted a "single scheme of criminal misconduct." As to that, it is possible to argue either way.

ICE, applying *Adetiba* and *Pacheco*, will argue that there had been a "substantial interruption," since X had had to leave the scene of the crime and then come back. He had had time to reflect.

X will argue that his activity was all part of a single scheme. Both restaurants were his, he wanted the same thing for both, he bribed the same official, his actions occurred on the same day, and his conduct was identical. He would advocate use of the Ninth Circuit view in *Gonzalez-Sandoval* and argue for a finding of fact that the crimes were planned at the same time. Alternatively, he might maintain, even under *Adetiba* and *Pacheco* there was no *substantial* interruption or adequate time for real reflection, because the two crimes occurred the same day.

e. Judicial Recommendations Against Deportation:

The text raises the question whether JRAD's should be restored. The theory of the JRAD is that Congress legislates only in general terms. It cannot consider the facts of individual cases. The potential harshness of a removal order makes accuracy and precision important. At some point in the process, the argument runs, someone should make an individualized assessment of whether the noncitizen's criminal conduct is serious enough to warrant that consequence. The law could authorize either the immigration authorities or the courts to make that judgment, but the sentencing judge is best situated because he or she has observed the defendant and knows the evidence. The downside of JRAD's is that deportability can hinge on which judge the defendant lands. The standards are unlikely to be uniform. Congress could build specific standards into a JRAD provision, but it would be difficult to fashion standards that are both flexible enough to take account of individual circumstances and concrete enough to be of practical use.

The text also asks about the merits of the United Kingdom approach. On the assumption that the judge's assessment should control, the question is how to allocate the risk of error. As to that, there are at least two subissues:

a. Which is worse -- removing a deserving noncitizen because the court did not know about JRAD's, or allowing a non-deserving noncitizen to stay because the court did not know that it could recommend in favor of removal?

b. Which type of error would be more frequent under either approach? Probably the former. If a noncitizen could be removed only upon an affirmative judicial recommendation to that effect, then ICE and possibly criminal prosecutors would make sure judges become aware of it, and the judges themselves would build it into their routines. In contrast, experience has shown that attorneys who represent noncitizens in criminal cases are less likely to be aware of JRAD's. Probably this is true because such attorneys are rarely immigration specialists and often not criminal law specialists either. More importantly, there is no government agency on the side of noncitizen criminal defendants in the same way that there is a government agency (ICE) charged with the responsibility for removing noncitizens. Either way, it would be possible and arguably desirable to give judges the discretion to waive the 30-day limit.

3. Drug Offenses

<u>Problems 20-21 (page 573)</u>:

Problem 20: A is deportable under INA § 237(a)(2)(B)(i) for having been convicted of violating a law relating to a controlled substance. The marijuana exception is inapplicable because his offense was sale, not possession for his own use.

If the material on aggravated felonies has not yet been assigned, the instructor could note that, alternatively, ICE might charge A with being deportable under INA § 237(a)(2)(A)(iii) as an aggravated felon. Since his offense consisted of selling a controlled substance, it might be found to be "illicit trafficking" within the meaning of INA § 101(a)(43)(B). If so, then as discussed in the next subsection other consequences attach (virtually no opportunity for discretionary relief, abbreviated procedures, lifelong inadmissibility unless he secures permission from the Attorney General to reapply for admission, etc.).

Problem 21: In case the students ask, driving under the influence of a controlled substance (at least under a statute that requires no mens rea greater than negligence) is neither a crime involving moral turpitude, see Gordon, Mailman & Yale-Loehr § 71.05[1][d], nor an aggravated felony, see *Leocal v. Ashcroft* (excerpted and discussed in the next subsection). Therefore the only possible deportability ground is INA § 237(a)(2)(B)(i) (controlled substances). As to that, there are two issues:

a. Is driving under the influence "relating to?" At least one court has said yes. See *Flores-Arellano v. INS*, 5 F.3d 360 (9th Cir. 1993) (and so is use).

b. Is this substance "controlled?" B will argue that ICE cannot prove it is a controlled substance within the meaning of the federal definition of that term, because the state definition is broader and the record of conviction does not specify the drug. The instructor can note an older case, *Matter of Paulus,* 11 I. & N. Dec. 274 (BIA 1965), in which a noncitizen convicted under California law of offering to sell a "narcotic" (the then applicable statutory term) was held not to be deportable because California's narcotic definition was broader than the federal definition, and the record of conviction had not revealed the specific narcotic. One possibility, which can be more fully assessed once the students have explored the material on pages 742-43 of the text, is that the immigration judge could force B either to testify as to which drug it was (the privilege against self-incrimination being inapplicable because she has already been convicted) or to suffer the drawing of adverse inferences.

4. Aggravated Felonies

General: The sweeping expansions of the aggravated felony definition, coupled with the far-reaching consequences for the person convicted of such an offense, have dramatically enhanced the importance of this material. There remain very few cases, for example, in which ICE needs to charge deportability based on crimes involving moral turpitude, since the vast majority of the moral turpitude crimes will now also meet the definition of aggravated felony. From a prosecutorial standpoint, the latter charge is easier because it does not hinge on the timing of the commission of the offense, there are very few opportunities to apply for discretionary relief, and the other consequences discussed in the text apply as well.

Leocal v. Ashcroft (page 576):

An LPR was convicted, in Florida state court, of driving under the influence of alcohol and causing serious bodily injury. He was sentenced to 2 ½ years in prison. The IJ found this crime to be a crime of violence and therefore (because the term of imprisonment exceeded one year) an aggravated felony under INA § 101(a)(43)(F). He was thus found deportable under INA § 237(a)(2)(A)(iii) and ordered removed. The BIA affirmed, and the Court of Appeals for the Eleventh Circuit dismissed his petition for review. The Supreme Court granted certiorari to resolve a circuit split on the question whether DUI is a crime of violence.

The term "crime of violence" is defined in 18 USC § 16 as any offense that either (a) "has as an element the use . . . of physical force against the person or property of another" or (b) is a felony and, . . . by its nature, involves a substantial risk that physical force against the person or property of another may be used in the course of committing the offense." The Court first interpreted that language to require a categorical determination of whether an offense is a crime of violence, rather than a determination that rests on the facts of the individual case. The Court then held that the statutory references to "use" and "used" (in both prongs of 18 USC § 16) contemplated the *intentional* use of force against the person or property of another. A statute that requires only the negligent use of force or no mens rea at all therefore does not qualify as a crime of violence. Since the Florida statute at issue here did not require any mens rea, the offense was held not to be a crime of violence. The Court expressly left open whether an offense that requires the *reckless* (but not intentional) use of force against the person or property of another qualifies as a crime of violence.

Notes and Questions Following Leocal (page 580):

Q1: As to the first question (the applicability of *Garcia-Lopez*), perhaps the Court does not believe the BIA has any advantage over the federal courts in interpreting the phrase "aggravated felony." The federal courts do, after all, interpret that term constantly in the criminal sentencing context.

As to the second question, the principal rationale for *Chevron* deference is the presumed expertise of the relevant administrative agency. The agency is immersed in the interpretation process of the particular statute and also has the chance to observe the practical effects of its interpretations. A secondary rationale might be that judicial deference to a centralized agency contributes to nationwide uniformity in the results. Both rationales can be linked to the assumption that Congress intended to delegate a certain amount of interpretive authority to the agency.

So suppose, as happened here, a court defers to an agency interpretation, and the agency later changes its view, but then the agency nonetheless follows the interpretation adopted by the relevant circuit, contrary to the agency's now preferred view? In effect, no one - not the agency, not the court - is making an independent decision as to the meaning of the statute. The court reaches a particular decision because it thinks that was what the agency wanted, and the agency then reaches the same result because it thinks that is what the court wanted. The agency's expertise is rejected, and the uniformity that *Chevron* deference might ordinarily promote is thwarted as well. More sensible, it seems, would be for the BIA to follow its new, preferred interpretation even in a circuit that has taken a contrary position, provided the court had reached that contrary position by deferring to the BIA's prior interpretation. Analytically, the BIA would be distinguishing the court's ruling. In the present case, for example, the BIA would be characterizing the court as having held that DUI is a crime of violence if the BIA so holds - a statement of the court's holding that would be perfectly consistent with the court's rationale. Since the BIA no longer so holds, there would be no conflict with the the ruling of the relevant circuit.

Q2: As for the statutory interpretation question, the Court's analysis seems convincing. It highlights the language of both section 16(a) ("an offense *that has as an element* ") and 16(b) (an offense that "*by its nature* involves a substantial risk . . .". Both terms strongly suggest categorical determinations.

As for the policy question, the categorical approach will normally be more administratively efficient. Once case law accumulates, the administrative and judicial decisionmakers will have clearer standards to follow and won't have to reexamine all the evidence from the criminal proceedings. A disadvantage of the categorical approach, however, is that it permits a person who in fact has committed the crime encompassed by the aggravated felony definition to escape removal just because some other *hypothetical* defendant could have violated the same criminal statute without falling within the aggravated felony definition.

Q3: First, the meaning the Court ascribed to the statutory text does seem compatible with ordinary English usage. One does not usually say that X has "used" force on someone else if X's actions were accidental. "Use" ordinarily assumes intention. Second, perhaps the Court thought DUI too commonplace for Congress to have wanted to assign such severe consequences - in contrast to the kinds of conduct the Court and society might be more prone to associate with "real criminals." Third, most of the contrary court of appeals decisions had been based on deference to the old (and now superseded) BIA position. The Supreme Court's decision is consistent with the current BIA view, although (as discussed in question 1 above) the Court did not invoke the principle of *Chevron* deference even as a makeweight.

Q4: Since the hypothetical statute doesn't require the "use" of the firearm, prong (a) of the "crime of violence" definition is clearly inapplicable. The issue would be the applicability of prong (b). Can one say that this offense, "by its nature, involves a substantial risk that physical force against the person or property of another may be used in the course of committing the offense?" The rationale for making this a crime in the first place probably is that the legislature regarded convicted felons as disproportionately likely to use firearms to commit crimes. Hence there might well be an inherent "substantial risk" of the person intentionally using force. But the last phrase of prong (b) ("in the course of committing the offense") seems significant. "The offense" to which that language refers appears to be the crime of violence of which the person was convicted, not some future crime. The question, therefore, is *not* whether there is a substantial risk that the person will use the firearm to commit a second crime. Rather, the question is whether there is a substantial risk the person will use force to acquire *possession* of the firearm in the first place.

Q5: It's hard to say whether the Supreme Court would accept the first of the two reasons given in *Jobson*. The Supreme Court in *Leocal* did not comment on whether the force that the crime of violence definition contemplates must be applied directly by the defendant, as the court in *Jobson* holds, or whether the Supreme Court would think it enough that the defendant's conduct created a substantial risk that force will be applied, by someone, in some way. If it had believed the latter, however, the Court in *Leocal* would probably have reached a different result, since it is hard to deny that DUI carries a substantial risk of force being applied to the person or property of others. As to the second reason offered in *Jobson*, the Supreme Court in *Leocal* expressly left open whether the reckless (as distinguished from the intentional) use of force would suffice.

From a policy standpoint, it is not clear whether the immigration laws should treat an intentional battery more harshly than a reckless killing. The former entails an intention to apply unlawful force to another, while the latter requires only recklessness, usually regarded as a lesser degree of moral culpability. But the latter involves endangering life, whereas a battery does not (at least not inherently).

Q12: Perhaps some students will maintain that as long as people choose to remain noncitizens and to commit crimes, and assuming the law provides fair notice, there is little cause for complaint. But the examples given will surely prompt most students to conclude that the results are unduly harsh.

<u>Problems 22-24 (page 585):</u>

Problem 22: The crime clearly involves moral turpitude, but X cannot be charged under INA § 237(a)(2)(A)(i) because he committed the crime more than five years after admission.

ICE will charge that X has been convicted of an aggravated felony. There are two possible routes to that result:

a. Obtaining property by false pretenses will be classified as a theft offense for purposes of INA § 101(a)(43)(G). The "term of imprisonment" must be at least one year. According to INA § 101(a)(48)(B), "term of imprisonment" refers to sentence imposed (not maximum possible sentence), and suspended sentences are considered imposed. So the 5-year maximum is irrelevant. His sentence is exactly one year, because the suspended portion of it counts, and "one year or more" is all that is required.

b. ICE might argue that his crime involved "fraud or deceit," under INA § 101(a)(43)(M)(i). The exact amount of the loss is not given. If it exceeds $10,000, then this charge also applies. The question will be one of proof. If the record of conviction does not reveal the amount, and if X does not concede the amount, ICE will be able to succeed only if the Supreme Court in *Nijhawan* allows proof of the amount of the loss through external means and ICE is able to obtain such proof.

Problem 23: Y is <u>not</u> deportable under INA § 237(a)(2)(A)(i). Even if this crime involves moral turpitude (which is doubtful), the crime was committed more than five years after admission. But is Y deportable under INA § 237(a)(2)(A)(iii) as an aggravated felon? There are two possibilities:

a. Subsection G covers "burglary," provided the "term of imprisonment" is at least one year. Since "term of imprisonment" refers to the sentence imposed, not the time actually served, Y's release before one year is irrelevant. She was still sentenced to one year. The problem would be one of defining burglary. The *Taylor* case and its progeny make clear that a uniform, federal, common law definition of burglary should be used. Normally "breaking and entering" falls short of burglary, which typically requires some specific intent at the time of entry, such as intent to commit a felony or a theft. If that definition is adopted, then breaking and entering would not suffice.

b. Subsection F requires a "crime of violence." Does this statute qualify? If so, then she has been convicted of an aggravated felony, because the sentence imposed was one year (see above). The term "crime of violence," in turn, is defined in 18 USC § 16, which is reproduced in the *Leocal* opinion. The breaking and entering statute that Y was convicted of violating falls within part (a) of that latter definition. To be guilty, one must "break" and enter the building. Therefore, the crime requires force to property; under part (a) of the statutory definition of "crime of violence," that is enough. Since the breaking that the statute requires is presumably intentional, the *Leocal* issue does not arise.

Note: The crime here is a misdemeanor, but as the text explains, even misdemeanors can be "aggravated felonies."

Problem 24: The real questions are whether Z will be inadmissible when he seeks to return and, if he is in fact admitted, whether he would be deportable.

It is not clear whether Z would even be regarded as seeking admission when he returns. On the one hand, though he is an LPR and will have been away less than 180 days, he "engaged in illegal activity" (the failure to appear) while away. Thus he might be regarded as seeking admission. See INA §§ 101(a)(13)(A), 101(a)(13)(C)(ii,iii). On the other hand, as discussed earlier in the chapter, the admission definition requires an "entry." That term is no longer defined anywhere in the statute. If *Fleuti* is applied, the short duration and the otherwise innocent purpose of the trip are positive factors that make the entry determination uncertain.

Even if he is regarded as seeking admission, however, he seems to be admissible. Failure to appear is probably not a crime involving moral turpitude, and conviction of an aggravated felony is not a ground for inadmissibility. Therefore Z should not have to worry about being readmitted. For the same reason, he should not have to worry later about being deportable on the ground of inadmissibility at the time of admission.

Once he is readmitted, though, will he become deportable as an aggravated felon? INA § 101(a)(43)(T) encompasses the offense of failure to appear, where the underlying charge is a felony punishable by two years of imprisonment or more. The felony charge for which he failed to appear carried a maximum term of 20 years. So it fits the description of an aggravated felony.

One other possible issue is what the phrase "for which a sentence of 2 years' imprisonment or more may be imposed," in INA § 101(a)(43)(T), modifies. Z might argue that it refers to the offense of failing to appear rather than to the underlying felony. If so, it would not matter whether Z accepted the 15-day jail term; his future deportability would rest, instead, on the maximum sentence for the offense of failure to appear. Since the quoted phrase immediately follows the word "felony," with no intervening punctuation, this interpretation is unlikely but arguable. Thanks are due to Professor Victor Romero and his students for the idea.

But there is one remaining factor. Near the end of INA § 101(a)(43) is a proviso that, for a foreign conviction to be an aggravated felony, the term of imprisonment has to have been "completed within the previous 15 years." So if Z accepts the 15-day sentence, he will become deportable as an aggravated felon and will remain so for 15 years. Presumably a foreign conviction cannot constitute an aggravated felony at all if there never was any imprisonment; it wouldn't make sense to remove someone as an aggravated felon if he or she has never been imprisoned, while sparing the person who was imprisoned in the past. On that assumption, Z should say *merci*, pay the fine, and avoid the imprisonment.

5. Miscellaneous Criminal Grounds

The instructor might wish to discuss in class the regulation under which a conviction of a "crime of violence" punishable by a year of confinement or more can constitute a failure to maintain nonimmigrant status. See page 586 of the text. Even with the recent expansions of the aggravated felony definition, this regulation could make a difference. For example, a person might be convicted of a crime of violence that does not involve moral turpitude (say, simple assault) and is punishable by a year or more, but the sentence actually imposed might be less than a year.

Is the regulation valid? The broad issue is what power DHS has to create new deportability grounds by making avoidance of particular conduct a condition of every nonimmigrant's stay. Opponents of this regulation might observe that, if such a regulation is valid, DHS can use this device to add almost any deportability ground it likes for nonimmigrants. The effect would be to read out of the statute the limitations on the deportability grounds that Congress created -- for example, the requirement that the crime involve moral turpitude, or that it be committed less than five years after admission, or that a sentence of at least one year actually be imposed. Defenders of the regulation might point out that INA § 214(a) expressly authorizes the Secretary of Homeland Security to prescribe the conditions of every nonimmigrant's stay. Opponents might respond by arguing that those conditions, surely, are not unlimited. Congress must have had in mind conditions that are consistent with the limitations built into the existing statutory grounds.

Statutory interpretation aside, the instructor might wish to take up this material in conjunction with the Comparative Law Note that follows it. *Should* DHS have the power to issue regulations of the type just discussed? See the analysis immediately below.

Note on Comparative Law: Separation of Powers and the Making of Immigration Policy

The instructor could either skip this material entirely, assign it solely as outside reading, or assign it with an eye toward discussing the subject matter in class. If the instructor wishes to allocate class time to this material, there is a choice of level at which to operate. One approach would be to focus solely on the United States, discussing *why* major national policymaking is usually congressional. Is it because Congress is popularly elected and therefore, at least in theory, representative of the views of the people? Is it representative in practice? Even if not, should it be treated as if it were? Who *are* the constituencies and interest groups that affect immigration legislation? Is it that Congress is institutionally better qualified? Probably not. If anything, the administrative agencies will be far more knowledgeable than Congress about the subject matter they regulate. Or is it that some agencies cannot be trusted? Is the DHS one of them? Is it possible to build in constraints? The law could, for example, require the Secretary of Homeland Security to submit proposed policies to Congress, either for its affirmative approval or under some type of non-objection procedure. That in fact is the practice in the United Kingdom when the Home Office issues Immigration Rules. This entire discussion could focus either on the allocation of power generally or on the allocation of power specifically within immigration.

Alternatively, the instructor could engage the class in a discussion of why the allocation of power (either generally or in immigration) varies so much as between the United States and some of the parliamentary countries. The instructor should explain to the students that, in many parliamentary countries, the voters elect their own local representatives (Members of Parliament), and those MP's who are in the majority then choose a Prime Minister and other Cabinet members from their own ranks. Thus, with respect to selection, the separation between the two "political branches" is greater in the United States than it is in some of the parliamentary democracies. Also, in most parliamentary democracies, party discipline is extremely tight. When the Cabinet proposes a bill, MP's in the ruling (majority) party seldom oppose it. As a result, a broad discretion delegated to the executive branch is consistent with the reality that the executive calls the shots anyway.

Even still, the students are likely to be struck by the British provision allowing the Home Secretary to expel a noncitizen whenever he or she deems it "conducive to the public good." The text asks the students whether they would favor a similar grant of power to the Secretary of Homeland Security. The question is rhetorical. Given the size of this country and the size of the noncitizen population, the Secretary obviously would not be able to make these expulsion decisions personally. They would have to be delegated to lower echelon officials. And it is hard to imagine a general grant of power to DHS officers to remove any noncitizens whenever they thought doing so would be "conducive to the public good."

6. The Merits of Removing Noncitizen Criminal Offenders

As for the general question whether noncitizens should *ever* be removed because of criminal activity:

a. As the Supreme Court held repeatedly in the cases discussed in chapter 2, deportation is not supposed to be punishment. Anyway, the criminal laws already impose whatever degree of punishment the legislature regarded as appropriate for the particular crime. Response: A greater sanction is appropriate for noncitizens because, by engaging in crimes, they abuse their hospitality.

b. Some might argue that the removal of noncitizen criminal offenders serves a deterrent function. Others would argue that the criminal deterrent is already sufficient. And if it is not, they would say, the legislature should increase the *criminal* penalty (rather than expand the deportability grounds) so that citizens too will be adequately deterred.

c. Deportation can be viewed as a device to rid the United States of noncitizens whose presence is harmful to the public welfare. Opponents of removing criminal offenders might argue that, if a person is still considered harmful even after completing his or her criminal sentence, the law should not have permitted his or her release at that time. Either the minimum sentences are too low to provide adequate incapacitation, in which case the minimum sentences should be increased, or they are not, in which case there is no more reason to continue the noncitizen's isolation from society (through removal) than there would be to continue the incapacitation of otherwise similarly situated citizen offenders. Or is deportation just a way of alleviating prison overcrowding?

d. Some also argue that the removal of a noncitizen criminal offender is justifiable because, at least in some cases, the noncitizen declined the opportunity to become naturalized. Response: Should a noncitizen have to naturalize in order to avoid being subjected to greater sanctions than our citizens for criminal behavior?

<u>Drafting Exercise on page 588</u>

The instructor could either require the students to draft a model statutory provision or have them simply map out their suggested criteria in general terms. The students usually enjoy writing statutes, and having to draft actual statutory language forces them to make concrete choices and, in the process, to acquire an appreciation for the problems of legislative drafting. Either way, the instructor could either have the students hand in the problems or use their notes as the basis for class discussion. The instructor could, for example, call on one student to provide his or her proposal and then have other students amend it. If the exercise is taken up in class, It might be more important to establish the variables (and the students' reasons for attaching importance to those variables) than to pin the students down on precisely how long the criminal sentence should have to be, or the exact length of the time period during which the crime should have to be committed, etc.

Among the variables are the following:

1. Should the statute require an actual conviction, or should the person's admission of the essential facts be enough? Or should the statute require only a showing that the person in fact committed the crime? If only the commission of the crime is required, then the immigration judge would have to make a finding. That approach would create problems. The facts could be complex; the facts might have occurred long enough ago that evidence is no longer available; there could be legal evidentiary issues; cross-examination might be necessary and yet impractical; etc. (Note that under any of these approaches a conviction should always be regarded as *sufficient*. If the person has been convicted, then either there was a guilty plea or its equivalent, or at trial the crime was proved beyond a reasonable doubt. As the students will see in chapter 9, the standard of proof on the issue of deportability is the lesser standard of "clear and convincing evidence." Thus, the real question is whether admission or commission should *also* be sufficient.)

2. Which crimes should qualify? Here there are several subissues:

a. Should the statute continue to single out drug crimes for special treatment?

b. Has Congress gone too far in expanding the definition of "aggravated felony?"

c. Should the criterion of "moral turpitude" be retained? That term is vague, but by now a large volume of case law has accumulated. Still, every time a legislature creates a crime with a new combination of elements, it automatically generates a new "moral turpitude" issue.

d. Should the statute, perhaps, require a "serious" (or some other adjective) crime? This approach would cause many of the same problems as the "moral turpitude" approach.

e. Should the statute require that the crime be a felony? One difficulty in doing so is the high degree of state-to-state variation in classifying crimes. One partial solution to that problem is to use the federal definition of felony – i.e., a crime punishable by more than one year of confinement. Of course, even that seemingly uniform rule leaves results dependent on the differing sentences that individual states attach to the crime.

f. Should the statutes simply list the specific crimes that will make a noncitizen deportable? The disadvantages of this approach are that it is all too easy to miss important crimes, and that the names and definitions of crimes can vary widely from state to state.

g. Should the statute list categories of crimes? For example, all violent crimes, or all fraud crimes, or all sexual assaults, could be made the bases for deportation. A disadvantage here is that Congress could miss some particularly bad crimes or include some particularly mild ones.

h. Perhaps Congress could make any crime the potential basis for deportation and address the seriousness problem by imposing a sentencing requirement. As to that, see the discussion that follows.

3. Should there be sentencing requirements? If so, what should they be? The theory here is that sentencing is a good indicator of seriousness. For that reason, a sentencing requirement might be unnecessary if the law adopts some other barometer of seriousness, such as moral turpitude, or classification of the crime as a felony, etc. If sentencing is adopted as a criterion, then an important additional issue arises: Should the determinant be the maximum potential sentence, the sentence *imposed*, or the sentence *served*? Each of these approaches has both advantages and disadvantages:

a. Potential sentence is a good indicator of how harmful the legislature thinks the crime is. A disadvantage of making deportation hinge on potential sentence, however, is that there will be much state-to-state variation for the same crime. In addition such a criterion would treat all those who violate that statute in the same way, even though the degree of moral culpability can very widely among the offenders.

b. The sentence imposed better reflects the degree of culpability of the particular individual, as well as the likelihood of recidivism and the likelihood of future harm to society. There are still state-to-state variations, however, and now, in addition, there will be judge-to-judge variations.

c. The sentence served best reflects the individual's most recent behavior, since the parole board can consider post-conviction conduct. Still, there remain state-to-state and judge-to-judge variations, and now there will also be parole board variations.

In general, the choice among these three types of sentencing criteria requires policymakers to balance the desirability of considering maximum information about the individual against the need for equal treatment.

4. Should the number of crimes be taken into account? Probably, as is true under the existing scheme, the number of crimes should determine what the other criteria should be. With all else equal, less should be required to remove the repeat offender than the first-time offender.

5. What time factors should be built into the substantive criteria? Should the law, for example, require that the crime be committed within a certain number of years after entry? Or should the law impose a statute of

limitations, requiring that removal proceedings be commenced within a certain number of years after the commission or the conviction of the crime? Or should there be some combination? For example, should the law require that proceedings be commenced within a certain number of years after entry (or of attainment of LPR status)? The last section of the chapter will explore the timing issue in greater depth.

6. Should the sentencing judge play a role in recommending either removal or non-removal on criminal grounds? On the one hand, the sentencing judge knows the evidence best. On the other hand, judges bring widely varying philosophies to the subject of removal, and at least some of the judges who hear criminal cases will likely hear too few removal cases to achieve a high degree of internal consistency. See the previous discussion of judicial recommendations against deportation (JRAD's).

SECTION E. POLITICAL AND NATIONAL SECURITY GROUNDS

Since almost all the key concepts in this short section were already covered in the corresponding materials on exclusion (in chapter 5, section B), the section can be assigned simply as background reading.

SECTION F. OTHER DEPORTABILITY GROUNDS

This two-paragraph description is also intended as background reading.

SECTION G. TIME LIMITS

The instructor might ask the students to discuss the pros and cons of each of the four types of time limitations that could be imposed on deportability.

A category I limitation (i.e., one that limits the time period from entry or admission to deportable act or event) has several advantages: It recognizes both the roots that grow with time spent in the United States and the hardship of severing those roots. It also reflects the notion that, the longer a person lives here, the more the person is a product of United States society and the less a person is a product of his or her original society.

Arguments against limiting removal in this way might include the following: The fact that a person fits within one of the deportability grounds means that Congress considered him or her undesirable, though perhaps less so than if the act had occurred more recently. The United States should encourage long-term resident aliens to become naturalized. And time limits are not necessary because (as the students will see in chapter 8) other discretionary remedies, such as cancellation of removal and registry, already provide some (limited) measure of relief.

Category II limitations are simply traditional statutes of limitations. At present, no deportability grounds are subject to such limits. The advantages of category II limitations would be as follows: They provide repose and certainty for the individual. Once time begins to elapse, witnesses become hard to locate and other evidence becomes stale. And the defendant hopefully will reform in time. The main disadvantage, of course, is that a person escapes legal consequences simply because a wrongful act was not promptly discovered (although it is possible to start the clock running at the time when the act was discovered or should have been discovered).

The objective of a category III limitation (i.e., one that limits the time period from entry or admission to start of proceedings) is, like the objective of a category I limitation, to recognize the individual's roots in society. Its advantage over a category I limitation is that a category III limitation better reflects the person's roots. If, for example, an LPR commits a crime of moral turpitude just one year after admission, and is immediately convicted, but ICE doesn't discover the conviction until thirty years later, a five-year category III limitation would prevent removal while a five-year category I limitation would not.

A category I limitation, however, does have a theoretical advantage over a category III limitation. Part of what a category I limitation implicitly says to the defendant is: "Since you were here X years before committing the crime, the influences that prompted you to do it are more likely American than foreign. Therefore we should not now send you to that foreign society." If the point in time at which the crime was committed were made irrelevant, as would be the case with the category III limitation, then a noncitizen who commits a crime soon after admission would be spared if enough time had gone by later, even though the crime could not realistically be ascribed to the influences of United States society.

A category IV limitation (enactment of deportability ground must precede conduct on which removal is based) is simply a prohibition of ex post facto deportability grounds. The principal advantage of this kind of limitation is fairness. Since the individual had no way to know that the act would some day be prohibited, there was no meaningful opportunity to conform his or her conduct to the law. (This argument is weaker if the act was criminally proscribed at the time of commission and only the addition of removal consequences was new.) The main disadvantage of a category IV limitation is that it can preclude the removal of a noncitizen whose conduct society now finds objectionable.

Problems 25-27 (page 592):

Problem 25: She seems to be deportable under INA § 237(a)(2)(B)(ii). ICE cannot show that she "is" an abuser or addict, but it can establish that, after (her first) admission into the United States, she "has been" an addict. The instructor might wish to note that, under the version of this provision that had been in force before the Immigration Act of 1990, she would not have been deportable. That provision covered only the person who "hereafter" at any time after entry has been a narcotic addict.

X would not be alternatively deportable under INA § 237(a)(1)(A) (inadmissibility at entry) on the basis that she had been inadmissible under INA § 212(a)(1)(A)(iv). That exclusion ground covers only current abusers or addicts, not those who once were. She did not fall within that ground at the time of either entry.

Problem 26: Y is not deportable. INA § 237(a)(2)(B)(ii) is inapplicable because he is not now an abuser or addict and was not an abuser or addict at any time *after* admission. Nor is Y deportable as one who had been inadmissible at the time of admission under INA § 212(a)(1)(A)(iv). At the time of his admission, he was not an abuser or addict.

Problem 27: Z does not seem to fit within INA § 212(a)(1)(A)(iv), since she is no longer an abuser or addict. She therefore appears to be admissible. Upon her readmission, however, it seems she will become deportable because, at some time after her (first) admission, she "has been" an addict. She might argue that, to avoid the anomaly of finding a person admissible only to have to find her deportable the moment she enters, a court should interpret the deportability ground (INA § 237(a)(2)(B)(ii)) to mean that the individual must be an abuser or addict at some time after his or her *latest* admission. The *Gunaydin* case (noted in Problem 7 on page 527 of the coursebook), will make that argument difficult. One final possibility is for a court to hold that, if the admission of a noncitizen would immediately render that person deportable, then he or she is inadmissible. See *Matter of O*, 8 I. & N. Dec. 291 (INS Ass't Comm'r & BIA, 1959) (inadmissible if would be immediately deportable upon admission).

CHAPTER 8
RELIEF FROM DEPORTABILITY

SECTION A. LASTING RELIEF

1. Cancellation of Removal

a. Cancellation of Removal: Part A (Permanent Residents)

The history is essential to understanding the how's and why's of the present provision. It is presented in the text in condensed form. We find it worthwhile to spend about 15 minutes of class time having the students reproduce the trilogy of cases on pages 596-98. Apart from the substantive value of this exercise, tracing the progression from *L* to *G.A.* to *Francis* enables the students to see why the courts would want to extend the provision beyond its original statutory language. The trilogy also illustrates how several logical steps, each one independently defensible, can cumulatively produce a result that travels far beyond the literal statutory text. The instructor might wish to ask the students to reread *Francis*, but we have found the summary paragraph sufficient for present purposes.

We also recommend spending at least a few minutes on *Hernandez-Casillas*, even though IIRIRA renders the ultimate conclusion moot. The case represents a classic tension between a literal (or at least relatively literal) reading that leads to the bizarre results discussed in the text and a more flexible reading that produces more rational results but deviates sharply from what Congress actually said.

<u>Questions on page 601:</u>

Q1: On one side are all the reasons Congress deports noncitizens in the first place. As discussed in chapter 7, these reasons include trying to correct errors or lapses in the admission process, holding noncitizens to the conditions imposed on them at the time of admission, deterring misconduct, and ridding society of people regarded as harmful to the national welfare. In the case of cancellation part A, where most applicants are noncitizens who are found deportable on crime-related grounds, some of the goals of criminal punishment are also logically relevant, even though removal itself has been held not to be punishment.

On the other side are all the reasons for affording relief. One is rehabilitation; the assumption is that even noncitizens who commit deportable crimes can rehabilitate with time. They have, moreover, paid their dues by serving whatever criminal sentence was imposed. And since cancellation part A is limited to LPRs who have resided continuously in the United States for seven years, the individual interests at stake, such as ties to family and businesses, integration into the community, and the costs to the individual of being removed to a country he or she may no longer consider home, are typically great; the weight to be placed on the pursuit of compassion is correspondingly high.

Q2: In chronological order, the possibilities include the following:

a. The occurrence of the act or event that made the person deportable.

b. The issuance of the Notice to Appear.

c. The decision of the immigration judge.

d. The BIA decision.

e. The decision of the reviewing court. (Note that INA § 242(a)(2)(B)(i), which the students will encounter in chapter 9, appears to bar judicial review of the decision denying cancellation of removal. But the person might well have succeeded in obtaining judicial review of the deportability decision, and even certain elements of statutory eligibility for cancellation appear to be reviewable. See chapter 9, § B.6.a.ii of the coursebook.)

f. The execution of the removal order (i.e., the physical removal of the person from the country).

The pros and cons of the various positions include the following:

a. The act or event that makes the person deportable. No court has yet adopted this position. The argument in favor would be that it was then that he or she first contravened the immigration laws, and therefore it is then that residence became unlawful. The argument against would be that the argument in favor is a nonsequitur. The residence did not become unlawful at that time; the individual just became deportable. Moreover, without any adjudication of removal, the person still has the legal right to remain in the United States.

b. The issuance of the Notice to Appear. Advantages of using this date to mark the end of lawful permanent residence are that the date is clear and that prolonging the removal proceedings will not affect eligibility. The disadvantage of this position is that the person is still in the United States lawfully, and thus his or her intent to remain permanently is still lawful at this time.

c. The issuance of the removal order by the immigration judge (or order of voluntary departure). No court has yet adopted this test. Its advantages would be as follows: First, there has now been a formal adjudication and an authoritative order that the person must leave. Second, if this test is used, delays resulting from an appeal to the BIA will not affect eligibility. Third, either the BIA will later affirm, in which case it will be possible to say with hindsight that the immigration judge was right, or the BIA will later reverse, in which case the decision of the immigration judge will have caused no prejudice. The disadvantages of this position are as follows: First, the individual has a legal right to file an administrative appeal. Under the regulations, he or she has a further right to remain in the United States while the appeal is pending. Thus, during this period, there is nothing unlawful about intending to remain permanently. Second, the fact that the decision of the immigration judge was later proved to be correct does not mean the person could not have had a lawful intent to remain in the United States before learning what the BIA decision would be.

d. The BIA decision ordering the individual removed. This is the position taken by the Justice Department regulations, in cases where the noncitizen in fact appeals to the BIA. Most of the arguments here are parallel to the arguments for and against using the immigration judge decision as the demarcation line. In certain respects, however, the analysis is different: As for advantages, *both* the immigration judge and the BIA are delegates of the Attorney General; therefore it makes sense to use the Attorney General's decision as a criterion. In appealed cases, the Attorney General's decision is that of the BIA, not the immigration judge. Second, by this point the person has had two rounds of de novo consideration and cannot argue that there has been no opportunity for full adjudication on the merits. Disadvantages of this approach include the following: First, under this view eligibility turns on the amount of administrative processing time for the BIA appeal. How important a consideration that is remains debatable; as noted above, whatever the length of that period, the person has the legal right to remain in the United States during that period.

e. The completion of judicial review of the deportability decision. Advantages include the following: First, once a court has adjudicated the case, there can be no possible complaint that the adjudication has not fully run its course. Second, since the person has a statutory right to judicial review and (if granted) a court-ordered stay pending that review, the person during that period can legitimately intend to remain permanently. Third, there is no analytical reason to distinguish administrative review from judicial review. Disadvantages include the following: Once the BIA has decided the case, the removal order becomes administratively final. Second, the decision of the Attorney General (including that of the BIA) is de novo; in contrast, the court will be reviewing under a narrower standard. Thus, there is a logical basis for distinguishing administrative review from judicial review. Third, allowing the noncitizen to count judicial review time as part of the required lawful permanent residence could encourage frivolous petitions for review. (A counter-argument here is that a court could hold, as one court did for purposes of the earlier lawful unrelinquished domicile requirement, see *Torres-Hernandez v. INS*, 812 F.2d 1262 (9th Cir. 1987), that any time needed to adjudicate a frivolous petition for review will not count.) Fourth, allowing this time to count would cause eligibility for relief to hinge arbitrarily on the amount of processing time required for judicial review.

f. The person's physical removal from the United States. Advantages: Until the person is actually removed, he or she might cling to the hope of being allowed to stay. Therefore, during this time, he or she is still lawfully resident. He or she is not breaking any law by awaiting execution of the removal order. Disadvantages: At that point, even though the noncitizen has a right to remain in the United States, it is stretching things to say that he or she can lawfully intend to remain *permanently*. Also, adoption of this test might encourage noncitizens to disregard removal orders, abscond, and then resurface after the necessary time has accumulated.

Problems 1-3 (page 601):

Problem 1: A has to have "resided continuously in the United States for 7 years." INA § 240A(a)(2). There are two issues:

a. Under INA § 240A(d)(1), continuous residence "shall be deemed to end when the alien is served a notice to appear." A received one such notice in 2007, only four years after his arrival. Since then, he has lived in the U.S. only three years. The immigration judge eventually terminated the proceedings based on that notice to appear, but the literal language of the statute doesn't say that the notice to appear must eventually lead to deportability in order for it to end one's continuous residence. Can Congress really have intended the literal meaning?

A would argue no. First, he would ask, why would Congress want a baseless charge to destroy eligibility for relief? Second, why give ICE an incentive to file baseless notices to appear? This provision, A would argue, should be interpreted as referring only to the particular notice to appear on which ICE bases the deportability from which the person is seeking relief.

The BIA reached such a conclusion in *Cisneros-Gonzalez*, the case cited in the text. (This case involved part B of cancellation of removal, not part A, but the language the Board was interpreting – INA § 240A(d)(1) – applies to parts A and B alike.) In *Cisneros-Gonzalez*, the Board said it was holding that the phrase "notice to appear" pertained only to the notice served in the present proceeding, not those served in any prior proceedings. But Cisneros-Gonzalez, unlike the person in Problem 1, had accumulated ten more years of continuous physical presence after returning (without inspection) from his prior deportation. Thus, all the BIA had to decide was whether one notice to appear would forever bar all future continuous presence. Here, the question is whether it merely stops and restarts the clock. On the other hand, the deportation that followed the first notice to appear in *Cisneros* was clearly lawful; here, the IJ in the first proceeding found the person *not* to be deportable.

b. A was away for 100 days, but nothing in the statute speaks to the effect that such an absence will have *on continuous residence*. Under INA § 240A(d)(2), an absence of more than 90 days will destroy *the continuous physical presence* required for cancellation part B, but there is no analogous provision for *residence* for purposes of *part A*. That limitation was clearly deliberate, because paragraphs d(1) and d(3), in contrast, refer to both continuous residence and continuous physical presence. Thus, the question whether a 100-day trip disrupts continuous residence has to be resolved without statutory guidance. (Possibly the court could look for analogies in some of the naturalization provisions, but it is not clear which way those provisions cut. To the extent they permit significant absences, A could argue similar policies should apply here. To the contrary, however, ICE could argue that the naturalization provisions show that Congress knows how to exempt temporary absences when it wants to, and it didn't do so here.)

Problem 2: Again the issue is continuous residence. From B's admission in April 2002 to her commission of the crime in May 2009, a total of 7 years (and one month) expired. But there are two issues:

First, did she "reside" in the United States during her first year? As a result of the BIA decision in *Blancas* (see coursebook page 580), time spent as a nonimmigrant (her first year) now counts toward the 7-year residence requirement.

Second, did she "reside" in the United States during her second year, when she was out of status? It seems so. INA § 240A(a)(2) requires only that the person "has resided in the United States continuously for 7 years after having been admitted in any status." It does not say the person needs seven years of lawful residence.

Problem 3: To qualify for relief, C had to be "an alien lawfully admitted for permanent residence for not less than 5 years." INA § 240A(a)(1). There are two issues:

First, was C *ever* "lawfully" admitted for permanent residence? Both the IJ and the BIA found that C's adjustment of status had been based on a fraudulent marriage. ICE will argue, therefore, that B's admission for permanent residence was not lawful. C might argue that the statute requires only an admission as a lawful permanent resident, as opposed, for example, to an admission as a nonimmigrant or no admission at all. But the BIA held in *Koloamatangi* (see coursebook at 579-80) that LPR status obtained by fraud does not satisfy the 5-year LPR requirement. His only hope, therefore, is judicial review; he would need to persuade a court that the BIA interpretation is incorrect. (Judicial review is now generally available to challenge a BIA determination that a person is statutorily ineligible for discretionary relief. See chapter 9 of the coursebook, § B.6.a.ii.)

Second, if C were treated as having been lawfully admitted for permanent residence in August 2004, the required five years in that status couldn't accrue until August 2009. In June 2009, however, the BIA affirmed the removal order. Did that order terminate C's lawful permanent residence? According to the Justice

Department regulations noted in the text, lawful permanent residence ends when the removal order becomes administratively final. And under INA § 101(a)(47)(B), BIA affirmance of a removal order makes the order administratively final. Invoking the policy arguments discussed in item 2 of the preceding Questions, C might argue that the Justice Department regulations wrongly interpret the statutory phrase "alien lawfully admitted for permanent residence," and that a correct interpretation would allow lawful permanent residence to continue at least until the removal order is *judicially* final (if not until physical removal). The court would have to decide whether, even allowing for *Chevron* deference, the BIA interpretation was wrong.

As for the additional requirement that C have "resided" continuously in the United States for seven years, his four years of nonimmigrant status are now fully counted. Thus he has been in the country for nine years. The sham marriage, however, was most likely a crime involving moral turpitude, because it evidenced dishonesty. If so, then the commission of that crime disrupted the continuity of his residence, INA § 240A(d)(1)(B) (not requiring a conviction), and since then he has resided in the United States for less than seven years. See the analysis of that issue in the previous Problem.

b. Cancellation of Removal: Part B

i. Continuous Physical Presence

<u>Questions on page 605:</u>

Q1: Congress enacted the suspension provision (now cancellation of removal, part B) out of compassion for those noncitizens who, although deportable, have acquired roots in the United States and whose deportations would produce special hardship. Congress required physical presence because the time spent here is at least a rough indicator of how deep those roots go. Congress required continuity because frequent significant absences would raise doubts about the significance of the person's roots. Since there is generally no reason to make deportation hinge on an innocent, casual, and brief departure that had no effect on either the degree of hardship that deportation would cause or the unexpectedness of deportation, it made sense to allow some room for temporary departures. As to how to delineate which interruptions will be permissible, a bright line test is administratively convenient, less susceptible to the whims of the adjudicator, and objectively more consistent. A flexible test would have the advantages of allowing the adjudicators to consider all the relevant indicators of hardship and giving them whatever weight the circumstances dictate.

Q2: There does seem to be a technical glitch. Maybe the courts will read some leeway into the word "immediately," interpreting "immediately preceding the date of application" to mean <u>almost</u> up to that point. Otherwise, it seems no one could ever qualify.

One possible amendment would be to require that the ten years be "immediately preceding service of the notice to appear or the commission of [the specified criminal offenses], whichever is earlier."

Problem 4: (page 605):

Since all the people in this Problem are LPRs, one should first ask whether they qualify for cancellation of removal part A. They meet the requirement of 7 years of continuous residence, because *Blancas* allows them to count their nonimmigrant years. The issue would be whether they have the required five years of LPR status. The notice to appear was served a little more than 4 years after they became LPRs, but nothing in section 240A says that a notice to appear terminates permanent resident status. Thus, if it takes more than about 10 months to obtain an administratively final removal order, recall 8 CFR § 1.1(p) (2008), they will accrue the requisite 5 years and, if otherwise eligible, could either apply for relief then or move to reopen, depending on how far the proceedings have progressed.

As for cancellation of removal, part B, the problem is showing ten years of *continuous* physical presence (immediately preceding the date of application). All had lived here slightly more than ten years by the time the notice to appear was served, but under INA § 240A(d)(2), continuity is broken if the applicant has departed from the United States for more than 180 days "in the aggregate." Here, they made 10 annual trips (summer 1997 through summer 2006, inclusive) of 21 days each, for an aggregate absence of 210 days. This seems to disqualify them. The instructor might ask the students whether this doesn't seem unduly harsh in the light of the statutory objectives.

ii. Hardship

INS v. Jong Ha Wang (page 608):

The Wangs, a married couple from Korea, were admitted as nonimmigrant treaty traders. They were ordered deported for overstaying. After a delay apparently occasioned by an unsuccessful application for adjustment of status, and after the seven years then required for suspension of deportation had accrued, the Wangs moved to reopen to apply for suspension. They alleged that deportation would cause extreme hardship (then the criterion) to their two young children because the children didn't speak Korean and therefore would lose educational opportunities. They also alleged economic loss from the forced sale of their home and business. The IJ denied reopening, and the BIA affirmed on the ground that the Wangs had failed to make a prima facie showing of extreme hardship. The Ninth Circuit reversed, holding that the stated facts constituted a prima facie case.

The Supreme Court ordered summary reversal on alternative grounds.

First, the Supreme Court held, the motion to reopen had not been accompanied by specific enough allegations or supported by affidavits. Second, the Ninth Circuit had usurped the power of the BIA to define "extreme hardship" narrowly if it wished. On these facts, the Supreme Court concluded, the BIA could reasonably have denied the motion to reopen.

Notes and Questions Following Jong Ha Wang (page 612):

Q1: The theory of *Chenery* is that Congress has delegated power to the agency to make a particular decision. If the agency makes a wrong decision because it has erred as a matter of law on one element of that decision, the court has no way to know whether the agency would have reached that same result but for the error. That the agency could have done so does not mean it would have done so. One exception to *Chenery* is that, if the agency was required as a matter of law to reach the decision it did (for some reason other than the one that actually led it to its decision), the court may affirm the agency decision. In such a case, a remand would be pointless.

The BIA's stated reason for its decision was that the Wangs had not established a prima facie case of extreme hardship. The Supreme Court gave two reasons for reversing the Ninth Circuit. The Supreme Court was clearly wrong to hold that the Ninth Circuit had erred in failing to affirm the BIA on the grounds that the allegations were conclusory and unsupported. The *Chenery* principle foreclosed that option. The second "error" of the Ninth Circuit is trickier. Is the Supreme Court saying that the BIA was within its rights to find a prima facie case lacking, or is the Court holding that the BIA has the discretion to deny reopening even when a prima facie case is presented? The first interpretation seems unlikely. The Supreme Court provided no discussion of what "prima facie case" means, or whether on this evidence the BIA could find the absence of a prima facie case. Rather, the Court appears to affirm the BIA decision on the ground that the existence of a prima facie case does not compel reopening. And that clearly was not the basis for the BIA's decision. Maybe the BIA would have reopened if it had found a prima facie case.

Q2: By analogy to either torts or criminal law, the term "prima facie case" probably means there is enough evidence of each of the elements of the underlying relief sought that a reasonable person could find eligibility. That is the position taken in the cited Ninth Circuit decision in *Abudu*, but the Supreme Court has reversed *Abudu*, and it is not clear whether the Ninth Circuit test is still viable. If it is viable, then the Supreme Court decision is problematic. It would be difficult to say that no reasonable person could find extreme hardship on those facts.

Perhaps, however, the phrase "prima facie case" refers to allegations which, if true, would actually result in the BIA granting suspension of deportation. If the BIA concludes that it would not grant suspension even if it finds the allegations to be true, then under this test there would be no need to reopen. If that is the test, and if the Board says it would not grant suspension even if the allegations were true, then a court should uphold that decision as long as a reasonable BIA *could* so conclude. But unless no reasonable BIA could find extreme hardship, the BIA should at least be required to state that that is the basis for its decision.

Q3 and Q4: These questions are best combined. Consider first the case in which the BIA denies reopening, despite the presence of a prima facie case, because there are negatives that the BIA feels would have led to a denial of suspension (now cancellation of removal, part B) on discretionary grounds in any event. Is that a sufficient basis for denying reopening?

The noncitizen would argue that, if there is enough evidence to permit reasonable minds to differ about eligibility for cancellation, then the importance of the individual interests should require at least a hearing, which is all the person is seeking when moving to reopen. That is especially true, the applicant will point out, when one considers that one of the elements of the prima facie case that the person will have had to establish is exceptional and extremely unusual hardship. Further, without holding a hearing, the BIA cannot really know it would reach a negative decision on the discretionary question. Perhaps a hearing would show that the assumed negatives are not true or that they at least are less aggravated than was first thought. A hearing might also demonstrate positive equities that would outweigh those negatives. ICE would respond that reopening entails not only a labor-intensive hearing, but also delay. ICE would argue that the BIA can reasonably conclude that, if it grants motions to reopen too freely, it will create encourage noncitizens to challenge decisions just to obtain delay. The BIA must balance the two factors and should have the discretion to say that in a given case the potential for delay outweighs the need for a hearing when the negative discretionary factors make the likelihood of success slight. The Supreme Court seems to agree. In footnote 5 of its opinion, it quotes Judge Wallace's comments approvingly.

Consider next the situation in which the BIA denies reopening because it regards the allegations as outlandish. It might be that the allegations would establish the requisite hardship if true, but that it is virtually certain they are not true. The noncitizen might argue that, despite the BIA's initial perception, one can never be certain that the allegations are false. ICE would likely respond that, surely, there are some allegations that one would not hesitate to label as preposterous. The noncitizen might respond that, assuming the existence of inherently preposterous allegations, a doctrine that permits the BIA to deny reopening on that basis requires the drawing of an unrealistically difficult line between the likely and the unlikely.

The hardest question is whether, if the allegations are not outlandish on their face and there are no negative factors that would clearly cause the BIA to withhold the favorable exercise of discretion, and the noncitizen has made out a prima facie case, the BIA should be *required* to reopen. The most common situation in which this issue would be expected to arise is where the BIA concludes that, even if the allegations are true, they do not add up to exceptional and extremely unusual hardship. As to that, the rhetorical questions in item 4 raise some of the advantages of a hearing even then. Hardship, after all, is a question of degree. The instructor might ask the students how they would respond to those rhetorical arguments. For example, the students might feel that, even though a hearing could possibly be helpful, the chances are slim enough to be outweighed by the negative consequences of reopening. These latter include more work for the BIA and a delay in executing the removal of a deportable noncitizen.

Q5: Judge Goodwin suggests that, under the Ninth Circuit view, a noncitizen would be able to enter the United States illegally, or enter as a nonimmigrant and overstay, have children, and then apply for suspension of deportation (now cancellation part B). Judge Goodwin is confusing the decision whether to reopen with the decision whether to grant relief on the merits. All that happens when the BIA reopens is that the person receives a hearing at which he or she may present evidence. If the application is frivolous, the person will not be permitted to jump the queue. If the applicant does eventually prevail on the merits, it will only be because he or she meets all the requirements and the BIA has exercised its discretion favorably. In the latter case, the result is precisely what Congress would have wanted.

Q6: This is a common problem in administrative law -- the proper judicial role in reviewing an agency interpretation of a broad statutory phrase that requires judgment. ICE would argue that Congress intended to empower the BIA to use its discretion in interpreting this phrase; that the BIA has more expertise than do the courts; and that the BIA is better situated than are the courts for promoting nationwide consistency. The noncitizen will argue that this is a question of law for the court. The noncitizen might argue alternatively that, even if this is a question of discretion, there are limits to the agency's discretion and the court must discharge its responsibility of reviewing for abuse of discretion. Moreover, the question here is not whether deportation would cause the requisite hardship, but simply whether a hearing is required. The issue, in other words, is one of <u>procedural</u> fairness, which a court is competent to decide and which Congress arguably intended the court to decide.

As for the maxim that doubts in deportation statutes should be construed favorably to the noncitizens, ICE might offer the following arguments: First, this is a relief provision, not a deportation ground. (Should that matter?) Second, this is a discretionary decision rather than a straight interpretation of law; it should be assumed, therefore, that the congressional intent was to allow the BIA to decide. Third, the Court is not interpreting the phrase "extreme hardship;" all the Court is saying is that it is up to the BIA to interpret this phrase. Fourth, to the extent the BIA is ultimately interpreting statutory language, its interpretation is entitled to *Chevron* deference.

Q7: The students might suggest any of the following statements of the Court's holding:

a. BIA denials of motions to reopen deportation proceedings, being "committed to" BIA discretion, are unreviewable. So radical a reading seems unlikely. The Supreme Court in *Giova v. Rosenberg*, 379 U.S. 18, 85 S.Ct. 156, 13 L.Ed.2d 90 (1964), had held that denials of motions to reopen are reviewable in the courts of appeals. The Supreme Court is highly unlikely to have overruled *Giova* without saying so.

b. BIA findings of no extreme hardship are unreviewable. That is in fact the law today (since IIRIRA in 1996), but at the time of the decision such a reading was highly unlikely. First, had the Supreme Court meant to go that far, it would surely have said so. Also, at one point the Court says the statute commits the definition of extreme hardship to the Attorney General and his delegates "*in the first instance*," implying that those decisions can, under proper circumstances, be overturned. The Court adds that a court should not overturn those decisions "simply because it may prefer another interpretation," again implying that in a proper case the decision can be overturned. (The instructor at this point could ask: "Is that really what the Ninth Circuit had held -- that the BIA was in error because, in the court's opinion, there was extreme hardship?")

c. The standard of judicial review of a BIA refusal to reopen is merely abuse of discretion. (If that was the holding, then the Ninth Circuit seems to be in agreement).

d. On this particular evidence, there was no abuse of discretion. At first glance it might seem doubtful that the Supreme Court would really grant certiorari to decide so fact-specific an issue. It is possible, however, that the Supreme Court meant to do precisely that. This holding has an *a fortiori* effect, requiring the affirmance of the BIA in all cases where the motion to reopen alleges facts that entail no more hardship than is present here. The present decision might be seen as a general measuring stick. It might simply be the Court's way of saying that, to reverse a BIA decision refusing reopening, one must show hardships more compelling than these.

e. The BIA may deny a motion to reopen even when the movant has established a prima facie case. Support for this interpretation could be gleaned from the Supreme Court's approving quotation of Judge Wallace in footnote 5. On the other hand, the Court never says there is a prima facie case here, and the BIA in fact decided the case on a different basis.

f. The BIA may construe "extreme hardship" narrowly if it wishes. (Alternatively, if the BIA denies reopening on the ground that inadequate hardship has been shown, a court may not reverse the BIA decision in the absence of very unusual facts.) Whether the Court intended so vague a principle, or even whether a principle that general can be of concrete use, is not clear.

Q10: The instructor could use *Hamid* as a vehicle for exploring whether it is an abuse of discretion for the BIA to deny reopening (and therefore a hearing) on the ground that it disbelieves the allegations in the moving papers. The decision in *Wang* seemed concerned with the problem of courts doubting the BIA interpretation of the phrase "extreme hardship." The Court was concerned, in other words, with the standard of review of a BIA conclusion that the allegations would not constitute "extreme hardship" even if true. In *Hamid*, in contrast, the BIA simply assumes that the allegations were not true.

Q11: This question is intended to introduce students to the stormy relationship between the Ninth Circuit and the Supreme Court in the early-to-mid-1980's -- a classic battle between two courts of strikingly opposite philosophy. The question for the students is what message the Supreme Court was trying to send with its summary reversal. Almost certainly, the Supreme Court intended a slap on the hand. The message might simply be that the Supreme Court does not want the Ninth Circuit interfering in the exercise of BIA discretion unless the abuse is crystal clear.

Q12: The decision might simply be the Supreme Court's way of conveying the general message that the BIA has the power to construe the phrase "extreme hardship" narrowly and that, whatever the exact location of the line between permissibly and impermissibly narrow interpretations, the hardship has to be greater than the level displayed by the Wang's before a court may set aside that discretionary judgment.

Matter of Recinas (page 618):

A mother and her two children, now ages 15 and 16, entered the U.S. on nonimmigrant visas 14 years ago and overstayed. She later bore 4 U.S. citizen children (age range now 5-12). Her parents and her siblings are all LPRs living in the United States. In removal proceedings she applied for cancellation of removal, alleging hardship to her four citizen children and her LPR parents. The immigration judge denied the application on the ground that the hardship did not meet the "exceptional and extremely unusual" standard.. She appealed to the BIA.

The BIA compares her case to what it regards as the two seminal cases on the hardship standard – *Monreal* (2001) and *Andazola* (2002). In both those cases, exceptional and extremely unusual hardship was not found. Distinguishing both cases on their facts, the Board finds the requisite hardship to the four U.S. citizen children in the present case, though just barely (saying this case represents the "outer threshold" for granting cancellation of removal). The main factors on which the Board relies are (1) Recina's entire family lives in the United States and (except for two of her children) are here lawfully and thus most likely permanently; no family members remain in Mexico, her country of origin; (2) She is a single mother, with no parental or financial support from the father; (3) Her mother cares for the children while Recina works; no comparable child care would be available in Mexico, thus making it even harder for her to support her children there; (4) the four U.S. citizen children have lived their entire lives in the United States and know very little Spanish; and (5) given the lengthy backlogs for family-sponsored 2B immigrants (unmarried adult sons and daughters of LPRs), there is no alternative short-term avenue for the mother to attain LPR status.

Notes and Questions Following Recinas (page 622):

Thanks are owed to Christina Kleiser and Becky Sharpless for suggesting the addition of *Recina* as a principal case.

Q2: Generally this factor will fortify the showing of hardship. Removal means the applicant loses these family members' companionship and possibly their services, including child care. The result is not only lost familial relations, but also loss of a service that makes it possible for the applicant to work.

In one sense this same factor cuts the other way as well. Having a family member who will stay behind in the United States might provide additional income, at U.S. earnings rates, that that family member will be able to remit to the applicant after he or she is returned to the country of origin.

Q3: The BIA in *Recinas* acknowledges that each case turns on its own facts, but it still uses *Monreal* and *Andazola* as its two "seminal interpretations" and, therefore, its starting points and bases for comparison. Even though the determinations are ultimately factual, the prior decisions can still serve a precedential function because (a) there are many commonly recurring, indistinguishable, fact situations; and (b) decisions can have *a fortiori* effects (i.e., if even X level of hardship is not considered "exceptional and extremely unusual," then the lesser level of hardship that the present applicant will suffer won't either; or vice-versa).

Q4: The hardship requirement itself could be relaxed in either of two ways: The narrow fix would be to add siblings (or perhaps siblings under a certain age) to the list of qualifying family members. The broader fix would be to return to the pre-1996 approach, in which the applicant's own hardship, if rising to the requisite level, would be enough; hardship to a U.S. citizen or LPR family member (or even *having* a U.S. citizen or LPR family member) would not be required. Since the hardship standard is so high (merely "extreme" hardship is no longer enough), humanitarian considerations alone suggest not deporting a person who can demonstrate such an exceptional level of hardship. And even when an applicant meets this high standard, relief remains subject to the immigration judge's or the BIA's discretion, so that compelling countervailing factors could still be considered.

Another possible solution is open to the immigration judge or the BIA even under the existing statute. T he Board observes at the end of its opinion that eventually the mother is likely to be granted cancellation of removal and, therefore, adjustment of status to permanent residence. The Board therefore instructs the immigration judge to hold the cases of the two undocumented children in abeyance until then. When the mother's status is adjusted, these two children will have an LPR parent and their applications for cancellation of removal can then proceed. Presumably, however, they will have to show that their *mother* will suffer "exceptional and extremely unusual hardship" if *they* are removed, and they will also have to establish the other statutory prerequisites. That will require an analysis very different from the sole-economic-support factor that played such a dominant role in the mother's case. This remedy therefore has the twin disadvantages of delay and uncertainty.

Perhaps a better solution, then, would be to simply add a provision for some kind of "derivative" cancellation of removal, analogous to INA § 203(d) (the "accompanying or following to join" provision for admitting preference immigrants). Congress could make the cancellation applicant's spouse, parents, and children eligible for cancellation upon the granting of cancellation to the principal applicant, rather than require them to meet all the cancellation requirements independently. As with the "accompanying or following to join" provision, the rationale would be the unification of preexisting families.

iii. Other Hurdles: Good Moral Character, Disqualified Groups, Discretion, and Reporting to Congress

This text is intended to be self-explanatory. The instructor might want to take up in class the question of structuring the exercise of IJ and BIA discretion. The instructor might note that the Justice Department once tried to issue such guidelines but gave up. The Department concluded that it could not list all of them and that listing only some, even with disclaimers, could create misunderstandings and undue rigidity. 46 Fed.Reg. 9119 (Jan. 28, 1981). The benefits of such guidelines would include uniformity, fairness, and predictability. One disadvantage is the potential for rigidity. Another is the inevitable uncertainty over whether the guidelines have the force of law, such that deviation from them might require judicial reversal.

2. Registry

The proposal by Gordon, Mailman & Yale-Loehr, described in the first paragraph of this section, might be worth discussing briefly in class. At least two arguments can be made on behalf of this proposal: First, under the present provision, relief becomes harder and harder with the passage of time and then suddenly easier when Congress, as is inevitable, amends the statute to advance the cutoff date. Second, the process of continually reevaluating the cutoff date and changing it requires unnecessary work by Congress. An opponent of the suggestion might argue that such a change would encourage illegal entry. Proponents might respond, however, that Congress invariably changes the registry cutoff date anyway. Besides, the waiting period is extremely long.

The text also asks the students to invent hypotheticals in which individuals are eligible for registry but not cancellation of removal, part B, and vice-versa. It is quite easy for someone to be eligible for registry but not cancellation. A person who has lived in the United States since before the cut-off, but who cannot demonstrate sufficient hardship, would be an example. Note also that registry, unlike cancellation, does not require continuous physical presence for the past ten years; residence, which permits more extensive absences than does physical presence, is enough.

The converse is also possible. First, the individual who has been in the United States more than ten years but not since 1972 would be the clearest case. Second, it is theoretically possible to have continuous physical presence without residence; the person might, for example, have lacked an intent to remain permanently. Third, a person might be ineligible for United States citizenship, usually from having exercised his or her exemption from military service. He or she would be ineligible for registry but not necessarily ineligible for cancellation.

3. Legalization

Analysis of this subject is deferred to chapter 12, section B.

4. Adjustment of Status

Since the students were already introduced to adjustment of status in chapter 6, the treatment of the subject in this chapter is brief and confined generally to the use of this remedy as a defense to removal.

5. Private Bills

This section too is generally intended as background reading, but the instructor might want to take up the policy question raised in the text. The theory behind private bills is that they can temper the rigidity of general legislation by permitting individualized consideration of exceptional cases. The down sides are that private bills increase the workload of Congress (as a practical matter, the immigration subcommittees of the two Houses), and that results frequently hinge on the political influence of the particular beneficiary or his or her family. Moreover, they can be abused as a device for delaying removal; ICE is not required to stay removal pending congressional consideration of a private immigration bill, but as a matter of courtesy it usually does.

SECTION B. LIMITED RELIEF

1. Deferred Action

Notes and Questions on Deferred Action (page 632):

Q1: As to the mandatory word "shall," perhaps the statutory phrase "upon the order of the [Secretary of Homeland Security]" qualifies the government's duty to remove deportable noncitizens. The question is whether the statute means (a) the Secretary must issue such an order if the person is deportable or only (b) if the person is deportable, the Secretary may issue such an order and, if he or she does, the person must then be removed. Second, the analogy to prosecutorial discretion in criminal proceedings is well accepted. Third, if Congress appropriated less money than it knows ICE would need for full enforcement, it can be inferred that Congress intended discretionary prosecution in the light of available resources and in accordance with legitimate criteria.

Even apart from the problem raised by the word "shall," the source of ICE's power is not clear. There remains the question, illustrated by the good moral character hypothetical, whether deferred action renders the limitations on the various statutory relief provisions meaningless. If the individual doesn't meet the requirements for cancellation of removal, or for adjustment of status, or for registry, or for legalization, etc., ICE could confer relief indirectly by exercising its discretion not to initiate removal proceedings. The result, it could be argued, is that ICE could always circumvent the deliberate statutory limitations on the other remedies. Maybe the key is that, although ICE can choose not to prosecute, it cannot formally grant resident status without an affirmative authorization to do so. ICE could allow the person to stay forever, but he or she would never have the security of knowing that fact for sure and in any event would not have the other rights of permanent residents -- e.g., the right to file a family-sponsored second preference petition, the right to apply for naturalization later, the (very limited) right to receive welfare, etc.

Q2: The theory for distinguishing between efficiency and compassion as rationales for deferred action is that prosecutorial discretion should not be judicially reviewable even for abuse of discretion, because it is a basic efficiency-driven administrative policy determination beyond the authority or the understanding of the court. If in contrast the program is considered just another "remedy" based on compassion, then a court should be able to review ICE's decision just as easily as it could review a decision to deny any other form of affirmative relief from removal.

Arguments for allowing judicial review of an ICE decision to prosecute might include the following: First, the prospect of judicial review forces the agency to consider each case carefully and to articulate legitimate reasons for its decision. Second, judicial review can correct errors. Third, judicial review can guide the development of future case law. Fourth, judicial review can assure equal treatment.

Arguments against judicial review of ICE's decision to prosecute might include the following: First, the courts are institutionally incompetent to review those decisions. Second, if ICE knows that its creation of an ameliorative program will subject every decision not to use it in a particular case to judicial review, then ICE might be less inclined to adopt the program in the first place.

2. Voluntary Departure

Questions on page 637:

Q1: Relief under subsection (b) requires everything subsection (a) requires, plus the following: one year of physical presence before service of the Notice to Appear; 5 years of good moral character; and a showing, by clear and convincing evidence, that the applicant has the financial means to depart. INA § 240B(b)(1)(A,B,D). Also, while both subsections (a) and (b) disqualify aggravated felons and terrorists, subsection (b) also disqualifies anyone who is deportable on any of the other national security grounds. Compare INA §§ 240B(a)(1) and 240B(b)(1)(C). Under subsection (a), bond is discretionary; under subsection (b), it is mandatory. Compare subsections (a)(3) and (b)(3). The maximum voluntary departure period permitted under subsection (a) is 120 days; under subsection (b), it is 60 days. Compare subsections (a)(2) and (b)(2). (Denials under both subsections are immune from judicial review, see INA § 242(a)(2)(B)(i), despite the confusing language in section 240B(f) that refers only to denials under subsection (b). See INA § 242(a)(2)(B)(i)).

Q2: Relief under subsection (a) is available only before removal proceedings begin, or at least before they conclude. The contrast between the provisions gives noncitizens an incentive to bypass their removal hearings. If they do so, they will qualify more easily for voluntary departure, and if it is granted, they might get up to 120 days.

Is it a good idea for Congress to create that incentive? Reducing the number of removal hearings obviously saves government resources, but it seems difficult to justify substantively penalizing a person for exercising a procedural right. The contrast potentially chills the exercise of the important right to a fair hearing by making the individual gamble in order to obtain an opportunity to request relief.

Problems 5-6 (page 637):

Problem 5: The following analysis reflects helpful comments from Michael Churgin, Susan Saab Fortney, Craig Mousin, and Victor Romero.

X has three basic options:

Option A: X could accept ICE's offer. But he has now been unlawfully present more than 180 days and less than one year. If he departs "prior to the commencement" of removal proceedings, as the offer contemplates, he will become inadmissible for three years under INA § 212(a)(9)(B)(i)(I). Since his priority date is expected to come up in two years, he would thus likely have to wait an extra year before returning. With an LPR spouse he might be eligible for a waiver under section 212(a)(9)(B)(v), but he would have to prove that his removal would cause extreme hardship to his spouse and that he merits the favorable exercise of discretion. As to those issues, more facts would be needed.

Option B: X could decline ICE's offer and then, once a Notice to Appear is issued, reapply for subsection (a) voluntary departure. Despite the inartful drafting noted in the text, the regulations permit such an application. ICE, desirous of avoiding a hearing, might be amenable. If so, then it could join X in moving the immigration judge to terminate the proceedings; if termination is ordered, ICE could then grant voluntary departure under subsection (a) of INA § 240B. Alternatively, under the regulations it could join with X in asking the immigration judge to grant voluntary departure himself or herself. Either way, assuming voluntary departure is granted, X could then leave the country and return as a permanent resident when his priority date becomes current. He would not be inadmissible under INA § 212(a)(9)(B)(i)(I) because his departure was not "prior to the commencement" of removal proceedings. The result seems odd, since, all else equal, there is no obvious policy reason to treat X *more* favorably after the filing of the Notice to Appear than before it. If anything, as the text notes, one would have expected Congress to encourage pre-commencement voluntary departures.

There is, of course, a risk in declining ICE's initial offer in the hope of reapplying after commencement of proceedings. ICE might change its mind and deny voluntary departure. If so, then X could still apply for subsection (a) voluntary departure to the immigration judge before or during the master calendar hearing. But if the immigration judge denies the application and proceeds to a full removal hearing, subsection (a) voluntary departure will be precluded (30 days after the master calendar hearing). At that stage, events would be the same as in option C below.

Option C: X could insist on exercising his right to a removal hearing, with the intention of applying for voluntary departure there. This would be a bad idea. X is clearly deportable as an overstay, and by the time a removal hearing is held he will be ineligible for both forms of voluntary departure. Subsection (a) will be precluded, assuming, as is realistic, that 30 days will easily have elapsed since the master calendar hearing. Subsection (b) will be precluded because X was physically present in the United States for less than a year immediately preceding the service of the Notice to Appear. (He was apprehended eight months after arrival; we assume here that it will not take ICE four additional months to serve the

Notice to Appear.) Therefore, he will be ordered removed. Once that happens, he will become inadmissible for another ten years under INA § 212(a)(9)(A)(ii), absent permission to reapply.

Problem 6: Now X has been unlawfully present for more than one year. Once he leaves the U.S., he will be inadmissible for 10 years, regardless of whether he voluntarily departs or is removed. That is because section 212(a)(9)(B)(i)(II), the one-year unlawful presence provision, applies to any "departure or removal."

As in Problem 5, X could apply for a waiver under INA § 212(a)(9)(B)(v). He has an LPR spouse. More facts would be needed on the issues of extreme hardship and discretion.

If X is ordered removed, then ten years of inadmissibility would also flow, alternatively, from section 212(a)(9)(A)(ii). Again, the Secretary of Homeland Security will later have the discretion to consent to X applying for readmission.

On these facts, then, there seems little reason to accept voluntary departure, other than to avoid a (possibly pointless, depending on the facts) removal proceeding and to avoid bond or detention.

3. Objections to Destination

Both the majority and dissenting opinions in *Jama* are skillfully written. The opinion is not reproduced in the book, but a teacher who would like to immerse the students in the intricate statutory interpretation analysis can photocopy and assign the case. It is not long.

Linnas v. INS (page 639):

Linnas was born in Estonia, served as Chief of the Nazi concentration camp in Tartu during World War II, and later entered the United States under the Displaced Persons Act by misrepresenting his past. He was eventually found out and denaturalized. The former INS then instituted deportation proceedings. He was found deportable and designated "the free and independent Republic of Estonia" as the country to which he wished to be deported. At the time (1983), Estonia was still part of the Soviet Union. Linnas apparently was referring to the office building in New York housing the Estonian representatives. After an initial decision by the IJ and a remand by the BIA, the IJ ordered Linnas deported to the Soviet Union. INA § 243(a) [now 241(b)(2)] required deportation to the country designated by the noncitizen (here, an impossibility because Estonia did not then exist as a sovereign state), then deportation to the country of citizenship (also impossible, for the same reason), and then to any of seven other choices, one of which is any country willing to receive the person. The Soviet Union was evidently the only country willing to receive Linnas.

The problem for Linnas was that the Soviet Union had already sentenced him to death (in absentia) for his war crimes and wanted him returned so that the sentence could be carried out. Linnas argued that deporting him to the Soviet Union was a disguised extradition that no extradition treaty authorized. The court rejected the argument, pointing out the differences between deportation and extradition and explaining why this was merely the former. Linnas also argued that Soviet procedures are so lacking in fairness that to deport him to the Soviet Union to face a death sentence imposed pursuant to Soviet procedures would violate due process. The court rejected his due process claim, equating it to an appeal for decency and expressing offense that a person who did what Linnas had done would appeal to the court's decency.

Notes and Questions Following Linnas (page 642):

Q4: Arguments in favor of providing more choice might include the following: First, nothing is gained by making the person gamble. Second, freedom of movement should be limited only to the extent necessary to fulfill the nation's interest in executing the removal order. There is no reason for the United States to decide in which country a person whom it removes should end up. Arguments against liberalizing INA § 241(b)(2) in the way suggested might include the following: Affording too many choices could cause delay if the United States government must keep checking sequentially with other countries. It would be possible to allow simultaneous designations and to do simultaneous checks, but that course would entail extra work both for the United States government and for the countries that are contacted. Second, a person might designate a far-away place to which transportation would be expensive. The United States should not have to pay for that preference. (Of course, this can happen even when only one designation is permitted).

Q5: On the one hand, Linnas's strategy seems pointless. Surely the immigration judge would not have been willing to deport him to New York. On the other hand, if no other country will accept him, he might have figured either that he had nothing to lose by trying or even that he should pursue the possibility, however slim, that he would not be deported at all if it proved impossible to honor his designation.

Generally, though, what *should* the immigration judge do when a designation is ambiguous? At a minimum, the immigration judge should press for further clarification. If the designation remains ambiguous despite those efforts, then of course the immigration judge can only do his or her best to select the appropriate destination, but little is lost by attempting to seek clarification. An advantage of the current system in which the immigration judge, rather than ICE, selects the country is that it affords the immigration judge the opportunity to press the noncitizen to elaborate. In this case, perhaps the immigration judge simply didn't spot the ambiguity; he might have assumed that Linnas truly had in mind the Republic of Estonia.

Q6: The Attorney General could have continued to search for a country willing to accept Linnas, but from the sound of things, that search was likely to prove futile. Depending on Linnas's whereabouts immediately before his original passage to the United States, options E(i), E(ii), or E(iii) might theoretically have been available. But even if such other countries existed and could have been identified, they were unlikely to accept Linnas. Of course the holding in *Jama* eliminates the U.S. domestic legal requirement of acceptance, but absent truly extraordinary circumstances the U.S. would not have sent Linnas to any such countries without their consent. Thus, removal would have been unlikely. That, in turn, would have put Linnas in a *Zadvydas* situation; see coursebook pages 206-23.

Q7: Nothing in United States law prevents her from doing precisely that (unless the statutory qualifier "prejudicial to the interests of the United States" is interpreted broadly enough to cover this situation). As a practical matter, however, Fiji would not accept her unless she meets Fijian immigration requirements. If she seeks to enter as a tourist, Fijian law would probably exclude her unless she has a return ticket to Canada. In any event, she would save only the difference between the round trip airfare and the one-way airfare, unless Fiji deports her (and at its own expense).

Q8: As to the first question, deportation and extradition differ in several respects:

a. Extradition criteria are specified by treaty; deportation criteria are specified by the domestic law of the deporting country.

b. Both citizens and noncitizens may be extradited (treaty permitting); only the latter may be deported.

c. The receiving state initiates extradition; the sending state initiates deportation.

d. The purpose of extradition is to return a criminal offender or suspect to a country for criminal prosecution or punishment; the purpose of deportation is to rid the sending country of the person's presence. Recall *Fong Yue Ting*, especially the discussions on pages 140 and 152-53 of the coursebook.

The second question is whether there is anything wrong with disguised extradition. If the noncitizen in fact is deportable, why should it matter that the real motive of the United States government in returning the person is to deliver him or her to a foreign government for criminal prosecution or sentencing? Some might say that such an action is wrong because that is not the purpose of deportation. But if extradition is a legitimate function of government, and the person in fact is deportable, what is wrong with killing two birds with one stone? The real problem is that extradition requires an international treaty, the limitations of which must be honored. If no treaty covers the particular crime, then using deportation as an indirect device to achieve extradition would enable administrative officials to circumvent the congressional and presidential policy decision not to allow extradition for this crime.

Less drastic than a disguised extradition is allowing the immigration judge, when making his or her discretionary decision concerning destination, to consider as one factor that a particular country wants this individual's return. Although the balancing might be slightly different, the analysis of this possibility is similar to that of disguised extradition, except that one could argue that both a desire to promote good foreign relations by helping an ally and a desire to see criminal justice done are legitimate discretionary considerations. Others might argue to the contrary, questioning whether that consideration should be relevant to the aims of deportation.

Q9: Potentially limiting facts include the following:

a. The impetus for Linnas's removal came from the United States, not the Soviet Union.

b. Linnas wasted his right to designate, probably because he knew that no other country would accept him.

c. The United States made a good faith effort to locate a country other than the Soviet Union.

The instructor might also note that these facts are not like the ones presented in question 10 below. There, another country was willing to receive the person and the deporting country refused to accommodate that choice.

Q10: This is a closer question than the one presented in *Linnas*. Here the person is willing to go to a particular country and that country is willing to receive him or her, but the sending country prefers to deliver the person to another country that seeks extradition. The *Soblen* problem could arise under United States law when the noncitizen for some reason cannot be removed to the country of designation or when removal to that country would be "prejudicial to the United States."

The *Soblen* case illustrates the issue. The British courts gave three reasons that the Home Secretary might have preferred to deport Soblen to the United States even though his preference was to go to Czechoslovakia and that country was willing to receive him. None of those reasons seems persuasive. The fact that the United States was the only country *required* by international law to accept Soblen is irrelevant since, as it turns out, another country was *willing* to receive him and he was willing to go there. The second stated possibility -- that the Home Secretary might simply have wanted to help an ally -- is equally problematic. The "help" consisted of the return of a criminal offender, which is exactly what extradition entails. (In fact the British Court of Appeal in *Soblen* acknowledged that, if the true purpose of the Home Secretary had been to extradite, then that purpose would have been improper.) The Home Secretary's last possible reason (deterring this method of entry) is both highly speculative and highly unrealistic. The United Kingdom is a pleasant place, but it is difficult to imagine people lining up to cut their wrists to gain a few days or a few weeks there.

In fact, the reasons offered by the various courts in *Soblen* were simply hypothetical. The Home Secretary declined to state any reasons. It is not evident why the courts did not simply require the Home Secretary to state a reason that they could then review for abuse of discretion.

Q11: The court's discussion of the irony of Linnas objecting to execution without due process reflects the court's lack of sympathy to his due process claim. That doesn't mean the court's conclusion is wrong, however, and one could even argue that that factor is not truly "external." It is arguably relevant to the court's rejection of Linnas's appeal to the court's sense of "decency."

<u>Problem 7</u> (page 644):

The designated country, Suriname, has turned him down. The second step, therefore, is to remove X to any country of which he is a subject, national, or citizen. There is no such country, however, because he renounced his Dutch citizenship and has lost his United States citizenship. The court must therefore choose from the seven other possibilities enumerated in section 241(b)(2)(E). The first possibility, and probably the second as well, in his case refer to Suriname. That country has already refused. The next four paragraphs refer to the Netherlands.

The seventh paragraph allows removal to "another country whose government will accept the alien into that country," but only if it is "impracticable, inadvisable, or impossible to remove the alien to *each* country described in a previous clause of this subparagraph [emphasis added]." Since the Netherlands, which is the country described in four of the preceding clauses, is willing to receive X, the seventh paragraph seems inapplicable and the immigration judge *must* choose the Netherlands as the country to which X will be removed. As a policy matter, it is not clear why Congress would want to force removal to one country when another country is willing to receive the person and the person prefers to go there (absent prejudice to the United States in the particular case).

If a student suggests that Canada is ruled out because it is contiguous to the United States, the instructor can point out that the contiguous country limitation applies only to step one -- the person's initial designation. INA § 241(b)(2)(B).

4. Stays of Removal

Although this material is generally intended only as background reading, the second paragraph asks about one of the more common situations in which noncitizens request stays of removal -- to pursue motions to reopen removal proceedings. The reason the government has not made stays pending motions to reopen mandatory is its fear of abuse. If such stays were mandatory, the person could always file for a stay even if the underlying motion to reopen is frivolous, thus delaying removal. As a practical matter, if the immigration judge or the BIA found the underlying motion to reopen frivolous, the usual response would be to promptly deny the motion to reopen itself, thereby mooting the stay request.

SECTION C. MISCELLANEOUS DEFENSES

This section too is intended as background reading, although the instructor might want to solicit the students' reactions to the reasons given by courts for rejecting the de facto deportation arguments.

SECTION D. A PERSPECTIVE ON RELIEF FROM DEPORTABILITY

The practical consequences of adopting the New Zealand system would be (a) to broaden the categories of cases in which affirmative relief is legally available and (b) to shift much of the policymaking authority in individual cases from the legislature to the administration. The theory of the United States system is that most of the statutory prerequisites to affirmative relief are attempts to generalize about which conditions will merit relief if other factors are favorable.

One advantage of the United States approach is that it diminishes the chance of unequal treatment. A second is that it reduces the number of cases the administrative authorities would otherwise have to handle. The United States approach also provides more certainty, at least for those people who <u>do</u> <u>not</u> meet the statutory prerequisites. On its face, the United States system does not provide any more certainty for those people who do qualify. They are then subject to the same sort of discretionary hurdle as are their counterparts in New Zealand. As a practical matter, however, a noncitizen who survives the statutory prerequisites for some of the remedies (not all) is fairly likely to receive the favorable exercise of discretion because the prerequisites are themselves often in the nature of equities -- e.g., hardship, character, length of stay, etc.

The New Zealand system also has considerable advantages. United States-style rules can be rigid; a person might fall through the holes even if he or she is worthy, since the prerequisites are necessarily general. Not all possible fact situations can be anticipated. Second, because the New Zealand system is less complex, a lower proportion of cases should require the services of lawyers or generate difficult technical questions of statutory eligibility that administrative tribunals and courts must ultimately resolve.

CHAPTER 9
DEPORTATION PROCEDURE

SECTION A. OVERVIEW

This Overview is designed mainly for perspective, so that the issues sampled later in detail will fit more easily into the broad scheme. The intent was to provide (a) an overall sense of the process; (b) the flavor and atmosphere of removal proceedings; and (c) some specific procedural information not detailed below. Although it is intended principally as background reading, there are a few issues that some instructors might wish to take up in class:

On pages 652-53, the coursebook asks why DHS would want to delay giving people warnings of their rights until after they have been interrogated. The obvious hope is that the noncitizens will blurt out statements that can be used against them in removal hearings. If noncitizens knew that they could remain silent and that any statements they choose to make could be used against them, many would remain silent. And if they knew they had the right to counsel and knew how to obtain free legal services, many would do so and the attorneys would advise them not to make statements to DHS. DHS sees all of these consequences as impediments to law enforcement. But the DHS strategy works only to the extent it keeps people ignorant of their rights. An official policy grounded on that premise seem hard to justify.

SECTION B. A SAMPLING OF SPECIFIC PROCEDURAL INGREDIENTS

The issues in this section are just a sampling. There is absolutely no attempt here to be exhaustive.

1. Immigration Judges

This material describes how the present adjudication process came into being. In doing so, it touches on the role of the Administrative Procedure Act in U.S. immigration law. It also deals with a variety of problems that are often lumped together under the headings "separation of functions" and "decisional independence."

Notes and Questions Following Rawitz (page 665):

Q2: Arrangement #1 has never characterized removal proceedings. It would clearly violate 5 USC § 554(d), if that section applied to removal proceedings. The dangers in this arrangement include at least two: First, the investigator can be privy to ex parte information to which the noncitizen has no chance to respond. That information might be unreliable and might bias the investigator. Second, allowing the investigator to adjudicate the case can create the appearance of unfairness.

Arrangement #2 used to exist in deportation proceedings but, as Rawitz points out, it no longer does. Today's immigration judges do only adjudication. This arrangement would not violate 5 USC § 554(d) even if that provision applied to removal proceedings. One danger of arrangement #2 is that an investigator/adjudicator could develop an enforcement bias. Another is that it might be awkward for an adjudicator to rule against his or her own prosecutor colleagues, who might later be deciding cases in which he or she is involved.

Arrangement #3 is partly true of removal hearings today. The immigration judge may do those things, but if deportability is contested the regulations require that DHS be represented by a trial attorney, in which event the immigration judge's role in the development of the record is typically secondary. But the immigration judge could be more assertive even then. To the extent that one of the immigration judge's functions is prosecutorial in nature, it is not clear whether his or her involvement is substantial enough that the APA would be violated if it applied. One danger in this arrangement is that an adjudicator could become so intent on developing the prosecutor's evidence that he or she loses objectivity. In addition the immigration judge in such a setting must either investigate or work with an investigator, and either way it is possible to become biased by unreliable ex parte information.

Arrangement #4 formally characterizes removal hearings at present. Immigration judges and BIA members are employees of the Department of Justice and therefore are subordinate to the Attorney General, who has both investigative and prosecutorial functions. With respect to the BIA there is the further problem of no statutory recognition. The Attorney General could dissolve the BIA, dismiss its members, or reverse its decisions. The first two options were once unthinkable, but the more liberal members were removed from the Board in 2003, as discussed in section B.4 of this chapter of the coursebook. And certainly attorneys general have reversed BIA decisions from time to time. As for immigration judges, at least until the events of 2001 described in question 3 below, few today really doubted their independence.

It is not clear whether this is enough of a supervisory relationship that the APA would be violated if it applied. This is really just a case of two agencies with differing functions in the same department.

There are several dangers: First, the supervisor, who might well have agendas other than the dispensation of justice, could overtly or even subtly try to influence the outcome of a case. That would be problematic because the adjudicator sees and hears the evidence and the argument and should judge the case on the record. Second, an adjudicator could wrongly fear such interference and decide cases to please the supervisor. Third, this arrangement could cause the parties to the litigation and the general public to perceive unfairness whether it exists or not. Again, consider the events described in question 3.

Q3: These actions clearly diminish the independence of these adjudicative officials. In the U.S. case of the immigration judge, the issue is somewhat blurred by the "administrative" component of the particular decision. Should calendaring be considered a "legal" ruling that an aggrieved party should challenge in the usual way, by appealing to the BIA? Or is it an "administrative" decision within the realm of the Office of the Chief Immigration Judge? In this case, the ruling hinged on whether the noncitizen was eligible for adjustment of status, a question that in turn depended on whether the former INS could legally defeat his eligibility by refraining from processing his visa petition. The IJ believed the INS had a legal duty to process the application and that, until it did, the only defense that the noncitizen would be able to present at a recalendared hearing would be effectively blocked. The issue certainly seems like a legal one that the INS could and should have raised by way of the usual appeal procedure rather than by an ex parte contact with the administrative office.

In the cases of both the BIA in the United States and the RRT in Australia, the two concerns are (a) the advance signal that tenure on the board is not secure and (b) the actual dismissal of selected members with no announced criteria. The first element leaves all the members uncertain how the decisions they render in the interim might affect their job security, with obvious implications for the integrity of the adjudicative process. The second element both distorts the composition of the board and sends a message to surviving (and future) Board members about the effects of their decisions on their future job security. The two situations are different, however, in at least one respect. In the Australian case, the Minister was explicit that it was the conclusions members reached in their opinions that would govern their continued service on the board. In the U.S., the Attorney General gave no explicit indication of his future decisional criteria at all, even though the strongly held suspicion (confirmed later by the selection of the particular members purged) was that the decisions would be heavily ideological.

In the Australian case, the Minister purported to nonrenew the offending tribunal members because they had "failed to follow the law." Of course, this is but another way of saying that their interpretation of the law differed from his. This is not an uncommon reaction by the losing party. The unusual part is that in this instance the losing party responded by firing the adjudicators! It is difficult to imagine that future RRT members will be oblivious to the risks of ruling against the Minister.

Still, one might observe, these are administrative tribunals, not article III courts or their Australian equivalents. Independence is just the flip side of accountability. Is independence desirable in this context, or are these decisions more in the nature of executive policymaking that should be within the purview of politically accountable officials? On the one hand, the courts remind us often that immigration is a quintessential policy decision that courts should approach with special sensitivity. And thinking of these decisions as executive policymaking permits the executive branch to bring all its immigration decisions – those made through rulemaking and those made through administrative adjudication – into a single coherent framework. The traditional view of separation of powers is that, when legislatures enact laws and the executive branch issues regulations, the policies demand political accountability. That is the essence of representative democracy. Still, once those policy decisions have been made, disputes about the meaning of those laws and their applicability to particular fact situations require independent judicial thought. (Of course, in an administrative state, the line that separates policymaking from adjudication is blurry. But arguably the basic principle should remain intact.) Certainly one can argue that the adjudicator should strive to base his or her findings of fact on the evidence presented, and the conclusions of law on his or her honest and thoughtful readings of the available legal evidence – not on the basis of the personal consequences to the judge or whether the judge's supervisors will be upset by the decision.

This issue is revisited in section B.4 in the specific context of the BIA.

2. Representation

a. Authorization to Practice

Notes and Questions Following 8 CFR §§ 1292.1, 1292.2 (2008) (page 671):

Q1: The specific question of law students (and law school graduates not yet admitted to the Bar) is taken up separately in question 2 below. Here, if the instructor wishes, the class can discuss any proposals for changing any of the other categories of representatives. The instructor could ask, for example, whether it would not be better simply to give the immigration judge the discretion to allow any individual to provide representation if the immigration judge believes the person is competent to do so (in addition to certain automatic categories such as licensed attorneys).

Q2: The real question here is whether first-year and second-year law students should be permitted to provide representation. Arguments in favor might include the following: First, noncitizens need the representation; having a first or second-year law student is better than no representation at all (assuming as a practical matter that that would be the alternative in many cases). Second, since an attorney will provide supervision, the differences in knowledge and legal experience between third-year law students and those in their first and second years are marginal. Third, the representation brings educational benefits to the students; they learn more about the process before embarking on their own. Fourth, such representation could encourage more students to go into the practice of immigration law after graduation and help fill a need.

Arguments against permitting first-year and second-year law students to represent noncitizens in immigration proceedings might include the following: First, precisely because the interests at stake for the noncitizen are so important, it is crucial that those who represent them have maturity and judgment. Second, even second-year law students are less likely than third-year law students to have taken certain specific courses that would be helpful in this setting -- immigration law, professional responsibility, evidence, and trial techniques. (Of course if that is the only barrier, then the law could simply condition the representation by second-year law students on their having passed such courses.)

Q3: It is probably not coincidence that the relaxation of the law school sponsorship and no-remuneration requirements occurred at the same time. Both of course, reflected the Justice Department's concern about the rising caseloads and the attendant need to expand the pool of potential representatives. More relevant to question 3, though, as long as law school sponsorship was required, the regulations might simply have reflected the law school tradition against students receiving pay and academic credit for the same work. The basis for that rule -- apart from the antipathy to double dipping -- might be that the educational purpose of law school clinics could be compromised if the employer feels justified in assigning work on the basis of the employer's needs rather than the student's learning experience. (Thanks to Karen Tokarz for that suggestion.) And that, in turn, is more likely to happen if the student is receiving a salary. At any rate, now that law school sponsorship is no longer required, that rationale disappears.

So why disqualify law students (and graduates not yet admitted to the Bar) if the client is the source of the remuneration but not if the organization is the source? Perhaps the idea is that the only reason nonlawyers are allowed to appear in immigration proceedings in the first place is that many noncitizens are financially unable to hire lawyers. If a noncitizen who wants representation can afford to pay for it, the argument would run, then he or she should hire a lawyer. One counterargument would be that there might well be people who can afford to hire nonlawyers but who cannot afford the higher fees charged by lawyers. Those individuals are better off being represented by competent nonlawyers who are supervised by faculty members or attorneys than not being represented at all. Moreover, the system itself runs more smoothly when there is a knowledgable representative to assist the noncitizen and help sort out the issues.

b. Lawyers for the Indigent

i. A Constitutional Right to Counsel?

Aguilera-Enriquez v. INS (page 673):

An LPR pleaded guilty to possession of cocaine. No one had advised him that the resulting conviction might lead to deportation. At his deportation hearing, Aguilera-Enriquez alleged indigence and requested appointed counsel. The IJ denied the request, denied voluntary departure (almost impossible in cases of criminal convictions), and ordered him deported. Aguilera then obtained an attorney, who appealed to the BIA on the ground that another attorney had filed a motion in state court to allow Aguilera to withdraw his guilty plea. The BIA dismissed the appeal, and Aguilera petitioned for review. He argued that due process requires the appointment of counsel for indigent noncitizens in deportation proceedings. (The Sixth Amendment right to counsel was inapplicable because deportation is a civil proceeding.)

The court held that due process does not require the appointment of counsel in deportation cases unless the facts of the particular case make it fundamentally unfair to proceed without counsel. That was not the case here, the court held. At the deportation hearing there was nothing counsel could have done, since at that time no motion to withdraw the guilty plea had yet been filed. And at the BIA stage Aguilera had competent counsel. The dissent would reject case-by-case analysis and hold that due process always requires the appointment of counsel for indigent indigent LPRs in deportation proceedings.

<u>Notes and Questions Following Aguilera-Enriquez</u> (page 678):

Q2: Among the variables that affect the magnitude of the individual interest are whether the individual is documented or undocumented; whether, if documented, he or she is an LPR or a nonimmigrant; the length of time the person has been in the United States; and the existence of family or other ties. The first two variables (and, to a more limited extent, the third) lend themselves to categorical determination. The last variable requires individualized judgment.

Q3: As to the first question, it is not clear how counsel would interfere with the flexibility of the decisionmaker. The principal role of counsel is to offer and object to evidence and to argue for particular results. The immigration judge will ultimately decide which evidence to accept and what findings and conclusions to reach.

As to the second question, a large part of the job of the immigration judge in removal proceedings is to decide applications for discretionary relief. Sometimes even the statutory prerequisites to those remedies themselves entail the exercise of discretion (e.g., assessments of "exceptionally and extremely unusual hardship" in cancellation of removal cases). In fact, as the students saw in chapter 8, noncitizens in the vast majority of removal cases concede deportability and request discretionary relief. So it is difficult to see removal proceedings as any less discretionary than proceedings to revoke probation or parole. (It is true that most of the determinations made by immigration judges are not "predictive," but it is not clear why predictive determinations are any more or less suited to the use of counsel than are any other decisions that require judgment. Moreover, as the students will see in chapter 11, asylum decisions require predictions as to the likelihood of future persecution). Of course, immigration judges in removal proceedings must also find facts and interpret law, both with respect to the deportability grounds and with respect to the statutory prerequisites to discretionary relief. Presumably, however, proceedings to revoke parole and probation are not entirely devoid of the need for similar decisionmaking.

Q4: With respect to factfinding, counsel can depose witnesses, otherwise investigate the facts before the hearing, assemble documents, line up witnesses, and cross-examine government witnesses. With respect to legal questions, counsel can spot issues (including possible defenses and bases for affirmative relief), research the law (including obtaining a sense of what showings have sufficed in other cases), inform the client of the available defenses, and argue the law.

Q5: The instructor might organize the answer along the lines of the three *Eldridge* factors. Those factors relevant to the magnitude of the individual interest might include whether there is the potential for a deprivation of liberty and, if so, the degree of seriousness of that deprivation. Those factors relevant to the governmental interest in dispensing with counsel might include the volume of cases, the expense associated with counsel per case, the availability of counsel, the costs of delay, and any detrimental effects of increased formality in the particular type of proceeding. Those factors relevant to the value of counsel might include whether the procedure is adversarial or inquisitorial, how formal the proceeding is, how complex it is, and whether the government is likely to be represented by counsel.

Q7: In this case, perhaps there would have been no point in reversing for lack of counsel. If there are any legal arguments that could have been made earlier, present counsel can make them now. If those arguments have merit, a court can reverse on that basis; if they do not have merit, then the fact there was no opportunity to raise the points below should be irrelevant. And if the argument is that the findings of fact might have been different, counsel can *now* indicate the new evidence that might have altered the findings (or any points he or she would have made at oral argument to the extent that was permitted).

The major counter-argument is that counsel might have cross-examined the witnesses more effectively. It is difficult to know whether they would have withstood vigorous cross-examination.

More important, however, even if it can be shown that the absence of counsel caused no injustice in this case, the real problem is with a general rule of law that will encompass future fact situations. Most people who are found deportable after hearings at which they were not represented by counsel either give up at that point or, if they appeal to the BIA, do so without counsel. These individuals never had the opportunity to find out what counsel would have done differently.

The instructor could also examine in class whether there is an equal protection argument: Wealthy noncitizens can secure counsel in removal proceedings, while poorer ones often cannot. There are analogous cases in other areas -- e.g., cases governing the provision of counsel to indigent criminal defendants on appeal when the state affords appeal as of right, court fees for divorce actions or for bankruptcy proceedings, etc.

ii. Legal Aid

The text here is intended to be self-explanatory, and the instructor can assign it solely as background reading. An instructor who wishes to do so, however, could use this material as a vehicle for a policy discussion of what the government's role should be with respect to the assistance of noncitizens in removal proceedings. If the government chooses to enact technically complex immigration laws, and if the reality is that the vast majority of noncitizens in removal proceedings are indigent, often uneducated, and certainly not legally trained, and if many such people are in fact eligible for the substantive relief set out in the statute, does justice require the provision of counsel at government expense? Or, rather, is immigration control, being a sovereign function, something the government may implement without concern for the representation of those who are alleged to have violated U.S. immigration laws? At any rate, do the 1996 restrictions (preventing LSC recipients from using even non-LSC funds to represent ineligible noncitizens) impermissibly constrain private giving? Or are they a necessary step to prevent LSC recipients from using creative bookkeeping to do an end run around the restriction?

iii. Pro Bono Legal Services

Once again the instructor can either assign this self-explanatory material as background reading or use it as a vehicle for discussing the role of the private Bar. Do lawyers have a general obligation to do pro bono work? Those who say yes generally stress the privileges of being an attorney and the unique ability that attorneys have to provide help. Those who say no emphasize the importance of the government providing necessary services and ask why lawyers should be singled out as having a duty to provide free services (as compared to physicians, plumbers, etc.). Also, does the analysis change when the client is a noncitizen (or a noncitizen who is undocumented)? Do noncitizens, or undocumented noncitizens, have lesser moral claims to free legal service? What degree of help should be provided? If the hearings are held in remote locations, as is particularly common in the case of noncitizen criminal offenders, what are the limits on the responsibilities of private attorneys?

iv. Equal Access to Justice Act

Notes and Questions on EAJA (page 683):

Q1: Policy arguments in favor of awarding attorney fees to the prevailing party in removal proceedings when the position of the United States is not "substantially justified" might include the following:

a. The government initiated these proceedings, thereby subjecting the noncitizen to great personal expense. If its position is not even "substantially" justified, then why should the innocent party bear the cost?

b. There is no reason to treat removal proceedings differently from any other agency proceedings that are in fact adversarial.

c. The government is represented in these proceedings, at least whenever deportability is contested. The noncitizen needs an attorney simply to avoid an imbalance. It is not fair to stack the deck.

d. Noncitizens have a special need for legal representation. They face language barriers, they have much at stake, and the proceedings can be complex.

e. One purpose of EAJA was to encourage private actions that will establish principles affecting the general public. That purpose applies with equal force to removal proceedings.

Arguments against awarding attorney fees in removal cases might include the following:

a. The individuals are not citizens. They seek only the "privilege" of remaining. If the United States thinks they are deportable, the United States should not have to pay to remove them.

b. Many removal cases are routine events in which attorneys are unnecessary. (Response: Not those in which the United States position is not "substantially justified.")

c. Discipline of Practitioners

Notes and Questions Following 8 CFR § 1003.102 (2008) (page 687):

Q1: The rationale for disciplining those who engage in frivolous behavior is clear -- to deter the kinds of legally frivolous strategies that aim solely to achieve delay. The danger is that such prohibitions are hard to draft in a way that will not chill the vigorous advocacy of positions that raise close issues. The test used by paragraph (j) is whether the person knows or reasonably should have known that the asserted position lacks an "arguable" basis. "Arguable" presumably means "reasonably arguable," and reasonableness tests are familiar in many legal settings. The indeterminacy is accepted. In this case, though, the indeterminacy requires practitioners who wish to venture unconventional arguments to risk their livelihoods. The danger is diminished by the language in j(1) that the position need only be "warranted by existing law or by a good faith argument for the extension, modification, or reversal of existing law or the establishment of new law." Thus, novel arguments are not precluded. Still, practitioners cannot know in advance whether administrative officials will find the position "arguable." The effect is to create a conflict of interest between practitioner and client. Some practitioners might resolve the conflict in favor of self-interest, by playing it safe.

Q2: That the disciplinary rules punished practitioners for going too far on behalf of their noncitizen clients but not for failing to go far enough probably illustrates the priorities of the Justice Department. Wasting government time and resources is seen as a worse evil than abusing one's commitment to represent the noncitizen diligently and competently.

As for the dangers, however, the combination of such a regulation with the one that bars "frivolous behavior" arguably puts counsel between a rock and a hard place. Sometimes, whether to put forward a particular defense requires judgment. If the practitioner makes the argument and a tribunal later concludes the argument was frivolous, he or she can be disciplined for frivolous behavior. But if the practitioner doesn't make the argument and a tribunal later finds that the argument should have been made, the practitioner is exposed to disciplinary action for ineffective assistance. The risk might even be enough to deter pro bono representation in some cases. Still, given the stakes, it seems that somehow DHS, the immigration judges, and the BIA should strive to prevent at least egregious failures to provide adequate representation. And lawyers do, after all, routinely comply with both sorts of obligations under the ABA Model Rules of Professional Conduct. There is no apparent reason that these duties would be any harder to satisfy in the immigration context.

Second, as the students will see in the subsection below on ineffective assistance, the ineffective assistance issue will initially be raised by the client, against the practitioner, typically in a motion to reopen. A practitioner who might otherwise have been inclined to admit his or her ineffectiveness to help the client (or former client) might now hesitate to do so, for fear of discipline.

Q3: A prejudice requirement makes sense when a criminal defendant seeks to withdraw a guilty plea or when a noncitizen moves to reopen removal proceedings. There is no reason to disturb a prior resolution when the only alleged errors were harmless. In the case of a disciplinary proceeding based on alleged ineffective assistance of counsel, however, the purpose is to punish the offender and deter similar misconduct by the same practitioner and by others. Those rationales seem applicable regardless of whether the misconduct caused any harm. An analogy might be made to the distinction between torts and criminal law. In most torts cases (not all) a plaintiff must show actual injury; in criminal cases, where the focus is on punishing the defendant rather than on compensating the victim, the absence of harm is not normally a defense.

Q4: Arguments in favor of the rules include (a) there might be particular practices specific to immigration that are best addressed through specialized disciplinary rules; (b) perhaps immigration specialists will be more familiar with rules that relate to their specialty than with generic rules; (c) the rules are necessary for non-attorney practitioners at any rate, and as long as they have to exist, there is no reason to hold attorneys to a lesser standard; and (d) since immigration law is exclusively federal, it makes sense to have a uniform set of ethical rules that all who practice in this federal area are bound to follow.

Arguments against applying the rules to attorneys include (a) there is always potential for conflicting interpretations as between the ABA rules and the Justice Department rules; (b) it is too burdensome to expect lawyers to be familiar with entire sets of disciplinary codes imposed by both the states in which they are licensed and possibly several different federal agencies; and (c) (as argued by the ABA) there is potential for unfair prosecution when the same agency that represents the opposing side in a proceeding has the power not only to file a complaint against the opposing lawyer but then to decide it.

d. Ineffective Assistance of Counsel

People v. Pozo (page 689):

Pozo, an LPR, pleaded guilty to sexual assault and to escape. As in *Parrino* (discussed in item 1 of the Notes and Questions), the INS instituted deportation proceedings and Pozo moved to withdraw his guilty plea on the ground that he had not realized the convictions would lead to deportation and would not have pleaded guilty had he known this. Unlike Parrino, Pozo had not been affirmatively misinformed; rather, the subject simply had not been raised. Also unlike Parrino, Pozo argued that his attorney's failure to advise him of the deportation consequences amounted to ineffective assistance of counsel, in violation of the Sixth Amendment.

The majority opinion acknowledged that *the court* is not required to advise a criminal defendant of the *collateral* consequences of a proposed guilty plea and that deportation is a collateral consequence. It held, however, that the Sixth Amendment requires the court to allow withdrawal of a guilty plea when *the defense attorney* failed to inform the defendant of the possibility of deportation, provided the attorney had reason to know that the defendant was a noncitizen and actual prejudice resulted. The dissent would deny motions to withdraw guilty pleas unless the defendants show they did not understand the direct consequences.

Notes and Questions Following Pozo (page 694):

Q2: Several views are possible. Many would argue that it is even more indefensible for an attorney who spots an issue not to bother researching it or to research it sloppily than it is for an attorney inadvertently to miss an issue in the first place. Others might disagree, saying that an attorney should not be penalized for spotting an issue. Still others would argue that, in either situation, the defendant should not be able to withdraw the plea. The attorney has been retained only for help in the criminal matter. Others would say either way the defendant should be able to withdraw the plea. At least if the attorney had reason to suspect that the client was a noncitizen, it makes sense to require the attorney to do at least preliminary research. Common sense suggests that the consequence in question will be extremely important for the client. If an authoritative answer is beyond the attorney's expertise, he or she can always consult, or at least refer the client to, a specialist.

As the text observes, many courts do in fact find this distinction relevant. There are conflicting views as to the duty to advise, but most courts now allow plea withdrawal when the attorney affirmatively misinforms a defendant. Ironically, however, Parrino was affirmatively misinformed and the court held that was not enough; Pozo and his lawyer never discussed the issue, and the court held that the failure to reveal the possibility of deportation was enough.

Q3: The instructor can ask the students to try to imagine themselves as criminal defense lawyers who have never taken a course in immigration law and are now defending a client who appears to be from another country. They can then be invited to consider honestly whether they think it would occur to them that a criminal conviction could affect the client's immigration status. The instructor can then ask for a show of hands. A majority will probably say the thought would have crossed their minds, but a sizeable minority are likely to admit candidly that they might not have spotted the issue. Perhaps other students will be too embarrassed to admit this in class, even with the instructor's soothing assurance that it's OK to vote no; also, a student who is this far into the course sometimes finds it hard to know what he or she would have thought about, had he or she not taken the course. Still, the vote is instructive for students and teacher alike.

Assume, however, that an attorney who has reason to believe that his or her client is a noncitizen should be expected at least to consider the possibility that a deportation issue exists. Once the thought crosses the attorney's mind, he or she cannot ethically ignore it. Consultation and referral are among the attorney's options. If the attorney decides to plunge into immigration law himself or herself, the logical starting point would be a treatise on immigration law. Surely any immigration specialist, and probably any law librarian asked for advice, would refer the attorney immediately to Gordon, Mailman & Yale-Loehr, or perhaps to Kurzban. In the treatise the lawyer would immediately find a chapter on deportation grounds and should easily discover some section or subsection on criminal grounds, as well as a citation to INA § 237(a). A brief look at the list of deportation grounds would get the attorney started. Once the attorney sees the subsection on crimes involving moral turpitude, or on aggravated felonies, or on drug offenses, etc., it would be obvious that there is at least the potential for deportation. At that point the attorney would have an obligation either to continue with the research or consult a specialist. It seems hard to imagine a diligent non-specialist missing the entire issue.

Q4: This question raises the ethical issue after the fact. If the client asks the attorney to continue the representation, it seems the least the attorney can do is accept the employment if he or she feels competent to handle the case. Continued representation would require either research by the attorney or consultation with a specialist. Eventually the attorney will have to decide whether the client is better off leaving the original plea intact, withdrawing it and substituting a guilty plea to another crime, or going to trial. If the attorney decides that it would be strategic to move to withdraw the guilty plea, he or she would have to submit an affidavit confessing the deficiencies in the original advice. The confession will be embarrassing, but ethically it seems the least the attorney should do under the circumstances.

If instead the client wants another attorney, the first attorney should still offer to submit the necessary affidavit. In fact, if that offer is not made, the defendant's new attorney would likely subpoena the first attorney to testify. So the first attorney might as well be gracious about it, as were the original lawyers in both *Parrino* and *Pozo*.

Q5: There are several possible answers. Two of them are (a) the defendant would not have pleaded guilty; and (b) the defendant would not have pleaded guilty and either (i) would have been allowed to plead guilty to a different offense that would not have led to deportation or (ii) the defendant would have gone to trial and there is a reasonable chance that at trial he or she would have been found not guilty.

The first paragraph of original footnote 8 of the majority opinion in *Pozo* implies that the Supreme Court in *Hill* required only showing (a) above. The dissenting opinion of Judge Rovira seems to make the same assumption.

The argument for requiring the stiffer showing described in view (b) above is that pleading not guilty would not have helped unless the court finds that the defendant would ultimately have been acquitted. Therefore the defendant should be required to demonstrate at least a reasonable probability of that outcome. The argument for view (a) above is that one can never really know what would have happened had the defendant pleaded not guilty. There is always a chance of acquittal, and the defendant should now be given that chance.

Q7: Both defendants might have been able to allege breaches of their attorneys' duties to exercise due care. In each case the legal standard is that of the reasonable attorney as measured by the custom in the profession. It might be that most criminal defense lawyers would have been unaware of the deportation consequences, in which case at least Pozo's attorney might be found not to have breached his duty. Parrino has a stronger case than Pozo, since Parrino specifically posed the question to his attorney, who was a former INS commissioner, and the attorney never bothered even to look up the statute. Parrino might therefore have a cause of action not just in negligence, but in recklessness. There is, of course, the logistical problem that, once a noncitizen is denied the opportunity to withdraw the plea, deportation might take place. And once the person is out of the country, the mechanics of litigation become more burdensome.

The liability and remedy issues overlap. To establish liability the plaintiff would have to demonstrate not only that the attorney acted negligently, but also that negligence caused some identifiable injury. The latter will be difficult to prove. The plaintiff would probably be required to show that it is more likely than not that, had the attorney provided proper advice, deportation would have been averted. If the plaintiff is able to make that and the other showings required for a cause of action, there would remain the issue of remedy. Money damages seem most likely, since the attorney has no power to bring the person back into the country, but how to measure the loss entailed by deportation is not clear.

Q9: There are at least three subissues here. First, should apparent authority be enough, or should actual authority be required? As the text notes, general agency law principles normally recognize apparent authority; i.e., if the promisee reasonably believes that the promisor has actual authority to make the promise, then the promise is binding. As the court in *San Pedro* observes, however, *government* promisors must have actual authority, or their promises will not be held binding.

Is that fair? On the one hand, law operates through careful delegation of power. To allow one government official to bind the entire United States government by making promises that he or she had no authority to make could not only disrupt the work of the affected agency but also concentrate power dangerously in the hands of a single official. Moreover, private parties are presumed to know the law; thus, as long as it is clear that the particular official lacks the power to make a particular promise, then the private party should not have relied on it. The public availability of law is what distinguishes government promises from those made by private parties acting on behalf of other private parties. And in this case the regulation makes the law publicly available. On the other hand, no one can really know all the law, and at any rate the law is not always clear. (It certainly wasn't in the cases described in the text. The Attorney General's regulation makes it clearer, but for reasons discussed in the next paragraph, even the regulation does not conclusively settle the question.)

Second, assuming actual authority is required (and note that actual authority can be either express or implied), do federal prosecutors have the authority to promise non-deportation? The Attorney General's regulation clarifies that the Department of Justice has not delegated, and in fact expressly disclaims having delegated, such an authority. But there remains the question whether Congress itself has implicitly delegated to prosecutors the power to promise not to deport. (The court in*Thomas* suggested Congress has done so.) If that is the case, the Attorney General is powerless to cancel that promise. If that is not the case, then there is no actual authority, express or implied.

Third, if a court is not willing to enforce the promise, should it at least allow rescission of the agreement, thus permitting the defendant to withdraw the guilty plea? This will not be a fully satisfactory solution even to the defendant, because it is possible that the defendant (Parrino, for example) has already performed all or part of his or her end of the bargain, including serving the sentence and cooperating with the government. Moreover, the defendant might feel that he or she deserves the benefit of the bargain. From the government's point of view, withdrawal might be better than specific performance, because it avoids the problem of one government official or agency binding another agency. If the plea is withdrawn, the government could still prosecute, provided the evidence is still accessible and it has a solid case. Otherwise, however, withdrawal of the plea could mean that prosecution is no longer practically possible or worthwhile, and in turn without the conviction there will likely be no ground for removal.

Matter of Compean (page 698):

In each of three consolidated cases, undocumented immigrants were ordered removed upon the BIA's denials of their applications for affirmative relief (cancellation of removal, adjustment of status, and asylum and related remedies). Each of the three moved the BIA to reopen on grounds of ineffective assistance of retained counsel. In each case the BIA denied the motion. Attorney General

Mukasey certified all three cases to himself for review.

The Attorney General first held that the sixth amendment, which applies only in criminal proceedings, supplies no right to the effective assistance of counsel in civil removal proceedings. Disapproving two earlier BIA precedents, the Attorney General then held that there is also no fifth amendment due process right to the effective assistance of counsel in removal proceedings. For the latter proposition, he offered two broad rationales. First, he reasoned, the courts have generally disavowed a right to the effective assistance of counsel in contexts where (as is true in removal proceedings) there is no constitutional right to government-appointed counsel. Second, the Attorney General concluded that the conduct of private counsel does not constitute government action for due process purposes. Nor, he next held, is there a *statutory* right to the effective assistance of counsel in removal proceedings. The INA guarantees the "privilege" of representation by counsel, but not at government expense, and the Attorney General concluded that the statutory right to counsel does not embrace a right to effective assistance.

He acknowledged, however, that, subject to various statutory constraints, immigration judges and the BIA have the discretion to reopen removal proceedings. The Attorney General also acknowledged that the "deficient performance" of counsel is a permissible ground for exercising that discretion, but he went on to impose two sets of prerequisites to granting motions to reopen based on ineffective assistance. The various requirements were modifications of the criteria previously announced by the BIA in *Matter of Lozada*, 19 I. & N. Dec. 637 (BIA 1988).

One set of requirements is substantive. Counsel's error must be "egregious;" the motion to reopen must have been filed within the relevant time limits unless the movant can show due diligence in discovering and seeking to cure counsel's errors; and the movant must establish that the lawyer's shortcomings prejudiced the outcome. The prejudice standard, the Attorney General held, requires a showing that, but for the errors of counsel, the movant "more likely than not" would have been "entitled to the ultimate relief he was seeking."

To meet the procedural prerequisites to filing a motion to reopen based on ineffective assistance, the movant must submit a detailed affidavit setting out all the relevant facts, including the lawyer's deficiencies and the harm they caused. In addition, the movant must submit five documents: (1) a copy of the attorney-client agreement or a statement in the affidavit describing what the lawyer had agreed to do; (2) a letter to former counsel setting out the alleged deficiencies and counsel's reply, if there was one; (3) a completed and signed (but not necessarily filed) complaint to the appropriate disciplinary authority; (4) a copy of the evidence or arguments that the movant faults counsel for failing to offer; and (5) a signed statement by the current attorney (if there is one) stating his or her belief that former counsel's performance fell below minimal professional standards.

Finally, the Attorney General announced that these requirements are mandatory;

that even if they are met, reopening remains discretionary; that this framework applies to immigration judges and the BIA even in circuits that have recognized a constitutional right to the effective assistance of counsel in removal proceedings; and that the BIA has the authority to reopen even when counsel's deficient performance occurred after the entry of an administratively final removal order.

<u>Notes and Questions Following Compean</u> (page 710):

Q1: One might argue that rationale (a) is a nonsequitur. Why should the fact that there is no right to have the government provide counsel mean that those noncitizens who obtain private counsel without the government's help have no right to effective assistance? Perhaps the Attorney General would respond that such a position functionally gives the wealthy a constitutional right that the indigent don't have. But the noncitizen might respond that it is not a question of differential treatment, simply the reality that the effective assistance issue doesn't arise in pro se cases. Moreover, the noncitizen might add, ineffective assistance can be *worse* than no assistance at all. Among other things, the immigration judge might feel a greater obligation to identify possible avenues of relief when people are unrepresented.

As for rationale (b), the Attorney General's invocation of *Shelley v. Kraemer* is ironic. He cites its dictum that due process does not reach private conduct but not its famous holding that the use of the courts to enforce a racially restrictive covenant would be state action. In the present context, the noncitizen could argue that the use of the immigration court and the BIA to effect a deportation resulting from the ineffective assistance of counsel would similarly be state action. If that state action renders the proceeding fundamentally unfair (a fact question), then due process should be held to have been violated.

Q2: The noncitizen would argue that the Attorney General's rationale in *Compean* does not apply to this case. The Attorney General had reasoned that there cannot be a due process right to effective assistance when there is no constitutional right to appointed counsel. Since the latter right exists in this case, there is no reason to deny the existence of the former.

The government might respond, first, that the Attorney General would not have accepted the holding of *Aguilera-Enriquez* in the first place. Second, it might add, the recognition of a right to appointed counsel in this case still does not address the alternative rationale for the Attorney General's decision in *Compean* – that the conduct of private counsel is not government action.

Q3: First, litigation is logistically (and financially) difficult once the person has been sent overseas. Second, even if successful, a malpractice suit won't get the person back to the United States.

Q4: The noncitizen has a legitimate expectation that his or her attorney's performance will meet the standards of the legal profession. Moreover, in removal cases the clients are especially likely to lack the linguistic and cultural knowledge of the general population and thus are particularly dependent on the competence and effort of the attorney.

The government has an interest in the finality of the proceeding. There are fiscal costs in re-doing a hearing and even in reconsidering a case on a paper record. In addition, granting motions to reopen too freely might create the incentive to file frivolous motions to reopen for the purpose of delaying removal.

Q5: As to the first issue, the Attorney General looks to the "ultimate relief" that the noncitizen was seeking – e.g. cancellation of removal, asylum, voluntary departure, etc. That seems fair. The law does not require a showing that the person would have received LPR status, rightly so in cases where LPR status was not sought – for example, when the person was seeking some lesser relief such as voluntary departure, or withholding of removal. On the other hand, one could argue that it should be enough to demonstrate some specified probability that the person would have received *some* more favorable outcome.

As to the second issue, the Attorney General prescribes a "clear and convincing" standard of proof. This is greater than a preponderance of the evidence standard, and much greater than a standard that requires only a "plausible" or "reasonable" likelihood of a different result. On the one hand, insisting on such a high standard of proof puts the noncitizen in a bind, since predictions about what would have happened if different evidence had been offered or if different arguments had been made or if deadlines had been respected are inherently hazardous. In addition, the consequences of error can be grave, an argument that favors reopening when there is little reason to be confident that the right result was reached. On the other hand, there are important government interests at stake as well, including finality and the avoidance of delay. Those interests might command extra weight in the present setting, where the noncitizen seeks to reopen a proceeding after it has gone through a full hearing and appeal.

Q6: The real test should be whether a reasonable lawyer would have raised the issue of filing a brief. If the attorney raised the matter and the client instructed the attorney not to file a brief, then conceivably the attorney could be forgiven for failing to do so, although in that event one would at least expect more substantive specificity in the notice of appeal. But if the lawyer never raised the issue, it would be unrealistic to expect a lay client to raise it. The client normally would not know the litigation process in general and certainly would not be expected to know the difference between a notice of appeal and a brief. The client has a right to expect the attorney to represent the client to the best of the attorney's ability. If effective representation requires a brief, the client should not have to advise the attorney to file it.

Q7: The courts should certainly feel free to reject the Attorney General's conclusion that due process does not require the effective assistance of counsel.

Unlike the requirement of *Chevron* deference on matters of statutory interpretation, or the limited scope of review of administrative findings of fact or the exercise of discretion, there is no particular reason for courts to defer to the constitutional interpretations of executive or administrative officials. Especially is this true, it would seem, when the particular constitutional issue is procedural due process, a subject squarely within the expertise and authority of a court.

In effect, however, the framework announced by the Attorney General in *Compean* was a blanket approach to be used in guiding the exercise of a statutory discretion to reopen removal proceedings. And discretionary decisions are normally subject to narrow standards of review, such as "arbitrary, capricious, an abuse of discretion." One question is whether blanket guidance on how to exercise discretion deserves the same judicial deference as individualized discretion. Beyond that, it remains open to a court to invoke due process to reverse the Board's denial of a motion to reopen that was founded on a claim of ineffective assistance of counsel. As noted above, deference to the Attorney General's statutory interpretation, fact-finding, and discretionary powers does not even come into play. A desire for nationwide uniformity might inhibit courts from doing so, but since it will almost always be clear in which circuit a petition for review would be filed, see INA § 242(b)(2), the need for uniformity does not seem any greater here than for any other issues on which the courts of appeals have divided.

3. Evidence and Proof

a. Admissibility of Evidence

INS v. Lopez-Mendoza (page 713):

In two consolidated cases, noncitizens were found deportable for having entered without inspection. Both argued that their arrests were unlawful (in violation of the 4th Amendment). One of the two maintained that the unlawful arrest required the termination of deportation proceedings. Both argued that in any event the statements they made to INS officers pursuant to their arrests should have been suppressed at their deportation hearings. The immigration judges and the BIA rejected both arguments. The Court of Appeals for the Ninth Circuit held the exclusionary rule (under which illegally obtained evidence is suppressible in a criminal proceeding upon the motion of the defendant) applicable in deportation proceedings. The court then reversed one of the two deportation orders outright, and remanded the other case to the BIA for a determination of whether the INS had violated the 4th Amendment.

The Supreme Court first held that the illegality of the arrest does not require termination of deportation proceedings. The Court pointed out that that is true even in criminal cases.

The harder issue was whether the exclusionary rule applies in deportation proceedings, which are civil. In *United States v. Janis*, decided in 1976, the Court had held the applicability of the exclusionary rule to a given type of civil proceeding is determined through a cost-benefit analysis. The chief benefits are deterring police misconduct and avoiding judicial complicity in unlawful activity. The chief costs are the loss of probative evidence and the possibility that an offender will go free as a result. The Court exhaustively identified and evaluated the various benefits and costs of applying the exclusionary rule to deportation proceedings and concluded that the costs would outweigh the benefits. Accordingly, it held the exclusionary rule inapplicable in deportation proceedings.

There were four separate dissenting opinions. All joined Justice White, who discussed each of the benefits and costs of applying the exclusionary rule in deportation proceedings and compared each of them to the corresponding benefits and costs in criminal proceedings. He found the overall balance to be roughly the same in the two kinds of proceedings and, consequently, believed the exclusionary rule should apply to deportation as long as it applies to criminal cases. Two of the dissenters went further, expressing their previously articulated views that the exclusionary rule is itself constitutionally mandated, as a means of avoiding judicial complicity in police lawlessness.

General: This very long case presents some good policy analysis of the nature of deportation proceedings and their relation to criminal proceedings. If the instructor skips this case, it is worth telling the class what the holding was. The instructor should be prepared for some students who will never have heard of the exclusionary rule. This book does not attempt to cover the substantive scope of the Fourth Amendment, even as applied to immigration. That subject is left to courses in criminal procedure.

Notes and Questions Following Lopez-Mendoza (page 728):

Q1: Lopez-Mendoza did not object merely to the introduction of evidence. Rather, he objected to the entire proceeding, on the ground he had been illegally arrested. That objection generally is not permitted even in criminal proceedings. Sandoval-Sanchez, in contrast, objected only to the introduction of the evidence that had been obtained as a result of an illegal arrest. That evidence would be suppressible in a criminal case, but the case would proceed if there is enough other evidence against the defendant.

Q2: The instructor could either skip this question or examine in class the extent, if any, to which the principal goals of the criminal justice system apply to deportation. These goals include retribution, general and specific deterrence, rehabilitation, and incapacitation. (Is ridding society of an undesirable noncitizen just a specific form of incapacitation? See pages 152-54 and 517-18 of the text.)

Q3: The majority simply compares the benefits of applying the rule in deportation proceedings against the costs of doing so. For Justice White, the starting point is that the Court applies the exclusionary rule in criminal proceedings, a decision that reflects the Court's belief that the benefits of the rule outweigh the costs in that setting. He asks, therefore, whether the benefits of applying the rule in deportation proceedings are any less than they are in criminal proceedings, and whether the costs of applying the rule in deportation proceedings are any greater than they are in criminal proceedings.

Q4: As to the benefits:

a. The majority admits the INS cannot successfully argue that the inadmissibility of the evidence in any corresponding criminal proceedings is already a sufficient deterrent. In only a small percentage of arrests and seizures by immigration officers does the subsequent evidence end up in a criminal proceeding. Consequently, the immigration officer will be motivated principally by the potential use of the evidence in deportation proceedings. Justice White agrees.

b. The majority argues that the INS will often be able to prove that the person is not a United States citizen even without the illegally seized evidence -- i.e., through silence and inference. Justice White responds that the same is true in criminal proceedings. He might have added that, if the majority's assumption is correct, it should not bother the INS that the evidence will be suppressible. (The INS, of course, might have responded that the principal problem in this regard is the need for additional paperwork and processing.)

c. The majority argues that very few noncitizens ever challenge the seizure. 97.5% obtain voluntary departure, and few of the others challenge its admissibility. Justice White responds, first, that the same is true of plea bargains in criminal proceedings. Second, he points out, the exclusionary rule deters not only the individual immigration officers, but also the agency itself. He might have added that, if it is true that only a tiny proportion of noncitizens will object anyway, then that fact reduces the costs as well as the benefits.

d. The majority argues that the INS has its own, sufficient deterrent scheme. It has issued regulations that require a reasonable suspicion before certain evidence can be seized. New immigration officers receive an education in Fourth Amendment law. Evidence that is intentionally seized illegally is excluded. And there is the prospect of intra-agency discipline. Justice White responds that the regulations to which the majority refers were issued at a time when the agency thought the exclusionary rule applied. Perhaps, therefore, the exclusionary rule is precisely what prompted the agency to issue the regulations. With respect to discipline, Justice White points out that the INS has cited not a single instance in which an officer was actually disciplined for a Fourth Amendment violation. See footnote 1.

e. The majority points out that civil actions for declaratory relief will be available if institutional patterns of abuse can be demonstrated. Justice White responds that noncitizens are removed from the United States before such actions can be brought and that the affected citizens are frequently too poor or too uneducated to sue. Since IIRIRA, there are additional limitations on actions for injunctive relief. See chapter 9, § B.6.c.ii of the text.

As for the costs:

a. The majority argues that, if as a result of the exclusionary rule a noncitizen is permitted to remain at large, the court would be sanctioning a continuing offense (INA §§ 262, 266) (unregistered presence). The Court assumes that in such a case the person was unregistered, because, if he or she were registered, the registration would have revealed the circumstances of the entry and the INS would not have needed the tainted evidence. See INA §§ 275, 276. Justice White responds by identifying limitations on the cited criminal provisions. INA § 262, for example, is not violated until 30 days have elapsed, and then only if the person is more than fourteen years old. INA § 266(a) punishes a noncitizen for violating INA § 262, but only if the violation was "wilful." There was no evidence of that in this case. Consequently, he concludes, there would not necessarily have been a continuing violation of INA § 262. INA § 275 (entry without inspection) has been held not to constitute a continuing offense. INA § 276 (entering, attempting to enter, or being found in the United States after a prior exclusion, deportation, or removal order), in contrast, is a continuing offense. But since it requires a prior exclusion, deportation, or removal order, the government would ordinarily have access to the record of the prior proceeding and therefore would not need the tainted evidence.

Note: If the instructor plans not to cover chapter 12 (Undocumented Imigrants), then this is a good opportunity to point out the existence of these criminal provisions. These provisions put some of the inadmissibility and deportability grounds into perspective as being merely <u>some</u> of the instruments by which Congress regulates immigration. The instructor could also ask the class whether, given the Court's reliance on the continuing violation rationale, the exclusionary rule should apply when *an LPR* is charged with being deportable on the basis of post-entry conduct (e.g., assisting illegal entry of other noncitizens, etc.). The answer is not clear. Such a person could distinguish *Lopez-Mendoza* on the ground that here there is no continuing violation. The INS might respond that that was only one of the rationales that the Supreme Court found persuasive in *Lopez-Mendoza*. In particular, the Court found other costs (discussed below) and concluded that, at any rate, the exclusionary rule would achieve little in the way of deterrence.

b. The majority argues that the exclusionary rule would complicate and lengthen deportation hearings. Justice White responds that the mechanism for suppression motions is already in place, because such motions will be allowed anyway when the illegality is egregious. He observes too that only 50 suppression motions were filed before *Sandoval*. Finally, he adds, the requirement of objective good faith imposed in *Leon* will reduce the number of motions.

c. The majority argues that hearing officers are not experts on the Fourth Amendment. Justice White reminds the majority of its argument that immigration enforcement officials have received a Fourth Amendment education. He asks rhetorically whether these law enforcement officials should be treated as knowing more than immigration judges about the Fourth Amendment.

d. The majority argues that the exclusionary rule will disrupt enforcement if immigration officers have to compile elaborate records and then attend hearings. Also, the majority argues, the exclusionary rule would hinder mass arrests of suspected noncitizens. Justice White responds by asking rhetorically how, then, it would be possible to rely on the civil suits cited by the majority as an alternative form of protection.

Q5: It's hard to say what the Court had in mind with this reference. The text might suggest that evidence is suppressible only if the violation is egregious <u>and</u> transgresses fundamental fairness, for example by undermining the probative value of the evidence. Arguably, regardless of whether the admission of illegally seized evidence would unwisely encourage illegal seizures in future cases, there is nothing fundamentally unfair about admitting such evidence if it is probative. The description of *Toro* in footnote 5 (page 722 of the text) might suggest, therefore, that the court will not suppress probative evidence even when it has been seized illegally.

The court's citations to the other two cases are not as revealing. In particular, it is not clear whether the Court is citing them as examples of cases in which the BIA has suppressed the evidence because the seizure violated the Fourth Amendment or because the circumstances cast doubt on whether the statements had been made under coercion, in which event they would not have been probative. In *Garcia*, it might be that the repeated deprivations of counsel simply wore the person down, until eventually he admitted being a noncitizen just to be left alone. If that was the case, then the evidence was probably non-probative. On the other hand, maybe Garcia's counsel would have encouraged him not to answer, in which case there is no reason to think his concession is untrue. The Ninth Circuit did hold the evidence suppressible in *Arguelles-Vasquez* (cited in the text of question 5), and one point the court made was that *Rochin* -- the very case the Supreme Court in *Lopez-Mendoza* had cited as an example of an "egregious" violation (a stomach-pumping case) -- involved *probative* evidence that the court nonetheless suppressed. In that case, in other words, the fact that the evidence was probative did not mean that the violation was not egregious.

Other Illegally Obtained Statements (page 730):

This material is intended as background reading. The questions raised concerning the privilege against self-incrimination and the burden of proof are taken up more generally in the coursebook pages cited in the text.

Note on Judicial Politics:

This material is also intended as background reading.

b. Burden of Proof and Sufficiency of the Evidence

Woodby v. INS (page 732):

This Supreme Court opinion covers two consolidated cases involving judicial review of deportation orders. In each, there was a contested fact question and some ambiguity as to the standard of proof that the immigration judge and the BIA had applied. The INA contained two provisions requiring "reasonable, substantial, and probative evidence." The question was whether these provisions referred to the standard of proof at the deportation hearing, as the former INS contended, or merely to the standard of judicial review, as the immigrants contended. The Court held that both provisions referred only to the scope of judicial review and that Congress had not addressed the proper standard of proof in deportation proceedings. Considering the latter question an open one, therefore, the Court had to decide which standard made the most policy sense. The immigrants urged the court to require proof beyond a reasonable doubt, as in criminal cases. The INS wanted the Court to require proof only by a preponderance of the evidence, as in most civil cases. The Court chose a middle course -- clear, unequivocal, and convincing evidence -- which it thought appropriate in light of the interests at stake for the immigrants.

The dissent agreed that one of the two existing statutory provisions referred to the scope of judicial review, but it believed that the other one referred to the standard of proof. The dissent interpreted the latter provision as requiring proof by a preponderance of the evidence.

Notes and Questions Following Woodby (page 738):

NOTE: IIRIRA essentially codified the holding in *Woodby*, but with some significant modifications discussed in items 9-11 of the Notes and Questions below. Some instructors might therefore wish to skip*Woodby* and simply tell the students that ICE now has the burden of proving deportability by clear and convincing evidence. INA § 240(c)(3)(A). There are, however, at least three real benefits to assigning *Woodby*. One is its value as a statutory interpretation / judicial process case. To interpret the statute the Court has to parse the literal language of two provisions, consider the legislative history, apply a "contextual" approach (selectively, as question 1 points out), decide whether a given interpretation of one provision would render another provision superfluous, and, once it concludes that neither provision settles the issue before the Court, create federal common law. Second, without the *Woodby* decision, it is doubtful that the students will be able to appreciate either the history or the policy behind the selection of this standard of review. And third, the Court's opinion contains some interesting discussion of how the standard of proof in deportation (now removal) cases should compare to those in expatriation and denaturalization cases.

Q1: The Court reasoned that the 1952 Act originally contained no section at all on the subject of judicial review. It is not significant, therefore, that Congress would consider a portion of INA § 242, which dealt with deportation procedure generally, to be as good a place as any in which to state a standard of judicial review. Its placement in that provision tells us nothing about Congress's intention on this issue.

Q2: The most obvious explanation is that the duplication was an oversight. To avoid it, Congress should simultaneously have repealed INA § 242(b)(4). It did not. The likely explanation is that this oversight occurred because INA § 106(a)(4) was just one of many subsections of section 106, all of which dealt with varying aspects of judicial review.

Q3: INS counsel should have asked the court to infer from that phrase that the standard in question goes to the proof at the deportation hearing, not to judicial review. It would be strange indeed for the Attorney General to issue a regulation specifying the standard by which a court should review the Attorney General's own determinations. It would be stranger still for Congress to authorize the Attorney General to issue such a regulation.

Q4: To prescribe "reasonable, substantial, and probative evidence" as the standard of *proof* in deportation cases would be truly extraordinary. Such a standard would not even rise to the level of a preponderance of the evidence, the standard familiar in most civil cases. An immigration judge in theory could find it much less likely than not that a person is deportable and still have to order removal simply because reasonable minds could differ. Given the stakes, such a standard is hard to imagine. Justice Clark in dissent suggests that adopting a "reasonable, substantial, and probative evidence" standard for the validity of the order is tantamount to requiring a preponderance of the evidence for the proof. That conclusion is a nonsequitur for which he offers no explanation.

Q5: To specify a standard of review equal to an (extremely non-demanding) standard of proof is theoretically possible, but that type of de novo review would be highly unusual. Ordinarily, (there are some exceptions), on questions of fact, the agency makes an original finding and the reviewing court simply determines the reasonableness of that finding. Again, the dissent might respond by suggesting that the standard of proof is a preponderance of the evidence, not just "reasonable, substantial, and probative evidence." See the analysis of question 4 above.

Q6: The cited passage, if anything, seems fairly clearly to support the majority opinion. An *appellate* court may not reverse simply because its judgment differs from that of the immigration judge. The requirement means only that a court may reverse when a reasonable person could not have reached the same conclusion as the immigration judge. This certainly sounds like judicial review. It also confirms that the standard of judicial review in these proceedings is narrower than the standard of proof.

Q7: The majority should also have considered the harm to society when a noncitizen who in fact is deportable is erroneously allowed to remain in the United States. The person could be dangerous, detrimental to the economy, etc. Then the court should have compared the magnitudes of the two opposing harms.

Q8: The phrase "dispel all doubt" implies even more than the phrase "beyond a reasonable doubt." The "clear, unequivocal, and convincing evidence" standard could not possibly mean that, especially since the Court in *Woodby* thought it was choosing a middle ground between the parties' opposing positions. In fact, it seems difficult to envision this standard as implying anything more than "clear and convincing evidence."

Q9:

(a) The Harlan formulation makes eminent sense even on the issue of burden of proof. If the party who has the burden of proof in fact satisfies the relevant substantive requirements but is unable to produce the evidence necessary to prove his or her case, then a social harm has occurred. Thus, the assignment of the burden of proof determines the relative frequency of error, just as the determination of the standard of proof does. Consequently, Justice Harlan might say, the decision as to burden of proof should similarly reflect the "comparative social disutility" of the various possible errors.

Another possibility is that the burden of proof should be assigned to whichever party would normally have easier access to the evidence. This approach would emphasize the probability of error rather than the gravity of error. In addition it would discourage parties from concealing evidence (or at least penalize them when they do).

A third possibility is to assign the burden of proof to whichever party seeks to alter the status quo.

(b) If Justice Harlan's approach is extended to the issue of burden of proof, the possible errors would include the removal of a noncitizen who in fact is not inadmissible or deportable, and the nonremoval of someone who is inadmissible or deportable. The *Woodby* decision reflects the implicit value judgment that the former kind of error is worse. Under that assumption, the burden of proof should be on ICE when it seeks to remove a person who is already present in the country, even if the charge is presence without admission. The same result would follow under the third approach listed above, since the government is the party that wishes to alter the status quo by removing a person who is already present.

Under the second approach, however, the burden should be placed on the noncitizen. When the charge is presence without admission, the person need only produce his or her entry papers. If the person really has been admitted, those should be easy to produce (unless they have been lost). It is harder for ICE to prove a negative -- i.e. that the person has not been admitted.

(c) The cases tend to fall into the third pattern. When the noncitizen seeks an affirmative benefit, such as admission or naturalization, he or she must generally prove eligibility. If the United States wants to take away a benefit, for example by deportation or by denaturalization, the government usually has the burden of proof. Whichever party wants a shift in the status quo ordinarily has the burden of proof, at least as to the prima facie case. (The opposite is true for affirmative defenses.)

A possible additional pattern might be the Harlan approach. Generally there will be more pain when a benefit is taken away (evicted from one's home in the United States, or stripped of United States citizenship) than when the benefit is denied in the first place (denied initial admission to the United States, or turned down for naturalization).

Problem 1 (page 743):

ICE would probably allege inadmissibility under INA § 212(a)(6)(A)(i) (presence without admission), knowing that it will be up to the noncitizen to prove a prior admission (or current admissibility). If he proves a prior lawful admission, and it has now expired, then ICE can always request permission to amend the Notice to Appear to allege deportability under INA § 237(a)(1)(B) (present in violation of INA) or, alternatively, INA § 237(a)(1)(C) (failed to comply with terms of nonimmigrant visa).

With respect to the statutory standard of proof: As just noted, the initial burden will be on the noncitizen. If that burden is not sustained, ICE will not have any standard of proof to worry about. If the burden is sustained, for example by evidence of a lawful admission as a nonimmigrant, then that evidence will reveal the expiration date. If the expiration date has passed, ICE will have proved by clear and convincing evidence that the person is within both of the deportability grounds mentioned above. (Of course, if the noncitizen shows that his or her original permission to remain has not expired, then ICE will not be able to meet its burden of proof. That is unlikely, since anyone who can easily demonstrate lawful presence would not normally remain mute, other than possibly as a high-stakes protest.)

The third question is hard to answer. As noted earlier, the courts have generally required the government to prove that the respondent is not a United States citizen before the respondent incurs the burden of proving anything. Again, however, it is possible a court would allow the immigration judge to infer the lack of citizenship from the person's silence. There is also, of course, the possibility that ICE can discover the person's identity from independent sources -- for example from an employer. In that case, possibly ICE will be able to track down the person's birth certificate and show a foreign birth.

4. Administrative Review: The Board of Immigration Appeals

Notes and Questions Following BIA Materials (page 752):

Q1: One reason the regulations prescribe summary dismissal when the appellant fails to specify the grounds for appeal on the notice of appeal is that, without a meaningful identification of the issues, the BIA would have to sift through the entire record itself to see whether anything was done improperly. The task of spotting errors in the original proceeding should be shouldered by the appellant or his or her lawyer, not the BIA. In addition, when a case is dismissed at that stage, EOIR avoids having to prepare a hearing transcript, and ICE avoids having to write a brief. In contrast, the purposes of single-member AWOs are to reduce the number of BIA members who will need to study the file, and to save the time that would have been required to write a reasoned opinion, in cases that seem unlikely to succeed.

The two measures also serve common objectives. At the most general level, they save government resources. They also permit speedier decisions, an important goal in itself but also a possible means to discourage baseless appeals by showing that they will not succeed in buying time. Note that the two sets of objectives are further related. Summary dismissal for failure to state adequate grounds for appeal in the notice of appeal might reflect an assumption that, if the lawyer did not identify the error, it is probably because there was none to identify. In such a case, the appeal might be regarded as lacking an arguable basis and thus the second ground might be present as well. A single-member summary dismissal without opinion might follow.

Q2: When the BIA summarily dismisses, the noncitizen loses both the opportunity to have the Board review the written transcript of the hearing and the opportunity to file a brief that could have set out the arguments more effectively. Also lost is the opportunity for independent, de novo review of the IJ's legal and discretionary determinations, as well as the (albeit narrower) "clearly erroneous" review of the findings of fact.

As for policy alternatives to summary dismissal in the insufficient notice of appeal cases:

a. The BIA could comb the record itself. But that is time-consuming and possibly futile. Arguably too, that is not the BIA's job.

b. The BIA could notify both the noncitizen and the lawyer (separately) and grant the noncitizen additional time in which to file a more meaningful notice of appeal, either pro se or through the same or a different lawyer. The disadvantage of this approach is that it delays the proceedings.

c. The BIA could order summary dismissal but stay the execution of the removal order for a short time to give the noncitizen an opportunity to move to reopen, possibly on grounds of ineffective assistance of counsel. The motion to reopen, of course, is subject to more stringent standards. And since ineffective assistance of counsel is now a ground for discipline, the first attorney might be less willing to admit ineffectiveness.

Q3: The first question is whether the specificity requirements are realistic without a hearing transcript. On the one hand, if the alleged error pertains to discretionary relief, it seems perfectly fair to require the appellant to specify whether the issue concerns eligibility or discretion or both. Those issues are separated fairly clearly at the hearing, and the decision of the immigration judge will be available at the time of the notice of appeal. The same conclusion can probably be reached with respect to the distinction between factual issues and legal issues. But requiring the attorney to research the case and supply authority for legal propositions within 30 days, and to provide the details of the factual arguments without yet having received a transcript, seem far less realistic.

As to the second question, the regulations could have taken the position that, as long as the notice of appeal and the brief together provide enough specificity to permit the BIA to decide the issue intelligently, the case would not be summarily dismissed. The problem is that the brief might be filed long after the notice of appeal. In the meantime, the appellant enjoys an automatic stay of removal. Probably, therefore, the idea is to weed out baseless appeals right away in order to remove any incentive to delay (and before resources are expended on a transcript).

Q5: As for one member versus three, there are several arguments to be made. (Some of the arguments below are made by Yale-Loehr in his congressional testimony, cited on page 745 n.58 of the casebook, at 9-10.)

a. With three members independently reviewing the record and the legal arguments, there is less chance of missing an error. (Some might argue that with three members, each one might wrongly assume the others are scrutinizing the record carefully; the counterargument would be that each member might pay closer attention in order to avoid the embarrassment of missing an obvious error that his or her colleagues pick up.)

b. With three members, the probability of ideological bias is reduced, since there is a greater chance that at least one of the members will lack the same bias.

c. There is benefit to deliberation.

d. Perhaps with three members the losing party and the public will be more likely to feel the process was taken seriously.

e. With only one member there is no possibility of a dissenting opinion to aid the thoughtful future development of the law.

f. As Yale-Loehr points out, 34% of the BIA caseload is pro se. In those cases the Board normally has no legal briefs to assist it, so the need for some exchange of ideas on the often complex legal questions can be especially great.

g. The elimination of judicial review accentuates the importance of investing the resources necessary to make the administrative appellate process fair and thorough; the interests are enormous.

As for the "without opinion" component:

a. To write a reasoned opinion, the Board has to consider the losing side's arguments with some care. Without an opinion, it is too easy for the member to affirm without serious consideration.

b. Without an opinion, no one can tell why the appellant's arguments were rejected. This leaves the appellant uncertain whether justice was done and frustrates his or her ability to write an effective brief for judicial review. For the same reasons, the reviewing court has little to go by, other than the opinion of the IJ, whose rationale might or might not have been the same as the BIA's.

c. When the IJ erred and the BIA failed to consider the claim of error adequately, the reviewing court has to spend time doing what the BIA should have done. This is not an academic point; as the materials in the next section of the coursebook illustrate, the result has been a spectacular increase in the caseloads of the courts of appeals.

Q8: The benefits and costs of decisional independence are laid out more fully in Stephen H. Legomsky, *Deportation and the War on Independence*, 91 Cornell L. Rev. 360 (2006). See also the analysis of question 3 in the Notes and Questions following the Rawitz excerpt in section B.1 above (concerning the willingness of the Chief IJ to supersede ex parte a decision that had been made by an IJ in open court).

As to the benefits:

a. The most obvious benefit is procedural fairness. Simply put, you want people who perform adjudicative functions to reach their decisions honestly. You want them to base their findings of fact solely on the evidence before them, and you want them to base their legal conclusions solely on their honest interpretations of all the relevant sources of law – not on the basis of which outcome they think is favored by the person who will be reappointing them. An adjudicator who fears that a particular outcome will jeopardize his or her job cannot possibly be disinterested.

b. Decisional independence is a way to protect unpopular individuals and minorities. In the particular case of review of congressional Acts for constitutionality, decisional independence helps protect those who aren't adequately protected by the political process.

c. Threats to decisional independence can create public *perceptions* of unfairness, which ultimately has to diminish public confidence in the legal system.

d. Independence also has implications for the equality interests that are at stake. To the extent possible, individuals who are similarly situated should be similarly treated. As it is, the indeterminacy of the law and the many differences among adjudicators already mean that to some unavoidable extent the outcome of any case will hinge on which adjudicator you happen to land. One's first reaction might be that, if anything, decisional independence is a centrifugal force, because it permits adjudicators to go off on their own. So the assumption might be that taking away decisional independence adds a centripetal, unifying force, because now everyone will gravitate toward the outcome preferred by the superior power. There is something to be said for that, but arguably it actually works the other way too. If adjudicators know that their decisions will affect their job security, they are likely to be influenced, but they will be influenced to varying degrees. How much they are influenced will depend on their varying personal circumstances, their own varying levels of integrity and courage, their own perceptions of how much their superiors are going to care about the particular issue before them, what reactions their superiors will have if they do care, and so forth. Thus, taking away decisional independence *possibly* increases the variance from one adjudicator to another.

e. Apart from all these sorts of fairness, equality, and public confidence concerns, there is a separation of powers concern. When independence evaporates, the same branch that decides on issues of arrest, detention, and prosecution effectively also controls the outcome of adjudication. The checks and balances that separation of powers principles were designed to provide are defeated to that extent.

As for the costs of decisional independence, independence is the flip side of political accountability. There is the issue of lawmaking by unelected officials who are not accountable either to the public at large or to other public officials, and there is the issue of judicial activism and the accompanying risk of political backlash. In addition, allowing the Attorney General to control the BIA decisionmaking permits an executive branch official (the Attorney General) to synthesize all of his or her immigration policymaking decisions – those made through rulemaking and those made through administrative adjudication – into a single coherent framework. The latter argument commands less weight now that the bulk of the Attorney General's immigration policymaking authority has been ceded to DHS.

5. Motions to Reopen or Reconsider

Question on Motions to Reopen or Reconsider (page 756):

The driving force behind the time and number limits on motions to reopen or reconsider removal orders is a congressional and Justice Department belief that such motions are too often filed solely to delay removal. The assumption has been that rarely will a noncitizen who has had the benefit of a full evidentiary hearing before an immigration judge and an appeal to the BIA (and the availability of judicial review) truly need to file two motions to reopen or reconsider. Apart from delaying removal while administrative authorities decide whether to stay the order pending consideration, the motions consume the time of ICE, the IJ's, the BIA, and the courts.

But the price is high. First, circumstances can easily change more than 90 days after the final administrative order or after a prior motion has been filed on a different issue. An absolute rule prohibiting noncitizens from calling the changed circumstances to the Board's attention could result in a miscarriage of justice. Since the stakes are high in removal cases, the degree of injustice could be large. What if the new circumstances give rise to the "exceptional and extremely unusual hardship" required for cancellation of removal, part B?

Second, it is not clear why so broad a rule is necessary. Stays are not mandatory. DHS has the power to remove a noncitizen while a motion to reopen or reconsider is pending, unless the IJ or the BIA, in their discretion, believe the motion is serious enough to warrant a stay. Moreover, as the students saw in the earlier materials on discipline of attorneys and accredited representatives, frivolous motions are already grounds for discipline. The prospect of discipline is arguably deterrent enough.

6. Judicial Review of Removal Orders

a. Petitions for Review

Most of the discussion in this subsection is intended as background reading. But the instructor might wish to discuss the judicial administration issues presented by the choice between district court review (with a right of appeal) and court of appeals review.

If every district court decision reviewing a given type of agency action were in fact appealed to the courts of appeals, then it would certainly be more efficient to assign the review function to the courts of appeals directly. District courts and courts of appeals ordinarily do the same things when they review agency action, and if the case will eventually end up in the court of appeals anyway, the district court might as well be spared the extra work. But as long as the appeal rate from district courts to courts of appeals in agency cases is less than 100%, different efficiency-related factors will have to be balanced.

One critical factor is that district court decisions are normally rendered by single judges, while court of appeals decisions are normally rendered by three-judge panels. The latter therefore require more judge time, though not three times as much because in most cases only one of the three judges writes the opinion. Also, it cannot be assumed that the time of one district judge has exactly the same value as the time of one court of appeals judge. To make that comparison, one would need to consider the caseloads, the time pressures, and the functions of both types of courts.

There is also a recurrent theme in the cases and commentary that district courts are better suited than courts of appeals to review those agency decisions that are reached in informal proceedings for which the administrative records are incomplete. The assumption seems to be that, when necessary, a district court can hold an evidentiary hearing more efficiently than a court of appeals can. That argument is problematic, however, because, as the Supreme Court observed in a nuclear regulatory case, *Florida Power and Light Co. v. Lorion*, 470 U.S. 729, 743-44, 105 S.Ct. 1598, 1606-07, 84 L.Ed.2d 643, 656 (1985), the reviewing court is not likely to hold such a hearing even when the existing record is inadequate. Rather, the reviewing court in that case would remand the case to the agency for further investigation or explanation. A court of appeals can issue a remand order just as easily as a district court can.

Finally, the sheer volume of a given type of case is sometimes so great that as a practical matter it would be impossible to assign the entire caseload to the courts of appeals. Sending social security disability cases to the district courts is probably the clearest example.

Another judicial administration (and practical immigration) topic for class discussion is the elimination of mandatory stays of removal pending the courts' decisions. Option (a) -- routinely denying stays without examining the merits of the underlying petitions and hoping DHS won't remove the petitioners before the courts can decide the cases -- seems unthinkable. It seems especially unthinkable in asylum cases, where there is little leeway for false negatives. Option (b), which is to grant stays routinely, was the practice under the analogous former provision for reviewing *exclusion* orders by habeas, without automatic statutory stays. The Ninth Circuit approach, which involves serious screening, is plausible, but whether busy judges and law clerks will really want to invest the time to look at the merits twice is questionable.

The instructor should emphasize to the class how sweeping the unreviewable categories are. The instructor might ask the students what they think should happen when noncitizens seek judicial review of administrative decisions that exercise a discretion conferred by *regulations* rather than by statute. This issue can arise, for example, when USCIS denies extensions of nonimmigrant stays, or permission for F-1 students to transfer schools, as well as in the contexts noted in the text - continuances and motions to reopen or reconsider. What if the only statutory authorization for the issuance of the particular regulation is itself within Title II of the INA? In such a case, can it be said that "the authority for" the decision or action "is specified under this title to be in the discretion of the Attorney General?"

As for those decisions that Title II clearly specifies to be in the discretion of the Attorney General, the text raises the question whether Congress really meant to bar review of all the prerequisites to relief, or just the discretion itself. The hypothetical about registry illustrates the point. What if registry is denied on statutory eligibility grounds (say, a finding of fact that the person entered the U.S. after 1972), rather than on discretionary grounds? Is the decision subject to judicial review? One could argue that it is. First, the literal language could be read as referring only to the "decision" to exercise discretion unfavorably. Second, the contrast between the wording of this bar and the analogous wording of other bars to judicial review mentioned in the text suggests that Congress deliberately confined the bar on review of Title II discretionary decisions to the discretion itself. The counter-argument would be that the natural reading of the phrase "decision or action" suggests a reference to the ultimate decision to deny relief, not to the rationale for that decision.

The instructor could also solicit the students' reactions to Congress's attempts to bar courts from reviewing agency regulations that are claimed to be ultra vires or even from reviewing the constitutionality of the statutory restrictions. These latter issues will also surface in the next subsection, however, and might be better handled in connection with the Henry Hart dialogue and the *St. Cyr* case.

b. Habeas Corpus

Question Following Hart Excerpt (page 775):

Maybe the answer depends on the type of challenge the person wishes to bring. First, does it matter whether the administrative decision is being challenged on factual, legal, or discretionary grounds? From the plenary power cases in chapter 2, it is clear that the Constitution doesn't require de novo trials of fact questions in article III courts (except for certain citizenship claims). Whether the Constitution requires judicial review of the *sufficiency* of the evidence to support a finding of deportability is a closer question. A fine analysis appears in Gerald L. Neuman, *The Constitutional Requirement of "Some Evidence,"* 25 San Diego L. Rev. 631 (1988).

Second, if the issue is one of law, does it matter whether the challenged conclusion rests on the Constitution or on some subordinate legal authority? The case for requiring judicial review of challenges to legal interpretations is strongest when the legal issue is itself one of constitutional stature. If Congress could insulate its own decisions from judicial review for constitutionality, then, as Hart suggests, the practical effect would be to neutralize the constitutional provision that is being challenged. (The counter-argument would be that Congress can interpret the Constitution just as well, and just as conscionably, as the courts can. But query whether Congress's political accountability makes such an assumption unrealistic.) The dangers of Congress immunizing *administrators'* decisions from judicial review seem even greater. As the students will see in item 4 of the Notes and Questions following *St. Cyr*, there seems to be an emerging judicial consensus that the federal courts retain habeas jurisdiction to review removal orders when "substantial constitutional questions" are presented. As a statutory matter, INA § 242(a)(2)(D), added by section 106(a)(1)(A)(iii) of the REAL ID Act, assures that the courts of appeals retain jurisdiction over all constitutional claims (not just "substantial" ones) and over other questions of law as well.

Can Congress constitutionally oust judicial jurisdiction to reject administrators' interpretations of the INA? Much of the Supreme Court case law allowing review of the constitutionality of congressional action rests on the premise, rooted in separation of powers, that it is the duty of the courts to say what the law is. The same rationale would seem to apply to nonconstitutional issues of law. Moreover, habeas jurisdiction has frequently been invoked to review the legality of executive action even when the underlying claims have been statutory rather than constitutional. But most habeas cases have themselves rested on interpretation of the statutory grant of habeas, rather than the constitutional grant. Whether the Constitution compels habeas review of administrators' statutory interpretation decisions (assuming the requisite liberty interest is at stake) is not yet clear.

INS v. St. Cyr (page 775):

NB: This decision was handed down before the REAL ID Act amended INA § 242(a)(2)(C) to bar statutory habeas expressly. Since the Court's statutory construction was heavily influenced by the constitutional implications of a contrary interpretation, however, the decision remains highly relevant.

St. Cyr, a citizen of Haiti, was admitted to the United States as an LPR. Ten years later, just before AEDPA or IIRIRA, he was convicted, upon a guilty plea, of selling a controlled substance. Under the then applicable law he would have been eligible for discretionary relief under former INA § 212(c). But AEDPA and IIRIRA repealed section 212(c), replaced it with cancellation of removal part A, and disqualified aggravated felons from the latter. He was found deportable for having been convicted of an aggravated felony and ineligible for cancellation of removal for the same reason. St. Cyr challenged his removal order by applying in federal district court for habeas corpus under 28 USC § 2241. His argument on the merits was that the 1996 amendments that preclude discretionary relief in situations like his were not meant to apply retroactively. The district court agreed and set aside his removal order. The Second Circuit affirmed. On petition of the INS, the Supreme Court granted certiorari.

The INS contended, first, that several provisions of the 1996 amendments eliminated the district courts' jurisdiction to hear the case, even via habeas. In a 5-4 decision, the Supreme Court rejected that argument. Relying on the strong presumption against repeal of habeas, the lack of an express statutory statement that habeas review is being eliminated, the practice of interpreting ambiguous statutory language to avoid substantial constitutional questions, the history of judicial reliance on habeas corpus in immigration cases, and the absence of an alternative forum for judicial review, the Court construed the 1996 amendments as not stripping the courts of the power to review removal orders via habeas corpus. In a portion of the opinion not excerpted in the book, the Court then proceeded to hold, on the merits, that noncitizens who pleaded guilty to crimes remained eligible for the discretionary relief that was available to them under then existing law. The four dissenters found the statutory preclusion of judicial review both clear and constitutional and thus would not have reached the merits of St. Cyr's claim.

Notes and Questions Following St. Cyr (page 784):

Q2: There are several arguable (and related) rationales:

a. The principle that only a clear statement by Congress will be construed as a repeal of habeas corpus is a specific application of the broader principle that courts should interpret statutes in ways that will avoid serious constitutional questions. The latter principle reflects several values. At least one of them does indeed relate to congressional intent. The assumption is that Congress itself does not want to violate the Constitution; thus, when the court locates a saving interpretation, it is most likely locating the interpretation that Congress intended. A separate rationale, however, is structural. Courts often accept legal fictions in order to serve overriding policy goals. Construing a statute to avoid constitutional doubts enables Congress to save face and staves off a confrontation between two branches of government.

b. Courts often see themselves as the ultimate (in the sense of final) guardian of individual rights. Attempts to eliminate access to court are therefore inherently unnerving. Habeas corpus thus occupies an especially important place in the pantheon of constitutional safeguards; it is a bulwark between the individual and the government. (The theory of judicial review is considered more generally at the conclusion of this section.)

Q3: New INA § 242(a)(2)(D), a result of the REAL ID Act, expressly exempts "questions of law" from the constraints of subsections B and C of INA § 242(a)(2). The issue is whether "question of law" is broad enough to embrace mixed questions of law and fact. In one sense, every question that comes before the appellate courts – even the questions of whether the evidence supports the findings of fact and whether discretion was abused – are questions of law. But that expansive an interpretation of subsection (D) would effectively read subsections A, B, and C off the books. Moreover, the degree of judgment required to apply broad statutory language to specific facts can make the exercise tantamount to discretion – a notion that courts have implicitly recognized when characterizing the hardship determinations in cancellation of removal cases as discretionary. It is doubtful, therefore, that Congress intended to allow review of such claims in petitions for review.

If that conclusion is right, then *statutory* habeas under 28 USC § 2241 is similarly precluded. The REAL ID Act is clear on one thing: Whenever INA § 242 bars review of a particular decision by way of petition for review, it means to bar 2241 review of that same decision. Either a decision is one that may no longer be challenged in a petition for review, in which case 2241 review is also barred, or the decision *may* be the subject of a petition for review, in which case there is no need for 2241 review. Either way, 2241 now seems unavailable as a means for challenging orders of removal.

The constitutional question then becomes crucial. On the one hand, the function of habeas corpus is to guarantee some vehicle to test the legality of a governmental restraint on liberty. If an agency's application of law to fact fails to meet minimum legal standards as defined by courts, then there is arguably as much reason for a court to assert habeas jurisdiction as there would be if the question were one of "pure law." On the other hand, the broader the statutory language, the more analytically difficult it becomes to distinguish its application to the facts from the more explicit brand of discretion also familiar in the administrative context.

Q4: As a matter of statutory interpretation, INA § 242(a)(2)(C) expressly deprives the courts of the jurisdiction to review crime-related removal orders. Section 242(a)(2)(D) exempts questions of law from that bar. If the issue of whether there is substantial evidence (or "some" evidence) were to be characterized as one of "law" for purposes of 242(a)(2)(D), then all that would remain of 242(a)(2)(C) would be a bar on discretionary decisions, and those decisions are already essentially nonreviewable under 242(a)(2)(B). Such an interpretation would emasculate section 242(a)(2(C).

That raises the constitutional issue. In the text that accompanies footnote 27, the Court says that in the pre-1952 habeas cases "courts generally did not review factual determinations made by the Executive." It cited *Vajtauer* as a qualifier, noting that for due process purposes courts did review to make sure there was "some" evidence to support the order. Whether a modern court, post-APA but also post-IIRIRA and post-REAL ID Act, would draw the habeas line between "no evidence" and "substantial evidence" in the light of *St. Cyr* is difficult to say.

Q5: Justice Scalia's assumption is probably right. One important element in the reasoning of the majority opinion was that, without habeas, INA § 242(a)(2)(C) would bar all judicial review of removal orders that are based on criminal convictions. The same is not generally true of other noncitizens ordered removed.

One other possible reason to limit habeas to those deportable noncitizens whose removal orders are based on criminal convictions concerns detention. As discussed earlier, noncitizens who are charged with being deportable on most criminal grounds are subject to mandatory detention from the beginning of the proceedings until the execution of the removal order (or termination of proceedings). Given both the deprivation of liberty and the financial cost to the taxpayer, it makes sense to use habeas to get a speedy resolution one way or the other. Nonetheless, perhaps this factor does not really distinguish criminal offenders, because detention is also mandatory for all noncitizens from the time of the removal order (regardless of ground) until actual removal.

As to the third question, delay is beneficial to some, but those people who are removable on the crime-related grounds to which section 242(a)(2)(C) applies are usually in detention. For them, delay just means more time behind bars. As for the second bite at the apple, it must be remembered that *either* side may appeal a district court habeas decision to the court of appeals. In habeas cases, therefore, the *government* also gets two bites at the apple.

Q6: Probably so. It sounds as if the majority will not recognize a statutory repeal of habeas, at least when repeal would leave the affected individuals with no means to test the legality of the order in court, unless Congress explicitly refers to "habeas corpus" or to "28 USC § 2241." It is difficult to imagine how Congress could have made its intent clearer without using those words. But that doesn't mean the majority got it wrong. Since

Congress is now (and arguably was previously) on notice that magic words are necessary to repeal habeas, it could easily have made its will known if repealing habeas was truly what it intended. In the REAL ID Act, Congress has now done so. (Whether a statute so construed leaves any constitutional gaps is another question.)

Q8: The Court could uphold the statute, since all it decided in *St. Cyr* was that a "serious" constitutional issue was presented. But for the 242(a)(2)(D) exemption, however, it seems likely, though not inevitable, that the same five Justices would find a violation of the suspension clause. At any rate the precarious 5-4 decision is always vulnerable to a change in the composition of the Court; a new Justice less enamored of habeas corpus (or immigrants) could observe that *St. Cyr* did not decide the constitutional question and could then conclude that the habeas preclusion is constitutional. With the 242(a)(2)(D) exemption, the remaining gaps for those noncitizens who are removable on criminal grounds are claims that rest on findings of fact, perhaps mixed questions of law and fact, and the exercise of discretion. As discussed in *St. Cyr*, it is not yet clear whether the Constitution guarantees judicial review in those cases.

Q9: On the face of it, that argument sounds odd. A permanent abolition of the writ would be more intrusive than a temporary suspension; thus, it seems unlikely that the framers intended such a result. Justice Scalia's argument, however, is that the framers feared most the selective deprivation of the writ to unpopular persons or classes, and that a wholesale elimination (while capable of oppressing) was not the particular evil at which the suspension clause was aimed.

Q10: Henry Hart argues that Congress cannot constitutionally immunize its own actions from constitutional review. Otherwise, the practical effect would be to neutralize the constitutional provision that is being challenged. (The counter-argument would be that Congress can interpret the Constitution just as well, and just as conscionably, as the courts can. But query whether Congress's political accountability makes such an assumption unrealistic.) At any rate, he argues, the Supreme Court has historically invoked habeas corpus to review deportation orders – long before Congress had provided any specific authority for judicial review of deportation.

Justice Scalia might accept Hart's position insofar as it applies to *constitutional* arguments. Justice Scalia clearly does not accept, however, that habeas is constitutionally required in cases where the challenge to the removal order is on nonconstitutional grounds (as in *St. Cyr*), particularly if the challenge is to a denial of discretionary relief.

Q11: At the same time that the Supreme Court was inventing and solidifying the plenary power doctrine, it was routinely utilizing habeas corpus to review deportation orders, at least when the challenges were based on nonconstitutional grounds and sometimes even when they were based on constitutional grounds. And all this happened without any affirmative authorization of judicial review from Congress. But that is a very different matter from proceeding in the face of an affirmative congressional attempt to bar habeas.

Perhaps, like *Chadha*, the present case reflects (and augurs) judicial discomfort with anything that erodes the courts' role in the constitutional scheme of separation of powers. It might be that this is just another chink in the plenary power doctrine – another limitation on the special judicial deference owed to Congress in immigration matters. As the material at the end of chapter 2 suggests, however, the number of qualifications to the plenary power doctrine is growing rapidly. Perhaps "PPD-lite"(the term used in the text) is taking hold, and the expanding catalog of exceptions to the PPD is becoming more important than the PPD itself.

c. Other Strategies

This is just background reading.

d. Consolidating Reviewable Claims

The first two editions of the coursebook included a line of cases in which the courts built and refined a set of criteria for determining which ancillary orders were reviewable only by petition for review. Apart from their historic value, these cases were a wonderful vehicle for illustrating the common law method and for practicing synthesis skills. In the wake of IIRIRA and other intervening developments, however, too much of this case law has become dated. Despite its pedagogical value, therefore, this material was deleted from the third edition on. Teachers who wish to continue teaching it will need to photocopy it from the second edition (1997).

e. The Theory and the Consequences of Judicial Review

<u>Question on page 790:</u>

The benefits and the costs are summarized in the cited article. Most of the benefits are familiar:

Some benefits fit within the category of correcting errors. The courts are a check on fallible agency officials. This is the benefit that first comes to mind for most students. They might cite cases they have read that illustrate the injustices that judicial review can prevent. The study by Schuck & Wang demonstrates that that benefit is real, not theoretical.

The instructor might ask the students how, exactly, judicial review helps avoid errors. If the judge's view differs from that of the agency official, what reason is there to believe that the judge is right and the official was wrong, rather than vice-versa?

As to that, one can cite the advantages that article III judges inherently possess. First, they are independent. As the prior readings illustrated, there is now serious doubt as to the decisional independence of at least the BIA members (see subsection 4 above) and even some question as to the freedom enjoyed by immigration judges (recall the adventures of Judge Van Wyke, on pages 665-68 above.) Second, judges provide the appearance of independence, which is vital to bolstering public confidence in the legal system. Third, judges are generalists; they can draw on a broader legal perspective and on analogies in other areas of law. Fourth, when courts review the decisions of administrative agencies, the courts have access to the agencies' written decisions, which contain the insights of a specialist tribunal. The court can then combine the product of specialist and generalist thinking (unlike the administrative tribunal, which will not have had the benefit of the court's thinking).

Other benefits might be classed under the heading of creating law for the future. By publishing precedential decisions, judges guide public officials and private practitioners alike. Administrative tribunals, of course, also can and do publish useful precedential decisions. But there is danger in making a single tribunal, which might have a particular ideological leaning, solely responsible for the creation of an entire body of case law. Judicial review spreads this huge power among many courts. (The practice of according deference to the administrative tribunal reduces the impact of this factor.)

Finally, just the prospect of judicial review furnishes an incentive for administrative officials to approach their cases thoughtfully, carefully, and with due regard to law.

As for costs:

Federal judges, being unelected and tenured for life, are not politically accountable (except to the extent they could be impeached for what Congress decides is misbehavior). BIA members, as just noted, must now consider the policy preferences of the Attorney General. It is not clear which way this factor cuts; accountability and independence are just two sides of the same coin.

One cost of judicial review is that it permits a nonspecialist to reverse the decision of a specialist. Whether that is good or bad depends partly on one's views of the pros and cons of specialized decisionmaking. In any case, as noted earlier, specialist insights can be transmitted through a written opinion. When they are, generalist judges are able to benefit from them.

Judicial review also sacrifices uniformity. Consistency is more likely to emerge from a single decisionmaker than from a network of courts. Of course, the flip side of administrative agency consistency is undue concentration of power in a single individual or small group. Moreover, generalist judges can actually achieve greater consistency in another sense -- locating fundamental principles that unite the various specialty areas.

Fourth, in the context of deportation, judicial review further delays the person's actual removal. Courts could minimize delay by routinely denying stays pending decisions, but the cost would be an increased rate of erroneous deportations. Given the stakes for the individuals, that price would be unacceptable.

Fifth, judicial review costs money. Judges, government attorneys, and other publicly funded personnel have to be paid.

SECTION C. A SIMULATED REMOVAL HEARING

This exercise has several purposes: Primarily, it immerses students in the procedure and mechanics of a removal hearing. Secondarily, it engages them in substantive and strategic issues in a way that exposure to abstract judicial opinions cannot. By involving the students in the conduct of the hearing, the exercise hopefully will make the issues from the preceding material come alive. Additionally, the exercise aims to develop students' abilities to convert analysis into advocacy, improve students' oral communication skills, enhance their understanding of the atmosphere of a removal hearing, and hone a skill frequently overlooked in law school -- factual analysis. In the process, it provides a review of some of the deportability grounds and waiver provisions studied in chapters 7 and 8. Depending on the format that the instructor chooses, the exercise can also supply experience in cooperative teamwork.

The instructor will have a good deal of flexibility. The logistical options include these:

(1) Research or Self-Contained? The exercise is meant to be self-contained; no student research is required. (But coverage of certain previous parts of this book is assumed -- see below). The instructor could convert the exercise into a research assignment simply by instructing the students to research any legal issues raised by the facts.

(2) Assignments and Amount of Class Time. If absolutely necessary, the hearing could be compressed into a single 50-minute class session. In that time frame, however, the hearing would be quite rushed. In 100 minutes, the hearing can be completed at a more comfortable pace with enough time left over for the instructor to provide a 10-15 minute critique at the end. One recommended approach is to devote the first hour to the immigration judge's preliminary tasks (see below) and the deportability segment of the case, and the

second hour to the affirmative relief segment, the immigration judge's oral decision, and (optionally) a critique.

If the class ordinarily meets in 50-minute sessions, one possible assignment sequence would be this: Have the students read the entire exercise at their leisure, but at any rate before the class immediately preceding the one designated for the actual hearing. The instructor could devote a portion of that class (i.e., the one before the hearing class) to providing guidance and answering questions about the assignment. At this class the instructor could divide the students into two groups: ICE trial attorneys and counsel for Mr. Godasse. Each student's assignment for the next class (i.e., the one in which the hearing begins) could then be to prepare his or her case. The required preparation would include making a list of the documents the student would offer as evidence, a list of the witnesses he or she would call, and an outline of the questions he or she would ask of those witnesses.

In selecting the student lawyers, the instructor has several options. Having required each student to prepare the case, the instructor could call one student from each side to conduct the hearing (either a volunteer or a conscript). Or the instructor could, well before the date of the hearing, select two or more students from each side (again, either volunteers or conscripts) to work as teams, letting them allocate the work between them as they wish. Since there will be exactly two witnesses during each phase, the instructor might suggest that each student examine one witness (with the understanding that co-counsel could add questions as the testimony progresses).

There are tradeoffs involved. Advance selection enhances the preparation levels and therefore the quality of the hearing. The down side of advance selection is that it reduces the incentive for the non-participating students to prepare carefully. If time permits, the instructor at the close of the hearing could invite non-participating students to volunteer additional questions or evidence or make other comments about what they would have done differently. The instructor could also have the class deliberate and decide the case in lieu of a decision by the immigration judge (see immigration judge instructions below).

(3) Assigning the Players. The hearing requires at least three players other than opposing counsel: the respondent (Arnaud Godasse); ICE agent Leslie Kinney (first name gender-neutral so that the instructor may choose either a male or a female); and Elizabeth Des Champs. An interpreter for Des Champs is optional. The instructor would normally be the immigration judge (see below).

Some instructors might wish to use students from the class to play some or all of these roles. The advantage of doing so is to broaden the class participation. Better, if possible, is to use strangers as witnesses. Students are sometimes less serious when they cross-examine their classmates. The presence of strangers makes the hearing seem more real. And strangers tend to add an element of productive tension.

Instructors might simply ask their own colleagues or other personal friends to play the roles of the witnesses. If the course is being taught at a University that has a drama department, drama students eager to volunteer are usually easy to find. To add a touch of realism, the instructor can try to dredge up two-French-speaking people (from the French Department or elsewhere): one, a female, to be Elizabeth Des Champs and to testify in French, and the other to interpret. Students enjoy that extra feature, which often helps them forget that this exercise is a simulation. If the instructor prefers, however, the hearing can be conducted entirely in English. Des Champs can be fluent in English, and Godasse will be testifying in English in any event. He is a doctoral candidate in literature at an American university and has made several articulate statements to others in English.

There is one other scheduling consideration. If, as recommended, the instructor elects to spread the hearing over two class hours (the first for deportability and the second for relief), every witness except one will be able to complete his or her work in a single session. ICE agent Kinney is needed only for the deportability segment; Elizabeth Des Champs and her optional interpreter are needed only for the relief segment. The one exception is Godasse himself, who will present testimony relevant to both issues. The actor who plays Godasse will therefore need to appear at both sessions.

Whoever plays the witnesses will require some minimal instruction. Written witness instructions are included below. To avoid the problem of witnesses failing to show up on the date of the hearing, it is also wise to select in advance, and to give copies of the witness instructions to, one student backup for each witness role.

As for the immigration judge: It is possible to select a student or an actor for this role as well, but this is not recommended. The exercise works best when the instructor either (a) plays this role herself or himself, or (b) recruits a real immigration judge or immigration lawyer to play this part.

(4) Recording the Hearing. The immigration judge might record the hearing on a tape recorder that he or she can stop and re-start at will. See 8 CFR § 1240.9 (2008). A tape recorder can enhance realism, sustain the students' seriousness level, and enable interested students (especially those who served as counsel) to hear themselves later.

Some instructors might like to videotape the hearing. Interested students (again, especially those who played the roles of counsel) could watch and learn from the exercise. The instructor could also play back portions of the video to the class as part of a critique, and could play it to the following year's class before their hearing date to give them a sense of what is expected.

(5) Formality Level. The instructor should decide on the desired formality level. The classroom could be arranged in the format of an actual immigration court, which today contains a raised dais for the immigration judge and two conference tables -- one for the respondent and his or her counsel, and one for the ICE trial attorney. The immigration judge could wear a robe as is now the practice (a plain graduation gown works fine) or could dress more casually.

(6) Optional Extra: BIA Brief. After the hearing, an instructor who wants to continue with this problem could draft and distribute to the class a written opinion of the immigration judge (and, optionally, a transcript of the tape recording of the hearing). If a written opinion is distributed, it should not contain great detail. The object is to make the students spot the issues and articulate the arguments; also, anything you distribute will inevitably make its way to future generations of students, thus affecting the preparation for future mock hearings. Half the students could represent the losing side and draft appellate briefs to the BIA. After those briefs are in, the other half could draft briefs in response.

(7) Prior Coverage. This exercise assumes coverage of the basic parts of chapters 7-9. It is especially desirable that the students have previously read the material on the mechanics of a removal hearing (section A.3 of this chapter). Although the intent requirements for F-1 student status are relevant and important, the students need not have covered any of chapter 4 to do this exercise. If they have not studied the portions of chapter 4 that deal with F-1 status (chapter 4, § B.1) and Intent to Remain Permanently (chapter 4, § F.1), then the instructor should tell them to read INA § 101(a)(15)(F) (spelling out the requirements for student status). The coursebook's introduction to this simulation exercise also includes a one-paragraph summary of the rules on duration of student stays. The instructor should also explain the doctrine of dual intent, which provides that it is permissible for a nonimmigrant to enter the United States with the following state of mind: "I might some day apply for lawful permanent residence and remain permanently *if it is granted*. But I intend to leave upon expiration of my authorized stay if permanent residence is not granted."

OUTLINE OF ISSUES AND STRATEGY

A. As to deportability: All the charges rest ultimately on whether, at some point, Godasse fraudulently concealed an intent to remain permanently.

1. If he had such an intent *at the time he procured his original F-1 visa*, then he arguably lied when he stated (see Document C, question 24) that he planned to stay in the United States only four years. Thus he would be deportable under INA § 237(a)(1)(A) as having entered while inadmissible under section 212(a)(6)(C)(i) (procured visa by fraud). Whether he lied is a

question of fact. Opposing counsel should ask him about the 2d paragraph of his August 6, 2010 statement (Document A), concerning why he sought an F-1 visa rather than an immigrant visa. Contrary inferences are possible. The ICE trial attorney should stress Godasse's comments about (a) an F-1 visa being quicker than an immigrant visa and (b) F-1 visas being renewable. Godasse's counsel should emphasize Godasse's comment about wanting to return to university to study American literature. His later extensions of stay are also relevant to, though obviously not dispositive of, his intent at the time he procured his original visa. In arguing the fact question, counsel should keep in mind the substantive law of dual intent (see above). Note that a section 237(a)(1)(H) defense is unavailable because Godasse never had an *immigrant* visa.

Note: If the IJ finds that Godasse fraudulently intended all along to remain permanently in the United States, then in a real case the government could lodge an additional inadmissibility charge under INA § 212(a)(7)(A) (no valid immigrant visa). Doing so would not add anything to the government's case, but a compassionate trial attorney might be willing to do so to avoid the permanent inadmissibility that removal under section 212(a)(6)(C)(i) would entail. (For classroom purposes, lodging of additional charges should probably not be permitted.) Thanks are due to Professor Huyen Pham for spotting the 212(a)(7)(A) possibility.

2. If Godasse intended to remain permanently *at the time he was admitted at a port of entry*, the analysis is roughly the same as above because section 212(a)(6)(C)(i) also covers fraudulent admissions. (He was admitted just two days after obtaining a visa; it is unlikely his intentions changed greatly during that interval).

3. If Godasse intended to remain permanently *at the time he obtained his extension of stay in May 2010*, then the extension was invalid because, under 8 CFR § 214.1(a)(3)(ii) (2008), an extension of an F-1 stay requires the person to "agree to depart the United States at the expiration of his or her authorized period of admission or extension . . ." ICE would argue that he could not truly have agreed to depart at the expiration of his extension if all along he was planning to remain in the United States permanently. And if the extension was invalid, then as soon as the existing authorization of stay expired (May 30, 2010), Godasse would have no lawful permission to remain and presumably would be deportable under INA § 237(a)(1)(B) ("present in the United States in violation of this Act").

As for the fact question of Godasse's intent at the time he obtained an extension of stay, students should question both him and ICE agent Kinney about the meaning of Godasse's statement at Jason's Bar and Grill and about his subsequent explanation of it. (See Document A.) Godasse claims he was simply emphasizing how happy he was to be here. Agent Kinney will testify that he or she interpreted Godasse's remarks more cynically. Godasse's references to "manag[ing] to keep my F-1 alive for 10 years so far" and to planning to "keep extending it until they throw me out" bolster Agent Kinney's interpretation. If Godasse's comment about "the geniuses at ICE" was sarcastic, the inference might be that he has outwitted them concerning his intentions. Godasse claims, however, that his comment was not sarcastic and that he truly meant to bestow a compliment. (This seems hard to believe.)

There is also the fact that Alliance Francaise developed an interest in hiring Godasse as a permanent employee even before he had applied for an extension of his temporary stay, and actually applied for labor certification for him only four days after he had requested the extension. Did Godasse change his intention during these periods? Is this another case of dual intent? What do these events say about Godasse's intentions? Counsel could question Godasse as to (a) *dual* intent; (b) *changing* intentions; and (c) whether Alliance Francaise applied for labor certification with Godasse's blessing.

What about the fact that Godasse had been dating an American woman? Godasse's counsel might ask Godasse whether she was a United States citizen. If she was, then marriage to her would have enabled Godasse to become a permanent resident. That they did not marry would seem odd if, as ICE claims, his intent all along had been to stay permanently. Perhaps opposing counsel will ask Godasse whether the decision to forego or defer marriage was his, hers, or mutual.

Occasionally a student asks why ICE didn't simply allege that his misrepresentation at the time he applied for the last extension rendered him inadmissible under INA § 212(a)(6)(C)(i) (obtained benefit by misrepresentation). ICE did, after all, make analogous allegations with respect to his representations at both the time of his original visa application and the time of his original admission. But even if ICE could establish inadmissibility, the inadmissibility would not be a ground for deportability under INA § 237(a)(1)(A) because it did not occur at or before his entry into the United States.

B. As to discretionary relief:

1. Godasse will apply for cancellation of removal, part B, under INA § 240A(b). See Documents D and E. Ten years continuous physical presence is not a problem, because he arrived on August 4, 2000, and the Notice to Appear was served on August 7, 2010.) But several other issues arise:

a. Exceptional and extremely unusual hardship? As a result of IIRIRA, the hardship to Godasse himself will not suffice; only the hardship to Paul, Godasse's United States citizen son, will count. Godasse will have to establish that, if he himself is removed to Switzerland, Paul will need to accompany him and will suffer exceptional and extremely unusual hardship. INA §

240A(b)(1)(D). If Godasse's life is really endangered, then of course Paul will suffer hardship as well -- both the loss of his father if the threat materializes and the constant fear, stress, and insecurity from the omnipresent danger. The latter hardship will occur even if Godasse is not endangered but believes he is. If this were an actual case, there would be a difficult strategic decision here. Should Godasse call Monique's sister, Elizabeth, as a witness? She will support Godasse's statement about her father's intention to kill Godasse; without her confirmation, the immigration judge might dismiss Godasse's story as self-serving or even far-fetched. But Elizabeth will also testify that she does not believe Godasse's denial of paternity. That testimony could damage not only Godasse's ability to establish the good moral character required for cancellation of removal and for voluntary departure (see below), but also his chances of obtaining the favorable exercise of discretion required for all the affirmative relief he seeks. These strategic questions are moot in this exercise, however, because the ground rules given to the students require Godasse's counsel to call Elizabeth Des Champs as a witness.

b. Good moral character for the past ten years? Three issues:

i. At the time Godasse applied for his 2010 extension of stay, he had to agree to depart the United States at the expiration of his authorized stay. Lingering doubts about the truthfulness of that representation, even though not rising to the level of "clear and convincing evidence," might dissuade an IJ from finding Godasse has good moral character. (Any alleged misrepresentations at the visa or admission stages were more than ten years ago.)

Both Huyen Pham and David Hudson spotted another sub-issue. If the immigration judge found Godasse removable, then the IJ must have found that his earlier representations were fraudulent. Since Godasse would have been asked about those statements at the removal hearing, he presumably denied having made fraudulent statements. This means Godasse most likely gave "false testimony" at the hearing itself. Under INA § 101(f)(6), that false testimony should preclude "good moral character." In other words, he lied about lieing. (Had he conceded deportability, this issue would not have arisen. Of course, he would not want to concede deportability if he thought that his earlier statements were unlikely to be found fraudulent.)

ii. Did he impregnate Monique? He claims he did not. If he did, does he honestly believe he did not? This is relevant to whether his failure to pay child support should be held against him on the issue of character. At any rate, he will argue, Monique has never requested support.

iii. He admits to having fathered a different child, Paul, out of wedlock and not getting married. It seems doubtful, however, that the fathering of the child would be enough to preclude good moral character (assuming the mother was not married to someone else at the time). Nor do we know whose decision it was to forego or defer marriage or the reasons for that decision.

c. If Godasse is found statutorily eligible for cancellation, should discretion be exercised in his favor? Many of the factors relevant to various prerequisites will also be relevant here.

2. If the IJ finds Godasse deportable and denies cancellation, Godasse should request voluntary departure under INA § 240B(b). His problems will be:

a. Good moral character for the past 5 years? Same analysis as for cancellation.

b. Discretion? The same factors are in place, but the balancing is different because the immigration judge would be doing much less for Godasse (allowing him to leave voluntarily) than in cancellation (which entails granting LPR status).

3. At the beginning of the hearing the immigration judge will have asked Godasse to designate the country to which he would prefer to be removed. Under INA § 241(b)(2)(A), Godasse need not designate Switzerland. Note, however, that under section 241(b)(2)(B) Godasse may not designate a country contiguous to the United States. Moreover, the designated country might refuse admission, in which case the immigration judge may choose from a list of other possibilities.

SUMMARY OF RELEVANT DATES

August 6, 1970	Godasse born.
April 2000	Monique becomes pregnant.
August 1, 2000	Godasse applies for student visa.

August 2, 2000	Obtains student visa.
August 4, 2000	Admitted to United States and enrolls at University of Texas (authorized to remain for duration of status).
May 30, 2004	Receives bachelors degree and officially enrolls in Ph.D. program. University extends his stay and notifies him and former INS that his expected completion date is May 30, 2008.
April 15, 2008	Requests another extension.
April 18, 2008	Extension granted. Expected completion date May 30, 2010.
October 2008	Paul is born.
May 15, 2010	Applies to University for third extension.
May 19, 2010	Alliance Francaise applies to DOL for labor certification.
May 21, 2010	Third extension granted. Expected completion date May 30, 2012.
August 6, 2010	Godasse is arrested and interrogated.
August 7, 2010	ICE issues Notice to Appear.
Sept. 15, 2010	Master calendar hearing.
Sept. 24, 2010	DOL denies labor certification.
Oct. 10, 2010	Removal hearing.

INSTRUCTING THE PLAYERS

Each of the three witnesses -- Godasse, Kinney, and Elizabeth Des Champs -- will need his or her own individualized "Witness Instructions." So, too, will the interpreter (if one is used). Included in the pages that follow are witness instructions that the instructor can photocopy and distribute to the witnesses.

In addition to giving each witness his or her individualized Witness

Instructions, Godasse will need photocopies of Documents A, D, and E, and Kinney will need document A. Neither Des Champs nor her optional interpreter will need any other papers.

Optionally, the instructor can ask the actor who plays Godasse whether it would be all right for the students who will be playing the roles of his attorneys to consult with him before the hearing. The same can be done with immigration inspector Kinney and the students representing ICE. It would then be up to the students whether to accept the invitation.

The instructor should make sure the witnesses are clear as to exactly where and when they are needed, and should emphasize that it is critical for them to be there on time. It is safest to confirm with the witnesses a day or two before their appearance and arrange for student backups just in case.

WITNESS INSTRUCTIONS FOR ARNAUD GODASSE

The project in which you are taking part is a mock hearing for removing a foreign student from the United States (formerly called a deportation hearing). Students enrolled in a course on immigration law will play the parts of the opposing lawyers. Some of them will represent a federal government agency called "Immigration and Customs Enforcement," or ICE. They will be trying to have the foreign student, a fictional Swiss national named Arnaud Marie Godasse, sent back to Switzerland. Other students will be the lawyers for Godasse; they will try to save him. The official who presides over the hearing is called an immigration judge.

You will be playing the part of Godasse. One of the (student) lawyers will call you as a witness. The Immigration judge will place you under oath, and the opposing student lawyers will take turns asking you questions. The immigration judge might occasionally ask you an additional question.

Godasse came to the United States in 2000, on a student visa, to do a bachelor's degree in American literature at the University of Texas. He completed his bachelor's degree in the usual four years, graduating in May 2004. On graduation day he enrolled in the University's Ph.D program in American literature, simultaneously obtaining a 4-year extension (to May 30, 2008) of his student visa. His doctoral work has been progressing slowly. Although he completed the required coursework in three years, his dissertation has been taking much longer than expected. "Conceptual problems" required him to modify his research topic. As a result he had to request two additional extensions. In May 2008 the University extended his stay to May 30, 2010. In May 2010, the University again extended his stay, this time to May 30, 2012.

There is one thing you need to know about immigration law. In order to be admitted to the United States as a foreign student, one must intend to leave the United States when his or her authorized stay expires. A person whose intention all along is to remain permanently in the United States is ineligible for a student visa. The same is true when a foreign student who is already here wishes to <u>extend</u> his or her authorized stay. If, at the time the person applies for an extension, his or her true intent is to remain permanently, then the extension is not supposed to be granted. If ICE eventually discovers that a foreign student intended, either at the time of the original entry or at the time of the extension, to remain permanently, then that student can be sent home. That is what Godasse is trying to avoid.

Godasse has done several things to cast suspicion upon himself. On August 6, 2010, while celebrating his fortieth birthday by drinking with friends at a place called Jason's Bar and Grill, Godasse made some indiscreet remarks that were overheard by an immigration officer named Leslie Kinney. Kinney arrested Godasse, brought him to ICE headquarters, read him his rights, and questioned him. Godasse, explaining the circumstances that had prompted him to come to the United States to study, made some comments to Kinney that created additional uncertainty about whether he had intended to remain permanently all along. Godasse also stated that, a few weeks before he applied for an extension of his student stay, the Alliance Francaise had expressed interest in hiring him for a permanent position. Finally, he said that, just four days after he requested the extension, the Alliance started the process of applying for his permanent residence. Those facts raise a question of whether Godasse intended to remain permanently even as he was applying for the extension; if he did, then he was ineligible for that extension. Kinney typed up a statement embodying everything Godasse had said. Kinney then asked Godasse to read it and, if it was accurate, to sign it. Godasse did so.

Under the immigration laws, some people who are deportable may nonetheless apply to the immigration judge for various kinds of discretionary relief. Godasse's lawyer will be doing that in this case. He or she will apply for a remedy called "cancellation of removal." To receive it, Godasse must persuade the immigration judge that Godasse is an honest person of good moral character and that deportation would cause "exceptional and extremely unusual" hardship to Godasse's son, Paul, who is a U.S. citizen. To prove the latter, Godasse's lawyer will present to the immigration judge an affidavit, signed by Godasse, that tells Godasse's story about certain dangers Godasse will face if sent back to Switzerland and the resulting hardships for Paul.

To prepare for your part, you should read the three attachments. The first is a copy of what you (Godasse) said to Kinney at ICE headquarters. The second is the standardized form that your lawyer had to fill out in order to apply for cancellation of removal. It contains some biographical data about you. And the third is the affidavit in which you describe the hardships that will occur if you are sent back to Switzerland. No one will expect you to remember exact dates off the top of your head, or to testify in technical terms. As long as you are reasonably informed about the character you are playing, you will do fine and will be performing a real service.

Finally, please try to be as believable as you can. You should avoid outlandish answers or a flamboyant persona. Don't be afraid to admit that you don't know the answer to a particular question or to give a vague answer occasionally. (In fact, vague answers can liven up the hearing, since the student who is questioning you will have to try to pin you down.) Occasionally, also, you might purposely either misunderstand a question or give an unresponsive answer, just as witnesses often do in real life. Above all, enjoy your performance. The instructor and the students alike will be extremely grateful for the time and effort you are giving them.

WITNESS INSTRUCTIONS FOR LESLIE KINNEY

The project in which you are taking part is a mock hearing for removing a foreign student from the United States (formerly called a deportation hearing). Students enrolled in a course on immigration law will play the parts of the opposing lawyers. Some of them will represent a federal government agency called "Immigration and Customs Enforcement," or ICE. They will be trying to have the foreign student, a fictional Swiss national named Arnaud Marie Godasse, sent back to Switzerland. Other students will be the lawyers for Godasse; they will try to save him. The official who presides over the hearing is called an immigration judge.

You will be playing the part of an immigration officer named Leslie Kinney. The student who is playing the part of the ICE attorney will call you as a witness. The immigration judge will place you under oath, and the opposing student lawyers will take turns asking you questions. The immigration judge might occasionally ask you an additional question.

There is one thing you need to know about immigration law. In order to be admitted to the United States as a foreign student, one must intend to leave the United States when his or her authorized stay expires. A person whose intention all along is to remain permanently in the United States is ineligible for a student visa. The same is true when a foreign student who is already here wishes to extend his or her authorized stay. If, at the time the person applies for an extension, his or her true intent is to remain permanently, then the extension is not supposed to be granted. If ICE eventually discovers that a foreign student intended, either at the time of the original entry or at the time of the extension, to remain permanently, then that student can be sent home. That is what Godasse is trying to avoid.

As an immigration officer, you work for ICE and are attached to its local district office in Austin, Texas. Your job is to find, apprehend and question any non-U.S. citizens who appear to be subject to removal (formerly called deportation). On the evening of August 6, 2010, while taking a coffee break at a place called Jason's Bar and Grill, you overheard a conversation. Godasse, who had been drinking with friends, made some indiscreet remarks about his immigration plans and some comments about ICE employees. You interpreted those remarks as suggesting an intention to remain in the United States more or less permanently. You also interpreted them as sarcastic comments about ICE officials, whom Godasse seemed to imply he had easily fooled. Consequently, you asked to see his papers, which he produced. When you saw he was here on a temporary visa, you arrested him, brought him to ICE headquarters, read him his rights, and asked him several questions, which he answered willingly and in great detail. You then prepared a typed statement containing the answers he had just given and asked him to read it over. He did so, found it accurate, and signed it. You also filled out the required paperwork.

To prepare for your part, you should read the attached Document A, which gives you a little more detail. You will not be expected to remember the exact dates off the top of your head, or to testify in overly technical terms. As long as you are reasonably informed about the character you are playing, you will do fine and will be performing a real service.

The ICE lawyer will probably ask you to describe the events of August 6, 2010 as they relate to Godasse. You should tell the lawyer about your coffee break, what you overheard, where you brought Godasse, etc. You might be asked whether you advised him of his rights (you did), whether it seemed to you that he understood those rights (it did), etc. Godasse's lawyer might ask you why you were eavesdropping in the first place. (You couldn't help it; Godasse was in a festive mood and had been talking in a loud voice.) If you are asked about your experience or qualifications, say you have a college degree and have completed an ICE training course. If you are asked about the details of your training, just make them up.

Finally, please try to be as believable as you can. You should avoid outlandish answers or a flamboyant persona. Don't be afraid to admit that you don't know the answer to a particular question or to give a vague answer occasionally. (In fact, vague answers can liven up the hearing, since the student who is questioning you will have to try to pin you down.) Occasionally, also, you might purposely either misunderstand a question or give an unresponsive answer, just as witnesses often do in real life. Above all, enjoy your performance. The instructor and the students alike will be extremely grateful for the time and effort you are giving them.

WITNESS INSTRUCTIONS FOR ELIZABETH DES CHAMPS

The project in which you are taking part is a mock hearing for removing a foreign student from the United States (formerly called a deportation hearing). Students enrolled in a course on immigration law will play the parts of the opposing lawyers. Some of them will represent a federal government agency called "Immigration and Customs Enforcement," or ICE. They will be trying to have the foreign student, a fictional Swiss national named Arnaud Marie Godasse, sent back to Switzerland. Other students will be the lawyers for Godasse; they will try to save him. The official who presides over the hearing is called an immigration judge.

You will be playing the part of Elizabeth Des Champs. The (student) lawyer who is representing Godasse will call you as a witness. The immigration judge will place you under oath, and the student lawyers will take turns asking you questions. The immigration judge might occasionally ask you an additional question.

Here is how you fit in: You are a Swiss citizen now living in Austin, Texas. You have a green card, having been admitted to the United States as a permanent resident. Your sister, Monique Des Champs, lives in Geneva, Switzerland. She and Arnaud Godasse dated for several months in 2000. (This was many years ago, and you cannot now remember exactly howlong they dated.) While they were still going out, Monique became pregnant. Arnaud denied paternity, claiming he and Monique had never had sexual intercourse. Your and Monique's father, however, did not believe him. Having a violent temper, your father tried to kill Arnaud, who escaped with his life. A few months later, Arnaud fled to the United States on a student visa. He enrolled as an undergraduate student in American literature at the University of Texas, in Austin. Several months later, the child (your niece) was born. She is now almost 10.

ICE wants to return Arnaud to Switzerland because it believes that he deceived the U.S. immigration officials. He obtained and then renewed his student visa, which is only a temporary visa, when ICE believes that all along Arnaud actually intended to remain permanently in the United States. By the time you take the witness stand, the immigration judge will already have reached the conclusion that Arnaud did indeed try to deceive ICE. But Arnaud will try to avoid removal (formerly called deportation) by persuading the immigration judge that he would be in danger if sent back to Switzerland. For that reason, his lawyer will want you to confirm that your father believes Arnaud is the one who impregnated Monique, that your father is ferocious, that he tried to kill Arnaud once, and that he would try again if given the chance. If asked, you should confirm all these facts.

Arnaud will also have to demonstrate that he is an honest person of good moral character. For that reason, the question whether he is actually the father of Monique's child becomes important. The ICE attorney will probably ask you whether you have any information on that question, but even if no one asks you, you should look for an opportunity to volunteer your opinion. You are firmly convinced that Arnaud is lying, and that he and your sister had a sexual relationship. Arnaud's lawyer will probably ask you whether Monique ever told you that, and you should admit that she never did. But you can say that you "sensed" it from some casual comments Monique had made to you, and, besides, Monique was sexually active and it is simply hard to believe she would have a non-sexual dating relationship for several months.

One of the lawyers might also ask you whether Monique was going out with any other men at the time she became pregnant. You should say she was not. If pressed, you should admit that you don't know for sure, but you can say that you and Monique were very close, and you can't imagine her having become involved with someone and not telling you. For all these reasons, you are certain Arnaud was the father, and you are angry at him for not offering to pay Monique child support (which you realize Monique has not requested).

To prepare for your part, please study carefully the information just provided. Be as believable as you can. You should avoid outlandish answers or an overly flamboyant persona. Don't be afraid to admit that you don't know the answer to a particular question or to give a vague answer occasionally. (In fact, vague answers can liven up the hearing, since the student who is questioning you will have to try to pin you down.) Occasionally, also, you might purposely either misunderstand a question or give an unresponsive answer, just as witnesses often do in real life. Above all, enjoy your performance. The instructor and the students alike will be extremely grateful for the time and effort you are giving them.

INTERPRETER INSTRUCTIONS

The project in which you are taking part is a mock hearing for removing a foreign student from the United States (formerly called a deportation hearing). Students enrolled in a course on immigration law will play the parts of the opposing lawyers. Some of them will represent a federal government agency called "Immigration and Customs Enforcement," or ICE. They will be trying to have the foreign student, a fictional Swiss national named Arnaud Marie Godasse, sent back to Switzerland. Other students will be the lawyers for Godasse; they will try to save him. The official who presides over the hearing is called an immigration judge.

You will be playing the part of an interpreter for a French-speaking witness named Elizabeth Des Champs. (She is from Geneva, Switzerland.) When it is Des Champs' turn to testify, the immigration judge will place both you and her under oath and ask you to serve as an interpreter. After that, each time one of the lawyers asks Des Champs a question, your job will be to translate the question into French, listen to her answer, and then translate that answer back into English. Please be sure to translate verbatim, rather than offer a smoother or more articulate version of the actual question or answer.

Enjoy your performance. The instructor and the students alike will be extremely grateful for the time and effort you are giving them.

THE IMMIGRATION JUDGE

As suggested earlier, the immigration judge should be played by the instructor or by someone else with knowledge of removal procedure (e.g., a real immigration judge or an immigration lawyer). The instructor as immigration judge can direct the hearing in a way that will bring out the elements the instructor wants to emphasize. The instructor/immigration judge can also regulate the pace of the hearing to reflect the amounts of time budgeted for, and in fact being consumed by, the various witnesses.

Most of the hearing mechanics are laid out in 8 CFR § 1240.10 (2008). The instructor can review section A.3 of this chapter for a summary of the mechanics.

The immigration judge should turn on the tape recorder and proceed in the following order:

Primary Matters

a. Announce the start: "This is a removal hearing in the matter of Arnaud Marie Godasse, file number A45 365 902. This hearing is being held on October 10, 2010, at the Immigration Court in Austin, Texas, before Immigration Judge ________________ ______________. The respondent, Mr. Godasse, is present. Appearing on his behalf is [are] ______________________________. Appearing for ICE is [are] ______________________________. [And appearing as the interpreter in the French language is ____________________]."

b. Ask Godasse whether he speaks English (and hope he says yes).

c. Show Godasse the Notice to Appear and ask him whether he received it. When Godasse answers yes, announce you are marking it Exhibit 1.

d. Ask Godasse's counsel whether Godasse will waive the immigration judge's reading of Godasse's rights. This request is routinely made and honored when the respondent is represented by counsel. Just in case counsel insists on the reading, however, the immigration judge should be ready to recite Godasse's rights. The following is adapted from 8 CFR § 1240.10(a) (2008), but you should check the most current version to see whether this provision has changed. Barring major change, the following should suffice:

[You have the] right to

> representation, at no expense to the Government, by counsel of [your] own choice authorized to practice in these proceedings; . . . [you] will have a reasonable opportunity to examine and object to the evidence against [you], to present evidence in [your] own behalf and to cross-examine witnesses presented by the Government.

e. Godasse has the right to have the IJ explain the allegations in nontechnical language. 8 CFR § 1240.10(a)(6) (2008). Ask counsel whether Godasse will waive this right. If not, explain the allegations to Godasse at this point.

f. Place Godasse under oath: "Do you solemnly swear or affirm that the testimony you give in this proceeding will be the truth, the whole truth, and nothing but the truth?"

g. Ask Godasse's counsel whether he or she will plead on behalf of Godasse. Then read the allegations one at a time, asking counsel how Godasse pleads. In this case the ground rules require counsel to admit allegations 1, 2, 3, and 6 but deny allegations 4, 5, 7, and 8. Finally, ask counsel whether deportability is conceded or denied. (Counsel should deny deportability in this case.)

h. Ask Godasse's counsel: "If I decide to order Godasse removed, to which country would he wish to be sent?" (Counsel may not designate Canada or Mexico. INA § 241(b)(2)(B)).

i. Say that you understand from the master calendar hearing that, in addition to contesting deportability, Godasse plans to apply for cancellation of removal. Ask whether Godasse will request voluntary departure as a last resort. Then announce that the hearing will proceed in two phases: a deportability phase and, if Godasse is found deportable, a relief phase.

<u>The Deportability Phase</u>

ICE, which has the burden of proving deportability, will present its case first. The ground rules for this exercise require ICE to introduce several documents and to call Kinney as a witness. ICE might also call Godasse as a witness. (After the ICE trial attorney has finished examining each witness,

Godasse's counsel will cross-examine that witness.) When ICE has concluded its case, Godasse has the opportunity to present his. If ICE called Godasse as a witness, Godasse might decline to present any case of his own (in this deportability phase), because Godasse's counsel might already have asked all of his or her desired questions during cross-examination of Godasse and Kinney.

At the conclusion of the deportability phase, the immigration judge can announce that he or she has found Godasse deportable and specify the ground(s). (If the immigration judge were to find Godasse not deportable, the whole relief phase would be mooted.) Alternatively, the IJ could simply say, at the conclusion of the deportability phase, "I am going to reserve my finding as to deportability and proceed to the requests for discretionary relief."

The Relief Phase

In this phase Godasse presents his case first. He has the burden of proving both that he is eligible for relief and that as a matter of discretion he should receive it. He must file with the judge the pertinent application materials for cancellation (documents D and E). 8 CFR §§ 1240.11(a), 1240.20 (2008). (Document E, the affidavit accompanying the cancellation application, would be unnecessary in a real case because Godasse can testify to all the stated facts. It is included in the file here as a way of getting the information to the students. The instructor can tell the students not to offer it into evidence if the instructor wishes.) The immigration judge should ask Godasse to sign the cancellation application then and there. Godasse may orally request voluntary departure in the alternative. 8 CFR § 1240.11(b) (2008).

Godasse and Elizabeth Des Champs will appear as witnesses. If there is an interpreter for Des Champs, the immigration judge can either administer an oath ("Do you solemnly swear or affirm that you will correctly, accurately, and impartially translate all questions addressed to the witness from English to French and all responses from French to English?") or, if the interpreter is a government employee rather than a private contractor, dispense with the oath. 8 CFR § 1240.5 (2008). Either way, the immigration judge should then ask the witness, through the interpreter, whether she speaks French. At that point the IJ can administer the oath to Des Champs, translated into French by the interpreter.

When Godasse has completed his case, ICE is permitted to present its case. Again, however, that might well prove unnecessary because the ICE trial attorney will already have had the chance to cross-examine Godasse and Des Champs, all pertinent documents will already have been introduced, and there are no witnesses left to call.

Ongoing Activities of Immigration Judge

The immigration judge

(a) will place every witness under oath;

(b) may ask questions of the witnesses; and

(c) is permitted to go off and on the record when appropriate. 8 CFR § 1240.9 (2008).

Decision of Immigration Judge

At the conclusion of a real removal hearing, the immigration judge either gives a spontaneous oral decision or, if a case is complex, adjourns to prepare a written (or sometimes oral) decision. In a real case the oral decision would be tape-recorded; the present hearing could be taped too. The opinion must include a finding as to inadmissibility or deportability, and it must state the reasons for granting or denying any request for discretionary relief. 8 CFR § 1240.12 (2008). It should direct either removal or voluntary departure or the termination of removal proceedings. If the immigration judge orders removal, he or she must specify the country. Id. § 1240.12(d). If the immigration judge grants voluntary departure, he or she must specify the time period (no more than 60 days, see INA § 240B(b)(2)).

One option here is for the immigration judge to prepare a tentative opinion in advance and to organize it along the lines of the issue outline provided earlier. The opinion will require modification to reflect the evidence introduced and, possibly, the performance of the student lawyers. After delivering the opinion, the immigration judge should explain the parties' rights to appeal to the BIA. The immigration judge at this point can become an instructor again and either offer a critique or invite the students to provide critiques or both.

As an alternative to an immigration judge decision, the instructor could break the decision down into components and have the class deliberate and then vote on each component: Is Godasse deportable on the first ground charged? The second? Is he eligible for cancellation? If so, should the immigration judge exercise discretion favorably? Is Godasse eligible for voluntary departure? Should it be awarded?

To complete the hearing in any of these suggested ways will require the IJ to leave time at the end of the class session. Each of the two phases can easily consume a full 50-minute session. An instructor who prefers to let each phase run its full course can either dispense with the disposition entirely or include it in the next class discussion.

SECTION D: EXCEPTIONS TO USUAL REMOVAL PROCEDURES

1. Expedited Removal

2. Criminal Cases

3. In Absentia Removal Proceedings

4. Noncitizens Reentering after Prior Removals

5. Crew Members

6. Terrorist Removal Proceedings

All six of the preceding subsections are intended mainly as background reading. All six describe procedures that Congress has substituted for the usual removal proceedings. And in each of those instances, Congress has consciously sacrificed some measure of procedural thoroughness for increased speed and efficiency. The instructor could take the first six subsections (or the first five, since the subject matter of subsection 6 will be detailed in chapter 10) as a unit and ask the students how they feel about the balances that Congress has struck. In the case of subsection 2 (criminal cases), the instructor could also explore with the students what they think the respective roles of DHS, the BIA, and the courts should be in deciding whom to remove. On that issue, see the material on crime-related deportability grounds in chapter 7.

7. Rescission of Adjustment of Status

Notes and Questions on Rescission of Adjustment of Status (page 814):

As explained in the text, rescission is much less important now that inadmissibility at the time of adjustment of status is a ground for deportability. The text proceeds to ask how rescission nonetheless can ever be of use today. There are at least two situations in which it might. First, the deportability ground, INA § 237(a)(1)(A), applies only when the person was *inadmissible* at the time of adjustment of status, not when the person was ineligible for adjustment for some other reason – for example, because he or she was out of status, or previously out of status, or otherwise falls within INA § 245(c). Second, even in a case where ICE could proceed directly under section 237(a)(1)(A), it might choose not to do so if the infraction was minor and the person will still have some time remaining on his or her original nonimmigrant visa. In that case ICE could still rescind the person's adjustment without triggering his or her immediate removal.

Q1: Arguments for requiring a showing of fraud would be that (a) rescission on the basis of strict liability is too harsh and (b) the person has now innocently relied on having attained permanent resident status. Arguments in favor of the status quo (i.e. fraud need not be shown) would include the following: First, rescission merely restores the person to the position he or she would have been in had the government followed the law by denying adjustment. Second, reliance is minimal because rescission can take place only during the first five years after adjustment. Third, if rescission would cause real hardship in a given case, and/or the person was innocent of any wrongdoing, the immigration judge has the discretion not to rescind.

Q2: The statutory language seems ambiguous on this point. The argument in favor of rescinding B's status might be as follows: Under the literal language of the statute, once adjustment has been rescinded, the person "shall thereupon be subject to all provisions of this chapter to the same extent as if the adjustment of status had not been made." By that language, it is clear that A would have been a nonimmigrant but for the adjustment of status. Therefore B would not have been eligible for adjustment at the time he received it because in fact he was not married to an LPR. The counter-argument would be that in fact A was, at the time of B's adjustment, an LPR. Therefore B was eligible for adjustment at the time he received it.

CHAPTER 10
IMMIGRATION AND NATIONAL SECURITY

SECTION A. THE DETENTION OF NONCITIZENS

Notes and Questions Following Subsection A.2 (page 823):

Q1: The cited article lays out the general pros and cons of detaining noncitizens (not just in the national security context). See the cited pages of the article for a fuller discussion.

For several reasons, punishment is not a legitimate purpose of preventive detention. Rather, the theories most frequently invoked by the government to support the detention of noncitizens (at least pending removal proceedings) have been (1) preventing individuals from absconding; (2) isolating those who pose a danger to the community; and (3) deterring noncitizens from engaging in undesirable conduct in the first place. All three theories obviously apply to suspected terrorists or to others who would endanger national security.

There are also substantial costs: (1) The loss of liberty; (2) the inability to work, go to school, socialize, interact with family members and friends, etc; (3) the deprivation of the family members' interest in maintaining their relationships with the detainees; (4) the economic losses to the detainees and their dependents as a result of the detainees' inability to work; (5) the practical barriers that detention poses to the detainees' abilities to prepare their cases (lack of access to counsel, interpreters, physical and documentary evidence, etc.); (6) the fiscal costs to the state of keeping people detained (buildings, personnel, food, medical care, etc.); and (7) the loss of income tax revenue in the cases of detainees who would otherwise be working.

Q2: The article cited in question 1 also lays out, at pages 544-58 of the original article, the general pros and cons of mandatory, categorical detention (as opposed to discretionary, case-by-case detention decisions). Generally, those arguments apply to the automatic-stay-on-appeal rule.

On the benefit side, making the detention mandatory avoids the expense of individual hearings. Under the new rule, there will be no need for a hearing to determine whether release should be stayed pending appeal, because release is stayed automatically. (A counterargument is that we willingly accept the analogous expense in the context of criminal proceedings.) Mandatory detention also avoids false negatives. If the immigration judge retained the discretion whether to release the person on bond pending appeal to the BIA, there would be a certain number of cases in which the IJ predicts that the person is not likely to abscond or to endanger the public but the prediction proves wrong. Automatic stays of the release decisions eliminate those false negatives. When terrorism is involved, the argument might run, the potential human and economic costs of those errors are unusually great. (The main counterargument, noted below, is that the automatic stays also assure a certain number of false positives – i.e., instances in which the person in fact could safely have been released). A third benefit is that the deterrence objectives of preventive detention – themselves controversial – are more likely to be realized when detention is mandatory than when the person knows detention is discretionary.

On the cost side, as just noted, automatic stays of release decisions generate false positives – i.e., instances in which there in fact was no need for the detainee, his or her family, and the public to bear all the human and economic costs of prolonged detention (discussed in the analysis of question 1 above). The wasted economic resources – both funds and physical facilities – could have been diverted to other programs for protecting national security.

A specific consideration applicable to the automatic stay rule is that we are dealing solely with cases in which immigration judges, having examined the evidence, have found release to be a safe option. Thus, there are built-in reasons to expect an unusually low incidence of false negatives and high incidence of false positives. Further, as the readings imply, the prosecuting officials end up with carte blanche to detain people for several months without having even to allege, much less prove, that there is any reason to expect the particular individual to abscond or to endanger the public. In contrast, in the analogous criminal setting, a stay normally requires showings that the appeal is likely to succeed on the merits and that release could cause irreparable harm.

Q3: The theory behind the rule is that (as Professor Ting says) monitoring attorney-client conversations is a small price to pay if it will help prevent the killing of thousands of innocent individuals in a terrorist act. The instructor can describe the safeguards. The information required to monitor a given inmate must come from the head of a federal law enforcement or intelligence agency. There must be "reasonable suspicion" that the attorney-client communications will be used to facilitate a terrorist act. Advance notice must be given to the inmate and his or her attorney unless a court orders otherwise; presumably a court would not permit monitoring without notice unless there is reasonable suspicion that the communication is meant to further a terrorist act, in which case the attorney-client communication wouldn't be protected anyway. And a firewall separates the investigators from the privilege team that monitors the conversation. The privilege team is not allowed to impart the information to the investigators without a court order unless it believes that violent or terrorist acts are "imminent."

The ABA and others have, however, marshaled strong arguments against the policy. The rule is unnecessary, they say, because the government already has the authority to seek a court order permitting monitoring of inmate-attorney communications in appropriate cases. To satisfy constitutional concerns, the judge's decision has to be made on the basis of the facts of the individual case, and the judge must find probable cause – not just "reasonable suspicion" – that the communication is meant to facilitate a crime. One might add that the policy purports to apply in any case where the relevant official has reasonable suspicion of *any* act of "terrorism" – a very broadly defined term. Thus, the argument would run, the worst-case scenario suggested by Professor Ting is not the typical setting in which the policy would be applied.

SECTION B. INTELLIGENCE-GATHERING

<u>Notes and Questions at end of section B</u> (page 831):

Q1: The government will argue that it has every right to obtain information from nonimmigrants, especially for reasons of national security, and that it also has every right to remove noncitizens who lack valid immigration status. It should not be required to choose between doing one or the other. Even though discovering overstayers was not the impetus for the NSEERS program, why, the government asks, should it not act on violations that happen to come to light?

On the other hand, the fear that complying with the registration requirements will result in one's removal from the United States puts the noncitizen in a practical bind. Whatever the rights and wrongs of the matter, the argument runs, the instinctive human tendency in such situations is not to come forward. While we know that 13,000 people who were subject to removal did in fact come forward, we do not know how many chose not to, especially after word got out that registration could spell detention and removal. We also do not know how many people made misrepresentations or produced false documents to avoid removal. The privilege against self-incrimination is founded partly on the desire to avoid subjecting individuals to the trilemma of conviction, contempt penalties for refusing to answer questions, or perjury. The privilege does not apply with respect to noncriminal penalties such as removal, but the underlying rationale has some force. Especially is this so, some would argue, when one considers that many of the nonimmigrants who were subjected to removal were soon-to-be LPRs, waiting for their priority dates to become current so that they could be legally reunited with nuclear family members. Humanity aside, there is the very real strategic question how to balance the desire for maximum participation and maximum information about potential terrorist activities against the desire for fuller enforcement of the immigration laws. If a practice of detaining and removing those registrants who are out of status in fact discourages significant numbers of nonimmigrants from registering, then the question is whether the removal practice is worth the cost.

Q2: The preoccupation with foreign students does seem baffling. Except for those hijackers who had used F-1 visas to attend U.S. flight schools (and flight schools could be, and now are, subjected to special requirements), almost all the September 11 hijackers had entered on simple tourist visas. There is no evidence that individuals holding F-1 visas are disproportionately predisposed to participate in terrorist activities. The fact that (apparently) two of the hijackers happened to enter on (non-flight school) F-1 visas seems no more relevant than would be an observation that X number of the hijackers were left-handed.

Perhaps the idea is that the commercial categories of nonimmigrants often already receive more scrutiny when they are first admitted. The H and L categories, for example, must go through the visa petition process. The E-nonimmigrants also must present certain documentary evidence unique to those categories. But that is not the case with B-1 business visitors, and even for the others it is not apparent that the initial screening for terrorist-related proclivities is any more intense than for students. At any rate, arguments based on initial screening would not explain why students are monitored more closely than tourists. Maybe tourists can be distinguished on the grounds that (a) they usually stay for much shorter durations than students; and (b) there are far too many of them to make a SEVIS-style record-keeping system feasible.

Or, maybe, the thinking is that the looseness of university studies gives even full-time students greater opportunity than commercial visitors to devote time to terrorist plots. That distinction too seems dubious, however, because in any of these categories the vast majority of the person's time would be his or her own.

Possibly it all comes down to political pragmatism. Universities don't like excessive government intrusion into their relationships with their students, but most universities simply don't have the political muscle to prevent it, especially in this post-September 11 era. Industry, in contrast, probably would not put up with it. Employers endure the bookkeeping and loss of privacy associated with the employer sanctions program (which the students will see in chapter 12), but corporations and other employers would almost certainly balk at SEVIS-level intrusion.

SECTION C. EXPANSION OF REMOVAL GROUNDS

This subject is detailed in chapter 5 (exclusion grounds).

SECTION D. SHRINKING PROCEDURAL RIGHTS

<u>Simulation Exercise</u> (page 835):

The big issue is what to do when (a) releasing even a summary of the evidence would entail great risk to public safety; (b) a summary can safely be released but it is too general to be helpful; or (c) the circumstances are such that only access to the actual evidence (not just the government's summary of it) would enable the person to discover errors but the government believes that allowing access to the evidence would endanger public safety. What if the government has exaggerated the risk? Worse, what if the government is just plain wrong? What if it is a case of mistaken identity, or a person's words or actions were misconstrued, or evidence has been maliciously manufactured? What if the government officials in the particular case (or systemically) were animated by either conscious or unconscious racial or religious prejudice?

The special attorney procedure furnishes some degree of protection, but that protection is constrained in at least two ways: First, only LPRs receive special attorneys. (Should nonimmigrants be included?) Second, the special attorney cannot disclose the information to his or her client. If, for example, the government wiretapped a conversation in which the person said such and such to so and so, and the statement was misunderstood, and the person would be able to clear up the confusion if he or she knew what the government had assumed was meant, how will the special attorney even spot the issue, much less clear up the mistake, without asking the client?

On the other hand, realistically, what else can Congress do? Release a dangerous person into society? Disclose classified information that would itself cause harm if released (e.g., the identity of undercover officers, methods of infiltrating terrorist organizations, etc.)? The special attorney procedure, while not fully protective of innocent noncitizens, at least provides some measure of protection. So, too, does the right of appeal (albeit again without access to the evidence) to the court of appeals.

If the terrorist court were actually used, a certain number of noncitizens who in fact are both innocent and harmless would be wrongly expelled. Some of those individuals might have been able to clear themselves if they had been advised of the evidence against them and given a chance to respond to it -- i.e., if they had received the very basics that due process requires in almost all other contexts in which significant liberty interests are at stake. Yet, if the government in all cases had to choose between disclosing classified information that it believes would jeopardize national security and releasing noncitizens whom it believes to be dangerous terrorists, harm to other innocent people could occur.

It all seems to come down to which kind of error one thinks is worse, and which kinds of error would be the most likely to occur under the various procedural alternatives. Put another way, the question is how to optimize procedural protection for the individual, freedom from ethnic or religious discrimination, and public safety and security.

<u>Notes and Questions at end of section D</u> (page 839):

Q1: At first glance the answer would seem to be no. The respondent, if sympathetic to terrorism, can always pass on the information to terrorist organizations, family, friends, etc. So, what good does it do to keep the information from the press? Perhaps the idea is that the respondent might choose not to do so – out of lack of sympathy for terrorism, or fear of repercussions from the government, or for any other reason. Also, the respondent might not recall every piece of information that surfaces at the hearing.

Q2: For one thing, the respondent's knowledge of sensitive information gives terrorist organizations an added incentive to approach him or her. For another, those approaches are more likely to be intimidating, especially if the respondent, who will be in detention during the proceedings, is later found not to be deportable and is released.

Q3: It's apples and oranges. In a closed hearing, the main interest being sacrificed is that of the public and the press in knowing that the government is treating people fairly (though one can argue that sunlight also protects the respondent from government overreaching). In contrast, in a secret evidence hearing the problem is that the respondent cannot properly present his or her case or rebut the government's case. The readings give concrete examples of how concealment of the evidence can hamper the respondent: (1) Not knowing the names, dates, or places of the respondent's supposed contacts with terrorist operatives prevents the respondent from offering innocent explanations or alibis. (2) Not knowing the names of sources of the government's evidence prevents the respondent from identifying problems with the sources' credibility. (3) The government's assertion might be based on simple error or misunderstanding that the respondent will be prevented from discovering or explaining. (4) Having to guess at what conduct or statements might have raised the government's suspicions requires the respondent to choose between remaining silent (which might be misconstrued as tacit acceptance of the government's inferences) and volunteering information about a range of other possibly suspicious acts (which carries other obvious risks). In addition to these factors, which increase the chance of an erroneous finding against the respondent, there is the risk (a realistic one in the present climate) that secret evidence rules will be invoked discriminatorily based on nationality, ethnicity, or religion. (On the other hand, unless the secret evidence hearing is also closed, at least the press will have the opportunity to expose egregious problems.)

SECTION E. VISAS AND OTHER OVERSEAS POLICIES
SECTION F. ENHANCED BORDER ENFORCEMENT

These sections are intended as background reading.

SECTION G. PROFILING

Notes and Questions at end of section G (page 850):

Q1: Much of Schuck's analysis draws specifically on the practical necessity of spontaneous decisions. The actor doesn't have the luxury of conducting empirical studies or investigating the life of each subject. But Schuck's basic utilitarian logic would seem to apply with equal force to instances in which policymakers are able to make more studied determinations. At any level of national security decisionmaking we are, at some point, forced to balance civil liberties against other collective national interests. Moreover, in predicting the likely effectiveness of a strategy and the accuracy of particular criteria, in the end we are forced to play the odds. Schuck's ultimate criteria – especially the probability and gravity of both false positives and false negatives and the practicability of more individualized inquiry – are as applicable to spontaneous decisionmaking as they are to more deliberative policymaking. (The degree of required spontaneity might very well affect the results, though.)

Note: The analyses of questions 2-11 below are elaborated more fully in Stephen H. Legomsky, *The Ethnic and Religious Profiling of Noncitizens: National Security and International Human Rights*, 25 Boston College Third World L.J. 161 (2005).

Q2: As to the argument made in the first paragraph of the excerpt, the counterargument might be that Cole is examining the wrong percentage. Assume he is right that only a minuscule percentage of persons who appear Arab and Muslim are involved with terrorism. The government might well argue that that is not the point. The more relevant figure, it would say, is the percentage of people involved in terrorism who appear to be either Arab or Muslim. If there is evidence that that percentage is abnormally high (relative to the U.S. population as a whole), then it is perfectly rational for the government to deploy its limited resources where they stand the greatest likelihood of apprehending terrorists.

The second paragraph of the excerpt actually contains two separate arguments. The first is that, "when one treats a whole group of people as presumptively suspicious, it means that agents are more likely to miss dangerous persons who do not fit the profile . . ." The counterargument would be this: The government simply does not have the resources to scrutinize *everyone,* at least not with the intensity required to ferret out terrorists. Therefore, it has to be selective. That means it has only two choices – either select people randomly or take into account those attributes that correlate positively with terrorist involvement. Either option has the unavoidable disadvantage that Cole identifies – i.e., the government will miss a certain number of terrorists – but the latter option at least mitigates that risk.

The other argument in the second paragraph is this: "[T]he fact that the vast majority of those targeted on the basis of their Arab or Muslim appearance will prove to be innocent will inevitably cause agents to let their guard down." The counterargument might be that this problem would be even greater without profiling. Unless the proportion of terrorists that the government would encounter through random sampling (or even nonrandom sampling that relies solely on non-race-related profiling) is higher than the proportion of terrorists in the Arab and Muslim sample, then the problem of officers letting their guard down because the sampled population is overwhelmingly innocent would be even greater without the race-related profiling. The real question is whether there is a positive correlation between terrorism and the attributes the government employs in its profiles. If there isn't, then all should agree the profiling is irrational. If there is, though, then the practice seems rational. (As the readings emphasize, however, "rational" does not necessarily mean "justified.")

Q3: There are two kinds of harms. First there are the harms associated with the particular deprivations. These are harms that would result even if the deprivations were nondiscriminatory – the person's removal, detention, arrest, questioning, prosecution, registration, etc. Second are the harms associated with the discrimination. These can include not only the core injustice of being treated less favorably than others for insufficient reasons, but also personal feelings of humiliation, a loss of dignity, a loss of confidence, a sense of being treated unfairly, a sense of being seen and treated as an outsider, etc.

Q4: They are not necessarily inconsistent. A person might believe that racial profiling is not always wrong and that evaluation requires a balancing of benefits and costs. On the benefit side, as discussed earlier, one main issue is whether there is a high statistical correlation between the particular attribute and the particular misconduct. If there is, then concentrating limited resources on those who possess the relevant attribute might well be rational. A person might also believe that such a statistical correlation exists in the national security context but not in the motorist context, or might feel that the magnitude of the benefit (preventing a terrorist attack) is more important than preventing whatever offenses the police have in mind when pulling over drivers. Conversely, one might place differing weights on the particular deprivations. Depending on the particular racial profiling in question, one might feel that the intrusion is less in some of the national security contexts (for example, the voluntary interviews) than in the driving context, for example because the latter is more likely to keep recurring more frequently. Generally, then, the magnitudes of the competing benefits and costs will vary as between the two contexts. Of course, one might well feel that the bar on government discrimination is absolute – i.e., that the kind of utilitarian balancing this analysis assumes is simply inappropriate. And at any rate, to say the two positions are not contradictory is not to suggest that ethnic profiling in the current context is appropriate.

Q5: By positing the admittedly unrealistic figure of 2/3 of the particular ethnic group being involved in terrorism, this question is designed to get students to decide how they feel about the general concept of ethnic profiling, without the added distractions of the citizen/noncitizen distinction or the problem of misleading physical appearances, intermarriages, etc. Some students will undoubtedly feel that ethnic profiling is simply wrong, no matter what the percentages and no matter how minor the intrusion (questioning as opposed to detention, criminal sanctions, removal, etc.) Others will prefer to balance the rationality of questioning a hypothetical group whose members are so disproportionately suspect against the harms associated with government-sponsored discrimination. Once students come to grips with that basic decision, they can start to focus on the refinements presented in the next series of questions. The second part of the question – hypothesizing that only 2 per cent of the members of the targeted ethnic group are involved in terrorism but that the corresponding percentage for the general population is much lower still

– is meant to get the students to think about whether the rationality of the targeting hinges on how *large* the yield is or on how *disproportionate* it is.

Q6: Now some of the same kinds of considerations that the students had to weigh in chapter 2 (the constitutional foundations of immigration law) come into play, even though this is a policy question rather than a constitutional one. To the extent noncitizens are thought of as mere guests (rather than full members of the political community), their interests might be seen as deserving of less weight, relative to national security needs. And if the government perceives that the particular ethnic subcategory of noncitizens is deriving support from the country or countries of origin, then the sensitive foreign policy concerns might prompt the students to give the United States government greater leeway than in a purely domestic context. On the other hand, the distinction in this hypothetical question is based on ethnicity, not country of citizenship or nationality. For several decades, even as the U.S. immigration laws have embodied several country-specific practices, the longstanding policy (at least officially) has been to prohibit distinctions based explicitly on ethnicity, even for noncitizens.

Q7: By basing its differential treatment on country of nationality rather than ethnicity, the government at the very least puts its policy on more respectable footing. On the assumption that countries which harbor terrorists might well be inclined to provide logistical or other support to their own nationals who are planning terrorist acts in the United States, the U.S. policy of targeting the nationals of such countries has a rational basis. Moreover, there might be foreign policy reasons to take a hard line against the nationals of a particular country. In contrast, policies that officially discriminate against particular ethnic groups are more inherently suspect.

The distinction should not be exaggerated, however. First, almost all the countries that the U.S. designates as harboring terrorists are predominantly Arab and Muslim nations. Thus, even if the U.S. policy is truly not driven by ethnicity or religion, the practical impact falls disproportionately on one ethnic group and one religious group. Second, as long as the impact is disproportionate, large segments of the population will perceive, rightly or wrongly, that the country-of-nationality distinction is merely a facade for anti-Arab or anti-Muslim sentiments – or, at least, that the same action would not have been taken had other ethnic groups been the ones affected. These considerations do not *ipso facto* make country-of-nationality profiling wrong, but they are negative consequences that have to be included in any weighing of the competing interests.

Q8: Most of the same considerations apply, including the offensiveness of treating people as suspects based solely on ethnicity or religion. Now, however, there are additional problems. First, the police can be wrong about the person's ethnicity or religion. When they are, the policy causes them to waste time on individuals whom there is no reason (individualized or statistical) to suspect. Second, every police force will comprise individuals of vastly different views and attitudes. Those police officers whose biases incline them toward harassment of particular ethnic or religious subgroups would now have an official excuse.

Q9: That change diminishes the danger somewhat but probably doesn't change the competing arguments. We are still left with the need to balance the perceived gains in the thoroughness and efficiency of the counterterrorism program against the harms to the targeted individuals.

Q10: The analysis probably doesn't change, but the weight to be placed on the harm to the targeted group obviously increases.

<u>Simulation Exercise</u> (page 853):

Given all the variables mentioned (and any others that the instructor and the students come up with), there are any number of possible student reactions to this bill. The instructor might simply conduct the exercise as if the House were in session and take on the role of speaker, calling on whichever students elect to speak (or call on non-volunteers). Or, during the preceding class session, the instructor could divide the class in half, designating one half of the class "generally in support" and the other half "generally opposed," and asking them to come to class prepared to make speeches consistent with those designations. After one or two short speeches on each side, the instructor could either let the process continue or call for any motions to amend the bill. One or more students could move amendments (the formality of a second could be omitted), the students would then speak on behalf of any amendments they offer, other speeches either for or against the amendment could be made, and (optionally) the class could vote on each amendment.

SECTION H. IMMIGRATION AND NATIONAL SECURITY IN PERSPECTIVE

Notes and Questions at end of section H (page 866):

Q1: Ryan's point is that there was nothing in most of the hijackers' past records or visa applications (no criminal record, no known association with terrorists, no suspicious answers, etc.), that would have given even the most careful examiner any reason to suspect terrorism. Therefore, she says, more rigorous and more labor-intensive screening would not have prevented their admission.

Krikorian responds in two ways. First, he says, according to Joel Mowbray, six current and former consular officers believed every application should have been rejected on its face because "every application was incomplete or contained patently inadequate or absurd answers." But even if we accept Mowbray's account of the consular officers' comments at face value (though described by Krikorian simply as an "investigative reporter," Mowbray is a passionate, highly acerbic anti-immigration commentator), and even if we assume the six consular officers were a representative sample and not pre-selected because of their views, we are never told what it was about the applications that left them "incomplete" or "patently inadequate" or "absurd." The real question is whether the problems, if any, were substantive ones that would ultimately have resulted in visa denials, or whether they were simply omissions that could easily have been cured by filling in any of the blanks. If the former, then Krikorian is probably right; if the latter, then Ryan is probably right.

Krikorian also argues that, "even if the applications had been properly prepared, many of the hijackers, including Mohammed Atta and several others, were young, single, and had little income" and therefore should have been rejected as likely to overstay. The "little income" part would require more information to analyze. If the incomes of the applicants were so low as to have made them likely to become public charges during their temporary stays in the United States, then, it is true, they should have been denied visas on that ground. Short of that, however, modest means are not a ground for exclusion. The question then becomes one of policy: Should U.S. consular officers really assume that all foreign nationals who are young and single – or even young, single, and having incomes that are sufficient to support their temporary stays but still "low" by U.S. standards – are likely to overstay, and therefore deny visas to all such applicants? Unless one answers yes (and CIS might), then Ryan is quite right that more rigorous screening would not have uncovered any reason to deny visas to the men who carried out the 9/11 attacks. Indeed, as the excerpt from Chishti et al observes, all but two of the 9/11 terrorists were well-educated men with no criminal records and no known connection to terrorism.

Q2: Immigration lawyers are bombarded with complaints of inexplicable visa denials, particularly from nationals of developing countries and particularly when the applicants wished to visit family members settled in the United States. There is a widespread feeling in the immigration bar that likelihood of overstaying can be found with surprising ease. Admittedly neither the rejected applicants nor their attorneys are the most objectively situated to judge whether the denials were really as arbitrary as they appeared; suffice it to say not many practitioners expressed surprise when the Brazil episode became public knowledge. At any rate, the doctrine of consular absolutism (no administrative or judicial review of visa denials) has exacerbated the difficulty of finding out.

As for incentives: Obviously, no consular officer would want to turn out to be the one who granted the visa to a terrorist. Denying a visa, especially in the light of the doctrine of consular absolutism, is a much safer course.

Q3: The instinctive answer is that a competent terrorist would seem less likely to do so. The last thing the terrorist wants is attention while the terrorist act is being planned. On the other hand, some might say, a terrorist also wants adequate planning time. Thus, there might be an incentive to overstay, or to drop courses if he or she has been admitted on a student visa, just to create the necessary time – even though a violation of status carries risks.

Q4: Perhaps the most effective tools would simply be more resources, both personnel and technology. Expanding the corps of consular officers (a process already in place) would permit more rigorous screening of all visa applicants. More vigorous targeting of likely visa violators in the United States, on mere speculation that terrorists are disproportionately present in that population (as distinguished from the population of noncitizens lawfully present), seems grossly inefficient, unless the actual main target is illegal immigration rather than terrorism.

Q5: On the one hand, there are so many different immigration statuses and so many different documents in use that confusion and mistakes seem inevitable. How good the employees would be at detecting fake documents is an additional issue. Still another is how much enthusiasm they would bring to the job, given that their main duty is service and that they want to attract business, not repel it. On the other hand, (a) employers perform analogous functions for purposes of the employer sanctions laws (see chapter 12 below); (b) perhaps the statuses and documentation could be simplified; and (c) maybe a certain error rate would be a tolerable price to pay if these sorts of checks appreciably improved U.S. national security (a premise examined in question 3 above).

Q6: Conform to the terms of their admission.

Q7: Since the causal connection between immigration violations and terrorism has yet to be demonstrated, and since the organizations that have been emphasizing the vulnerabilities of U.S. immigration controls in the terrorism debate are generally the same organizations that have been lobbying the most intensely for immigration restrictions for many years, the motive question is a natural one to ask. But that doesn't mean the restrictionists are wrong. One who either subscribes to the causal links that Krikorian asserts between immigration violations and terrorism or simply believes that immigration should be further restricted for independent reasons might well favor his suggestions. Those who do not find the causal links convincing and who regard the benefits of most of the U.S. immigration policies as outweighing the costs would be more likely to find the two succeeding writings more persuasive.

Q8: There is certainly truth to that assertion. The vast majority of the measures discussed in the preceding sections of this chapter are directed exclusively to noncitizens. The real question is whether the focus on noncitizens is appropriate. Many would say that the laws of any country *should* treat citizens of that country more favorably than noncitizens. (This debate is the focus of chapter 13, section C above.) Moreover, it is true that the overwhelming majority of the individuals believed to have carried out major terrorist acts in the United States have been noncitizens (the two principals in the Oklahoma City being the exception, not the norm), even though the noncitizen population of the country is only a minority. (The effectiveness of targeting particular subclasses of noncitizens on the basis of country of nationality, ethnicity, or religion is a separate question and the subject of section G above.)

Q9: Justice and morality aside, and all else equal, it is certainly better to have all communities on board than to turn particular communities into enemies. The dilemma lies in balancing that strategic benefit against law enforcement gains that a *particular* targeting strategy is expected to produce. As for the tactical question of which strategies will produce the best long term results, the verdict is still out.

Q10: Krikorian's piece does not acknowledge any of the costs of his proposed immigration control mechanisms. The costs include not only the fiscal resources, but also the effects on immigrants who seek admission for reasons that relate to either economic or compassionate value – helping industry and consumers, family reunification, and safety for refugees. (Of course the policies that underlie specific admissions programs, as well as the computation of how the benefits stack up against the costs, are the subject of legitimate debate. But few would claim the benefits are trivial.) Other costs include possible congestion and longer queues at consulates, at ports of entry, and at the places where the proposed immigration status checks would take place – banks, DMV offices, etc.

The MPI and Cole writings, in contrast, while emphasing the civil liberties side of the ledger, acknowledge the national security issues and address them. Indeed, a central thesis of both excerpts is that certain of the immigration-related national security strategies, in addition to infringing on civil liberties, have not even been effective in apprehending suspected terrorists.

CHAPTER 11
REFUGEES

Note: There are some excellent instructional videos that contain simulated or actual footage of attorney-client and asylum officer-applicant interviews, plus related materials. They are described, along with ordering information in some cases, in this Teacher's Manual (this chapter, § B.8 below, Check List item 3). We mention them now because ordering requires lead time.

SECTION A. OVERSEAS REFUGEES.

Notes and Questions on page 888:

These Notes and Questions pull together the various readings contained in Section A.

Q1: One factor that could augur an increase in the number of refugees is the rapid population growth of the Third World, a phenomenon that will exacerbate competition for land and resources. Second, there is evidence that the inequalities of wealth, if anything, are widening. Third, since the Suhrke article, emigration restrictions have been eased in eastern Europe, the Soviet Union, China, and from time to time in Cuba. The Soviet and Eastern European liberalizations have been felt particularly by the traditional receiving nations of western Europe.

Other factors might suggest a future decrease in refugee numbers. The growth of democracy in eastern Europe and elsewhere is one of them. Suhrke also suggests there will be fewer wars of independence. Her article, however, was written in 1983, before the breakups of the Soviet Union and Yugoslavia and the rash of subsequent independence movements.

There remain many unknowns. No one can safely predict the number, scale, and nature of future secession movements. Nor is it always possible to predict how the governments of newly independent states will treat ethnic and religious minorities. If Suhrke is right to suggest that refugee movements have a "pull" component in addition to a "push" component -- and that premise is itself controversial because some feel that such a characterization minimizes the interests at stake for refugees -- then another relevant unknown will be the receptiveness of other nations and international organizations to the acceptance and resettlement of refugees.

Q2: One vehicle is economic aid to stabilize the country of origin. A second possibility is withholding support from despotic regimes, though there is much debate about when this helps and when it hurts. Military intervention always remains an option of last resort but an option nonetheless.

Q3: The after-the-fact remedies have traditionally been grouped into the three categories described in question 3. Third-country resettlement is an important remedy, but the problem is that the countries wealthy enough to receive significant numbers of refugees are, in fact, absorbing only a small fraction of the world's refugees, especially those from Africa. Voluntary repatriation is the ideal solution when it is truly "voluntary." Refugees might be persuaded to return if conditions have changed -- for example, if a totalitarian government has either accepted democratic reforms or been overthrown. The large refugee-receiving countries might condition reconstruction aid to those governments on improvements in human rights. Local integration in the country of first asylum is sometimes a viable option, but the major problem is that most countries of first asylum are developing nations that lack the resources to resettle massive numbers of refugees on a permanent basis. Many of those countries are themselves politically unstable. The wealthier nations could, of course, step up their economic aid, but the hurdles include domestic taxpayer resistance, finding a way to make sure the aid gets to the intended beneficiaries, and avoiding the perception that the donor is "paying off" other countries to accept the particular group when the donor freely admits large numbers of other ethnic groups.

Q5: Those who advocate using ideology or foreign relations as criteria for selecting refugees might make the following arguments: First, a charitable donor has the right to decide whom it wishes to benefit. Second, since the United States cannot admit all refugees, it must somehow select some legitimate refugees over others. There is nothing wrong with considering national self-interest in making that judgment. Third, the United States has a special relationship with those who are fleeing Communism. In addition to fighting a common "enemy," the United States publicly encouraged a liberal Soviet emigration policy and therefore has a responsibility to accept a significant number of those who are permitted to leave. Fourth, INA § 207(a)(3) specifically directs the government to prioritize those refugees who are of "special humanitarian concern" to the United States. The government could rationally conclude that ideological soulmates fit that description.

Opponents of ideological refugee selection might make the following arguments: First, from a domestic legal perspective, the whole point of the Refugee Act of 1980 was to get away from ideological discrimination. INA § 207(a)(3) should be interpreted with that goal in mind. Second, although proponents of ideological selection criteria might suggest that such criteria do no harm because the United States can admit only a limited total number anyway, not all else is equal. There are degrees of persecution. The result of ideology-based refugee selection is that the United States accepted many refugees from Communism (or from governments who are otherwise U.S. adversaries) who are less severely persecuted than are many of the refugees from right-wing governments who are not accepted. Third, the primary purpose of a refugee program should be humanitarian. It should be administered without regard to political considerations. Fourth, even one who believes that foreign policy is a relevant consideration in a refugee selection system might conclude that in the United States the present system is tilted toward foreign policy to an unhealthy extreme. Fifth, such heavy emphasis on foreign policy signals those of our allies whose governments are repressive that the United States will overlook their human rights abuses. Sixth, if all nations did this, there would be no one to take care of those refugees who lack powerful allies. Seventh, many would question whether the United States practice of foreign policy-based refugee selection is in our national interest. Cynically using refugee policy as a tool in a political war creates adverse international publicity. Moreover, it creates a quandary when changes in foreign governments alter the relationship between those governments and that of the United States (as has happened, for example, in Iran, the Philippines, and Nicaragua).

Q6: Most of the arguments for and against country-specific refugee policy are analogs of the arguments for and against considering ideology in refugee selection. In addition, one can argue that ad hoc legislation permits a prompter response to particularly important groups when there is a glitch in the system that it would be either too time-consuming or politically infeasible to cure generically.

Q7: One argument for retaining a strong Presidential power in this area is that the President can react more promptly to world events than Congress can. Congress might delay action for a variety of reasons. Moreover, refugee policy has foreign affairs implications. Some would argue that it is especially important for the President to maintain consistency in foreign policy. Finally, some might contend that the present system is fine. If the President seriously offends Congress one year, Congress can always amend the statute, although admittedly it would have to worry about a presidential veto.

Proponents of a stronger congressional role in the refugee process might emphasize congressional responsibility for foreign affairs (even if it is conceded that foreign affairs should be a factor in refugee decisions).

The cited article argues that an independent refugee board would combine the deliberative qualities of Congress, the speed of the executive branch, and the impartiality of the judiciary.

Q8: This question should be deferred until section C unless the instructor plans to skip that section.

Q10: The argument for a longer adjustment of status period would probably emphasize the advantages of voluntary repatriation. Repatriation -- if truly voluntary -- is often better for the refugee, for the refugee's country, and for the receiving country, which can then use its finite resources to admit other refugees. Once adjustment is granted, the receiving country implicitly is giving up on voluntary repatriation. A longer qualifying period for adjustment might help to encourage voluntary repatriation.

Proponents of a shorter adjustment period (or elimination of the waiting period entirely) would argue that truly voluntary repatriation is usually unrealistic unless conditions change, which is unlikely in the short term. In the meantime, the refugees have to rebuild their lives, a hard enough job that is made harder while they are kept in limbo. Nor does the granting of adjustment of status preclude a truly voluntary repatriation later.

SECTION B. ASYLUM AND NONREFOULEMENT

1. Persecution or Fear of Persecution

Matter of Acosta (page 895):

Acosta, a Salvadoran, appeals to the BIA from an IJ's denial of asylum and nonreturn. Acosta testified that he and other taxi drivers in San Salvador had formed a co-op called COTAXI, in which drivers contributed earnings in order to buy their own taxis. The guerrillas, hoping to disrupt life in the capital, carried out threats to kill COTAXI members who refused to strike. After being beaten and assaulted, Acosta fled to the United States. He asserts a well founded fear that he would be killed by the guerrillas if he returns. Alternatively, Acosta believes he would be persecuted by the government, which perceives COTAXI as a socialist organization.

The BIA found Acosta's testimony credible and found he genuinely feared persecution. The Board also acknowledged that persecution need not be at the hands of the government; private sector persecution can also suffice. Nonetheless, the Board denied asylum. First, it held, his fear of persecution, while honest, was not well-founded. His concerns about the government's motives were not factually based, and his concerns about the guerrillas were no longer valid because the guerrillas' strength had diminished, taxi drivers were no longer in danger, and at any rate he did not plan to return to driving. Second, in a portion of the opinion that was omitted (because the issue is discussed in the next subsection of the chapter), the Board held that any persecution Acosta claimed to fear could not be said to be on account of political opinion or social group (the two categories he had alternatively alleged). And third, the Board held, Acosta had failed to prove he could not avoid the persecution by relocating to another part of the country of origin. For the same reasons, Acosta was held ineligible for withholding.

<u>Notes and Questions Following Acosta</u> (page 901):

General: This case was included mainly to introduce the concept of "persecution," but the portions that are reproduced here also consider the requirement of "fear." It is possible to use this case as a vehicle for discussing whether asylum should require persecution at all (rather than some more generalized danger, such as war, natural disaster, etc.), but it is better to defer that subject to section C of this chapter unless the instructor plans to skip section C. At this stage the instructor should also avoid detailed discussion of the requirement that the fear be "well founded" and related standard of proof issues. These issues are discussed in the full version of *Acosta*, but that portion of the case has been superseded by *Cardoza-Fonseca* and *Mogharrabi*, discussed in section B.3 of this chapter of the text; that portion of *Acosta* was therefore edited out.

Q1: The requirement that fear be the primary motivation seems stricter than what the statute requires. INA § 101(a)(42) refers only to one "who is unable or unwilling to return to ... that country because of ... a ... fear of persecution ...." The statute does not say that such a fear has to be the applicant's “primary” reason for being unable or unwilling to return. It could be argued, however, that this language should be interpreted even more strongly, to mean that the fear of persecution must be the applicant's only motivation. Also, the UNCHR Handbook is based on other signatories' interpretations. Those interpretations which were rendered before 1980 might be relevant to the congressional intent at the time of the Refugee Act of 1980.

As a matter of policy, should asylum be available to someone who primarily fears poverty, but who secondarily fears persecution? Some would say no, because there are too many such people for the United States to accommodate. Others would argue yes. They would say that, if the applicant in fact has a well-founded fear of persecution on the basis of one of the five statutory grounds, the fact that he or she would face additional, even more compelling hardships should not be seen as a strike against the person. And if the problem is one of numbers, a ceiling would be preferable to an outright disqualification.

Q4: Those who interpret "persecution" to require a danger different from that faced by a large segment of the population might make the following arguments: First, the very word "persecution" implies that the harm must be individualized. Second, there is a concern for numbers; Congress could not have intended to make entire national populations eligible.

Those who oppose reading in a requirement that the threatened harm not be faced by a large segment of the country might offer the following arguments: First, persecution indeed requires a threat based on the attributes of the particular individual, but the fact that there are other individuals in the same boat does not mean this particular individual is not in danger of persecution. Second, the requirement in question would preclude asylum for people who in fact would be persecuted, simply because the persecutor's focus was too broad. Such a broad focus is common in countries where human rights problems are serious. Third, some of the statutory bases for persecution -- race, nationality, and membership in a particular social group -- are always defined by group characteristics. Even the others -- religion and political opinion -- at least usually are group characteristics. Thus, persecution is almost always on account of characteristics that the individual shares with others. Fourth, if the only problem is high volumes, then the proper response is either to change the statutory definition (to the extent treaty obligations permit) or impose quotas.

The instructor can illustrate this point by hypotheticals. If, for example, a student believes that an applicant should not have to be threatened in a way that distinguishes him or her from society at large, the instructor might ask the student whether United States law requires asylum in a situation where half the country is persecuted on account of race. (In Fiji, for example, a 1987 coup resulted in widespread government discrimination against Fijian citizens of Indian ancestry, even though ethnic Indians make up about half the population of that country.) The student's answers might be that in such a situation the solution is, in fact, to grant asylum to any Indian from that country who arrives here and applies for it or, alternatively, to change the law (either by changing the statutory definition of refugee to the extent international treaty obligations permit or by imposing quotas). Conversely, if the student believes that a danger distinct from that faced by the general population is required, the following hypothetical might be posed: Suppose the pre-Apartheid South African government had decided to exterminate the entire black population of the country. If a black South African made it to the United States and claimed persecution on account of race, should the United States have denied asylum on the ground that the threatened harm is common to a major segment of the population? Faced with such a hypothetical, the student might say that that is not what "individualized" actually means. The student might retreat enough to suggest that it requires only a targeting of an individual who possesses a particular characteristic and that that requirement is met in this hypothetical. But in *Bolanos-Hernandez*, discussed in the text, there was individual targeting and the court still denied relief on the ground that too many others had also been personally targeted.

Q5: The regulations make clear that the applicant does not have to be uniquely exposed to the risk of persecution. Nor does the regulation expressly disqualify anyone solely because the persecuted group of which he or she is a member is very large. But part (B) does require the applicant to establish that "his or her fear of persecution upon return is reasonable." Arguably, the larger the group, or the smaller the percentage of group members actually persecuted, the less reasonable the fear of persecution will be, even for one who is clearly a member of the persecuted group. In that way, group size seems relevant but not conclusive.

Q6: Those who argue that such a practice does not constitute persecution might stress that the government is not punishing the individual because of a belief or a characteristic that the government seeks to overcome, to use the definition formulated in *Acosta*. The penalties are there just to enforce a law that is applied uniformly to everyone.

Those who believe such practices do constitute persecution might argue that, even if the policy is facially neutral, and even if it is not selectively enforced, a consequence that is innocuous for some can be severely debilitating for others. Also, the two examples might be analytically different. The whole point of the dress code is to force particular religious practices on those who do not subscribe to them, with severe penalties for noncompliance. The same cannot quite be said about a military draft, since its purpose is not to require draftees to follow a particular religious practice or to hold a particular political opinion, etc.

Q8: Those who believe that the severity of the threatened harm must reach a certain level before it constitutes persecution would probably argue that, however obnoxious the practice is, the United States should save its limited absorption resources for people who face greater dangers. Others would argue that, although the deprivation might be slight, it is still persecution aimed purposely at a particular group based solely on their religion, or race, etc. The government should not attempt to draw lines based on <u>how</u> bad the persecution is.

The second hypothetical, in which the persecutors are private citizens rather than government officials, might be different for that reason. Those who oppose the granting of asylum in such cases might argue, in addition to the points discussed above, that if persecution were to be found whenever a private group not controllable by the government discriminates in insulting but intangible ways, almost anyone would qualify for asylum. Others might respond that an otherwise innocuous practice like a stream of insults becomes serious when it reflects a widespread hostility that the government is either unable or unwilling to subdue.

Q10: Of course any requirement beyond well-founded fear of persecution – say, a requirement that the person be left-handed – will reduce the number of people who qualify for refugee status, thus mitigating the burden on receiving states. But the question is whether the particular limitation discussed here – a nexus to one of the five Convention grounds – makes sense.

If the guiding impulse behind the asylum laws is simply to provide humanitarian relief from suffering, then the additional limitation is counter-productive. If the harm is severe enough to rise to the level of persecution, then the degree of suffering is not diminished by the fact that the persecution will be inflicted for reasons other than those enumerated in the Convention. It is persecution just the same.

But humanitarian relief is not the only goal of the refugee regime. If it were, there would be no reason to distinguish suffering that results from persecution from suffering that results from any other cause – armed conflict, natural disaster, poverty, etc. Rather, the refugee regime is also meant to protect individuals from violations of human rights. That being the case, one could argue that persecution, because it is directed at particular individuals and groups for unjustifiable reasons and because by definition it must rise to a certain level of severity, is inherently a human rights violation – whether or not the persecutors' motives are among the five listed in the Convention. The counter-argument might be that, bad as persecution is, it is worse still when inflicted on one of the grounds listed in the Convention, since the discrimination involved (as in the case of race, religion, or nationality) or the constraints on freedom of expression (in the case of political opinion) constitute additional violations of human rights. That being so, the argument would run, the nexus requirement is a rational dividing line.

Matter of Izatula (page 907):

In exclusion proceedings, Izatula applied to an immigration judge for asylum. In Afghanistan, he had given supplies to the Mujahedin rebels, who were seeking to overthrow the Soviet-sponsored government. Izatula feared that, if returned, he would be punished severely (imprisonment, and possibly torture or even death), both for aiding the rebels and for refusing to serve in the Afghan army. The IJ denied asylum (and withholding). He rejected the claim that was based on punishment for refusing to serve in the army, because the Soviet army had since withdrawn from Afghanistan; and he rejected the argument that was based on punishment for aiding the rebels, because such punishment was criminal prosecution rather than political persecution. Izatula appealed.

The BIA agreed with the IJ that the Soviet troop withdrawal eliminated Izatula's draft resistance argument. The Board disagreed, however, with the remainder of the IJ's opinion. The rulers of Afghanistan did not permit a peaceful change of government through democratic means. Violent overthrow was thus the only practical instrument for change. Consequently, punishing those who attempt violent overthrow constituted persecution. (The BIA went on to find a well founded fear of persecution and granted asylum. It did not discuss whether the persecution was on account of political opinion.)

Board member Vacca wrote a concurring opinion. He felt it was not the place of the BIA to judge which governments were legitimate and which ones weren't. Even a totalitarian regime, he argued, has the right to punish armed insurrection. For him, the key point was that the particular punishment was likely to be excessive, an indicator that the criminal prosecution was just a pretext for persecution on account of political opinion. Accordingly, he too would have granted asylum.

Notes and Questions Following Izatula (page 911):

Q1: The viewpoint of the BIA majority is a pragmatic one. If the government shuts off all opportunity for peaceful democratic change, then the only option for dissenters is force. In that case, armed rebellion becomes legitimate and the government's attempts to punish it should be regarded as persecution. The example of the German Resistance during World War II highlights the usefulness of that principle in that case, although most likely one would find persecution under Mr. Vacca's approach as well.

Arguments for the viewpoint of Mr. Vacca (and possible responses to those arguments) might include the following: First, the United States should not impose its own norms on other governments. The fact that a government is not democratic does not mean it has no right to protect itself by punishing attempts at violent overthrow. Second, Mr. Vacca argues, the majority approach undermines the President's authority to conduct foreign affairs. (Response: The BIA is simply interpreting the statutory word "persecution." Nothing it does is binding on the President. The Attorney General may always reverse an objectionable decision of the BIA). Third, Mr. Vacca might argue that the BIA is not competent to make the kinds of foreign policy judgments that its formulation requires. (Response: The human rights reports and other evidence in the record permit knowledgeable factfinding. It is true that these facts are "legislative" in character rather than "adjudicative," but as long as the information necessary for making those findings is contained in the human rights reports, the BIA is competent to proceed.)

Q2: The first question concerns the relationship between the second and third sentences of paragraph 85. "Excessive or arbitrary punishment" can be probative evidence of a "pretext for punishing the offender for his political opinions."

In the *Izatula* case, it is difficult to find "pretext." Izatula admits he aided the rebellion; this is not a trumped-up charge. Still, the word "pretext" might cover more than simply trumped-up charges. Perhaps it also encompasses excessive punishment or selective prosecution. Either might indicate a motive to persecute. Here, a sentence of torture, although not advertised as government policy, is excessive. That being the case, there is good reason to think it could be a pretext for punishing rebels more severely for their political views. Mr. Vacca's decision is based at least in part on that exception. He says Izatula "would suffer punishment disproportionate to his crime." Without the torture and with a fair trial, the only question would be whether capital punishment is excessive for treason. For an American court, such a holding would be difficult.

Q4: The two holdings do seem inconsistent. If attempting to overthrow a totalitarian government is a legitimate form of political expression -- and the BIA majority suggests it is-- then the <u>less</u> drastic act of merely refusing to take up arms in support of the government seems no less legitimate. The reasoning employed by Mr. Vacca in his concurring opinion seems equally inconsistent. If the punishment that Izatula would receive is disproportionate to the offense of aiding the overthrow of the government, then *a fortiori* it would seem disproportionate to the offense of draft resistance.

Question on Coercive Population Controls as Persecution (page 915):

If the BIA was right to find that the Changs would experience nothing more than higher taxes and other economic consequences (rather than forced abortion or sterilization, as they alleged), then in theory the Changs could return home and continue to follow their religious beliefs. In practice, however, even merely "economic" sanctions can be devastating. The question is one of degree, and we would need to know more. Still, is that persecution or just economic hardship? They could certainly argue persecution based on religion, but ICE would contend that a country has a legitimate right to limit even religiously motivated acts if those acts cause damage to the economy and, hence, to the welfare of others.

If, despite the findings of the BIA, the fact is that the Changs would indeed be subjected to forced sterilization or abortion, then of course the basis for finding persecution is stronger. Even then, though, the BIA might have been right to say that the Changs were not being treated any differently from the rest of the population. The policy is facially neutral but has a disproportionate adverse impact on Roman Catholics. If the Changs are not Catholic, they would still be adversely affected but would have to argue that the "persecution," if any, is based on political opinion or social group, rather than on religion. See the next subsection for that discussion. The 1996 amendment discussed below now moots this latter point.

The larger question is the legitimacy of coerced abortions and sterilizations as population control devices. The tension is between solving a compelling national problem and respecting basic human rights. That the U.S. Constitution would not permit a particular practice doesn't mean the practice would violate international human rights norms (or vice-versa). Here the instructor could pose questions about the comparative merits of cultural relativism (deferring to the cultural norms of other countries) versus universalism (emphasizing the universal nature of international human rights). If one concludes, as the BIA did, that even coerced abortions and sterilizations would be permissible responses to China's population crisis (and, again, Congress has now answered that question), then the UNHCR Handbook suggests that the inquiry is whether the punishment is excessive.

2. "On Account of Race, Religion, Nationality, Membership in a Particular Social Group, or Political Opinion"

a. Race, Religion, and Nationality

This brief description is intended only as background reading.

b. Political Opinion

INS v. Elias-Zacarias (page 918):

In deportation proceedings, a Guatemalan who had entered without inspection applied for asylum. Guerrillas had come to his and his parents' home, requesting that Elias-Zacarias (and his family members) join them. Fearing retaliation by the government, the family refused. The guerrillas threatened to (and eventually did) return. Elias-Zacarias fled to the United States.

The IJ and the BIA denied asylum. The Ninth Circuit reversed, holding that forced recruitment by the guerrillas would constitute persecution on account of political opinion. The court reasoned that the resister is expressing a political opinion hostile to the persecutor and that the persecutor's motive is political.

The Supreme Court, by a vote of 6-3, reversed the Ninth Circuit. The Court expressed some doubt that Elias-Zacarias's refusal to join the guerrillas was the expression of a political opinion at all. His decision might simply have reflected a fear of combat or a desire to remain in civil life. The Court also questioned, but did not decide, whether neutrality could constitute political opinion. In addition, the Court left open whether imputed political opinion would ever suffice; it found that at any rate there was no evidence that the persecutors had imputed any particular opinion to Elias-Zacarias. Ultimately, though, the Court refrained from deciding whether Elias-Zacarias had expressed a political opinion. In the Court's view his claim failed for a different reason: To establish persecution on account of political opinion, the Court held, it is not enough to prove that the persecutors had a political objective; rather, one must prove that the persecutors' motive had been to persecute the claimant *because of the claimant's political opinion.* That showing had not been made in this case.

Justice Stevens, dissenting, would have held that political opinion can be expressed through inaction and that one's motives for taking a particular political position -- ideological conviction, a simple desire to live an ordinary life, or fear -- are irrelevant. He would also have recognized a persecution claim based on political opinion when the persecutors' actions are in response to a person's "overt manifestation" of a political opinion, such as refusing to join the ranks of the guerrillas.

<u>Notes and Questions Following Elias-Zacarias</u> (page 922):

Q2: If asylum policy is conceived in humanitarian terms, persecution motivated by the political strategy of the persecutors should suffice. To the asylum claimant, it will seldom matter whether the persecutors will act because they dislike the claimant's political opinion or because they believe the action will promote their own political objectives. Either way, the claimant fears suffering and the suffering is politically related. If, however, asylum policy is more narrowly conceived as an instrument for promoting human rights, then one can argue that the claimant who is persecuted because of his or her own political views has extra reason to be protected. In addition to the alleviation of suffering, asylum in this case helps to protect freedom of expression.

Q3: To be consistent, the Court would probably have to deny relief in the union hypothetical. Just as the guerrillas don't care why Elias-Zacarias refused to join them, the government won't care why the union leaders sought or received their positions. In each case, all that can be said is that the persecution promoted the political objectives of the persecutors.

The BIA in *Izatula* seems simply to have assumed that the feared persecution would be on account of political opinion. After *Elias-Zacarias*, that assumption is dubious. The government of Afghanistan probably didn't care whether Izatula was politically sympathetic to the rebel cause or just acting out of fear or self-interest. Either way, it would probably have wanted to punish him for aiding armed insurrection. The Supreme Court in *Elias-Zacarias* suggests that under those circumstances the required link between the persecution and applicant's political opinion is not present.

To demonstrate that its holding does not drain the political opinion prong of all significance, the Court perhaps would distinguish words from action. One who is persecuted for making anti-government statements, or for his or her associations, might still be eligible for asylum, while one who is persecuted only for actions -- even if those actions were prompted by political conviction -- might not. The dissent takes a broader view. Quoting from *Bolanos-Hernandez* (excerpted below on pages 925-27 of the text), the dissent characterizes the refusal to join the guerrillas as "an act that constitutes an overt manifestation of a political opinion."

Taken to its logical conclusion, though, wouldn't the *Elias-Zacarias* formulation bar asylum on political opinion grounds even in the political statements or political associations contexts? After all, one could make a speech or join an association for any number of reasons. It might be to express genuine political conviction, but it could also be to acquiesce to a threat, to bond with a group, or to impress a friend. The government probably won't care what beliefs or opinions the dissidents actually held; all the government would care about is that the statements were made or the associations formed, whether sincerely or not. It is hard to know, therefore, how Justice Scalia could draw any line that would be consistent with the result he reaches in *Elias-Zacarias* and at the same time not read the political opinion prong off the books.

Q4: Elias-Zacarias's claim seems the stronger of the two. Izatula faced persecution for aiding an armed insurrection against his government, while Elias-Zacarias faced persecution for refusing to do so. The former INS was therefore able to argue that Izatula faced only criminal prosecution, not persecution. That argument was not available to the INS in *Elias-Zacarias*. See also footnote 6 of the dissent.

Perhaps the BIA would seek to reconcile its decisions by observing that Izatula had sought to dislodge a totalitarian government. But the only reason that fact was thought relevant was that the totalitarian nature of the government precluded peaceful and legal means of effecting change. And if that was the idea, then Elias-Zacarias can observe that he had no lawful alternative either.

Q5: To argue against recognizing imputed political opinion, one might observe that the reason for granting asylum to a person who fears persecution based on political opinion is that one should not have to choose between suppressing his or her ideas and risking persecution. That rationale, the argument would run, does not apply when the person does not actually hold the viewpoint in question.

The arguments in favor of recognizing imputed political opinion might include the following:

a. The consequences to the individual are just as severe when the political opinion is imputed as they are when the political opinion is real. (Response: That argument is too far-reaching. The consequences could be just as severe even if the danger had nothing to do with political opinion at all or even with persecution.)

b. Just as one should not have to suppress his or her actual opinions, so too a person should not have to hold back on innocuous conduct just because it could be misunderstood as reflecting an objectionable political opinion.

c. Asylum is designed to protect the individual whose own government cannot or will not confer such protection. This rationale does not depend on a showing that the opinion imputed to the individual is real.

Q7: The reasons for recognizing imputed political opinion partly apply even when the imputation is cynical. The fact that the imputation is cynical does not render the consequences for the individual any less severe (although, again, the severity of the consequences might not be the proper test). Again, a person should not be required to refrain from innocent conduct just because he or she will be accused of holding subversive opinions. Also, the individual to whom a political opinion is cynically imputed is still just as unable to turn to his or her own country for protection. The main argument against recognizing cynically imputed political opinion is that the applicant in fact is being persecuted only for something that has nothing to do with politics (assuming that is the case on the particular facts), and the persecutor is merely using the political system as a tool.

Notes and Questions Following Note on Neutrality as Political Opinion (page 928):

Q1: Another possible interpretation is that Bolanos made a decision not to take action for either side but that he never really made a decision to remain politically neutral. Perhaps, for example, he sympathizes with one of the two other sides but was unwilling to get involved. Another possible interpretation is that Bolanos simply has no opinion at all. The government might argue that in such a case he could not claim persecution on the basis of political opinion because he would be no different from the vast majority of the rest of the populace.

Q2: Judge Reinhardt's opinion does not address that concern. Possible answers he might give include the following:

a. The vast majority of the population would not be likely to qualify because they would not be persecuted for their neutrality unless they openly articulate it.

b. The whole population is not going to arrive in the United States.

c. This consideration is legally irrelevant in any event. The law should be interpreted in a way that lets the chips fall where they may. If the consequence of this law is unacceptable, Congress can change it. The court should not do so.

Q3: Those who believe that neutrality should not be recognized as political opinion might argue that the purpose of granting asylum based on persecution on account of political opinion is to help those people who are in danger for standing up for their convictions, not to reward those who take positions out of expedience. One who holds that view might therefore disagree with Judge Reinhardt's first reason for recognizing neutrality as political opinion – that it is improper for the government to inquire into the motives that underlie an individual's political decisions. Opponents of recognizing neutrality might argue, in other words, that it is perfectly proper for the government to inquire into the motives when those political views are the basis on which a noncitizen seeks to enter or remain in the United States.

Judge Reinhardt also relied on the fact that the persecutor did not care what had motivated the individual's neutrality. Opponents of recognizing neutrality as political opinion might respond by observing that United States law does not protect against all persecution -- only against that which is based on political opinion or on one of the other four protected grounds.

Judge Reinhardt's other argument is more solid. He points to the practical difficulties of distinguishing economic, political and other motives. For the same reason, it is difficult to distinguish political opinion from political strategy. If the government persecutes members of a particular political party, should asylum really be denied simply because the applicant joined that party for selfish reasons?

Q4: There is something to what Judge Reinhardt has said here, but at the same time neutrality should not be equated with moderation. One could, for example, be neutral because one's beliefs are <u>more</u> radical than those of either of the two major sides.

Q5: Even if Judge Sneed had done his homework, he might have been skeptical that the BIA or a court could accurately determine whether an individual's choice was conscious and deliberate. There might be cases in which the evidence simply does not permit a confident assessment of whether the person has made a conscious choice or simply had no opinion at all. But there are indeed factors that could guide such a decision. The person might be able to produce evidence of prior political involvement. In *Bolanos*, for example, the court observed that the applicant had been a member of the right-wing political party, had severed his ties with that party, had been recruited by the guerrillas, and had refused to help them despite threats on his life.

Q7: The majority opinion says that "not taking sides" will not "ordinarily" be the affirmative expression of a political opinion. The implication is that there might be cases to the contrary. The Court seems to say that political opinion is to be distinguished from "indifference, indecisiveness and risk-averseness." Left open, therefore, is the possibility that a conscious preference for political neutrality will be treated differently from simple apathy. The dissent clearly recognizes neutrality as political opinion and suggests, moreover, that political neutrality can be sufficiently demonstrated through inaction.

<u>Refugees Sur Place</u>

The instructor who assigns this brief description could either use it as background reading or take up in class the question posed at the end: Which of the described classes of refugees sur place should be held eligible for asylum? The latter question could be discussed both as a matter of statutory interpretation and as a matter of policy.

As for statutory interpretation, categories (2) and (3) should clearly qualify if there is no independent barrier. Nothing in the refugee definition or in the terms of INA § 241(b)(3) disqualifies those applicants whose post-departure actions triggered the danger of persecution. With respect to category (1), the issue is whether this is persecution on the basis of political opinion or prosecution for a crime. Generally, nations may legally enforce emigration restrictions. Exceptionally, however, such restrictions could constitute persecution if the punishment is excessive or if the law is applied discriminatorily based on political opinion, as the court holds in *Rodriguez-Roman*. See also the Notes and Questions that follow *Izatula*.

As for policy, the government might argue that the applicant's predicament was self-induced; he or she could have remained silent. But there is no more reason in policy to require such silence after departure than there would be to require it before departure. The special problem with category (1) is that, unlike the applicants in categories (2) and (3), the applicant in category (1) broke the law. Again, the question is whether either the law as written or the law as applied is unjust. See above. Finally, with respect to category (2), those who oppose granting asylum to refugees sur place will argue that the law should not create an incentive for a noncitizen to file an unfounded asylum claim out of hope that, if it is denied, the denial will provide the foundation for a valid claim. At the same time, however, the law should not deter genuine refugees from filing claims out of fear that, if they are erroneously denied, the person will now be in even more serious trouble upon return.

c. "Particular Social Group"

i. General Definitions of "Social Group"

There are two reasons to assign this material. One is its growing practical importance, especially with respect to gender and sexual orientation. The other reason is that, of all the recognized bases for persecution, the "social group" prong generates the most serious policy discussions of the reasons for granting, and the reasons for limiting, asylum. Coverage of this material will also enhance the usefulness of Problems 1-5 on pages 997-99 of the text; those Problems, in turn, are an aid to bringing together the material on the substantive criteria for asylum.

Matter of Acosta (page 931):

This is the same case that opened the asylum section of this chapter, but the excerpt is a different one. Acosta alleged persecution on account of membership in a particular social group. The group consisted of members of COTAXI (the taxi co-op described earlier). Applying the principle of "ejusdem generis," the Board scanned the other four prongs of the statutory refugee definition and discerned that all dealt with immutable characteristics. It therefore held that "social group" means a group in which membership is determined by an immutable characteristic. The Board defined "immutable" to mean that the trait is either literally unchangeable or so fundamental to personal identity that the law should not require a person to change it. Since COTAXI members can avoid persecution by changing jobs, the Board reasoned, they do not comprise a social group.

Notes and Questions Following Acosta and Helton (page 934):

Q1: Probably the Board felt that, if a person will be persecuted because of membership in a group, and the person can easily end his or her membership in that group by eliminating that characteristic, then he or she can avoid persecution. In such a case, the argument would run, there is no real need to grant asylum. If in contrast the characteristic is one that literally cannot be changed, or it is so fundamental to personal identity that the law cannot conscionably require the person to change it, then asylum will be the applicant's only viable means of protection.

The main down side of the *Acosta* test is the practical problem of defining when a characteristic will be "fundamental" to personal identity. Is the test subjective or objective? Either way, judges will simply have to do their best. Perhaps it is no more difficult to decide whether a trait is fundamental to personal identity than to determine whether a particular deprivation is persecution.

Q3: The status seems immutable as the Board used that term in *Acosta*, since there is *now* no way to change his past and thus no way to avoid persecution. As a policy matter, he has committed a serious wrong but has served his sentence, and the past wrong seems an inadequate reason to expose him to further harm severe enough in magnitude to constitute persecution (unless his conviction renders him ineligible for asylum under one of the exceptions, discussed separately below.)

Q4: The refugee definition does refer to a "*particular social* group" (emphasis added), and perhaps that literal language is what inspired the BIA to add the social visibility and particularity requirements. But the policy reasons for denying refugee status on either ground (whether they are seen as requirements or merely factors to be weighed) are elusive. As for social visibility, perhaps the idea is that, if society does not perceive the alleged individuals as a group, there is less reason to believe they will be persecuted because of their membership in that group. But if any perception of group is to be treated as relevant to the probability of persecution, it should be the persecutors' perception, not that of the larger society. More important, it is superfluous to require even a showing that the persecutors perceive enough of a group to make it likely they will persecute individuals for membership in that group, because the refugee definition already requires that the fear of persecution be "well-founded." If in a given case neither society nor the persecutors regard the alleged group as a group and are therefore unlikely to persecute them on that basis, then there will be no "well-founded" fear of persecution. So the social visibility requirement seems unnecessary. And if the fear of persecution is well-founded notwithstanding the group's lack of social visibility, then denying asylum for lack of social visibility leaves the affected group unprotected.

As for particularity, it is understandable that an adjudicative body would want some objective basis for judging whether a given individual meets the group definition. But the fact that there is some room for subjective judgment at the edges does not seem a convincing reason to deny protection in cases where it is clear that the individual fits the definition.

Q8: If read literally, the UNHCR definition embraces every group (except a group defined solely by the fact that the group members are persecuted). The qualifier "who share a common characteristic" adds nothing, because every group capable of being described will necessarily have at least one common characteristic and therefore will qualify under the first prong. It is true that other passages in the Guidelines emphasize immutability even though the actual definition does not say it is required; possibly, therefore, UNHCR intended to require it (for the first prong). On the other hand, the wording of the definition appears to distinguish intentionally between facts that are required and facts that will "often" be present. It is a strange formulation.

Q10: If the word "social" had been omitted, Helton's interpretation would clearly be correct. It would be necessary only to show a well-founded fear of persecution on account of membership in a particular group. Even with the insertion of the word "social," a similar conclusion is possible. Perhaps the term came to mind because the particular examples that prompted the Swedish representative and others to propose it happened to be groups whose activities had social implications, and no limitation along those lines was intended.

If the drafters meant what Helton suggests they meant, better wording might have been "well-founded fear of persecution, including, but not limited to, that based on race, religion, etc."

As for the UNHCR definition, even a literal reading still requires persecution because of membership in some group. It would not be enough, for example, to prove that the persecution will be prompted by a personal grudge unique to the applicant. Therefore even the literal reading (see the analysis of item 8 above) would not technically render the other four Convention grounds superfluous. But it would certainly make them a lot less significant.

Q11: The second quoted sentence from *Estrada-Posadas* seems inadequate as a rationale. Congress did not list *any* of the specific classes that might constitute a social group. By the court's reasoning, therefore, there would be no social groups at all (except possibly those defined by race, religion, nationality or political opinion-- i.e., groups whose members do not need to establish "social group" because they are already expressly covered).

Under a pure *Acosta* test, one's own immediate family easily constitutes a social group, since family membership is immutable, whether the relationships are blood relationships that cannot be altered or marriage relationships that are fundamental to personal identity. Some would even call family the paradigm "social group." The imposition of a social visibility requirement probably would not alter that result, since almost any society would perceive the family as a group. Particularity might theoretically be a problem, since reasonable minds could differ as to which family relationships are too distant to be included, but even as to that, nothing prevents an adjudicator from making individualized judgments.

Whether the family members of similarly situated others meet the various social group definitions is a closer question. Immutability is not at issue, since, again, family membership is either literally unchangeable or at least fundamental to personal identity. But social visibility could be problematic, as society might not perceive the family members of army deserters, for example, as a discrete group. If the family members band together in some observable way, the case might well be strengthened. The particularity question is similar to the one just discussed; the main issue would be whether the lines that separate qualifying and non-qualifying family relationships are clear enough.

Q12: Under *Acosta*, people with HIV would clearly be a social group because the disease is not yet curable; therefore the trait is immutable. Social visibility and particularity would not seem problematic either. The policy question turns largely on the nature of the persecution. If the persecutors' actions are sufficiently targeted, and the consequences are serious enough, then there is no obvious reason not to find that the refugee definition has been met. As for discretion, the competing interests are (a) compassion and (b) medical costs and the risk of spreading the disease.

ii. Sexual Orientation and "Social Group"

Matter of Toboso-Alfonso (page 940):

A gay man from Cuba applied, in exclusion proceedings, for asylum and withholding. Because of a drug conviction, the IJ denied asylum in the exercise of discretion. The IJ granted withholding, however, and the INS appealed. Toboso alleged that both the Cuban government and the private sector persecute homosexuals, whom he characterized as making up a particular social group for purposes of the refugee definition. The claimed persecution took the form of general harassment (including periodic detention and interrogation), a specific threat to imprison him if he did not leave in 1980 on the Mariel boatlift, and mob violence. By a 3-2 vote, the BIA held that homosexuals constitute a social group because homosexuality is immutable, and it found that his life or freedom would be threatened because of his homosexuality. Thus, it granted withholding of removal. The two dissenters did not believe he would face as much danger or as much harassment as he claimed.

Notes and Questions Following Toboso-Alfonso (page 943):

Q2: It is not clear what result the BIA would have reached. The INS had argued that, because particular homosexual acts are illegal, the Board should not recognize gays as a social group. In rejecting that argument, the Board specifically relied on the fact that Toboso was being persecuted solely because of his status, not because of his acts. Later in the opinion the Board again emphasized that this was not a case of enforcing the laws that prohibit homosexual activity. This does not mean the BIA would have rejected a claim based on punishment for homosexual acts. It means only that *Toboso-Alfonso* is distinguishable.

The distinction between status and acts is relevant to at least two elements of the refugee definition -- persecution and social group. As for the former, the question is whether the sanctions amount to mere criminal prosecution rather than persecution. From *Izatula* and the Notes and Questions following it, the students should remember that courts usually resolve the characterization question by asking whether the punishment is a pretext for persecution. One way to establish pretext is to show that the punishment is disproportionate to the crime. We would need to know the prohibited act and the punishment.

As for social group, the Board relies on the immutability of sexual orientation. Here the instructor might refer the students to the earlier empirical readings, on pages 276-82 of the text, concerning the nature of homosexuality. Punishment for prohibited acts presents a more difficult issue. The government might argue that, while one cannot change or be expected to change his or her sexual orientation, one can refrain from engaging in prohibited physical acts. The asylum claimant might respond that when the law prohibits consensual sexual acts it makes demands that are fundamental to basic personal identity. Under that reasoning, engaging in prohibited consensual sexual acts might well be an immutable characteristic in the second sense in which *Acosta* used that term, and those who engage in such acts might thus constitute a social group.

Q3: Yes, the BIA did hold precisely that. By applying the *Acosta* test and finding homosexuality immutable, the Board held gays and lesbians to be a social group. As the cited cases illustrate, there remain several obstacles to the success of individual claims: The claimant must establish that the feared consequences qualify as persecution; that the fear that those consequences will materialize is well founded; and that they will occur because of the claimant's sexual orientation. All these showings will vary with country of origin and with the circumstances of the individual claimant.

Q4: The arguments in favor of granting asylum on this basis are that the persecution of gays and lesbians in many countries can be unusually vicious and that the immutable nature of sexual orientation makes persecution almost impossible to avoid without giving up relationships central to one's identity.

The main argument against recognizing asylum claims based on sexual orientation is that the enactment of laws prohibiting even consensual homosexual acts reflects societal disapproval of homosexuality. The counterargument would distinguish between persecution based on status and persecution based on acts.

iii. Gender and "Social Group"

Notes and Questions Following Greatbatch (page 949):

Q2: Possible explanations include the following:

a. There might be a concern that the volume of cases is simply too great for the United States (or even the world) to handle.

b. Maybe national and international leaders don't take gender-based persecution seriously enough to think that adding gender is important or even a good idea.

c. Some might believe that gender roles are a matter for each culture to work out on its own.

d. There might be a belief that adding gender to the list would leave the definition too vulnerable to judicial activism. (Analogous arguments were made by opponents of the Equal Rights Amendment to the United States Constitution).

Fatin v. INS (page 950):

Fatin applied for asylum and withholding in deportation proceedings, alleging (at the BIA stage) that she would be persecuted in Iran because of her membership in a social group -- westernized women who found it offensive to be forced to conform to Muslim teachings, including the compulsory wearing of the chador. At her hearing she implied that, if returned to Iran, she would wear the chador rather than openly disobey the law. The IJ and the BIA both denied her applications on the ground that she had not established a great enough likelihood of persecution. She petitioned the court of appeals for review.

Deferring to the BIA, the court adopted the immutability test announced in *Acosta*. The court then held that, in order to qualify for either asylum or withholding based on membership in a particular social group, a person must (1) identify a particular social group; (2) establish his or her membership in that group; and (3) establish that he or she would be persecuted because of that membership.

The court acknowledged that under the *Acosta* test women constitute a social group, because gender is immutable. It held, however, that if the claimed social group were defined as all women, Fatin would fail to satisfy element 3 because, in the court's view, not all women are persecuted in Iran; only those whose convictions are so strong that they would defy the religious laws would be persecuted. Confining the social group to women who find it offensive to be forced to wear the chador would produce the same result, the court held, because the court did not regard a dress code as persecution. And if the social group were defined still more narrowly, to embrace only those women whose convictions are so strong that they would disobey the law requiring the wearing of the chador, then persecution could be established but Fatin would fail element 2 because the evidence did not prove that she would refuse to comply. All of the possible social group claims would therefore fail for one reason or another. (In another portion of the decision, edited out, the court rejects a parallel claim based on political opinion.)

<u>Notes and Questions Following Fatin</u> (page 955):

Q1: The pertinent social group could be defined as all women, since gender is immutable. And obviously Fatin is a member of that group. The court holds, however, that Fatin could not establish persecution based *solely* on gender because, as the court sees it, not all women in Iran are persecuted. Only those women who would actually defy the dress code (or maybe some subcategory of women whose objections reach a certain level of intensity but fall short of outright disobedience) are persecuted.

If the claimed social group is narrowed to include only those women who find the dress code offensive, the court suggests that Fatin would fail to satisfy element 3. The claimed group might well be a social group, but she has not shown that, for her, being forced to wear the chador is so deeply abhorrent to her beliefs as to constitute persecution.

Finally, if the group is further narrowed to encompass only those women whose convictions are so strong that they would defy the law and risk the severe punishment, then the trait is fundamental enough that membership is immutable and the group qualifies as a social group. Fatin, however, has not established that she meets that test.

Q2: This issue is mentioned at this point because it figured in the court's analysis. The instructor might ask the class whether there would have been any statutory interpretation or other policy reason to deny asylum had the court regarded forced adherence to the dress code as persecution. Put another way, if a government persecutes some women, and it would not have persecuted them had they been men, is it not engaging in persecution on account of gender?

More detailed class discussion is probably best deferred to the subsection that deals with the meaning of "on account of."

Q3: To reject the proposition that the court assumes *arguendo* would be asking a lot. One can accept the premise that not all discrimination, and not all intrusions on personal autonomy, rise to the level of persecution, and one can accept the court's specific conclusion that forced adherence to a dress code is not per se persecution, and still feel that a willingness to defy the law is too high a standard. Arguably, a person should not have to risk his or her life in order to show that a belief is abhorrent enough to make a practice persecution.

Q4: These questions have a common theme. Should a person be denied asylum when he or she can avoid persecution by sacrificing a human right? Some would argue that, regardless of whether asylum is conceived as primarily a humanitarian project or a human rights project, the answer depends on the importance of the particular right. Others would take a purist approach, arguing that the deprivation of any human right rises to the level of persecution and that one should not be required to trade off one human right to receive another.

Q5: The government might make two arguments. One would be that the woman is making a conscious decision. If she chooses to resist, the argument runs, then she should accept the consequences. Such is the nature of civil disobedience. She should not be able to force the United States to grant asylum by choosing a course of action that she knows will lead to persecution. Moreover, the government might argue, violation of the dress code is a criminal act. The ensuing punishment is simply criminal prosecution, not persecution. Thus, the only issue is whether the punishment is selectively imposed because of her race, religion, etc., disproportionate to the crime, or otherwise pretextual.

The court ends up applying a test that requires <u>both</u> a subjective and an objective showing. See original footnote 10 of the court's opinion.

Q8: There does seem to be a difference in degree. Those who object to the dress code normally object because of the compulsion, and its attendant intrusion on personal autonomy and dignity, not because they think it would be immoral to wear the chador. In contrast, those who are denied the freedom to practice their own religion object not only because of the compulsion but also because the religion itself is fundamental to their beliefs.

Matter of Kasinga (page 959):

Kasinga, a 19-year-old native and citizen of Togo, was about to be subjected, against her will, to female genital mutilation (FGM), in preparation for an arranged polygamous marriage. She fled Togo and eventually made her way to the United States, applying for asylum at the port of entry. She provided extensive testimony and documentary evidence detailing the FGM procedure used by her tribe, as well as the relevant country conditions. Her claim was that the FGM that she would be forced to undergo in Togo was persecution on account of her membership in a particular social group. The opinion does not make clear precisely how Kasinga formulated the applicable social group, but the BIA, on appeal from the IJ's denial, describes the group as consisting of young women of her particular tribe who have not yet undergone FGM as practiced by that tribe and who oppose that practice.

The former INS stipulated that FGM *can* amount to persecution on account of membership in a social group, but it asked the Board to adopt a comprehensive framework for deciding future cases and it asked for a remand in the present case on issues of credibility. The BIA rejected both INS requests. The Board found Kasinga credible, found that her fear of FGM was well-founded, held that the particular form of FGM that she feared constituted persecution (though it did not indicate what the relevant factors were), found that the group it had posited met the definition of a social group because intact genitalia are fundamental to identity and therefore immutable, and found that the persecution would occur on account of membership in that social group. In the exercise of discretion, the Board granted asylum.

Board Member Filppu's concurring opinion, joined by Member Heilman, elaborated on why it was proper not to formulate the comprehensive roadmap that the INS had requested. He also questioned whether the group hypothesized by the majority opinion constituted a social group, hinting that the *Sanchez-Trujillo* test might have some (unspecified) relevance.

Board Member Rosenberg emphasized that the Board's opinion did not deviate from any settled principles of asylum law. She doubted, though, that it was necessary to qualify the social group definition by reference to Kasinga's opposition to FGM, an element that Member Rosenberg saw as more relevant to whether the practice amounted to persecution. She also lamented the failure of the INS to cite or otherwise apply its own Gender Guidelines.

Notes and Questions Following Kasinga (page 967):

Q2: As for the first question, there is no obvious reason to add the qualifiers it did. Perhaps the Board thought that a broader definition of "social group" would have made it too hard for Kasinga to establish a causal link between the persecution and the social group. If that was the sole concern, it seems misplaced for reasons discussed in item 11 of the Notes and Questions and in subsection d (the meaning of "on account of").

The Board's use of the *Fatin* decision is questionable. The court in that case hypothesized three different social groups. The Board here ignores the two parts that seem directly relevant and cites, without explanation, the only part that doesn't. The one part the Board cites is the part in which the court held that a person who suffers great harm for *refusing* to conform with a cultural norm that goes against the applicant's conscience might make out a case of persecution on account of social group. Since Fatin did not claim she would refuse, the court held, she was ineligible for asylum. That doesn't help Kasinga.

In contrast, the other two portions of the *Fatin* analysis seem relevant. In the first part, the court held that women constitute a social group, an argument that Kasinga could have made here. (But the court held that that theory would not avail Fatin, for reasons discussed in items 5 and 11 below and possibly applicable here.) And in the second part, which is most closely analogous to the theory the majority ultimately adopts in *Kasinga*, the court in *Fatin* defined the group as consisting of women who found the feared harm (in that case, the mandatory dress code) offensive. So defined, however, the group was not a social group, the court said, because merely taking offense is not fundamental enough to be considered immutable. Somehow, therefore, the Board needed to distinguish *Fatin*, not just cite it. Perhaps it could have done so by emphasizing the difference between the dress code in *Fatin* and the permanent loss of sexual sensation and the safety risks associated with FGM. Since the court in *Fatin* did not consider forced compliance with the dress code onerous enough to constitute persecution, it was only the consequences associated with noncompliance that would rise to that level. FGM, because of its intrusiveness, its painfulness, and its permanence, is different. Alternatively, the Board in *Kasinga* might have been able to argue that Kasinga found FGM not only “offensive” but “abhorrent.” The court in*Fatin* did not hold that that would suffice, but at least it refrained from deciding the issue, opting instead to assume it *arguendo* and find Fatin had failed to establish her abhorrence.

Q3: Board Member Filppu's concurrence is puzzling. He argues that the social group should not be "defined principally in relation to the harm feared by the asylum applicant." By that he seems to mean that one's opposition to FGM should not "principally" define the social group. It is difficult to quibble with that proposition. If the social group could be defined to consist of all individuals who will incur particular persecution, then by definition any form of persecution could be characterized as being on account of its own tailor-made social group. That is the approach subsequently repudiated by the Justice Department’s proposed regulations.

The difficulties with Mr. Filppu's social group analysis, however, are twofold. First, arguably he is attacking a straw person. It is not at all evident that the harm feared was the principal -- let alone the only -- element of the majority's social group definition. Probably the main elements were gender and (in the Board's view) tribal membership. Second, Mr. Filppu does not stop with that observation. Citing *Sanchez-Trujillo*, he goes on to lament that the Board does not have more information about the degree of affiliation and homogeneity among the group members. Before that, he suggests that it is important to know whether Togolese society views the members of the proposed social group as a distinct body. None of those considerations is relevant under the *Acosta* formulation that had been thought to be firmly in place; the *Acosta* test asks only whether group membership is immutable. The Filppu approach does, however, foreshadow the emergence of the social visibility requirement discussed on pages 934-35 above.

Q4: That Kasinga is a member of the Kchamba-Kunsuntu tribe is relevant both to whether she will be subjected to FGM and to what form the FGM is likely to take. And the particulars of this tribe's surgical procedures are relevant, if at all, only to whether the practice can be termed a form of persecution. (As to the last point, see item 6 below.) If there is something to be gained by including these factors again in the social group definition, it is not apparent.

Q5: The proposed approach certainly is simpler. The Board's approach leaves great uncertainty as to which elements ought to be included in the social group definition. Further, once the elements are chosen, each one requires an immutability check. If the social group is defined in such a way that the persecution would not occur but for membership in that group, that should be enough. See item 11 below.

Q6: One possible answer is that as a matter of law involuntary FGM is always persecution. The argument would be that the harm is inherently severe since it entails a loss of sexual fulfillment, for the rest of one's life, and for the purpose of enabling males to exert dominion over females. Moreover, it is involuntary. Another possible answer is that FGM is never persecution; it is merely a cultural norm and a tribal ritual. A third possible approach is a multi-factor test. Factors could include the degree of safety and sanitation with which the procedure is performed and how painful the surgery is (including whether an anesthetic is used).

Q7: The real question is how severe the harm must be in cases (like the typical FGM case) in which the person administering the harm has no malignant or punitive intent. The INS proposal was that in such cases the action must "shock the conscience." On the one hand, it could be argued that all human rights violations should shock the conscience; otherwise the interest being infringed would probably not have risen to the level of a universal human right in the first place. On the other hand, there is a spectrum of seriousness even within the class of interests recognized as human rights -- surely murder and torture are on a different scale from suppression of speech. To the extent that asylum is seen as a vehicle for promoting human rights, then, the line might be drawn below the "shock the conscience" level. On this point, see the Hathaway argument noted in item 2 of the Notes and Questions following *Acosta* in the "Fear of Persecution" section, above.

Q8: U.S. law normally allows parents to make significant decisions for their young children, subject to various constraints. There is no apparent reason to deviate from that principle in this case. Thus, the child should be treated as having refused. If the case is otherwise indistinguishable from *Kasinga*, the result should therefore be the same. The INS took the position that a young child who has experienced FGM should not be regarded as a victim of past persecution, but the opinion does not reveal what the INS position would be in instances of future FGM administered to a young child whose parents are opposed to it.

As to the asylum claim of the parent, there have been many cases in which asylum has been granted based on the harm that would befall a family member. Courts recognize that harm to one family member can be severe enough to be considered persecution of others. The result of the *Olowo* decision is that the mother has to choose between abandoning her daughter and subjecting her to FGM.

Q9: Male circumcision seems different in several respects. First, it does not destroy the sexual function, as FGM (designedly) does. Second, it is not intended as a means for one gender to exert power over another gender or as a means for one gender to repress the sexuality of another gender. Third, male circumcision is not normally a practice that is forced on the parents. It is the forcible nature of FGM that raises the issue. Fourth, when the applicant is a baby, the consent issue becomes more complicated, as discussed above.

Q10: There is no scientific answer to the general question; it is all a matter of the relative weights to be attached to human rights and respect for cultural norms repugnant to our own, and of one's reaction to the specific practice of FGM. As for the hypothetical, it is not clear how those who reject an asylum claim based on FGM would come out. Perhaps they would reach a similar result. Or, perhaps they would distinguish FGM from castration on the ground that the latter permanently prevents procreation.

Q13: How much guidance to provide is always a difficult judgment call. Comprehensive guidance is usually best provided by statute or regulation rather than in the written opinion of an adjudicative tribunal. Apart from the superior accountability of the political branches, judges receive most of their information from the opposing counsel, who seldom have either the time or the incentive to do careful research on issues that their cases do not present.

Here, though, the BIA does seem to have gone to the opposite extreme. It accepts the parties' stipulation that FGM *can* constitute persecution, but it says nothing about how one can tell when it will and when it won't. Perhaps readers of the opinion would have been able to infer that the BIA was applying a particular test if the BIA at least had explained precisely what it was about the present facts that led it to conclude that the FGM feared by Kasinga was persecution. But the Board did not do even that. Maybe the BIA believed that involuntary FGM is always persecution, as a matter of law, but it did not say that. If, as is likely, the BIA concluded that sometimes FGM is persecution and sometimes it isn't, then what made the FGM in this particular case persecution? Without explanation, immigration judges, ICE, and the practicing bar will have no way to know.

Q14: One of the most important functions of a draft dissent is to persuade one or more panel members to change their minds. Another is to persuade a reviewing court to reverse the decision on appeal. Still another is to persuade adjudicators in other cases not to accept the majority opinion if they don't have to (e.g. higher courts in the same jurisdiction or courts in other jurisdictions). Yet another audience is whichever person or group has the power to supersede the decision -- in the present context, the Attorney General or the Congress. A dissent can also provide ammunition for advocates in future cases, as they argue either for overruling or for a narrow interpretation. Finally, a dissent can be written out of professional pride; the dissenter wants to disassociate himself or herself from the reasoning of the majority and wants the public to know that the reasons for the dissent are convincing.

<u>Notes and Questions Following Moore and Anker Articles</u> (page 983):

Q1: The theory for insisting on a link to the state is that the state is supposed to protect individuals within its territory. The theory of asylum is that it is only when that supposition breaks down, because of either inability or unwillingness on the part of the state, that asylum becomes a necessary substitute. This, it might be argued, is an inevitable result as long as we live in a world of sovereign states.

The counter-argument might be that, if the feared private persecution takes place, it has to be because the state is either unable or unwilling to prevent it. There is no third possibility. If the state were both willing and able to prevent it, then obviously the act would not take place. That logical argument aside, one might argue that the goals of asylum - promoting human rights, avoiding unnecessary suffering, etc. - do not hinge on the identity of the persecutors. Whoever the perpetrators are, granting asylum to the applicant who demonstrates a well-founded fear of persecution on a protected ground serves both human rights and the humanitarian relief of suffering.

This question implicates the public sphere / private sphere distinction raised at the outset of this section. Women's asylum claims, the argument runs, are especially likely to occur in the private sphere, where the difficulty of establishing a link to the state is disproportionately likely to occur. Men's asylum claims, in contrast, are more likely to involve state actors.

Q2: The *Horvath* approach appears to require a showing that the state fails to make *reasonable* efforts to prevent the feared persecution. The New

Zealand approach does not require that the state be at fault; the approach resembles strict liability. If the applicant establishes a well-founded fear of persecution because of one of the protected grounds, the fact that the state made or would make a "reasonable" but ultimately unsuccessful effort to prevent it is irrelevant to asylum.

A proponent of *Horvath* might argue, again, that in asylum law the focus should be on the state as the primary source of protection. No one can preempt all conceivable harm, but if the country of origin makes reasonable efforts to prevent persecution, it has done all the international community could rightly ask of it.

An advocate of the New Zealand approach might respond that the preceding argument misses the point. Whether to grant an asylum claim is not about holding the country of origin accountable. It is about whether to grant refuge to a person who reasonably fears persecution on one of the protected grounds. Neither the likelihood nor the magnitude of the feared harm will depend on whether the state's failure to prevent it reflected reasonable or unreasonable efforts by the state.

Q3: If one otherwise accepts the New Zealand approach - i.e., that "unable to protect" really does mean precisely that, and not merely "unwilling to exert reasonable effort" - then the rest of Chairperson Haines's position follows. If the state stands on the sidelines and refrains from acting out of a desire to allow persecution on one of the protected grounds, then it seems easy to characterize the private actor as an agent of state persecution. Conversely, if the private actor is motivated by a desire to persecute on one of the protected grounds, then that alone should satisfy the requirements for asylum, since the harm that might occur is precisely the harm that the asylum laws were meant to avoid.

Q4: Anker's empirical premise is that domestic violence is meant "to keep . . . wives in their place," and is "fueled by stereotypical sex-role expectations for 'their' women."

Modern sociological studies certainly suggest that those motives underlie much of the domestic violence prevalent at least today. But motives can vary. What if the batterer is simply a violent bully who has no specific ill will toward women, would use force against anyone he can to get his way, and picks mainly on his wife solely because her proximity and his greater physical size enable him to get away with it?

Accepting the empirical premise as generally valid, however, one might posit any of several rules of law, including the following:

a. The law could adopt a conclusive presumption that physical assault by a male against his female partner is on account of gender (and therefore social group). If the actual correlation is felt to be strong enough, then any error that will occur in a minority of cases might be thought less important than avoiding false negatives in which the motive was in fact gender-related but the applicant is unable to provide the proof.

b. The law could adopt a rebuttable presumption along the same lines. Once the applicant demonstrates a well-founded fear of persecution by her male partner, the burden would shift to ICE to prove that the partner is motivated by something other than one of the five protected grounds.

c. The law could adopt a permissible inference. The rule could be that a well-founded fear of persecution by one's male partner permits, but does not require, the factfinder to conclude that the persecution was gender-motivated.

Q6: The regulation does seem self-contradictory. The decisionmaker is instructed only that he or she "should consider whether the government takes *reasonable* steps to control the infliction of harm or suffering and whether the applicant has *reasonable* access to the state protection that exists" [emphasis added]. All of the specific evidence that the regulation then lists goes only to whether the government is doing what it is supposed to do – not to whether, despite the government's best efforts, the fear of persecution on one of the protected grounds remains reasonable. To avoid the self-contradicting feature of the regulation, a court could give plain meaning effect to the phrase "unwilling or unable" and hold that the list of factors, being relevant only to "unwilling," was not meant to be exhaustive.

d. "On Account Of"

Islam v. Sec. of State for the Home Dept. (page 990):

See the synopsis of the facts in the coursebook.

Notes and Questions Following Islam (Shah) (page 995):

Q2: Lord Hoffmann points out that only a subset of a protected racial group is being persecuted – not all Jews, only those Jews who are perceived as having violated certain norms. Nonetheless, he concludes, it is still persecution based on race. Lord Millett agrees that the Jews in this hypothetical are being persecuted on account of race.

Lord Hoffmann implies that the same analysis should guide the present case. Just as the persecution (hypothetically) was directed only at those Jews who were believed to have violated certain norms, so too the persecution here is being directed only at a subcategory of women. In neither case should the fact that only a subset of a protected group is targeted preclude a finding of persecution on account of that protected ground.

Lord Millett distinguishes the present case. He acknowledges that women are generally *discriminated against* in Pakistan, but argues that only a subcategory of women – those who are thought to have violated social norms – are *persecuted*. He distinguishes the Jewish example by stressing that the particular norm that the persecuted group was violating – the requirement of conspicuous identification as Jews – was in fact used for the very purpose of setting them up to be persecuted. Yet couldn't the same thing be said here? The threat to falsely accuse the women of adultery was specifically intended to set them up to be persecuted.

Q3: In the present case, the persecution might or might not reflect a specific animus toward women, but even if it doesn't, the point is that the government's refusal to protect women makes the private actor's persecution possible. In each case, therefore, Lord Hoffmann's point is that government-sponsored discrimination is what motivates the private actors to target their respective victims.

Q4: It is not clear why this hypothetical claim should fail. Private actors are singling out women, and only women, for persecution, and the government is unable to prevent these acts from taking place. The real issue this hypothetical presents is whether the law should require an asylum claimant to prove that the government is failing to exert a reasonable effort. One who believes that such a showing should be required would reject this hypothetical claim for that reason, but not because of dissatisfaction with the but-for test. If indeed only women are targeted, then it is hard to see why "common sense" would require a conclusion that the persecution is not on account of gender.

Q5: The first part of the question returns us to the "university students of Asian descent" hypothetical offered in the essay that precedes the *Islam* case. The individuals are being persecuted on two grounds – being university students and being of Asian descent. The fact that they have two strikes against them, not just one, should hardly weaken their asylum claim, from either a policy or an interpretation standpoint. As to the second part of the question, there is no inherent inconsistency in finding that in a given society both men and women are persecuted because of gender. As long as each gender is expected to follow a different set of norms, and as long as individuals are persecuted for failing to comply with those gender-specific norms, there is nothing illogical in finding persecution on account of gender. To dismiss the women's claim on the speculation that men might also be persecuted for violating social norms ignores the fact that the particular norms in question were themselves imposed only on women.

Q6: The courts' test and the Justice Department's proposed test seem inherently irreconcilable, as Anker suggests. If a persecutor has two motives, and the more dominant motive is not related to a protected characteristic but the other motive is, then the applicant presumably would fail a centrality test but pass the "at least in part" test. The instructor can ask the students whether that is a good result. On the one hand, some might argue, finite asylum slots should be reserved for claimants who would be persecuted mainly for the especially pernicious reasons listed in the Convention and statute. On the other hand, if the protected characteristic were the only motive, the person would clearly qualify; why the additional motive for persecution should work *against* the applicant is not clear.

A but-for test might well solve this problem too. If the Justice Department's concern is that a motive that contributes only in a trivial way to the persecution should not be accorded legal significance, a but-for test could be a way to weed out such claims. If the protected characteristic was important enough to the persecutor that without it the persecution would not occur – i.e., if it made the difference between persecution occurring and not occurring – then it cannot be dismissed as trivial.

<u>Problems</u> <u>1-5:</u> (page 997):

These Problems bring together the material covered up to this point on the substantive criteria for asylum. The students will generally have to decide whether there has been persecution and, if so, whether that persecution is "on account of" one of the five protected grounds.

Problem 1: The first question is whether the consequence she faces constitutes "persecution." As to that, there are two issues:

a. Is the hardship severe enough? She would have the choice of either risking her life (because of her heart condition) if she does farm labor, or being taken away and killed if she resists. Even if she is exaggerating the health risks, what she faces might well be persecution simply because she is given no choice of work and is losing her career. Economic loss alone, however, is generally held not to be enough for persecution, and she is apparently being paid enough to survive. Still, combined with the loss of her career, the difficult conditions might rise to the level of persecution.

b. Is she being singled out? The operation is not specifically targeted at her, but the government efforts might be systematic enough that she can be sure she would be included.

c. Is this really persecution rather than prosecution for violating the legal obligation to move to the countryside? She can certainly argue that the punishment -- being taken away and probably killed -- is disproportionate to the offense.

Assuming she would suffer "persecution," is it "on account of" one of the five protected grounds? One possibility is political opinion. She could argue that by resisting relocation she is manifesting her political opinion that she should not be forced to relocate and to do agricultural labor. Under *Elias-Zacarias* that argument would probably fail, since the government might not care what political opinion is prompting her to resist. Alternatively, she might argue that the government is likely to impute an adverse political opinion to her if she resists relocation. ICE's response to both arguments would probably be that, if she refused to cooperate, her government would merely be punishing her for violating the law.

She might also argue that lawyers constitute a "social group." Under *Acosta*, the question is whether being a lawyer is so fundamental to her personal identity that she should not be required to make that change. The BIA in*Acosta* rejected a similar argument by a taxi driver, holding that one has no right to a job of his or her choice. She might attempt to distinguish *Acosta* by arguing that, as a professional, she has invested considerable time and training, to a much greater degree than has a taxi driver. Is that a valid basis for distinction, or is it just elitism? If a social visibility requirement is superimposed, the question would be whether her country's society perceives lawyers as a group.

Problem 2: Here there are at least two consequences on which a persecution claim might be based: the danger posed by the private groups (including his being driven out of business) that the government is either unable or unwilling to control, and a possible prosecution for sodomy. Evidence of the first fear will include the note on his door and the firebombing of a nearby business. This evidence would seem to establish both the necessary degree of severity and any necessary singling out.

Is that persecution "on account of" membership in a "social group?" Applying the immutability test of *Acosta*, the BIA in *Toboso-Alfonso* held that homosexuals are a social group. If social visibility is also required, the fact question would be whether society perceives gays as a group. Possibly there could even be "particularity" issues, since not everyone is neatly categorized as straight or gay.

An additional difficulty is that he is not willing to disclose his sexual orientation. Therefore we do not know whether he is in fact a member of the group. The argument, then, would have to be that the government would impute homosexuality. By analogy to the cases on political opinion, that should be enough.

Finally, he might argue he would be persecuted on account of his political opinion. His business, after all, is a bookstore, and putting him out of business would stop the spread of ideas. He might also argue that, in his country, persecutors impute to homosexuals a political opinion critical of the government position on homosexuality.

Although the persecution discussed thus far is by private actors (at least not proven otherwise), the facts suggest that the government is doing little if anything to prevent it. If anything, the government seems to be fanning the flames. Under those circumstances, it is fairly easy to conclude that the government is at least "unwilling" to control the private conduct.

The veiled threat to prosecute him for sodomy requires a separate analysis. It is not clear whether the threatened prosecution will occur, since he is not willing to reveal his sexual orientation and therefore is unlikely to engage openly in homosexual acts. If the prosecution does occur, however, is it persecution? Prosecution for criminal activity is not ordinarily persecution, but as discussed earlier it can be if either the punishment is excessive or the law is being enforced discriminatorily on the basis of one of the five protected grounds. Here he would probably not be able to show that criminal punishment for this offense is inherently excessive, because sodomy is still punished in many states of the United States. Rather, he would argue that the particular punishment -- ten years imprisonment -- is excessive. It is not clear how a court would respond.

Assuming persecution, would it be on account of one of the five protected grounds? One possibility, again, is social group. See the analysis above. He probably would not be able to demonstrate persecution on account of political opinion, unless he can demonstrate that he is being selectively prosecuted because he is outspoken or because he owns a bookstore.

Problem 3: Economic disadvantage is usually not enough to constitute persecution. The cultural bias against women in her country might also not be strong enough to be persecution, since otherwise almost any group that is the object of popular prejudice would be refugees. But official government discrimination against women in university grants is a stronger factor. Although discrimination alone is usually not enough to establish persecution, this particular form of discrimination is fundamental because it affects her ability to earn a living and because the action the government has taken systematically perpetuates inequality.

If any of the above arguments lead the court to find a well-founded fear of persecution, and if the particular court accepts *Acosta*, then women will be a particular social group and she should have little difficulty establishing eligibility for asylum. Again, however, courts that adopt a social visibility requirement will have to determine whether society perceives women as a group.

Problem 4: The couple must choose among prison, abstention from sex even during marriage, or taking the chance of having children against their will. All are significant restrictions on personal freedom, although there might be some difficulty in establishing persecution if the particular court requires a singling out of the individual.

They might argue persecution based on religion. Their position would be that the law discriminates against non-Catholics. The government might argue that the law is facially neutral and that it does not become discriminatory simply because it has a disproportionate impact on non-Catholics. The government might also argue that the law punishes only actions, not beliefs, and that it therefore amounts to nothing more than criminal prosecution.

It is difficult to separate religion from political beliefs. They would assert they hold the political opinion that they should be free to use birth control. Again, however, ICE would argue they are being punished not for believing this practice should be permitted, but for their actions if they use birth control in violation of law.

Finally, they might argue they are being persecuted because of their membership in a particular social group – married couples who prefer to remain childless. Under the *Acosta* test, although it is possible to change their status (either by divorcing or by having children), the traits that define membership in this group seem fundamental to personal identity. Married couples who prefer to remain childless come from all walks of life, however, and thus might not be perceived by society as a single group.

Problem 5: Executing her for speaking out would obviously be persecution on account of political opinion. The government would argue, however, that the question here is merely whether she should be required to remain silent, thus avoiding punishment, rather than be granted asylum. Can a person be eligible for asylum based on something she would do if sent back? Generally, the courts are not as receptive to post-departure conduct as a basis for asylum because, if they were, people might deliberately create risks of persecution and thereby qualify for asylum.

She might offer three arguments in response: First, being silenced is itself a form of persecution. Second, her feelings now are so intense that she might be literally unable to remain silent any longer. Third, even if she is capable of restraining herself but chooses not to, she could analogize to *Fatin*. There, the court made clear that a woman whose convictions were so strong that she would willingly defy the dress code and accept the punishment could establish persecution on account of social group.

3. "Well-Founded" Fear and "Would be Threatened:" Standards of Proof

<u>Notes and Questions on page 1000:</u>

Q1: The Court in *Cardoza-Fonseca* made the point that anyone who establishes eligibility for withholding of removal receives it automatically. In contrast, asylum requires not only eligibility (admittedly easier than for withholding), but also the favorable exercise of discretion. The government suggested that in practice the discretionary hurdle is rarely a problem. The Court countered by citing two cases in which discretion was outcome-determinative.

Q2: First, one could argue that, even if persecution never materializes, simply living under constant *fear* of persecution is too cruel a fate to permit. The requirement that the fear be well-founded confines this theory within manageable bounds. Second, if the case is that close, returning the person entails a high probability of error; the argument would be that the social harm in erroneously returning a person to persecution is worse than the social harm that occurs when a person is erroneously allowed to remain in the United States even though the feared persecution would not have materialized.

Q3: It could be argued that the sort of retreat envisioned in the asylum context is even more costly to the individual than that envisioned in the criminal law or torts context. The persecuted victim is being required to give up his or her home, job, and other community ties, and to do so for the long-term, not just for the few minutes or hours until the attacker leaves, as in criminal law or torts. In the case of asylum, however, the person has retreated already. The only question is whether the retreat will be to a safe part of the person's own country or to a brand new country. If the former is a viable option, why use up a limited asylum spot? Also, voluntary repatriation should be encouraged as a way to rebuild the country of origin and to challenge human rights abuses.

Q4: When the BIA requires a person to show country-wide persecution, it is because the person will have to move somewhere whether it grants asylum or not. The rationale is that there is no particular reason to allow the person to move to the United States when the person could avoid persecution by moving elsewhere in the country of origin. Whether the same is true within the European Union is less clear. While freedom of movement is allowed (subject to some exceptions related to criminality, national security, etc.), and while Europeans differ widely as to the nature of the association, most will agree that the EU is not yet a true federation in the way most federal states are. Migration to another EU nation, where the language and culture are likely to differ from those of the country of origin in most cases, is no more or less logical than migration to the United States.

<u>Problem 6</u> (page 1002):

Realistically, there are at least three ways an immigration judge might react:

a. Follow the law and deny all relief -- asylum in the exercise of discretion, and withholding of removal because there is not a "clear probability" of persecution. The immigration judge would then order removal to the third country and gamble that it will admit the person.

b. The immigration judge could grant asylum despite his or her misgivings about the exercise of discretion, because the alternative entails a risk that the person will be removed to the country of possible persecution in the event the third country says no.

c. Despite his or her feelings about the facts, the immigration judge might enter a finding that the applicant faces a clear probability of persecution but deny asylum in the exercise of discretion and order the applicant removed to a third country. Under that approach, the immigration judge knows DHS will be prohibited from returning the person to the country of persecution in the event the country to which removal was ordered says no.

4. Methods of Proof

a. Material Facts

This material is intended as background reading.

b. Relevant Evidence

i. The Applicant's Own Testimony

Damaize-Job v. INS (page 1007):

A Nicaraguan Miskito Indian in deportation proceedings applied for asylum or withholding of removal. He introduced evidence that the Sandinistas persecute Miskitos and supporters of former President Somoza and testified that he fit both descriptions. He further testified to prior persecution in the forms of imprisonment, beatings, torture, and threats to kill him if he were found again. He testified he fled to Costa Rica and stayed there a year, returning to Nicaragua only to help gain the release of his uncle and his sister, who had been captured by the Sandinistas. When he learned they had been killed, he fled to the United States. The IJ denied asylum, both on the ground that he did not find the applicant to be a credible witness and on the ground that, even if true, his testimony did not establish he had been singled out for persecution because of his race or his political opinion. The BIA affirmed, and Damaize-Job petitioned for review.

After rejecting the IJ's conclusion that the evidence would not establish either a clear probability of persecution or a well-founded fear of persecution even if it was true, the court turned to the credibility issue. The court said that an IJ who makes an adverse credibility finding must offer specific, articulable reasons. Here, the IJ offered three reasons that the court found wanting. There were discrepancies in some of the dates to which Damaize-Job had testified, but they were minor and could not possibly have been intended to mislead because they were on extraneous matters. Damaize-Job had not married the mother of his children, but that fact said nothing about his credibility and at any rate was a personal choice that he had the right to make. He had not sought asylum in any of the countries that he transited en route to the United States, but again, once he was free of the Sandinistas, his preference for the United States says nothing about the genuineness or reasonableness of his fear. Ultimately, the court ordered that Damaize-Job be granted withholding of removal and found eligible for asylum, and it remanded to the BIA for a discretionary decision as to the latter.

<u>Notes</u> <u>and</u> <u>Questions</u> <u>Following</u> <u>Damaize-Job</u> (page 1009):

Q2: INA § 208(b)(1)(B)(iii) does indeed make inconsistencies relevant, but it adds the important qualifier "considering the circumstances under which the statements were made." The circumstances would of course include the physical setting and time pressures involved, but arguably they should also include whether the applicant had a motive to misrepresent. If there is no conceivable motive to misrepresent the particular facts (the case here), then a reasonable assumption would be that the inaccurate or inconsistent statement was inadvertent, not deliberate. Under that interpretation, the current provision would similarly have permitted the court to reverse.

The same statutory provision adds that these factors apply "without regard to whether an inconsistency, inaccuracy, or falsehood goes to the heart of the applicant's claim." While the fact that a false statement goes to the heart of the claim might be thought to increase the likelihood that the falsity was deliberate, perhaps a more telling factor would be whether the applicant *believed*, rightly or wrongly, that the falsehood was material. In this case, however, the birth years of the applicant's children could not have been relevant or even believed by the applicant to be relevant.

Q3: The court was clearly right to reject that reason, which seems entirely extraneous. Apart from the questionable assumption that a decision not to get married evidences immorality, the problem is that the inference of immorality that the judge draws is not even probative of the applicant's honesty as a witness. Nor is there anything in section 208(b)(1)(B)(iii) that would have made this factor relevant to credibility.

Q4: INA § 208(b)(1)(B)(iii) does list the applicant's "candor" as one factor relevant to credibility. Its argument here would probably be that this evidence shows Damaize-Job will lie whenever he feels that doing so will bring immigration benefits. Moreover, the government might suggest, the reason he wanted to go to Mexico rather than El Salvador might be that it is easier to reenter the United States surreptitiously from Mexico.

Q6: Under INA § 208(b)(1)(B)(iii), one factor relevant to credibility is whether the applicant's statements are consistent with U.S. State Department reports on country conditions. If the country is a democracy with a good human rights record, a request for corroboration might well be reasonable. Even without a specific flaw in the testimony, statements that are unlikely to be true can permit an immigration judge to conclude that the applicant has not discharged his or her burden of proof (discussed below). In*Dass*, the applicant was a Sikh who made sweeping accusations of human rights violations by the government of India. The BIA held that, without background reports showing India persecutes Sikhs, the immigration judge would be unable to put the applicant's testimony in context. Relief was denied.

Q7: The question is whether credible testimony should require corroborating evidence. The government might argue that, if there is reason to expect corroborating evidence, what's wrong with asking the person to produce it or explain why he or she cannot? That is the approach taken in INA § 208(b)(1)(B)(ii). The applicant might offer some of the following counter-arguments:

a. Witnesses more often than not tell the truth. Absent evidence to the contrary, the immigration judge should therefore assume that this applicant is telling the truth. (Is that presumption realistic in the case where there is a powerful motive to misrepresent?)

b. Cross-examination can root out falsities. At least when it fails to do so, the immigration judge should presume that the witness has testified truthfully (again, absent other affirmative reason to have doubts).

c. As discussed earlier, an erroneous denial of asylum is far worse than an erroneous grant.

d. A request for corroboration might seem reasonable, but if the applicant is unable to produce it, and a reviewing court wrongly concludes that it should have been produced, a person will be sent back to face the very persecution that Congress (and the international community) sought to prevent.

ii. State Department Opinions

The instructor could either assign this subsection as background reading or discuss in class the propriety of admitting State Department opinions into evidence. With respect to State Department information concerning general country conditions, the main argument for admission would be that the State Department has both expertise and information from sources not otherwise accessible to the asylum officer or immigration judge. The principal argument against admission of such evidence is the problem of accuracy. The State Department has knowledge, but it also has a conflicting mission -- foreign relations. Without cross-examination, the applicant will be denied any opportunity to discover the basis for the opinion. In addition, the DHS documentation center now makes the State Department information less critical.

With respect to admitting State Department opinions about the merits of individual cases, the government would again emphasize the State Department's expertise and information. Seeing the basis for the claim, and knowing the practice of the particular country, the State Department might well have insights that are worth receiving. But there remains the problem of filtering out the State Department's inescapable concerns about foreign affairs. And in any event the State Department, unlike the asylum officer and the immigration judge, has not seen all the evidence in the case.

iii. Advice from UNHCR

The question here is what role, if any, UNHCR should play in the adjudication of asylum cases. Some would say it should play no role at all. Whether to grant asylum in an individual case is purely a matter of national sovereignty. (In the case of withholding of removal, the United States has agreed to limit that sovereignty by binding itself to the 1967 Protocol and therefore the 1951 Convention.)

The principal advantage of including UNHCR as a participant is that its expertise is considerable and should be tapped. Unlike the State Department, UNHCR does not have conflicting obligations between protecting refugees and conducting foreign affairs. (Some would emphasize, however, that UNHCR does face an analogous conflict between protecting refugees and maintaining friendly relationships with those nations on which it depends for funding.)

UNHCR lacks the resources to participate in every asylum case, but one possibility would be to notify it of all cases and permit it to (a) submit a recommendation; (b) intervene; or (c) decide the case, either initially or as an appellate authority (depending on how significant a role the nation wants UNHCR to have). The UNHCR could also perform a monitoring function, coming to asylum hearings unannounced for spot checks. See Helton's examples of how other countries use UNHCR.

iv. Other Sources of Information

This paragraph is intended as background reading.

5. Exceptions to Eligibility

a. Firm Resettlement

This material is intended as background reading.

b. Past Wrongdoing

Matter of Carballe (page 1018):

A Marielito who had been paroled into the United States in 1980 was later convicted of two counts of armed robbery and related offenses. At his exclusion hearing, he conceded inadmissibility and applied for asylum or withholding of removal. Without deciding whether Carballe was a refugee, the IJ denied both claims on the ground that the armed robberies were "particularly serious crimes" that made him a danger to the community. That finding made Carballe ineligible for withholding of removal and, under the then existing version of the regulations, ineligible for the favorable exercise of discretion needed for asylum.

On appeal, Carballe argued that the disqualification in question required two separate findings -- that he had been convicted of a particularly serious crime and that, as a result, he remains a danger to the community. The BIA disagreed. It interpreted the statutory disqualification to mean that a conviction of a "particularly serious crime" automatically makes the person a "danger to the community." No separate showing of the latter is required. The Board explained that that interpretation does not make the "danger" requirement meaningless. Only by considering the danger that a given crime poses can a court determine whether that crime is "particularly serious." Here, the Board held, armed robbery is inherently "particularly serious." Consequently, the IJ did not err by declining to admit evidence of rehabilitation.

<u>Notes and Questions Following Carballe</u> (page 1021):

Q1: At least two practical consequences turn on this issue. First, some might differ over whether a person who is convicted of a "particularly serious crime" necessarily posed a danger to the community even at the time of the conviction. Second, and probably of more practical importance, there is a question whether the person who was convicted of such an offense many years ago but who no longer poses a danger to the community should automatically be disqualified from asylum. If the answer is no, then evidence of rehabilitation becomes relevant and important.

On the merits, several items of evidence are available. With respect to the literal language, the government in *Carballe* argues that, if Congress had meant to impose two independent requirements, it would have said "and." Instead, the language Congress chose implies that the very fact of a conviction of a "particularly serious" crime requires a conclusion that the person is dangerous to the community. Carballe responds that the word "constitutes" is in the present tense, and therefore Congress must have meant to require that the person <u>now</u> be a danger. Carballe could also argue that, if the government interpretation were right, Congress would simply have said "convicted of a particularly serious crime," without specifying any requirement concerning danger. Congress, in fact, did precisely that in the case of various crime-related grounds for both inadmissibility and deportability. Thus, the reference to danger would be superfluous under the government's interpretation. The government (and the court) respond to this latter point by arguing that Congress added the reference to "danger" in order to aid the determination of whether a crime is "particularly serious."

With respect to legislative history, the government in <u>Carballe</u> points to a sentence from the House Judiciary Committee Report referring to those "who have been convicted of particularly serious crimes *which* make them a danger . . ." (emphasis added by BIA). Under the government's view, this language shows that Congress meant that a conviction of a particularly serious crime is what makes a person dangerous. The instructor might ask the class how Carballe could respond. In particular, the instructor could invite the students to consider the punctuation in the cited Report. The argument would be that in the quoted sentence there is no comma after the phrase "particularly serious crimes." Thus the phrase "which makes them a danger" is a restrictive clause. Congress, the argument would run, was referring only to those particularly serious crimes that make the offender dangerous -- not to all particularly serious crimes.

As a policy matter, the government might emphasize that the exception requires a "particularly serious" crime, not just any crime. When a crime is that serious, the government might say, the offender either (a) will always be dangerous or (ii) has misbehaved so badly that he or she will never deserve relief. Carballe could respond that the crime might have been committed so long ago that the threat to life or freedom, in a given case, outweighs the present danger or the need for further retribution. He might also stress that in any event the ineligibility goes to withholding of removal, not merely to asylum. Whatever reservations the court might have about allowing a noncitizen who has committed a particularly serious crime to remain in the United States, Carballe would argue, it would be disproportionate to return him to the country of persecution, especially if the crime was committed in the distant past. The government might respond that, if no third country is willing to take the person (a strong possibility when there has been a particularly serious crime), then withholding of removal can amount to de facto asylum.

Q2: The majority approach to "moral turpitude" determinations and to "aggravated felony" determinations is at least theoretically more favorable to the noncitizens than is the BIA approach to "particularly serious crime" determinations. Under the majority approach to moral turpitude, discussed earlier in chapter 6, a crime will not be held to involve moral turpitude unless moral turpitude could be found in *every* fact situation constituting that crime. It is not enough, in other words, that the actions of the particular individual involve moral turpitude.

Q5: The reason for the question is that, at first glance, paragraph (ii) seems to require more than paragraph (iii) requires. A conviction, for example, requires more than simply "serious reasons for considering that the alien has committed a crime." The phase "particularly serious" demands more than simply "serious." And paragraph (ii) requires a danger to the community, although in *Carballe* the BIA holds this requirement is subsumed within the phrase "particularly serious crime."

But paragraph (iii) has at least two requirements that paragraph (ii) does not. For paragraph (iii) to operate, the crime must be "nonpolitical," and it must be committed "outside the United States prior to the arrival of the alien in the United States." So paragraph (ii) would disqualify someone who is convicted of a particularly serious nonpolitical crime and represents a danger to the community, even though paragraph (iii) would not have done so. The same is true if the person is convicted of <u>any</u> particularly serious crime, political or otherwise, committed within the United States.

Q6: The argument for a relative approach is that some forms of persecution are too harsh to visit even upon a person who has been convicted of a particularly serious crime; others are not. The argument for an absolute approach is that a relative approach would necessitate a discretionary determination and the consideration of evidence concerning the likelihood of persecution merely to adjudicate a section 241(b)(3) claim. The proponents of a relative approach might counter that such evidence will be necessary in any event to adjudicate the section 208 claim that invariably is filed simultaneously.

Q7: Once the students see that there is a difference between the balancing test and the "incident to rebellion" test, the two questions contained here can be considered.

As for the first question, the court distinguishes extradition from deportation on the basis that deportation is an internal matter for the United States while extradition requires consideration of the relations between the United States and a foreign country. The court says that the purpose of deportation is merely to rid the country of undesirables and that it does not matter where the person goes as long as it is to some place else. At best, the relevance of that rationale seems limited to asylum, not withholding of removal. The whole point of nonrefoulement is that the person seeks a destination other than the country of deportation. The issue is not whether to deport, but where.

With respect to the second question, there does seem to be a great inconsistency. As the students saw in chapter 2, the basic premise for judicial deference to Congress in immigration matters is that these decisions inherently involve foreign affairs considerations into which courts should not intrude. Yet, here, the court says just the opposite to distinguish deportation from extradition. The suggestion here is that deportation differs from extradition precisely because deportation is purely an internal matter for the United States. The court might attempt to distinguish the two contexts by observing that in constitutional cases the noncitizen is challenging an act of Congress, while here he or she is challenging only the application of a statute by an immigration judge in an individual case. But certainly these particular individual cases can affect foreign relations because, by their nature, they reflect judgments about particular countries' human rights practices.

Q8: The exception contained in INA § 241(b)(3)(B)(ii) (for those who have persecuted others) seems compatible with the restrictions contained in article 1.F(a, c) of the Convention. Article 1.F(a) covers "a crime against peace, a war crime, or a crime against humanity." Article 1.F(c) covers the person who has been "guilty of acts contrary to the purposes and principles of the United Nations." The latter presumably includes persecution, which is condemned by this very treaty.

The exception contained in INA § 241(b)(3)(B)(II) ("particularly serious crime") is word for word the same as the exception contained in article 33.2 of the Convention. But the combination of the provision that regards all "aggravated felonies" for which five-year sentences are imposed as "particularly serious crimes" and the expansion of the "aggravated felony" definition greatly broadens the practical scope of the statutory disqualification. The question would be whether, given that broadened scope of "particularly serious crime," the statutory restriction is still compatible with the Convention.

The exception contained in INA § 241(b)(3)(B)(iii) for "serious nonpolitical crimes" is the same as that contained in article 1.F(b) of the Convention.

The exception in INA § 241(b)(3)(B)(iv) (danger to security) is the same as that provided in article 33.2 of the Convention.

The instructor might also note that article 33.1 of the Convention prohibits only the return of certain "refugees." Therefore article 1.F, which limits the definition of "refugee," also limits the obligations under article 33.

6. Discretion in Asylum Cases

This subsection was intended as background reading, but there are at least two questions that an instructor who wishes to take up this material in class can discuss:

First, the instructor can explore the merits of Anker's approach, which rejects manner of entry as a significant discretionary factor and focuses instead on whether the applicant poses a serious danger to the United States and on whether he or she was firmly resettled in a third country. The advantages of the Anker approach are outlined in the text. The instructor might invite counter-arguments. One, for example, would be that not all fraudulent entries by asylum claimants are the products of desperation. An applicant could, for example, be safely out of the country of origin but simply prefer the United States to the third country in which he or she currently resides. In such a case, the negative factors should include not only the firm resettlement, but also the dishonesty that the alleged fraud evidences. Second, an advantage of considering fraudulent entry as a negative factor is that doing so might discourage entry fraud in the first place. The students can decide which set of competing arguments they find more persuasive.

Second, the instructor might wish to discuss the last two paragraphs of the excerpt from *Pula* and the hypothetical concerning applicants A and B following *Pula*. A is precisely the person discussed in the next-to-last paragraph of the excerpt, from the second sentence on. A established eligibility for asylum but not for withholding of removal, so removal to the country in which he or she has a well-founded fear of being persecuted is possible. And since there are no *egregious* adverse factors, A will receive asylum. B does not fit within that paragraph because he or she is eligible for withholding of removal. Absent adverse factors, the BIA in *Pula* says B would receive asylum, but the problem here is that there are adverse factors and no positive equities. Presumably, therefore, B will not receive asylum. The net result is that A receives asylum while B receives only withholding of removal.

The instructor might ask the students whether that combination of results makes sense. If one were to start from scratch, the answer would certainly be no. The two individuals are exactly alike except that the one who faces a higher probability of persecution must leave the United States (albeit for a third country) while the other is permitted to remain. Yet there is clearly some logic in considering, as a factor bearing on the discretionary decision whether to grant asylum, the fact that a denial of asylum could entail returning the person to the country in which he or she has a well-founded fear of persecution. The real source of the anomaly is the differing standards of proof announced in Stevic and Cardoza-Fonseca.

7. Procedure

Notes and Questions on Page 1040:

Q2: Many of the following pros and cons of specialized adjudication are taken from chapter 1 of *Specialised Justice*, cited in the text of the question.

Advantages of Specialized Justice:

a. The most obvious advantage is the specialized expertise of the adjudicators themselves. This expertise stems both from the selection process (relevant experience can be made a priority) and from the expansion of the adjudicators' expertise as they take on more cases and from their continuing professional education (which they will have an incentive to do since they are specialists).

b. A specialized office has the ability to hire a specialized staff. All this diminishes the need to rely on opposing attorneys, the State Department, and other experts for basic information.

c. With a corps of specialists, productive collegial interchange becomes more realistic.

d. A body of specialized precedent might be easier to build.

e. In the asylum context, all this expertise can be brought to bear in achieving familiarity with a complex domestic statutory scheme and with common international interpretations of the refugee definition, understanding country conditions, understanding the international human rights underpinnings of refugee law, knowing what sorts of questions to ask, and developing the necessary cultural sensitivities.

f. Expertise breeds greater uniformity, at least within the universe of the particular specialty. This is mainly because specialists are more likely to be familiar with related cases than are generalists who have to keep up with additional areas of law. In addition, when the cases are entrusted to specialists, there will be fewer people making the decisions, simply because each person will devote full time to that specialty; fewer people, in turn, should mean fewer decisions to have to reconcile.

g. Specialized expertise introduces efficiencies. The adjudicator doesn't require staff and opposing lawyers to educate him or her on basic principles before every case. The procedure can be tailored to the specific attributes of the specialty area.

h. When judicial review becomes necessary, a specialist tribunal, through its written opinion, can alert the generalist court to special considerations that it is important for the court to know about.

Disadvantages of Specialized Justice:

a. Probably the greatest disadvantage is the loss of the generalist perspective. That is important both because generalists can often find solutions in analogous areas of the law and because generalists would be expected to harbor fewer narrow biases about the specialized area. Generalists are also better situated to make the case law in the specialized area consistent with that in other areas. In the case of asylum, for example, adjudicators might well benefit from knowledge of non-asylum cases that deal with credibility assessments, administrative procedure, etc. Generalist adjudicators could also strive to achieve consistency between asylum law and other areas of immigration law or, more broadly, administrative law.

b. Faced with a steady diet of asylum cases, asylum specialists could become too calloused. They might become too inclined to discount the severity of the consequences the applicant faces.

c. Although specialized asylum adjudicators will obviously be more knowledgeable about asylum than generalist adjudicators would be, the public at the same time might perceive them as more biased.

d. A narrow mix of cases can hamper the recruitment and retention of talented people, given the monotony of the work.

e. The more highly specialized the adjudicators will be, the more opportunity and the more incentive lobbyists will have to influence the appointment process. In the case of asylum, both ethnic lobbies and government (especially the State Department) would have great interest in the selection of the adjudicators.

f. The more specialized the adjudicators, the less flexible the system will be in its capacity to adjust to volume fluctuations in various cities. The broader the range of cases, the less drastic those fluctuations in volumes are likely to be.

Q3: Assessing the optimum level of specialization requires the students to apply some of the general pros and cons of specialization discussed in the analysis of question 2 above. Among the competing considerations are the following:

a. The specialization level will affect the range of resulting expertise and the pace at which that expertise is able to develop. Adjudicators could, for example, be trained generally in immigration law with an emphasis on asylum law and, to the extent resources permit, an emphasis on the economies, political structures, and cultures of selected countries -- all depending on precisely how narrow their specialized jurisdiction will be.

b. A country-specialist or region-specialist is more likely to be biased. Would a China expert, for example, really be likely to be neutral and detached, or would that person be likely to have a bias in one direction or the other about the Chinese system? The same questions could be asked about Balkan specialists, Middle East specialists, etc. There is the potential here for a dangerous concentration of power.

c. Specialization can have mixed effects on consistency. As the level of specialization increases, one might expect more consistency within a specialized area (both because there are fewer adjudicators for such cases and because those adjudicators should be more knowledgeable about their common specialty), but less consistency from one area to another. Is it more important that all Iraqi cases, for example, be decided under the same standards, or that Iraqi and Chinese cases be analyzed under the same general criteria?

d. Specialization can also have mixed effects on efficiency. On the one hand, there is an efficiency gain in not having to educate the adjudicator about the empirical facts relevant to the country or region involved in the particular case. On the other hand, the more specialized the adjudicators are, the more vulnerable the system is to changes in caseloads and the more difficult it becomes to respond to those changes by transferring personnel.

Q4: Professor Martin lays out the pros and cons of requiring that adjudicators be lawyers. See his footnote 255, which reads as follows:

"255. Several persons interviewed for the study (most of whom were from countries other than the United States) stated that characteristics other than legal training may be most important in identifying good asylum adjudicators. They urged that serious thought be given to hiring nonattorneys. Canada has taken this approach for the majority of the adjudicators (Immigration and Refugee Board members) recruited for its new system, even though the position carries a salary that would be sufficient to attract attorneys. In an early draft of this study, I thus suggested recruitment among nonattorneys with the requisite international experience and sensitivity, without, of course, precluding lawyers. This suggestion, however, drew a strongly negative reaction, from government officials and refugee advocates alike. Not only will the adjudicators have to follow fairly complicated developments in the burgeoning American case law on asylum, but also, and perhaps more importantly, they will very often be dealing with lawyers for the applicants, in the course of conducting the proceedings and constructing the factual record. That record, in turn, is meant to be the basis for both the initial decision and further review, which will be entirely under the stewardship of lawyers. I have therefore withdrawn the suggestion. At least for the American administrative context, dominated as it is by lawyers and infused with the American cultural preference for an adversarial form of justice, asylum adjudicators should be trained attorneys."

Q5: The main reason for eliminating NOID's was to speed asylum officers' disposition of cases. Formerly, an asylum officer not only had to spend time drafting the NOID, but also had to return to the case to review the applicant's response. Apart from the work time of the asylum officer, the extra response time delayed the final decision. Writing out reasons for decisions required further time from the asylum officers.

The main advantage of NOIDs was that they enabled applicants to know what potential problems had to be addressed. The earlier they become aware of what the government thought the problems were, the sooner they could remedy any omissions that turned out to be curable. In addition, the very process of writing the NOID forced the adjudicator to think through, carefully, what the decision should be. Sometimes it is not until one has to articulate an analysis in writing that flaws come to light.

Q6: The disadvantages of a system that allows two bites at the apple are obvious. But such a system also has at least two advantages. First, it allows two chances to detect error. Martin might well be right that, if the first and second decisionmakers differ, the first one is just as likely to be right as the second one. But the counter-argument is that the second adjudicator will have the benefits of another person's insights *in addition* to his or her own. That issue aside, there is some benefit in having both a non-adversarial procedure in which reticent applicants might feel more comfortable relating sensitive facts, *and* an adversarial hearing during which opposing counsel can more fully develop the facts.

Q7: The major consequences of decisions concerning the degree of independence of the adjudicators are how insulated those adjudicators will be from political pressure and how insulated the general public and the affected constituencies will perceive them to be. Therefore, much of the decision as to how much independence to confer rests on how one feels asylum decisions should be made. Should they follow the adjudicative model, one that requires disposition based solely on the law and the facts of the case? Or should they be seen as policy decisions that also reflect foreign affairs and other national policy interests?

The analysis of these questions might very well differ as between asylum and withholding of removal. The latter presents the clearer case for an adjudicative model. Withholding of removal is mandatory under the 1951 Convention, the 1967 Protocol, and INA § 241(b)(3). There is lacking the broad discretionary component that might strengthen the argument for taking political factors into account. Asylum, being discretionary, is inherently more policy-oriented. (Of course there remains the question which policy considerations are permissible to consider even in the case of asylum.)

Q8: The advantages of a non-adversarial approach include the following:

a. Some applicants might feel more comfortable with an adjudicator who is trying to examine the case neutrally than they would with two opposing lawyers, one trying to help and the other trying to oppose. The applicant might particularly feel more at ease in testifying.

b. In a nonadversarial proceeding, the adjudicator would be better situated to proceed without counsel if counsel cannot be secured.

c. A nonadversarial system saves government resources because a USCIS trial attorney will not be needed in every case.

The principal advantage of an adversarial proceeding is a fundamental one. The theory of the adversary dialectic -- the model used in court and most frequently studied in law school -- is that the truth is most likely to emerge when there are two opposing sides, each with an incentive to present those sides most effectively.

Q9: The advantages of counsel are enormous. First, counsel can spend much more time investigating the facts, drawing out the applicant's story, doing legal research, and arguing the various legal theories than can the adjudicators -- even under the new system. The excerpt from *Castro-O'Ryan* illustrates what can happen when counsel is not available. (Admittedly that kind of horror story should be less likely to occur in a system where the asylum adjudicators are more knowledgeable about asylum than Judge Nail was.) Second, an asylum applicant is more likely to trust his or her own counsel than to trust an adjudicator whom the applicant might well perceive as an arm of the government. Third, not all adjudicators will be sufficiently conscientious or inclined to press hard to find possible substantiation for the applicant's claim, especially if case loads are heavy (as they are likely to be for the foreseeable future).

There are, however, some advantages to proceeding without counsel. Doing so can minimize delay. The procedures can be simpler, less formal, and possibly less intimidating for the applicant. In addition, the process will generally be less expensive.

Q10: For a fuller discussion, see the cited article. It discusses the benefits and costs of judicial review of administrative action generally, and then it applies those considerations to asylum.

The principal advantages of permitting judicial review of asylum decisions are as follows:

a. Judges are both independent and perceived as independent. They can feel secure when deciding cases on the merits. Now that the decisional independence of the BIA can no longer be assumed, that factor commands particular weight. Judges are also far less likely to be tainted by foreign affairs considerations than, for example the Department of State. To the extent that either immigration judges or asylum officers rely on the opinions of the Department of State (much less a factor today), then they too are ultimately less independent than article III judges. The individual interests at stake in asylum cases are great enough that both independence and the appearance of independence are important. They are important for the additional reason that asylum applicants, like other noncitizens, generally lack access to the usual political channels.

b. Judicial review by the general courts brings a generalist perspective to the case. Judges will ordinarily have a broader knowledge of the law, an advantage that will enable them to analogize to other areas. They also will generally have less bias in the specialized area and might be less calloused in evaluating the likelihood of persecution.

c. The very prospect of judicial review can encourage careful and rational decisions in the first instance. This factor is especially important because only a tiny proportion of cases actually get to court. (Admittedly, however, the fact that the percentage is tiny reduces the magnitude of this incentive.)

d. Courts can create case law. Without courts, all case law in this subject area would be pronounced by the BIA. That consequence would not only produce an unhealthy concentration of power, but also eliminate the opportunity for dialogue between and among different appellate bodies.

The disadvantages of judicial review of asylum decisions include the following:

a. Some asylum cases present policy issues (including foreign affairs considerations), and judges are not politically accountable. (Response: This factor seems generally inapplicable to questions of pure fact and even to questions of pure technical law. And even when there is a discretion to be exercised, it is important to have checks on that discretion.)

b. Non-experts should not reverse decisions of experts. (But note that the scope of review is limited.)

c. Since there are so many courts, judicial review will inevitably produce splits of authority. The result will be unequal treatment of similarly situated litigants and forum-shopping. Moreover, it is inefficient to have more than one body deciding the same issues.

d. Judicial review adds delay and, to the extent the person is detained pending judicial review, expense.

e. Judicial review entails fiscal costs, including both court costs and the time of government counsel. Moreover the federal bench is already overburdened. (Response: That argument could be made for any category of judicial review. Why single out asylum cases?)

Q11: That would seem highly unlikely. Asylum applicants at ports of entry are subjected to expedited removal, which entails mandatory detention until the person has established a credible fear of persecution and discretionary detention thereafter. The applicant will be questioned at length about his or past and anything else relevant to the asylum claim. There are intensive background checks before asylum can be granted, the last thing a terrorist would want to undergo. Ample documentation will ordinarily be required; a paper trail, again, is not what a competent terrorist would want to provide. And of course the vast majority of asylum claims are ultimately denied. Approval rates for tourist, student, temporary worker and other visas are much higher, and these visa applications attract far less attention.

Barring or Discouraging Access to Asylum Systems

Each of the devices discussed in this subsection is treated in greater detail in the "New Techniques" article cited in the coursebook (opening footnote to this subsection). The instructor can consult the article for descriptions of the pros and cons of the various strategies, and then ask the students for their views on some or all of those strategies. Some instructors might prefer to relegate this subsection to background reading, or skip it entirely, depending on how much emphasis they wish to place on the policy debate over asylum procedure.

Sale v. Haitian Centers Council (page 1065):

In 1992, President (George H.W.) Bush issued an executive order instructing the Coast Guard to interdict vessels on the high seas if they were suspected of illegally transporting Haitians to the United States. Under the terms of the order, no passengers were interviewed for possible refugee claims. All occupants were to be returned to Haiti. HCC, an organization serving interdicted Haitians, sued to enjoin enforcement of the Executive Order. HCC argued that the Order violated both INA § 243(h) [now 241(b)(3)] and article 33 of the 1951 U.N. Refugee Convention. The former then prohibited the Attorney General from "return[ing]" [now "remov[ing]" refugees to places where their lives or freedom would be threatened on account of race, religion, etc. The district court denied a TRO, ruling that the statutory provision was inapplicable in international waters and that the treaty provision was not self-executing. The Second Circuit reversed, holding that the statutory bar on refoulement applies extraterritorially. Because the Eleventh Circuit had ruled contra, the Supreme Court granted certiorari to resolve the conflict.

After considering the literal statutory language, the presumption against extraterritorial statutory application, the effects of alternative interpretations on related statutory provisions, the legislative history of the Refugee Act of 1980, and the negotiating history of article 33 (including a comparison of the French word "refoulement" and the English word "return"), the majority concluded that then section 243(h) was not intended to have extraterritorial effect. It therefore reversed the Second Circuit.

Justice Blackmun dissented. Relying mainly on the literal statutory language, the language and history of article 33 (which he stressed was the impetus for enactment of the statutory withholding of removal provision), and the policy underlying the prohibition of returning refugees to their persecutors, he would have interpreted the statute as barring such returns whether or not the United States government officials were physically within U.S. territory.

Notes and Questions Following Sale (page 1080):

Q1: There are probably several motivating factors:

a. Interdicting vessels and returning the occupants promptly is cheaper than affording removal hearings, possible administrative review, and possible judicial review.

b. With so many Haitians arriving at once, detention of all the arriving Haitians would have been impossible. Most would have been at large during the long interval between filing and final disposition. That, in turn, led to fears (i) that many would abscond; and (ii) that the long periods of freedom (and probably work authorization) would encourage others to come and file asylum claims.

c. Presidents Bush and Clinton both stressed the perils of the Haitians' voyages in arguing for interdiction as a deterrent and as a potential rescue strategy for those who are not deterred.

One other option, used both before and since *Sale* (see item 3), is interdiction followed by interviews. This affords greater procedural fairness and spares the return of a certain number of genuine refugees. But (i) shipboard space is limited; (ii) space on Guantánamo is limited; (iii) other extraterritorial resources are limited by the willingness of 3rd countries to allow use of their soil; (iv) access to counsel and other safeguards are problematic; and (v) questions will persist why the Haitians are being treated differently from other asylum claimants.

Another option was economic pressure -- either unilateral or multilateral -- to remove the coup leaders and restore President Aristide, followed by large scale economic assistance to help rebuild the country. In fact, President Clinton did try various economic sanctions before resorting to military force. The disadvantages of economic pressure are that it might be ineffectual and that it creates hardship for the general population.

Military intervention -- ultimately used in Haiti -- can entail loss of life (though it did not in this case), can meet much resistance from the United States public, can raise questions about the role of the United States in the world, and can leave the problem of how to keep the peace once the military action is completed.

Q2: Many critics charged racial discrimination, as noted in item 2 of the Notes and Questions. It was commonly observed that Cubans who arrived in the United States were welcomed, sometimes as heroes, while Haitians were interdicted and returned. Others would argue that it was the Cubans (not the Haitians) who were treated specially, as a result of Cold War politics and the Cuban Adjustment Act of 1966. Today, as the students saw in chapter 2, Cubans are interdicted too. That specific comparison aside, however, the instructor could ask the students to imagine boatloads of Europeans fleeing in rickety vessels across the Atlantic, and the U.S. Coast Guard intercepting them and returning them to the kinds of dangers that prevail in Haiti. What would the footage look like on the evening news? What would the general public's (not necessarily the Administration's) reaction be?

Q4: The Haitians stress the phrase "deport or return," argue that "return" is precisely what the government is doing, and point out that the statute contains no exception for the high seas. The government fixes on the language "Attorney General," arguing that nothing in the statutory text limits the actions of the President or the Coast Guard.

Q5: The Haitians argue that the purpose of the presumption is to avoid conflicts between United States law and foreign law. If that is the purpose, they observe, there would be little reason to apply the presumption here, since the events in question are occurring on the high seas, not in a foreign jurisdiction. The Court responds, however, that the presumption is built on a "broader" foundation. It never tells us what those broader purposes are, content instead to cite *Smith*.

The instructor could tell the students that, in *Smith*, a private contractor employed by the United States government was accidentally killed on the job in Antarctica. His widow brought a wrongful death action against the United States under the Federal Tort Claims Act (FTCA). That statute is expressly inapplicable to claims arising "in a foreign country." Antarctica (like the high seas and outer space) belongs to no sovereign state. The Court in *Smith* held nonetheless that Antarctica is a foreign country for purposes of the FTCA. To reach that result, it invoked the presumption against extraterritoriality and suggested one function of the presumption -- to give effect to "the common sense notion that Congress generally legislates with domestic concerns in mind."

What it meant by that is not clear. Perhaps the Court was saying that Congress generally legislates for the purpose of protecting the interests of Americans. Since the plaintiff was a United States citizen seeking compensation for precisely the type of loss that would have been compensable had the accident occurred in the United States, however, that explanation would not fully account for the result. In the context of section 243(h), the Court might have felt that extraterritorial application would not address any identifiable domestic concerns. But does the provision serve any domestic concerns even when it is applied to noncitizens in the United States? Or is it geared more toward serving human rights and humanitarian goals?

Q6: The Haitians interpret "return" to mean "send back to the place the person came from." The government argues for a narrower meaning, something like "exclude a person who is at a United States port of entry."

The Court reasons that "deport" refers only to individuals who have already entered the United States. Therefore, if "return" encompassed sending back any person, no matter where that person was located, it would extend to those who had already entered the United States interior. And if that is what Congress had meant by "return," there would have been no need for Congress to add the word "deport." The Haitians could counter-argue that sometimes Congress <u>is</u> redundant. That is especially likely in a context like this one, where there was no particular reason at the time for Congress to think about the distinction between refugees at the border and refugees interdicted on the high seas.

Congress's consistent use of the word "exclude" elsewhere in the INA, to mean the turning away of a person who is physically at a port of entry, should have made it harder for the Court to conclude that in section 243(h) Congress decided to use the word "return" to express exactly that concept. Had that argument been made, the government perhaps would have countered that Congress wanted to track the language of article 33 of the U.N. Convention, which uses the word "return." That counter-argument would be weak, however, because article 33 says "*expel* or return (refouler)," yet Congress substituted the United States technical term "deport" for "expel." Why would Congress have had any qualms about substituting "exclude" for "return" when it was willing to substitute "deport" for "expel?"

Q7: The Haitians appear to be urging the direct application of article 33, arguing that the Court should enjoin the interdiction program if it violates article 33. To make that argument, however, the Haitians would also need to establish that article 33 was self-executing -- i.e., not simply a directive for the state party to implement the agreement by enacting legislation. (The Court escaped that issue because article 33 was held not to have extraterritorial effect.)

The Haitians might also have been making the narrower argument that the Convention should at least inform the interpretation of the statute. U.S. courts will often interpret statutes so as to make them conform to treaty obligations.

Q8: The Court's argument is that article 33.1 prohibits refoulement and that article 33.2 creates an exception for the person who endangers the security of "the country in which he is . . ." If article 33.1 were to be applied extraterritorially, the Court reasons, the person who poses a security danger would be ineligible if apprehended within the country but not if apprehended on the high seas. That, the Court concludes, would be anomalous.

The Haitians' counterargument would be that there is nothing anomalous about that result. The drafters did not expect a country to keep a person who is *in its territory* and is a danger to the state. It does not follow that the drafters would want to permit a state to go out onto the high seas, intercept people forcibly, and affirmatively bring them to the country of persecution. The exception in 33.2 is a concession to national sovereignty and thus is inapplicable on the high seas.

Justice Blackmun in dissent responds with an interesting hypothetical: Suppose 33.2 had excepted individuals who were dangers to their families. Would that really mean 33.1 is inapplicable to claimants without families?

Q9: The Court finds that the French word "refouler" connotes something different from the English word "return." The word "refouler," the Court concludes, does not contemplate any particular destination; it envisions only a defensive action of repelling, or pushing back.

Of the French words that the dictionary lists for the English word "return," the one that most closely resembles the Haitians' suggested interpretation seems to be "renvoyer," or "send back." Thus, the government might have argued, the drafters would have used "renvoyer" -- not "refouler" -- if they had meant what the Haitians say they meant.

The Haitians would still have three counter-arguments. First, the premise that "return" and "refouler" express different concepts is shaky. As the dissent observes, even the French press was using the word "refouler" to describe the U.S. actions. Second, even if one accepts that refouler does not mean return, why should a U.S. court assume that, in the event of conflict, Congress drew its understanding from the French version rather than the English version? Third, in this case there is particular reason to credit the English language meaning. The whole point of article 33 was to prohibit states from sending refugees to particular destinations. The English word captures precisely that concept. Article 33 has nothing to do with purely defensive actions.

Q10: The Court's conclusion is that several states signed the Convention on the understanding that article 33 would not apply extraterritorially. There seem, however, to be three possible interpretations of the comments of the Swiss representative: (a) Once a state admits a refugee, we agree it should not be permitted to deport the person to a place of persecution, but a similar prohibition should not apply to the refugee who is at the border, seeking admission (i.e. deportation versus exclusion); (b) We agree that even the person who is at the border should not be returnable to the country of persecution, but we should not be affirmatively required to admit the person to our territory (i.e. nonrefoulement versus asylum); or (c) Even the person who is at the border should not be returnable to the country of persecution, but a person apprehended on the high seas or otherwise far away from the border should be returnable to the country of persecution (i.e. exclusion versus interception on the high seas or in some third country).

Interpretations (a) and (b) both seem plausible. The quoted language would lend itself to either of these interpretations, and under either interpretation the practical concerns seem realistic and understandable. If (a) was intended, however, it is clear that the Swiss position was rejected; even the Court acknowledges that the refugee at the border cannot legally be returned to the country of persecution. If (b) was intended, then the Swiss position was honored, since the Convention does not obligate states to grant asylum; only withholding of removal is at issue in the present case. The Swiss comments prove the Court's point only if (c) was intended, and that seems highly unlikely. For one thing, the quoted language draws no distinction between the person at the border and the person who has not yet reached the border. More important, Switzerland is landlocked. It is hard to believe that the Swiss representative was worried that the Convention would prohibit his government from intercepting refugees on the high seas (or perhaps in some other country) before they could reach the coast of Switzerland!

8. A Simulated Attorney-Client Asylum Interview (page 1085):

This is a simulated attorney-client initial consultation. It will require anywhere from 1 to 3 hours of class time, depending on which of the options (described below) the instructor chooses. One or more students play the role(s) of the immigration lawyer(s). One or more other individuals (who could also be students or could be outsiders) play the role of the client. The exercise is meant to take about 50 minutes of class time.

Like the simulated removal exercise in chapter 9, this exercise has several purposes. Primarily, it exposes students to the give-and-take of an initial consultation between an attorney and an asylum seeker. It also engages students in substantive and strategic issues in a way that exposure to abstract judicial opinions cannot. It forces them to think about the sorts of questions that an attorney must ask (and how to ask them) in order to flush out the relevant facts and prepare an asylum application. In the process, it provides a review of substantive asylum law.

This exercise works best after completion of the subsection on asylum procedure. (On these facts an alternative claim under the Convention Against Torture is possible, but the exercise raises enough other issues that you might wish to skip the CAT claim. If you want students to discuss it, however, then you should first assign all or part of section C.1 below.)

This section of the Teacher's Manual contains the following parts:

Synopsis of the Facts

Synopsis of the Facts

The client, Maria Ortiz, has fled Oquito, a tiny fictional country in Central America. She is in danger there because of the political activities of Pedro Tejada, with whom she lived for many years. She is interested in applying for asylum in the United States. More detailed facts appear in the "Instructions to Maria," below. In case the students whom the instructor wants to select to play the client include some males, however, the materials have been designed to make it easy for the facts to be reversed; i.e., Pedro can be the client, and he can be seeking asylum based on the dangers resulting from Maria's political activities.

Options on How to Conduct This Exercise

You (the instructor) will have two main decisions to make at the outset. The first one is how much you want to accomplish with this exercise, which in turn will largely depend on how much class time you want to allocate to it. The interview itself should be manageable in one class hour, and you could do just that and nothing more. But you might wish to devote all or part of a second class hour to a group critique of the interview, focusing on interviewing technique, the kinds of questions that were asked or could have been asked, the interviewer's manner, style, and sensitivity, etc. It is possible to allocate a third class to the several substantive issues raised by the facts. A middle option is to do the interview in one class hour and then allocate just one more class hour for a combined discussion of the interviewing techniques and the substantive issues.

Whether or not you decide to allot additional class time for a follow-up discussion, you have to make a second major choice between two ways of conducting the interview component itself. One approach is a demonstration model, in which only one interview takes place (involving one or more students) and the rest of the class observes (and, optionally, also critiques). The other approach is to arrange for multiple simultaneous interviews that involve all the students in the class as active participants. There can be sub-variations of either approach.

One advantage of the one-interview demonstration model is that only one client is needed. That makes it easy for the instructor to recruit a person not known to the students to play that role. To the students in the class, a stranger will likely be a more believable asylum applicant than would a fellow student. In addition, using an outsider as the client means that the instructor doesn't have to distribute client instructions to students, with the risk that they will hand down the materials to future students and possibly spoil the exercise for future use. (Of course, it might be possible to recruit a large number of outsider volunteers to play the client roles at simultaneous interviews. Perhaps an undergraduate drama class or regional studies class could be a good source. Still, having to recruit, coordinate, and ensure the appearances of so many people is a major hassle.) A third advantage of the demonstration model is that the whole class can watch the same interview and critique it; if instead all the students are involved in their own interviews, then the only feedback they can receive on their performances will be from the other participant(s) in their own interviews unless some of the interviews are videotaped. To increase the number of students involved in each interview, you could start with one student attorney but then stop the interview from time to time and substitute new student attorneys. There is a risk, though, that interview will become disjointed.

But the great advantage of the multiple interviews/full class participation approach is that the students will be much more engaged and will have to think more carefully about the issues and the interview techniques. Most likely the lessons they learn from the experience will also be more enduring.

Under either approach, each interview will require a minimum of two players – an attorney and a client. One option is to use teams of two student-attorneys, so that each interview will involve three people. If the multiple interviews/ full class participation model is used, than an additional option is to assign one student as an observer for each interview; the observer would be expected to take notes and later critique the interview. (There is no reason to do this if the demonstration model is used, since the whole class will be observers.) So if the multiple interviews/ full class participation model is used, each interview would require 2-4 students – i.e., 1 or 2 attorney(s), 1 client, and possibly 1 observer (unless outsiders are recruited for the client roles). If teams of 2 attorneys are used, and if observers are also used, then in effect the class would be divided into pods of 4 people each – two attorneys, a client, and an observer. Since a no-show by a client would ruin the exercise for that client's attorneys, one or more reliable students should be assigned special roles. They would be instructed to prepare for both the client and the observer roles and to see the instructor at the start of the class. They can then be assigned as substitute clients if needed, otherwise as second observers for randomly chosen pods.

One additional option under the full class participation model is to require the students to conduct their interview outside of class (in which case they should be required to report, orally or in writing, on their interviews) and then use class time to discuss the experiences and the issues. This would save class time. If this is done, you can have one or more of the interviews videotaped so that relevant snippets can be shared with the class.

Since the materials have been prepared in such a way that the client can be either Pedro or Maria, you do not have to worry about being forced to select only male students, or only female students, to play the client role or, even more awkward, requiring males to play female roles or vice-versa.

A few optional extras:

1. Research or Self-Contained? The exercise is meant to be self-contained; no student research is required. (But coverage of certain previous parts of this book is assumed – see below). You could convert this exercise into a research assignment simply by telling the students to research any legal issues raised by the facts.

2. An Interpreter? To add further realism, you might try to recruit two Spanish-speakers, perhaps from the Spanish Department. One would play the role of the client and be interviewed in Spanish; the other would interpret. If you use an interpreter, he or she will also need instructions; they appear below. Using an interpreter has one large disadvantage: It reduces the effective interviewing time by half, and time will be short as it is. So interpreters are not recommended unless you are willing to allocate two class hours to the actual interview.

3. Taping the Interview? You can videotape (or audiotape) the interviews. Interested students (especially the direct participants) could watch and learn from this experience. A student who misses the class would also then have a chance to observe. You can also play back portions of the video to the class as part of a critique and can put the video on reserve for next year's students to watch before they do their own interviews (though the educational videos described below are better for that purpose).

Instructing the Players

The instructions for the student(s) who play the attorney role appear in the coursebook. The clients' instructions appear next in this Teacher's Manual. (There are alternative client instructions – "Instructions for Maria" and "Instructions for Pedro," depending on whether the person who plays the client is a woman or a man.) There are separate Instruction sheets for the observers, the special role students, and the interpreters (if any).

You should make sure all the players are clear as to exactly where and when they are needed, and you should emphasize how critical it is for them to be there on time. It's a good idea to confirm with the players a day or two before their appearance and, as noted earlier, to arrange for student backups just in case.

INSTRUCTIONS FOR MARIA

This project is a simulated attorney-client consultation. A student enrolled in a course on immigration law will be your attorney. (It's possible you will have a team of two students as your attorneys; if so, they will interview you together.) You will be playing the part of the client. This is the first time you and your attorney have met. Before the interview, all your attorney knows about you is that your name is Maria Ortiz, that you are from a tiny Central American country called Oquito, and that you are thinking about applying for asylum in the United States. Your attorney might also have some general preexisting knowledge about the political conditions in Oquito.

Here is your story:

You and Pedro Tejada lived together for ten years in the town of Puebla. You are not legally married (Oquito does not recognize common law marriages), but everyone in the town refers to you as Mr. and Mrs. Tejada. Puebla is a small, poor agricultural town in Oquito, a tiny Spanish-speaking country in Central America.

Pedro is very active in a local action group called Cambio para Puebla (Change for Puebla), or CPP. In fact, before the incidents in question here, he served as the leader of CPP. The mission of CPP is to improve the educational, cultural, and economic opportunities in Puebla. CPP meets weekly to discuss future goals and work on its ongoing projects. You yourself are not politically active, were never a CPP member, and never attended its meetings, but you are aware of its goals and have always supported Pedro in all he does.

Two years ago CPP completed a new library for the town. Practically the whole town turned out for the dedication ceremony. Proud and joyful over CPP's achievement, Pedro gave an emotional speech recounting CPP's efforts to fund and build the new library. He got a bit carried away, however, adding, "The Gonzalez regime has done nothing for this town. When we asked for a library, they instead brought weapons with which to terrorize us. The Gonzalez regime has driven this country into despair. They have taken away our jobs and our dreams. It's time for a change! This library is just the first step."

CPP held its weekly meeting two days after the dedication ceremony. Seven heavily armed men dressed in the country's military fatigues stormed the meeting. Confusion ensued. Some CPP members escaped. Others, including Pedro, were trapped and savagely beaten. The assailants also threatened to punish those trapped in the room for their anti-Gonzalez rhetoric. The assailants told the others in the room that their anti-Gonzalez rhetoric would not be tolerated, that they had a list of CPP members, and that, if the CPP members did not leave the country immediately, the military would hunt them down and kill them and their families.

After the armed men left, Pedro returned home to find the apartment had been ransacked. Thankfully, you were not home during the ransacking. When you returned home later that night, Pedro told you what had happened. Although you were both shaken, you both decided to remain in Oquito.

Two weeks later, a group of five masked men attacked one of the other CPP members, Juan, in his home. Unlike the first group of assailants, these men were not dressed in military fatigues, but they were armed with assault weapons. They rounded up Juan and his family in the kitchen. One of the masked men aimed an assault rifle at Juan and threatened him, saying, "We know what you've been doing, and we will kill you and your precious family if you don't get out of Oquito now!" Then two of the masked men took turns kicking and punching Juan in front of his family while the others watched and laughed. Juan and his family fled the country that day and have not returned. Another CPP member, Felipe, and his family suffered a similar experience two weeks later. They too fled the country within hours.

But Pedro refused to leave. He continued to lead the (now much smaller) monthly CPP meetings in secret at your and Pedro's apartment. Fearing for both of your lives, you repeatedly begged Pedro to quit CPP. He has refused. Finally, about a year after the attacks, you decided you could not live in fear any more and fled to the United States. It took you a week to travel here by land. You crossed the U.S. border approximately ten months ago by evading inspection in the middle of the night. You were and remain undocumented. Since your arrival in the U.S., you have been working in a restaurant.

Pedro remained behind in the same town (Puebla), but just after you left he moved to a new apartment in order to avoid detection. He continues to lead the secret CPP meetings there. You have been able to speak to him intermittently by phone.

Three weeks after your arrival in the United States, the Gonzalez regime was overthrown in a military coup. While the new regime has promised to reform the government and the military, the verdict is still out. The new President and a majority of the other leaders were fiercely opposed to Gonzalez. Nonetheless, some of the leaders of the Gonzalez regime have been absorbed into the leadership of the new administration.

You are now scheduled for an initial consultation with your attorney concerning a possible asylum application. To prepare for your part, please study this story carefully; don't consult the script during the interview because that would detract from the realism. You won't be expected to remember exact dates, but you should go into the interview with at least a rough idea of when the key events occurred. The attorney will probably ask you an open-ended question like "How can I help you?" If so, you should explain that you have fled from Oquito because you are in danger there and that you want to apply for asylum here in the U.S. At that point the attorney will probably ask you to describe what happened and explain why you are fearful. Without going into much more detail, you should explain that there are people who want to harm Pedro and his family because of his political activities with CPP and that they have already beaten him and other CPP members, ransacked your home, and warned him that if he didn't leave Oquito they would kill him and his family. Once you have said that much, the attorney will probably start to ask you more specific questions. Feel free to make up additional details spontaneously, as long as they aren't inconsistent with the given facts. At some point near the end of the interview, if your attorney hasn't already offered an assessment, ask your attorney what your chances are.

Finally, try to be as believable as you can. Try to stay in role and avoid outlandish answers or a flamboyant persona. Don't be afraid to admit that you don't know the answer to a particular question or to give a vague or disorganized answer occasionally. (In fact, vague or disorganized answers can liven up the interviews, since the attorney will then have to ask you questions to clarify the story.) Occasionally, also, you might purposely either misunderstand a question or give an unresponsive answer, just as clients often do in real life. Above all, enjoy your performance.

INSTRUCTIONS FOR PEDRO

This project is a simulated attorney-client consultation. A student enrolled in a course on immigration law will be your attorney. (It's possible you will have a team of two students as your attorneys; if so, they will interview you together.) You will be playing the part of the client. This is the first time you and your attorney have met. Before the interview, all your attorney knows about you is that your name is Pedro Tejada, that you are from a tiny Central American country called Oquito, and that you are thinking about applying for asylum in the United States. Your attorney might also have some general preexisting knowledge about the political conditions in Oquito.

Here is your story:

You and Maria Ortiz lived together for ten years in the town of Puebla. You are not legally married (Oquito does not recognize common law marriages), but everyone in the town refers to you as Mr. and Mrs. Tejada. Puebla is a small, poor agricultural town in Oquito, a tiny, Spanish-speaking country in Central America.

Maria is very active in a local action group called Cambio para Puebla (Change for Puebla), or CPP. In fact, before the incidents in question here, she served as the leader of CPP. The mission of CPP is to improve the educational, cultural, and economic opportunities in Puebla. CPP meets weekly to discuss future goals and work on its ongoing projects. You yourself are not politically active, were never a CPP member, and never attended its meetings, but you are aware of its goals and have always supported Maria in all she does.

Two years ago CPP completed a new library for the town. Practically the whole town turned out for the dedication ceremony. Proud and joyful over CPP's achievement, Maria gave an emotional speech recounting CPP's efforts to fund and build the new library. She got a bit carried away, however, adding, "The Gonzalez regime has done nothing for this town. When we asked for a library, they instead brought weapons with which to terrorize us. The Gonzalez regime has driven this country into despair. They have taken away our jobs and our dreams. It's time for a change! This library is just the first step."

CPP held its weekly meeting two days after the dedication ceremony. Seven heavily armed men dressed in the country's military fatigues stormed the meeting. Confusion ensued. Some CPP members escaped. Others, including Maria, were trapped and savagely beaten. The assailants also threatened to punish those trapped in the room for their anti-Gonzalez rhetoric. The assailants told the others in the room that their anti-Gonzalez rhetoric would not be tolerated, that they had a list of CPP members, and that, if the CPP members did not leave the country immediately, the military would hunt them down and kill them and their families.

After the armed men left, Maria returned home to find the apartment had been ransacked. Thankfully, you were not home during the ransacking. When you returned home later that night, Maria told you what had happened. Although you were both shaken, you both decided to remain in Oquito.

Two weeks later, a group of five masked men attacked one of the other CPP members, Juan, in his home. Unlike the first group of assailants, these men were not dressed in military fatigues, but they were armed with assault weapons. They rounded up Juan and his family in the kitchen. One of the masked men aimed an assault rifle at Juan and threatened him, saying, "We know what you've been doing, and we will kill you and your precious family if you don't get out of Oquito now!" Then two of the masked men took turns kicking and punching Juan in front of his family while the others watched and laughed. Juan and his family fled the country that day and have not returned. Another CPP member, Felipe, and his family suffered a similar experience two weeks later. They too fled the country within hours.

But Maria refused to leave. She continued to lead the (now much smaller) monthly CPP meetings in secret at your and Maria's apartment. Fearing for both of your lives, you repeatedly begged Maria to quit CPP. She has refused. Finally, about a year after the attacks, you decided you could not live in fear any more and fled to the United States. It took you a week to travel here by land. You crossed the U.S. border about ten months ago by evading inspection in the middle of the night. You were and remain undocumented. Since your arrival in the U.S., you have been working in a restaurant.

Maria remained behind in the same town (Puebla), but just after you left she moved to a new apartment in order to avoid detection. She continues to lead the secret CPP meetings there. You have been able to speak to her intermittently by phone.

Three weeks after your arrival in the United States, the Gonzalez regime was overthrown in a military coup. While the new regime has promised to reform the government and the military, the verdict is still out. The new President and a majority of the other leaders were fiercely opposed to Gonzalez. Nonetheless, some of the leaders of the Gonzalez regime have been absorbed into the leadership of the new administration.

You are now scheduled for an initial consultation with your attorney concerning a possible asylum application. To prepare for your part, please study this story carefully; don't consult the script during the interview because that would detract from the realism. You won't be expected to remember exact dates, but you should go into the interview with at least a rough idea of when the key events occurred. The attorney will probably ask you an open-ended question like "How can I help you?" If so, you should explain that you have fled from Oquito because you are in danger there and that you want to apply for asylum here in the U.S. At that point the attorney will probably ask you to describe what happened and explain why you are fearful. Without going into much more detail, you should explain that there are people who want to harm Maria and her family because of her political activities with CPP and that they have already beaten her and other CPP members, ransacked your home, and warned her that if she didn't leave Oquito they would kill her and her family. Once you have said that much, the attorney will probably start to ask you more specific questions. Feel free to make up additional details spontaneously, as long as they aren't inconsistent with the given facts. At some point near the end of the interview, if your attorney hasn't already offered an assessment, ask your attorney what your chances are.

Finally, try to be as believable as you can. Try to stay in role and avoid outlandish answers or a flamboyant persona. Don't be afraid to admit that you don't know the answer to a particular question or to give a vague or disorganized answer occasionally. (In fact, vague or disorganized answers can liven up the interviews, since the attorney will then have to ask you questions to clarify the story.) Occasionally, also, you might purposely either misunderstand a question or give an unresponsive answer, just as clients often do in real life. Above all, enjoy your performance.

INSTRUCTIONS FOR STUDENT OBSERVERS

This project is a simulated attorney-client consultation. Two of your classmates will be attorneys working as a team. A third classmate will be a client whom they are interviewing for the first time. Your role is that of observer.

Before the interview, the only information the attorneys have are the name of the client (Maria Ortiz if she is a woman, Pedro Tejada if he is a man), the fact that the client is from a tiny Central American country called Oquito, and the fact that the client is thinking about applying for asylum in the United States. The attorneys might also have some general preexisting knowledge about the political conditions in Oquito.

As an observer, you should not talk during the interview. It's OK to take notes, but otherwise be as unobtrusive as possible. Your job will be to offer comments, during the next class session, on your observations and reactions. So that all the observers will have a chance to speak, and so that there will still be enough class time to hear the impressions of some of the attorneys and clients as well, please keep your classroom critiques extremely brief - ideally under 2 minutes.

Among the issues you might choose to comment on (you won't have time to comment on all of these, so be selective) are the following:

Are there any substantive questions that the attorneys failed to ask but should have? Are there any questions that were asked that should *not* have been asked because they were either irrelevant ("I didn't understand where you were going with that.") or inappropriate (too personal)? Did the attorneys listen to the client? Did they give the client enough space to add information or ask questions of his or her own? Too much space? Did the attorneys create an environment in which the client could be as comfortable as possible, given the inherent stresses of both refugee trauma and the attorney-client setting? Were the attorneys respectful? Did the attorneys explain things in terms that would be comprehensible to a lay client, without being patronizing?

The keys here:

1. Read the assigned materials carefully.
2. Enjoy the interview; you're not being graded, so you can just focus on the learning experience and the drama.
3. PLEASE BE SURE TO SHOW UP ON TIME FOR THE INTERVIEW. IF YOU DON'T SHOW, OR YOU SHOW UP LATE, IT WILL MESS UP THE OTHER THREE CLASSMATES IN YOUR POD!

INSTRUCTIONS FOR STUDENTS PLAYING SPECIAL ROLE

You actually have two roles. If one of the clients fails to show up on the day of the interviews, you will be asked to serve as that client. If all the clients show up, you will be assigned to one of the other pods as a second observer.

This means you will need to prepare both roles and therefore will receive both the client instructions and the observer instructions. Until we start, I won't know which pod is going to need you, so please see me at the very beginning of the class session. Thanks very much in advance for your flexibility.

INTERPRETER INSTRUCTIONS

The project in which you are taking part is a mock attorney-client consultation. One or two students enrolled in a course on immigration law will play the part(s) of the attorney(s). Someone else will play the part of the client, whose name will be either Pedro or Maria. He or she is from Oquito, a (fictional) Spanish-speaking country in Central America, and has consulted this attorney in order to apply for asylum in the United States. This is their first meeting.

You will be playing the part of the interpreter. The attorney speaks only English, and Pedro or Maria speaks only Spanish. So each time the attorney says something, you should translate the statement or question into Spanish. And each time Pedro or Maria says something, you should translate his or her statement or question into English. It's important that you translate verbatim; don't try to offer a smoother or more articulate version of what was said.

Enjoy your performance. The instructor and the students alike will be extremely grateful for the time and effort you are giving them.

Check List for Setting Up the Interviews

1. Make the two basic decisions: (a) which components to do (interview, critique of interviewing technique, and/or class discussion of substantive issues), and the amount of class time to allocate to each; and (b) whether to use the one-interview/demonstration model or the multiple interviews/full class participation model (and whether to use single students or two-student attorney teams and whether to add an observer to each interview).

2. Make sure the class will have covered the essential parts of the chapter before the interview – the main elements of the refugee definition and at least a skimming of the subsection on asylum procedure. If you want the students to consider alternative claims under the Convention Against Torture (not recommended), then section C.1 should also have been covered.

3. Introductory materials: There are some excellent videos that could be shown to students in the classes that precede the interviews (or you could simply place them on library reserve depending on the availability of class time). The Epidavros Project has produced a documentary film entitled "Well-Founded Fear" (2000) (a bit under 2 hours), which takes the viewer inside the asylum process. Using other archive footage shot for "Well-Founded Fear," the Epidavros Project has also produced two offshoots, both in 2004, entitled "Tales from Real Life" (5 vignettes, of 15 minutes each, of 5 asylum seekers' cases) and "Practicing Asylum Law" (footage of actual asylum officer interviews, plus commentary). The latter two videos are accompanied by written materials. To order, you can either visit the website at http://www.wellfoundedfear.org and click on "Products," or write to the Epidavros Project Inc., 141 West 28th Street, Suite 6-B, New York, New York 10001, or phone them at 212-594-2127. The website posts all the prices.

In addition, Professor Philip Schrag, under the auspices of the Center for Applied Legal Studies at the Georgetown University Law Center, has produced a superb instructional video showing a simulated interview of an asylum claimant by a law student in a clinical setting. There are accompanying written materials. The simulation deliberately includes errors that students and lawyers commonly make when interviewing potential asylum claimants. There is ample opportunity for class discussion of strategic decisions. The video is about 30 minutes long but with class discussion requires a total of about 90 minutes of class time. The same Center has produced another excellent video reproducing excerpts of a removal hearing (involving asylum) before an immigration judge, in which actors follow the script of an actual hearing. It is called the "Metara Tape." It runs 15 minutes and requires a total of about 75 minutes of class time. The Center supplies these tapes without charge to teachers of immigration or refugee law. To contact the Center, see the website:

http://www.law.georgetown.edu/clinics/cals or write to Center for Applied Legal Studies, Georgetown University Law Center, 111 F Street, N.W., Suite 332, Washington, DC 20001, or phone 202-662-9565.

Finally, ALI-ABA (with credit to Michele Pistone) recently produced a four-hour DVD and accompanying written materials that track the fictional asylum case of an unaccompanied child from Guinea, from initial intake through an asylum hearing before an immigration judge, and including expert commentary. The DVD is entitled "Best Practices in Representing Asylum Seekers." For more information, visit the ALI-ABA website: http://www.ali-aba.org/aliaba/rdvd01.asp or call 215-243-1613.

4. At least a few days before the actual interview(s), you should alert the students to the upcoming exercise and provide general guidance. That is also a good time at which to (a) suggest (or require) that the students watch one or more of the instructional videos (if you have them); (b) assign them to read section B.8 of the coursebook (which contains the instructions for the exercise, the DOS Country Report on Oquito, and the excerpts from "Interviewing a Client"); (c) assign the student roles (you can have them sign up for their preferred roles and/or preferred interview teams, or you can make the assignments randomly); (d) tell those students who play the attorney role that their instructions are all included in the text; (e) tell all the other students that they will soon receive written instructions that they will need to study carefully and that they may not reveal any information from those stories to any other students before the interviews; and (f) once all the roles are set, distribute the instructions (reproduced below).

5. If you are going to use any outsiders (for clients and/or interpreters), line them up well in advance and give each a copy of his or her instructions. (They appear below and can be photocopied.) To avoid the problem of an outside actor failing to show up on the date of the interview, it is also a good idea to select a backup for each outsider's role (attorney, client, interpreter). The client and interpreter backups will also need copies of their respective instructions.

6. Decide where to hold the interview(s). If you use the one interview/ demonstration model, the regular classroom should be fine. If you use the multiple interviews/full class participation model, the regular classroom will probably still be fine, but if small interview rooms are available for at least some of the interviews, so much the better.

7. If you plan to videotape the interview(s), make advance arrangements for the equipment.

<u>Instructions for Follow-Up Class Sessions</u>

A. Critiques of Students' Interviewing Techniques

It is possible simply to have an unstructured class discussion in which students offer whatever comments occur to them, but one alternative is to invite self-critiques from the students who did the interviewing, then critiques from the client(s), then critiques from the observers who were assigned to specific interviewers if you used that approach, and, finally, critiques from anyone else in the class.

Another way to structure the discussion is by posing specific questions: Are there any questions that the attorneys failed to ask but should have? Are there any questions that were asked that should not have been asked because they were either irrelevant ("I didn't understand where you were going with that.") or inappropriate (too personal)? Did the attorneys listen to the client? Did they give the client enough space to add information or ask questions of his or her own? Too much space? Did the attorney create an environment in which the client could be as comfortable as possible, given the inherent stresses of both refugee trauma and the attorney-client setting? Were the attorneys respectful? Did the attorneys explain things in terms that would be comprehensible to a lay client, without being patronizing?

B. Discussion of the Substantive Issues

As for discussion format, any of the usual classroom methodologies would work well. One possibility is to convert the class into a giant immigration court in which half the students represent the asylum applicant, the other half act as ICE trial attorneys, and the two sides take turns summarizing their cases to the teacher as immigration judge (on the assumption that the applicant's testimony has already been given). Alternatively, the students could represent the opposing sides in oral argument before the BIA (rare nowadays) or a court of appeals. A USCIS asylum officer interview is a third possible setting, but from a substantive standpoint it might tend to duplicate most of what was said during the attorney-client interview(s).

The substantive issues are discussed in the following outline:

<u>Outline of Issues and Strategy</u>

[This outline assumes that Maria is the client and that Pedro is her partner who stayed behind in Oquito. If you assign the client role to one or more males, however, then Pedro becomes the client and Maria becomes the partner who stayed behind. In that latter case, simply read all the references in this Outline to Pedro and Maria as if they were reversed.]

A preliminary issue is whether Maria should even file an asylum application. By doing so, she will be revealing her identity, her presence, her undocumented status, and her whereabouts to USCIS, thus exposing herself to possible removal if her application fails. At this point she is already removable and, even if she were to leave the United States on her own, she would be inadmissible for another 3 years under INA § 212(a)(9)(B)(i)(I) for having been unlawfully present more than 180 days but less than a year. If she is formally ordered removed, which could happen if she applies for asylum and her application is ultimately denied, she will become inadmissible for longer (10 years) because of the removal order. Maria therefore needs to balance the likelihood and benefits of asylum against the likelihood and detriment of a removal order or even a voluntary departure order.

The student playing the attorney interviewer might feel uneasy about that aspect of the case. Should an attorney even raise with Maria the possibility of remaining in the United States without applying for asylum? Would that amount to counseling the client to violate the law, something a lawyer obviously is barred from doing? It is perfectly appropriate, however, for the attorney to explain the legal consequences of different courses of action – e.g., explanations about what asylum requires, what consequences flow from removal, etc.

The attorney/student should also point out to Maria that she needs to file her asylum application within one year of arrival. That would be approximately two months from now. Without pressuring the client, the attorney needs to make clear that with the lead time necessary to prepare a convincing asylum case, Maria will need to decide soon whether she wants to file for asylum.

The main job of the attorney in this exercise will be to elicit all the relevant facts. In order to do that, and also to evaluate Maria's claim, the attorney will need to spot the potential issues. To be eligible for asylum under INA § 208, Maria must show that she is a "refugee," within the meaning of INA § 101(a)(42) (and must receive the favorable exercise of discretion). To be a refugee, she must prove persecution or a well-founded fear of persecution on one of the five Convention grounds. To qualify for withholding of removal under INA § 241(b)(3), she must show that her life or freedom would be threatened on one of the five Convention grounds. Except as noted below, the two claims will raise the following common issues:

A. Are the harms that Maria fears "persecution?"

There is no unique authoritative definition of "persecution," but the BIA in *Matter of Acosta,* 19 I. & N. Dec. 211 (1985), defined it as "either a threat to the life or freedom of, or the infliction of suffering or harm upon, those who differ in a way regarded as offensive." Ultimately, whether conditions rise to the level of persecution is a question of fact. The student should elicit from Maria exactly what she fears will happen to her if she is returned to Oquito. She will probably say she fears that armed men will assault her, ransack her home, and possibly torture or even kill her. By any standard, these acts would be serious enough to constitute persecution.

As for the "singling out" that some decisionmakers have required, the attorney will need to emphasize the assault on the CPP members following the library dedication, the direct threat to Maria's life as the common-law wife of a CPP member, the ransacking of her home, and the threats and assaults on Juan, Felipe and their families in their own homes. The attorney will also want to establish that these are not threats the average Oquitoan faces. Rather, it will have to be shown that CPP members and their families have been singled out for their criticism of the Gonzalez government. The information in the DOS Country Report supports the singling out of dissidents.

The persecution must be inflicted by the government or by a party that the government is unable or unwilling to control. The student should ask Maria exactly who she believes is threatening her. There is ambiguity here. It is unclear whether the Gonzalez government was responsible for the persecution. The armed, masked men who raided the CPP meeting were dressed in the country's military fatigues, but they never indicated they were part of the military or acting on behalf of the Gonzalez government. The armed, masked men who terrorized Juan and Felipe similarly revealed no group or government affiliation, and they did not even wear military uniforms. Still, even if none of the armed men was officially part of the Gonzalez regime, they might have been part of a private group that the Gonzalez government was unable or unwilling to control. The student will need to inquire whether the government was aware of the situation and whether it took any steps to prevent further threats and violence.

B. Is Maria's fear of persecution "well-founded?"

The Supreme Court in *INS v. Cardoza-Fonseca*, 480 U.S. 421 (1987), vaguely construed the term to require something short of "more likely than not." The Justice Department regulations, adopting the approach taken by the BIA and several lower courts, require a "reasonable possibility of suffering such persecution." See 8 CFR § 208.13(b)(2)(B) (2004). In contrast, the Supreme Court has set the standard of proof for withholding of removal as a "clear probability," by which it meant that persecution must be more likely than not. See *INS v. Stevic*, 467 U.S. 407 (1984).

Two of the ways to prove a well-founded fear of persecution are to establish (a) past persecution; or (b) a "pattern or practice" of the country persecuting a group of people and the applicant's inclusion in that group, "such that his or her fear of persecution upon return is reasonable." 8 CFR § 208.13(b)(2)(iii) (2008).

1. Past Persecution: Past persecution creates a rebuttable presumption of a well-founded fear of future persecution. While Maria herself was never physically persecuted, her husband was physically assaulted. The attorney might explore whether the resulting mental suffering of Maria was extreme enough to be persecution. In addition, the home that was ransacked was hers as well as Pedro's. If these factors together rise to the level of past persecution of Maria, then she is entitled to a rebuttable presumption of a well-founded fear of future persecution.

2. Pattern or Practice of Persecuting a Group of People: As explained in section C below, Maria might be able to show persecution on account of either political opinion or membership in a particular social group. The student should examine whether there is a pattern or practice of persecuting the families of anti-Gonzalez dissidents or CPP members. For this purpose the DOS Country Report will be instructive (though not conclusive).

3. Other Evidence

The attorney should ask Maria why she fears for her safety when Pedro has managed to carry on with his CPP activities undisturbed for the past year. While Pedro has moved to a new apartment and conducts CPP meetings in secret, presumably would-be persecutors still see him on the streets of Puebla and hear of him from other residents. The attorney will also want to know whether there have been any more incidents involving threats or violence toward CPP members and their families. If there have been no further incidents, perhaps the danger has passed.

The attorney should also explore whether the incidents involving Juan, Felipe and their families can even be connected to the attacks at the CPP meeting. While these incidents all appear similar, the armed, masked men who threatened Juan, Felipe and their families did not wear the same military uniforms as those who interrupted the CPP meeting, as noted above. This should raise the question of whether the armed men were actually connected to those at the CPP meeting or whether they were simply a random group of thugs. The attorney should also elicit more details of the threats Juan and Felipe received. The armed men made very vague statements concerning why Juan and Felipe were targeted. Although both were CPP members, there was no indication that "We know what you've been doing" referred to CPP activities. This statement alone is not conclusive as to whether Juan, Felipe and their families were targeted for their CPP membership. These might have been simply random attacks that could have happened to anyone in Puebla. But if no other explanation emerges, the inference that they were selected because of their CPP activities seems fair.

The attorney might also ask Maria why she thinks the armed men attacked and threatened Juan and Felipe but not Pedro, who was, after all, the leader of CPP at the time (as well as being the person whose public statement at the library dedication ceremony had set off the whole chain of events). Maria will probably say she doesn't know. She might speculate that the assailants simply weren't aware Pedro was the leader.

Since Pedro and Maria were never formally married, the attorney might additionally explore whether Maria would really be targeted as "family" if she were returned to Oquito. She will probably reply that the entire village knows that she and Pedro have lived together as a married couple for ten years and regards them as married for all practical purposes.

The changed country conditions are yet another concern. Since Maria's departure, the Gonzalez regime has been unseated in a coup. While Maria might have had a well-founded fear under the Gonzalez regime, the attorney should ask why her fear persists now that Gonzalez is gone. The attorney should also ask whether any similar assaults on Gonzalez opponents or CPP members have occurred since Caleros's rise to power. On this point, the DOS Country Report supplies further guidance. It indicates that, although the Caleros government has rejected a formal policy of targeting political dissidents, it continues to imprison those who criticize the Government. Of particular importance is the finding that Gonzalez loyalists within the military and police forces similarly threaten, imprison and physically abuse those who today or in the past have criticized the Gonzalez regime. The report indicates that the Caleros government has done little to control these abuses.

Finally, there is the question of internal flight options. Before asylum will be granted, it must be established that Maria would not be safe in a different area of the country. Questions the attorney might ask include: "Do you have any relatives or friends in Oquito?" and "What do you think would happen if you simply moved to a different town?" Maria might say that she could not relocate safely in a different part of the country because Oquito is so small. The attorney should also ask whether the Gonzalez loyalists exist throughout the country. Even if the loyalists do exist throughout the country, the attorney would want to establish that the loyalists would seek out and discover Maria if she were to move to a different part of Oquito.

C. Is the persecution that Maria fears "on account of race, religion, nationality, membership in a particular social group, or political opinion?"

Here, the possibilities include political opinion and social group.

1. Political Opinion: Maria herself has not expressed a political opinion. She is not a part of the CPP and has not made any statements in opposition to the Gonzalez government. Still, the attorney should consider whether Maria is eligible for asylum on the basis of her *imputed* political opinion. The idea of imputed political opinion is well accepted in the United States. Imputed political opinion occurs when the persecutor believes the asylum applicant holds a particular view and intends to persecute the person because of it. It does not matter whether the person actually holds that political opinion. Maria should be asked how the threats arose. She will most likely trace them to Pedro voicing his anti-Gonzalez political opinion at the library dedication ceremony. By threatening to kill the CPP members and their families, the persecutors were imputing the anti-Gonzalez opinions of some CPP members to all CPP members and their families – or, at the very least, to Pedro's family.

A counter-argument to Maria's imputed political opinion argument is that the would-be persecutors did not actually believe the dissidents' family members held any particular political opinion. Rather, the argument would run, the would-be persecutors were threatening the CPP members' families only to intimidate the CPP members themselves and to gain leverage.

2. Membership in a Particular Social Group: The attorney must decide whether Maria fits into a particular social group. Maria can argue that she will be persecuted because of her membership in the social group that consists of family members of political dissidents or, as a more specific alternative, families of CPP members. She might also argue that Pedro's family comprises its own smaller social group.

The main test is still *Acosta*, where a social group was defined by reference to an "immutable" characteristic – i.e., one that either cannot be changed or is so fundamental to the applicant's identity that she should not be required to change it. The immutable characteristic shared by all of these potential social groups is family. Maria and Pedro are not blood relatives and are not legally married. Certainly, however, Maria can argue that her long-term relationship with Pedro, even though not formally enshrined in marriage, is fundamental to her identity and something she cannot and should not be expected to change. Since the BIA or the court might also require social visibility, the attorney should ask Maria whether her community in Oquito thinks of family members of political dissidents, or families of CPP members in particular, as a group.

Finally, the attorney should explore whether the feared persecution is actually "on account of" Maria's membership in the social group. The masked men at the original CPP meeting warned that they had a list of CPP members and that, if the members did not leave, the armed men would kill the members and their families. In addition, Maria's and Pedro's home was ransacked, very likely by the same armed men. These facts appear to indicate that Maria was threatened because of her relationship with Pedro and would be targeted because of her status as the wife of a CPP member should she return to Oquito. Maria might also point to the incidents involving Juan's and Felipe's families as evidence that she would be persecuted because of her membership in the social group. The attorney should specifically ask Maria whether she thinks the threats and attacks against Juan, Felipe, and their families can be connected to the incident at the CPP meeting.

Convention Against Torture [Optional]: If the Convention Against Torture has already been covered in the course, the attorney might wish to elicit any additional factual information relevant to that claim and might also wish to explain and recommend this additional option to Maria. The main advantage to Maria is that she would no longer have to prove that the feared harm is linked to one of the five Refugee Convention grounds. On the other hand, (1) torture requires more than persecution; (2) the probability of its occurrence must be more than 50% (under U.S. law); and (3) the successful applicant is not necessarily allowed to remain in the U.S. (she would only be protected from refoulement).

Under the U.S. Senate resolution ratifying the Convention against Torture, and under regulations codified in 8 CFR § 208.18(a)(5) (2008), an act qualifies as torture only if it is "specifically intended to inflict severe physical or mental pain or suffering." Mental pain or suffering is defined in the Resolution, and in *id.* § 208.18(a)(4), as "prolonged mental harm caused by or resulting from . . . (iii) the threat of imminent death; or (iv) the threat that another person will imminently be subjected to death, severe physical pain or suffering . . . ." Whether the harms to which Maria would be subjected in Oquito rise to the level of torture under CAT is a question of fact. The threats to Pedro and Maria are relevant to this assessment. Both Maria and Pedro were threatened with death if they remained in Oquito. It is possible, therefore, that Maria will be subjected to severe physical suffering and even death if sent back to Oquito. There is the additional risk that, even if she is not hunted down and killed, she would still suffer from prolonged mental pain as a result of the threat of imminent death to herself and to Pedro. The attorney should try to get a sense of the degree of mental suffering Maria would incur.

The torture must also be "inflicted by or at the instigation of or with the consent or acquiescence of a public official or other person acting in an official capacity." 8 CFR § 208.18(a)(1) (2008). The Senate Resolution and the regulations in turn define "acquiescence" to require "awareness" by the public official and a breach of his or her "legal responsibility to intervene to prevent such activity." *Id.* § 208.18(a)(7). There is some ambiguity in the facts concerning exactly who is responsible for the threats to Maria. See section A above. In addition, the Country Report indicates that pro-Gonzalez loyalists in both the local police forces and the military have threatened, detained, and/or physically assaulted anti-Gonzalez dissidents. Maria will eventually have to prove that at the very least public officials acquiesced in the intimidation and physical violence.

The Senate Resolution and the regulations further limit torture to acts that are "directed against a person in the offender's custody or physical control." 8 CFR § 208.18(a)(6) (2008). It is unclear who the "offender" is in cases involving government acquiescence in private acts. If the public official is the one who is said to offend by acquiescing, the claim might fail because the official lacks custody or control over the victim. And if the offender is the private actor, the claim might fail because the private actor is not a public official. But that combination of results would render the "acquiescence" language meaningless. Nonetheless, early United States cases have been disinclined to find government acquiescence. For example, in *Matter of S.V.*, 22 I. & N. Dec. 1306 (BIA, 2000), the Board held that the actions of rebel guerrillas did not constitute torture because the government could not be said to have acquiesced in those acts.

SECTION C. BEYOND PERSECUTION: PROTECTION FROM OTHER DANGERS

1. The Convention Against Torture

Notes and Questions on Page 1104:

Q2: CAT article 1.1 defines "torture" as "*any* act by which severe pain or suffering, whether physical or mental, is intentionally inflicted on a person for such purposes as . . ." [emphasis added]. To the extent that the Senate Understanding purports to limit the torture definition to specified threats and harms, therefore, it does indeed seem to fall short of what the Convention requires.

Perhaps prong # 2 will be given a saving construction. Read literally, it includes as torture the administration or threatened administration of "procedures calculated to disrupt profoundly the senses or the personality." Almost any form of mental torture that one could envision would seem to fit that description. Under that interpretation, then, prong 2 alone seems coextensive with the Convention definition. ICE might counterargue that the literal interpretation was not intended. First, ICE might say, prong 2 seems concerned with torture via mind-altering substances; the reference to "other procedures . . ." should be construed as referring to similar techniques. Second, ICE might add, the literal (broad) interpretation of prong (2) would render the other three prongs superfluous. All of them describe techniques "calculated to disrupt profoundly the senses or the personality."

Being generally wary of conflicts between treaties and the Senate's understandings in ratification resolutions, courts might look for ways to reconcile the two definitions. This effort could follow either of two paths. A court could interpret the Convention as contemplating definitional refinements like the one the U.S. Senate has imposed. Or the court could broadly interpret prong 2 of Understanding 1(a) so as to bring the ratification resolution into conformity with the plain language of the Convention.

Q4: There is no obvious answer to this question. See the analysis of Problem 9 below.

Q5: (a) The language recommended by the Committee made clear that sanctions would not be "lawful" for CAT purposes if they clearly violated international law. The amendment replaced that qualifier with narrower language to the effect that a state could not use domestic sanctions that would defeat the purpose of CAT to prohibit "torture."

(b) Torture is merely one of many possible violations of international human rights law. The amendment therefore expands the range of activities in which a would-be violator could engage without technically committing torture. (As discussed in (c) below, a literal reading of the amendment <u>might</u> have even more sweeping effects.)

(c) If interpreted literally, Understanding # 1(c) arguably permits a state party to engage in any actions it wishes, without violating CAT, as long as it first passes enabling legislation. The state may not use domestic sanctions to "defeat the object and purpose of the Convention to prohibit *torture*" [emphasis added]. But "torture" in turn is defined not to cover "lawful sanctions," which, according to the first sentence of Understanding # 1(c), encompass "enforcement actions authorized by United States law." If the assumption is that other states parties could announce reciprocal restrictions -- i.e. provisions to the effect that sanctions are lawful if authorized by *their* laws -- then the "nonetheless" clause accomplishes nothing, and in the process the recommended "international law" constraint has been lost.

Perhaps a more sensible, and equally literal, interpretation of the Understanding, therefore, is that the Senate truly meant to use United States law as the litmus test for judging the lawfulness of a foreign government's sanctions. That interpretation, while shamelessly chauvinistic, would do less damage to the torture definition than a circular reading that effectively condones any foreign actions enshrined in domestic law.

Q7: The reading seems strained. CAT article 3 doesn't refer to substantial grounds for believing that the person "would be tortured." It is enough that there are substantial grounds for believing that the person "would be in danger" of torture.

Q9: Section 2242(a) does use words like "expel" and "return," the same words the Supreme Court in Sale construed as inapplicable on the high seas. But unlike section 241(b)(3) or the predecessor version interpreted in Sale, section 2242(a) ends with the explicit phrase "regardless of whether the person is physically present in the United States." Consequently, CAT clearly applies on the high seas.

Q10: Possibilities include the following:

a. Examples of cases in which the feared harm constitutes torture but doesn't constitute persecution on account of one of the five protected grounds might include these:

i. The harm will be inflicted because of a personal grudge;

ii. The harm will be inflicted to punish someone for a crime, see CAT art. 1.1, and for some reason the claim does not survive the prosecution / persecution distinction read into the refugee definition for asylum purposes;

iii. The harm is inflicted in order to obtain information or a confession (see CAT art. 1.1); or

iv. Perhaps CAT claims will succeed in some cases of gender-related violence when the omission of gender from the list of the five protected "refugee" grounds, combined with either restrictive readings of the "social group" category or broad readings of the non-state actor limitation, cause an asylum claim to fail. If the only difficulty is that a court is unwilling to recognize women or a subgroup of women as a "social group," then a CAT claim solves the problem, because there is no need to link the torture to a particular protected ground. But if the problem is the non-state actor limitation, then the early decisions in *S.V.* and *Ali*, discussed in item 5, could augur high hurdles in the domestic violence cases. See Problem 9.

b. The Supreme Court's decision in *Sale* is clearly inapplicable to CAT claims. See item 10 above. So interdictions on the High Seas could be an example, assuming the particular harm feared rises to the level of torture.

c. The criminal, national security, and persecutor exceptions to eligibility for both asylum, INA § 208(b)(2)(A), and persecution-related nonrefoulement, INA § 241(b)(3)(B), will not defeat CAT claims, though they will relegate the claimant to "deferral of removal" rather than "withholding of removal." See items 9 and 14 of the Notes and Questions.

d. Neither nonrefoulement for persecution nor nonrefoulement for torture requires the exercise of discretion; nor is either type of nonrefoulement claim subject to a one-year filing deadline. Thus, both types of nonrefoulement differ from asylum.

Q11: There are several possibilities:

a. The feared harm constitutes persecution but doesn't rise to the level of torture. Possible examples:

i. Imprisonment and even death, even when they constitute persecution, do not necessarily entail torture.

ii. Actions by rebels or other private groups. Senate Understandings 1(b) (concerning custody or control) and 1(d) (concerning the meaning of "acquiescence") might make it hard to press CAT claims against nongovernmental torturers. See item 5 of the Notes and Questions and especially the *Ali* case that it cites. It might be somewhat easier to win asylum cases in which the alleged persecutors are private actors.

iii. As item 6 of the Notes and Questions illustrates, Senate Understanding 1(c) potentially broadens the "lawful sanctions" qualification in CAT. This development could make CAT claims problematic in situations where municipal legislation condones the particular alleged torture. The analogous issue in asylum law is the prosecution / persecution distinction, which seems more flexible than the Senate's version of the "lawful sanctions" definition.

b. As noted in item 7 of the Notes and Questions, past persecution is a basis for asylum (but not 241(b)(3)); past torture is not a basis for a CAT claim.

c. You saw earlier that the standard of proof for persecution-based nonrefoulement is "more likely than not." The same is true for CAT nonrefoulement. Senate Understanding # 2. (Asylum, in contrast, requires only a "well-founded fear," interpreted to mean merely a "reasonable" fear.)

Q14: (a) The language in section 2242(d) that deals with review of individual claims doesn't say that no court has jurisdiction. In sharp contrast to the clause that precedes it (the one dealing with review of the regulations themselves), the claims clause says merely that "nothing in *this* section shall be construed as *providing* jurisdiction . . ." The contrast is clear, and it seems deliberate. Thus, if some other source of jurisdiction were available (perhaps habeas corpus, or general federal question jurisdiction before the REAL ID Act), the quoted language would not have ousted it.

If a contrary conclusion were otherwise inferrable from that language -- i.e., if the quoted language were interpreted as not only not creating non-242 review but actually barring it -- the "notwithstanding" clause would become relevant. As the students saw in the habeas materials in chapter 9, §

B.6.b of the coursebook, implied repeal of habeas is highly disfavored. Even "notwithstanding any other provision of law" language has been construed to mean "except for habeas corpus." But new INA § 242(a)(4), added by the REAL ID Act in 2005, now makes clear that the petition for review in the court of appeals is the exclusive avenue of judicial review of denials of CAT claims; even (statutory) habeas corpus is expressly excluded.

(b) On this issue the statute is ambiguous. The provision, including punctuation, is in the form: Notwithstanding A, and except for B, no court shall have jurisdiction over C, and nothing here shall be construed as conferring jurisdiction over D, except as part of a 242 proceeding. The "except" clause at the end of the provision clearly modifies the preceding clause, which concerns the review of individual claims raised under the Convention or the implementing statute. Thus, judicial review of the denial of CAT claims is generally available under INA § 242 as part of the review of the resulting removal order. But does this "except" clause additionally modify the earlier language concerning nonreviewability of the regulations themselves? That is not clear. As Kristen Rosati notes in the cited passage, the "except" clause is preceded by a comma. She argues that that means it does indeed modify both parts, not just the clause that precedes it. This is most likely right, but not necessarily so. The absence of a comma would certainly have suggested that the "except" clause modifies only the preceding phrase, but the presence of the comma doesn't necessarily establish the converse, because the clause relating to the reviewability of the regulations is also set off by commas. Who on earth drafted this provision, and who was his or her legal writing teacher?

(c) The first "except" clause is extraordinary. First, one would think that Congress itself, subject to any applicable constitutional limitations (such as habeas corpus), has the responsibility to decide the jurisdiction of the federal courts. This doesn't seem like a decision it could delegate to an administrative agency, much less a law enforcement agency. Second, it seems inappropriate to authorize any agency to decide whether its own regulations will be subject to judicial review. Whatever one might think about Congress's power to bar the courts from reviewing the legality of Congress's own enactments, it seems more radical still to delegate to a law enforcement agency the power to decide whether its own regulations will be subject to judicial review. If the agency regulations exceed the authority conferred by the statute, or if they violate the treaty that Senate ratification makes the "Law of the Land," the agency should not be able to enforce unlawful action by barring judicial review. (Note that the government in any event does not appear to have done so.)

Q15. (a) Article 20 allows the Committee, on its own initiative, to investigate any state party when there is evidence of systematic torture, unless the state party affirmatively opts out under article 28. The U.S. has not opted out, so it has accepted the Committee's competence under article

20. But this power would rarely be exercised with respect to individual claims.

(b) Article 21 contemplates claims by states parties that other states parties have violated the Convention, but only if both states parties have declared that they recognize the competence of the Committee to consider such communications. In Declaration # 2 of the Senate ratification resolution, the United States has so declared. Consequently the Committee may consider claims against the United States, provided they are brought by other states parties who have similarly recognized the competence of the Committee under this provision.

(c) Article 22 empowers the Committee to investigate complaints brought by individuals, but, again, only if the state party against whom the complaint is filed has declared its recognition of the Committee's competence under this article. The United States has not made such a declaration, so individuals who seek nonrefoulement under CAT article 3 (or who claim torture at the hands of United States officials) may not go to the Committee Against Torture to complain against the United States.

<u>Problems</u> <u>7-9</u> (page 1113):

Problem 7: Under the CAT definition it seems clear that A has been tortured. His tormentors have inflicted severe mental suffering (for the purposes of obtaining information), and the Convention does not limit the methodology.

Under Senate Understanding 1(a), the answer is less certain. Prong 1 seems inapplicable because, while they have threatened to kill him in his sleep, they have not really threatened severe physical pain or suffering. Prong 2 is arguably applicable under a literal interpretation, since they have used a "procedure" that was "calculated to disrupt profoundly the senses or the personality." As discussed in the analysis of Question 3 above, however, it is not clear whether a literal, expansive interpretation was intended. Prong 3 is probably inapplicable, because a death that might still be months away is probably not "imminent." And Prong 4 is inapplicable, despite the false statements about having killed his family, since this prong contemplates only threats of *future* death or severe pain to others.

Problem 8: B is statutorily ineligible for asylum, because INA § 208(b)(2)(A)(ii) disqualifies anyone who, having been convicted of a particularly serious crime, constitutes a danger to the community. Under INA § 208(b)(2)(B)(i), an aggravated felony is automatically considered a "particularly serious crime." (If a student asks about the element of "danger to the community," the instructor can observe that courts and the BIA have construed this requirement as being automatically satisfied once the crime is found to be "particularly serious.")

B is also statutorily ineligible for withholding of removal under INA § 241(b)(3). Subsection 241(b)(3)(B)(ii) contains the same "particularly serious crime" exclusion, and the language that follows provides that an aggravated felony will be a particularly serious crime whenever the offender was sentenced to five years or more, as B was. (At any rate, B is ineligible for withholding under section 241(b)(3) because his life or freedom is no longer threatened. Past persecution does not make out a case for withholding.)

His criminal conviction will not bar relief under CAT. As the students have seen, CAT does not contain the exceptions that the 1951 Convention does, and the regulations protect even those who have been convicted of crimes, albeit only through "deferral of removal" rather than the more secure "withholding of removal." His CAT claim will fail nonetheless. Unlike the "refugee" definition, which covers both past persecution and a well-founded fear of future persecution, CAT article 3 prohibits refoulement only when "there are substantial grounds for believing that he would be in danger of being subjected to torture." See item 7 of the Notes and Questions. Since the threat has now passed, article 3 does not apply. [The main purposes of this Problem are to highlight the past torture vs. future torture distinction and to illustrate that some people will fall through one gap in the asylum law and another gap in CAT law.)

Cancellation of removal is also inapplicable, since B has been in the United States less than the required ten years. INA § 240A(b)(1)(A).

Deferred action is always possible. Since removal proceedings have already started, ICE would first need permission from the immigration judge to dismiss the case.

A private bill is also a possibility, but these have become exceedingly rare.

Problem 9: As for asylum, the verdict is still out. She clearly has a well-founded fear of persecution. One major hurdle will be demonstrating that the persecution is on account of her membership in a social group (women). With an emerging consensus that the feared persecution cannot be made an element of the social group, a claim that the group consists of all women who are domestic violence victims will probably fail. She will also need to prove that she has no reasonable internal flight alternative. A final hurdle will be the non-state actor problem. Under the regulations, she must prove the government was unable or "unwilling" to protect her. With *Matter of R-A-* vacated (and reconsideration pending at the time of this writing), there seems a reasonable chance the BIA or a court could find the government "unwilling" on these facts. The police appear to have turned a blind eye to the violence. See generally the material on gender-related asylum claims and in particular the discussion of the non-state actor issue on coursebook pages 973-84.

As for a CAT claim, there is no question that the husband has intentionally inflicted severe pain. Possibly he has been abusing her for one of the purposes listed in CAT article 1.1 (intimidation, or gender discrimination), but in any event the listed purposes are not exclusive; they are merely examples. See item 4 of the Notes and Questions.

But there are two related problems:

First, CAT article 1.1 requires at least the "acquiescence" of a public official (or other person acting in an official capacity). Senate Understanding # 1(d) defines "acquiescence" to require "awareness" and a breach of the official's "legal responsibility." See item 5 of the Notes and Questions.

The "awareness" requirement should not be a problem here. As noted, the Senate Foreign Relations Committee report makes clear that "wilful blindness" suffices. Here, we are told that her screams and her bruises made her situation obvious to everyone, including the police. They chose to ignore the abuse.

The "legal responsibility" requirement is more ambiguous. By failing even to investigate, the police might well have breached a legal duty under municipal law. Beyond that, "legal" responsibility seems to include duties imposed by international law, including CAT itself. CAT article 12, for example, requires each State Party to ensure that its competent authorities investigate promptly "wherever there is reasonable ground to believe that an act of torture has been committed" in its territory. See also CAT article 13 (states must protect torture complainants against intimidation). But "torture" in turn requires acquiescence by a public official, and that is precisely what is at issue.

Second, Senate Understanding # 1(b) states that the torture definition applies "only to acts directed against persons in the offender's custody or physical control." As discussed in item 5 of the Notes and Questions, it is not clear to which "offender" the Senate was referring. C can certainly argue that in a very real sense she was within the "physical control" of her husband, who made clear that she could not leave and that he would find her if she tried. She would have to argue further that, in a case of torture resulting from the acquiescence (as opposed to the instigation) of a public official, Senate Understanding # 1(b) must view the actual torturer as the "offender."

C must also show "substantial grounds for believing that [s]he would be in danger of being subjected to torture." On the assumption that the kind of abuse she has already suffered qualifies as "torture," the question is how likely the torture is to recur if she returns. This is a question of fact. Her husband claims he will track her down if she comes back.

If her CAT claim is administratively denied because of any of the definitional hurdles added by Senate Understandings 1(b) or 1(d), she may petition the court of appeals for review under subsection 2242(d) of the implementing statute. In that proceeding she of course can make arguments concerning the meaning of the Senate "Understandings" themselves. In addition, she can argue that CAT is self-executing, that the Senate has ratified it, that it is therefore the "law of the land," and that the relevant "understandings" were inaccurate interpretations of CAT article 1. Since courts typically defer to the Senate's interpretations contained in treaty ratification resolutions, however, this latter argument will be difficult to win. See item 2 of the Notes and Questions and the corresponding analysis in the Teacher's Manual.

2. Temporary Protection

a. United States Domestic Law: Temporary Protected Status and its Predecessors

<u>Notes and Questions on page 1119</u>:

Q1: Two practical motives for the United States to treat Convention "refugees" more favorably than those fleeing more generalized violence are the large volumes of the latter and the fact that the 1951 Convention requires protection only for those who face "persecution."

Whether the two groups *should* be treated differently is another question. Many would argue that the law should treat both groups in the same way, since both face threats to life or freedom and, arguably, can therefore assert similar moral claims. Moreover, the theory for granting asylum to "refugees" is that the country of origin is either unable or unwilling to protect them. This rationale would seem to apply with equal force to those who flee armed conflict; in that situation, the breakdown in public order has rendered the country of origin at least "unable" to protect its citizens.

Those who believe that individuals fleeing generalized danger should not be treated as favorably as those who flee "persecution" would assert the practical concerns noted earlier (volumes and treaty obligations). In addition, they would say, this difference in treatment is the main consequence of distinguishing humanitarian objectives from human rights objectives. The former would dictate relief of suffering in both settings, while the latter is aimed principally at deterring and responding to persecution and selected other violations of human rights. Some might also believe that in the civil war context asylum is less critical because a safe area of the country of origin is more likely to be available. But even asylum will be denied if the applicant can live safely in another region of his or her country of origin, and there is no reason a similar condition could not be attached to TPS.

Protection of individuals fleeing national economic collapse certainly seems politically infeasible in the present climate, and one can argue it would be bad policy in any event. The principal concern would be numbers, but again the numbers problem could be addressed by a numerical ceiling. The issue would then be one of distribution, not total admissions. Probably the most principled argument against accepting those who flee economic collapse is that, at least more so than persecution, economic emergencies can be addressed through economic assistance.

Q2: One consequence of amending the refugee definition in the manner proposed by Heyman is that Congress would also be expanding the class of individuals who qualify for the overseas refugee admission program. This is a more drastic step than expanding eligibility for asylum because the result would be to make more people eligible to enter rather than simply to allow those who are already here to stay. Further, once refugees are admitted under the overseas program, their eventual adjustment of status is extremely likely. Of course, if the President does not raise the refugee quota, the effect of expanding the classes eligible for admission would, at most, be one of redistribution rather than additional immigration.

Expanding the refugee definition would also expand eligibility for asylum -- not just temporary safe haven, and not just withholding of removal. The question is whether the United States should not only refrain from sending a person back to a war zone or other dangerous area, but also (a) allow the person to remain in the United States rather than depart for a third country and (b) make a person eligible for adjustment of status, which is the inevitable consequence of expanding the refugee definition if conditions do not change in the country of origin within one year. (TPS does not provide for adjustment of status.) Some might fear that these benefits would attract future asylum claimants.

Q3: This question gets one step more specific. It distinguishes, within TPS, between armed conflict and environmental catastrophe. Under INA § 244(b)(1)(B)(i,ii), the biggest difference in treatment is that in the case of environmental catastrophe the foreign State must officially request designation.

The argument for uniform treatment of these two different classes is that their claims are on the same moral footing. Each faces a threat to life or freedom. Arguments in favor of the present distinction might be twofold: First, in the case of an environmental hazard, there are often alternative ways to provide assistance, such as airlifting food and supplies, sending money, etc. Second, nations are more likely to admit to their inability to cope with an environmental disaster, which is beyond their control, than they are to admit an inability to prevent their own people from rebelling. Consequently, if United States law insisted on a nation requesting designation in the case of war, the nation might well decline to do so even when the need in fact was acute.

Q4: There are several sources of discretion in the country designations:

a. The greatest is that the Secretary of Homeland Security "may" designate a foreign state if certain criteria are met. There are no constraints on whether the Secretary should do so except that he or she is required to consult first with the appropriate government agencies.

b. Each of the three specific categories of country conditions itself requires a subjective judgment. The "armed conflict" prong requires a determination whether the threat posed is "serious." That determination, in turn, entails both a factual prediction about the probability of harm and a discretionary characterization of that level of probability as "serious" or not. The "environmental disaster" prong requires findings that the disruption is "substantial" and that the State is unable to handle the return "adequately." And the third and final prong requires a finding of "extraordinary" conditions, as well as an even broader judgment whether TPS would be "contrary to the national interest of the United States."

The Secretary also has the discretion to decide how long a period to specify for TPS (although the period must be at least six months and may not initially exceed 18 months). And the Secretary has the discretion, analogous to that in the original designation decision, either to terminate or to extend a designation.

Apart from the designation decisions, the Secretary has at least two sources of discretion in adjudicating individual cases. First, the Secretary "may" grant TPS to a qualified individual. Second, the Secretary has the discretion to waive selected exclusion grounds.

Are these various discretionary components desirable? As for the designation decision, the breadth of the Secretary's discretion seems just as great for TPS as it was for EVD. The statutory language seems broad enough to permit the designation of almost any State beset by the kinds of conditions present in previous EVD grants, and the word "may" assures that the Secretary will not have to designate such a State even then. But it is difficult to see how that discretion could be confined without boxing the Secretary into a corner. One possibility would have been to authorize the Secretary merely to perform investigations and to file factfinding reports.

Congress could then have reserved for itself the final decisions whether to designate, as it did in effect for El Salvador in section 303 of the Immigration Act of 1990.

As for the broad discretion to deny TPS in individual cases, the analysis is quite different. One could argue that low-echelon immigration officers should not be given an open-ended discretion to deny TPS to individuals. First, there is no need to give them that discretion, since the grounds for ineligibility are comprehensive. Second, low-level officials should not be permitted to apply personal values in deciding whom to send back to life-threatening conditions.

Q5: This question admittedly is not very neutrally worded, but it does illustrate the extreme results that are possible when discretion is foreclosed. The instructor can ask what USCIS would be likely to do if such a case ever arose. Hopefully, USCIS would simply use its prosecutorial discretion and not institute removal proceedings. The instructor can also ask how the statute should be amended. Some students might want simply to substitute "may" for "shall;" others might prefer to retain "shall" but make a discretionary exception for category (C) only.

Q6: This question addresses an interesting parliamentary maneuver by the drafters of the TPS provision. The instructor might ask the students why Congress did not simply provide that "any future law to grant adjustment of status to (TPS) recipients shall require a 3/5 majority, as will any future law to amend this section itself." The answer, of course, is that a future Congress inclined to do so could, by a simple majority vote, repeal, or create an exception to, any provision that purports to require a supermajority.

Since Congress could not lawfully enact such an entrenched provision, it decided instead to change only the procedural rules of the Senate. The statute provides that the Senate shall not "consider" any such bill without a 3/5 vote. Without Senate consideration, a bill can never become law. Yet the enacted provision acknowledges the "constitutional right of the Senate to change" its rules at any time. This language is a reference to U.S. Const. art. I, § 5, cl.2, which says that each House "may determine the Rules of its proceedings." Given that acknowledged power, a simple majority of the Senate could vote to change the rule that section 244(h) purports to enact. Therefore, INA § 244(h) has no apparent legal consequences. Its only real significance is that the parties to the compromise might feel morally bound to respect the agreement.

Q7: The instructor might note initially that there is nothing philosophically inconsistent about doing both. Congress might believe that either it or the executive branch, upon finding conditions in a particular country so dangerous that no one should be sent back, should have the power to allow that country's nationals to remain temporarily in the United States. In terms of practical politics, at least two consequences really attach to the difference between generic legislation and country-specific legislation:

a. Who decides? Generic legislation like that contained in INA § 244 delegates power to the executive branch, while legislation like that contained in section 303 of the Immigration Act of 1990 reflects the substantive preferences of Congress (and of the President to the extent he or she could veto legislation and withstand an attempt to override the veto).

b. Which policies will drive the decision? The principal motivation for section 303 was the safety of Salvadorans. The assumption was that, if the decision were left to the executive branch, it would be made on foreign policy grounds and El Salvador would not be designated.

b. Global and Regional Approaches to Temporary Protection

Notes and Questions Following Fitzpatrick (page 1127):

Q1: From the standpoints of refugee advocates, the attractions are (a) TP reaches displaced populations many of whose members might not qualify as Convention refugees; (b) it provides immediate relief in cases of mass influx, giving governments time to fashion longer-term solutions; and (c) it offers supplementary group-based determinations. Concerns are that TP can give governments an excuse to bar access to the individualized asylum determination system, to avoid bestowing on the beneficiaries the rights available under the 1951 Convention, and to repatriate the beneficiaries before the dangers have sufficiently subsided.

From the standpoints of the governments of the major destination states, TP can be a way to minimize the duration of the beneficiaries' stays and to avoid having to provide the fuller range of social and economic benefits awarded to Convention refugees. Both factors reduce the domestic political barriers to providing refuge. The main concern of these governments has been that programs intended to provide only temporary safe haven often have a way of becoming permanent resettlement programs, especially if the conditions that spurred the exodus in the first place persist for a long period. (The Kosovo experience was probably atypical.) The longer the beneficiaries remain in the TP country, the more likely it is they will want to stay permanently and the less conscionable involuntary repatriation becomes.

Q2: Much depends on the forces that prompted the particular refugee flow and on subsequent events in the countries of origin. In the particular case of ethnic cleansing, there is a difficult moral question for potential states of refuge, as Fitzpatrick points out. On one side is the moral impulse to permit TP beneficiaries to begin to rebuild their lives in their new countries. On the other side is the desire not to contribute to the ethnic cleansing by facilitating the permanent expatriation of the expelled group. More generally, whatever trauma prompted the exodus, the sending state might lack the resources or the infrastructure (housing, transportation, jobs, etc.) to accommodate large numbers of returning refugees. Conversely, depending on the state of the economy and other conditions, countries of origin might especially need the labor and talents of their expatriates to rebuild.

Q3: It depends on what the terms of the convention might be. There might well be benefit in a convention that spells out certain threshold requirements for any state that provides temporary refuge, including nonrefoulement and certain social and economic rights. One danger is the race to the bottom, as states insist on the least rigorous requirements as a condition for signing. The opposite danger is that rigorous requirements could discourage states from granting TP in the first place.

Q4: By a "formalized" regime, Fitzpatrick means a regime established by states acting in concert, as distinguished from leaving TP entirely to the domestic laws of the destination states. Such an agreement in theory could take almost any form, including one that simply lays out certain threshold requirements that each signatory is obligated to meet to protect the welfare of its TP beneficiaries. A "responsibility-sharing" arrangement is one specific, and more ambitious, species of formalized regime. Under such an arrangement, the states parties agree to share responsibility for the temporary protection of designated individuals or groups. The agreements might bind the states parties to accept specified numbers or proportions of TP applicants under a prescribed formula, might differentiate among TP groups based on regional or other factors, and might entail mutual financial or other resource-sharing commitments.

Q5: Fitzpatrick observes, convincingly, that mass influx does not correlate well with whether protection should be short-term or long-term. The armed conflicts that frequently give rise to mass influx are not inherently likely to be any shorter in duration than the persecution that gives rise to Convention-based refugee status. Still, a mass influx can make orderly decisionmaking under the asylum determination system impractical. In such a case, TP can be a useful way to respond to immediate needs. But eventually, Fitzpatrick argues, even in cases of mass influx there must be reasonable opportunity for each individual who claims persecution on one of the five Convention grounds to receive an asylum determination. At worst, such determinations might be group-based, at least in the short term.

Q6: On the one hand, for many people who are in danger of serious harm, external relocation is the only realistic option. In other contexts, such as natural disaster, economic aid to the country of origin might be a viable substitute. On the other hand, states are generally far more hesitant to transport overseas refugees (whether Convention or non-Convention) than to allow people already within their territories to remain.

Q7: Analytically, TP beneficiaries have some of the attributes of asylees (both forcibly displaced from their homes by traumatic events), and some attributes of nonimmigrants (admitted on the assumption the stay will be temporary). Still, the reality is that in many armed conflict or natural disaster contexts, the TP beneficiaries will live in the host state for a long period of time. At some point they need to get on with their lives, and of course even in the short term they need a means of support. It might be employment authorization, it might be eligibility for government assistance, and it might be both. Another issue is whether and, if so, when their family members will be permitted to join them (and if so, which ones). As Walter Kälin observes on page 905 of the report cited in item 9 of the Notes and Questions, the longer people are present and the harder it is for them to gain access to the regular asylum determination system, the broader all these rights should be. Again, however, there is a political tradeoff. The more extensive the rights, the less likely it is that a state will feel inclined to grant TP in the first place.

3. Other International Law Protection Mechanisms

T.I. v. United Kingdom (page 1131):

The following facts are taken from the synopsis that appears in the coursebook: T.I., a Sri Lankan man, applied for asylum in Germany. There he testified in detail about his imprisonment and repeated torture first by Tamil terrorists and later by government soldiers. Two German courts denied asylum, in the first instance because the court would not recognize persecution by non-State actors and did not regard the soldiers' actions as those of the state, and in the second instance because his story was not believed. He fled Germany and made his way to the United Kingdom, where he again applied for asylum. Under the Dublin Convention, signatory States in Europe have agreed on rules for determining which state is responsible for deciding asylum cases when the applicants have traveled through more than one state. (A regulation of the Council of the European Union has now superseded the Dublin regime. See Council Reg. (EC) No. 343/2003, establishing the criteria and mechanisms for determining the Member State responsible for examining an asylum application lodged in one of the Member States by a third-country national (18 Feb. 2003)). The U.K. and Germany agreed that the present case was Germany's responsibility. Consequently, the U.K. ordered T.I. removed to Germany. T.I. sought review of that decision in the U.K. courts, mainly on the ground that Germany was not a safe country because its laws permitted refoulement to non-State persecutors. While his request for judicial review was pending, T.I. gathered expert medical evidence concluding that his many physical scars and psychological symptoms show "very little doubt" that his injuries were caused in the way he had described. The U.K. domestic courts ultimately denied relief nonetheless and approved the removal order to Germany. He then applied to the European Court of Human Rights, alleging, among other things, a violation of article 3 of the European Convention.

Article 3 of the European Convention says "No one shall be subjected to torture or to inhuman or degrading treatment or punishment." The European Court of Human Rights has consistently interpreted article 3 as not only barring states parties from directly torturing or inflicting inhuman or degrading treatment or punishment, but also from sending anyone to another country in which he or she would suffer such treatment. The test for the latter, the European Court of Human Rights holds, is whether there is a "real risk" of that happening. Here, although Germany does not interpret the 1951 Refugee Convention to bar refoulement to non-State persecutors, German domestic law gives the relevant authorities the discretion not to deport when there is "a substantial danger for life, personal integrity or liberty." The applicant emphasized the discretionary, and therefore uncertain, nature of this relief. Observing that German case law makes clear that "a grave danger involving a serious risk to life and personal integrity" dictates the favorable exercise of discretion, however, the Court found no real risk that refoulement to Germany would result in the applicant suffering treatment contrary to article 3.

<u>Notes and Questions Following T.I.</u> (page 1137):

Q1: Article 33 speaks explicitly to the act of expelling or returning a person to a place where he or she will face certain dangers, whereas article 3 speaks only to the harms themselves. But even article 3 has been interpreted to forbid the expulsion or return of a person to a country that in turn will subject the person to the prohibited acts. The leading case is *Soering v. United Kingdom*, 161 Eur. Ct. H.R. (Ser. A), 11 E.H.R.R. 439 (Euro. Ct. Human Rights 1989) (holding UK could not extradite German murder suspect to United States to face inhumane conditions of death row).

Most importantly, as many commentators have pointed out, nothing in the text of either provision distinguishes between private and state actors or even refers to state actors at all. About the only arguable relevant difference is that article 33 speaks of return to "frontiers," a term that could perhaps be stretched to imply State border authorities. But a stretch is what it would have to be.

Q2: On the one hand, both decisions make clear that the European Convention forbids states parties to refoule anyone to non-State torture or inhumane or degrading treatment or punishment. Both cases hold that this is not an issue on which the Convention admits of different interpretations. On the other hand, the *T.I.* case affords States significant wiggle room to employ alternative remedies that are less certain and less durable than nonrefoulement.

Thus, it is still to the advantage of a well-informed asylum claimant who fears persecution by non-State actors to enter Europe in protection states rather than accountability states (if any of the latter even remain). To the extent they do so, the fair and orderly distribution of asylum claims that the Dublin Convention hoped to achieve will be impaired. To the extent they do not do so, either because they are unaware of the differences in viewpoint or for other reasons, the probability of success will vary by asylum country, another result that the Council regulation on uniform substantive criteria and the general drive for harmonization hope to avoid.

Since some substantive and procedural differences among European States will inevitably persist, the hard question is which differences the Council Regulation can live with and which ones it cannot. Jennifer Moore, in the cited article, has argued that the non-State actor issue, being as fundamental to the very applicability of the European Convention as it is, demands uniform resolution, an argument that seems now to have been accepted.

Q3: In the present case, Germany provided assurances that, even though article 53(6) is discretionary, those who would face torture abroad are "entitled" to 53(6) relief. Those assurances seemed to satisfy the Court. Whether they should have is not clear. On the one hand, Germany supplied several examples of its having refused to return Sri Lankans who faced the sorts of dangers that T.I. alleged. On the other hand, Germany could cite no examples of the same being true for failed asylum claimants. The broader question is whether the Court ought to adopt a flat rule like the one hypothesized here or whether the Court should treat the matter as one of probabilities. It is not clear how probable the event has to be before the Court considers the risk "real," because here the Court seemed to feel that Germany had essentially committed to nonrefoulement if they find the applicant is telling the truth. The other safety net is that, if Germany were to go back on its word, the applicant could always file a new application with the European Court of Human Rights and hope that his refoulement is stayed pending the Court's decision.

Q4: Absent a showing of bad faith, this would not seem a valid basis for barring removal to Germany. EU member states will inevitably bring different degrees of openness and skepticism to their asylum determinations; to declare a state party unfit to adjudicate classes of asylum cases on that basis might strain the threshold level of comity the EU and the Council Regulation assume. As for article 3 of the European Convention, the *T.I.* case suggests the test is whether there is a "real risk" of the person being returned to the proscribed dangers. That one state is at the low end in terms of credibility assessments might be evidence that the risk is real, but by itself that evidence is probably insufficient.

CHAPTER 12
UNDOCUMENTED IMMIGRANTS

Because of the recent dramatic increase in interest in the subject of illegal immigration, particularly the flurry of state and local activity, this chapter has been substantially expanded and otherwise revised. Still, informal feedback from a number of immigration law instructors suggests that, while many teachers would like to include basic coverage of undocumented immigrant and law enforcement issues, time is short even in three-unit courses. The material on the origins, scale, and impact of unauthorized immigration is still designed mainly as background reading, but the material on the various strategies Congress and DHS have used in responding to illegal immigration, as well as the material on other proposed policy responses, has been reorganized, enhanced, and updated in this edition. The chapter also includes a few fact problems on employer sanctions and the anti-discrimination provisions that will require the students to delve into the statute. The Problem sets can be supplemented by a class discussion of the need for, the effectiveness of, and the dangers presented by, employer sanctions. The class might also discuss whether existing safeguards against discrimination are adequate and, if not, what else the law might do. The chapter additionally considers some of the basic issues regarding undocumented immigrants' eligibility for public benefits, education, and drivers' licenses, with particular emphasis on the REAL ID Act of 2005. Finally, the chapter devotes a section to state and local efforts to regulate immigration or immigrants in some way–a topic that has received renewed scholarly attention and has become an important subject of litigation in response to state and local efforts to crack down on employers and landlords in their dealings with undocumented immigrants.

SECTION A. ENFORCEMENT OF THE IMMIGRATION LAWS

1. Immigration Offenses Generally

This material is intended as background reading.

2. IRCA and Employer Misconduct

a. Employer Sanctions

Depending on the time constraints, the instructor might want to draw the students into a discussion of the pros and cons of employer sanctions. Such a debate would necessarily require some thinking about the importance of the goal -- diminishing the undocumented population -- and about the feasibility of accomplishing that goal through other means. If both the goal and the theoretical benefits of an employer sanctions system are accepted, then other questions arise: How effective are employer sanctions in practice? Some of the literature highlighted in this edition emphasizes that the sanctions have failed to serve their purpose and have worsened labor conditions to boot (see the Wishnie and Pham articles). What are the practical impediments to effectiveness, and can those impediments be removed without undue economic or human costs? What are the disadvantages of employer sanctions? [Here the class could discuss the administrative burdens on both the government and the employer, the discriminatory impact of sanctions on authorized United States workers (see the GAO Report), and the dangers (see the Strojny article) that could arise if employer sanctions and document fraud eventually prompt Congress to create a permanent centralized data bank and/or a national ID card.]

In discussing whether sanctions can be made effective, instructors might focus on the social security no-match letter regulation adopted by DHS in the final years of the Bush administration. As of this writing, the regulation was still enjoined, and the Obama administration was considering whether to defend it. But if the regulation survives legal challenge, would it give employers greater incentives to police the immigration status of their workers? Would it make enforcement easier and more effective for DHS? Even if the regulation deters the hiring of undocumented workers, are the costs too high, especially if the result of the regulation is that employers fire workers for whom no-match letters are issued? As for the computerized national registry, the Strojny article is highly recommended because he spells out, in some detail, the specific scenarios that most alarm him.

<u>Problems</u> <u>1-7</u> (page 1170):

Problem 1: The initial hiring was legal, but A has violated INA § 274A(a)(2) by continuing to employ the person, knowing he or she was unauthorized "<u>with respect to such employment.</u>" The 30- hour weeks exceeded the authorization.

Problem 2: First, B has clearly violated INA § 274A(a)(1)(B). He hired someone without complying with the paperwork requirements. B has verified identity but has neither examined one of the documents from list B or list C (work authorization), nor attested to such examination. INA § 274A(a)(1)(B) doesn't expressly specify any particular mens rea, and the relatively light penalties make it likely that Congress intended to impose strict liability (or, at the very least, that negligence is enough).

Whether B has violated INA § 274A(a)(1)(A) (a more serious offense) is not clear. Did B hire the person "knowing" he was not authorized to work? B lacked actual knowledge. Did he have constructive knowledge, which *Mester* and *New El Rey* said was enough? Both cases had in mind a deliberate decision not to investigate. Neither case addressed whether a merely negligent failure of the type involved here would qualify, and *Collins Foods* implies that constructive knowledge requires wilful blindness.

Problem 3: Again, assuming INA § 274A(a)(1)(B) (paperwork) imposes strict liability, C is guilty. She in fact did not inspect any document that demonstrated work authorization.

As for INA § 274A(a)(1)(A) (knowingly hiring an unauthorized worker), the defense this time would be mistake of law. Although mistake of law ordinarily is not a defense to a criminal prosecution, the students might remember from criminal law that it can be a defense when it negates the mental element required for the crime. At least that is true when the mental element is expressly included in the statutory definition of the crime. C knew the employee had B-1 status. If C erroneously believed that the law authorizes B-1 visitors to work, then C cannot be said to have hired this employee "knowing" she was unauthorized.

Problem 4: Under the literal language of the statute, yes. D has hired Justin for employment without doing the required paperwork. But the regulations define "employment" to exclude "casual employment by individuals who provide domestic service in a private home that is sporadic, irregular, or intermittent." 8 C.F.R. § 274a.l(h) (2008). The employment here seems casual enough. It is not clear whether it constitutes "domestic" service in a private house, which sounds more like housecleaning, maid service, or some other indoor activity. But there are no obvious policy reasons for drawing indoor/outdoor distinctions. There might also be a question whether this employment is "irregular" enough, since there was a regular schedule that continued through a full summer. Of course, this is not the kind of activity that ICE would target for enforcement, but that is a different matter. The instructor can ask whether using a regular baby-sitter is casual employment and whether it matters that there is a standing arrangement for the person to sit every Saturday night.

Problem 5: Until Benito resumed work in April 1991, no charges could have been brought against E. IRCA § 101(a)(3)(A) renders INA § 274A(a)(1) (knowingly hiring, and failing to verify) inapplicable if the hiring occurred before the enactment of IRCA. That is the case here. In any event, Benito was authorized to work at the time of his hiring. Similarly, IRCA § 101(a)(3)(B) makes INA § 274A(a)(2) (continuing to employ) inapplicable if the hiring took place before the enactment date.

E, therefore, will be safe unless Benito's resumption of work is considered a new, post-IRCA hire. If it is, then E would likely be charged under both INA § 274(a)(1)(A) (assuming E knows Benito's status has expired) and INA § 274A(a)(1)(B) (paperwork). At this writing, there is little case law on what kind of break will disrupt the continuity of an employment relationship. By analogy to *Fleuti*, however, the length and purpose of the visit and the degree of casualness might all be relevant. Perhaps a court would consider whether E had been keeping Benito on its employee list, what Benito's intentions were when he left the United States, etc.

Problem 6: F's first decision is whether to fire Helen. F now knows that

Helen is not authorized to work. If he continues to employ her, he will clearly be violating INA § 274A(a)(2). It is even possible that, just by letting her work these past two days, he has already violated that subsection. If that is the case, then he probably doesn't hurt himself appreciably by continuing that violation, except to the extent that the ALJ has some discretion in setting the amount of the fine. In any event F cannot be sure he would be found guilty for failing to fire Helen within two days. (*Mester* and *New El Rey* allow a "reasonable" period). Obviously the lawyer cannot ethically counsel F to continue his violation of the law.

F's more difficult decision is whether to apply for labor certification. If he applies, he will be alerting the Labor Department that he has been employing someone whom he at least now knows is not an LPR. As the readings indicate, the Labor Department is likely to pass that information on to ICE, which might then prosecute F. In theory the filing of an application for labor certification does not necessarily mean F knows Helen is unauthorized, since some noncitizens who are not permanent residents are authorized to work. As a practical matter, however, if ICE decides to investigate, it will surely discover at the very least that F's company failed to properly inspect Helen's documents and, perhaps, that F had also committed a substantive violation by continuing to employ Helen once she informed him she lacked authorization. F, therefore, would be taking a chance by applying for labor certification. He would have to decide whether that chance is worth taking.

The ethical problem for the attorney is that F and Helen have potentially conflicting interests. In deciding whether to apply for labor certification, F has to balance the benefit (keeping a valued employee if the application is granted) against the risk (being prosecuted for a hiring violation). For Helen, the benefit is attaining LPR status if the application is granted, and the risk is detection and removal. F faces a roughly similar tradeoff with respect to the decision whether to fire Helen, while for Helen the principal benefit is keeping her job, and there seems little risk to her in continuing to work. The attorney has to decide whether those conflicting interests are reconcilable and, if they are not, which client (if either) to represent.

Problem 7: The initial hiring clearly was not a violation. John was then a citizen, so G never did hire an "alien," as INA § 274A(a)(1)(A) requires. Nor would G have broken any then existing law even if John had been an "alien."

But what about INA § 274A(a)(2), which makes it unlawful "after hiring *an alien* for employment to continue to employ the alien in the United States knowing the alien is (or has become) an unauthorized alien . . . [emphasis added]"? There are two subissues. First, has G violated this provision? Under the literal language, no. The statutory wording "after hiring an alien" is not satisfied, because G never did hire an "alien." Arguably, that interpretation violates the spirit of this subsection, since G is knowingly continuing to employ an unauthorized worker. Second, if John's continued employment otherwise violates section 274A(a)(2), does the grandfather clause -- IRCA § 101(a)(3)(B), reproduced on page 1159 of the text -- eliminate the violation? The grandfather clause makes this section inapplicable "to continuing employment of an alien who was hired before the date of the enactment of this Act." How much does the phrase "before the date of the enactment" modify? If Congress meant that the employee before enactment had to be "an alien who was hired", then the literal wording does not apply here, because before enactment John was not an "alien." But if Congress meant only that the employee must be an "alien" and that the employee was hired before enactment, then it applies here; John is now an "alien," and he was hired before enactment.

Note: Someone might ask, "What if the the employer fires John and it later turns out that continued employment would not have violated section 274A? Will the company now have to worry about liability under the antidiscrimination provisions (citizenship status)?" The answer is no, for reasons that the students will see for themselves when they get to the next section (if it is covered). First, the antidiscrimination provision, INA § 274B, doesn't apply to unauthorized immigrants, which John is. Second, the specific bar on citizenship status discrimination can be invoked only by "protected individuals," which John isn't.

b. Prohibitions on Discrimination

General: The text of this section is intended as background reading, but the instructor might want to take up the particular question of disparate treatment versus disparate impact, discussed at the end of the text. In addition to the statutory interpretation arguments considered in the text, a number of policy considerations are relevant here: During the debates that preceded the enactment of IRCA, many people expressed concern that, if employer sanctions were enacted, employers would discriminate against "foreign-looking" individuals out of a misplaced belief that they had to do so in order to avoid liability. INA § 274B was a response to that fear. Given the legislative purpose, a broad reading that would prohibit actions that have disparate impact (absent sufficient explanation by the employer) might well be justifiable. The employer, for example, might adopt an English- language requirement precisely because it mistakenly thinks this is a good way in which to weed out undocumented workers. It is also possible, however, to argue that INA § 274B reflected only the narrower fear that employers would use employer sanctions as a pretext for intentionally discriminating on the basis of national origin. Under that view, the statute might be read to prohibit only intentional discrimination.

Problems 8-12 (page 1177):

Problem 8: A discriminated against X because of X's citizenship status. But X is not a "protected individual" within the meaning of INA § 274B(a)(3) because she did not apply for naturalization within six months of becoming eligible (2007). Therefore X has no claim under INA § 274B.

A discriminated against Y on the basis of Y's national origin. Unlike citizenship status discrimination, national origin discrimination is a basis for a claim by anyone other than an unauthorized worker. Thus, Y has a valid claim.

Note: The fact that the workforce is ten employees is a new fact, added to the 4th edition in order to avoid the 274B(a)(2)B) restriction. The latter bars claims that are already covered by 42 U.S.C. § 2000e-2 (employment discrimination under Title 7 of the Civil Rights Act of 1964). Since Title 7 applies only to employers of 15 or more, a claim under Title 7 would not have been possible here. Thanks to Cindy Buys for the insight that prompted that change.

Does this combination of results make for good policy? Some might argue that X should receive protection. First, she is an LPR and has applied for naturalization. Second, even if she had no intent of ever becoming a United States citizen, federal law authorizes her to work. More importantly, there is no *need* to discriminate.

Those who approve of withholding protection from X might offer any of the following arguments:

a. She could have applied for naturalization; the fact that she waited so long might evidence either disloyalty or opportunism.

b. She might well be rejected for naturalization.

c. The law should permit employers to prefer United States citizens. Citizenship is part of a common bond. (See chapter 13, Section C).

d. Although federal law gives LPRs the right to work, it does not give them the right to work for particular employers.

e. Giving more rights to United States citizens than to LPRs might have the beneficial effect of encouraging naturalization.

Problem 9: W is a "protected individual," having applied for naturalization within six months of becoming eligible for it. But there are two issues:

a. What mens rea does INA § 274B require? B has intentionally discriminated against a protected individual on the basis of citizenship status. But the question is whether INA § 274B requires knowledge that the employee <u>is</u> a protected individual. The statutory text is ambiguous on this point.

b. The "equally qualified" exception in INA § 274B(a)(4) applies only to hiring, recruiting, and referring – not to discharging. Thus it is inapplicable here even if (question of fact) the employer rejected W in favor of an equally qualified United States citizen.

Problem 10: There are 3 claims to consider:

a. She has no citizenship status discrimination claim because, as a nonimmigrant, she is not a "protected individual."

b. She might claim national origin discrimination. She would have to prove either intentional discrimination (the excessive documentation requirement being a pretext for national origin discrimination) or disparate impact on individuals of her national origin. If she can prove only the latter, she would also have to persuade the administrative authorities or a reviewing court that IRCA covers disparate impact claims based on national origin. (Again, the 274B(a)(2)(B) restriction is inapplicable because fewer than 15 are employed.)

c. She could file a claim under INA § 274B(a)(6), which prohibits employers from requiring more documentation than is required by INA § 274A. As a result of IIRIRA, however, V will have to prove intentional discrimination. In addition, one ambiguity in the statute is relevant here. Do you have to be a "protected individual" to have a claim under subsection (a)(6)? (V is not.) The provision itself does not expressly require this, and it says that the request for excessive documentation "shall be treated as an unfair immigration-related employment practice" (if done with the requisite purpose or intent). If the provision had said merely that such a request constitutes a form of discrimination (again, if done with the requisite intent), then under subsection (a)(1) the complainant would still have to prove either that the discrimination was because of national origin or that she is a protected individual (and V is not). But subsection (a)(6) doesn't merely establish discrimination; it establishes an "unfair immigration-related employment practice." On the other hand, the qualifying phrase at the end reads "if made for the purpose or intent of discriminating against an individual *in violation of paragraph (1)*" [emphasis added]. If the complainant is not a protected individual, then the intended discrimination would not be in violation of paragraph 1 unless it is because of national origin discrimination.

If subsection (a)(6) is construed as limited to protected individuals, does it add anything? Arguably yes. If the request for documents is excessive but the person is ultimately hired, then (a)(6) might be the person's only recourse under IRCA. Subsection (a)(1)(A) would not cover the claim, even if the request for excessive documentation was based on national origin, because that provision requires that the discrimination be with respect to hiring, recruiting, referring, or discharging (unless the "hiring" decision is interpreted broadly to include the document request).

Problem 11: The personnel officer has to walk a thin line. On the one hand, if she rejects this person and cannot articulate the problem, she might not be believed when she denies that she was discriminating on the basis of national origin or possibly even citizenship status. Along the same lines, if she asks for another document, she might be violating INA § 274B(a)(6) (overdocumenting). On the other hand, if she accepts the person, and the document proves to be fraudulent, and the defect that was bothering her is ultimately identified, it might be found that the document did not "reasonably appear on its face to be genuine." See INA § 274A(b)(1)(A). Her best bet, if in doubt, is to jot down the identifying number that appears on the card and call DHS for verification, provided she can get through and DHS is willing to do this. If her employer participates in E-Verify (see the description in the employer sanctions readings), she can inquire electronically.

Problem 12: The problem here is one of selecting the proper remedy. One cannot simultaneously file discrimination claims under Title 7 of the Civil Rights Act of 1964 and IRCA. See INA § 274B(b)(2). The complainant must elect.

T's claim of national origin discrimination might be based on either intentional discrimination or disparate impact. If he is confident he will be able to show that the policy was a pretext and that there was an intent to discriminate (a showing that will depend on what E claims as the rationale for the policy), then T should probably file a claim under INA § 274B. As long as E has more than three employees, the Office of the Special Counsel will have jurisdiction. But if the evidence of discriminatory intent is shaky, his disparate impact claim will become more crucial, and OCAHO has not embraced disparate impact claims under IRCA.

If instead he files his claim with the EEOC, then he will clearly be able to argue disparate impact. But if the EEOC finds that E had fewer than 15 employees at the time of the discriminatory act, it will lack jurisdiction over his claim.

Before the OSC-EEOC Memorandum of Understanding mentioned in the text, claimants like T were in a bind. If they claimed under one of the statutes and lost, the 180-day limit on both EEOC claims and IRCA claims might have expired by the time they received a decision. Perhaps some sort of equitable tolling would have given them extra time to claim under the other statute, but they certainly could not depend on that possibility. Now, as a result of the Memorandum of Understanding, T can simply file in what he believes is the more favorable venue. If the tribunal rejects the claim but feels he has a valid claim under the other statute, it can refer the case to the latter. The original filing date will be preserved. In this case, therefore, if he files with the EEOC and it is later determined that the employer had fewer than 15 employees, he will still be able to pursue his IRCA claim. Conversely, if he files with the OSC and it is determined that IRCA does not cover disparate impact claims (and he cannot prove intentional discrimination), then he can file his Title 7 claim with the EEOC. He will not be penalized for failing to guess the facts or the law.

SECTION B. LEGALIZATION

Questions on page 1186:

Q1: Depending on how hot an issue legalization becomes or remains, the instructor might wish to discuss the general merits of legalization in class. As a practical matter, the 1986 legalization reflected the congressional recognition that the huge numbers of undocumented immigrants were likely to remain permanently in the United States and the additional recognition that regularizing their status would be not only humane but also beneficial in eliminating the negative effects of an underground subculture. From a political standpoint, the 1986 coalition of legalization proponents and employer sanctions proponents was critical to the passage of both. The main concerns about a legalization program were (a) the potential unfairness of treating undocumented migrants more favorably than those who had been waiting outside the country for lawful admission under the quota system (the "queue-jumping" problem); and (b) a fear by some that enactment of the legalization program would spur hope of future legalizations and thus encourage further illegal immigration.

As the excerpt illustrates, the same sorts of competing concerns, and others, are aired today, albeit in a very different political environment. The instructor could use the arguments contained in the fictional dialog on coursebook pages 1179-86 as a springboard for the policy discussion. In discussing legalization, instructors might wish to consider simultaneously the alternative methods of addressing the undocumented population, since the absence of reasonable alternatives is often given as a justification for legalization. If so, the discussion of the pros and cons of legalization could be delayed until students have read the material in Sections A and C.

Q2: The advantages, of course, are the opportunities for cultural integration and employment. On the negative side was a concern that these requirements would discourage many otherwise eligible individuals from applying. Moreover, opponents of the English language requirement pointed out, such a requirement is not imposed on other applicants for LPR status. The response to that latter point was that legalization applicants are different; they sought to cut ahead of others in the queue.

Q3: On the one hand, family unity is central to many of our other immigration policies, as the students will have seen in chapter 3. Moreover, the law should encourage family unification as a basis for enhancing both the welfare and the productivity of all permanent residents. On the other hand, some people question why spouses and children of those who attained LPR status by legalization should receive preference over the spouses and children of other LPRs. The latter have many of the same problems and have waited longer for family-sponsored second preference visas. A partial response to that question is that the preference system does allow spouses and children "accompanying or following to join" the principal immigrant to acquire LPR status at the same time as the principal immigrant, though only if the relationship was formed before the principal's admission as an LPR.

SECTION C. THE RIGHTS OF UNDOCUMENTED IMMIGRANTS AND THE SELF-DEPORTATION STRATEGY

1. The Legal and Social Identities of Undocumented Immigrants

This material is meant to be background reading.

2. Undocumented Immigrants and Public Assistance

This subsection is also meant to be background reading. The instructor could use it to discuss under what general circumstances undocumented immigrants should qualify for public assistance, or it could be used simply to set the stage for the more specific legal and policy questions raised in subsection A.3 below and to defer the subject of noncitizens and welfare to chapter 13, section C below.

3. Undocumented Immigrants and Public Education

Plyler v. Doe (page 1194):

A Texas statute authorized local school districts to bar undocumented children and withheld state funds for the education of any undocumented children whom a school district chose to enroll. In two cases that were eventually consolidated before the Supreme Court, undocumented children sued to enjoin enforcement of the statute. They argued that the statute violated equal protection and intruded into congressionally preempted subject matter. In each case, both the district court and the court of appeals struck down the statute on equal protection grounds. The Supreme Court granted certiorari.

After holding that undocumented immigrants are "persons" entitled to invoke the equal protection clause, the Court turned to the main issue -- whether the Texas statute violated equal protection. For that purpose, the Court first had to determine the standard of review. The Court had invoked strict scrutiny in several prior equal protection challenges to state action discriminating against noncitizens, but those cases had all involved LPRs, a suspect class. Undocumented immigrants, the Court held, were not a suspect class. Nor was education a fundamental interest. Therefore, the rational basis test would apply. Still, because education is vitally important to assuring permanent equal opportunity, and since the individuals being singled out were innocent children who had no control over their status, the Court held that any interest the state was asserting would have to be substantial in order to meet the rationality standard.

In the present case, the Court went on to hold, the interests that the state was asserting were not substantial enough. Reducing state fiscal burdens was certainly a legitimate state interest, but the state's challenge was to provide a rational basis for the particular classification -- undocumented children. As to that, the state offered several possibilities. The statute did not help deter undocumented immigrants from coming, the Court concluded, because the undocumented generally come for employment, not for education. Instead, the state could have prohibited employers from hiring undocumented workers. The Court similarly found that excluding undocumented children would not improve the overall quality of education in the state. Nor was it enough to speculate that undocumented children were less likely to remain permanently in Texas and thus less likely to contribute the benefits of their education. All that would result from the Texas statute, the Court said, is the creation of a permanent underclass of people unable to fend for themselves, and that would not rationally further any legitimate state objective. Nor was the state merely reinforcing a federal policy, since there was no evidence of a federal desire to exclude undocumented children from public schools (in contrast, for example, to a federal policy decision not to authorize undocumented immigrants to work). For all those reasons, the Court invalidated the Texas statute on equal protection grounds. (The Court did not decide whether the statute was additionally invalid on preemption grounds.)

Five Justices formed the majority. Three of them (Justices Marshall, Blackmun, and Powell) wrote separate concurrences, though only Justice Blackmun's is reproduced in the book. Justice Blackmun explained why he believed education was unique. When a state provides an education to some and denies it to others, he argued, it creates permanent class distinctions that deny equal protection.

The Chief Justice (Burger) and three other Justices dissented. While expressing grave reservations about the wisdom of the Texas statute, the dissenters found it "rational" for the state to withhold state funds for those children who were not supposed to be in the United States at all, in order to conserve their resources for those who were lawfully present. To insist on more, the dissenters argued, was to usurp the policy role that the Constitution delegates to Congress.

Notes and Questions Following Plyler v. Doe (page 1207):

Ql: It does seem likely that the majority's decision to invoke an intermediate level of scrutiny affected the outcome of the case. Had the Court invoked minimal scrutiny, it might well have held that a rational legislature could have concluded that excluding undocumented children from the public schools would deter undocumented immigrants from coming, or would free up resources that could then be used to educate lawfully resident children, etc.

On the one hand, the narrow combination of facts that led the Court to intermediate scrutiny might well have been an example of result orientation. On the other hand, the fact that a test is outcome-determinative does not mean the court's selection of that test was motivated by a desire to reach a particular result. Ultimately, the Court said that the combination of two elements -- innocent children as victims and the life consequences of denial of education -- was sufficient to trigger more than the usual level of judicial scrutiny. What reason is there to think the Court didn't believe precisely what it said?

As for the Chief Justice's strange language, maybe by "senseless" and "folly" he really meant merely "a bad idea but one on which reasonable minds could disagree."

Q2: As the materials preceding the case point out, several Supreme Court decisions have held that "alienage" is a suspect class, and that state action discriminating against members of that class is subject to strict scrutiny. As was also noted, however, all those cases involved LPRs. Should strict scrutiny also apply to state action discriminating against undocumented immigrants?

In footnotes 14 and 19 of the majority opinion, the Court lays out some of the factors that have led it to classify certain groups as suspect. As applied to undocumented immigrants, these factors cut both ways. On the one hand, there is the historical pattern of "deep-seated prejudice;" if even LPRs have been found to have satisfied this requirement, a fortiori undocumented immigrants do so. In addition, undocumented immigrants certainly suffer from the political powerlessness that prevents them from relying on the political process for protection.

On the other hand, the fact that undocumented immigrants' very presence is the product of a violation of law (at least in the case of those who entered without inspection -- no law prohibits overstaying, which is a deportability ground but not a punishable offense) is not an "irrelevancy," as the Court points out. Moreover, the Court argues, membership in a suspect class is usually beyond the person's control; undocumented immigrants made voluntary decisions to enter or remain in the United States and could terminate their status simply by leaving. (One could argue that racial minorities enjoy the protection of strict scrutiny even though they too could simply leave, but undocumented immigrants are different, both because they have no legal right to remain and because, unless stateless, they have a country to which they can count on being readmitted.) Of course, the argument that the class members can simply leave has no direct application to young children, unless parents are treated as making voluntary decisions on behalf of their children.

Q3: Counsel would probably argue that, on the question of economic impact, opinion is divided and the Court should therefore allow the State to decide which evidence is more persuasive. As for the deterrence issue, counsel might suggest that, whatever undocumented immigrants' principal motives for coming to the United States might be, surely some come for education. In any event, counsel could argue, even one whose sole motive for coming to the U.S. is employment might decide not to come if doing so meant sacrificing the education of his or her children.

As for the second question, the Court's conclusion does rest on a finding that the asserted state interests are not rational. If a state can demonstrate that the presence of undocumented immigrants is causing a net economic loss, then this portion of the Court's analysis would lose its force. That does not mean the state action would be upheld. Intermediate scrutiny allowed the Court to judge the rationality by reference to the total impact of the statute. The creation of a permanent underclass of uneducated youth (eventually adults) would be economically and socially disastrous. Perhaps that factor would be enough to persuade the Court to adhere to its decision in *Plyler* even if the empirical evidence is later found to demonstrate that the economic impact of undocumented immigrants is negative.

Q4: It is difficult to answer this question without examining the empirical evidence in the case. The Court seems to suggest that the effect the State was describing was negligible. Maybe the State could rationally conclude that expending the same resources for fewer children would enhance the product it could offer each remaining child and that, even if the quality increase is small, every little bit helps. But that result is not inevitable, because the cost savings from reducing the school population would have to be set off against whatever additional costs the State and local governments would incur in having to deal with a school-age population that is not in school and, eventually, uneducated adults.

Q5: Texas argued that undocumented immigrants are less likely to remain in Texas permanently and that the State is thus less likely to reap the benefits of the education it is providing them. The Court finds the correlation between undocumented status and likelihood of remaining too tenuous, especially in light of the then pending (later successful) proposals to legalize the status of many undocumented immigrants. Apart from that, perhaps the State could argue that, like any other State, its fortunes are tied to those of the nation; thus, supporting a national goal is ipso facto a legitimate interest. On that basis, the State might argue that, by deterring undocumented immigrants from coming to the United States in the first place, it is helping the national government achieve a goal reflected in the INA. The Court does not explicitly reject such an argument, but it does insist on a more particularized showing, observing that the federal government has not demonstrated any desire to withhold education as a deterrent measure.

Q6:

(a) As for standard of review, the two dominant themes in *Plyler* were the fact that the disqualified class consisted of innocent children who had not chosen their status and the essential role of education in shaping one's life opportunities. To the extent that a state law excluded undocumented children from specified welfare programs, the first of the two themes would be just as present. The applicability of the latter factor (education as essential to life opportunity) is not quite as clear. It is hard to imagine anything resembling equal opportunity when people lack access to food, medical services, and other necessities. Justice Blackmun's concurrence, however, emphasizes the permanence of the impact of denying an education. Depending on the specific facts of the case and the specific parameters of the welfare program, the permanence factor might or might not be present.

(b and c) Texas offered three specific state interests in discriminating against undocumented immigrants. One was deterring them from coming to the United States in the first place. A similar deterrence argument could be made in the welfare context (and frequently was, during the public debates that preceded both welfare reform legislation and IIRIRA in 1996). Just as the Court in *Plyler* suggested that undocumented immigrants generally come for employment rather than education, many argued in 1996 that undocumented immigrants come for welfare. The question concerning the net economic impact of undocumented immigrants (and therefore the importance of the goal of stemming their influx into the particular state) remains significant.

Texas also argued that withholding education from undocumented children would preserve more of its resources for its other resident children. Certainly an analogous argument could be made in the context of welfare. The Court in *Plyler* had empirical doubts about the practical magnitude of the improvement and about the offsetting social and economic costs of creating a large uneducated class. Similar empirical questions arise when a large class is denied food, medical treatment, and other needs.

Finally, Texas argued it was rational to invest its resources in people who were likely to reside in Texas permanently. The same argument could be made with respect to welfare, but again the Court might have analogous empirical doubts about the strength of the correlation between present immigration status and long-term residence.

Q7: The first issue is whether the standard of review should change when it is the federal government, rather than a state, that is imposing the disqualification. On the one hand, the two factors that prompted the Court in *Plyler* to raise the standard of review to intermediate scrutiny still exist. The children are still innocent and powerless to change their status, and education is still vital to life opportunity. On the other hand, as the students saw in chapter 2, the plenary power doctrine continues to restrict the judicial role when the federal government enacts immigration laws. The cited articles explore, among other things, the question whether the plenary power doctrine fully applies to federal legislation regulating noncitizens outside the context of admission and expulsion. The leading case is *Mathews v. Diaz*, 426 U.S. 67, 96 S.Ct. 1883, 48 L.Ed.2d 478 (1976), where the Court, relying on the plenary congressional power over immigration, upheld a federal statutory provision disqualifying certain LPRs from various welfare programs. Similarly, in footnote 19 of its opinion in *Plyler*, the

Court in dictum sounded some of the familiar plenary power themes – especially foreign affairs and sovereignty – in the context of federal legislation directed against undocumented immigrants.

The federal governmental interests asserted as justifications would be virtually identical to those invoked by the State of Texas, except that the discussion of undocumented immigrants' net economic impact would focus on the nation rather than the state. The threshold level of persuasiveness that a given interest would have to reach would be lower in the case of federal legislation, for the reasons given in the paragraph above.

Q8: Such a law would be halfway between a federal prohibition on free public education for undocumented students and an independent state prohibition. On the one hand, *Plyler* held that the state legislation violated the equal protection clause; opponents of the Gallegly amendment might argue, therefore, that the amendment is an unconstitutional attempt by Congress to authorize states to violate the equal protection clause. On the other hand, proponents of Gallegly might argue that it was only the absence of federal authorization that caused the Texas statute to violate equal protection in the first place. They would find support in footnote 5 of the Court's opinion. There the Court pointed out that in a previous case, *De Canas v. Bica*, a state statute prohibiting undocumented immigrants from working was upheld because the federal immigration statute reflected a policy of protecting the United States labor force. In contrast, the footnote added, the district court in *Plyler* "discerned no express federal policy to bar illegal immigrants from education." The Gallegly amendment, if passed, would eliminate that premise. And in the third paragraph of section IV of the Court's opinion in *Plyler*, the Court acknowledged the authority of the states "to act with respect to illegal aliens, at least *where such action mirrors federal objectives* and furthers a legitimate state goal" (emphasis added).

Q10: On the one hand, the Court emphasizes the harm that society will incur if large numbers of poor, uneducated adults are allowed to roam the community. One would not have to regard undocumented immigrants as members of the community in order to fear them. On the other hand, much of the opinion turns on the importance of education to the individual, a factor that would seem irrelevant if the interests of that individual didn't count. That the Court deems the individual interests worthy of consideration at all suggests, as Professor Bosniak says, that the Court regards undocumented immigrants as having at least some attributes of membership. In addition, the Court alludes to the reality that many undocumented immigrants will end up living in the community for a long time, either legally or illegally.

<u>Notes and Questions on Postsecondary Education</u> (page 1212):

Q1: Arguments against allowing undocumented residents to qualify for in-state resident tuition rates at public colleges and universities include these:

1. They're not even supposed to be here.

2. Conferring benefits on undocumented immigrants encourages more to come illegally and discourages them from leaving.

3. It is regrettable that young people will be disadvantaged by the actions of their parents, but that was the decision their parents made when they came here illegally, and they should be held to it. Besides, the students can always attend college in their countries of origin.

4. The fiscal burdens of subsidizing undocumented students will fall on U.S. citizens and lawful residents. That is unfair.

5. Those burdens will fall disproportionately on taxpayers in the states with the greatest number of undocumented immigrants. If American taxpayers are going to subsidize these costs, the burden should be on the federal government, whose immigration policies have created the situation. That way, the costs will be spread more equitably throughout the entire population.

Counter-arguments include:

1. Undocumented immigrants are still residents of the state in every sense of the word, notwithstanding that they have violated federal immigration laws.

2. They are usually minors even now, and typically were not only minors but very young children when their parents brought them to the United States. They are not morally culpable and should not be penalized because of their parents' actions.

3. The vast majority will remain permanently in the United States at any rate; both they and the country will gain if they are permitted to realize their full potential.

4. Their parents pay federal and state income tax, sales tax, fuel tax, and (directly or indirectly, depending on whether they own homes or rent) property tax, just like anyone else.

5. Postsecondary education is probably at least as essential to life opportunity today as secondary education was in former times.

6. Barring them from in-state tuition rates will not discourage illegal immigration. Nobody suggests that in-state tuition (which almost certainly is still much greater than tuition rates in most undocumented students' countries of origin) will be a significant factor in decisions to immigrate illegally.

Q2: The implication appears to be that it is anomalous to grant benefits to undocumented immigrants while denying the same benefits to U.S. citizens. But the point is that the state would simply be granting preference to its own residents over the residents of other states, all else equal. Since the state's own residents generally provide the tax revenues that provide these and other benefits, distinguishing based on residence rather than citizenship or immigration status is perfectly rational.

Q3: Hard to say. On the one hand, the Court emphasizes frequently that it is dealing with the interests of children. Arguably, the individual interest is less compelling when the issue concerns adults (which most high school graduates are). On the other hand, the Court also stressed the innocence of the affected students. The children had no input into the decisions that led to their undocumented status and could not be faulted in any way. The same rationale will ordinarily apply to postsecondary education, with caveats. On the assumption that the applicants attended at least high school in the state, one can usually assume they were brought to the United States, while still under age, by their parents. They might even have been brought to the United States at very young ages – certainly innocent of wrongdoing at the time of entry and generally present long enough that they cannot be faulted for not returning to their countries of origin now. In addition, the Court stressed the practical importance of elementary and secondary education to the students' life opportunities. Today, similar statements could be made about college education, though obviously not to the same degree.

4. Undocumented Immigrants and Labor Law

Instructors could assign this material with the material on IRCA and employer sanctions from section A.2 to underscore that unauthorized workers are protected by many of the labor laws. In 2002, however, the Supreme Court limited the reach of those protections in *Hoffman Plastic Compounds* (discussed below).

Hoffman Plastic Compounds, Inc. v. NLRB (page 1214):

In a five to four decision, the Supreme Court held that federal immigration policy as expressed in IRCA foreclosed the National Labor Relations Board from awarding backpay to an undocumented worker who had never been authorized to work in the United States. The case began when the NLRB found that Hoffman had violated section 8(a)(3) of the National Labor Relation Act for laying off four workers, including one unauthorized worker, to "rid itself of known union supporters." In an opinion written by Chief Justice Rehnquist, the Court acknowledged that the NLRB possessed broad authority to select and fashion remedies for violations of the NLRA but emphasized that the Board's remedial discretion was limited by federal immigration policy, which the Board has no authority to enforce or administer. The Court observed that the Board's holding would "award backpay to an illegal alien for years of work not performed, for wages that could not lawfully have been earned, and for a job obtained in the first instance by a criminal fraud." The Court reasoned that awarding backpay under these circumstances would encourage and condone future violations.

Writing for the four dissenters, Justice Breyer disputed the majority's assumption that the possibility of a future backpay award would enhance the incentives for illegal immigration, because "so speculative a future possibility" could not realistically influence a person's decision to migrate. Instead, denying the Board the power to award backpay could very well increase the magnetic force of employment by lowering the cost to the employer of an initial violation of the labor law. The dissent concluded by emphasizing that, regardless of whether its analysis of the effects of backpay awards on the policies of IRCA was accurate, the Court should have deferred to the Board's careful and reasonable consideration of labor and immigration law, citing *Chevron U.S.A. Inc. v. Natural Resources Defense Council, Inc.* (1984).

<u>Notes and Questions Following Hoffman Plastic</u> (page 1223):

Q1: The majority and the dissent debate whether awarding unauthorized workers backpay would encourage or discourage employers from hiring them. Instructors might use these claims to structure a debate among students, underscoring that the outcome of the case appears to turn on the Justices' own policy assumptions with respect to incentives. Whereas the majority focuses on the incentives of would-be undocumented immigrants, the dissent focuses on the incentives of employers. Is it possible to take both perspectives into account and come to a coherent conclusion? Instructors interested in exploring the implications of *Hoffman* for deference regimes in administrative law might also pose the question of whether the Court should have given *Chevron* deference to the Board's decision to issue a back pay award. The Board arguably was doing nothing more than interpreting the labor laws, over which it has expertise, in the context of a particular set of facts, with only speculative consequences for the enforcement of IRCA. The Board did not interpret any substantive provisions of IRCA itself.

Q2: To test the arguments of both the majority and the dissent, instructors might explore whether the answer to question 1 varies depending on the labor law remedy at issue. Would awarding undocumented immigrants wages for work already done have the same effect the majority predicts with respect to back pay? If so, why might the majority nonetheless permit the NLRB to award wages not paid for work already done? The Thirteenth Amendment's prohibition of slavery and involuntary servitude might provide all the justification necessary. As for the second question, the employer's knowledge would not seem to change the majority's analysis of the incentives created for undocumented immigrants, but the employers more "culpable" conduct might justify striking the balance less favorably to employers. This same question is raised by the *Balbuena* case, though it is not exactly clear why the employer's knowledge should affect the outcome in that case.

Q3: Whether state law remedies for tortious or actionable conduct by employers are preempted in light of *Hoffman* raises questions similar to those posed above with respect to federal remedies. Instructors might wish to return to these cases after assigning the federalism materials in section E.

5. Undocumented Immigrants and Drivers' Licenses

Questions on Drivers' Licenses (page 1231):

Q1: On the one hand, the driver's license, even if specially marked to reveal the bearer's unlawful immigration status, is a document that can be shown to a police officer if a driver is pulled over. It's better than being pulled over and not having a license. In addition, although the document cannot be used to board an airplane or for other federal identification purposes, it can be used for identification if the person is dealing with any state agency or with a private actor, such as opening or withdrawing money from a bank account. A passport would already serve the identification function, but possibly banks, other private institutions, and state agencies will want some proof of state residence, which a passport would not provide.

On the other hand, as soon as the person displays the specially color-coded license marked "not for federal identification," it will usually be obvious that he or she is undocumented. That revelation could prompt whoever is doing the checking to contact the immigration authorities. Whether undocumented immigrants will choose to take that risk remains to be seen.

Q2: A foreign terrorist who is in lawful immigration status could obtain the regular state-issued driver's license or identification card, and might decide to do so in order to avoid encounters with the police in connection with routine traffic violations. The license or card might also facilitate his or her daily transactions, including financial transactions. The risk will be that, to obtain the license, the person will now have to supply a great deal of information, leaving a paper trail in the process. That is usually the last thing a prospective terrorist would want to do.

If the terrorist is undocumented, then all of the same considerations apply except that now the person also has to worry that anyone who sees his or her license or card will inform the police. The terrorist would have to decide whether his chances of coming to the attention of the law enforcement authorities will be greater with the "undocumented immigrant" license or card, or without it.

Q3: Obviously it will be very difficult, and unless staff resources are multiplied several times over, these determinations will have to be made very quickly. There are not only many different immigration statuses, but also many different documents that cover various combinations of them. Some of the statuses recognized by the REAL ID Act, § 202(c)(2)(B), are irregular categories for which Congress nonetheless has elected to allow the issuance of licenses – *pending* applications for asylum, TPS, or adjustment of status, or approved deferred action status. Expecting state DMV officials to understand and apply all those distinctions seems unrealistic. The Act does require states to make arrangements with DHS to use the SAVE system, see § 202(c)(3)(C), but whether that system can consistently yield reliable data on the several million noncitizens present in the United States, and the constant changes in their statuses, remains to be seen.

D. REDUCING FUTURE FLOW BY CREATING ALTERNATIVES TO ILLEGAL IMMIGRATION

This section could be assigned as background reading for a broad-based policy discussion on how best to address future illegal immigration. Instructors might wish to reserve (or revisit) the discussion of the morality of immigration restriction, presented in Chapter 1. Instructors might also(re)introduce some of the moral questions through a discussion of the legitimacy and desirability of guest worker programs. It is also worth getting students to see that investment in the development of source countries and temporary worker programs are not mutually exclusive. In fact, temporary worker programs may be defended as one component of a longer-term development strategy.

<u>Questions Following Material on Guest Worker Programs</u> (page 1238):

Q1: Among the strategies that have been proposed for ensuring that guest workers return home after their visas expire is withholding some of their wages or benefits until they return. Failure to return might also provide a basis for barring re-entry in the future. Given that millions of immigrants, under the status quo, assume the risks of being undocumented, do these compliance strategies have any chance of success?

Another possibility, explored by Eleanor Brown in the article cited on coursebook page 378 n.12, is to outsource part of the guest worker selection function to trusted community leaders overseas.

Q2: Business lobbies appear reluctant to give up the employer sponsorship requirement for labor migration, thus presenting a political obstacle to the implementation of a portable visa. The portability idea raises many additional design questions. Should temporary workers be required to stay within a particular industry, or should portability extend across numerous industries? For how long may a temporary worker remain in the United States while in search of a new job? Should changing jobs be permitted only under certain circumstances, such as violations of the labor law by the employer?

Q3: In the spring of 2009, two major labor unions—Change to Win and the AFL-CIO—announced their opposition to a temporary worker program as a component of comprehensive immigration reform. In the 2006 and 2007 debates over reform, the unions had taken different positions from one another. Employers groups and organizations such as the Chamber of Commerce, however, support temporary worker programs. Instructors might wish to explore whether room for compromise exists, or whether the failure to find common ground on this issue might doom immigration reform more generally. Instructors might also wish to explore how the fact that the U.S. maintains small-scale temporary workers programs in agriculture and other industries should inform this debate.

Q4: Whether a transnational labor visa will reduce illegal immigration and protect the rights of immigrant workers depends, on some level, on whether enough visas will be made available to satisfy demand, as well as on whether immigrant workers stand to make more money, or otherwise maximize their interests, outside the context of the program. What is more, if enforcement of labor laws remains weak, the incentives to hire unauthorized workers will not decrease. The advantage of increasing the availability of permanent visas is that permanent status would make workers even more secure and therefore better able to stand up for their rights by challenging employers' unlawful practices. But if migration from Mexico tends to be cyclical, then workers may not opt into the visa system, hoping instead to work for short periods of time and then to return home. In addition, an increase in permanent visas commensurate with demand is likely to be more politically difficult to pass than a temporary worker program. Regardless of the strategy adopted, however, it may be impossible to prevent illegal immigration altogether, especially in boom times, given the strong economic logic behind it.

Q5: The answer to this question depends on what a guest worker program is supposed to accomplish, how the implementation of such a program plays out in practice, and on one's views concerning the desirability of immigration. For example, if a guest worker program does not succeed in reducing illegal immigration, the decline in public confidence in government might be steeper than if the government were simply to tolerate (and make enforcement noises against) illegal immigration. This decline in public confidence could lead to greater long-term suspicion of immigration and immigrants and make subsequent immigration reform more complicated as a matter of political economy. If the long-term effect of a guest worker program is to create ever-larger classes of temporary laborers with no possibility for integration into society, that result might be inferior morally, or from the perspective of democratic theory, to accepting high levels of illegal immigration and adopting occasional regularization programs that provide immigrants with a path to citizenship. Finally, if one's interest is in keeping immigration and naturalization levels low, then a guest worker program–particularly one that puts temporary workers on a path to citizenship–might be less desirable than tolerance of illegal immigration, since undocumented immigrants are easier to remove through formal and informal mechanisms.

E. FEDERALISM AND THE REGULATION OF UNDOCUMENTED IMMIGRANTS

Most of the state and local laws discussed in this section directly address illegal immigration and can fruitfully be explored as a dimension of that phenomenon. That said, instructors might decide to present this material in conjunction with Chapter 2, because it fleshes out the federal exclusivity component of the plenary power and introduces the basics of alienage jurisprudence, which is itself shaped by the plenary power. With a brief introductory lecture to IRCA, students who have read Chapter 2 but have not yet read the remainder of Chapter 12 should be equipped to handle the material in this section.

1. The general legal framework

Graham v Richardson and *DeCanas v Bica* together lay out the basic framework for evaluating state regulation of immigrants and immigration and are probably most effective as teaching tools when assigned together. *Graham* seems to rest primarily on the holding that the Equal Protection Clause of the Fourteenth Amendment restricts states' authority to discriminate against noncitizens—at least lawfully present noncitizens—but the Court also suggests that the federal immigration power limits states' authority to adopt laws that resemble immigration regulation. *De Canas* makes clear that immigration regulation, as a constitutional matter, is an exclusively federal power, but it also lays out the general statutory preemption framework that applies to state laws that regulate in an area where Congress has regulated as well. Together, these cases will help students understand the difference between constitutional and statutory preemption. They also both raise the question of what exactly it means to regulate immigration. *De Canas* emphasizes that not every regulation that affects immigrants constitutes immigration regulation. The scope of this statement is unclear, but the distinction between the two types of regulation can be used to frame the material in this chapter. Drawing the line between a law that regulates immigration and a law that affects immigrants in some way is central to evaluating the state laws explored in this section. Perhaps because the distinction is so difficult to draw, however, the statutory preemption framework is crucial to courts' evaluation of all state and local laws that touch on immigration, making *De Canas* a significant case.

Graham v. Richardson (page 1244):

In *Graham v. Richardson*, the Supreme Court strikes down an Arizona law that established a 15-year residency requirement for LPRs to receive state-administered Medicaid benefits, as well as a Pennsylvania law that denied state public assistance entirely to otherwise eligible LPRs. In Part II of its opinion, the Court offers an equal protection analysis, noting that alienage classifications are subject to close judicial scrutiny, because noncitizens represent prime examples of "discrete and insular" minorities. The Court concludes that the states' justifications for their restrictions on noncitizens' eligibility for public services–to preserve limited state resources for their own citizens, or "fiscal integrity"–were not compelling and therefore could not save the classifications. In Part III of its opinion, the Court offers an alternative federalism rationale for its holding. According to the Court, Congress has not seen fit to impose any burdens or restrictions on noncitizens who become indigent after their admission into the United States. State statutes that deny noncitizens access to public benefits therefore impose "auxiliary burdens" on noncitizens and thus discourage entry into or continued residency within the states that have adopted such restrictions. The Court concludes that the denial of welfare benefits is tantamount to the denial of entrance and abode and that the state laws at issue thus encroach upon Congress's exclusive federal power to regulate immigration.

<u>Notes and Questions Following Graham v. Richardson</u> (page 1250):

Q1: The term "discrete and insular" comes from the famous footnote 4 of *Carolene Products.* There, the Supreme Court sketched a new framework for judicial review in the post-New Deal period, in light of the Court's conclusion that socioeconomic legislation was presumptively constitutional. The Court has since applied the "discrete and insular" formulation to determine whether legislation burdening a particular group should receive strict scrutiny from the Court, with the category of race serving as the paradigm case of discrete and insular status. Among the indicia the Court has used over time to determine whether a group qualifies are: (1) Has the group been subject historically to discrimination or subordination; (2) Is the characteristic that defines the group immutable, or constructively immutable; (3) Is the characteristic that defines the group either morally relevant, or relevant to public policy in some way; and (4) is the group politically powerless? Immigrants pretty easily meet criterion (1), but it is less clear that criteria (2) and (3) apply, given that many lawful immigrants can eventually naturalize, and that status as a noncitizen has long been considered relevant to the rights and privileges immigrants can claim vis-à-vis the state, including the right to vote. How should the fact that immigrants pay taxes and are subject to conscription factor into this analysis? Moreover, instructors might ask students what they make of the fact that immigrants are politically powerless. Though they lack the vote, they are not entirely powerless, because they might well be voters eventually. Moreover, in today's world, the Latino electorate and interests groups such as business and labor can be strong advocates for immigrants' interests.

Q2: The Court's application of rational basis review to federal laws that discriminate against noncitizens can be justified on the ground that citizenship status is relevant to the rights and privileges to which one is entitled, because noncitizens have not yet been formally integrated into the polity–a decision existing members of any nation state have the authority to control. The federal government routinely makes membership decisions, theoretically speaking for the people as a whole. Strict scrutiny applies to state laws that discriminate, however, because states have no role to play in the process of defining and distributing membership, or so the argument goes. Recent scholarly literature cited at the beginning of this section challenges these assumptions.

Q3: Instructors at this stage might revisit *Plyler v. Doe* and ask students whether the outcome in that case would/should have been different had the context involved adult undocumented immigrants. On the one hand, undocumented immigrants are highly vulnerable to exploitation by employers and coercive treatment by the state. Historically they have been subject to at least as much, if not more, discrimination and prejudice that authorized immigrants. On the other hand, undocumented immigrants are present in the United States without the consent of the polity and in violation of its laws. This "culpability," which the Court in *Plyler* declines to apply to minors, renders undocumented status morally relevant, justifying discrimination by the state on the basis of that status.

Q4: Courts disagree over whether the federal government can constitutionally authorize states to deny access to Medicaid. The cases are complex but might be useful supplemental reading for instructors who wish to think through whether devolution is permissible. The justifications for devolution include that Congress should be permitted to rely on state officials to administer its programs, and that as long as state laws adopt federal guidelines, they do not present a threat to uniformity. *See, e.g., Doe v. Comm'r of Transitional Assistance*, 773 N.E.2d 404, 526 (Mass. 2002) ("strict scrutiny does not apply to state laws that merely adopt uniform guidelines"). The courts that have been skeptical of devolution have continued to apply strict scrutiny to state alienage classifications, even if the classifications are authorized by federal statute. *See, e.g., Erlich v. Perez*, 908 A.2d 1220 (Md. 2006) (holding that failure to appropriate funds to medical benefits program for resident alien children and pregnant women fails strict scrutiny, despite apparent authorization under federal law); *Aliessa v. Novello*, 96 N.Y.2d 418 (N.Y. 2001) (invalidating New York social services law limiting lawful immigrants' access to state Medicaid).

De Canas v. Bica (page 1251):

In 1976, the California Labor Code prohibited employers from knowingly hiring noncitizens unauthorized to live in the United States if such employment "would have an adverse effect on lawful resident workers." In *De Canas v. Bica*, the Supreme Court considers whether this state law was preempted either by the Constitution, as an attempt to regulate immigration and naturalization, or by the INA. On the constitutional question, the Court begins by emphasizing that, even though immigration regulation is an exclusive federal responsibility, not every state enactment that deals with immigrants constitutes a regulation of immigration According to the Court, the California law sought to strengthen the state's economy and adopted federal standards in imposing criminal sanctions on state employers who hire noncitizens with no right to employment within the country. Even if the law indirectly affects immigration, the Court reasons, it would not be an invalid incursion into federal power, absent congressional action.

The Court then considers whether the INA occupies the field and thus implicitly preempts the California law. The Court frames its analysis by emphasizing that states possess broad authority under their police powers to regulate the employment relationship. As a result, the Court will not presume that Congress intended to oust state authority to regulate employment when it passed the INA; such ouster must have been the "clear and manifest purpose" of Congress. Nothing in the text or legislative history of the INA, the Court observes, reveals such an intent. The Court also points to affirmative evidence that Congress sanctioned concurrent state legislation in the area covered by the California statute and underscores that there would not appear to be a predominant federal interest in an area in which state law has been fashioned to remedy local problems. The Court concludes by observing that a conflict preemption question remains. It must be determined whether the state law presents an obstacle to the execution of the objectives of the INA. The Court remands the case to the California courts to address this question in the first instance, noting that it does not have an adequate record to make the determination itself.

Notes and Questions Following De Canas v. Bica (page 1256):

Q1-2: One way to define immigration regulation is that it constitutes defining the terms of admission, expulsion, and legal status. That definition could be expanded to include laws that affect immigrant movement within the United States, but it's not clear that such a definition is consistent with *De Canas*. The articles cited in footnote 73 of this chapter discuss the difficulty of distinguishing immigration regulation from other laws that affect immigrants or immigrant movement. Most of the court decisions that have dealt with state laws related to immigration have been decided on statutory grounds, perhaps reflecting the difficulty of defining constitutional preemption with precision, coupled with the steadily wider and more detailed scope of federal regulation.

Q4: Though this question effectively transports students to a different (pre-IRCA) time and legal regime, it encourages them to explore arguments based on obstacle preemption grounds. The question is whether California's penalties on employers posed an obstacle to the federal government's pursuit of its own enforcement priorities.

Q5: The statement in *De Canas* that not all regulation that affects immigrants constitutes immigration regulation would seem to survive the passage of IRCA, because even at the time of *De Canas*, an extensive federal regulatory scheme existed, and the Court nonetheless contemplated that some immigrant-affecting state legislation would be permissible. The more difficult question is whether and how much state regulation of the employment of undocumented workers is permitted. This question is explored in section C.4 and the discussion of *Hoffman Plastic*, and it is explored in section E.2 through an application of the *De Canas* framework to current state laws that apply penalties to employers who hire undocumented immigrants.

Q6: In *Toll*, the Court appears to be invoking constitutional preemption, but the decision itself is based on conflict preemption grounds. The Maryland state law undermined the policies embodied in the federal statutes, international agreements, and treaties governing G-4 visa holders. Those policies included the tax exempt status enjoyed by G-4 visa holders, which the Court reasoned was designed to enable international organizations to employ noncitizens in the U.S. without being encumbered by tax obligations. As for whether states can constitutionally extend rights or benefits to immigrants that are more generous that what the federal government has given, it seems clear that states cannot confer lawful status where it does not exist or otherwise alter a noncitizen's status. But the alienage cases that police discriminatory state laws are concerned with preventing states from imposing burdens on noncitizens without compelling reason, not on ensuring that states do not extend benefits beyond those that exist under federal law. That said, extending such benefits to immigrants could create incentives for immigrants to move to the benefit-granting state, including by crossing the border into the United States. But as long as the noncitizen acquires a visa from the federal government, state laws that create incentives for people to come to the U.S. would not seem to interfere with the federal government's immigration power.

Q7: The Court in *Toll* certainly reads *De Canas* narrowly, but it is difficult to read *De Canas* itself as hinging on the observation regarding the Farm Labor Contract Act. In his dissent in *Toll*, then-Justice Rehnquist writes: "The Court's dicta seems to me inconsistent with our prior cases, and its conclusion about the effect of the statutes and treaties [regarding G-4 visa holders] is strained at best. In short, the Court reaches a result that I find quite out of step with our normal approach to federal pre-emption of state law." 458 U.S. 1, 26 (Rehnquist, J., dissenting). He goes on to contend that the Court reverses the presumption that normally applies in preemption cases by suggesting in dicta that any state law that discriminates against lawfully admitted aliens is void, regardless of the strength of the state's justification. In his view, *Graham v. Richardson* is not consistent with the Court's apparent assumption in *Toll* that all state laws that burden aliens conflict with the "amorphous" federal power over immigration. *Id.* at 26-30.

2. State regulation of employers and landlords

Instructors might choose to focus on either the state employer sanctions laws or the local laws regulating landlords. The employer sanctions laws are arguably more consequential, because they have been adopted at the state level and have been upheld by at least one court of appeals, whereas the landlord laws, while notorious, have appeared only in a handful of localities and have been struck down in every court challenge at the time of this writing. It is possible that the cost of defending and enforcing these provisions will lead some states and localities to rescind their laws, such that the importance of engaging this material in depth will diminish over time. Nonetheless, the *Lozano* case and the notes that follow are useful in exploring how the legal framework outlined in section E.1 is applied.

Lozano v. City of Hazleton (page 1259):

In 2006, the town of Hazleton, Pennsylvania enacted a series of ordinances to sanction employers who hire unauthorized workers and landlords who rent to undocumented immigrants (IIRA). In *Lozano v. City of Hazleton*, the federal district court held that federal law preempts both sets of regulation.

With respect to the employment provisions, the court first concludes that IIRA is preempted by IRCA, which expressly preempts any "State or local law imposing civil or criminal sanctions (other than through licensing and similar laws) upon those who employ, or recruit or refer for a fee for employment, unauthorized aliens." The court rejects the City's claim that its ordinance, which would suspend the business permit of an employer found to be in violation of the act, constituted a licensing law, rather than a criminal or civil sanction. The court reasons that the suspension of a business permit would constitute the "ultimate sanction," and that Congress could not have intended to prohibit criminal and civil penalties but permit states to impose far greater penalties. The court alternatively concludes that IIRA is field-preempted, because the federal government possesses an especially strong interest in immigration, and because IRCA is a comprehensive scheme that leaves no room for state regulation. The court also concludes that IIRA conflicts with IRCA, because the former pursues objectives similar to the latter's but uses means that are distinct. For example, whereas IRCA requires employers to verify potential employees' documents, IIRA requires the employer to present documents to a city office, which then contacts the federal government to determine the worker's status. Whereas IRCA does not require employers to participate in E-Verify, IIRA makes participation mandatory in some circumstances.

The court also held that the housing provisions were preempted. The housing provisions: (1) made it unlawful to harbor an undocumented immigrant, defining harboring as letting, leasing, or renting a dwelling unit to an undocumented immigrant, and (2) required any person who seeks to occupy a rental unit to obtain an occupancy permit from the city by providing proof of legal citizenship or residency, and prohibited landlords from allowing occupancy to any person without a permit. The court concludes that both provisions were in direct conflict with federal law, because they were based on two incorrect assumptions: (1) that the federal government seeks removal of all noncitizens who lack legal status, and (2) that it can be conclusively determined that a person may not remain in the United States outside of a formal removal hearing. The court notes that the federal government retains discretion with respect to whom to remove, that even noncitizens ordered removed may nonetheless be permitted to remain inside the U.S., and that regularization of status is a complex process. The court then explains that the registration provision was additionally preempted because it calls upon employees of the city to determine immigration status–a determination that can be made only by a federal immigration judge.

Notes and Questions Following Lozano v. City of Hazleton (page 1271):

Q1: The *Lozano* court interprets IRCA's savings clause as limited to those licensing actions taken against employers "found to have" violated IRCA. The implication of the court's distinction between an employer found to have violated the local ordinance and an employer found to have violated IRCA is somewhat obscure. Given that the Hazleton law defines "illegal alien" as an alien not lawfully present according to the terms of the INA, the court's implication must be that the savings clause comes into play only in instances in which the federal government has found liability under the procedures laid out in IRCA. The legislative history does not reveal whether Congress thought a state or locality could itself find that an employer has violated IRCA. If a state or local statute incorporates the provisions of the INA for determining whether an employer has hired an unauthorized worker, it is at least reasonable to conclude that a violation of the state statute constitutes a violation of IRCA.

Q3: On the one hand, it is arguably sufficient to avoid conflict preemption for a state or local law to incorporate the standards of the INA; under these circumstances, enforcement of the state or local law would not conflict with federal law, because it would be tantamount to enforcing federal law. On the other hand, even if a state or local law incorporates federal standards, the state or locality might set different enforcement priorities from the federal government, prosecuting employers whom the federal government has chosen not to. In addition, a state tribunal applying federal immigration standards might not have the necessary expertise to act as an acceptable agent for the federal government.

Q4: The Arizona and Illinois E-Verify preemption holdings are consistent with one another in that they both advance the federal government's interest in ensuring that E-Verify be available for employer use. Congress's rationale for making E-Verify voluntary at the national level was arguably to ensure the gradual roll-out of the program. If all fifty states were to make participation in E-Verify mandatory, this objective might be thwarted. Even if that were the case, however, the holding in the Illinois case seems sound, given Congress's clear intent to make E-Verify available and to encourage its expansion to all fifty states.

Q5: The employer and landlord ordinances call for the application of the same preemption framework. The existence of IRCA, however, necessarily makes the conflict preemption inquiry more detailed, but perhaps more sound, in the employment context. Because the harboring provision in the INA does not obviously address the landlord-tenant relationship and has not been applied to the sorts of instances implicated by the Hazleton ordinance, the argument that the Hazleton statute conflicts with this specific provision of the INA would be difficult to make (and perhaps unwise, as well, given that it would depend on defining the harboring provision quite broadly). The analysis of the landlord provisions, therefore, would either have to depend on a more general statement of conflict–that the landlord ordinances, by forcing immigrants out of communities, interferes with the federal government's articulation of its own enforcement priorities–or on field preemption, a claim that is more difficult to make in light of *De Canas*. That said, the fact that Congress has not authorized state and local governments to use landlord-tenant sanctions, but has contemplated some room for state and local governments to regulate employers in IRCA's savings clause, might support a preemption claim against the landlord ordinances.

Q7: One reading of *Villas at Parkside* is that, had Farmers Branch used federal immigration standards to determine to whom landlords could rent, the city ordinance would not have been preempted. That said, the court could still have concluded that the purpose of the ordinance was to regulate immigrants' movement by preventing them from residing in Farmers Branch. The city's reliance on HUD standards simply made it easier for the court to conclude that the city was regulating immigration in a manner that conflicted with federal law. The court also could have followed the *Lozano* court's lead and concluded that, even if the ordinance incorporated federal standards, it still would have required city officials to determine immigration status in order to prosecute violators of the ordinance–a determination that can only be made definitively by the appropriate federal officials. Indeed, this same argument could be made in response to state and local laws that require employers to verify status, whether through the use of E-Verify or other procedures. But given that federal law contemplates that employers will screen potential workers, thus making final determinations with respect to a potential employee's status to work (not hiring those who cannot prove their authorization), this argument is weak. That said, it would make sense for courts to require state and local laws, at the very least, to provide employers and employees with opportunities to challenge findings of no authorization comparable to opportunities provided by federal law.

Q8: Given that the licensing savings clause appears in IRCA, a statute wholly focused on the employment relationship, the claim that the savings clause covers landlord-tenant licensing is implausible. The fact that the Arizona law requires employers to use E-Verify, whereas the Farmers Branch ordinance relies on property owners and managers to determine immigration status, matters because E-Verify is a federal database and therefore ensures that employers under the Arizona law are relying on federal information to determine a worker's status. But given that IRCA permits employers to use the documents listed in the I-9 forms to confirm authorization to work, it is not clear that the failure of the Farmer Branch ordinance to require landlords to use E-Verify should be dispositive.

3. State and local participation in immigration policing

Instructors might choose to assign this material, rather than the employer and landlord sanctions material, to explore the legitimacy of state and local involvement in immigration regulation. This section does not raise many statutory preemption questions, so the *De Canas* framework is less relevant. But it does present questions with respect to the constitutionality of devolving federal immigration authority, as well a claim not yet seen in this chapter–that states have inherent authority, absent explicit congressional preemption–to enforce federal immigration law.

4. State regulation of public benefits

Notes and Questions Following State Regulation of Public Benefits (page 1285):

Ql: Most of the arguments in favor of barring undocumented children from public schools are set out in *Plyler*, since the Court had to examine the various interests asserted by Texas in support of (somewhat) similar legislation. To those purposes might be added a symbolic one: The voters of California perhaps wanted to "send Washington a message." The message might be twofold -- that the federal government should do more to stem illegal immigration, and that, until it does, the federal government should reimburse California for the costs the state incurs.

The arguments against Proposition 187 occupy a wide field. They include the following:

a. It is wrong to punish the children; they had no say in the matter.

b. The kind of punishment being imposed -- taking away their education -- is too cruel for a civilized society. It results in heavy permanent damage to their life opportunities.

c. It puts teachers in an impossible bind. How can they forge any kind of bond with a child when they are seen as adversaries from whom the child has to conceal information? And how can they get parents involved in the education of their children if the parents have to fear contact with the teacher?

d. The initiative will create a permanent underclass that will haunt California for decades.

e. Undocumented immigrants pay taxes too. They pay federal and state income taxes, sales taxes, gasoline taxes, and, either directly or indirectly (depending on whether they own their own home or rent), property taxes.

f. It won't get people to leave. First, as long as there is so great a disparity between the standards of living in the United States and Mexico, the temptation to immigrate will be too powerful to resist. Those who have already been here, who have experienced the greater economic opportunities here, and who have grown roots are especially unlikely to leave. Second, if necessary, people will produce false documents if that is what it takes to stay in school; schoolteachers and principals will not have the training to detect counterfeit documents.

Q2: Uniformity would certainly seem to be an issue. If some states barred undocumented children from public schools and others didn't, obviously a certain number of undocumented families would move to states that allowed their children to attend public school. The effect could be a race to the bottom, where each state, in order to avoid absorbing a disproportionate fiscal burden, tries to be at least as restrictive as its neighbors.

Embroilment is an issue as well. Mexico reacted angrily to Proposition 187. One response of the Mexican government to Proposition 187 (and to other measures perceived as anti-Mexican) was to announce that Mexican nationals who became naturalized U.S. citizens would no longer lose their Mexican citizenship. The hope was that the action would encourage Mexican nationals living in the United States to naturalize, and thereby both protect themselves from harsh immigration laws and obtain the right to vote. Clearly, an increase in naturalizations has national, not just local, impact (e.g., increasing the number of immediate relative filings).

Q3: As for the policy question, state adjudication does seem dubious. The students saw in chapters 7-9 how complex both the substantive criteria and the procedures for determining deportability can be. Entrusting those decisions to school, welfare, and social work officials who have not been trained in the nuances of immigration law is problematic. Proponents of 187 would argue, however, that the state officials are not making final decisions. When an official reports a person's name to the federal immigration officials, it would be up to the latter to decide whether to initiate removal proceedings, and eventually up to the immigration judge and maybe the BIA to decide whether to order removal. Still, serious harm would result if the state official wrongly denies a welfare benefit or social service to which the applicant in fact is entitled, or if a school official wrongly expels from school a student who in fact is a United States citizen or a lawfully present noncitizen.

As for the preemption question, the plaintiffs pointed out that Congress had created an elaborate system for adjudicating disputes over citizenship and deportability. The system includes formal evidentiary hearings before immigration judges, the right of appeal to the BIA, and the possibility of judicial review. In asylum cases, the system also provides in most instances for an interview with an asylum officer. All these officials are highly trained to make these various determinations. It seems doubtful that Congress would, by implication, allow state officials to circumvent that process. Again, however, proponents of 187 would argue that state officials are deciding only eligibility for public benefits, not the right to remain in the United States. Opponents would respond that the state officials have to decide deportability in order to make their eligibility determinations.

Q4: The argument for exclusive federal decisionmaking is that, realistically, a decision as fundamental as whether children may attend public school could have a significant impact on immigration patterns -- at the very least, on the distribution of immigrants' final destinations among the fifty states. In Plyler, Texas acknowledged that one of its goals was to deter undocumented immigrants from coming to Texas.

The argument for state power would be that, just as immigration has traditionally (though not always) been a federal responsibility, education has traditionally been a state and local responsibility. Moreover, as Professor Spiro argues in the article cited in the preceding materials, the impact of undocumented immigrants undeniably varies considerably from state to state. It is only fair, the argument might run, that states have input into decisions that affect them in significant ways.

Q5: On the one hand, one cannot blame California for wanting other states to share the cost of educating undocumented children. On the other hand, this question again raises the spectre of a race to the bottom, see item 1 above, and illustrates the benefits of federal regulation.

Q6: First, the preemption issue is one of congressional intent: Did Congress intend for states to have the power to bar undocumented children from the public schools? Had the Gallegly amendment never been introduced, the State of California might have been able to argue that Congress simply never thought about the issue one way or the other and that therefore there is no evidence of an intent to preempt. Now, however, Congress has consciously considered whether to authorize the states to bar undocumented children from public schools, and it has made a purposeful (and highly visible) decision not to do so. Second, by way of contrast, Congress has specifically authorized states not to provide most other public benefits to undocumented immigrants. (See the preceding discussion of both the Welfare Act and IIRIRA.) The plaintiffs would ask a court to read significance into Congress's decision to authorize one type of bar but not the other (after having considered and debated both).

Q8: One possibility is to urge a straight overruling of *Plyler*. The vote in that case was 5-4, and since then the composition of the Court has changed substantially.

As for distinctions, the California initiative if anything was even more extreme than the Texas statute struck down in *Plyler*. Proposition 187 absolutely prohibited school districts from enrolling undocumented children, while the Texas statute merely gave the school districts the discretion to do so (though it also withheld state funds for undocumented students). Proposition 187 also established a complex enforcement mechanism that relied on a network of state employees making deportability decisions and communicating them, without hearings of any kind. And Proposition 187 did more than deny education to the children; it also required the education officials to investigate the children's parents. Consequently, even United States citizen children were for all practical purposes barred from school if they had undocumented parents (unless they were willing to turn their parents in to the former INS).

California might be able to argue changed circumstances. The Court in *Plyler* expressly relied on both (a) Texas's failure to demonstrate that undocumented immigrants had a net negative economic impact on the State; and (b) the availability of alternative strategies, including specifically employer sanctions. California might argue that today the empirical evidence of a negative economic impact on the State is clearer, and that now Congress has in fact prohibited the employment of undocumented workers. Of course the two factors on which the Court placed the greatest reliance -- the innocence of the children and the centrality of education to life opportunity -- are just as significant today as they were then.

Q9: Virtually every action the federal government takes will have more practical impact on some states than on others. The system would grind to a halt if the federal government had to calculate the impact of every decision on every state and provide reimbursement for every loss. Even then, the system would not be fair unless, conversely, states that gained by federal action had to reimburse the federal government.

With respect to illegal immigration, however, there are at least two other arguable elements: The federal government has exclusive power to regulate immigration, and the federal government has failed to prevent large numbers of noncitizens from entering the United States unlawfully or overstaying. From the point of view of those states that experience heavy economic losses from undocumented immigrants, the status quo is responsibility without power. That, essentially, is the point of footnote 1 of the dissent in *Plyler*. Still, it is hard to know how to identify federal "failure." All significant policy decisions involve tradeoffs. Deciding what resource level to invest in the enforcement of the nation's immigration laws is no exception.

CHAPTER 13
CITIZENSHIP

Introduction to the text points out, citizenship is a core concept to both theoreticians and practitioners. Some instructors might wish to take up some of this material (particularly the section C material on the significance of citizenship and portions of the section A material on acquisition of citizenship) at an earlier stage of the course. Doing so would facilitate the students' understanding of the immigrant selection system. One workable plan would be to cover this subject matter in conjunction with the material on the morality of immigration restrictions (chapter 1, section B). On the other hand, covering citizenship at the end of the course also works well, because the students will already have acquired a basic understanding of what it means *not* to be a citizen. In addition, the material on the meaning and significance of citizenship (section C) is a satisfying way to end the course.

SECTION A. ACQUIRING CITIZENSHIP

1. Citizenship Acquired at Birth

a. Jus Soli

This brief subsection is intended only as background reading. In section A.5, however, the concept of jus soli will be revisited, in the context of the debate over the proposed constitutional amendment.

b. Jus Sanguinis

Problems 1-3 (page 1295):

Problem 1: On the first question, despite what the Passport Office thought, both Frank and Maria were, and are, United States citizens. To establish their claims, however, they need to demonstrate that their father - not only their mother - was a United States citizen. If he was, then under all applicable laws they acquired citizenship at birth because they had two citizen parents, at least one of whom (their mother) had resided in the United States before Frank and Maria were born. All applicable laws also exempt them from the condition subsequent when both parents were United States citizens.

The reason their father was a United States citizen is as follows: Their paternal grandfather became a United States citizen by birth in the United States. Their father was born in 1913. His citizenship, therefore, is determined by the law described in the first row of the Chart. Under that law, their father acquired United States citizenship at birth because his father (i.e., Frank's and Maria's grandfather) had been a United States citizen who had lived in the United States as a child, before the birth of Frank's and Maria's father.

As for the second question, the employee of the Passport Office most likely assumed Frank had a United States citizen mother (by birth) and a noncitizen father. Frank was born on May 3, 1941. The law then in effect determines whether he is a United States citizen. Under that law (third row of chart), his mother would have to have lived in the United States for at least ten years before Frank's birth (which she did). In addition, however, five of those years would have to have come after she had turned 16 (and before Frank's birth). The five-year requirement was not met because she went to Mexico at age 16 and did not return to the United States until after Frank's birth. Probably on the basis of the (erroneous) assumption that Frank had only one U.S. citizen parent, therefore, the Passport Office denied his application.

As for the third question, on the basis of what he or she knew, the same passport officer would also have denied a passport to Maria, but for different reasons. She was born in June 1934. Therefore the law applicable to her is the one that appears in the second row of the chart. With a United States citizen mother who had resided in the United States before Maria's birth, Maria became a United States citizen at birth. There was no requirement of ten years residence or five years after age 16, etc. Her problem was the condition subsequent. Unlike Frank, she did not remain in the United States. She left at about age 15 1/2 (December 20, 1949 minus June 25, 1934), and returned at about age 26 1/2 (December 30, 1960 minus June 25, 1934). Therefore, between ages 14 and 28, she spent two different 1 1/2 periods in the United States. The total stay was approximately three years, but the statute applicable to her required two years of *continuous* presence. Therefore, as the Passport Office probably saw it, she lost her United States citizenship. Today, as a result of the 1994 amendment, she could regain her citizenship easily by taking an oath of allegiance.

[Note: At first blush one might think that the Child Citizenship Act, discussed in section A.2.b of this chapter of the coursebook, provides an alternative route to citizenship for both Frank and Maria. While under age 18 they were brought to the U.S. by their U.S. citizen mother, presumably as LPRs. See INA § 320. But the Child Citizenship Act was not retroactive. The beneficiaries had to have been under age 18 at the time of enactment. See Daniel Levy, *The Child Citizenship Act of 2000* , 6 Bender's Immigration Bulletin 293 (Mar. 15, 2000).]

Problem 2: The first question is whether Guillermo acquired United States citizenship at birth. Guillermo's paternal grandfather became a citizen by birth in the United States. Guillermo's father was born before 1934. The applicable law, therefore, is the one described in the first row of the Chart. Under that law Guillermo's father became a United States citizen at birth because *his* father (i.e., Guillermo's paternal grandfather) had been a United States citizen who had resided in the United States before Guillermo's father's birth. Guillermo himself was born in 1937. The applicable law for him, therefore, is the one described in the second row. Under that law Guillermo similarly became a citizen because his father had been a citizen and had lived in Arizona as a child. (Arizona became a state in 1912, but the facts say that the children - i.e., Guillermo's father and Guillermo's father's siblings -- moved there in 1905 and were raised there.)

The only issue here is the condition subsequent. Under the law described in the second row of the Chart, Guillermo needed two years of continuous physical presence between ages 14 and 28. The facts state that Guillermo attended high school in Michigan for "two years." If he literally spent two years (or more) in the United States, then he satisfied the condition subsequent, provided those two years occurred after age 14 -- a likely event even if they were his freshmen and sophomore years. But if his actual stay was only two academic years and the one intervening summer, he could fall short. Even in that latter event, he could now reinstate his citizenship by taking an oath of allegiance.

Mautino's main reason for including this Problem was to discuss the practical difficulties of proving the necessary facts. Many of the relevant events occurred long ago, at a time when records of vital events were not always kept and retained. The instructor might ask the students for their ideas as to how a lawyer might go about proving the necessary facts in this case. Here, the easiest way to prove Guillermo's two years of residence would be to obtain a copy of his high school transcript or, possibly, a statement from the family's landlord. To establish some of the older events, Mautino effectively used Census records from the National Archives. In general, other possibilities include employer records, tax or social security records, and military service (or pension) records. Birth certificates in the United States are usually not that difficult to obtain. Sometimes the attorney must prove that a child was born in wedlock, a fact that will affect the requirements for obtaining citizenship by descent. Proving legitimacy often means unearthing old marriage certificates, sometimes from foreign countries.

Problem 3: This Problem was heavily paraphrased because the original wording mixes the answer in with the question.

Mary's great-grandfather acquired citizenship by birth in the United States. Under the pre-1934 law, Mary's grandfather also became a United States citizen at birth. (*His* father - i.e., Mary's great grandfather - had been a United States citizen who had resided in the United States before Mary's grandfather's birth).

Mary's father was born in 1930. His citizenship, therefore, is governed by the same law. Under that law, Mary's father also acquired citizenship at birth because *his* father had been a United States citizen who had previously (1889-92) resided in the United States.

But Mary herself is not a United States citizen. Born in 1953, she must look to the citizenship law that appears in the 4th row of the chart (first prong). Her father was a United States citizen, but he never resided in the United States or even physically set foot there before Mary's birth. (This analysis assumes that Mary's mother is not also a United States citizen. There are no facts to indicate that she is). Since Mary is not a United States citizen, it also follows that David will not be an immediate relative.

Still, Mary is the married daughter of a United States citizen. Her father can therefore file a family-sponsored third preference visa petition on her behalf. In theory, David will be eligible for LPR status as an "accompanying spouse." The major problem will be the backlogs. The April 2009 Visa Bulletin on page 266 of the coursebook shows a third preference wait of about 8 ½ years. Unless that period shortens, and depending on how many years David has remaining on his temporary work visa, this wait is likely to be problematic.

Once again there are some difficult proof problems. Mautino used a creative mix of traditional birth records when they could be found, employer records, and, because the great-grandfather had fought in the Civil War, some military pension records from the Veterans Administration.

<u>Jus Sanguinis and the Constitution</u> (page 1296):

Chapter 2 examined and evaluated the principle of plenary congressional power as it applies to the admission and the expulsion of noncitizens. Many students will feel that the plenary power doctrine is inappropriate even in those contexts. Here, it might be best to ask the students to accept the plenary power doctrine as a given and to focus on whether the various justifications for it are either stronger or weaker in the contexts of citizenship than they are in the contexts of admission or expulsion. Among the plenary power doctrine theories examined in chapter 2 (whether persuasive in that context or not) are the following:

1. The constitutionality of immigration legislation is a political question because foreign affairs are potentially implicated. One could probably argue that foreign affairs concerns are at least as likely to surface in citizenship cases as they are in admission and expulsion cases. This is particularly true with issues concerning citizenship by descent because in those cases claims of dual citizenship are especially frequent and therefore conflicts as to loyalty are more likely to surface.

2. Decisions as to whom to admit and whom to expel are essential

components of a nation's sovereignty. One could argue that the same is true a fortiori with respect to citizenship. The political branches should be at least as free to define who is a member as they are to decide which non-members may enter and remain.

3. Just as courts say it is a "privilege" for a noncitizen to enter and to remain in the United States (rather than a "right"), one could similarly argue that the acquisition of citizenship (at least citizenship by descent, which is not constitutionally compelled) is merely a "privilege."

4. The Constitution is inapplicable to exclusion cases because, by definition, the noncitizens in these cases are outside the United States. This argument might or might not apply to citizenship, since the claimant could be either outside or inside the United States.

5. The noncitizen in removal proceedings lacks full constitutional protection because he or she has elected to maintain an ambiguous allegiance. That argument is clearly inapplicable to the person who is seeking citizenship.

2. Citizenship Acquired After Birth

a. Administrative Naturalization

Citizenship USA (page 1302):

This is just background reading to introduce the students to the politics of naturalization.

i. Substantive Criteria

In re Petition for Naturalization of Vafaei-Makhsoos (page 1308):

An Iranian national adjusted his status to that of lawful permanent resident in December 1977. Thereafter, he made two temporary trips to Iran. The second one lasted two years because, while he was there, the United States embassy was stormed and Iran temporarily banned all travel to the United States. In deportation proceedings, an immigration judge held that, because his prolonged stay in Iran had been involuntary, Vafaei-Makhsoos had not abandoned his permanent residence. In June 1983, he applied for naturalization. The former INS recommended denial on the ground that he had not shown five years continuous residence immediately preceding the filing of the petition, as required by INA § 316(a). Under section 316(b), an "absence" from the United States for more than one year breaks the continuity of the residence for naturalization purposes.

The district court agreed with the INS and denied naturalization. The literal statutory language was on point, and it makes no exception for involuntary absences. Other language in the statute allows an applicant who was away for 6-12 months to prevail by proving he or she had not abandoned permanent residence, so the absence of similar language for the applicant who is away more than a year is revealing. Moreover, the court reasoned, the purpose of the five-year requirement is to make sure the applicant has been sufficiently exposed to United States institutions; an exception for involuntary absences would undercut that purpose. Nor, the court held, did it matter that the immigration judge had found the applicant had not abandoned his residence for deportation purposes; the residence issue for naturalization purposes requires a different determination.

Notes and Questions Following Vafaei-Makhsoos (page 1311):

Q1: The residence requirements of INA § 316(a) include the following – continuous residence in the United States for at least five years after admission for permanent residence and immediately preceding the application for naturalization; at least three months of residence (not necessarily continuous) in the state or INS (now USCIS) district in which the application was filed; and continuous residence in the United States from the filing of the application to the grant of naturalization. The same provision requires physical presence for at least half of the five-year period immediately preceding the filing of the application.

INS Interp. 316.1(b)(2)(iii) is difficult to reconcile with INA § 101(a)(33). But for the INS inclusion of the word "continuing" and the qualifier "following a lawful admission for such purpose," one might say that the applicant need only have an intent to remain permanently at the time he or she applies for naturalization -- not necessarily for the entire preceding five-year period. But those qualifiers seem to preclude that explanation.

Q2: a. Even the present court does not seem to regard the literal language as the end of the inquiry. It might possibly think involuntary departures present different policy considerations from voluntary absences that are involuntarily prolonged.

b. Congress obviously intended to treat the person who left for a year more harshly than the person who left for six to twelve months. It does not follow, however, that Congress intended to subject even the former to an absolute bar. It might not be enough to show that the former person did not abandon his or her residence, but it might be enough to show he or she was physically prevented from returning.

c. The list of exceptions was not necessarily meant to be exhaustive. Possibly Congress thought of those specific exceptions but wanted to leave to the courts the discretion to read in other exceptions when necessary to further the policy objectives of INA § 316.

e. All three of the purposes described in this question would seem to be fostered more effectively by a physical presence requirement than by a residence requirement. Maintaining a residence in the United States won't enhance the person's exposure to American institutions or help a person learn English or demonstrate an inclination to obey our laws, if he or she is physically absent. Further, if the person is absent, the fulfillment of these policies will not depend on whether the absence is voluntary or involuntary, much less on whether, if involuntary, the involuntary element was the departure or the prolongation of the stay.

Q3: Maybe because the consequences of finding an abandonment are generally more severe. One who abandons his or her permanent residence thereby loses the basis for being readmitted to, or remaining in, a country in which he or she has acquired roots. In contrast, even when a court finds no continuous residence for purposes of naturalization, the applicant may continue to remain in the United States and, once the five-year requirement is met, reapply for naturalization.

Q4: A petitioner needs five years of continuous residence. He last returned from Iran on June 1, 1981. He is permitted to count up to one year of absence toward the continuous residence requirement. Thus he can count the period from June 1, 1980 to June 1, 1981 and then the four succeeding years spent in the United States. That brings him to June 1, 1985.

Q5: The statutory silence, when compared to the explicit congressional directions on how to count absences of six to twelve months and absences of one year or more, presumably means that an absence of less than six months does not destroy continuity.

Q6: The court in *Castrinakis* said, 179 F.Supp. at 445, that one of the purposes of the state residence requirement "is to facilitate the investigation" of character, constitutional attachment, etc., and also to facilitate the testimony of witnesses before the court in the event questions arise (by minimizing distance and jurisdictional problems). The problem is not as burdensome as it might seem because, if the person moves, the only consequence is that he or she must wait a few more months before reapplying for naturalization.

Q7: The petition was filed on June 9, 1983. The pertinent five-year period therefore runs from June 9, 1978 to June 9, 1983. The petitioner was absent from July 1978 until May 1979, and then again from June 1979 to June 1981, for a total of more than 2 1/2 years during the five-year period that immediately preceded the filing of the petition. Most likely, the court forgot about the first trip. Under INA § 316(a), the applicant had to be physically present in the United States for at least half of that period, and he was not. Thus it appears that he was ineligible on that ground alone, and the court could have avoided the continuous residence issue (unless possibly the first trip was not counted for *Fleuti* reasons, by analogy to the old suspension of deportation cases like *Kamheangpatiyooth*).

Q8: The standard of review is difficult to predict. In*Bellei* and *Elias*, both discussed on pages 1297-99 of the text, the courts seemed to assume that they had the power to review only for arbitrariness. In *Elias*, in fact, the court applied the even more deferential *Mandel* standard (*facially* legitimate and bona fide reason). And in those cases, the courts emphasized, the adversely affected parties were United States citizens. Here, in contrast, the adversely affected parties are noncitizens seeking naturalization. Moreover, the courts would be dealing here with an express congressional power - i.e., the naturalization clause.

On the other hand, as discussed in chapter 2, the fact that a power exists does not mean that it is unlimited. Moreover, while the plaintiffs are not United States citizens, they are LPRs (although that did not seem to mean much in *Harisiades*, discussed in chapter 2). In addition, race is a suspect classification even with respect to federal action, and the court in *Elias* hinted that racial classifications could be devoid of all valid purposes. If that is so, however, then it is difficult to explain cases like the *Chinese Exclusion Case*, *Fong Yue Ting*, etc. An additional complication is that a nationality determination, probably even more than an admission or expulsion decision, looks like a foreign policy judgment. In such cases, therefore, the argument for characterizing the constitutionality of the statute as a political question becomes stronger.

ii. Procedure

This description of the naturalization process is intended as background reading.

b. Miscellaneous Forms of Naturalization

This brief description is also meant for background reading.

c. A Swiss Perspective

More background reading.

3. **Dual Nationality** (page 1317)

The instructor could either assign this subsection as background reading or take up in class the arguments for and against dual citizenship that are discussed in the text. Views on dual nationality tend to reflect, among other things, the relative values that particular students assign to state sovereignty and personal autonomy and how they feel more generally about the institution that we have come to call "citizenship." The more normative significance one attaches to sovereignty and to both geographic and demographic borders, and the more strongly one subscribes to citizenship and nationality as indicia of community membership or as criteria for defining rights, the more one tends to resist dual allegiance and dual nationality. Those who place less weight on state sovereignty and on the state as the source of individual rights, and relatively greater weight on free will and the universality of human rights, seem generally less bothered by dual nationality and often affirmatively drawn to it.

4. Statelessness (page 1320)

This subsection too was intended mainly as background reading.

5. Who Should Be a United States Citizen?

Notes and Questions Following Schuck & Smith and Neuman (page 1333):

Q2: Professors Schuck & Smith interpret "subject to the jurisdiction thereof" as referring to a consensual (public law) jurisdiction. Under this interpretation, the government has complete, direct power over the individual, and at the time of birth there is a reciprocal relationship such that the government consented to the individual's presence and status and offered him or her complete protection. Using that formulation, the authors explain the result reached with respect to Indians by asserting that tribes had obtained by "mutual consent a measure of sovereignty." (Therefore, the reciprocal relationship required for "subject to the jurisdiction thereof" is lacking.) They explain the grant of citizenship to children of illegally imported slaves by asserting that, although the slaves were illegally imported (and therefore the United States cannot really be said to have "consented" to their presence), the slaves eventually became United States nationals by virtue of an "enduring conquest." Therefore, the argument runs, their children were born "subject to the jurisdiction" of the United States. The instructor could ask at this point: "If I go to Mexico and kidnap a Mexican national, and keep the person in the United States as a slave, does he or she become a United States national? Or is that different?" The third conclusion – that children born in the United States to undocumented parents do not become United States citizens – flows from reading the Fourteenth Amendment to require the government's consent to an individual's presence.

Professor Neuman construes "subject to the jurisdiction thereof" as meaning "actual subjection to the lawmaking power of the state." He regards Indians born within tribal authority as not so subject, given the level of quasi-sovereignty that they enjoy. (Schuck and Smith reject that characterization.) Neuman explains the grant of citizenship to the United States-born children of illegally imported slaves by observing that they were in fact subjected to the lawmaking power of the State. He believes the Schuck and Smith formulation is incompatible with that result because the United States never consented to the presence of the slave parents. Neuman reaches the same results for the children of undocumented parents as for the children of illegally imported slaves. In each case, the parent was subject to the State's lawmaking authority.

Q3: The real question here is whether the consent principle is consistent with the grant of citizenship even to children born in the United States to citizen parents. The argument in favor of the legal fiction admittedly employed by Schuck and Smith is that, since no conscious decision was made one way or the other, the law should strive to obtain what the parents would have decided had they thought about it. And surely the parents would have wanted citizenship for their children. The arguments against the use of such a legal fiction might be twofold. First, the fact remains that the parents *did not* think about it. Second, even if the parents had spotted the issue and had insisted on citizenship for their children, the thesis of Professors Schuck and Smith demands mutual consent. Even under that thesis, therefore, the question remains whether the government would have granted citizenship as desired. Schuck and Smith believe the answer to that latter question is yes, and probably it is.

Q4: The argument based on longstanding policy would seem to apply with equal force to the United States-born children of undocumented parents. Those children have long been regarded as United States citizens.

The consideration that rests on the tradition of openness is probably more applicable to children of LPRs than to the children of undocumented parents, since the United States has been more open to permanent residents than to undocumented ones. Still, the United States has not been closed to the *United States-born children* of undocumented parents, at least in this century.

Professors Schuck and Smith might argue that the children of LPRs could more easily become citizens because these children are most likely LPRs themselves. But if, as Schuck and Smith imply in their response to the fifth objection, children born in the United States to undocumented parents would also become LPRs, then naturalization seems as likely an eventual option for those children as it does for LPRs.

Q5: The children, of course, have done nothing illegal. All they did was to have been born to parents who have violated United States immigration laws. The question is whether to treat them adversely because of the misconduct of their parents -- a question central to the analysis of Schuck and Smith. But see question 8 and the analysis below.

Q6: Professor Neuman would probably respond that such recognition would not limit the power of the nation -- only the power of Congress, which is but one organ of the nation. The question, in other words, is one of internal allocation of power as between Congress and the Constitution. Ultimately, of course, the real question is one of allocating power between the majority and the minority. Limitations on other powers are often seen as necessary for protecting vulnerable minorities. Schuck and Smith argue that this particular minority interest -- becoming a member -- should not be insulated from majority rule.

Q7: Since descent is also an accident of birth, citizenship by descent would seem vulnerable to the same criticism. Schuck and Smith might respond by emphasizing that at least a statute conferring citizenship by descent reflects a conscious congressional choice and is therefore "consensual." Still, that point goes only to the consent objection, not to the objection that citizenship should not rest on accident of birth. They do suggest that citizenship based on parentage differs from citizenship based on geography (for reasons discussed earlier in the analysis of question 2).

Q8: As to the first point, Neuman might argue that, even if one accepts the premise that inherited citizenship is no worse than inherited wealth, it would not follow that citizenship by birth on United States soil is not also morally acceptable. As for the second point, it seems difficult to distinguish between citizenship as a "prize" and mere "nondiscrimination." The only thing that distinguishes these children from those to whom the authors would encourage Congress to give birthright citizenship (i.e., children born abroad to citizen parents) is the conduct of their parents. If both groups are granted citizenship, then citizenship *is* "mere nondiscrimination," not a prize. Even if one elects to call it a "prize," however, the question remains why this prize should be given to others but withheld from them.

As for the third point, the options open to the children seem problematic. Schuck and Smith say the children have the option of "continuing in illegal status." The fact remains, however, that they have done nothing "illegal," and the "more limited equal protection and due process rights" include susceptibility to deportation from the only country where they have ever lived to one that they do not know. The second option -- "seeking to obtain legal status" -- would be quite difficult unless Congress admits them as LPRs, as the authors previously suggested (in which event they would not have been living in "illegal status"). And the last option -- "returning to their home countries" -- overlooks the reality that, for them, the United States *is* home.

9. As to the first question: Since the child was born in the United States, the only issue is whether he or she is "subject to the jurisdiction thereof." Under conventional analysis, citizenship seems clear. This is not the child of enemy occupiers or foreign diplomats. Perhaps it could be argued (a) that the child's status is the functional equivalent of that of a person born on an enemy warship in U.S. waters; and (b) that the latter, in turn, is akin to an enemy

occupier. But both links are at least questionable. The mother has been brought to the United States, by United States officials, for the specific purpose of subjecting her to U.S. jurisdiction. And even under the consent-based approach of Schuck and Smith, she is undeniably in the U.S. with the consent of the U.S. So she seems subject to U.S. jurisdiction in every sense of the term.

The harder question is the normative one. The child lacks any meaningful connection to the United States, but unless the principle of jus soli is to be jettisoned, a meaningful connection is not required. There is, of course, the practical question of what to do with the child if the mother is imprisoned for life or executed, but (a) that's always a problem when the mother is imprisoned and no other family member is available; and (b) it would be a problem whether the child is a U.S. citizen or not. Obviously the child is innocent of wrongdoing, but so are the children of undocumented parents, and those who favor denying citizenship to the latter (not Schuck and Smith, who argue merely that the Constitution should be interpreted as empowering Congress to decide the issue) seem not to be deterred by the innocence of the child; for them, the combination of lack of meaningful ties and the fact that the parents were not supposed to be in U.S. territory in the first place is reason enough to withhold citizenship. Even those who favor withholding jus soli citizenship from children born to undocumented parents would have to acknowledge, however, that the mother has not violated any U.S. immigration laws. At bottom, is this child really any different from any other child born in the United States to a noncitizen parent who has committed a serious crime?

Q10: Schuck and Smith might favor such an amendment, but they would not have to. Reasons that they might not advocate such an amendment include the following:

a. They might stress they are not making a normative argument for a consent theory. They are advancing only a consensual theory of constitutional interpretation. Thus there is no need to amend the Constitution.

b. Amending the Constitution has stability costs that would have to be balanced against the perceived desirability of the new provision.

c. Citizens are presumed (conclusively or rebuttably) to condition their acceptance of citizenship upon the nation's tacit promise to give citizenship to their children. Legislation is not needed to manifest consent. (But why leave this to implication?)

d. The Constitution itself could be a form of consent, and reasonable minds can differ over whether a given class of citizens ought to be "constitutional" citizens or merely "statutory" citizens.

SECTION B. LOSING CITIZENSHIP

1. Revocation of Naturalization

Kungys v. United States (page 1338):

Kungys applied successfully for an immigrant visa in 1947, was admitted to the United States, and in 1954 obtained naturalization. In 1982 the government brought proceedings in district court to revoke his naturalization on the alternative grounds that his naturalization (a) had been illegally procured (meaning that in actual fact he had been ineligible for naturalization because he had lied under oath and therefore lacked good moral character); and (b) had been procured by willful misrepresentation (which all courts had interpreted to require materiality). Kungys admitted having wilfully made the alleged misrepresentations but denied they were material. The misrepresentations concerned the date and place of his birth and his wartime address and occupation. (The government believed he had assisted in wartime atrocities and that that was why he had told various lies, but the evidence of his participation in those atrocities was not strong enough - hence, the reliance on the misrepresentation and moral character grounds.) The district court found that the charges had not been proved. The court of appeals reversed, holding his naturalization had been procured by willful misrepresentations.

The Supreme Court divided along several lines. Different combinations of Justices formed majorities or pluralities on several different issues; those issues, and a summary of the Justices' rationales, appear in the analysis of Question 1 below.

Notes and Questions Following Kungys (page 1354):

General: This is an incredibly long and complicated series of opinions. The main value of this case is as an exceptional vehicle for developing statutory interpretation skills. The instructor who wishes to focus on policy would probably do best either to skip this case entirely or to assign it but focus on the policy questions raised by question 7.

Q1: Here is the scorecard:

a. With respect to "illegally procured:"

i. The Justices seem unanimous in accepting the *Fedorenko* holding that naturalization was "illegally procured" if, at the time of naturalization, the applicant was in fact ineligible for it.

ii. With respect to Kungys himself, the eligibility issue

concerned "good moral character." As to that, the question was whether Kungys had given "false testimony for the purposes of obtaining any benefits under" the INA, thus precluding "good moral character" under INA § 101(f)(6).

(A) Five Justices (Scalia, Rehnquist, Brennan, White, and O'Connor) hold that the false testimony need not be material in order to trigger section 101(f)(6). White suggests that whether false testimony precludes good moral character requires a balancing test in which materiality is relevant. Three Justices (Stevens, Marshall, and Blackmun) hold that section 101(f)(6) requires a material falsity.

(B) The Justices seem to agree that "testimony" means oral evidence given under oath and that section 101(f)(6) also requires a subjective intent to obtain immigration or naturalization benefits.

(C) The Scalia group favors remanding for determinations of whether Kungys's misrepresentations were "testimony" and, if so, whether they were made for the purpose of obtaining immigration or naturalization benefits. White and O'Connor think the existing record produces yes answers to both.

b. With respect to "procured by * * * willful misrepresentation:"

i. All Justices agree that this prong requires a material misrepresentation.

ii. The Scalia group, along with White and O'Connor, agree that a misrepresentation is material if it has a "natural tendency" to produce a conclusion by the INS that the applicant was eligible for naturalization. The Stevens group adheres to the *Chaunt* test, which requires that the true facts, if known, either themselves would have warranted denial or might have been useful in an investigation that in turn might have led to the discovery of other facts warranting denial. (Whether they interpret *Chaunt* to require an actual disqualifying fact is unclear.)

iii. The Scalia group holds that, if the government proves a material misrepresentation, then the applicant will be rebuttably presumed to have been ineligible for naturalization. Brennan joins in that conclusion with the understanding that the presumption will arise only if there is enough evidence to raise a "fair inference" that a statutory disqualifying fact existed.

iv. There is disagreement over whether Kungys's misrepresentations were material. The Scalia group concludes that under the "natural tendency" test the misrepresentations concerning date and place of birth were not material, and that the district court on remand should decide whether the other misrepresentations (wartime address and occupation) were material. The Stevens group reaches the same result under the *Chaunt* test. White and O'Connor, while purporting to apply the Scalia test, find material misrepresentations concerning the date and place of birth, both during the visa process and during the naturalization process.

v. As to whether naturalization was "procured by" the misrepresentations:

(A) White and O'Connor believe it is enough that the *visa* was procured by fraud, since the visa was a necessary step in eventually securing naturalization. The Scalia group believes the misrepresentation must occur as part of the naturalization process.

(B) The Scalia group, along with White and O'Connor, conclude that "procured by" does not require the government to prove that the applicant would have been eligible but for the misrepresentation. The Stevens group disagrees.

c. All the Justices seem to agree that "concealment of a material fact" requires willful concealment.

Q2: Justice White concludes that INA § 101(f)(6) does not require materiality. Yet he acknowledges that there do indeed exist misrepresentations that under section 101(f)(6) would preclude good moral character if material but not if immaterial. His position would be perfectly plausible if he were purporting to interpret the phrase "good moral character" generally, without reference to section 101(f)(6). Section 101(f), after all, does not exhaust the ways of finding a lack of good moral character. Thus, if none of the prongs of section 101(f) applied, the materiality of the misrepresentations might well be a legitimate factor to weigh in assessing good moral character. The problem is that White purports to be interpreting section 101(f)(6), which expressly precludes good moral character during any period in which one has given false testimony for the purpose of obtaining benefits under the INA. If this provision does not require materiality (as he concludes), and if the representation qualifies as testimony and is false, and it was made for the purpose of obtaining benefits under the INA, then how can White avoid a finding that the applicant lacked good moral character?

Q3: If anything, there is even greater reason to apply the contrast technique to the phrase "concealment of a material fact or * * * willful misrepresentation," where the contrasting language is found within a single statutory phrase, than there is to apply the technique to the contrast between "naturalization procedures by" and "false testimony for the purpose of obtaining any benefits" language in INA § 101(f)(6), which is part of the "good moral character" definition applicable to a whole range of immigration and nationality issues. Still, there would seem to be little reason for Congress to denaturalize someone for nonwillful concealment while declining to denaturalize someone for non-willful misrepresentation. So it makes sense to assume Congress wanted the willfulness requirement to apply to both. Further, the line that separates misrepresentation from concealment is blurry in any event; attaching legal consequences to that distinction would therefore create additional problems. The same reasoning might explain why a materiality requirement would be read into the misrepresentation prong, although there it is possible to argue that Congress viewed affirmative misrepresentations as being more culpable than mere failures to provide information, and thus might have wanted to require additional showings for the latter.

Q4: Perhaps a "natural" tendency is just a "foreseeable" one. Maybe, in other words, the *Kungys* test is whether a reasonable person would think that a misrepresentation would improve his or her chances of receiving naturalization. In contrast, it is not clear whether the *Chaunt* test requires proof of an ultimate disqualifying fact. If it does, then it requires more than the *Kungys* test does. For example, if the applicant reasonably but mistakenly believes he or she is ineligible for naturalization, or at least is uncertain, and therefore misrepresents the facts, and it turns out the true facts would not have destroyed eligibility, the *Kungys* test would probably lead to denaturalization. The *Chaunt* test, if interpreted to require an ultimate disqualifying fact, would not.

Q5: The important point here is that knowledge of the true facts (actual date and place of Kungys's birth) would have had no independent relevance. For Justice White, the value of knowing the true facts is that they would have exposed an inconsistency that might have prompted further investigation. Scalia argues that under White's approach an otherwise irrelevant misrepresentation acquires relevance by being repeated. White, however, sees such an inconsistency as evidence of possible dishonesty.

Q6: As to the first question: Scalia observes that in *Fedorenko* the Court held that, even absent a misrepresentation or concealment, a showing that the applicant was in fact ineligible for naturalization when he or she received it establishes the naturalization was "illegally procured." Thus if the government, in order to show that naturalization was procured by misrepresentation, had to prove that the applicant would not have qualified for naturalization under the true facts, it would be required to prove precisely what it would have had to prove under the "illegally procured" prong. Therefore the "procured by misrepresentation" prong would be superfluous.

Justice Stevens responds that Fedorenko does not literally make "every newly discovered noncompliance" a basis for finding citizenship "illegally procured." Some kinds of noncompliance might be too trivial to justify denaturalization. But, in answer to the second question, it is not clear how Stevens would draw the line. He implies through his examples that a willful misrepresentation would probably be enough but that an innocent misrepresentation probably would not. Still, even if Stevens is right to assume that non-willful misrepresentations would not make procurement illegal, that observation does not help him because the willful misrepresentation prong also doesn't reach such cases.

As for the third question, Scalia does seem to attach enormous weight to the maxim that a court should not construe one statutory phrase in a way that will leave another one superfluous. Here, however, there are at least two possible explanations for this seeming redundancy:

a. The Court in *Fedorenko* misinterpreted the phrase "illegally procured." Perhaps the word "illegally" requires more than mere ineligibility. For example, INA § 246 provides for rescinding a grant of adjustment of status upon a showing that, at the time the person received adjustment, he or she "was not in fact eligible" for it. Using the contrast technique, a court might ask why Congress would not use similar language for denaturalization if, as Justice Scalia believes, that is what Congress meant.

b. Probably more important, perhaps there is some unnecessary repetition in INA 340(a). Congress is not perfect.

Q7: The argument for generally making it more difficult to denaturalize someone than to deny naturalization as an original matter is that roots and reliance interests grow with time. Moreover, it should be more difficult to alter the status quo (by taking away what has already been conferred) than to preserve the status quo. In addition, once a person has taken an oath renouncing all former allegiances, as U.S. law requires, denaturalization can leave the person stateless. Finally, once the person has been naturalized, the lives of other people can also be affected. Many of these arguments are analogous to those that would apply to the distinction between inadmissibility and deportability grounds.

Two arguments might be advanced for making the criteria for denaturalization congruent with the criteria for denying naturalization originally. First, the naturalization requirements reflect Congress's substantive judgment about the traits a person should possess in order to attain membership in the political community. If a person lacked that trait (and still does), the passage of time does not eliminate the problem. Second, the law should not create an incentive for a person to lie to obtain naturalization, knowing that it will be more difficult to remove naturalization once it is granted.

A more specific question is whether the grounds for denaturalization should relate to ineligibility for original naturalization, or to dishonesty, or to both. One argument for emphasizing original ineligibility is the same as the above arguments for generally making denaturalization as easy as a denial of original naturalization. Even if the fact that initially made the applicant ineligible no longer exists, the argument based on avoiding incentives to lie will still apply.

The more difficult question is whether dishonesty should be an independent basis for denaturalization (i.e., whether a willful misrepresentation should be a ground for denaturalization if it turns out the applicant would have been eligible under the true facts). The arguments in favor of denaturalizing such a person are (a) dishonesty is itself a bad quality for a prospective member of the political community and (b) the law should deter misrepresentations. The argument against denaturalizing such an individual is that no real harm was done if the misrepresentation was indeed immaterial. The sanction of denaturalization is disproportionate to the transgression.

2. Expatriation

Vance v. Terrazas (page 1360):

Terrazas, born in the United States to citizens of Mexico, acquired dual citizenship at birth. At age 22, while studying in Mexico, he applied for a certificate of Mexican nationality. For this he had to swear allegiance to Mexico and expressly renounce allegiance to all other countries, including specifically the United States, which he knowingly did. Under INA § 349(a)(2), one loses United States citizenship by voluntarily and formally declaring allegiance to a foreign state. Accordingly, the State Department issued a certificate of loss of nationality (CLN), and the Board of Appellate Review (BAR) affirmed, finding he had taken the oath voluntarily. He sued and lost in district court, but the court of appeals reversed, holding that the Constitution required the government to prove an intent to renounce citizenship, and to prove it by clear, unequivocal, and convincing evidence. (The district court had not imposed either requirement.)

Interpreting *Afroyim*, the Court held that expatriation requires both the voluntary commission of one of the statutory expatriating acts and an intent to relinquish citizenship. (The Court then adopted a saving interpretation of the statute.) It also held, however, that neither the due process clause nor the 14th amendment citizenship clause of the Constitution requires the "clear, unequivocal, and convincing evidence" standard of proof; Congress could constitutionally prescribe a preponderance standard and had done so. Finally, the Court upheld the constitutionality of then section 349(c) [now 349(b)], which creates a rebuttable presumption that a person who commits one of the statutory expatriating acts does so voluntarily. The effect was to make duress an affirmative defense. The Court emphasized that there is no analogous presumption of an intent to relinquish citizenship.

Justice Marshall agreed with the majority that the Constitution requires a showing of intent to relinquish citizenship, but he dissented from the conclusion that a preponderance of the evidence would be enough. He would have held that the Constitution mandates the "clear, unequivocal, and convincing evidence" standard of proof. Justice Stevens reached the same conclusions as Justice Marshall, except that Justice Stevens found it impossible to read the statute as requiring an intent to relinquish citizenship and thus would have rested his result solely on the Constitution. Justice Brennan dissented. He argued that a formal oath of renunciation is the only constitutionally permissible way to surrender citizenship, and he concluded that the oath Terrazas had taken did not qualify.

<u>Notes and Questions Following Terrazas</u> (page 1368):

Q2: The cited pages of the Aleinikoff article contain a thorough discussion of all four theories and their limitations. His major points include the following:

a. The Rights Perspective:

i. Citizenship is of fundamental importance; the deprivation of it is a serious loss.

ii. Proponents of a rights-based theory would argue that conceptualizing citizenship as a right justifies the asymmetry. One can voluntarily waive a right, but ordinarily it cannot be taken away involuntarily.

iii. But the source of this right is debatable. Section 1 of the Fourteenth Amendment is usually assumed to be the source, but it is not clear whether that assumption is correct. This provision might be merely a definition rather than the conferral of a right. Substantive due process is another possibility, but in denationalization cases there is no balancing of individual and governmental interests as there usually is in substantive due process cases.

iv. Citizenship is important, but not as important as the Supreme Court implies. LPRs also have many legal rights. It is true that the practical effect of denationalization can itself be the loss of residence, but the person will still be permitted to live somewhere. Nor does denationalization always result in statelessness. Sometimes it means merely that one who was formerly a dual citizen will be left with only one citizenship.

v. Citizenship should be thought of as a relationship with the state, not a right held against the state.

b. The Consent Perspective:

i. The consent argument is inconsistent with the asymmetrical nature of the *Terrazas* doctrine. If a relationship is based on mutual consent, it cannot be true that the individual may end the relationship while the state may not.

c. The Contractarian Perspective:

i. Our social contract is framed in the Constitution.

ii. One possible frame of reference would be the actual intent of the framers. Originally, the consent of the sovereign was a prerequisite to losing one's citizenship. There is little evidence of any actual intent on the subject of denaturalization.

iii. Another frame of reference would be what a hypothetical group of constitutional drafters would say today. Most likely, they would allow for some right of expatriation. Probably this hypothetical group of drafters would not want to allow denationalization on public order grounds, at least without a very strong justification. To do so would create unlimited potential for tyranny. Maybe, however, they would allow denationalization on grounds that evidence a lack of allegiance. That approach would be similar to excommunication of a person opposed to the core principles of an institution. It is not clear whether a hypothetical group of framers today would even oppose denationalization for transferred or divided allegiance (e.g., foreign naturalization or dual nationality).

d. The Communitarian Perspective:

i. The social ties that form with time mean that denationalization can cause great hardship. It can intrude on one's conception of "self." Therefore it should be subject to stringent limits.

ii. The community helps to shape a person's values; thus, the community should not easily be able to renounce that person.

iii. At some point, however, a citizen might condemn the community. If the condemnation demonstrates a lack of allegiance, then the community should be able to terminate that relationship.

iv. Dual nationality is a closer call, but if there is an actual conflict in allegiance the community should be permitted to require the citizen to make a choice.

Q3: The greatest danger (as Aleinikoff acknowledges, at page 1500 of his article) is that denationalization based on loss of allegiance could lead to intrusive government investigations of the loyalty of individual citizens. History shows how real those dangers can be. Also, people hold different views about what allegiance means. The concept can be manipulated.

To minimize the danger, Aleinikoff would insist on the identification of "specific acts." He also stresses that a court ought not defer to congressional judgments about what constitutes a loss of allegiance. See the original article at 1500.

Among the activities he would include in the list is the voluntary renunciation of United States nationality, especially if done as part of a foreign naturalization process. Generally, joining the army of a country that has invaded the United States and seeking the violent overthrow of the United States government would also be accepted as evidence of lack of allegiance. Foreign naturalization by itself would not be enough. Nor would it be sufficient that the person has voted abroad, served in a foreign military unit, or served in a foreign government.

For Aleinikoff, the most significant benefit of the change is that it would allow denationalization in the case where the individual lacked any intent to renounce citizenship but in which the loss of allegiance was great enough to be incompatible with retention of citizenship. His theory thus fits in with all of the citizenship perspectives that he has identified to the extent they are based on relationships -- relationships with the state, relationships with the rest of the citizenry, and relationships with the society. It is not clear whether his proposal would be compatible with the constitutional right perspective.

Q4: Arguments for expatriation include:

1. The core meaning of citizenship is loyalty. While the person should not be required to demonstrate positive acts of civic sacrifice, it is not too much to expect the person who claims a legal bond to a country at least to refrain from affirmatively attempting to harm it. By analogy, in international law the country's right to protect an individual is usually assumed to correlate with the individual's allegiance to the country.

2. The main harm associated with expatriation is usually assumed to be a severing of the roots that citizens have formed with time. A person who wants to harm the country (as a positive desire, not merely as an unfortunate side effect of some other project) can be assumed not to have those sorts of close bonds.

Arguments against expatriation include:

1. The core meaning of citizenship is not loyalty; it is simply the legal rights and obligations associated with a tie to a particular country. To the extent the individual has breached those obligations, criminal punishment is appropriate, but there is no basis for terminating his or her citizenship.

2. The bond between the individual and the state is mutual. Only by agreement, therefore, can it be severed.

3. Unless the person happens to be a dual national, the consequence of expatriation is statelessness, which is universally disfavored.

Q5: If a right to retain citizenship is of constitutional stature, then this approach would not seem permissible unless (a) the waiver of the constitutional right is truly voluntary and (b) the benefit that the individual is relinquishing citizenship in order to keep is not itself a constitutional right. Under any of the other perspectives -- consent, contractarian, or communitarian -- a voluntary decision to choose some other (not constitutionally compelled) benefit seems to present no difficulty.

As a policy matter, however, the basic question remains whether the United States should put a person to that choice. The real issue is whether there are any benefits that the United States should tell a person he or she simply cannot have without giving up United States citizenship.

Q7: The argument against Justice Brennan's formulation is that, even absent a formal oath of renunciation, some acts are so inherently inconsistent with an intent to retain citizenship that if the acts are done voluntarily a court could reasonably infer an intent to relinquish. Brennan would probably respond that, in light of the stakes, such an intent should not be left to inference. A formal renunciation oath is much more reliable.

As for the facts of this case, Terrazas did more than just swear allegiance to Mexico. He also expressly renounced all foreign citizenships, including specifically that of the United States.

Q8: It is not clear why the law generally requires travel abroad in order to renounce United States citizenship. Perhaps the idea is purposely to make the process burdensome in order to discourage a person from taking such drastic action impulsively. Possibly, too, the idea is that, once a person renounces citizenship, it is better for the person not to be in the United States. (Although the consequence of renunciation will be that the person is now a noncitizen and therefore subject to all the deportability grounds, there will not ordinarily be any obvious deportability ground.)

But there are strong arguments for allowing renunciation to take place in the United States. If a person truly wants to renounce, the law should not make it expensive for him or her to sever a relationship that the person never chose in the first place.

As for the proposal to furnish renunciation forms at age 18, the obvious problems are the immaturity of individuals at that age and the possibility of rash decisions that people will later regret. That concern is paternalistic, but for 18-year olds paternalism might be appropriate. Professors Schuck and Smith emphasize both that individuals will not take this action lightly because of the high stakes and that in any event the law could permit such individuals to retain LPR status. As Martin points out, however, little is gained by affirmatively encouraging young people to renounce their United States citizenship; nor is it clear why the United States would want to allow renouncers to remain permanently in the United States.

Q12: One could easily argue that more harm is done when someone's United States citizenship is erroneously taken away than when it is erroneously preserved. If that value judgment is accepted, then Justice Harlan's formulation would call for increasing the standard of proof to some level beyond the "preponderance of the evidence" test -- perhaps to "clear and convincing evidence" or even to "proof beyond a reasonable doubt."

The majority reasons that the criminal and involuntary commitment cases are distinguishable because "expatriation proceedings are civil in nature and do not threaten a loss of liberty." But involuntary commitment proceedings are also civil. And as for the loss of liberty, the dissenting opinion of Justice Marshall is persuasive.

There is one other perspective from which the instructor could explore this problem. Is the balance of comparative social disutility any different here from the corresponding balancing of interests in criminal cases? What about deportation cases?

Q13: Proponents of such a presumption might argue as follows:

a. All that is presumed is that the act was done voluntarily; it is not presumed that the act was done with an intent to relinquish citizenship. So understood, the rebuttable presumption reflects common experience. More often than not, proponents would argue, individuals who engage in the listed acts do so voluntarily. Thus the Supreme Court was right to treat this presumption as simply a common sense evidentiary rule that the government has the authority to prescribe.

b. Rules that assign burdens of proof also commonly reflect judgments about the parties' relative access to the evidence. Here, the individual is more likely than the government to know whether his or her act was the product of free will or duress.

Opponents of the presumption might observe that the burden of proof typically lies with whichever party wants to alter the status quo. In this case, that party is the government.

SECTION C. THE SIGNIFICANCE OF CITIZENSHIP

<u>Questions on Citizenship and Welfare Reform</u> (page 1381):

Q1: The pros and cons are laid out in the cited article, 42 UCLA L.Rev. at 1462-70, and thus are not repeated here. Some of those arguments are specific to LPRs, some are specific to undocumented immigrants, and some apply to all noncitizens.

One point worth emphasizing is that students will be tempted to make arguments that prove too much. If, for example, a student argues that the government should not expend limited funds on people who are not "our own" citizens, the instructor might ask the student whether he or she favors providing police protection, or fire protection, or emergency medical aid after a car accident - even if the victims are immigrants. Almost any student would answer that such protection of course should be provided. Depending on the particular example used, the student's reason might be either that that is an unusually compelling human need or that in that particular case protecting the individual is necessary to protecting the larger society. (For example, fires can spread, criminals should be apprehended so that they don't later harm citizens, etc.) Or, the student might justify the expenditure on the basis that there is no practical, on-the-spot method of ascertaining the victim's citizenship status. Under any of those scenarios, the point is that it would be untenable to argue that the government should *never* spend public funds on noncitizens; rather, the question is almost always one of degree. Thus, whether a given benefit should be reserved for citizens can seldom be answered by a simple reference to conserving public resources for the members of the community (even assuming, as Schuck and Aleinikoff show is not inevitable, that citizenship equals membership).

Q2: The answer is not at all clear. The LPRs would argue that state action discriminating against LPRs has generally been subjected to strict scrutiny, and ultimately struck down as violative of equal protection, unless the subject matter falls within the political function exception (and welfare does not). *Graham v. Richardson*. They will further argue that the federal authorization is invalid because the federal government cannot constitutionally authorize a state to violate the federal Constitution.

The state might respond that even if strict scrutiny is applied, the state legislation meets that demanding test because Congress has declared that state action of the type taken is necessary to further a compelling governmental interest. The state might argue also that strict scrutiny is inapplicable at any rate, because the state is merely acting as the federal agent, pursuant to an express delegation of power, and thus is entitled to the same deference that the federal government received in *Mathews v. Diaz*. Under the latter theory, the federal government is not authorizing the state to violate the Constitution; rather, the federal government's blessing causes the state action not to *be* a violation. If a rational basis test is found applicable, the state might argue that its fortunes are linked to those of the nation; thus, helping the federal government to further a national goal is itself a rational state interest. On that point, see the discussion following *Plyler v. Doe* in chapter 12 (especially the reconciliation of *Plyler* with *De Canas v. Bica)*.

Under either standard of review, the state at some point has to articulate a legitimate (and maybe compelling) *state* interest. Whether it can do so depends in part on the nature of the federal power. If the exclusivity of the federal power is thought to be merely a matter of preemption under the supremacy clause, then a clearly expressed congressional decision to permit state action solves the problem. If, however, the exclusivity is thought to be constitutionally based, as the early cases suggested, then Congress cannot delegate the power to the states. In *Henderson* and *Chy Lung*, discussed in chapter 2, § A.4 of the text, the rationales for an exclusive constitutional power were the need for uniformity and the desire not to allow a single state to embroil the United States in a foreign policy dispute. The first rationale clearly applies here, since differing state welfare policies for LPRs could have the effects of altering migration patterns and triggering a race to the bottom among states eager to divert noncitizens to other states. As for the second rationale, a state that adopts stringent restrictions on noncitizens' eligibility for public benefits could easily antagonize a country whose nationals make up a large chunk of the state's noncitizen population. Witness Mexico's reaction to California Proposition 187.

Notes and Questions Following Schuck and Aleinikoff (page 1392):

General: The excerpts from Schuck and Aleinikoff ideally should be assigned as a unit. If the instructor prefers, however, either article can be assigned without the other. If the Schuck article is not assigned, the teacher should instruct the students to skip item 1 of the Notes and Questions. If the Aleinikoff article is omitted, the teacher should instruct the students to skip items 3 and 4 of the Notes and Questions. (A few other items in this set of Notes and Questions refer to either Schuck or Aleinikoff but are sufficiently self-contained that the students will be able to analyze them without having read the articles.)

Q1: a. Schuck's response might be twofold. First, he might say, many such individuals -- particularly those who lack formal educations -- might not understand either the legal consequences of declining citizenship or the potential for economic exploitation. Second, and less paternalistically, even if the particular individuals are no worse off keeping their old citizenship, society might be worse off. (Schuck mentions this in connection with the fourth danger, the "emotional" one.) Excluding the underclass can cause alienation and friction.

b. As to part (i), Schuck might argue that, although the correlation is not perfect, encouraging naturalization would at least be one way to induce more people to learn English and civics. As to part (ii), Schuck might contend that newcomers who do not learn English or acquire knowledge of American traditions and institutions jeopardize the well-being of their new society by diminishing their own capacities to contribute. The weight of this argument hinges, of course, on the degree to which one views moral principles in individual or collective terms.

c. As to part (i), Schuck might argue that citizens at least have a moral duty to society to vote and to participate in the democracy. (Of course, an LPR could still become naturalized and not vote. Therefore, it is not an unwillingness to assume the obligations of citizenship that keeps them from attaining naturalization.) As to part (ii) - the argument that a person's willingness to share communal burdens is likely to depend much less on citizenship than on personal values and relationships - Schuck might acknowledge the point but observe that citizenship might add a psychological impetus and at any rate can't hurt.

d. The two points made here relate to the lack of empirical evidence connecting citizenship with either (i) emotionally meaningful ties to others in society and (ii) one's self-image as an "American." Schuck's response might be that there is also no empirical evidence to the contrary, and that all we can therefore go by is intuition. As to that, it seems plausible that a common goal can enhance communal feelings within a group of individuals who have gone through the process, and that, if worked for, a reward is more likely to influence self-definition and self-image.

Q3: Aleinikoff acknowledges the argument, see pages 16-17 of the original article, but does not respond directly. A possible response is that naturalization requires renouncing one's existing citizenship. For many people, that is very painful. Some who are perfectly loyal to the United States nonetheless view renunciation of original citizenship as an act that would either feel to them, or be perceived by others, as a betrayal of heritage or family. Thus a hesitance to naturalize does not evidence a lack of loyalty.

Q4: For the reasons given in the text, the opinion of Justice Blackmun contains no internal contradiction. That fact does not weaken Aleinikoff's basic thesis that LPRs should be regarded as "members." It simply adds a further reason, independent of membership theory, for holding states to a higher standard when they seek to justify discrimination against LPRs.

Q5: The quoted statement is clearly incorrect. As the students will have seen by this point, noncitizens enjoy a range of statutory and even constitutional rights. It's just that those rights aren't as extensive as the rights of citizens.

Q6: This question and the next one ask, respectively, who should be thought of as "members" and whether the law really needs a concept of "citizenship."

The Aleinikoff article does not address the general question of what the criteria for "membership" ought to be, probably because the author believes that membership should not be the test for the standard of constitutional review in any event. The instructor might simply ask the students to identify the possible factors on which membership decisions could be based. Among the factors that the students might deem either necessary or sufficient (or, in some cases, both) would be the following: citizenship, permanent resident status, physical presence, lawful physical presence, duration of stay, employment, and family relationships.

Q7: Even with respect to domestic law, most students will instinctively resist the abolition of citizenship. In most cases, that intuition will reflect the citizens-as-members philosophy that Aleinikoff rejects. For some, the need for a membership-based status will follow from one or more of the intangible effects described by Schuck. One way to explore these questions is to ask the students whether, if the legal concept of citizenship were suddenly abolished, they would feel any less "American" (or an analogous question if the student is of some other citizenship). Most American students will probably respond that their identities as Americans have been shaped more by their having grown up in the United States, having lived here, being part of the culture of the country, etc.